The Sociology of Juvenile Delinquency

Nelson-Hall Series in Sociology

Consulting Editor: Jonathan H. Turner
University of California, Riverside

The Sociology of Juvenile Delinquency

Edited by
Ronald J. Berger
University of Wisconsin—Whitewater

Nelson-Hall Publishers
Chicago

Project Editor: James Cambias
Text Designer: Tamra Campbell-Phelps
Illustrator: Bill Nelson
Compositor: Precision Typographers
Manufacturer: R.R. Donnelley & Sons
Cover Painting: *Psyche,* Leah Sosewitz, Oil on Canvas

Library of Congress Cataloging-in-Publication Data

The Sociology of Juvenile Delinquency / edited by Ronald J. Berger.
   p. cm. — (Nelson-Hall series in sociology)
   ISBN 0-8304-1212-3
  1. Juvenile delinquency—United States. 2. Juvenile delinquency—
United States—Prevention. 3. Juvenile delinquents—United States—
Psychology. 4. Juvenile justice, Administration of—United States.
I. Berger, Ronald J. II. Series.
HV9104.S375 1990   90-32880
364.3'6'0973—dc20   CIP

Manufactured in the United States of America.

10 9 8 7 6 5 4 3 2

TM The paper used in this book meets the
minimum requirements of American
National Standard for Information
Sciences—Permanence of Paper for
Printed Library Materials, ANSI
Z39.48-1984.

To Ruthy, Corey, Chad, and Kelly

Contents

Preface

There are currently a large number of texts available for sociology, criminology, and criminal justice courses on juvenile delinquency. Several of these texts are "encyclopedic" in scope, attempting to cover nearly everything that has been written on the topic. While the books may differ in minor respects (for example, some offer more chapters on particular types of delinquency such as drug use, gangs, and female delinquency; some focus on the juvenile justice system or practical applications; and some present more historical material), the content and organization of these books are quite similar. A few of the available texts are relatively short. Although they are less comprehensive, some instructors are attracted to shorter texts, presumably because they are less expensive, and thus allow instructors the option of using them along with one or two other books.

As an instructor of upper division sociologically-oriented juvenile delinquency courses for a number of years, my experience with some of the available texts has not always been satisfactory. From an instructor's point of view, a book of readings allows greater freedom and creativity in the organization of courses because the readings may be easily re-ordered to conform to one's preferences. In addition, evaluations from my upper division courses indicate that students find reading articles to be more interesting and informative than reading traditionally organized textbooks. Students also report a greater appreciation for the sociological research enterprise by reading a piece in its entirety.

Unfortunately there are very few readers available for juvenile delinquency courses. When I decided to put this book together, there were only three "textbook" readers published in the 1980s that were appropriate for a student, rather than scholarly, audience. In an attempt to please everyone, two of the available readers included over forty articles. In an attempt to be brief, one included only fourteen articles. In terms of length, I have designed this reader to fall somewhere in the middle. It includes twenty-seven articles, a few of which were written especially for this book.

As the title makes clear, this book is intended to provide a *sociological* perspective on juvenile delinquency. The readings are divided into six topical sections: The Social Construction of Juvenile Delinquency; The Measurement and Social Distribution of Delinquency; The Social Psychology of Delinquency; Social Structural and Institutional Influences on Delinquency; The Delinquent Experience: Girls, Guys, and Gangs; and The Juvenile Justice System. The articles have been selected to provide comprehensive coverage of the field, and the section introductions and conclusion fill in any significant gaps that remain. The book is designed to be used either as a main text or as a supplemental text for students taking delinquency courses in sociology, criminology, and criminal justice programs. The articles include theoretical, empirical, and applied/practical pieces that provide students with an understanding of how sociological theory and research can be both insightful and relevant. The readings are taken from varied sources—professional journals, edited anthologies, monographs, and popular magazines. This variety is intended to help maintain student interest by avoiding the monotony that students often feel after reading material of similar style and format. Many of the articles, particularly the ethnographic research and journalistic accounts, will be especially enjoyable for students to read and will sensitize readers to the day-to-day life experiences of delinquent youth.

I would like to thank Stephen Ferrara, President of Nelson-Hall, and Jonathan Turner, Sociology editor at Nelson-Hall, for their support of this project. I would also like to thank Dorothy Anderson, Senior Editor at Nelson-Hall, and James Cambias, Assistant Editor.

PART 1
The Social Construction of Juvenile Delinquency

Adults of every generation have often complained about the unruly conduct of youth. Even the ancient philosopher Aristotle remarked that the "young are . . . ready to carry any desire into action, . . . [and are] apt to be carried away by their impulses . . . [and] carry everything too far" (cited in Hall, 1905:523). But while youths have long been known for their tendency to be rowdy, to fight with one another, to drink excessively, and to be sexually active, the concept of "juvenile delinquency" as a phenomenon distinct from adult criminality is a relatively recent social invention (Aries, 1962; Empey, 1982). In fact, the first specialized juvenile court in the United States was not created until 1899 in Illinois when specialized legal codes dealing with juvenile misconduct began to expand.

Earlier societies did not make the distinctions between childhood, adolescence, and adulthood that we make today. Children were believed to be miniature adults, as was illustrated by early paintings and sculptures that portrayed them as "mature midgets" (Empey, 1982:37; Aries, 1962). Moreover, the many years of schooling required by modern societies have extended the period of adolescence (the ages between the onset of puberty and full adult status) into the late teens and early twenties.

Modern families are often child-centered and especially protective of their children. This was not the case in earlier times. Indeed, as late as the eighteenth century, infanticide, the deliberate killing of unwanted infants, particularly females, was not uncommon and was viewed as casually as abortion is today (Empey, 1982; Mause, 1974). Unwanted children were also abandoned and sold into slavery, indentured servitude, and prostitution; and children in general were both economically and sexually exploited. In addition, mothers with the economic means hired wet-nurses to feed their babies who consequently died at higher rates than

1

mother-fed infants because wet-nurses were often malnourished. Swaddling, a method of wrapping children entirely in bandages (feces and all) so that they could not move, was also practiced. And a large number of children could be considered ''battered'' in light of the harsh physical punishment they received. Thus children lived under difficult and unhealthful conditions and suffered from much disease. The average life expectancy as late as the seventeenth century was not more than thirty years (Bremner, 1970; Gillis, 1974).

However, as western civilization emerged from the Middle Ages many of these practices began to fade. By the late sixteenth and seventeenth centuries, reformers became critical of the way children were treated, and in colonial America a modern conception of childhood began to develop. Religious moralists believed that while children were inherently sinful (original sin), they were also fragile and innocent. Since they were easily corrupted, they needed to receive special training in the family, church, and school. In other words, children ''were both wicked and worth saving'' (Empey, 1982:39; Aries, 1962). According to Puritan reformers, the ''ideal child'' had to be extensively supervised and disciplined (''spare the rod and spoil the child''), absolutely obedient to authority, sexually chaste, and impressed with the moral virtues of hard work (''idle hands are the devil's workshop'') (Bremner, 1970; Empey, 1982).

The Puritans, however, continued to believe in the apprenticeship system, which was considered ''part of the normal upbringing'' of children up to the eighteenth century (Binder et al., 1988:51). Though highly exploitative, apprenticeships were seen as offering ''safeguard[s] against parental overindulgence'' (pp. 51-2). Under the apprenticeship system, as Binder et al. note:

> young men and women bound themselves to masters for a set period of years, during which they would work for their masters and learn their trades. In return, the masters were expected to provide their apprentices with food, shelter, and clothing . . . [But the] apprentice's life was not . . . easy . . . Though a youth, he or she was still expected to work hard . . . and was often quite harshly treated and subjected to brutal punishments.

Gradually, however, a more nurturant view regarding children began to take hold. Good behavior in children was increasingly seen as a product of parental affection rather than of fear and strict punishment (Binder et al., 1988). The family began to be perceived more as ''an emotional unit'' and as a refuge from the outside world (p. 54). Obedient children were still the ideal, but they were obedient ''not because they were forced to behave'' but because they wanted to behave (p. 55).

The social construction of the ''ideal child'' and the changes in family life set the stage for the concept of juvenile delinquency. Yet until the end of the nineteenth century, there was no distinct legal category of ''delinquency.'' Americans relied on English common law which specified that children under age seven were incapable of criminal intent and thus absolved of guilt for serious crimes. Children ages seven through thirteen were presumed innocent unless proven otherwise, but children fourteen and older were treated as adults. A separate juvenile justice system designed to deal with young people did not exist yet (Empey, 1982; Thornton et al., 1987).

In colonial America, the community had been tightly knit and organized around the church which "set strict standards . . . and related obedience to eternal rewards and punishments" (Empey, 1982:55). By the nineteenth century, however, life in the United States underwent dramatic change with the rise of industrialization and urbanization. Foreign immigration and rural-urban migration increased the size of city populations and people were concentrated under conditions of considerably poverty in urban slums. Under these circumstances, the social controls characteristic of traditional community arrangements were less effective in regulating deviant behavior. Middle-class Protestant Americans were increasingly troubled by these changes and were concerned that immigrant and lower class families were failing their children (Binder et al., 1988).

Institutional confinement emerged as the preferred method of dealing with both youthful and adult offenders, replacing earlier methods of swift corporal punishment such as "public whippings, confinement in stocks or pillories, forms of mutiliation such as cropping the ears, [and] . . . death" (Binder et al., 1988:209). Incarceration was considered a progressive and humane alternative to the brutality of earlier methods, and for the first time special places of confinement for juveniles were created in *Houses of Refuge*. Reformers supported Houses of Refuge in order to prevent children from being exposed to the corrupting influence of adult criminals.

The first Houses of Refuge appeared in New York and Philadelphia in the 1820s and were designed not just for youthful criminals, but for a variety of problem children including runaways, vagrants, and other disobedient youth who were vulnerable to the corruption of urban life (Binder et al., 1988; Empey, 1982). As such, Houses of Refuge became institutions designed to induce ungracious and unruly lower class children to conform to the niceties of the "ideal child" (Schlossman, 1977). They operated on the basis of strict discipline, hard work, and "tight daily schedules, with regular hours for rising and retiring, meals at set times, and regular periods set aside for workshop training, . . . schooling . . . [and] religious observances and prayers" (Binder et al., 1988:211; Bremner, 1970).

By the mid-nineteenth century, however, Houses of Refuges, along with orphan asylums, began to be perceived as prison-like warehouses that often bred rather than prevented criminality. Reformers were also critical of the use of corporal punishment in these institutions, and began to look for alternative methods of reforming problem children. One of the most important of the new inventions was the *cottage system*. First introduced in Massachusetts and Ohio in the 1850s, the cottage system placed juveniles in small family-like environments from one to three dozen occupants under the supervision of a surrogate parent. The cottage system was believed to be superior to more congregate systems of confinement because they provided closer and presumably higher quality supervision (Binder et al., 1988).

The modern system of juvenile justice and the juvenile court was, of course, the most significant event in the development of alternative institutional approaches to the problem of delinquency. The first two readings in this section of the book address this new institutional mechanism. Both authors, Anthony Platt in "The Child-Saving Movement and the Origins of the Juvenile Justice System" (Chapter 1) and Ellen Ryerson in "The Ideal Juvenile Court" (Chapter 2), connect the development of the juvenile justice system to the *Progressive Era* of late nineteenth and early twentieth century United States. Progressivism is generally associated with a liberal political movement designed to clean up some of the problems and injustices associated with the early stages of industrialization and urbanization. As Siegal and Senna (1988:371) write:

> The Progressive Era was marked by a great deal of social change prompted by appeals to the conscience of the nation. Reformers were shocked by exposés of how society treated its less fortunate members. They were particularly concerned about what was going on in prisons and mental institutions. The poor, ill, and unfortunate were living in squalor, beaten, and mistreated by their 'keepers.' Progressive reformers lobbied legislators and appealed to public opinion in order to force better conditions. Their efforts helped establish the probation and parole system and other liberal correctional reforms (see Rothman, 1980).

Within the social science community, debate has occurred over whether Progressivism was in fact a movement of humanitarian reform, or whether it was a means by which dominant groups in the United States began to consolidate their economic and political power and attempt to regulate people and social practices that threatened the orderly transition of society from a competitive "laissez-faire" capitalist system to an economy increasingly dominated by large powerful corporations. In the first reading, Platt argues that the juvenile justice reforms associated with the "child-saving" movement "tried to do for the criminal justice system what industrialists and corporate leaders were trying to do for the economy—that is, achieve order, stability, and control while preserving the existing class system and distribution of wealth." Platt believes that the child-saving reformers could not have succeeded "without the financial and political support of the wealthy and powerful." He suggests that the informality associated with the new juvenile court system was a means by which the state expanded its jurisdiction over an increasing number of juveniles without providing them with constitutional due process protections against unfair governmental intrusion in their lives. According to the doctrine of *parens patriae,* adopted from English common law, the state could act in the "best interests" of children and take control of their lives before any serious crime occurred.[1] Importantly, the new system of juvenile justice established many status offenses, behaviors that were illegal only because the individual was under a certain age (typically eighteen). Juveniles could now be held in violation of the law for offenses such as truancy, drinking alcohol, running away from home, and curfew violations, as well as for vague transgressions such as immoral behavior and being incorrigible or habitually disobedient.

Platt's interpretation of the developing juvenile justice system utilizes a *conflict theory* of society. According to conflict theory, society is divided into conflicting groups, and the group that holds the economic power is also able to "control the law and the agencies that administer" the law (Siegal and Senna, 1988:198; Turk, 1966). Moreover, the "law is differentially administered to favor the rich and powerful and control the have-not members of society" (p. 198). Thus, according to conflict theory, the new juvenile justice system directed its control functions primarily against the less privileged (i.e., lower- and working-class) youth of society. Similarly, a *Marxian* version of conflict theory emphasizes group conflicts associated with the antagonism between the capitalist class, which owns and controls the major means of economic production, and the working class, which labors for and is exploited by the capitalist class (Quinney, 1977). Platt believes that the juvenile justice reforms were in part a means of "preparing youth as a disciplined and devoted work force" that would promote the expansion of corporate capitalism in the United States.

In the second reading in this section, Ryerson recognizes limitations of the early juvenile court reforms, but is more positive than Platt about the genuineness of the child-savers' humanitarian desire to help children and prevent crime through a program of individualized treatment, family revitalization, and probation rather than incarceration. In her view, a more balanced interpretation of the rise of the juvenile justice system recognizes its "inherently double nature." While some aspects "appear 'conservative' because they emphasized social control, . . . other aspects appear 'reformist' because they emphasized the rehabilitative ideal and found new ways to pursue it."[2]

Both Platt and Ryerson discuss juvenile delinquency as a social construction. Both recognize that a number of historical changes and social preconditions had to occur before society was able to identify a distinct category of individuals who were "delinquent" and who were deemed appropriate for processing through a separate system of juvenile justice. In the field of sociology, the concept of delinquency as a social construction has been understood in terms of *labeling theory.* According to labeling theory, deviance is not a property inherent to any particular act. Rather "social groups create deviance by making the rules whose infraction constitutes deviance, and by applying those rules to particular people and labeling them as outsiders" (Becker, 1963:9). Moreover, negative labeling of juveniles by authorities stigmatizes youth, facilitates the development of a delinquent self-image, and results in a self-fulfilling prophecy whereby an initial pattern of rule-violation (primary deviance) is transformed into a stable pattern of rule-violation (secondary deviance) (Lemert, 1951; Schur, 1971; Tannenbaum, 1938).

In the third reading in this section (Chapter 3), William Chambliss' "The Saints and the Roughnecks" illustrates how processes of societal labeling and differential selection practices operate in contemporary times. In his observational study, Chambliss describes the behaviors of two groups of boys from different class backgrounds. He notes how the delinquency of one group was ignored by authorities while the delinquency of the other group brought forth community condemnation. His analysis illustrates how the delinquent careers and "outsider" status of some individuals are produced by societal labeling, while the non-delinquent careers and "law-abiding" status of others are maintained through avoidance of such labeling.[3]

Notes

1. Literally *parens patriae* means "the state is the father." The doctrine goes back to the Middle Ages when the King invoked his power to protect the inheritance rights of children and when the state asserted the right to assume wardship of children when "the natural parents or testamentary guardians were adjudged unfit to perform their duties" (Binder et al., 1988:213).

2. See Hagan and Leon (1977) for a critique of Platt's interpretation.

3. Additional empirical literature on the effects of juvenile justice labeling will be considered in the conclusion of this book.

References

Aries, P. 1962. *Centuries of Childhood.* Translated by R. Baldick. New York: Knopf.

Becker, H.S. 1963. *Outsiders: Studies in the Sociology of Deviance.* New York: Free Press.

Binder, A., G. Geis, and D. Bruce. 1988. *Juvenile Delinquency: Historical, Cultural, Legal Perspectives.* New York: Macmillan.

Bremner, R.H. (ed.). 1970. *Children and Youth in America: A Documentary History.* Cambridge: Harvard University Press.

Empey, L.T. 1982. *American Delinquency: Its Meaning and Construction.* Second edition. Homewood, IL: Dorsey.

Gillis, J.R. 1974. *Youth and History.* New York: Academic Press.

Hagan, J. and L. Leon. 1977. ''Rediscovering delinquency: Social history, political ideology and the sociology of law.'' *American Sociological Review* 42:587–98.

Hall, G.S. 1905. *Adolescence: Its Psychology and Its Relationship to Physiology, Anthropology, Sociology, Sex, Crime, Religion, and Education.* New York: Appleton.

Lemert, E.M. 1951. *Social Pathology.* New York: McGraw-Hill.

Mause, L. 1974. *The History of Childhood.* New York: Psychohistory Press.

Quinney, R. 1977. *Class, State, and Crime.* New York: McKay.

Rothman, D. 1980. *Conscience and Convenience.* Boston: Little, Brown.

Schlossman, S.L. 1977. *Love and the American Delinquent.* Chicago: University of Chicago Press.

Schur, E. M. 1971. *Labeling Deviant Behavior: Its Sociological Implications.* New York: Harper and Row.

Siegel, L.J. and J.J. Senna. 1988. *Juvenile Delinquency: Theory, Practice, and Law.* Third edition. St. Paul, MN: West.

Tannenbaum, F. 1938. *Crime and the Community.* New York: Columbia University Press.

Thornton, W.E., L. Voigt, and W.G. Doerner. 1987. *Delinquency and Justice.* Second edition. New York: Random House.

Turk, A.T. 1966. ''Conflict and criminality.'' *American Sociological Review* 31:338–52.

The Child-Saving Movement and the Origins of the Juvenile Justice System

1

Anthony Platt

Traditional Perspectives on Juvenile Justice

The modern system of crime control in the United States has many roots in penal and judicial reforms at the end of the nineteenth century. Contemporary programs which we commonly associate with the "war on poverty" and the "great society" [of the 1960s] can be traced in numerous instances to the programs and ideas of nineteenth century reformers who helped to create and develop probation and parole, the juvenile court, strategies of crime prevention, the need for education and rehabilitative programs in institutions, the indeterminate sentence, the concept of "half-way" houses, and "cottage" systems of penal organization.

The creation of the juvenile court and its accompanying services is generally regarded by scholars as one of the most inno-

From "The Triumph of Benevolence: The Origins of the Juvenile Justice System in the United States," in Richard Quinney (ed.), *Criminal Justice in America* (Boston: Little, Brown, 1974), pp. 362–383. Reprinted by permission of the author.

vative and idealistic products of the age of reform. It typified the "spirit of social justice," and, according to the National Crime Commission, represented a progressive effort by concerned reformers to alleviate the miseries of urban life and to solve social problems by rational, enlightened and scientific methods.[1] The juvenile justice system was widely heralded as "one of the greatest advances in child welfare that has ever occurred" and "an integral part of total welfare planning."[2] Charles Chute, an enthusiastic supporter of the child-saving movement, claimed that "no single event has contributed more to the welfare of children and their families. It revolutionized the treatment of delinquent and neglected children and led to the passage of similar laws throughout the world."[3] Scholars from a variety of disciplines, such as the American sociologist George Herbert Mead and the German psychiatrist August Aichhorn, agreed that the juvenile court system represented a triumph of progressive liberalism over the forces of reaction and ignorance.[4] More recently, the juvenile court and related reforms have been characterized as a "reflection of the humanitarianism that flowered in the last decades of the 19th century''[5] and an indication of ''America's great sense of philanthropy and private concern about the common weal.''[6]

Histories and accounts of the child-saving movement tend either to represent an "official" perspective or to imply a gradualist view of social progress.[7] This latter view is typified in Robert Pickett's study of the House of Refuge movement in New York in the middle of the last century:

> In the earlier era, it had taken a band of largely religiously motivated humanitarians to see a need and move to meet that need. Although much of their vision eventually would be supplanted by more enlightened policies and techniques and far more elaborate support mechanisms, the main outlines of their program, which included mild discipline, academic and moral education, vocational training, the utilization of surrogate parents, and probationary surveillance, have stood the test of time. The survival of many of the notions of the founders of the House of Refuge testifies, at least in part, to their creative genius in meeting human needs. Their motivations may have been mixed and their oversights many, but their efforts contributed to a considerable advance in the care and treatment of wayward youth.[8]

This view of the nineteenth century reform movement as fundamentally benevolent, humanitarian and gradualist is shared by most historians and criminologists who have written about the Progressive era. They argue that this reform impulse has its roots in the earliest ideals of modern liberalism and that it is part of a continuing struggle to overcome injustice and fulfill the promise of American life.[9] At the same time, these writers recognize that reform movements often degenerate into crusades and suffer from excessive idealism and

moral absolutism.[10] The faults and limitations of the child-saving movement, for example, are generally explained in terms of the psychological tendency of its leaders to adopt attitudes of rigidity and moral righteousness. But this form of criticism is misleading because it overlooks larger political issues and depends too much on a subjective critique.

Although the Progressive era was a period of considerable change and reform in all areas of social, legal, political and economic life, its history has been garnished with various myths. Conventional historical analysis, typified by the work of American historians in the 1940s and 1950s, promoted the view that American history consisted of regular confrontations between vested economic interests and various popular reform movements.[11] For Arthur Schlesinger, Jr., "liberalism in America has been ordinarily the movement of the other sections of society to restrain the power of the business community."[12]

. . . Conventional histories of progressivism argue that the reformers, who were for the most part drawn from the urban middle classes, were opposed to big business and felt victimized by the rapid changes in the economy, especially the emergence of the corporation as the dominant form of financial enterprise.[13] Their reform efforts were aimed at curbing the power of big business, eliminating corruption from the urban political machines, and extending the powers of the state through federal regulation of the economy and the development of a vision of "social responsibility" in local government. They were joined in this mission by sectors of the working class who shared their alienation and many of their grievances.

. . . The political and racial crises of the 1960s, however, provoked a reevaluation of this earlier view of the liberal tradition in

American politics, a tradition which appeared bankrupt in the face of rising crime rates, ghetto rebellions, and widespread protests against the state and its agencies of criminal justice. In the field of criminology, this reevaluation took place in national commissions such as the Kerner Commission and President Johnson's Commission on Law Enforcement and the Administration of Justice. Johnson's Crime Commission, as it is known, included a lengthy and detailed analysis of the juvenile justice system and its ineffectiveness in dealing with juvenile delinquency.

The Crime Commission's view of the juvenile justice system is cautious and pragmatic, designed to "shore up" institutional deficiencies and modernize the system's efficiency and accountability. Noting the rising rate of juvenile delinquency, increasing disrespect for constituted authority and the failure of reformatories to rehabilitate offenders, the Commission attributes the failures of the juvenile justice system to the "grossly overoptimistic" expectations of nineteenth century reformers and the "community's continuing unwillingness to provide the resources—the people and facilities and concern—necessary to permit [the juvenile courts] to realize their potential. . . ."[14]

. . . In the following pages we will argue that the above views and interpretations of juvenile justice are factually inaccurate and suffer from a serious misconception about the functions of modern liberalism. The prevailing myths about the juvenile justice system can be summarized as follows: (1) The child-saving movement in the late nineteenth century was successful in humanizing the criminal justice system, rescuing children from jails and prisons, developing humanitarian judicial and penal institutions for juveniles, and defending the poor against economic and political exploitation. (2) The

child-savers were "disinterested" reformers, representing an enlightened and socially responsible urban middle class, and opposed to big business. (3) The failures of the juvenile justice system are attributable partly to the overoptimism and moral absolutism of earlier reformers and partly to bureaucratic inefficiency and a lack of fiscal resources and trained personnel.

These myths are grounded in a liberal conception of American history which characterizes the child-savers as part of a much larger reform movement directed at restraining the power of political and business elites. In contrast, we will offer evidence that the child-saving movement was a coercive and conservatizing influence, that liberalism in the Progressive era was the conscious product of policies initiated or supported by leaders of major corporations and financial institutions, and that many social reformers wanted to secure existing political and economic arrangements, albeit in an ameliorated and regulated form.

The Child-Saving Movement

Although the modern juvenile justice system can be traced in part to the development of various charitable and institutional programs in the early nineteenth century,[15] it was not until the close of the century that the modern system was systematically organized to include juvenile courts, probation, child guidance clinics, truant officers, and reformatories. The child-saving movement—an amalgam of philanthropists, middle-class reformers and professionals—was responsible for the consolidation of these reforms.[16]

The 1890s represented for many middle-class intellectuals and professionals a period of discovery of "dim attics and damp cellars in poverty-stricken sections of populous towns" and "innumerable haunts of misery throughout the land.''[17] The city was suddenly discovered to be a place of scarcity, disease, neglect, ignorance, and ''dangerous influences.'' Its slums were the ''last resorts of the penniless and the criminal''; here humanity reached the lowest level of degradation and despair.[18] These conditions were not new to American urban life and the working class had been suffering such hardships for many years. Since the Haymarket Riot of 1886, the centers of industrial activity had been continually plagued by strikes, violent disruptions, and widespread business failures.

What distinguished the late 1890s from earlier periods was the recognition by some sectors of the privileged classes that far-reaching economic, political and social reforms were desperately needed to restore order and stability. In the economy, these reforms were achieved through the corporation which extended its influence into all aspects of domestic and foreign policies so that by the 1940s some 139 corporations owned 45 percent of all the manufacturing assets in the country. It was the aim of corporate capitalists to limit traditional laissez-faire business competition and to transform the economy into a rational and interrelated system, characterized by extensive long-range planning and bureaucratic routine.[19] In politics, these reforms were achieved nationally by extending the regulatory powers of the federal government and locally by the development of commission and city manager forms of government as an antidote to corrupt machine politics. In social life, economic and political reforms were paralleled by the construction of new social service bureaucracies which regulated crime, education, health, labor and welfare.

The child-saving movement tried to do for the criminal justice system what industrialists and corporate leaders were trying to do for the economy—that is, achieve order, stability and control while preserving the existing class system and distribution of wealth. While the child-saving movement, like most Progressive reforms, drew its most active and visible supporters from the middle class and professions, it would not have been capable of achieving significant reforms without the financial and political support of the wealthy and powerful. Such support was not without precedent in various philanthropic movements preceding the child-savers. New York's Society for the Reformation of Juvenile Delinquents benefited in the 1820s from the contributions of Stephen Allen, whose many influential positions included Mayor of New York and president of the New York Life Insurance and Trust Company.[20] The first large gift to the New York Children's Aid Society, founded in 1853, was donated by Mrs. William Astor.[21] According to Charles Loring Brace, who helped to found the Children's Aid Society, ''a very superior class of young men consented to serve on our Board of Trustees; men who, in their high principles of duty, and in the obligations which they feel are imposed by wealth and position, bid fair hereafter to make the name of New York merchants respected as it was never before throughout the country.''[22] Elsewhere, welfare charities similarly benefited from the donations and wills of the upper class.[23] Girard College, one of the first large orphanages in the United States, was built and furnished with funds from the banking fortune of Stephen Girard,[24] and the Catholic bankers and financiers of New York helped to mobilize support and money for various Catholic charities.[25]

The child-saving movement similarly enjoyed the support of propertied and powerful individuals. In Chicago, for example, where the movement had some of its most notable successes, the child-savers included Louise Bowen and Ellen Henrotin who were both married to bankers.[26] Mrs. Potter Palmer, whose husband owned vast amounts of land and property, was an ardent child-saver when not involved in the exclusive Fortnightly Club, the elite Chicago Woman's Club or the Board of Lady Managers of the World's Fair;[27] another child-saver in Chicago, Mrs. Perry Smith, was married to the vice-president of the Chicago and Northwestern Railroad. Even the more radically-minded child-savers came from upper-class backgrounds. The fathers of Jane Addams and Julia Lathrop, for example, were both lawyers and Republican senators in the Illinois legislature. Jane Addams' father was one of the richest men in northern Illinois, and her step-brother, Harry Haldeman, was a socialite from Baltimore who later amassed a large fortune in Kansas City.[28]

The child-saving movement was not simply a humanistic enterprise on behalf of the lower classes against the established order. On the contrary, its impetus came primarily from the middle and upper classes who were instrumental in devising new forms of social control to protect their privileged positions in American society. The child-saving movement was not an isolated phenomenon but rather reflected massive changes in productive relationships, from laissez-faire to monopoly capitalism, and in strategies of social control, from inefficient repression to welfare state benevolence.[29] This reconstruction of economic and social institutions, which was not achieved without conflict within the ruling class, represented a victory for the more "enlightened" wing of corporate leaders who advocated strategic alliances with urban reformers and support of liberal reforms.[30]

Many large corporations and business leaders, for example, supported federal regulation of the economy in order to protect their own investments and stabilize the marketplace. Business leaders and political spokesmen were often in basic agreement about fundamental economic issues. . . . "Few reforms were enacted without the tacit approval, if not the guidance, of the large corporate interests." For the corporation executives, liberalism meant "the responsibility of all classes to maintain and increase the efficiency of the existing social order."[31]

Progressivism was in part a businessmen's movement and big business played a central role in the Progressive coalition's support of welfare reforms. Child labor legislation in New York, for example, was supported by several groups, including upper-class industrialists who did not depend on cheap child labor. According to Jeremy Felt's history of that movement, "the abolition of child labor could be viewed as a means of driving out marginal manufacturers and tenement operators, hence increasing the consolidation and efficiency of business."[32] The rise of compulsory education, another welfare state reform, was also closely tied to the changing forms of industrial production and social control. Charles Loring Brace, writing in the mid-nineteenth century, anticipated the use of education as preparation for industrial discipline when, "in the interests of public order, of liberty, of property, for the sake of our own safety and the endurance of free institutions here," he advocated "a strict and careful law, which shall compel every minor to learn and read and write, under severe penalties in case of disobedience."[33] By the end of the century, the working class had imposed upon them a sterile and authoritarian educational system which mirrored the ethos of the corporate workplace and was designed to provide "an increasingly refined training and selection mechanism for the labor force."[34]

While the child-saving movement was supported and financed by corporate liberals, the day-to-day work of lobbying, public education and organizing was undertaken by middle-class urban reformers, professionals and special interest groups. The more moderate and conservative sectors of the feminist movement were especially active in anti-delinquency reforms.[35] Their successful participation derived in part from public stereotypes of women as the "natural caretakers" of "wayward children." Women's claim to the public care of children had precedent during the nineteenth century and their role in child rearing was paramount. Women, generally regarded as better teachers than men, were more influential in child-training and discipline at home. The fact that public education also came more under the direction of women teachers in the schools served to legitimize the predominance of women in other areas of "child-saving."[36]

The child-saving movement attracted women from a variety of political and class backgrounds, though it was dominated by the daughters of the old landed gentry and wives of the upper-class nouveau riche. Career women and society philanthropists, elite women's clubs and settlement houses, and political and civic organizations worked together on the problems of child care, education and juvenile delinquency. Professional and political women's groups regarded child-saving as a problem of women's rights, whereas their opponents seized upon it as an opportunity to keep women in their "proper place." Child-saving became a reputable task for any woman who wanted to extend her "housekeeping" functions into the community without denying anti-feminist stereotypes of woman's nature and place.[37]

For traditionally educated women and daughters of the landed and industrial gentry, the child-saving movement presented an opportunity for pursuing socially acceptable public roles and for restoring some of the authority and spiritual influence which many women felt they had lost through the urbanization of family life. Their traditional functions were dramatically threatened by the weakening of domestic roles and the specialized rearrangement of the family.[38] The child-savers were aware that their championship of social outsiders such as immigrants, the poor and children, was not wholly motivated by disinterested ideals of justice and equality. Philanthropic work filled a void in their own lives, a void which was created in part by the decline of traditional religion, increased leisure and boredom, the rise of public education, and the breakdown of communal life in large, crowded cities. "By simplifying dress and amusements, by cutting off a little here and there from our luxuries," wrote one child-saver, "we may change the whole current of many human lives."[39] Women were exhorted to make their lives useful by participating in welfare programs, by volunteering their time and services, and by getting acquainted with less privileged groups. They were also encouraged to seek work in institutions which were "like family-life with its many-sided development and varied interests and occupations, and where the woman-element shall pervade the house and soften its social atmosphere with motherly tenderness."[40]

While the child-saving movement can be partly understood as a "symbolic crusade"[41] which served ceremonial and status functions for many women, it was by no means a reactionary and romantic movement, nor was it supported only by women and members of the old gentry. Child-saving also had considerable instrumental significance for legitimizing new career openings for women. The new role of social worker combined elements of an old and partly fictitious role—defender of family life—and elements of a new role—social servant. Social work and professional child-saving provided new opportunities for career-minded women who found the traditional professions dominated and controlled by men.[42] These child-savers were members of the emerging bourgeoisie created by the new industrial order.

It is not surprising that the professions also supported the child-saving movement, for they were capable of reaping enormous economic and status rewards from the changes taking place. The clergy had nothing to lose (but more of their rapidly declining constituency) and everything to gain by incorporating social services into traditional religion. Lawyers were needed for their technical expertise and to administer new institutions. And academics discovered a new market which paid them as consultants, elevated them to positions of national prestige and furnished endless materials for books, articles and conferences.

. . . While the rank and file reformers in the child-saving movement worked closely with corporate liberals, it would be inaccurate to simply characterize them as lackeys of big business. Many were principled and genuinely concerned about alleviating human misery and improving the lives of the poor. Moreover, many women who participated in the movement were able to free themselves from male domination and participate more fully in society. But for the most part, the child-savers and other Progressive reformers defended capitalism and rejected socialist alternatives. Most reformers accepted the structure of the new industrial order and sought to moderate its cruder inequities and reduce inharmonies in the existing system.[48] Though many child-savers were "socialists of the heart"

and ardent critics of society, their programs were typically reformist and did not alter basic economic inequalities.[44] Rhetoric and righteous indignation were more prevalent than programs of radical action.

Images of Crime and Delinquency

. . . The child-savers viewed the "criminal classes" with a mixture of contempt and benevolence. Crime was portrayed as rising from the "lowest orders" and threatening to engulf "respectable" society like a virulent disease. Charles Loring Brace, a leading child-saver, typified popular and professional views about crime and delinquency:

> As Christian men, we cannot look upon this great multitude of unhappy, deserted, and degraded boys and girls without feeling our responsibility to God for them. The class increases: immigration is pouring in its multitudes of poor foreigners who leave these young outcasts everywhere in our midst. These boys and girls . . . will soon form the great lower class of our city. They will influence elections; they may shape the policy of the city; they will assuredly, if unreclaimed, poison society all around them. They will help to form the great multitude of robbers, thieves, and vagrants, who are now such a burden upon the law-respecting community. . . .[45]

This attitude of contempt derived from a view of criminals as less-than-human, a perspective which was strongly influenced and aggravated by nativist and racist ideologies.[46] The "criminal class" was variously described as "creatures" living in "burrows," "dens," and "slime"; as "little Arabs" and "foreign childhood that floats along the streets and docks of the city—vagabondish, thievish, familiar with the vicious ways and places of the town";[47]

and as "ignorant," "shiftless," "indolent," and "dissipated."[48]

The child-savers were alarmed and frightened by the "dangerous classes" whose "very number makes one stand aghast," noted the urban reformer Jacob Riis.[49] Law and order were widely demanded:

> The "dangerous classes" of New York are mainly American-born, but the children of Irish and German immigrants. They are as ignorant as London flashmen or costermongers. They are far more brutal than the peasantry from whom they descend, and they are much banded together, in associations, such as "Dead Rabbit," "Plug-ugly," and various target companies. They are our *enfant perdus,* grown up to young manhood. . . . They are ready for any offense or crime, however degraded or bloody. . . . Let but Law lift its hand from them for a season, or let the civilizing influences of American life fail to reach them, and, if the opportunity offered, we should see an explosion from this class which might leave this city in ashes and blood.[50]

These views derived considerable legitimacy from prevailing theories of social and reform Darwinism which . . . proposed that criminals were a dangerous and atavistic class, standing outside the boundaries of morally regulated relationships. Herbert Spencer's writings had a major impact on American intellectuals and Cesare Lombroso, perhaps the most significant figure in nineteenth century criminology, looked for recognition in the United States when he felt that his experiments on the "criminal type" had been neglected in Europe.[51]

Although Lombroso's theoretical and experimental studies were not translated into English until 1911, his findings were known by American academics in the early 1890s, and their popularity, like that of Spencer's

works, was based on the fact that they confirmed widely-held stereotypes about the biological basis and inferior character of a "criminal class." A typical view was expressed by Nathan Allen in 1878 at the National Conference of Charities and Correction: "If our object is to prevent crime in a large scale, we must direct attention to its main sources—to the materials that make criminals; the springs must be dried up; the supplies must be cut off."[52] This was to be achieved, if necessary, by birth control and eugenics. Similar views were expressed by Hamilton Wey, an influential physician at Elmira Reformatory, who argued before the National Prison Association in 1881 that criminals had to be treated as a "distinct type of human species."[53]

Literature on "social degradation" was extremely popular during the 1870s and 1880s, though most such "studies" were little more than crude and racist polemics, padded with moralistic epithets and preconceived value judgments. Richard Dugdale's series of papers on the Jukes family, which became a model for the case-study approach to social problems, was distorted almost beyond recognition by anti-intellectual supporters of hereditary theories of crime.[54] Confronted by the evidence of Darwin, Galton, Dugdale, Caldwell and many other disciples of the biological image of behavior, many child-savers were compelled to admit that "a large proportion of the unfortunate children that go to make up the great army of criminals are not born right."[55] Reformers adopted and modified the rhetoric of social Darwinism in order to emphasize the urgent need for confronting the "crime problem" before it got completely out of hand. A popular proposal, for example, was the "methodized registration and training" of potential criminals, "or these failing, their early and entire withdrawal from the community."[56]

Although some child-savers advocated drastic methods of crime control—including birth control through sterilization, cruel punishments, and life-long incarceration—more moderate views prevailed. This victory for moderation was related to the recognition by many Progressive reformers that short-range repression was counter-productive as well as cruel and that long-range planning and amelioration were required to achieve economic and political stability. The rise of more benevolent strategies of social control occurred at about the same time that influential capitalists were realizing that existing economic arrangements could not be successfully maintained only through the use of private police and government troops.[57] While the child-savers justified their reforms as humanitarian, it is clear that this humanitarianism reflected their class background and elitist conceptions of human potentiality. The child-savers shared the view of more conservative professionals that "criminals" were a distinct and dangerous class, indigenous to working-class culture, and a threat to "civilized" society. They differed mainly in the procedures by which the "criminal class" should be controlled or neutralized.

Gradually, a more "enlightened" view about strategies of control prevailed among the leading representatives of professional associations. Correctional workers, for example, did not want to think of themselves merely as the custodians of a pariah class. The self-image of penal reformers as "doctors" rather than "guards," and the medical domination of criminological research in the United States at that time facilitated the acceptance of "therapeutic" strategies in prisons and reformatories.[58] Physicians gradually provided the official rhetoric of penal reform, replacing cruder concepts of social Darwinism with a new optimism.

Admittedly, the criminal was "pathological" and "diseased," but medical science offered the possibility of miraculous cures. Although there was a popular belief in the existence of a "criminal class" separated from the rest of humanity by a "vague boundary line," there was no good reason why this class could not be identified, diagnosed, segregated, changed and incorporated back into society.[59]

By the late 1890s, most child-savers agreed that hereditary theories of crime were overfatalistic. The superintendent of the Kentucky Industrial School of Reform, for example, told delegates to a national conference on corrections that heredity is "unjustifiably made a bugaboo to discourage efforts at rescue. We know that physical heredity tendencies can be neutralized and often nullified by proper counteracting precautions."[60] E. R. L. Gould, a sociologist at the University of Chicago, similarly criticized biological theories of crime as unconvincing and sentimental. "Is it not better," he said, "to postulate freedom of choice than to preach the doctrine of the unfettered will, and so elevate criminality into a propitiary sacrifice?"[61]

Charles Cooley, writing in 1896, was one of the first American sociologists to observe that criminal behavior depended as much upon social and economic circumstances as it did upon the inheritance of biological traits. "The criminal class," he observed, "is largely the result of society's bad workmanship upon fairly good material." In support of this argument, he noted that there was a "large and fairly trustworthy body of evidence" to suggest that many "degenerates" could be converted into "useful citizens by rational treatment."[62]

Although there was a wide difference of opinion among experts as to the precipitating causes of crime, it was generally agreed that criminals were abnormally conditioned

by a multitude of biological and environmental forces, some of which were permanent and irreversible. Strictly biological
theories of crime were modified to incorporate a developmental view of human behavior. If, as it was believed, criminals are
conditioned by biological heritage and
brutish living conditions, then prophylactic
measures must be taken early in life. "We
must get hold of the little waifs that grow up
to form the criminal element just as early in
life as possible," exhorted an influential
child-saver. "Hunt up the children of poverty, of crime, and of brutality, just as soon
as they can be reached."[63] Efforts were
needed to reach the criminals of future generations." They are born to crime," wrote
the penologist Enoch Wines, "brought up
for it. They must be saved."[64] New institutions and new programs were required to
meet this challenge.

Juvenile Court and the Reformatory System

The essential preoccupation of the child-
saving movement was the recognition and
control of youthful deviance. It brought attention to, and thus "invented" new categories of youthful misbehavior which had
been hitherto unappreciated. The efforts of
the child-savers were institutionally expressed in the juvenile court which, despite
recent legislative and constitutional reforms, is generally acknowledged as their
most significant contribution to progressive
penology. There is some dispute about
which state first created a special tribunal
for children. Massachusetts and New York
passed laws, in 1874 and 1892 respectively, providing for the trials of minors
apart from adults charged with crimes. Ben
Lindsey, a renowned judge and reformer,
also claimed this distinction for Colorado
where a juvenile court was, in effect, estab-

lished through an educational law of 1899.
However, most authorities agree that the
Juvenile Court Act, passed by the Illinois
legislature in the same year, was the first
official enactment to be recognized as a
model statute by other states and countries.[65] By 1917, juvenile court legislation
had been passed in all but three states and
by 1932 there were over 600 independent
juvenile courts throughout the United
States.[66]

The juvenile court system was part of a
general movement directed towards developing a specialized labor market and industrial discipline under corporate capitalism
by creating new programs of adjudication
and control for "delinquent," "dependent" and "neglected" youth. This in turn
was related to augmenting the family and
enforcing compulsory education in order to
guarantee the proper reproduction of the labor force. For example, underlying the juvenile court system was the concept of
parens patriae by which the courts were authorized to handle with wide discretion the
problems of "its least fortunate junior citizens."[67] The administration of juvenile justice, which differed in many important respects from the criminal court system, was
delegated extensive powers of control over
youth. A child was not accused of a crime
but offered assistance and guidance; intervention in the lives of "delinquents" was
not supposed to carry the stigma of criminal
guilt. Judicial records were not generally
available to the press or public, and juvenile hearings were typically conducted in
private. Court procedures were informal
and inquisitorial, not requiring the presence of a defense attorney. Specific criminal safeguards of due process were not applicable because juvenile proceedings were
defined by statute as civil in character.[68]

The judges of the new court were em-
powered to investigate the character and so-

cial background of "predelinquent" as well as delinquent children; they concerned themselves with motivation rather than intent, seeking to identify the moral reputation of problematic children. The requirements of preventive penology and child-saving further justified the court's intervention in cases where no offense had actually been committed, but where, for example, a child was posing problems for some person in authority, such as a parent or teacher or social worker.

The role model for juvenile court judges was doctor-counselor rather than lawyer. "Judicial therapists" were expected to establish a one-to-one relationship with "delinquents" in the same way that a country doctor might give his time and attention to a favorite patient. Juvenile courtrooms were often arranged like a clinic and the vocabulary of its participants was largely composed of medical metaphors. "We do not know the child without a thorough examination," wrote Judge Julian Mack. "We must reach into the soul-life of the child."[69] Another judge from Los Angeles suggested that the juvenile court should be a "laboratory of human behavior" and its judges trained as "specialists in the art of human relations." It was the judge's task to "get the whole truth about a child" in the same way that a "physician searches for every detail that bears on the condition of the patient."[70] Similarly, the judges of the Boston juvenile court liked to think of themselves as "physicians in a dispensary."[71]

The unique character of the child-saving movement was its concerns for predelinquent offenders—"children who occupy the debatable ground between criminality and innocence"—and its claim that it could transform potential criminals into respectable citizens by training them in "habits of industry, self-control and obedience to law."[72] This policy justified the diminish-

ing of traditional procedures and allowed police, judges, probation officers and truant officers to work together without legal hindrance. If children were to be rescued, it was important that the rescuers be free to pursue their mission without the interference of defense lawyers and due process. Delinquents had to be saved, transformed and reconstituted. "There is no essential difference," noted a prominent child-saver, "between a criminal and any other sinner. The means and methods of restoration are the same for both."[73]

The juvenile court legislation enabled the state to investigate and control a wide variety of behaviors. As Joel Handler has observed, "the critical philosophical position of the reform movement was that no formal, legal distinctions should be made between the delinquent and the dependent or neglected."[74] Statutory definitions of "delinquency" encompassed (1) acts that would be criminal if committed by adults; (2) acts that violated county, town, or municipal ordinances; and (3) violations of vaguely worded catch-alls—such as "vicious or immoral behavior," "incorrigibility," and "truancy"—which "seem to express the notion that the adolescent, if allowed to continue, will engage in more serious conduct."[75]

The juvenile court movement went far beyond a concern for special treatment of adolescent offenders. It brought within the ambit of government control a set of youthful activities that had been previously ignored or dealt with on an informal basis. It was not by accident that the behavior subject to penalties—drinking, sexual "license," roaming the streets, begging, frequenting dance halls and movies, fighting, and being seen in public late at night—was especially characteristic of the children of working-class and immigrant families. Once arrested and adjudicated, these "delinquents" became wards of the court and eligible for salvation.

It was through the reformatory system that the child-savers hoped to demonstrate that delinquents were capable of being converted into law-abiding citizens. Though the reformatory was initially developed in the United States during the middle of the nineteenth century as a special form of prison discipline for adolescents and young adults, its underlying principles were formulated in Britain by Matthew Davenport Hill, Alexander Maconochie, Walter Crofton and Mary Carpenter. If the United States did not have any great penal theorists, it at least had energetic administrators—like Enoch Wines, Zebulon Brockway and Frank Sanborn—who were prepared to experiment with new programs.

The reformatory was distinguished from the traditional penitentiary in several ways: it adopted a policy of indeterminate sentencing; it emphasized the importance of a countryside location; and it typically was organized on the "cottage" plan as opposed to the traditional congregate housing found in penitentiaries. The ultimate aim of the reformatory was reformation of the criminal, which could only be achieved "by placing the prisoner's fate, as far as possible, in his own hand, by enabling him, through industry and good conduct to raise himself, step by step, to a position of less restraint. . . ."[76]

Based on a crude theory of rewards and punishments, the "new penology" set itself the task of re-socializing the "dangerous classes." The typical resident of a reformatory, according to one child-saver, had been "cradled in infamy, imbibing with its earliest natural nourishment the germs of a depraved appetite, and reared in the midst of people whose lives are an atrocious crime against natural and divine law and the rights of society." In order to correct and reform such a person, the reformatory plan was designed to teach the value of adjustment, private enterprise, thrift and self-reliance. "To make a good boy out of this bundle of perversities, his entire being must be revolutionized. He must be taught self-control, industry, respect for himself and the rights of others."[77] The real test of reformation in a delinquent, as William Letchworth told the National Conference of Charities and Correction in 1886, was his uncomplaining adjustment to his former environment. "If he is truly reformed in the midst of adverse influences," said Letchworth, "he gains that moral strength which makes his reform permanent."[78] Moreover, reformed delinquents were given every opportunity to rise "far above the class from which they sprang," especially if they were "patient" and "self-denying."[79]

Reformation of delinquents was to be achieved in a number of different ways. The trend from congregate housing to group living represented a significant change in the organization of penal institutions. The "cottage" plan was designed to provide more intensive supervision and to reproduce, symbolically at least, an atmosphere of family life conducive to the re-socialization of youth. The "new penology" also urged the benefits of a rural location, partly in order to teach agricultural skills, but mainly in order to guarantee a totally controlled environment. This was justified by appealing to the romantic theory that corrupt delinquents would be spiritually regenerated by their contact with unspoiled nature.[80]

Education was stressed as the main form of industrial and moral training in reformatories. According to Michael Katz, in his study on nineteenth-century education, the reformatory provided "the first form of compulsory schooling in the United States."[81] The prominence of education as a technique of reform reflected the widespread emphasis on socialization and assimilation instead of cruder methods of social control. But as Georg Rusche and Otto Kirchheimer observed in their study of the relationship between economic and penal policies, the rise of "rehabilitative" and educational programs was "largely the result of opposition on the part of free workers," for "wherever working-class organizations were powerful enough to influence state politics, they succeeded in obtaining complete abolition of all forms of prison labor (Pennsylvania in 1897, for example), causing much suffering to the prisoners, or at least in obtaining very considerable limitations, such as work without modern machinery, conventional rather than modern types of prison industry, or work for the government instead of for the free market."[82]

Although the reformatory system, as envisioned by urban reformers, suffered in practice from overcrowding, mismanagement, inadequate financing and staff hiring problems, its basic ideology was still tough-minded and uncompromising. As the American Friends Service Committee noted, "if the reformers were naive, the managers of the correctional establishment were not. Under the leadership of Zebulon R. Brockway of the Elmira Reformatory, by the latter part of the nineteenth century they had co-opted the reformers and consolidated their leadership and control of indeterminate sentence reform."[83] The child-savers were not averse to using corporal punishment and other severe disciplinary measures when inmates were recalcitrant. Brockway, for example, regarded his task

as "socialization of the anti-social by scientific training while under completest governmental control."[84] To achieve his goal, Brockway's reformatory became "like a garrison of a thousand prisoner soldiers" and "every incipient disintegration was promptly checked and disinclination of individual prisoners to conform was overcome."[85] Child-saving was a job for resolute professionals who realized that "sickly sentimentalism" had no place in their work.[86]

"Criminals shall either be cured," Brockway told the National Prison Congress in 1870, "or kept under such continued restraint as gives guarantee of safety from further depredations."[87] Restraint and discipline were an integral part of the "treatment" program and not merely expediencies of administration. Military drill, "training of the will," and long hours of tedious labor were the essence of the reformatory system and the indeterminate sentencing policy guaranteed its smooth operation. "Nothing can tend more certainly to secure the most hardened and desperate criminals than the present system of short sentences," wrote the reformer Bradford Kinney Peirce in 1869.[88] Several years later, Enoch Wines was able to report that "the sentences of young offenders are wisely regulated for their amendment; they are not absurdly shortened as if they signified only so much endurance of vindictive suffering."[89]

Since the child-savers professed to be seeking the "best interests" of their "wards" on the basis of corporate liberal values, there was no need to formulate legal regulation of the right and duty to "treat" in the same way that the right and duty to punish had been previously regulated. The adversary system, therefore, ceased to exist for youth, even as a legal fiction.[90] The myth of the child-saving movement as a humanitarian enterprise is based partly on a superficial interpretation of the child-savers' rhetoric of rehabilitation and partly on a misconception of how the child-savers viewed punishment. While it is true that the child-savers advocated minimal use of corporal punishment, considerable evidence suggests that this recommendation was based on managerial rather than moral considerations. William Letchworth reported that "corporal punishment is rarely inflicted" at the State Industrial School in Rochester because "most of the boys consider the lowering of their standing the severest punishment that is inflicted."[91] Mrs. Glendower Evans, commenting on the decline of whippings at a reform school in Massachusetts, concluded that "when boys do not feel themselves imprisoned and are treated as responsible moral agents, they can be trusted with their freedom to a surprising degree."[92] Officials at another state industrial school for girls also reported that "hysterics and fits of screaming and of noisy disobedience, have of late years become unknown. . . ."[93]

The decline in the use of corporal punishment was due to the fact that indeterminate sentencing, the "mark" or "stage" system of rewards and punishments, and other techniques of "organized persuasion" were far more effective in maintaining order and compliance than cruder methods of control. The chief virtue of the "stage" system, a graduated system of punishments and privileges, was its capacity to keep prisoners disciplined and submissive.[94] The child-savers had learned from industrialists that persuasive benevolence backed up by force was a far more effective device of social control than arbitrary displays of terrorism. Like an earlier generation of penal reformers in France and Italy, the child-savers stressed the effi-cacy of new and indirect forms of social control as a "practical measure of defense against social revolution as well as against individual acts."[95]

Although the child-saving movement had far-reaching consequences for the organization and administration of the juvenile justice system, its overall impact was conservative in both spirit and achievement. The child-savers reforms were generally aimed at imposing sanctions on conduct unbecoming "youth" and disqualifying youth from the benefit of adult privileges. The child-savers were prohibitionists, in a general sense, who believed that social progress depended on efficient law enforcement, strict supervision of children's leisure and recreation, and enforced education. They were primarily concerned with regulating social behavior, eliminating "foreign" and radical ideologies, and preparing youth as a disciplined and devoted work force. The austerity of the criminal law and penal institutions was only of incidental concern; their central interest was in the normative outlook of youth and they were most successful in their efforts to extend governmental control over a whole range of youthful activities which had previously been handled locally and informally. In this sense, their reforms were aimed at defining, rationalizing and regulating the dependent status of youth.[96] Although the child-savers' attitudes to youth were often paternalistic and romantic, their commands were backed up by force and an abiding faith in the benevolence of government.

The child-saving movement had its most direct impact on the children of the urban poor. The fact that "troublesome" adolescents were depicted as "sick" or "pathological," imprisoned "for their own good," addressed in paternalistic vocabulary, and exempted from criminal law processes, did not alter the subjective experiences of control, restraint and punishment. It is ironic, as Philippe Ariès observed in his historical study of European family life, that the obsessive solicitude of family, church, moralists and administrators for child welfare served to deprive children of the freedoms which they had previously shared with adults and to deny their capacity for initiative, responsibility and autonomy.[97]

Notes

1. See, for example, The President's Commission on Law Enforcement and Administration of Justice, *Juvenile Delinquency and Youth Crime* (Washington, D.C.: U.S. Government Printing Office, 1967), pp. 2–4.

2. Charles L. Chute, "The Juvenile Court in Retrospect," 13 *Federal Probation* (September, 1949), p. 7; Harrison A. Dobbs, "In Defense of Juvenile Court," *Ibid.*, p. 29.

3. Charles L. Chute, "Fifty Years of the Juvenile Court," *National Probation and Parole Association Yearbook* (1949), p. 1.

4. George H. Mead, "The Psychology of Punitive Justice," 23 *American Journal of Sociology* (March, 1918), pp. 577–602; August Aichhorn, "The Juvenile Court: Is It a Solution?," in *Delinquency and Child Guidance: Selected Papers* (New York: International Universities Press, 1964), pp. 55–79.

5. Murray Levine and Adeline Levine, *A Social History of Helping Services: Clinic, Court, School, and Community* (New York: Appleton-Century-Crofts, 1970), p. 156.

6. Gerhard O. W. Mueller, *History of American Criminal Law Scholarship* (New York: Walter E. Meyer Research Institute of Law, 1962), p. 113.

7. See, for example, Herbert H. Lou, *Juvenile Courts in the United States* (Chapel Hill: University of North Carolina Press, 1927); Negley K. Teeters and John Otto Reinmann, *The Challenge of Delinquency* (New York: Prentice-Hall, 1950); and Ola Nyquist, *Juvenile Justice* (London: Macmillan, 1960).

8. Robert S. Pickett, *House of Refuge: Origins of Juvenile Reform in New York State, 1815–1857* (Syracuse: Syracuse University Press, 1969), p. 188.

9. See, for example, Arthur M. Schlesinger, *The American as Reformer* (Cambridge: Harvard University Press, 1950).

10. See, for example, Richard Hofstadter, *The Age of Reform* (New York: Vintage Books, 1955), and Joseph R. Gusfield, *Symbolic Crusade: Status Politics and the American Temperance Movement* (Urbana: University of Illinois Press, 1963).

11. R. Jackson Wilson (Ed.), *Reform, Crisis, and Confusion, 1900–1929* (New York: Random House, 1970), especially pp. 3–6.

12. Arthur M. Schlesinger, Jr., *The Age of Jackson* (Boston: Little, Brown, 1946), p. 505.

13. Hofstadter, *op. cit.*, chapter IV.

14. The President's Commission on Law Enforcement and Administration of Justice, *op. cit.*, pp. 7, 8.

15. For discussions of earlier reform movements, see Pickett, *loc. cit.* and Sanford J. Fox, "Juvenile Justice Reform: An Historical Perspective," 22 *Stanford Law Review*, (June, 1970), pp. 1187–1239.

16. The child-saving movement was broad and diverse, including reformers interested in child welfare, education, reformatories, labor and other related issues. This paper is limited primarily to child-savers involved in anti-delinquency reforms and should not be interpreted as characterizing the child-saving movement in general.

17. William P. Letchworth, "Children of the State," *National Conference of Charities and Correction, Proceedings* (St. Paul, Minnesota, 1886), p. 138.

18. R. W. Hill, "The Children of Shinbone Alley," National Conference of Charities and Correction, *Proceedings* (Omaha, 1887), p. 231.

19. William Appleman Williams, *The Contours of American History* (Chicago: Quadrangle Books, 1966), especially pp. 345–412.

20. Pickett, *op. cit.*, pp. 50–55.

21. Committee on the History of Child-Saving Work, *History of Child-Saving in the United States* (National Conference of Charities and Correction, 1893), p. 5.

22. Charles Loring Brace, *The Dangerous Classes of New York and Twenty Years' Work Among Them* (New York: Wynkoop and Hallenbeck, 1880), pp. 282–83.

23. Committee on the History of Child-Saving Work, *op. cit.*, pp. 70–73.

24. *Ibid.*, pp. 80–81.

25. *Ibid.*, p. 270.

26. For more about these child-savers, see Anthony Platt, *The Child-Savers: The Invention of Delinquency*, (Chicago: University of Chicago Press, 1969), pp. 75–100.

27. Louise C. Wade, *Graham Taylor: Pioneer for Social Justice, 1851–1938* (Chicago: University of Chicago Press, 1964), p.59.

28. G. William Domhoff, *The Higher Circles: The Governing Class in America* (New York: Random House, 1970), p. 48 and Platt, *op. cit.*, pp. 92–98.

29. "The transformation in penal systems cannot be explained only from changing needs of the war against crime, although this struggle does play a part. Every system of production tends to discover punishments which correspond to its productive relationships. It is thus necessary to investigate the origin and fate of penal systems, the use or avoidance of specific punishments, and the intensity of penal practices as they are determined by social forces, above all by economic and then fiscal forces." Georg Rusche and Otto Kirchheimer, *Punishment and Social Structure,* (New York: Russell & Russell, 1968), p. 5.

30. See, for example, Gabriel Kolko, *The Triumph of Conservatism: A Reinterpretation of American History, 1900–1916* (Chicago: Quadrangle Books, 1967); James Weinstein, *The Corporate Ideal in the Liberal State, 1900–1918* (Boston: Beacon Press, 1969); Samuel Haber,

Efficiency and Uplift: Scientific Management in the Progressive Era, 1890–1920 (Chicago: University of Chicago Press, 1964); and Robert H. Wiebe, *Businessmen and Reform: A Study of the Progressive Movement* (Cambridge: Harvard University Press, 1962).

31. Weinstein, *op. cit.*, pp. ix, xi.

32. Jeremy P. Felt, *Hostages of Fortune: Child Labor Reform in New York State* (Syracuse: Syracuse University Press, 1965), p. 45.

33. Brace, *op. cit.*, p. 352.

34. David K. Cohen and Marvin Lazerson, "Education and the Corporate Order," 8 *Socialist Revolution,* (March–April, 1972), p. 50. See, also Michael B. Katz, *The Irony of Early School Reform: Educational Innovation in Mid-Nineteenth Century Massachusetts,* (Cambridge: Harvard University Press, 1968), and Lawrence A. Cremin, *The Transformation of the School: Progressivism in American Education, 1876–1957,* (New York: Vintage, 1961).

35. It should be emphasized that child-saving reforms were predominantly supported by more privileged sectors of the feminist movement, especially those who had an interest in developing professional careers in education, social work and probation. In recent years, radical feminists have emphasized that "we must include the oppression of children in any program for feminist revolution or we will be subject to the same failing of which we have so often accused men: of not having gone deep enough in our analysis, of having missed an important substratum of oppression merely because it didn't directly concern *us.*" Shulamith Firestone, *The Dialectic of Sex: The Case for Feminist Revolution,* (New York: Bantam, 1971), p. 104.

36. Robert Sunley, "Early Nineteenth Century American Literature on Child-Rearing," in Margaret Mead and Martha Wolfenstein (Eds.), *Childhood in Contemporary Cultures* (Chicago: University of Chicago Press, 1955), p. 152; see, also, Orville G. Brim, *Education for Child-Reading* (New York: Free Press, 1965), pp. 321–49.

37. For an extended discussion of this issue, see Platt, *loc. cit.* and Christopher Lasch, *The*

New Radicalism in America, 1889–1963: The Intellectual as a Social Type (New York: Alfred A. Knopf, 1965), pp. 3–68.

38. Talcott Parsons and Robert F. Bales, *Family, Socialization and Interaction Process* (Glencoe, Illinois: Free Press, 1955), pp. 3–33.

39. Clara T. Leonard, "Family Homes for Pauper and Dependent Children," Annual Conference of Charities, *Proceedings* (Chicago: 1879), p. 175.

40. W. P. Lynde, "Prevention in Some of its Aspects," *Ibid.*, pp. 165–166.

41. Joseph R. Gusfield, *Symbolic Crusade, loc. cit.*

42. See, generally, Roy Lubove, *The Professional Altruist: The Emergence of Social Work as a Career, 1880–1930* (Cambridge: Harvard University Press, 1965).

43. Williams, *op. cit.*, p. 373 and Weinstein, *op. cit.*, p. 254.

44. Williams, *op. cit.*, pp. 374, 395–402.

45. Committee on the History of Child-Saving Work, *op. cit.*, p. 3.

46. See, generally, John Higham, *Strangers in the Land: Patterns of American Nativism, 1860–1925* (New York: Atheneum, 1965).

47. Brace, *op. cit.*, pp. 30, 49; Bradford Kinney Peirce, *A Half Century with Juvenile Delinquents* (Montclair, New Jersey: Patterson Smith, 1969, originally published 1869), p. 253.

48. Nathan Allen, "Prevention of Crime and Pauperism," Annual Conference of Charities, *Proceedings* (Cincinnati, 1878), pp. 111–24.

49. Jacob A. Riis, *How the Other Half Lives* (New York: Hill and Wang, 1957, originally published in 1890), p. 134.

50. Brace, *op. cit.*, pp. 27, 29.

51. See, for example, Lombroso's comments in the Introduction to Arthur MacDonald, *Criminology* (New York: Funk and Wagnalls, 1893).

52. Allen, *loc. cit.*

53. Hamilton D. Wey, "A Plea for Physical Training of Youthful Criminals," National Prison Association, *Proceedings* (Boston,

1888), pp. 181–93. For further discussion of this issue, see Platt, *op. cit.*, pp. 18–28 and Arthur E. Fink, *Causes of Crime: Biological Theories in the United States, 1800–1915* (New York: A. S. Barnes, 1962).

54. Richard L. Dugdale, *The Jukes: A Study in Crime, Pauperism, Disease, and Heredity* (New York: G.P. Putnam's Sons, 1877).

55. Sarah B. Cooper, "The Kindergarten as Child-Saving Work," National Conference of Charities and Correction, *Proceedings* (Madison, 1883), pp. 130–38.

56. I.N. Kerlin, "The Moral Imbecile, "National Conference of Charities and Correction, *Proceedings* (Baltimore, 1890), pp. 244–50.

57. Williams, *op. cit.*, p. 354.

58. Fink, *op. cit.*, p. 247.

59. See, for example, Illinois Board of State Commissioners of Public Charities, *Second Biennial Report* (Springfield: State Journal Steam Print, 1873), pp. 195–96.

60. Peter Caldwell, "The Duty of the State to Delinquent Children," National Conference of Charities and Correction, *Proceedings* (New York, 1898), pp. 404–10.

61. E.R.L. Gould, "The Statistical Study of Hereditary Criminality," National Conference of Charities and Correction, *Proceedings* (New Haven, 1895), pp. 134–43.

62. Charles H. Cooley, " 'Nature' in the Making of Social Careers," National Conference of Charities and Correction, *Proceedings* (Grand Rapids, 1896), pp. 399–405.

63. Committee on the History of Child-Saving Work, *op. cit.*, p. 90.

64. Enoch C. Wines, *The State of Prisons and of Child-Saving Institutions in the Civilized World* (Cambridge: Harvard University Press, 1880).

65. Helen Page Bates, "Digest of Statutes Relating to Juvenile Courts and Probation Systems," 13 *Charities* (January, 1905), pp. 329–36.

66. Joel F. Handler, "The Juvenile Court and the Adversary System: Problems of Function and Form," 1965 *Wisconsin Law Review* (1965), pp. 7–51.

67. Gustav L. Schramm, "The Juvenile

Court Idea," 13 *Federal Probation* (September, 1949), p. 21.

68. Monrad G. Paulsen, "Fairness to the Juvenile Offender," 41 *Minnesota Law Review* (1957), pp. 547–67.

69. Julian W. Mack, "The Chancery Procedure in the Juvenile Court," in Jane Addams (Ed.), *The Child, the Clinic and the Court* (New York: New Republic, 1925), p. 315.

70. Miriam Van Waters, "The Socialization of Juvenile Court Procedure," 21 *Journal of Criminal Law and Criminology* (1922), pp. 61, 69.

71. Harvey H. Baker, "Procedure of the Boston Juvenile Court," 23 *Survey* (February, 1910), p. 646.

72. Illinois Board of State Commissioners of Public Charities, *Sixth Biennial Report* (Springfield: H. W. Rokker, 1880), p. 104.

73. Frederick H. Wines, "Reformation as an End in Prison Discipline," National Conference of Charities and Correction, *Proceedings* (Buffalo, 1888), p. 198.

74. Joel F. Handler, *op. cit.*, p. 9.

75. Joel F. Handler and Margaret K. Rosenheim, "Privacy and Welfare: Public Assistance and Juvenile Justice," 31 *Law and Contemporary Problems* (1966), pp. 377–412.

76. From a report by Enoch Wines and Theodore Dwight to the New York legislature in 1867, quoted by Max Grünhut, *Penal Reform* (Oxford: Clarendon Press, 1948), p.90.

77. Peter Caldwell, "The Reform School Problem," National Conference of Charities and Correction, *Proceedings* (St. Paul, 1886), pp. 71–76.

78. Letchworth, *op. cit.*, p. 152.

79. Committee on the History of Child-Saving Work, *op., cit.*, p. 20.

80. See Platt, *op. cit.*, pp. 55–66.

81. Katz, *op. cit.*, p. 187.

82. Rusche and Kirchheimer, *op. cit.*, pp. 131–132.

83. American Friends Service Committee, *op. cit.*, p. 28.

84. Zebulon R. Brockway, *Fifty Years of Prison Service* (New York: Charities Publication Committee, 1912), p. 393.

85. *Ibid.*, pp. 310, 421.

86. *Ibid.*, pp. 389–408.

87. *Ibid.*

88. Peirce, *op. cit.*, p. 312.

89. Enoch Wines, *op. cit.*, p. 81.

90. On informal cooperation in the criminal courts, see Jerome H. Skolnick, "Social Control in the Adversary System," 11 *Journal of Conflict Resolution* (March, 1967), pp. 52–70.

91. Committee on the History of Child-Saving Work, *op. cit.*, p. 20.

92. *Ibid.*, p. 237.

93. *Ibid.*, p. 251.

94. Rusche and Kirchheimer, *op. cit.*, pp. 155–156.

95. *Ibid.*, p. 76. For a similar point, see American Friends Service Committee, *op. cit.*, p. 33.

96. See, generally, Frank Musgrove, *Youth and the Social Order* (London: Routledge and Kegan Paul, 1964).

97. Philippe Ariès, *Centuries of Childhood: A Social History of Family Life* (New York: Vintage Books, 1965).

The Ideal Juvenile Court

2

Ellen Ryerson

The juvenile court movement emerged from frustration with the dominant modes of dealing with child offenders. But the willingness to dispense with the old did not itself give form to the new. Those who condemned the old system as harsh and ill conceived had still to define a specific program, both more humane and more effective than the criminal law and the penal system. . . . As the nearest approximation of a concrete model, . . . they had the example of the state of Massachusetts.

Beginning in 1869, Massachusetts law had provided for the participation of visiting agents or officers of the State board of Charities in juvenile cases: these agents investigated juvenile cases and made recommendations to the judges for disposition. Between 1870 and 1877, a series of measures established separate hearings, dockets, and records for children under sixteen,

Excerpt from *The Best-Laid Plans: America's Juvenile Court Experiment* by Ellen Ryerson. Copyright © 1978 by Ellen Ryerson. Reprinted by permission of Hill and Wang, a division of Farrar, Straus and Giroux, Inc.

and a program of visitation by probation officers to homes in which delinquent children had been "placed out." With separate hearings for children and a rudimentary probation system, Massachusetts had gone further than any other state in modifying criminal procedure and criminal sanctions in children's cases. It had not gone far enough, but it provided an example on which to build a system which would relieve child offenders of the undeserved burden of criminal responsibility and yet prevent them from going astray again.

Perhaps the most influential idea in shaping the juvenile court system was the thesis that the defect which produced juvenile crime lay not so much in the child as in the environment from which he had come and, therefore, that no child should be treated as a criminal. The child, naturally or at least potentially innocent and moral, learned antisocial behavior from contact with corrupt adults. Accordingly, the first principle of the new court apparatus and its ancillary institutions was to separate the child from adult offenders at all times. The notion that child saving depending on sepa-

27

ration of children from adults was not new to the progressive period: the house of refuge had been organized on the same principle in the early nineteenth century. But the persisting incarceration of juveniles with adults in detention and correctional facilities and their commingling in the courtroom led progressive reformers to carry to its logical conclusion the effort to disentangle juvenile justice from adult justice. In this cause, juvenile court legislation usually prohibited the confinement of children with adults, and occasionally made nonsegregated confinement itself punishable as a misdemeanor. In the literature and the laws, founders of the juvenile court demanded not only separate reformatories but separate detention centers, and separate sessions or courtrooms as well.

Mandatory age segregation made implicitly the accusation that adult criminals were one cause of childhood corruption. Noncriminal adults also had to share the responsibility. In 1903, the Colorado legislature passed the first state law holding parents and guardians legally responsible for contributing to the delinquencies of their children.[1] Judge Ben Lindsey, pioneer of the Denver juvenile court and leader among reformers and defenders of wayward youth, claimed that the contributing-to-delinquency law "has done more than anything else to solve the problems of delinquency with us."[2] He considered the fining and jailing of citizens who encouraged or permitted delinquency in children under their charge his state's greatest contribution to the movement. Many localities followed Denver in coupling their juvenile court laws with provisions giving the court jurisdiction over contributing adults. These provisions gave institutional expression to the theory that the child was not ultimately responsible for his acts.

The reformers sought further expression of that theory and further detachment from the criminal law by trying to dispel from juvenile court proceedings the atmosphere of blame and recrimination which they detected in criminal proceedings. They hoped to remove entirely from the juvenile court process the implication that the child was capable of criminal intent or subject to criminal sanctions. In this they began at the beginning—with the mode of initiating cases. Ideally, initiation by petition was to replace initiation by complaint. By this process any reputable person might bring to the attention of the court a child he had reason to believe delinquent within the meaning of the law or in need of the court's supervision. Unlike the complainant, the petitioner need have had no direct connection with the case, and was presumably engaged in securing help for the child rather than seeking revenge. The reformers hoped that this change would bring more needy and troublesome children into court, and make apparent to such children that the court took action out of interest in their welfare and not out of anger. Behind this change in procedure one senses an image of community involvement with the welfare of children that bears greater resemblance to disappearing village life than to the urban disorder with which the juvenile court was supposed to cope. But whether the right of petition was placed in the public at large or only in a probation staff which would screen referrals, the process was in contrast to criminal procedure in its emphasis on sympathetic rather than accusatory initiations. A similar purpose animated the recommended shift from a warrant for arrest to a summons as the court's means of compelling the appearance of a child who had been brought to its attention.

To realize the constructive potential of court control, the founders recommended that at some time between petition and hearing an officer of the court conduct a preliminary investigation into the background of the child. The officer's mission was to unearth information which might point to the source of the child's misbehavior and suggest the proper remedy. While in a criminal case the preparation for trial would focus upon evidence concerning the commission of a specific prohibited act, here the preparation for a hearing was to give full scope to a systematic and sympathetic inquiry which could form the basis for a disposition based on the circumstances of the child's life rather than on the question of guilt or innocence. The reformers hoped to effectuate as well as to symbolize the fusion of the interests of the child with those of society by placing responsibility for this investigation in the hands of the probation officer, who was by law required to represent the child, and at the same time to serve the court. The functions of defense counsel and prosecuting attorney, so far as they remained, now fell to a single individual.

That person also assumed responsibility for the accused during the detention period. In contrast to criminal proceedings, where the right to bail might postpone the impact of the state upon the accused until guilt had been proven beyond a reasonable doubt, juvenile court proceedings included the option of a constructive detention period that could serve as the opening stage of a reformation process for children whose hearings had not even commenced. Before the child appeared in court he might be separated from his parents and placed in the charge of a probation officer or in a detention home, not because he was otherwise unlikely to appear at his hearing, but because the reformers presumed that he would benefit by state supervision whether he proved to be delinquent or not, and because the detention period would allow the gathering of important data for the hearing.

In order that every stage of the child's experience with the court contribute to the reformation of his character, the founders set to work to modify courtroom procedure as well. They intended to sweep away all elements of criminal trials "so that an intimate, friendly relationship [might] be established at once between the judge and the child."[3] The reformers so favored procedural informality that they made it a crucial test of the adequacy of a juvenile court system. They insisted that the true juvenile court could not be criminal at all, that its proceedings had to be civil in fact as well as in form. While a few reformers in some states thought it wise to allow for jury trials and defense counsel on demand, they did so "in order to avoid constitutional difficulties or attacks upon the law" and not because they believed that "any such provisions are necessary."[4] Generally, juvenile court reformers regarded juries and lawyers as unnecessary restraints upon the flexible pursuit of the best interests of the child.

The elimination of procedural formality in the courtroom presumably freed the judge to employ all available resources in gaining the child's confidence and thereby beginning the resocialization process. In this context, the kind of person who served as juvenile court judge became extremely important. Participants in the movement frequently stated their conviction that the success of the juvenile court turned upon the capability of the judge.

Juvenile court literature exhibited relatively little concern with the qualities usually associated with a judge—a thorough knowledge of the law, an independent and even-handed sense of justice. Rather, it asserted the desirability of a judge who would appeal personally to the youngsters brought before him. Judge Ben Lindsey believed that "more is accomplished through love than by any other method,"[5] and most of the court's supporters agreed that the emphasis belonged on sympathy rather than on legal learning. In the juvenile court movement, Lindsey's own brand of friendly and fatherly involvement in the lives of delinquent children served as a model for the approach which Stephen Schlossman has called "affectional discipline."[6] The emphasis on personal qualities of wisdom and kindness did not, however, imply that the juvenile court judge might be an amateur at his duties: the reformers conceived of the juvenile court judgeship as a fulltime specialty demanding the exclusive and long-term attention of the person who filled it.

The judge's task was, of course, to weigh all available evidence of the child's circumstances and to prescribe a treatment if treatment were in order. In collecting data about the child, the judge could and should allow testimony of any sort, irrespective of such constraints from criminal procedure as the rule against hearsay evidence. No scruples about the legal appropriateness of testimony in a criminal court could have outweighed in the founders' minds the potential value of knowing everything there was to know about the child and his environment.

The reformers overhauled court procedure in an effort, they said, to minimize future negative repercussions in the life of the offender. In order to prevent society from unjustly stigmatizing children who had appeared in court the reformers recommended the exclusion of all persons from juvenile court hearings except those directly involved in the case. The constitutional guarantee of a public trial seemed to them to carry more danger than protection. As a further precaution, the architects of the court suggested that only officials have access to the records of juvenile court proceedings and that evidence gathered in connection with such cases be inadmissible in

any other court. Finally, the reformers recommended that juvenile courts make general adjudications of delinquency rather than of specific offenses, also in the hope that such general adjudications would be less stigmatizing.

Once having found the child delinquent, the court still had before it the most important part of its job—the formulation of an intelligent course of treatment, which meant by definition a course that took its direction from the specific needs of the child in question. Punishment to fit the crime might be uniform, but treatment to fit the child had to be individualized, and treatment rather than punishment was the business of the juvenile court. In 1884, John Peter Altgeld made a classic statement of the medical analogy which persuaded so many reformers of the appropriateness of individualized justice:

> If the state were to enforce a system of medical practice and were to provide that but one prescription should be given for all the ills that afflict the flesh, it would not be more absurd than is the present system of treating offenders.[7]

In 1926, the director of the Psychopathic Clinic in Detroit expressed the continuing scorn of juvenile court supporters for the notion that a "uniform system of treating all crime is going to be any more successful than a uniform system of treating all fevers would be."[8]

In pursuit of the ideal of individualized treatment, the reformers seemed to imagine an infinite range of choice in tailoring the disposition to fit the child. Nevertheless, both practical considerations and the premises of the movement itself circumscribed the judge's choice.

One of the distinctive features of the juvenile court movement was its primary, if not exclusive, commitment to probation as the most desirable disposition for child offenders. Where other generations had channeled their dissatisfaction with correctional institutions into redesigning such institutions, the progressives concentrated on developing an alternative which could occupy the foreground of juvenile corrections while the last resort (or threat) of institutionalization remained in the background. With the exception of a diagnostic detention period, a cardinal rule of the juvenile court movement and of child-welfare work in general in this period was that whenever possible the child should receive what care he needed in a home—either his own or some other—rather than in an institution.

The preference for home rehabilitation still left the judge the choice of returning the child to his own home under the supervision of a probation officer or of having him placed in a new one. In this choice the reformers, and frequently the laws, guided the judge to make the first effort with the parents and to place a child in a foster home only if necessary. If the child was to be placed with another family, it was desirable that the relationship as closely as possible approximate a natural family setting. But except for the differences inherent in institutional and home living, the location and duration of the child's treatment were the only variables with which the courts could work directly. Whatever manipulation of the child's environment was actually to take place was likely to fall to the judgment and skill of the probation officer.

Regardless of the disposition of particular cases, the reformers intended that the child's experience with the court be free of accusation and full of constructive and friendly discipline. In all its dealings with delinquent children, the court was to take as its model the protective attitude of the state toward children who were abandoned or neglected or abused by their parents or guardians. A finding of delinquency might focus on the behavior of the child, while a finding of dependency or neglect focused on the behavior of his parents, but the former was only a symptom of the latter. The distinctions between dependent, neglected, and delinquent children were less important than their common need for state supervision in the manner of a wise and devoted parent. To each other and to the public the reformers pictured the court as a clinic for moral ills, an agent of moral and intellectual improvement, a school for the offending child and for the community. They proudly agreed that the juvenile court embodied a new understanding of the problem of delinquency and a new ideal of the relationship between society and its lawbreakers. Looking back over the first twenty years of the juvenile court movement, the executive secretary of the Ohio Humane Society wrote in 1922: "Against the old herd instinct we have a newer and more altruistic impulse in which all society gets together in an effort of reclamation."[9]

The reformers continually made these aims explicit and constantly put them in the foreground of their literature. But the tone of juvenile court propaganda and the implications of juvenile court techniques suggest that the goals of the reformers and the significance of the movement did not fit solely under the heading of more humane and effective treatments for child offenders. Or rather, the heading is too vague to convey fully the assumptions of the juvenile court movement or to reveal how its assumptions have made it vulnerable to criticism in spite of the general appeal of its stated goals.

The juvenile court promised the community that it would purge delinquents of their antisocial tendencies by giving them specialized treatment. The reformers pursued the ideal of such treatment by collecting data on the child's home life, school record, physical health, economic status, and so on. This aspect of the evidence, which reformers called "social" testimony, became so important to court supporters that they allowed and even encouraged it to overshadow evidence bearing upon questions of "guilt" or "innocence"—words which they rarely permitted to pass their lips. This studied disinterest in the facts of the alleged act of delinquency was often explicit. Julian Mack, the second judge of the Chicago juvenile court and an active participant in the movement, addressed an American Bar Association audience in 1909:

> The problem for determination by the [juvenile court] judge is not, has this boy or girl committed a specific wrong, but what is he, how has he become what he is. . . .[10]

A survey of juvenile courts published in 1920 found:

> . . . the fundamental purpose of juvenile court proceedings is not to determine whether or not a child has committed a specific offense, but to discover whether he is in a condition requiring the special care of the State. . . .[11]

While the literature customarily justified disinterest in specific offenses by a higher interest in providing children with needed guidance, and while this disinterest was in a way consistent with the movement's stated aim of benefiting the child, it suggested another aim as well. It suggested that the founders and supporters of the juvenile court were not exclusively or perhaps even primarily interested in juvenile offenders as that term had been understood before the passage of juvenile court laws

but in a far broader area of jurisdiction, both over the child and over his family.

For the most part, before 1899, a child offender was a person who had broken a law or ordinance and who also happened to be a minor: his age, not his act, differentiated him from the adult offender. However, by minimizing questions of guilt and innocence of specific criminal acts, the founders changed the focus of correctional efforts. Far from simply trying to secure better treatment for children who had been convicted of illegal acts, they were directing their efforts to a newly defined and greatly enlarged class of children—those who seemed to need the state's care whether or not they had in a strict sense committed an offense, and who might never have otherwise come within the reach of the law. While undertaking to extend to child criminals the protection which had previously been afforded neglected or dependent children, the juvenile court reformers were also casting a net that could catch children who might hitherto have eluded legal sanction: children who were neither dependent nor neglected nor guilty of a criminal offense. A manual for probation officers in New York State explained the virtues of unofficial probation for children who had not so much as appeared in court by pointing out:

> In many cases the delinquency is so incipient or the family circumstances are such that unless the cases could be dealt with unofficially they would never come to the attention of the court, or if they should, not until it was too late to secure the results possible through early unofficial treatment.[12]

The ideal juvenile court and probation system was to be available for rehabilitative work with children even where official court action was unwarranted.

The definition of delinquency which eventually prevailed in juvenile court laws illustrated more graphically the reformers' desire to reach beyond juvenile criminals to influence the lives of other "unfortunate" children. Only a few juvenile court statutes stopped at the boundaries of old definitions—with children who had violated laws or ordinances. Reformers criticized such statutes, including the original Illinois law, and sought to amend them. They much preferred laws that included such offenses as smoking cigarettes, fighting, using profane language, habitually walking along railroad tracks, frequenting houses of prostitution, associating with thieves, running away from home, growing up in idleness, idly wandering the streets at night, or being "incorrigible." Grace Abbott's 1910 abstract of juvenile court laws declared:

> Better laws make the definition much more inclusive so that the court will not be unable, because of any technical lack of jurisdiction, to place a child under the care of the court . . . if that seems to be for the best interest of the child.[13]

It is true that before the passage of juvenile court laws techniques were available to reach children who did some of the things which were now named as noncriminal conduct warranting a finding of delinquency. In some states "incorrigibility" had been grounds for commitment to a house of refuge, and disorderly-conduct laws undoubtedly brought to the criminal courts children who committed no independently criminal offense. Julia Lathrop described the juvenile clientele of the Chicago police courts just before the Illinois juvenile court act came into effect:

> 332 boys between the ages of nine and sixteen years were sent to the city prison. Three

hundred and twenty of them were sent up on the blanket charge of disorderly conduct, which covered offenses from burglary and assault with a deadly weapon to picking up coal on the railway tracks, building bonfires, playing ball in the street, or "flipping trains," that is, jumping on and off moving cars. . . . Out of the 332 cases sent to the Bridewell during the first half of the year 1899, nearly one-third were pardoned by the mayor.[14]

This was the dilemma which provoked juvenile court reformers: the criminal law gave the alternatives of commitment to correctional institutions which had proven cruel failures, or of pardon (or acquittal) to avoid commitment. While the reformers undoubtedly wished through probation to avoid incarceration, they also wished to avoid the alternative of non-intervention. The lengthening list of noncriminal acts which warranted a finding of delinquency was intended to bring within the purview of the juvenile court the many children who were " 'left off' by the justice or pardoned by the mayor" and on whose behalf, consequently, "no constructive work was done."[15]

By blurring the distinctions between dependent, neglected, and delinquent children, by minimizing questions of guilt or innocence of specific acts, and by including in the definition of delinquency noncriminal conduct, the juvenile court reformers were intentionally advocating a jurisdiction for the court which would augment the power of the state to intervene in the lives of children and in the relationships between the children and their parents.

Some scholars, Anthony Platt most notable among them, have implied that this expansiveness in the definition of delinquency gives the lie to the humanitarian claims of the juvenile court movement.[16] There is much to learn from this and other signs of the reformers' desire to expand state intervention into the lives of children and their families, but it is not direct evidence on the question of how "humane" were the intentions of juvenile court reformers. The usefulness of the question is mitigated by the danger that we are using more than one meaning of "humanitarian." First, the expansive definition of delinquency may have been largely intended to bring within the jurisdiction of the juvenile court acts which otherwise would have been gathered into the criminal courts under the label of disorderly conduct, as they were in Chicago just before the juvenile court law took effect. It is worth noting that the same behavior in juvenile court might bring years of probation until the age of majority was reached, while they might be followed by no action at all in criminal court or by sentences quite limited in time. But unless the definition of "humane" is irrevocably linked to nonintervention, even this observation does not give the lie to the reformers. Their definition of humanitarian treatment of children certainly was not mere leniency or nonintervention: it was constructive discipline, and this is not or was not an altogether implausible definition, even if it has little appeal in the present.

If the reformers had been accused of overextending juvenile court jurisdiction, they might have countered that such expansion of state intervention would prevent crime by bringing children within the scope of the law before their delinquent tendencies became criminal. And, indeed, prevention of crime counted among the founders' avowed intentions. Stephen Schlossman finds this aspect one of the few that really distinguish the ideas of the juvenile court movement from reform efforts on behalf of child offenders in the early nineteenth century.[17]

The defense of extended jurisdiction as a preventive measure against crime would have constituted an interesting though somewhat elliptical claim, since it omitted the vital demonstration of what represented a symptom of future criminality. The literature lacked any tightly reasoned argument to the effect that the commission of one of the new offenses indicated a propensity for the commission of genuine crimes later in life or to the effect that, in specific terms, boys who wandered around railroad tracks or used profane language were more likely than most eventually to rob banks. Nor was there any serious effort in the literature to make the more indirect connection between such behavior and laxness of parental control, which was in turn regarded as the breeding ground of more serious offenses. The issue of what constituted proto-criminal behavior was either too complicated or too self-evident to discuss. Or perhaps the relative silence on the subject reveals that the reformers were as dedicated to controlling these acts as an end in itself as they were to using them to detect potential criminals. While ostensibly legislating on matters of crime and punishment, they also legislated their preferences in the realm of manners and morals. By allowing noncriminal behavior on the part of children to trigger the intervention of a probation officer into family life, the juvenile court reformers were placing their movement among a number of others which were, in the progressive period, sending numerous missionaries from the dominant culture to the lower classes to acculturate immigrants, to teach mothers household management, and to supervise the recipients of charity.

Occasionally, the notions of individualized justice and positivist criminology were frankly linked by their advocates to the aim of stricter social control. But on a less explicit and philosophical plane, there were many indications that juvenile court supporters intended more than the mere control of criminal behavior in children and more even than the prevention of criminal behavior in future adults. Judge Lindsey wanted not only "to teach children how and why they should obey the law" but also to make the children "really patriotic in spirit, protectors of the state and upholders of its laws."[18] Others hoped to direct the delinquent's thoughts into "pure channels and higher ideals for virtue and pure manhood," and to teach an "appreciation of the true, the beautiful, and the good," "neatness, cleanliness and correctness, and . . . a love and respect for other people's property and opinions."[19] Such statements elevated the mores of the middle class to the level of universal values, but even if these mores had been universally shared, they were not the usual business of a court of law, and went well beyond the stated aim of discouraging crime. Although the scholarship of the twentieth century has accustomed us to consider definitions of deviance in a sociological framework, the lengths to which these middle-class reformers were willing to go in reproducing an image of themselves in "unfortunate" children is indeed striking. One did not have to be clean and neat, correct and patient to stay within the law; one did not have to protect the state in order to stay out of its jails. The Reverend Malcolm Dana saw the rehabilitation of wayward youth as an occasion for a probation officer to become "practically a member of the family, and by lessons in cleanliness, and decency, of truth and integrity . . . he can transform the entire family into something the State need not be ashamed to own as its citizens."[20] In such declarations of purpose, the reformers

exhibited a desire not simply to improve upon the criminal justice system but to retrain the child offender and his family in life patterns that were more acceptable to the middle class.

The dual role of the juvenile court system—a humanitarian gesture toward the downtrodden and a means of consolidating and protecting the safety and status of the more fortunate—is characteristic of reform as opposed to revolutionary movements, and many of the reform activities that occupied progressives exhibited the same duality. As Roy Lubove points out in his work on tenement-house reform, the miserable conditions of slum life prodded reformers into action not only because slums represented objective violations of universal standards of decency but also because they made the values of the middle class impossible to achieve.[21] The temperance movement aimed to rescue mankind from hideous dependence on alcohol as well as to ensure the reliability and productiveness of the work force. The public-health reformers exhibited solicitude for the physical condition of the poor *and* reflected the desire to protect the native population from contamination by unhealthy alien peoples.[22] The work of people interested in the process by which immigrants entered American life vacillated between the celebration of "immigrant gifts," of pluralism, and the anxious desire to remake foreigners in the safe and familiar image of Americans. The birth-control movement tried to provide individual families with the means of controlling their own destinies, but also sometimes seemed to provide the means by which the dominant middle class might preserve itself from the rampant fecundity of the lower orders, native and foreign.[23]

It is not mere conjecture to see similarly in the juvenile court movement elements of class and ethnic antagonism or of an effort to avoid them. According to the movement's own analysis, parental attitudes and home environment constituted the prime forces in molding a child's character. Also, according to that formula, ''most of the children who come before the court are, naturally, the children of the poor.''[24]

Responsibility for delinquency lay with the social and economic conditions of the lower class—conditions from which the reformers could easily sense their separateness. The men in the movement were usually lawyers, often judges, sometimes doctors and clergymen; the women, often well but less well educated and married to members of the same social status, were sufficiently free of domestic duties to devote much of their time to philanthropic causes. An awareness of their own good fortune was a virtual precondition of their efforts on behalf of others. Many saw that their mission involved crossing ''that yawning chasm . . . dividing into hostile classes the rich and poor.''[25] And they proposed to cross that chasm by offering delinquents and their families ''those higher gifts that we are able to bestow.''[26]

The reformers' sense of class differences between themselves and the objects of their philanthropy produced on occasion unconcealed disdain. Some court workers seemed convinced that no home deficient enough to produce a delinquent could command a child's—even a delinquent child's—affection. Henry Thurston, the chief probation officer of the Chicago juvenile court from 1906 to 1908, wrote about his reactions to the children and their families:

> Looking into their little faces, and watching them as they are taken away from their old unwholesome surroundings to be placed among environments that will lift them up and make them noble men and women in-

stead of burdens upon society, one wonders how much these little ones really feel, and how deep their suffering really is when they are snatched away from home and parents.[27]

It did not seem at all likely that a delinquent would have parents worthy of love.

The theory that the cause of delinquency lay in lower-class environments, physical and cultural, translated into the practice of probation as uplifting contact between the delinquent and his social betters. Such contact was the very essence of probation at the beginning of the juvenile court movement, and probation lay at the heart of the ideal juvenile court.

What is novel about progressive attitudes toward child offenders is not the concern to mitigate class differences. Early nineteenth-century managers of the houses of refuge, as Stephen Schlossman points out, had seen their role in the lives of child offenders as inducing confirmation to middle-class standards.[28] Rather, what is distinctive about the awareness of class differences in the progressive period is that the juvenile court movement contemplated not so much lifting the child out of his lower-class milieu as entering and transforming that milieu, not only for the child, but for his family, too.

The reformers' preference for returning the delinquent to his home did not jibe, at least superficially, with their conviction that the home had produced the delinquency in the first place. Nevertheless, for several reasons the reformers could live with this apparent contradiction. First, on the negative side, was their experience with institutional care as too rigid for individualized treatment and, more serious, as an environment more likely to teach the skills of criminality than good citizenship. Second, removing the child from his home in order to place him in another raised serious if not insurmountable legal, moral, and practical questions.

But the enthusiasm with which juvenile court reformers contemplated the probation system and its focus upon environmental as well as individual uplift cannot be accounted for by negative concerns about the alternatives alone. Schlossman believes that the juvenile court reformers' interest in a family setting for rehabilitative efforts was "one manifestation of a newly heightened sensitivity in the progressive period to the emotional bonds and educational possibilities in all families, even those in fairly dismal straits."[29] The faith in these possibilities is difficult to explain, since it seems to have emerged not from a belief in the growing strength and stability of family life but, on the contrary, from a concern that the family could not survive the effects of industrialization and the competition of other institutions—mainly educational and recreational—in socializing children.

It would appear that somehow progressive faith in the potential of family life outstripped the fear that the reality of family life was in decline. Juvenile delinquency was to provide an occasion to rejuvenate the family, and the rejuvenated family was to be an "ally"[30] in the reformation of the delinquent. Such optimism characterized to a remarkable degree the attitude of juvenile court reformers to the task of rehabilitation. The literature of the juvenile court movement contained many brief statements or summaries of the regeneration process, often presenting the task as one of impressive and even inspiring simplicity.

> There is such a thing as an instantaneous awakening of the soul to the realization of higher and better things by the magnetic influence of one soul reacting upon another.[31]

Thus, the process might have been as elementary as placing the delinquent in touch with a law-abiding citizen, or as simple as reasoning with him. Judge Lindsey wrote:

> We never release a boy on probation until he is impressed with the idea that he must obey. It is explained what the consequences will be if he does not obey and keep his word. It is kindly, but firmly, impressed why all this is so, and why after all it is for him we are working and not against him. We arouse his sense of responsibility.[32]

Lindsey seemed to suggest that hostility to society and its laws was just an error of judgment, a mistake that the child would recognize and correct if only someone took the trouble to point it out to him. This typical statement resembles an argument about madness made by a character in Dostoevsky's *Crime and Punishment*:

> In Paris they have been conducting serious experiments as to the possibility of curing the insane, simply by logical argument. . . . The idea is that there's really nothing wrong with the physical organism of the insane, and that insanity is, so to say, a logical mistake, an error of judgment, an incorrect view of things.[33]

This view of insanity implied that there existed a standard of reason not only universal in meaning but universally powerful in its appeal. The child-study movement took a similar position when it suggested that an appreciation of accepted morality inhered universally in human beings. The assumption that such standards of behavior had a natural hold on all human beings appeared subtly in many juvenile court articles. The superintendent of the Indiana Reform School for Boys told the National Conference of Charities and Correction in 1902:

> We must place our boy under the guidance of an affable, firm, prudent master who will

help by his own example. The courteous re-
plies and gentlemanly ways of an officer
have a tendency to draw as a magnet the respect and admiration of a boy.[34]

The reformers assumed that the child offender had a "smoldering ambition" to be
like the good men and women who worked
for the court,[35] that he had within him all the
while the potential and the desire to be an
upstanding citizen, and that he needed only
the example of "discreet persons of good
moral character" to transform that potential into reality.

Only the assumption that accepted behavioral codes were inherent in the child
could have explained the confidence with
which the reformers contemplated the probation system. As originally conceived,
probation treatment consisted of visits from
a probation officer to the child and reports
to the court by the child himself or by the
probation officer. The visits and reports
constituted the entire probation system,
"the keystone which supports the arch of
the juvenile law,"[36] the "cord upon which
all the pearls of the juvenile court are
strung."[37] The reformers expected the probation officer to show tact and patience and
common sense, but they did not expect him
to have professional skill or training. As
with the judge, personal qualities mattered
most. "The probation process is a process
of education by constructive friendship."[38]
"The friendly side of the probation officers' work is the important side."[39]

> There is no more potent influence over a
> boy than a good man or woman. . . . The
> way to make a good boy is to rub him
> against a good man.[40]

By expecting a casual, friendly relationship between a delinquent and a more fortunate adult to solve the child's behavioral
problems, the reformers revealed a singu-
lar faith in the powers of spontaneous
moral regeneration.

Thus, for all their concern about delinquency, the reformers' picture of the
problem was rather rosy: whereas the
child offender was clearly atypical in that
he did not abide by the moral code natural
to man, he was readily returned to normality; whereas for the moment he presented
society with a problem, he would soon
count as one of society's assets. Whatever
his impulses toward crime and destruction, they were not basic, for as a normal
human being his basic impulses by definition led him to preserve the social order.

The invention of the juvenile court was
largely the work of the old middle class responding to one of the urban problems
which troubled people in the 1890's, particularly after the panic of 1893. In a sense
their response resembles what Wiebe
would have considered an effort to imitate
in the impersonal, urban world the informal patterns of social control which belonged to disappearing village life. The reformers' hope that disinterested observers
in the community would petition the juvenile court on behalf of children is one point
of resemblance. The importance of a fatherly judge in face-to-face contact with
the children and their families is another.
The initial commitment to volunteer probation service by people whose main qual-
ification for the work was their social status is a third. As Geoffrey C. Hazard, Jr.,
has recently written, "It often seems that
juvenile law is operating on an unarticu-
lated wish that young people would behave as though they were members of an
integrated and static society living in untroubled times."[41]

On the other hand, the institution that
this old middle class invented embodied
much of what is characteristic of progres-

sivism. It invited the kind of administration by the kind of people—the new middle class—which Wiebe associates with progressivism and Brown associates with modernization. While the emphasis on a judge with personal involvement in his work seems to have been genuine and to have endured, it also demanded specialization in juvenile court work. The emphasis on a personal approach in probation was clearly less enduring and probably made a virtue of necessity—the political necessity to avoid burdening juvenile court proposals with expensive probation systems, and the more mundane necessity to get along with amateurs, since social work itself had not yet become a profession and the social sciences were only just emerging. When social work did become professional and the social sciences became better developed, there was already a place for them in the juvenile court system.

The emphasis of the earliest reformers on the importance of "social" testimony in juvenile cases made that place. The vagueness of definitions of delinquency had moved the decision as to what a delinquent was out of the legislature, which made the criminal law, and into the court. The lack of a time limit, except the achievement of majority, on dispositions in juvenile court gave full scope to the discretion of specialists who from the moment of petition (and even without one) had flexible, continuous control. This scope was augmented by the disinclination to institutionalize children: children who went to reform schools passed out of the control of the juvenile court: children who went home on probation did not. Juvenile courts, unfettered by the rules of criminal procedure, took delinquency out of the adversary process much as other progressive reforms took issues out of the contentious, unpredictable world of electoral politics.

Although the founders of the juvenile court did not fit comfortably into the new middle class to which Wiebe attributes progressivism, and although in its first manifestation the juvenile court idea had aspects which also make the fit not quite perfect, Wiebe himself counts the juvenile court among progressive institutions. He associates it with developments in law generally which tended to replace fixed rules with processes that adapted better to shifting contingencies. He associates it, correctly, with the emergence of sociological jurisprudence "which would adjust legal decisions to inductive, social evidence."[42]

That some aspects of the movement appear "conservative" because they emphasized social control and drew upon experiments already made, and that other aspects appear "reformist" because they emphasized the rehabilitative ideal and found new ways to pursue it, ought not to mystify us. As F.A. Allen has said, "No institution as complex as the juvenile court emerges suddenly and fully formed."[43] And the juvenile court reformers like most reformers were anxious to prove both that they had discovered something new which should be tried and that the trial would not be overly risky because it was related in spirit or form to tradition. It is also characteristic of the reformer, almost by definition, that he seeks to eliminate abuses in the system while preserving the system in its fundamentals. No one should be surprised to find in a reform program, particularly in the realm of penology, signs of such conservatism. Given the inherently double nature of reform movements, it makes little sense to seize excitedly upon one aspect or the other as its essence. This is as true of progressivism in general as it is of the juvenile court movement in particular.

That the juvenile court movement

made an easy fit with progressivism is clear from its reception. The juvenile court idea was received as the height of social justice and "was one of the most popular innovations in an era renowned for its solicitous attention to children."[44] Optimism for the fulfillment of its promise pervaded the movement as it pervaded all the progressive era.

Notes

1. Laws of Colorado (1903), chap. 94.

2. From a discussion reported in *Procs. of NCCC*, XXXI (1904), p. 632.

3. Grace Abbott, "Topical Abstract of Juvenile Court Laws," in *Juvenile Court Laws in the United States Summarized*, ed. Hastings H. Hart (New York, 1910), p. 129.

4. Benjamin Lindsey, *The Problem of the Child and How Colorado Cares for Him* (Denver, 1904), pp. 47–48.

5. "The Reformation of Juvenile Delinquents through the Juvenile Court," *Procs. of NCCC*, XXX (1903), p. 213.

6. Op. cit.

7. *Our Penal Machinery and its Victims* (Chicago, 1884), p. 47.

8. A.L. Jacoby, M.D., "The New Approach to the Problem of Delinquency: Punishment vs. Treatment," *Proc. of NCSW*, LIII (1926), p. 179.

9. Ruth Workum, "The Relation Between Functions of the Juvenile Court and Those of General Child-Rearing Agencies," *Procs. of NCSW*, XLIX (1922), p. 144.

10. "The Juvenile Court," *Report of the American Bar Association*, XXXIV (1909), p. 470.

11. Evelina Belden, *Courts in the United States Hearing Children's Cases*, U.S. Children's Bureau Publication #65 (Washington, D.C., 1920), p. 8.

12. *Manual for Probation Officers in New York* (Albany, 1918), p. 58.

13. Op. cit., p. 126.

14. Introduction to Sophonsiba Breckenridge, *The Delinquent Child and the Home* (New York, 1912), pp. 2–4.

15. Ibid.

16. Op. cit., pp. 135, 139.

17. Op. cit., pp. 57, 62.

18. From a discussion reported in *Procs. of NCCC*, XXIX (1902), p. 425.

19. Arthur MacDonald, *Abnormal Man* (Washington, D.C., 1893), p. 53.

20. "Remedial Work on Behalf of our Youth," *Procs. of NCCC*, XXII (1895), p. 237.

21. *Progressivism and the Slums: Tenement House Reform in New York City 1890–1917* (Pittsburgh, 1962), pp. 2, 7.

22. David M. Kennedy, *Birth Control in America: The Career of Margaret Sanger* (New Haven, 1970), p. 15.

23. Ibid.

24. Mack, op. cit., p. 465.

25. Reverend Malcolm Dana, op. cit., p. 237.

26. Mary E. McDowell, "Friendly Visiting," *Procs. of NCCC*, XXIII (1896), p. 253.

27. "One Day in Juvenile Court," *Juvenile Court Record*, II, No. 1 (1900), quoted in his *Concerning Delinquency: Progressive Changes in Our Perspectives* (New York, 1942), p. 95.

28. Op. cit., p. 24.

29. Ibid., p. 69.

30. Ibid., p. 69–78.

31. J. J. Kelso, "Reforming Delinquent Children," *Procs. of NCCC*, XXX (1903), p. 231.

32. *The Problem of the Child*, p. 35.

33. From the speech of Lebeziatnikov to Rodya, p. 365 of the Bantam paperback edition of Feodor Dostoevsky's *Crime and Punishment*.

34. E.E. York, "The Cultivation of Individuality," *Procs. of NCCC*, XXIX (1902), p. 262.

35. MacDonald, op. cit., p. 53.

36. Timothy D. Hurley, "Juvenile Probation," *Procs. of NCCC,* XXXIV (1907), p. 225.

37. Henry Thurston, "Third Day in Juvenile Court" (1900), in *Concerning Delinquency,* p. 99.

38. Robert Baldwin, quoted in Hastings H. Hart, *Preventive Treatment of Neglected Children* (New York, 1910). p. 272.

39. Homer Folks, "Juvenile Probation," *Procs. of NCCC,* XXXII (1906), p. 118.

40. Walter Wheeler in discussion, *Procs. of NCCC,* XXXI (1904), p. 570.

41. "The Jurisprudence of Juvenile Deviance," in Margaret Rosenheim, ed., *Pursuing Justice for the Child* (Chicago, 1976), p. 8.

42. Op. cit., p. 150.

43. *The Borderland of Criminal Justice: Essays in Law and Criminology* (Chicago, 1964), p. 46.

44. Schlossman, op. cit., p. 66.

The Saints and the Roughnecks

3

William J. Chambliss

Eight promising young men—children of good, stable, white upper-middle-class families, active in school affairs, good pre-college students—were some of the most delinquent boys at Hanibal High School. While community residents and parents knew that these boys occasionally sowed a few wild oats, they were totally unaware that sowing wild oats completely occupied the daily routine of these young men. The Saints were constantly occupied with truancy, drinking, wild driving, petty theft and vandalism. Yet not one was officially arrested for any misdeed during the two years I observed them.

This record was particularly surprising in light of my observations during the same two years of another gang of Hanibal High School students, six lower-class white boys known as the Roughnecks. The Roughnecks were constantly in trouble with police and community even though their rate of delinquency was about equal with that of the Saints. What was the cause of this dis-

Reprinted from *Society*, Vol. 11, No. 1, 1973, pp. 341–355, by permission of Transaction Publishers. Copyright © 1973 by Transaction Publishers.

parity? the result? The following consideration of the activities, social class and community perceptions of both gangs may provide some answers.

The Saints From Monday to Friday

The Saints' principal daily concern was with getting out of school as early as possible. The boys managed to get out of school with minimum danger that they would be accused of playing hookey through an elaborate procedure for obtaining "legitimate" release from class. The most common procedure was for one boy to obtain the release of another by fabricating a meeting of some committee, program or recognized club. Charles might raise his hand in his 9:00 chemistry class and ask to be excused—a euphemism for going to the bathroom. Charles would go to Ed's math class and inform the teacher that Ed was needed for a 9:30 rehearsal of the drama club play. The math teacher would recognize Ed and Charles as "good students" involved in numerous school activities and would permit Ed to leave at 9:30. Charles would return to his class, and Ed would go to Tom's English class to obtain his release. Tom would engineer Charles' escape. The strategy would continue until as many of the Saints as possible were freed. After a stealthy trip to the car (which had been parked in a strategic spot), the boys were off for a day of fun.

Over the two years I observed the Saints, this pattern was repeated nearly every day. There were variations on the theme, but in one form or another, the boys used this procedure for getting out of class and then off of the school grounds. Rarely did all eight of the Saints manage to leave school at the same time. The average number avoiding school on the days I observed them was five.

Having escaped from the concrete corridors the boys usually went either to a pool hall on the other (lower-class) side of town or to a cafe in the suburbs. Both places were out of the way of people the boys were likely to know (family or school officials), and both provided a source of entertainment. The pool hall entertainment was the generally rough atmosphere, the occasional hustler, the sometimes drunk proprietor and, of course, the game of pool. The cafe's entertainment was provided by the owner. The boys would "accidentally" knock a glass on the floor or spill cola on the counter—not all the time, but enough to be sporting. They would also bend spoons, put salt in sugar bowls and generally tease whoever was working in the cafe. The owner had opened the cafe recently and was dependent on the boys' business which was, in fact, substantial since between the horsing around and the teasing they bought food and drinks.

The Saints on Weekends

On weekends, the automobile was even more critical than during the week, for on weekends the Saints went to Big Town—a large city with a population of over a million 25 miles from Hanibal. Every Friday and Saturday night most of the Saints would meet between 8:00 and 8:30 and would go into Big Town. Big Town activities included drinking heavily in taverns or nightclubs, driving drunkenly through the streets, and committing acts of vandalism and playing pranks.

By midnight on Fridays and Saturdays the Saints were usually thoroughly high, and one or two of them were often so drunk they had to be carried to the cars. Then the boys drove around town, calling obscenities to women and girls; occasionally trying (unsuccessfully so far as I could tell) to pick girls up; and driving recklessly through red lights and at high speeds with their lights out. Occasionally they played "chicken." One boy would climb out the back window of the car and across the roof to the driver's side of the car while the car was moving at high speed (between 40 and 50 miles an hour); then the driver would move over and the boy who had just crawled across the car roof would take the driver's seat.

Searching for "fair game" for a prank was the boys' principal activity after they left the tavern. The boys would drive alongside a foot patrolman and ask directions to some street. If the policeman leaned on the car in the course of answering the question, the driver would speed away, causing him to lose his balance. The Saints were careful to play this prank only in an area where they were not going to spend much time and where they could quickly disappear around a corner to avoid having their license plate number taken.

Construction sites and road repair areas were the special province of the Saints' mischief. A soon-to-be-repaired hole in the road inevitably invited the Saints to remove lanterns and wooden barricades and put them in the car, leaving the hole unprotected. The boys would find a safe vantage point and wait for an unsuspecting motorist to drive into the hole. Often, though not always, the boys would go up to the motorist and commiserate with him about the dreadful way the city protected its citizenry.

Leaving the scene of the open hole and the motorist, the boys would then go searching for an appropriate place to erect the stolen barricade. An "appropriate place" was often a spot on a highway near a curve in the road where the barricade would not be seen by an oncoming motorist. The boys would wait to watch an unsuspecting motorist attempt to stop and (usually) crash into the wooden barricade. With saintly bearing the boys might offer help and understanding.

A stolen lantern might well find its way onto the back of a police car or hang from a street lamp. Once a lantern served as a prop for a reenactment of the "midnight ride of Paul Revere" until the "play," which was taking place at 2:00 A.M. in the center of a main street of Big Town, was interrupted by a police car several blocks away. The boys ran, leaving the lanterns on the street, and managed to avoid being apprehended.

Abandoned houses, especially if they were located in out-of-the-way places, were fair game for destruction and spontaneous vandalism. The boys would break windows, remove furniture to the yard and tear it apart, urinate on the walls and scrawl obscenities inside.

Through all the pranks, drinking and reckless driving the boys managed miraculously to avoid being stopped by police. Only twice in two years was I aware that they had been stopped by a Big City policeman. Once was for speeding (which they did every time they drove whether they were drunk or sober), and the driver managed to convince the policeman that it was

simply an error. The second time they were stopped they had just left a nightclub and were walking through an alley. Aaron stopped to urinate and the boys began making obscene remarks. A foot patrolman came into the alley, lectured the boys and sent them home. Before the boys got to the car one began talking in a loud voice again. The policeman, who had followed them down the alley, arrested this boy for disturbing the peace and took him to the police station where the other Saints gathered. After paying a $5.00 fine, and with the assurance that there would be no permanent record of the arrest, the boy was released.

The boys had a spirit of frivolity and fun about their escapades. They did not view what they were engaged in as "delinquency," though it surely was by any reasonable definition of that word. They simply viewed themselves as having a little fun and who, they would ask, was really hurt by it? The answer had to be no one, although this fact remains one of the most difficult things to explain about the gang's behavior. Unlikely though it seems, in two years of drinking, driving, carousing and vandalism no one was seriously injured as a result of the Saints' activities.

The Saints in School

The Saints were highly successful in school. The average grade for the group was "B," with two of the boys having close to a straight "A" average. Almost all of the boys were popular and many of them held offices in the school. One of the boys was vice-president of the student body one year. Six of the boys played on athletic teams.

At the end of their senior year, the student body selected ten seniors for special recognition as the "school wheels"; four of the ten were Saints. Teachers and school officials saw no problem with any of these boys and anticipated that they would all "make something of themselves."

How the boys managed to maintain this impression is surprising in view of their actual behavior while in school. Their technique for covering truancy was so successful that teachers did not even realize that the boys were absent from school much of the time. Occasionally, of course, the system would backfire and then the boy was on his own. A boy who was caught would be most contrite, would plead guilty and ask for mercy. He inevitably got the mercy he sought.

Cheating on examinations was rampant, even to the point of orally communicating answers to exams as well as looking at one another's papers. Since none of the group studied, and since they were primarily dependent on one another for help, it is surprising that grades were so high. Teachers contributed to the deception in their admitted inclination to give these boys (and presumably others like them) the benefit of the doubt. When asked how the boys did in school, and when pressed on specific examinations, teachers might admit that they were disappointed in John's performance, but would quickly add that they "knew he was capable of doing better," so John was given a higher grade than he had actually earned. How often this happened is impossible to know. During the time that I observed the group, I never saw any of the boys take homework home. Teachers may have been "understanding" very regularly.

One exception to the gang's generally good performance was Jerry, who had a "C" average in his junior year, experienced disaster the next year and failed to graduate. Jerry had always been a little more nonchalant than the others about the liberties he took in school. Rather than wait for someone to come get him from class, he would offer his own excuse and leave. Although he probably did not miss any more classes than most of the others in the group, he did not take the requisite pains to cover his absences. Jerry was the only Saint whom I ever heard talk back to a teacher. Although teachers often called him a "cut up" or a "smart kid," they never referred to him as a troublemaker or as a kid headed for trouble. It seems likely, then, that Jerry's failure his senior year and his mediocre performance his junior year were consequences of his not playing the game the proper way (possibly because he was disturbed by his parents' divorce). His teachers regarded him as "immature" and not quite ready to get out of high school.

The Police and the Saints

The local police saw the Saints as good boys who were among the leaders of the youth in the community. Rarely, the boys might be stopped in town for speeding or for running a stop sign. When this happened the boys were always polite, contrite and pled for mercy. As in school, they received the mercy they asked for. None ever received a ticket or was taken into the precinct by the local police.

The situation in Big City, where the boys engaged in most of their delinquency, was only slightly different. The police there did not know the boys at all, although occasionally the boys were stopped by a patrolman. Once they were caught taking a lantern from a construction site. Another time they were stopped for running a stop sign, and on several occasions they were stopped for speeding. Their behavior was as before: contrite, polite and penitent. The urban police, like the local police, accepted their demeanor as sincere. More important, the urban police were convinced that these were good boys just out for a lark.

The Roughnecks

Hanibal townspeople never perceived the Saints' high level of delinquency. The Saints were good boys who just went in for an occasional prank. After all, they were well dressed, well mannered and had nice cars. The Roughnecks were a different story. Although the two gangs of boys were the same age, and both groups engaged in an equal amount of wild-oat sowing, everyone agreed that the not-so-well-dressed, not-so-well-mannered, not-so-rich boys were heading for trouble. Townspeople would say, "You can see the gang members at the drugstore night after night, leaning against the storefront (sometimes drunk) or slouching around inside buying cokes, reading magazines, and probably stealing old Mr. Wall blind. When they are outside and girls walk by, even respectable girls, these boys make suggestive remarks. Sometimes their remarks are downright lewd."

From the community's viewpoint, the real indication that these kids were in for trouble was that they were constantly involved with the police. Some of them had been picked up for stealing, mostly small stuff, of course, "but still it's stealing small stuff that leads to big time crimes. Too bad," people said. "Too bad that these boys couldn't behave like the other kids in town; stay out of trouble, be polite to adults, and look to their future."

The community's impression of the degree to which this group of six boys (ranging in age from 16 to 19) engaged in delinquency was somewhat distorted. In some ways the gang was more delinquent than the community thought; in other ways they were less.

The fighting activities of the group were fairly readily and accurately perceived by almost everyone. At least once a month, the boys would get into some sort of fight, although most fights were scraps between members of the group or involved only one member of the group and some peripheral hanger-on. Only three times in the period of observation did the group fight together: once against a gang from across town, once against two blacks and once against a group of boys from another school. For the first two fights the group went out "looking for trouble"—and they found it both times. The third fight followed a football game and began spontaneously with an argument on the football field between one of the Roughnecks and a member of the opposition's football team.

Jack had a particular propensity for fighting and was involved in most of the brawls. He was a prime mover of the escalation of arguments into fights.

More serious than fighting, had the community been aware of it, was theft. Although almost everyone was aware that the boys occasionally stole things, they did not realize the extent of the activity. Petty stealing was a frequent event for the Roughnecks. Sometimes they stole as a group and coordinated their efforts; other times they stole in pairs. Rarely did they steal alone.

The thefts ranged from very small things like paperback books, comics and ballpoint pens to expensive items like watches. The nature of the thefts varied from time to time. The gang would go through a period of systematically lifting items from automobiles or school lockers. Types of thievery varied with the whim of the gang. Some forms of thievery were more profitable than others, but all thefts were for profit, not just thrills.

Roughnecks siphoned gasoline from cars as often as they had access to an automobile, which was not very often. Unlike the Saints, who owned their own cars, the Roughnecks would have to borrow their parents' cars, an event which occurred only eight or nine times a year. The boys claimed to have stolen cars for joy rides from time to time.

Ron committed the most serious of the group's offenses. With an unidentified associate the boy attempted to burglarize a gasoline station. Although this station had been robbed twice previously in the same month, Ron denied any involvement in either of the other thefts. When Ron and his accomplice approached the station, the owner was hiding in the bushes beside the station. He fired both barrels of a double-barreled shotgun at the boys. Ron was severely injured; the other boy ran away and was never caught. Though he remained in critical condition for several months, Ron finally recovered and served six months of the following year in reform school. Upon release from reform school, Ron was put back a grade in school, and began running around with a different gang of boys. The Roughnecks considered the new gang less delinquent than themselves, and during the following year Ron had no more trouble with the police.

The Roughnecks, then, engaged mainly in three types of delinquency: theft, drinking and fighting. Although community members perceived that this gang of kids was delinquent, they mistakenly believed that their illegal activities were primarily drinking, fighting and being a nuisance to passersby. Drinking was limited among the gang members, although it did occur, and theft was much more prevalent than anyone realized.

Drinking would doubtless have been more prevalent had the boys had ready access to liquor. Since they rarely had automobiles at their disposal, they could not travel very far, and the bars in town would not serve them. Most of the boys had little money, and this, too, inhibited their pur-

chase of alcohol. Their major source of liquor was a local drunk who would buy them a fifth if they would give him enough extra to buy himself a pint of whisky or a bottle of wine.

The community's perception of drinking as prevalent stemmed from the fact that it was the most obvious delinquency the boys engaged in. When one of the boys had been drinking, even a casual observer seeing him on the corner would suspect that he was high.

There was a high level of mutual distrust and dislike between the Roughnecks and the police. The boys felt very strongly that the police were unfair and corrupt. Some evidence existed that the boys were correct in their perception.

The main source of the boys' dislike for the police undoubtedly stemmed from the fact that the police would sporadically harass the group. From the standpoint of the boys, these acts of occasional enforcement of the law were whimsical and uncalled for. It made no sense to them, for example, that the police would come to the corner occasionally and threaten them with arrest for loitering when the night before the boys had been out siphoning gasoline from cars and the police had been nowhere in sight. To the boys, the police were stupid on the one hand, for not being where they should have been and catching the boys in a serious offense, and unfair on the other hand, for trumping up "loitering" charges against them.

From the viewpoint of the police, the situation was quite different. They knew, with all the confidence necessary to be a policeman, that these boys were engaged in criminal activities. They knew this partly from occasionally catching them, mostly from circumstantial evidence ("the boys were around when those tires were slashed"), and partly because the police shared the view of the community in general that this was a bad bunch of boys. The best the police could hope to do was to be sensitive to the fact that these boys were engaged in illegal acts and arrest them whenever there was some evidence that they had been involved. Whether or not the boys had in fact committed a particular act in a particular way was not especially important. The police had a broader view: their job was to stamp out these kids' crimes; the tactics were not as important as the end result.

Over the period that the group was under observation, each member was arrested at least once. Several of the boys were arrested a number of times and spent at least one night in jail. While most were never taken to court, two of the boys were sentenced to six months' incarceration in boys' schools.

The Roughnecks in School

The Roughnecks' behavior in school was not particularly disruptive. During school hours they did not all hang around together, but tended instead to spend most of their time with one or two other members of the gang who were their special buddies. Although every member of the gang attempted to avoid school as much as possible, they were not particularly successful and most of them attended school with surprising regularity. They considered school a burden—something to be gotten through with a minimum of conflict. If they were "bugged" by a particular teacher, it could lead to trouble. One of the boys, Al, once threatened to beat up a teacher and, according to the other boys, the teacher hid under a desk to escape him.

Teachers saw the boys the way the general community did, as heading for trouble, as being uninterested in making something of themselves. Some were also seen as being incapable of meeting the academic standards of the school. Most of the teachers expressed concern for this group of boys and were willing to pass them despite poor performance, in the belief that failing them would only aggravate the problem.

The group of boys had a grade point average just slightly above "C". No one in the group failed either grade, and no one had better than a "C" average. They were very consistent in their achievement or, at least, the teachers were consistent in their perception of the boys' achievement.

Two of the boys were good football players. Herb was acknowledged to be the best player in the school and Jack was almost as good. Both boys were criticized for their failure to abide by training rules, for refusing to come to practice as often as they should, and for not playing their best during practice. What they lacked in sportsmanship they made up for in skill, apparently, and played every game no matter how poorly they had performed in practice or how many practice sessions they had missed.

Two Questions

Why did the community, the school and the police react to the Saints as though they were good, upstanding, nondelinquent youths with bright futures but to the Roughnecks as though they were tough, young criminals who were headed for trouble? Why did the Roughnecks and the Saints in fact have quite different careers after high school—careers which, by and large, lived up to the expectations of the community?

The most obvious explanation for the differences in the community's and law enforcement agencies' reactions to the two gangs is that one group of boys was "more delinquent" than the other. Which group *was* more delinquent? The answer to this question will determine in part how we explain the differential responses to these groups by the members of the community and, particularly, by law enforcement and school officials.

In sheer number of illegal acts, the Saints were the more delinquent. They were truant from school for at least part of the day almost every day of the week. In addition, their drinking and vandalism occurred with surprising regularity. The Roughnecks, in contrast, engaged sporadically in delinquent episodes. While these episodes were frequent, they certainly did not occur on a daily or even a weekly basis.

The difference in frequency of offenses was probably caused by the Roughnecks' inability to obtain liquor and to manipulate legitimate excuses from school. Since the Roughnecks had less money than the Saints, and teachers carefully supervised their school activities, the Roughnecks' hearts may have been as black as the Saints', but their misdeeds were not nearly as frequent.

There are really no clear-cut criteria by which to measure qualitative differences in antisocial behavior. The most important dimension of the difference is generally referred to as the "seriousness" of the offenses.

If seriousness encompasses the relative economic costs of delinquent acts, then some assessment can be made. The Roughnecks probably stole an average of about $5.00 worth of goods a week. Some weeks the figure was considerably higher, but these times must be balanced against long periods when almost nothing was stolen.

The Saints were more continuously engaged in delinquency but their acts were not for the most part costly to property. Only their vandalism and occasional theft of gasoline would so qualify. Perhaps once or twice a month they would siphon a tankful

of gas. The other costly items were street signs, construction lanterns and the like. All of these acts combined probably did not average $5.00 a week, partly because much of the stolen equipment was abandoned and presumably could be recovered. The difference in cost of stolen property between the two groups was trivial, but the Roughnecks probably had a slightly more expensive set of activities than did the Saints.

Another meaning of seriousness is the potential threat of physical harm to members of the community and to the boys themselves. The Roughnecks were more prone to physical violence; they not only welcomed an opportunity to fight; they went seeking it. In addition, they fought among themselves frequently. Although the fighting never included deadly weapons, it was still a menace, however minor, to the physical safety of those involved.

The Saints never fought. They avoided physical conflict both inside and outside the group. At the same time, though, the Saints frequently endangered their own and other people's lives. They did so almost every time they drove a car, especially if they had been drinking. Sober, their driving was risky; under the influence of alcohol it was horrendous. In addition, the Saints endangered the lives of others with their pranks. Street excavations left unmarked were a very serious hazard.

Evaluating the relative seriousness of the two gangs' activities is difficult. The community reacted as though the behavior of the Roughnecks was a problem, and they reacted as though the behavior of the Saints was not. But the members of the community were ignorant of the array of delinquent acts that characterized the Saints' behavior. Although concerned citizens were unaware of much of the Roughnecks' behavior as well, they were much better informed about the Roughnecks' involvement in delinquency than they were about the Saints'.

Visibility

Differential treatment of the two gangs resulted in part because one gang was infinitely more visible than the other. This differential visibility was a direct function of the economic standing of the families. The Saints had access to automobiles and were able to remove themselves from the sight of the community. In as routine a decision as to where to go to have a milkshake after school, the Saints stayed away from the mainstream of community life. Lacking transportation, the Roughnecks could not make it to the edge of town. The center of town was the only practical place for them to meet since their homes were scattered throughout the town and any noncentral meeting place put an undue hardship on some members. Through necessity the Roughnecks congregated in a crowded area where everyone in the community passed frequently, including teachers and law enforcement officers. They could easily see the Roughnecks hanging around the drugstore.

The Roughnecks, of course, made themselves even more visible by making remarks to passersby and by occasionally getting into fights on the corner. Meanwhile, just as regularly, the Saints were either at the cafe on one edge of town or in the pool hall at the other edge of town. Without any particular realization that they were making themselves inconspicuous, the Saints were able to hide their time-wasting. Not only were they removed from the mainstream of traffic, but they were almost always inside a building.

On their escapades the Saints were also relatively invisible, since they left Hanibal and traveled to Big City. Here, too, they were mobile, roaming the city, rarely going to the same area twice.

Demeanor

To the notion of visibility must be added the difference in the responses of group members to outside intervention with their activities. If one of the Saints was confronted with an accusing policeman, even if he felt he was truly innocent of a wrongdoing, his demeanor was apologetic and penitent. A Roughneck's attitude was almost the polar opposite. When confronted with a threatening adult authority, even one who tried to be pleasant, the Roughneck's hostility and disdain were clearly observable. Sometimes he might attempt to put up a veneer of respect, but it was thin and was not accepted as sincere by the authority.

School was no different from the community at large. The Saints could manipulate the system by feigning compliance with the school norms. The availability of cars at school meant that once free from the immediate sight of the teacher, the boys could disappear rapidly. And this escape was well enough planned that no administrator or teacher was nearby when the boys left. A Roughneck who wished to escape for a few hours was in a bind. If it were possible to get free from class, downtown was still a mile away, and even if he arrived there, he was still very visible. Truancy for the Roughnecks meant almost certain detection, while the Saints enjoyed almost complete immunity from sanctions.

Bias

Community members were not aware of the transgressions of the Saints. Even if the Saints had been less discreet, their favorite delinquencies would have been perceived as less serious than those of the Rough-necks.

In the eyes of the police and school officials, a boy who drinks in an alley and stands intoxicated on the street corner is committing a more serious offense than is a boy who drinks to inebriation in a nightclub or a tavern and drives around afterwards in a car. Similarly, a boy who steals a wallet from a store will be viewed as having committed a more serious offense than a boy who steals a lantern from a construction site.

Perceptual bias also operates with respect to the demeanor of the boys in the two groups when they are confronted by adults. It is not simply that adults dislike the posture affected by boys of the Roughneck ilk; more important is the conviction that the posture adopted by the Roughnecks is an indication of their devotion and commitment to deviance as a way of life. The posture becomes a cue, just as the type of the offense is a cue, to the degree to which the known transgressions are indicators of the youths' potential for other problems.

Visibility, demeanor and bias are surface variables which explain the day-to-day operations of the police. Why do these surface variables operate as they do? Why did the police choose to disregard the Saints' delinquencies while breathing down the backs of the Roughnecks?

The answer lies in the class structure of American society and the control of legal institutions by those at the top of the class structure. Obviously, no representative of the upper class drew up the operational chart for the police which led them to look in the ghettoes and on streetcorners—which led them to see the demeanor of lower-class youth as troublesome and that of upper-middle-class youth as tolerable. Rather, the procedures simply developed from experience—experience with irate and influential upper-middle-class parents insisting that their son's vandalism was simply a prank and his drunkenness only a momentary "sowing of wild oats"—experience with cooperative or indifferent, powerless, lower-class parents who acquiesced to the law's definition of their son's behavior.

Adult Careers of the Saints and the Roughnecks

The community's confidence in the potential of the Saints and the Roughnecks apparently was justified. If anything, the community members underestimated the degree to which these youngsters would turn out "good" or "bad."

Seven of the eight members of the Saints went on to college immediately after high school. Five of the boys graduated from college in four years. The sixth one finished college after two years in the army, and the seventh spent four years in the air force before returning to college and receiving a B.A. degree. Of these seven college graduates, three went on for advanced degrees. One finished law school and is now active in state politics, one finished medical school and is practicing near Hanibal, and one boy is now working for a Ph.D. The other four college graduates entered submanagerial, managerial or executive training positions with larger firms.

The only Saint who did not complete college was Jerry. Jerry had failed to graduate from high school with the other Saints. During his second senior year, after the other Saints had gone on to college, Jerry began to hang around with what several teachers described as a "rough crowd"—the gang that was heir apparent to the Roughnecks. At the end of his second senior year, when he did graduate from high school, Jerry took a job as a used-car salesman, got married and quickly had a child.

Although he made several abortive attempts to go to college by attending night school, when I last saw him (ten years after high school) Jerry was unemployed and had been living on unemployment for almost a year. His wife worked as a waitress.

Some of the Roughnecks have lived up to community expectations. A number of them were headed for trouble. A few were not.

Jack and Herb were the athletes among the Roughnecks and their athletic prowess paid off handsomely. Both boys received unsolicited athletic scholarships to college. After Herb received his scholarship (near the end of his senior year), he apparently did an about-face. His demeanor became very similar to that of the Saints. Although he remained a member in good standing of the Roughnecks, he stopped participating in most activities and did not hang on the corner as often.

Jack did not change. If anything, he became more prone to fighting. He even made excuses for accepting the scholarship. He told the other gang members that the school had guaranteed him a "C" average if he would come to play football—an idea that seems far-fetched, even in this day of highly competitive recruiting.

During the summer after graduation from high school, Jack attempted suicide by jumping from a tall building. The jump would certainly have killed most people trying it, but Jack survived. He entered college in the fall and played four years of football. He and Herb graduated in four years, and both are teaching and coaching in high schools. They are married and have stable families. If anything, Jack appears to have a more prestigious position in the community than does Herb, though both are well respected and secure in their positions.

Two of the boys never finished high school. Tommy left at the end of his junior year and went to another state. That summer he was arrested and placed on probation on a manslaughter charge. Three years later he was arrested for murder; he pleaded guilty to second degree murder and is serving a 30-year sentence in the state penitentiary.

Al, the other boy who did not finish high school, also left the state in his senior year. He is serving a life sentence in a state penitentiary for first degree murder.

Wes is a small-time gambler. He finished high school and "bummed around." After several years he made contact with a bookmaker who employed him as a runner. Later he acquired his own area and has been working it ever since. His position among the bookmakers is almost identical to the position he had in the gang; he is always around but no one is really aware of him. He makes no trouble and he does not get into any. Steady, reliable, capable of keeping his mouth closed, he plays the game by the rules, even though the game is an illegal one.

That leaves only Ron. Some of his former friends reported that they had heard he was "driving a truck up north," but no one could provide any concrete information.

Reinforcement

The community responded to the Roughnecks as boys in trouble, and the boys agreed with that perception. Their pattern of deviancy was reinforced, and breaking away from it became increasingly unlikely. Once the boys acquired an image of themselves as deviants, they selected new friends who affirmed that self-image. As that self-conception became more firmly entrenched, they also became willing to try new and more extreme deviances. With their growing alienation came freer expression of disrespect and hostility for representatives of the legitimate society. This disrespect increased the community's negativism, perpetuating the entire process of commitment to deviance. Lack of a commitment to deviance works the same way. In either case, the process will perpetuate itself unless some event (like a scholarship to college or a sudden failure) external to the established relationship intervenes. For two of the Roughnecks (Herb and Jack), receiving college athletic scholarships created new relations and culminated in a break with the established pattern of deviance. In the case of one of the Saints (Jerry), his parents' divorce and his failing to graduate from high school changed some of his other relations. Being held back in school for a year and losing his place among the Saints had sufficient impact on Jerry to alter his self-image and virtually to assure that he would not go on to college as his peers did. Although the experiments of life can rarely be reversed, it seems likely in view of the behavior of the other boys who did not enjoy this special treatment by the school that Jerry, too, would have "become something" had he graduated as anticipated. For Herb and Jack outside intervention worked to their advantage; for Jerry it was his undoing.

Selective perception and labelling—finding, processing and punishing some kinds of criminality and not others—means that visible, poor, nonmobile, out-spoken, undiplomatic "tough" kids will be noticed, whether their actions are seriously delinquent or not. Other kids, who have established a reputation for being bright (even though underachieving), disciplined and involved in respectable activities, who are mobile and monied, will be invisible when they deviate from sanctioned activities. They'll sow their wild oats—perhaps even wider and thicker than their lower-class cohorts—but they won't be noticed. When it's time to leave adolescence most will follow the expected path, settling into the ways of the middle class, remembering fondly the delinquent but unnoticed fling of their youth. The Roughnecks and others like them may turn around, too. It is more likely that their noticeable deviance will have been so reinforced by police and community that their lives will be effectively channelled into careers consistent with their adolescent background.

PART 2

The Measurement and Social Distribution of Delinquency

In this section of the book, we examine issues related to the measurement and social distribution of delinquency. The most widely used measure of the social distribution of delinquency in the United States comes from official governmental statistics published in the Federal Bureau of Investigation's *Uniform Crime Reports (UCR)*. Since the 1930s, the FBI has compiled annual data from police departments across the country on "crimes reported to the police" (or known to the police) and on "arrests" for various types of offenses. The most information is available for the "Part 1 Offenses" or "Index Crimes"—the violent crimes of homicide, forcible rape, robbery, and aggravated assault; and the property crimes of burglary, larceny-theft, motor vehicle theft, and recently arson.[1] Data on "Part 2 Offenses" such as non-aggravated assaults, embezzlement and fraud, drug and liquor violations, vandalism, disorderly conduct, running away, and many other crimes are also available, though in less detail. Data from the *UCR* have been used to measure trends in criminal behavior for the society as a whole and for different subgroups (e.g., age, racial, or gender groups) in the population.

The data on crimes reported to the police are more appropriate than arrests for estimating the actual level of crime in any given year since not all crimes that are committed result in arrest. However, for learning about rate variations for different subgroups arrest data must be used since only after an arrest do the characteristics of the offender become known. The FBI publishes arrest data by age, race, and gender. Arrest data by social class are not recorded, although estimates of the social class distribution of arrests are often inferred from race statistics since minority groups are disproportionately represented in the lower social classes in the United States.

The accuracy of the *UCR* as a basis for generalizing about crime has been questioned by many criminologists. These data are influenced not only by the actual behavior of criminals, but also by police department classification systems and policies regarding enforcement of particular laws, by police officers' discretionary decision-making in the field, and by citizens' crime-reporting behaviors (Sheley, 1985). Variations in police or citizen reporting practices can produce changes in crime statistics independent of criminals' behavior. Consequently, criminologists have supplemented *UCR* data with alternative sources when making observations about the social distribution of delinquency. Two primary alternative data sources come from *self-report* and *victimization surveys*. In self-report surveys, respondents are asked to complete questionnaires indicating their personal involvement in various types of offenses. In victimization surveys, respondents are asked to report on their personal experiences as victims of crime.

Age and Crime

One central issue pertaining to the social distribution of delinquency involves whether juveniles, as compared to adults, account for a disproportionate share of the crime problem in the United States. Siegal and Senna (1988) reported that while juveniles age thirteen to eighteen made up only 9 percent of the U.S. population, they accounted for over 32 percent of arrests for index crimes and 19 percent of all arrests (Part 1 and Part 2 offenses combined).[2] They also noted that the peak age for property crimes occurred at about age sixteen and the peak age for violent crimes at about age eighteen. Similarly, Steffensmeier et al. (1989:806) observed that "most crimes peak in adolescence or early adulthood [and] then decline fairly steadily." They explained this pattern in terms of:

> the increased sources of criminogenic reinforcement experienced by young people . . . [and] the powerful institutional pressures for conformity that accompany adulthood. Juveniles have not as yet developed either a well-defined sense of self or strong stakes in conformity. . . . They are barred from many legitimate avenues for achieving socially valued goals; their dependent status insulates them from many of the social and legal costs of illegitimate activities; and their stage of cognitive development limits prudence concerning the consequences of their behavior (pp. 806–7).

In addition, Steffensmeier et al. (1989) reported that the peak ages for crime rates in the 1980s were generally lower than they were for the previous four decades, perhaps because of worsening conditions associated with the causes of youth crime. They also noted, however, that peak ages and rates of decline varied for different offenses. For instance, low-yield, high-risk offenses such as burglary, robbery, and vandalism receive more reinforcement among juveniles and thus peaked earlier and declined more rapidly with age. High yield, low-risk offenses such as embezzlement and fraud, or crimes involving an expressive or emotional character such as homicide or assault, that are "less susceptible to rational withdrawal and [that] have greater cultural supports," peaked later and declined more slowly (p. 808).

Because young people appear to account for a disproportionate amount of crime, the dramatic increase in the youthful population associated with the post World War II "baby boom" is believed to have accounted for the large increase in crime rates in the 1960s and early 1970s (Sheley, 1985). But as the size of the youthful population began to diminish, crime rates stabilized and started to decline in the 1980s (Cohen and Land, 1987; Steffensmeier et al., 1987).

Data from self-report studies regarding the age distribution of crime has suggested that the peak age for some crimes may actually be lower than is indicated in official statistics (Ageton and Elliott, 1978). Perhaps police use their discretionary authority to be more lenient with younger children, or perhaps they concentrate their enforcement activities against older youth (Empey, 1982). In any case, some self-report studies also found that older adolescents committed more serious crimes than younger adolescents (Hirschi, 1969; Williams and Gold, 1972). In addition, victimization surveys confirmed findings from *UCR* data that teenagers' rates of offending were higher than the rates for adults, especially for crimes such as robbery and personal larceny (Laub et al., 1987).

Race, Class, and Delinquency

In addition to issues pertaining to the age distribution of crime, one of the most controversial debates in criminology has occurred over the question of whether juveniles from minority racial groups and lower class backgrounds have higher rates of offending than other youths. *UCR* data indicate that, generally, black youths' rates of arrest have been disproportionately higher than white youths' rates. For example, Siegal and Senna (1988) reported that while black citizens constituted about 12 percent of the U.S. population, black youths accounted for about 34 percent of arrests for index crimes and about 27 percent of all arrests.[3] Rates of offending for black youths were especially high, in comparison to white youths, for violent crimes. On the other hand, black vs. white rates for crimes such as vandalism, disorderly conduct, and running away were proportional to their representation in the overall population, and whites' rates were disproportionately higher than blacks' for liquor law violations and public drunkenness.

Although *UCR* data are not available by social class for the U.S. as a whole, some studies are available to examine the social class distribution of arrests in particularly communities. The most well known research of this nature was a study conducted by Wolfgang, Figlio, and Sellin (1972) of a Philadelphia birth cohort.[4] Wolfgang et al. followed the delinquent careers of nearly ten thousand boys who were born in the city of Philadelphia in 1945. While over one-third of these boys had some police record by age eighteen, boys from lower-class census tracts were more likely to be delinquent than boys from higher-class tracts (45 percent of lower-class boys were delinquent vs. 27 percent of higher-class boys).

Wolfgang et al. also reported that about 54 percent of the delinquent boys had more than one police contact, over 36 percent had two to four contacts, and 18 percent had five or more contacts. This later group of "chronic offenders" constituted about 6 percent of the total youths in the cohort. Moreover, lower-class boys were more likely than higher-class boys to be among the chronic offender group.

Finally, Wolfgang et al. also found that race was the most significant predictor of delinquency in the cohort (50 percent of nonwhites were delinquent vs. 29 percent of whites). Their study indicated, however, that nonwhite youths were disproportionately represented in the lower-class census tracts (84 percent of nonwhites were lower-class vs. 31 percent of whites). Such overrepresentation of nonwhites among the lower-class has led many criminologists to conclude that the apparently greater involvement of nonwhites in delinquency can be best attributed to conditions associated with lower-class social status. For instance, Yablonsky and Haskell (1988:31) attributed this pattern to "unequal socioeconomic starting points and . . . employment opportunities" for minorities, as well continuing "prejudice and discrimination, . . . a sense of alienation from the larger society by minority group children, . . . [and] problems related to assimilation into the larger culture" (see Duster, 1987).

As indicated above, however, many criminologists have questioned the accuracy of official statistics as a means of making generalizations about the race or social class distribution of delinquency. Beginning in the late 1950s, self-report surveys consistently failed to confirm the relationship between race, class, and delinquency that had been apparent in official statistics (see Hindelang et al., 1981; Tittle et al., 1978). These studies have led some observers to conclude, as Chambliss did in "The Saints and the Roughnecks" (see Chapter 3), that police discriminate or focus their enforcement activities against minority and lower-class youth and that much middle-class delinquency remains hidden. (For further discussion of police bias, see Chapter 22, "Legal and Extra-Legal Influences on Police and Court Processing of Juveniles.")

On the other hand, many criminologists have continued to view the social patterns observed through official statistics as indications of greater minority group and lower-class involvement in much criminal behavior. For instance, Brownfield (1986) demonstrated a relationship between class and self-reported violent delinquency with some, though not all, measures of class; and Hindelang (1978) analyzed victimization survey data and concluded that blacks were overrepresented in *UCR* data because they did in fact commit more crimes (see

Braithwaite, 1981). In any case, the controversy over the race-class-delinquency relationship has important theoretical and practical significance. For if delinquency is viewed primarily as a minority group or lower-class problem, then the causes of delinquency will be seen as rooted primarily in the social conditions associated with lower-class minority communities. If, on the other hand, there is little relationship between race, class, and delinquency, then the causes will be seen in factors that cut across and affect all social groups.

Reconciliation of the controversy stemming from the discrepant findings of official and self-reported measures of delinquency was first suggested by Hindelang, Hirschi, and Weis (1979). They argued that the discrepancy was "largely illusory" because the two types of data did not "tap the same domain of behavior" (p. 995). Researchers administering self-report surveys had generally asked respondents about a wider range of behaviors than were reported in official statistics, and the surveys were skewed toward less serious forms of delinquency that remained largely "outside the domain of behavior that elicits official attention" (p. 996). Thus, Hindelang et al. suggested that there was virtually no relationship between race, class, and less serious delinquency, but that official measures of delinquency provided valid indications of the social distribution of the more serious youthful offending that is of primary concern to law enforcement authorities.

The first reading in this section (Chapter 4), Delbert Elliott and Suzanne Ageton's "Reconciling Race and Class Differences in Self-Reported and Official Estimates of Delinquency," pursues the line of investigation suggested by Hindelang et al. (1979). Elliott and Ageton review and attempt to overcome some of the problems inherent in the self-report survey method. This article is extremely valuable for understanding the construction of self-report surveys, and would be especially useful for students who wish to construct their own questionnaires. Elliott and Ageton carefully examine race and class differences for different categories of offenses: predatory crimes against persons, predatory crimes against property, illegal service, public disorder, and status offenses. They find significant race and class differences (i.e., higher rates for black and lower-class juveniles) only for some crimes, and primarily for high frequency or chronic offenders. They conclude that the differences between their findings and those of earlier self-report studies are "the result of differences in the specific [self-report delinquency] measures."

Analyses of class differences in similar self-report data for later years produced comparable results (Elliott and Huizinga, 1983). And while analyses of race differences in later years yielded inconsistent findings (Huizinga and Elliott, 1985), some researchers found that black male delinquents substantially underreported the extent of their delinquency records (Hindelang et al., 1981). After reviewing the literature on self-report vs. official measures of delinquency, Binder et al. (1988:32) concluded that official data do reflect "actual differences in oc-

currence of serious criminal acts,'' although the differences are ''not as dramatic
as those data make it seem.''

Finally, Elliott and Ageton's study points to an important distinction relevant to the social distribution of delinquency between the *prevalence* of offending
and the *incidence* of offending. Prevalence refers to the proportion of a particular
group that has engaged in delinquency, while incidence refers to the frequency of
offending by the active members of a group (Paternoster and Triplett, 1988). The
theoretical significance of this distinction has been stated by Blumstein and
Graddy (1982:265):

> It is reasonable to expect . . . that one set of factors distinguishes between those
> persons who become involved in crimes the first time and those who do not, and that
> a different set of factors distinguishes those who persist in crime once involved,
> from those who discontinue criminality at an early stage.

Gender and Delinquency

Unlike the race and class distribution of delinquency, one of the most consistent
findings in the delinquency literature has been that males are more involved than
females in most forms of delinquent activity (see Harris, 1977). Indeed, prior to
the 1970s most researchers treated females as marginal to the study of juvenile
delinquency. For example, Albert Cohen (1955:144), well known for his study
of male delinquent subcultures, paid only token attention to females, proposing
that male delinquency was ''versatile,'' while female delinquency was ''specialized'' and limited to ''sexual crimes.'' He concluded that girls became delinquent because they were preoccupied with establishing sexual relationships
with boys.

Most sociologists have used the concept of gender role socialization to explain the lower rates of female delinquency. Gender roles involve the socially
expected behaviors associated with being male and female that are learned from
the sociocultural environment and that are rooted in the organization of social institutions, particularly the family and occupational structure (see Messerschmidt,
1986). Some observers believe that as the position of women in society began to
change over the last two decades, the traditional patterns of female v. male delinquency also changed. By the mid-1970s, studies began to indicate that female
crime and delinquency were rising and that a new type of female offender had
emerged who was more violent and aggressive than her predecessors (Adler,
1975). These claims were fueled by media reports of women in militant revolutionary groups such as the Weather Underground and the Symbionese Liberation
Army (Patricia Hearst), of women participating in the killings orchestrated by
Charles Manson, and of Lynette Fromme's and Sara Jane Moore's attempts to

assassinate President Gerald Ford (Datesman and Scarpitti, 1980). Popular media began to proclaim that increased female crime was the negative side of women's liberation (Woodward and Malamud, 1975), providing propaganda for those who opposed the women's movement.

A large volume of scholarly literature has developed that has attempted to measure and explain the alleged changes in the volume and character of female law-breaking. Debate has centered around whether females have remained traditional and nonviolent in their patterns of crime and delinquency, whether the observed changes (if they exist at all) are real or the result of changing societal reaction (labeling) to female misconduct, and whether female law-violators have been "masculinized" or in other ways influenced by the women's liberation movement or changing roles. In the second article in this section (Chapter 5), "Contemporary Trends in Female Delinquency: Stability or Change?," Ronald Berger addresses these issues in an attempt to understand gender as a major component of the social distribution of delinquency. (In Chapter 14, Berger considers other sociological theories that have been advanced as explanations of contemporary female delinquency.)

Notes

1. Arson was added to the list of index crimes in 1979 (Sheley, 1985)
2. Data from Siegal and Senna are for 1985.
3. Siegal and Senna (1988:57) report that that arrest rates for Hispanic youths "seem to be proportional to their representation in the population."
4. For other birth cohort studies, see Shannon (1982) and Tracy et al. (1985).

References

Adler, F. 1975. *Sisters in Crime: The Rise of the New Female Offender.* New York: McGraw Hill.

Ageton, S.S. and D.S. Elliott. 1978. *The Incidence of Delinquent Behavior in a National Probability Sample of Adolescents.* Boulder, CO: Behavioral Research Institute.

Binder, A., G. Geis, and D. Bruce. 1988. *Juvenile Delinquency: Historical, Cultural, Legal Perspectives.* New York: Macmillan.

Blumstein, A., and E. Graddy. 1982. "Prevalence and recidivism in index arrests: A feedback model." *Law and Society Review* 16:265–90.

Braithwaite, J. 1981. "The myth of social class and criminality reconsidered." *American Sociological Review* 46:36–57.

Brownfield, D. 1986. "Social class and violent behavior." *Criminology* 24:421–38.

Cohen, A.K. 1955. *Delinquent Boys: The Culture of the Gang.* New York: Free Press.

Cohen, L.E. and K.C. Land. 1987. ''Age structure and crime: Symmetry versus asymmetry and the projection of crime rates through the 1990s.'' *American Sociological Review* 52:170–83.

Datesman, S.K. and F.R. Scarpitti (eds.). 1980. *Women, Crime, and Justice.* New York: Oxford University Press.

Duster, T. 1987. ''Crime, youth unemployment, and the black urban underclass.'' *Crime and Delinquency* 33:300–16.

Elliott, D.S. and D. Huizinga. 1983. ''Social class and delinquent behavior in a national youth panel.'' *Criminology* 21:149–77.

Empey, L.T. 1982. *American Delinquency: Its Meaning and Construction.* Second edition. Homewood, IL: Dorsey.

Harris, A. 1977. ''Sex and theories of deviance.'' *American Sociological Review* 42:3–16.

Hindelang, M.J. 1978. ''Race and involvement in common law personal crimes.'' *American Sociological Review* 43:93–109.

Hindelang, M.J., T. Hirschi, and J. G. Weis. 1981. *Measuring Delinquency.* Beverly Hills, CA: Sage.

_____. 1978. ''Correlates of delinquency: The illusion of discrepancy between self-report and official measures.'' *American Sociological Review* 44:995–1014.

Hirschi, T. 1969. *Causes of Delinquency.* Berkeley, CA: University of California Press.

Huizinga, D. and D.S. Elliott. 1985. *Juvenile Offenders Prevalence, Offender Incidence and Arrest Rates by Race.* Boulder, CO: Institute of Behavioral Science.

Laub, J., D. Clark, L. Siegel, and J. Garofalo. 1987. *Trends in Juvenile Crime in the United States: 1973–1983.* Albany, NY: Hindelang Criminal Justice Research Center.

Messerschmidt, J.W. 1986. *Capitalism, Patriarchy, and Crime: Toward a Socialist Feminist Criminology.* Totowa, NJ: Rowman and Littlefield.

Paternoster R. and R. Triplett. 1988. ''Disaggregating self-reported delinquency and its implications for theory.'' *Criminology* 26:591–625.

Shannon, L. 1982. *Assessing the Relationship of Adult Criminal Careers to Juvenile Careers: A Summary.* Washington, DC: U.S. Department of Justice.

Sheley, J.F. 1985. *America's ''Crime Problem'': An Introduction to Criminology.* Belmont, CA: Wadsworth.

Siegal, L.J. and J.J. Senna. 1988. *Juvenile Delinquency: Theory, Practice, and Law.* Third edition. St. Paul, MN: West.

Steffensmeier, D.J., E.A. Allan, M. D. Harer, and C. Streifel. 1989. ''Age and the distribution of crime.'' *American Journal of Sociology* 94:803–31.

Steffensmeier, D.J., C. Streifel, and M.D. Harer. 1987. ''Relative cohort size and youth crime in the United States, 1953–1984.'' *American Sociological Review* 52:702–10.

Tittle, C., W. Villemez, and D. Smith. 1977. ''The myth of social class and criminality: An empirical assessment of the empirical evidence.'' *American Sociological Review* 43:643–56.

Tracy, P., M. Wolfgang, and R. Figlio. 1985. *Delinquency in Two Birth Cohorts.* Washington, DC: U.S. Department of Justice.

Williams, J.R. and M. Gold. 1972. ''From delinquent behavior to official delinquency.'' *Social Problems* 20:209–29.

Wolfgang, M., R. Figlio, and T. Sellin. 1972. *Delinquency in a Birth Cohort.* Chicago: University of Chicago Press.

Woodward, K. and P. Malamud. 1975. ''Now, the violent woman.'' *Newsweek,* October 6.

Yablonsky, L. and M.R. Haskell. 1988. *Juvenile Delinquency.* Fourth edition. New York: Harper and Row.

Reconciling Race and Class Differences in Self-Reported and Official Estimates of Delinquency

4

Delbert S. Elliott
Suzanne S. Ageton

Problems of conceptualization, definition, and measurement continue to plague researchers interested in the epidemiology and etiology of delinquency. While most would acknowledge the conceptual distinction between delinquent behavior and official responses to delinquent behavior, these distinctions are not clearly maintained in the measurement of delinquency or in the interpretation and analysis of specific delinquency data. This problem is clearly illustrated in the current controversy over the validity of self-reported (as compared with official) estimates of the incidence and distribution of delinquency in the general adolescent population. Put simply, there are those who argue that police and arrest records provide more accurate and reliable estimates of the social correlates of delinquent behavior than do self-report surveys; others hold the opposite view.

Self-report measures of delinquency provide a different picture of the incidence and distribution of delinquent behavior

From *American Sociological Review*, Vol. 45, No. 1, 1980, pp. 95–110. Reprinted by permission of the American Sociological Association and the authors.

than do official arrest records. Both types of data indicate significant age and sex differentials, but the magnitude of these differences is much smaller with self-reported data than with official arrest data (Williams and Gold, 1972; Gold and Reimer, 1974; Elliott and Voss, 1974; Illinois Institute for Juvenile Research, 1973; Bachman et al., 1970; 1971; 1978).

At the center of the controversy, however, is the fact that self-report studies generally find no differences in delinquent behavior by class or race (Gold and Reimer, 1974; Elliott and Voss, 1974; Williams and Gold, 1972; Hirschi, 1969; Bachman et al., 1970; 1971; 1978; Illinois Institute for Juvenile Research, 1973), while studies relying upon police and court data report significant differences by both class and race (Wolfgang et al., 1972; Elliott and Voss, 1974; Williams and Gold, 1972; Gordon, 1976; West, 1973; Short and Nye, 1957–1958).

To date, attempts to reconcile this apparent discrepancy between official and self-reported findings have taken one of two approaches. Most recently, researchers have challenged the strength of the empirical evidence for the class differential in official data. Tittle and Villemez (1977) and Tittle et al. (1978) reviewed earlier published research findings and concluded that the class differences in official data are not clearly established and that the widespread belief in an inverse relationship between class and crime is not based upon sound empirical research findings. Hindelang et al. (1978) have also concluded that police records of juvenile offenses are not strongly or even moderately related to socioeconomic status.[1] On the other hand, the race differential in official data has not been seriously challenged, to our knowledge.

The second and more frequent approach has been to challenge the methodological adequacy of the self-report technique and the adequacy of self-report research. Specifically, critics of self-report research contend:

1. There are problems inherent in the method itself which make it inaccurate and unreliable. These problems include deliberate falsification, inaccurate recall, and forward and backward telescoping.
2. There are problems with the construction of measures used in self-report research and with the procedures for administering the measures. These problems concern the lack of respresentativity in items, item overlapping, imprecise response sets, and the lack of anonymity of respondents.
3. There are problems with generalizing from self-report studies, due to the almost exclusive reliance upon small, unrepresentative samples.

This paper is concerned with this second approach to reconciling official and self-reported findings with respect to class and race. We will not deal with those problems inherent in the self-report method itself, except to note that available research seems to support both the validity and reliability of

the method (Nye and Short, 1956; Erickson and Empey, 1963; Hirschi, 1969; Gold, 1966; Dentler and Monroe, 1961; Hardt and Bodine, 1965; Hardt and Hardt, 1977; Farrington, 1973; Elliott and Voss, 1974; Clark and Tifft, 1966). Instead, we will deal with the correctable problems, i.e., the construction of measures and their administration, as well as representativity and sample size. The general question we will address here is whether or not the satisfactory resolution of these methodological issues in the construction and administration of self-report measures will result in greater consistency between self-reported and official data. More specifically, will the satisfactory resolution of these problems produce race and class differentials in self-reported estimates of delinquent behavior?

The discussion that follows will focus on: (1) the methodological criticisms of previous self-report delinquency (SRD) research; (2) the use of a new SRD measure in a national youth study; (3) a comparison of the race/class findings of this study with previous SRD research and with official arrest data; and (4) the epidemiological and theoretical implications of these findings.

Problems with SRD Research

Instrument Construction

Much of the controversy over self-report measures involves problems with instrument construction. Primarily, criticism centers on three issues: (1) the question of the representativeness of items employed in SRD measures; (2) problems of item overlap; and (3) limited or ambiguous response sets.

The major criticism concerns the unrepresentativity of the items selected (Hindelang et al., 1975; Nettler, 1974; Farrington, 1973). Trivial and nonserious offenses (e.g., cutting classes and disobeying parents) are often overrepresented, while serious violations of the criminal code (e.g., burglary, robbery, and sexual assault) are frequently omitted. In addition, many SRD measures tend to overrepresent certain behavioral dimensions (e.g., theft) to the exclusion of other relevant delinquent acts. As a result of such selection processes, most existing SRD measures have a restricted focus and do not represent the full range of delinquent acts; this limits the appropriateness of these scales as general measures of delinquent behavior.

Another problem is the overlapping nature of items often included in SRD measures, which results in inaccurate estimates of frequency due to duplicate counts of certain events. For example, many SRD measures include a "shoplifting" item, a "theft under $5" item, and a "theft $5–50" item. A single theft event could logically be reported on two of these items. The presence of both a "cutting school" and a "cutting class" item represents another form of measurement redundancy since cutting school necessarily involves cutting classes. This problem is not easily overcome, since a given behavioral event in fact may involve more than a single offense. Nevertheless, item overlapping creates a potential source of error in estimating the volume of delinquent behavior from SRD measures.

The type of response sets typically employed with SRD measures has been another source of criticism. One major concern has been the frequent use of normative response categories such as "often," "sometimes," and "occasionally." This type of response set is open to wide variations in interpretation by respondents, and precludes any precise count of the actual number of acts committed.

Other response sets used to estimate the number of behaviors (e.g., "never,"

"once or twice," and "three times or more") have been challenged on the grounds that they are not precise categories for numerical estimation, and that numerical estimates based upon such categories may severely truncate the true distribution of responses. With the above set, for example, any number of behaviors in excess of two is collapsed into a single "high" category. While this procedure may allow for some discrimination between youth at the low end of the frequency distribution, it clearly precludes any discrimination at the high end. Thus, a youth involved in three shoplifting offenses during the specified period receives the same "score" as a youth involved in 50 or 100 shoplifting events during the period. This limited set of categorical responses appears particularly problematic when the reporting period involves a year or more and when such items as using marijuana; drinking beer, wine or liquor; and carrying a concealed weapon are included in the SRD measure.

Administration Procedures

The manner in which the measures are administered is also a problematic area for self-report delinquency research. Here the issue concerns: (1) anonymous vs. identified respondents, and (2) questionnaire vs. interview formats.

Many researchers have argued that anonymity has to be guaranteed or youth will not admit certain offenses—probably the more serious, stigmatizing ones. Research on this question suggests that there is slightly more reporting of offenses under conditions of anonymity, but that anonymous/identified differences are slight and statistically insignificant (Corey, 1937; Christie, 1965; Kulik et al., 1968). These findings have led Dentler (as cited in Hardt and Bodine, 1965) to comment that the necessity for anonymity is overemphasized, and that it may in fact lead to reduced involvement by respondents and careless or facetious answers.

On the matter of interview vs. questionnaire formats, the discussion again involved the issue of anonymity, and the belief that self-administered questionnaires are more likely to produce accurate responses than personal interviews. One recent self-report delinquency research study compared results from structured interviews and self-administered check lists, where anonymity was guaranteed under both conditions (Krohn et al., 1974). While seven of the eight offenses were admitted more often under check-list conditions than under interview conditions, none of the differences was significant at the .05 level. Even when education, sex, class, and IQ were controlled, no significant differences were obtained.

Some researchers, most notably Gold (1966), have argued that the interview format has significant advantages for delinquency research in that it permits clarification of specific behaviors and, consequently, the ability to more correctly classify illegal acts. In general, however, there is still controversy over the effects of specific administration procedures when the research is directed toward illegal or socially disapproved behaviors.

Sampling Design and Generality

Another problematic area for self-report delinquency research is that of the generality of findings. Here the question focuses primarily on the adequacy of the sampling designs for: (1) inferences to the adolescent population, and (2) comparisons with official data.

In most cases, SRD measures have been administered to small, select samples of youth, such as high school students in a particular local community or adolescents processed by a local juvenile court. The samples are rarely probability samples, and generalizations (about the adolescent populations sampled) cannot be made with any known degree of accuracy. Only two published studies involve national probability samples.[2]

A further concern is that few cohort studies using normal populations have incorporated a self-report measure in their instruments. This means that the age and sex gradients of SRD measures are not known, a critical fact if this measurement approach is to become more refined and useful. Furthermore, since the studies using self-report measures have almost always been cross-sectional ones, little is known about the dynamics of self-reported behavior over time.

Finally, Empey (1978) notes that national self-report studies have not been conducted on an annual basis and, as a result, it is not possible to discern trends across time or to make direct comparisons with other standard delinquency data such as the Uniform Crime Reports (UCR) or the National Crime Panel (NCP).

The National Youth Survey

We will now report on a national youth study in which we have attempted to deal with the previously noted methodological criticisms of self-report delinquency research. Our aim will be to see if these improvements in the quality of self-report research have an impact on self-report findings relative to findings from official data.

The National Youth Survey involves a five-year panel design with a national probability sample of 1,726 adolescents aged 11–17 in 1976.[3] The total youth sample was selected and initially interviewed between January and March, 1977, concerning their involvement in delinquent behavior during the calendar year 1976. The second survey was completed between January and March, 1978, to obtain delinquency estimates for the calendar year 1977. The third, fourth, and fifth surveys will also be conducted between each January and March of the years 1979, 1980, and 1981.

The data reported herein are taken from the first survey, completed in 1977. The estimates presented are thus for delinquent behavior during the calendar year 1976.

Construction of New SRD Measure

In constructing the SRD measure for this study, we attempted to obtain a representative set of offenses. Given our interest in comparing SRD and UCR estimates, we began by listing offenses included in the UCR. Any specific act (with the exception of traffic violations) involving more than 1% of the reported juvenile arrests for 1972–1974 is included in the SRD measure.

In addition to the list of specific offenses, the UCR contains a general category, "all other offenses," which often accounts for a high proportion of the total juvenile arrests. To cover the types of acts likely to fall within this general category, and to increase the comprehensiveness of the measure, two general selection criteria were used to choose additional items. First, items which were theoretically relevant to a delinquent lifestyle or subculture as discussed in the literature were selected for inclusion in this measure (Cohen, 1955; Cloward and Ohlim, 1960; Miller, 1958; 1966; Yablonsky, 1962; Short and Strodtbeck, 1965). Thus, additional items—such as gang fighting, sexual intercourse, and carrying a hidden weapon—are included.

Second, a systematic review of existing SRD measures was undertaken to locate items that tapped specific dimensions of delinquent behavior not previously included.

We believe the resulting set of 47 items to be both more comprehensive and more representative of the conceptual universe of delinquent acts then found in prior SRD measures used in major, large-scale studies. The item set includes all but one of the UCR Part I offenses (homicide is excluded); 60% of Part II offenses; and a wide range of "other" offenses—such as delinquent lifestyle items, misdemeanors, and some status offenses. The vast majority of items involve a violation of criminal statutes. (See Appendix A.)

Two separate response sets are being used. Respondents initially are asked to indicate how many times during the past year they committed each act. If an individual's response to this open-ended question involves a frequency of 10 or more, interviewers then ask the youth to select one of the following categorical responses: (1) once a month, (2) once every 2–3 weeks, (3) once a week, (4) 2–3 times a week, (5) once a day, or (6) 2–3 times a day.[4] A comparison of the two response sets indicates high agreement between frequency estimates given in direct response to the open-ended question and frequency estimates based upon the implied frequency associated with the midpoint of the category selected.[5]

A specific attempt was also made to eliminate as much overlap in items as possible. None of the items contains a necessary overlap as in "cutting school" and "cutting class." Although some possible overlap remains, we do not feel it constitutes a serious problem with this SRD measure.

The SRD measure asks respondents to indicate how many times, "from Christmas a year ago to the Christmas just past," they committed each offense. The recall period is thus a year, anchored by a specific reference point relevant to most youth. The use of a one-year period which coincides almost precisely with the calendar year allows for direct comparison with UCR data, NCP victimization data, and some prior SRD data. It also avoids the need to adjust for seasonal variations, which would be necessary if a shorter time period were involved.

Administration Procedures

For the present study, the research design (a longitudinal panel design) precludes a guarantee of anonymity. Therefore, our major concern is to guarantee respondents that their answers will be confidential. This assurance is given verbally as well as being contained in the written consent form signed by all youth and their parents. In addition, a Certificate of Confidentiality from the Department of Health, Education, and Welfare guarantees all respondents that the data and the interviewers will be protected from legal subpoena.

The interview format was selected over the self-administered questionnaire format for several reasons. First, we share Gold's belief that the interview situation (if properly structured to protect confidentiality) can insure more accurate, reliable data. Second, the necessity of securing informed consents from all subjects and the complexity of the present research require, in our judgment, a personal contact with the respondents. Once this contact is made, it seems logical to use the interviewer to facilitate the data collection process and to improve the quality of the data obtained. Finally, some of our previous research suggests that the differences in responding to SRD items in a questionnaire as opposed to an interview format are not significant (Elliott et al., 1976).

The Sample

The 1977 National Youth Survey employed a probability sample of households in the continental United States based upon a multistage, cluster sampling design. The sample contained 2,375 eligible youth aged 11–17 in 1976. Of these, 1,726 (73%) agreed to participate in the study and completed interviews in the 1977 survey.[6] A comparison of the age, sex, and race of eligible youth not interviewed with participating youth indicates that the loss rate from any particular age, sex, or racial group appears to be proportional to that group's representation in the population. Further, with respect to these characteristics, participating youth appear to be representative of the total 11 through 17-year-old youth population in the United States as established by the U.S. Census Bureau (Huizinga, 1978).

Summary of New Measure

In sum, the current SRD measure addresses many of the central criticisms of prior SRD measures.[7] It is more representative of the full range of delinquent acts than were prior SRD measures and involves fewer overlapping items; it also employs a response set which provides better discrimination at the high end of the frequency continuum and is more suited to estimating the actual number of behaviors committed. The choice of a one-year time frame with a panel design involving a one-year time lag is based upon both conceptual and practical concerns. Compared with the other SRD measures, the measure involves a moderate recall period, captures seasonal variations, and permits a direct comparison with other self-report and official measures which are reported annually. And, finally, the study involves a national probability sample of youth aged 11–17.

Analysis of Data

Subscales

An earlier paper (Ageton and Elliott, 1978) presented design effects and estimates of the frequency of each specific item on the SRD measure with .95 confidence intervals for the total sample and by age, sex, race, and class. The analysis in this paper focuses upon the total SRD measure and a set of specific subscales. The frequency estimates are based upon the open-ended response set, which provides slightly more conservative frequency estimates than does the categorical response set.

The subscales are based upon Glaser's (1967) offense typology. This particular classification scheme was selected because it offers a logical categorization of offense types while permitting a clear distinction between serious and nonserious crimes.

Glaser's typology encompasses four major types of crime: (1) predatory crimes, (2) illegal service crimes, (3) public disorder crimes, and (4) crimes of negligence. With the exception of category four, all Glaser's types were used.[8]

Furthermore, Glaser acknowledges an additional category called status crimes to encompass those behaviors which at special times and/or for particular classes of people have been illegal. The status crimes category in this national youth study includes all behaviors in the SRD measure which are illegal only when the individual involved is a minor.

In addition, a separate category entitled hard drug use was created to distinguish this type of drug involvement from that of alcohol and/or marijuana use, which are subsumed within the status crimes category and public disorder crimes category, respectively.

Finally, within the predatory crimes category, a distinction was made between crimes against persons and crimes against property. This differentiation separates violent crimes against people from other serious offenses which do not involve confrontation with another person.

Thus, the final offense typology is composed of the following six subscales:

1. predatory crimes against persons (sexual assault, aggravated assault, simple assault, and robbery);
2. predatory crimes against property (vandalism, burglary, auto theft, larceny, stolen goods, fraud, and joyriding);
3. illegal service crimes (prostitution, selling drugs, and buying/providing liquor for minors);
4. public disorder crimes (carrying a concealed weapon, hitchhiking, disorderly conduct, drunkenness, panhandling, making obscene phone calls, and marijuana use);
5. status crimes (runaway, sexual intercourse, alcohol use, and truancy);
6. hard drug use (amphetamines, barbiturates, hallucinogens, heroin, and cocaine).

Table 4.1 presents the mean frequency of self-reported delinquency by race[9] and class[10] for the total SRD measure and for each of the subscales. The statistical tests involve a one-way analysis of variance on these means.[11]*

Race and Class Differentials

Unlike most previous self-report studies, we find significant race differences for total SRD and for predatory crimes against property. Blacks report significantly higher frequencies than do whites on each of these measures. In both cases, the differences in means are substantial. With respect to total offenses, blacks report three offenses for

---

*Editor's Note: See Appendix 1 for a brief discussion of "analysis of variance."

every two reported by whites. For crimes against property, blacks report more than two offenses for every offense reported by whites.

While there is a substantial difference in mean scores on the crimes against persons scale, it is not statistically significant. The difference in the total SRD score appears to be primarily the result of the very high level of property crimes reported by blacks.

We also observe a class differential for total SRD and for predatory crimes against persons. For total SRD scores, the difference is between lower socioeconomic status youth and others; i.e., there does not appear to be any difference between working- and middle-class group means.

The differences are greater, and the trend is more linear, for the crimes against persons scale means than for total SRD.

Table 4.1
Mean Frequency of Self-Reported Delinquency by Race and Class

	Total Self-Reported Delinquency			Predatory Crimes Against Persons		Predatory Crimes Against Property	
	N	$\bar{X}$	SD	$\bar{X}$	SD	$\bar{X}$	SD
Race							
White	1357	46.79	161.37	7.84	58.42	8.93	42.87
Black	259	79.20	277.38	12.96	76.59	20.57	106.27
F		6.68		1.50		8.79	
Probability		≤.01		NS		≤.001	
Class							
Lower	717	60.42	220.24	12.02	72.68	13.50	78.60
Working	509	50.63	186.19	8.04	67.12	9.40	38.68
Middle	494	50.96	79.88	3.32	11.31	7.25	23.17
F		2.94		3.11		1.94	
Probability		≤.05		≤.05		NS	

	Illegal Service		Public Disorder		Hard Drug Use		Status Offenses	
	$\bar{X}$	SD	$\bar{X}$	SD	$\bar{X}$	SD	$\bar{X}$	SD
Race								
White	1.85	22.36	14.98	62.37	1.26	14.03	14.84	49.21
Black	1.71	22.83	16.50	67.78	.18	1.35	16.19	53.94
F	.09		.13		1.55		.16	
Probability	NS		NS		NS		NS	
Class								
Lower	2.19	30.29	14.32	58.75	1.20	14.64	14.27	46.54
Working	1.36	10.92	16.21	78.92	.73	4.02	14.47	42.36
Middle	1.56	14.07	13.81	42.44	1.37	15.68	15.66	58.33
F	.25		.22		.35		.13	
Probability	NS		NS		NS		NS	

Lower-class youth report nearly four times as many offenses as do middle-class youth and one-and-one-half times as many as working-class youth. There is also a substantial class difference in the mean number of crimes against persons, but this difference is not statistically significant. There are clearly no substantial differences in means for any of the remaining subscales.

A two-way analysis of variance (race × class) was also completed with the total SRD measure and each of the subscales. In every case, the direct effects observed in the one-way analysis of variance were replicated and no significant interaction effects were observed.

Comparisons with Prior Studies

Our basic concern in this analysis will now be to ascertain: (1) the comparability of the general findings reported here with other SRD findings, and (2) the extent to which these findings might offer some insight into the discrepancy between self-report and official measures of delinquency.

While we have not reported findings from this study relative to the age and sex distribution of delinquent behavior, they are generally consistent with those from other large-scale self-report studies (Hirschi, 1969; Williams and Gold, 1972; Illinois Institute for Juvenile Research, 1973; Gold and Reimer, 1974; Elliott and Voss, 1974). However, the findings relative to the distribution by race and class are not consistent with these earlier studies, none of which report significant differences in the mean frequencies of self-reported offenses by race or class.[12]

In this study, the black/white differential in total offenses is nearly 2:1; and for predatory crimes, over 2:1. Class differences in total offenses are significant and, while the differences are not large, they are

in the traditionally expected direction, with lower-class youth reporting higher frequencies. The trend in the previously referenced self-report studies is generally in the opposite direction.

In this study, class differences are clearer on the predatory crimes against persons scale than for total SRD scores; the trend is more linear, in the expected direction, and of greater magnitude (lower:middle = 3:1).

In an effort to determine if this basic difference in findings is due to the differences in the SRD measures employed, we undertook several additional analyses. We "rescored" the frequency estimates in two ways to approximate the frequency ranges used in the earlier studies. Since our focus is upon those scales where significant class and race differences are observed, our discussion will be limited to the total self-report measure and the two predatory subscales.

First, a comparison of the proportions of youth reporting one or more offenses on each of these scales reveals no statistically significant class or racial differences. Second, all frequencies of three and above on each item in the SRD measure were rescored as a 3 to approximate the frequency ranges used in the Richmond Youth Study (Hirschi, 1969), the Delinquency and Dropout Study (Elliott and Voss, 1974), and the 1967 and 1972 National Surveys of Youth (Williams and Gold, 1972; and Gold and Reimer, 1974). Frequency scores on items were then summed across items to generate new scale frequencies and means. With one exception, an analysis of race and class differences on these frequency scores reveals no significant differences. The one exception involves a small (but significant) class difference on the predatory crimes against persons scale.[13] The class differential in this case is in the same direction but substantially smaller than that observed with the original scoring.

These two analyses indicate that the extended frequency range used in this study does, in fact, contribute to the difference in findings relative to race and class. Had we used the proportion of youth committing one or more offenses, or a 0-3 range similar to that used in the 1967 and 1972 National Surveys of Youth, our conclusions relative to class and race differences would have been similar to those reported for the earlier self-report studies.

High-Frequency Offenders

Since the above analyses indicate that differences were not occurring at the low end of the frequency distribution (with one exception), we examined race and class differences at several points along the original frequency distribution, with a particular interest in the high end of the frequency continuum. The results of this analysis are presented in Table 4.2.

The data in Table 4.2 indicate that the original differences, by both race and class, are due in large part to the relative differences at the high end of the frequency continuum. For example, at the low end of the frequency distribution, the white/black ratios are close to 1:1; but at the high end of the continuum the ratios are greater than 1:2.[14] For class, the lower-class to middle-class ratios at the low end are again close to 1:1; but at the high end the ratio is 2:1 for total SRD and over 3:1 for predatory crimes against persons.

Not only are the relative *proportions* of blacks and lower-class youth higher at the high end of the frequency continuum but also, within the high category, blacks and lower-class youth report substantially higher *frequencies* than do whites and middle-class youth.

Table 4.2
Percentage of Respondents Reporting Specific Levels of Delinquency by Race and Class

	Total Self-Reported Delinquency				
Number of	Race		Class		
Offenses	White	Black	Lower	Working	Middle
Reported	%	%	%	%	%
0–24	71.8	67.6	71.7	72.3	70.9
25–49	11.0	8.1	10.6	9.4	11.5
50–199	13.1	15.4	11.4	14.4	14.4
200+	4.1	9.8	6.3	3.9	3.2

	Predatory Crimes Against Property		Predatory Crimes Against Persons		
Number of	Race		Class		
Offenses	White	Black	Lower	Working	Middle
Reported	%	%	%	%	%
0–4	70.6	70.7	77.3	80.0	84.6
5–29	24.1	22.7	18.2	16.1	13.8
30–54	3.4	2.4	1.7	2.1	.8
55+	1.9	4.2	2.8	1.8	.8

Lower-class youth in the high category on the total SRD measures (scores $\geq$ 200) report over one-and-one-half times as many offenses as do middle-class youth in this category. On the predatory crimes against persons scale, lower-class youth in the high category (scores $\geq$ 55) report nearly three times as many offenses as do middle-class youth in this category. Among those in the high category on the predatory property scale, blacks report over one-and-one-half times as many offenses as do whites.

The one exception to the above generalization is that blacks and whites within the high category on the total SRD measure have approximately the same mean frequencies. The black/white differential on this measure thus appears to be more simply the result of differences in proportions of blacks and whites in the high category.

In any case, blacks and lower-class youth are found disproportionately among high frequency offenders. Prior self-report measures were unable to detect this differential involvement because they used response sets which are sensitive to differences only at the low end of the frequency continuum. We thus conclude that the use of open-ended frequency responses does, in fact, contribute to our finding both class and race differentials.

Range of Offenses in SRD Measure

We also believe that the broader range of offenses included in our SRD measure has some effect on these findings. An item-by-item analysis indicates that the particular set of items included in a measure can have a major impact on observed ethnic and class differentials. For example, the predatory crimes against persons scale includes four types of offenses: sexual assault, aggravated assault, simple assault, and robbery. Mean frequencies, by race, on the three types of assault offenses are as follows:

Offense Type	Whites	Blacks	Ratio
Sexual Assault	.03	.15	1:5
Aggravated Assault	.12	.50	1:4
Simple Assault	2.07	1.05	2:1
Total Assault	2.22	1.70	1:1

With respect to all three types of assault, these data indicate a major difference in frequency, by race. They suggest that measures which include only simple assault items do not have a proper representation of assault items. Given the tendency of prior self-report studies to exclude the more serious assault items, findings from such stud-

ies are likely to minimize the racial differences regarding assaultive behavior.

Even when all three types of assault are represented, an analysis involving a summary assault measure would obscure, in this case, important differences by type of assault. For example, the magnitude of sexual and aggravated assault offenses is so small, compared with that of simple assault offenses, that the inclusion of the latter in a summary measure conceals major differences in the other items and even reverses the direction of the differential.

While assault items have been used for illustrative purposes, we believe the problem to be a general one. The inclusion of both very high and very low frequency items in a single measure may obscure important differences, often differences in seriousness. This is because nonserious offenses tend to be reported frequently, while serious offenses are reported infrequently.

Weighting SRD Items

For some purposes, it may be instructive to weight each item so that its potential contribution to the total score is the same as that of any other item. In this case, no single high frequency item can dominate the overall score. One procedure for accomplishing this weighting is to transform item frequency scores into standard scores and then add them into a total scale score. This transformation was performed, and the results are presented in Table 4.3.

With respect to class differences, this transformation confirms the earlier findings observed with raw frequencies. Significant class differences are observed for total SRD scores and predatory crimes against persons scores, but not for predatory crimes against property scores. In both cases, the significance levels are higher

Table 4.3

Mean Standardized Scores for Selected Scales
by Race and Class

	Total Self-Reported Delinquency	Predatory Crimes Against Persons	Predatory Crimes Against Property
Race			
White	−.2452	−.0860	−.0072
Black	1.5317	.4038	−.0117
F	3.870	8.179	.001
Probability	≤ .05	≤ .005	NS
Class			
Lower	.7375	.2194	−.0905
Working	.1131	−.0746	.1501
Middle	−1.3341	−.2486	.080
F	3.771	5.159	1.975
Probability	≤ .02	≤ .006	NS

when item scores are transformed into standard scores prior to summing.

With regard to racial differences, the black/white difference on the total SRD measure remains, but it is weaker than that observed with raw frequency scores. More importantly, with this transformation the race difference on the predatory property crimes scale (observed earlier) is not replicated. There is essentially no black/white difference in property crimes when separate property offenses are adjusted so as to have the same magnitudes. This change suggests that the higher raw frequency predatory property scale mean for blacks is largely the result of higher frequencies on selected offense items. A review of item specific means confirms that this is indeed the case.

The mean number of vandalism offenses reported by blacks is over three times that of whites, and their mean number of evading payment offenses is over five times that of whites. These two nonserious offenses are relatively high frequency offenses for

all youth. The individual item means for blacks are equal to or lower than those of whites on all serious offenses (felonies) included in this scale. Further, with one exception (family theft), means for blacks on all theft items are equal to or lower than those of whites. Thus, the initial racial differences on predatory property offenses are the result of large differences in vandalism (property destruction) and evading payment offenses, and not differences in theft offenses or serious property offenses.

Whereas there are no statistically significant racial differences in predatory crimes against persons offenses when unadjusted frequencies are used, the use of standard scores results in significant differences, with blacks reporting significantly higher scores. The direction of the racial differential is the same as that observed with the use of unadjusted frequencies, but the differential is stronger and statistically significant when standard scores are used.

As noted earlier in the discussion of specific assault items, simple assault is a relatively high frequency offense compared with the other offenses against persons, and whites report substantially higher frequencies than blacks on this offense. On the more serious offenses against persons, magnitudes are relatively low, but blacks report substantially greater frequencies than do whites on most of these items. The only exception involves robbery; here, the black and white means are identical. The transformation of item scores thus results in a greater racial differential than that observed with unadjusted frequencies.

The review and analysis of prior SRD studies by Hindelang et al. (1978) led them to conclude that racial differentials increase with the severity of the offense. The data in our National Youth Survey provide only partial support for that generalization. With respect to offenses against persons, the

Table 4.4

Two-Way Analysis of Variance: Mean
Predatory Crimes Against Persons Scale
Scores (Standardized) by Race and Class

Race	Class		
	Lower	Working	Middle
White	.013	− .030	− .267
Black	.828	− .253	− .143

Main Effects	Sum of Squares	DF	F	Significance Level
Race	39.818	1	6.256	≤ .01
Class	45.149	2	3.547	≤ .03
Interaction Race × Class	40.944	2	3.216	≤ .04

black/white differential is indeed greater
for serious (as compared with nonserious)
offenses. However, with respect to property offenses this is not the case. In fact, the
opposite is true; i.e., the differential is
greater for nonserious property offenses.

When unadjusted item scores are used,
there are no significant class by race interactions on any of the self-reported delinquency scales. With the transformation to
standard item scores, a significant class by
race interaction is observed on the predatory crimes against persons measure. The
results of the two-way analysis of variance
are presented in Table 4.4.

Main effects are observed for both race
and class. For whites, the major class difference is between middle-class youth and
others (as was the case with unadjusted frequency scores). For blacks, the differences
between lower-, working-, and middle-
class youth are relatively greater, but the
major difference is between lower-class
youth and others. Working-class black
youth report relatively fewer offenses
against persons than do middle-class
blacks, but this difference is not great. The
interaction effect appears to be primarily

the result of the relatively higher mean
score for lower-class black youth. This
analysis suggests a relatively high involvement of lower-class black youth in serious
offenses against persons.

Implications of Findings

Item Selection and Response Sets

Three major points need to be considered
relative to the selection and analysis of
items in a self-report measure. First, it is
critical that the items selected be representative of the offense areas to be covered.
Special attention should be directed to this
selection process, since the inclusion (or
exclusion) of specific items appears to have
implications for research findings, at least
with regard to the social correlates of delinquent behavior.

Second, when attempting to make incidence estimates, it is important that response sets reflect the total frequency
range. In this study, significant class and
race differences were found only at the high
end of the frequency range and, in most
cases, would not have been observed had
the traditional response sets been employed.

Third, from both theoretical and epidemiological perspectives, there is a danger
in summarizing items into general categories. The present data indicate that using
summary measures may obscure important
differences by type of offense, and suggest
that a more accurate picture is obtained by
employing offense specific as well as summary measure analyses.[15]

It seems clear, from our data presentation and discussion, that the criticism of
many SRD measures is well-founded; and,
further, that generalizations about the social correlates of "delinquent behavior" as
derived from measures with a limited re-

sponse set and item representativity may be very misleading and are probably unwarranted. In addition, the way in which specific items are combined into summary measures has some bearing upon outcomes, and caution must be exercised in the interpretation of general summary measures.

Relationship between SRD and Official Data

In sum, it appears likely that the differences between the findings reported here and those from earlier self-report studies are, in fact, the result of differences in the specific SRD measures employed. The findings also suggest a logical connection between self-report and official measures of delinquency which, at least in part, accounts for the observed differences in the class and race distributions of these two measures.

The consistent findings of earlier self-report studies have led many sociologists and criminologists to the conclusion that race and class differences in arrests are primarily the result of processing biases and have little or no basis in behavior (Turk, 1969; Quinney, 1970; Williams and Gold, 1972; Taylor et al., 1974). The findings from the 1977 National Youth Survey suggest some behavioral basis for the observed class and race differences in official processing. In this sense, the National Youth Survey data are more consistent with official arrest data than are data from most prior self-report studies.

Further, these findings provide some insight into the mechanism whereby official actions produce exaggerated race and class (as well as age and sex) differences in delinquent behavior when compared with self-reported differences in normal adolescent populations. On both logical and empirical grounds, it seems reasonable to argue that

the more frequent and serious offenders are more likely to be arrested (Short and Nye, 1957–1958; Erickson and Empey, 1963; Illinois Institute for Juvenile Research, 1973; Elliott and Voss, 1974; Empey, 1978), and that the youth population represented in official police statistics is not a representative sample of all youth.

Self-report studies are capturing a broader range of persons and levels of involvement in delinquent behavior than are official arrest statistics. Virtually all youth report some delinquent activity on self-report measures, but for the vast majority the offenses are neither very frequent nor very serious. Police contacts, on the other hand, are most likely to concern youth who are involved in either very serious or very frequent delinquent acts. Police contacts with youth thus involve a more restricted segment of the general youth population.

The findings discussed previously indicate that race and class differences are more extreme at the high end of the frequency continuum, that part of the delinquency continuum where police contacts are more likely.[16] In fact, at this end of the frequency continuum, self-report and official correlates of delinquent behavior are relatively similar. While we do not deny the existence of official processing biases, it does appear that official correlates of delinquency also reflect real differences in the frequency and seriousness of delinquent acts.

The results of this self-report delinquency study also have implications for previous tests of theoretical propositions which used SRD data. Stated simply, earlier self-report measures may not have been sensitive enough to capture the theoretically important differences in delinquency involvement. Given the truncated frequency distributions and the restricted behavioral range of earlier self-report measures, the only distinctions possible were fine gradations between relatively nonde-linquent youth.

For example, earlier distinctions were typically among (1) youth with no reported offenses; (2) those with one or two offenses; and (3) those with three or more offenses. Given the extensive frequency distribution observed in this study, there is reason to question whether or not such a trichotomy would capture meaningful distinctions among offending youth. The most significant difference may not be between the nonoffender and the one-time offender, or even between the one-time and multiple-time offender. Equal or greater significance may be found between those reporting over (or under) 25 nonserious offenses, or between those reporting over (or under) five serious offenses.[17]

The ability to discriminate more fully among many levels and types of involvement in delinquent behavior introduces much more variance into the delinquency measure. That ability also allows for the identification of more extreme groups of offenders, and that identification may be particularly relevant for tests of theoretical propositions.

Appendix A

Self-Reported Delinquency and Drug-Use Items as Employed in the National Youth Survey

How many times in the last year have you:

1. purposely damaged or destroyed property belonging to your *parents* or other family *members.*
2. purposely damaged or destroyed property belonging to a *school.*
3. purposely damaged or destroyed *other property* that did not belong to you (not counting family or school property).
4. stolen (or tried to steal) a *motor vehicle,* such as a car or motorcycle.
5. stolen (or tried to steal) something worth more than $50.
6. knowingly bought, sold or held stolen goods (or tried to do any of these things).
7. thrown objects (such as rocks, snowballs, or bottles) at cars or people.
8. run away from home.
9. lied about your age to gain entrance or to purchase something; for example, lying about your age to buy liquor or get into a movie.
10. carried a hidden weapon other than a plain pocket knife.
11. stolen (or tried to steal) things worth $5 or less.
12. attacked someone with the idea of seriously hurting or killing him/her.
13. been paid for having sexual relations with someone.
14. had sexual intercourse with a person of the opposite sex other than your wife/husband.
15. been involved in gang fights.
16. sold marijuana or hashish ("pot," "grass," "hash").
17. cheated on school tests.
18. hitchhiked where it was illegal to do so.
19. stolen money or other things from your *parents* or *other members of your family.*
20. hit (or threatened to hit) a *teacher* or other adult at school.
21. hit (or threatened to hit) one of your *parents.*
22. hit (or threatened to hit) other *students.*
23. been loud, rowdy, or unruly in a public place (disorderly conduct).

24. sold hard drugs, such as heroin, cocaine, and LSD.
25. taken a vehicle for a ride (drive) without the owner's permission.
26. bought or provided liquor for a minor.
27. had (or tried to have) sexual relations with someone against their will.
28. used force (strong-arm methods) to get money or things from other *students.*
29. used force (strong-arm methods) to get money or things from a *teacher* or other adult at school.
30. used force (strong-arm methods) to get money or things from *other people* (not students or teachers).
31. avoided paying for such things as movies, bus or subway rides, and food.
32. been drunk in a public place.
33. stolen (or tried to steal) things worth between $5 and $50.
34. stolen (or tried to sell) something at school, such as someone's coat from a classroom, locker, or cafeteria, or a book from the library.

35. broken into a building or vehicle (or tried to break in) to steal something or just to look around.
36. begged for money or things from strangers.
37. skipped classes without an excuse.
38. failed to return extra change that a cashier gave you by mistake.
39. been suspended from school.
40. made obscene telephone calls, such as calling someone and saying dirty things.

How often in the last year have you used:
41. alcoholic beverages (beer, wine and hard liquor).
42. marijuana—hashish ("grass," "pot," "hash").
43. hallucinogens ("LSD," "Mescaline," "Peyote," "Acid").
44. amphetamines ("Uppers," "Speed," "Whites").
45. barbiturates ("Downers," "Reds").
46. heroin "Horse," "Smack").
47. cocaine ("Coke").

Notes

1. Hindelang et al. (1978) have also recently studied the extent to which sex and race are differentially related to self-reported and official records of delinquency, and some of their conclusions with regard to the race discrepancy will be cited later.

2. These are Gold's 1967 and 1972 National Surveys of Youth and the Youth in Transition Study (Bachman et al., 1970; 1971; 1978). Both studies are limited by a restricted set of SRD items and truncated response sets. The Youth in Transition Study also has problems associated with overlapping reporting periods for its reported SRD measures.

3. The National Youth Survey is funded by the Center for Studies of Crime and Delinquency, NIMH (MH27552), and the National Institute for Juvenile Justice and Delinquency Prevention, LEAA (78-JN-AX-0003). Current

funding covers the first three of the five projected annual surveys. The first survey was funded solely by NIMH, the second and third by NIMH and LEAA jointly.

4. The categorical response set has led to the identification of some highly episodic events, e.g., 20 shoplifting offenses, all occurring within a two-month period during the summer (an initial response of 20; a categorical response 2-3 times a week, and an interviewer probe revealing that the offenses all occurred during the summer).

5. The only exception involves the last two (high frequency) categories. At this end of the frequency continuum, estimates based upon the midpoint of the category are substantially higher than the frequency response given directly. The open-ended frequency measure thus appears to provide a more conservative estimate of number

of delinquent acts, and the estimates reported here are based upon this response.

6. At each stage, the probabilities of selection were established to provide a self-weighting sample. Seventy-six primary sampling units were selected, with probability of selection being proportional to size. This sampling procedure resulted in the listing of 67,266 households, of which approximately 8,000 were selected for inclusion in the sample. All 11- through 17-year-old youth living in the selected households were eligible respondents for the study. The selected households generated a total of 2,375 eligible youth. Of these, 649 (27%) did not participate in the study due to (1) parental refusal, (2) youth refusal, or (3) the youth being considered inappropriate for inclusion in the study (e.g., severely mentally retarded). In general, based upon a comparison with 1976 U.S. Census Bureau estimates, the resulting sample of participating youth does appear representative of American youth with respect to age, sex, and race (U.S. Bureau of the Census, 1977). For a detailed description of the sample, see Huizinga, 1978, and Ageton and Elliott, 1978.

7. While we are concerned with the issues of validity and reliability of the self-report method, we will not deal with these issues here beyond reporting that: (1) we are obtaining data on official police contacts for each respondent and intend to compare self-reports of delinquent behavior with official records of police contact and arrest; and (2) the reliability (internal consistency) of the new SRD measure is quite high (Alpha = .91) for the 1977 survey. We are planning further validity tests with these data, but have nothing to report, yet.

8. Category Four, crimes of negligence, was excluded because it contains predominantly automobile infractions which were not included in the SRD measure.

9. Because of the small number of Mexican-American respondents (N = 72) and some obvious clustering effects for this ethnic group, the accuracy of the estimates of variances is questionable, and we have not included this group in the analysis. The same situation holds for the residual "other" category (N = 32). Comparisons are, thus, limited to whites (Anglos) and blacks.

10. The social class measure employed in this analysis is the Hollingshead two-factor index (Hollingshead and Redlich, 1958) as applied to the principal wage earner in each youth's family. Hollingshead Classes I and II—involving primarily professional managerial occupations and college level educations—are collapsed to make the "middle" class category. Class III—primarily owners of small businesses, clerical workers, and persons in sales occupations and skilled manual occupations, with high school or some college work completed—constitutes the "working" class category.

Classes IV and V—primarily semiskilled persons and those in unskilled manual occupations with high school or lower levels of education—make up the "lower" class category.

11. It should also be noted that the statistical tests are based upon a simple random sample design. The effect of our departure from this design is probably in the direction of inflating the F values. However, the design effects are small, suggesting that the effect of this departure is not a serious one. For example, the average design effects on items in the total SRD measure are as follows: Males = 1.13; Females = 1.12; 11-12-years-olds = 1.14; 13-15-year-olds = 1.08; 16-17-year-olds = 1.05; Middle Class = 1.05; Working Class = 1.22; Lower Class = 1.09; Whites = 1.14 and Blacks = 1.15. Further, unless otherwise specified, statistical significance refers to probabilities $\leq .05$. Because of our sample sizes, the statistical tests employed are rather powerful. An examination of Table 1 indicates very large variances and, even when significant differences in means are found, it is clear that the distributions being compared overlap substantially.

12. Williams and Gold (1972) report a white/black race differential for seriousness of self-reported delinquency behavior, but no difference in frequency. They also report a significantly higher seriousness for higher socioeconomic status (SES) boys, but no differences in frequency by SES. We have not considered seriousness here but, to the extent that our predatory crime subscales reflect the more serious offenses, our data would support the race differen-

tial and contradict the direction of the class differential in seriousness as reported by Williams and Gold.

13. Mean frequencies were as follows: Lower = 2.02; Working = 1.74; Middle = 1.38.

14. For purposes of discussion, the low end of the frequency distribution refers to total SRD scores ≤ 24 and predatory crimes against persons and property scores ≤ 4. The high end refers to total SRD scores ≥ 200 and predatory crimes against persons and property scores ≥ 55.

15. While summary measures are reported herein, offense-specific analyses were presented in a previous paper (Ageton and Elliott, 1978).

16. Although we have not presented the data here, age and sex differences are also greater at the high end of the SRD frequency continuum.

17. For example: for 1976, 5-10% of the most frequent offenders reported over 200 total offenses each, including over 30 serious offenses against persons.

References

Ageton, Suzanne S. and Delbert S. Elliott. *The Incidence of Delinquent Behavior in a National Probability Sample of Adolescents.* Project Report Number 3. HEW Grant Number MH27552, *The Dynamics of Delinquent Behavior: A National Survey.* Boulder: Behavioral Research Institute, 1978.

Bachman, Jerald G., Swayzer Green, and Ilona D. Wirtanen. *Youth in Transition: Vol. II.* Ann Arbor: Institute for Social Research, University of Michigan, 1970.

_____. *Youth in Transition: Vol. III.* Ann Arbor: Institute for Social Research, University of Michigan, 1971.

Bachman, Jerald G., Patrick O'Malley, and Jerome Johnston. *Youth in Transition: Vol. VI.* Ann Arbor: Institute for Social Research, University of Michigan, 1978.

Christie, Nils. "Summary of His Report to the Conference." Pp. 1-3 in Robert H. Hardt and George E. Bodine. *Development of Self-Report Instruments in Delinquency Research: A Conference Report.* Syracuse: Syracuse University Youth Development Center, 1965.

Clark, John P. and Larry L. Tifft. "Polygraph and interview validation of self-reported deviant behavior." *American Sociological Review* 31:516-23 (1966).

Cloward, Richard A. and Lloyd E. Ohlin. *Delinquency and Opportunity.* Glencoe, Ill.: Free Press, 1960.

Cohen, Albert K. *Delinquent Boys: The Culture of the Gang.* Glencoe, Ill.: Free Press, 1955.

Corey, Stephen M. "Signed versus unsigned questionnaires." *Journal of Educational Psychology* 28:144-8 (1937).

Dentler, Robert A. and Lawrence J. Monroe. "Social correlates of early adolescent theft." *American Sociological Review* 26:733-43 (1961).

Elliott, Delbert S. and Harwin Voss. *Delinquency and Dropout.* Lexington, Mass.: D. C. Heath, 1974.

Elliott, Delbert S., Suzanne S. Ageton, Margaret Hunter, and Brian Knowles. *Research Handbook for Community Planning and Feedback Instruments (Revised).* Vol. 1. Prepared for the Office of Youth Development. Department of Health, Education, and Welfare. HEW-OS-74-308. Boulder: Behavioral Research and Evaluation Corporation, 1976.

Empey, LaMar T. *American Delinquency.* Homewood, Ill.: Dorsey, 1978.

Erickson, Maynard L. and Lamar T. Empey. "Court records, undetected delinquency and decision-making." *Journal of Criminal Law, Criminology and Police Science* 54:456-69 (1963).

Farrington, David P. "Self-reports of deviant behavior: predictive and stable?" *Journal of Criminal Law and Criminology* 64:99-110 (1973).

Glaser, Daniel. "National goals and indicators for the reduction of crime and delinquency." *Annuals of the American Academy of Political and Social Science* 371:104–26 (1967).

Gold, Martin. "Undetected delinquent behavior." *Journal of Research in Crime and Delinquency* 3:27–46 (1966).

Gold, Martin and David J. Reimer. *Changing Patterns of Delinquent Behavior among Americans 13 to 16 Years Old—1972. Report Number 1 of the National Survey of Youth, 1972.* Ann Arbor: Institute for Social Research, University of Michigan, 1974.

Gordon, Robert A. "Prevalence: the rare datum, in delinquency measurement and its implications for the theory of delinquency." Pp. 201–84 in Malcolm W. Klein (ed.). *The Juvenile Justice System.* Beverly Hills: Sage, 1976.

Hardt, Robert H. and George E. Bodine. *Development of Self-Report Instruments in Delinquency Research: A Conference Report.* Syracuse: Syracuse University Youth Development Center, 1965.

Hardt, Robert H. and Sandra Peterson-Hardt. "On determining the quality of the delinquency self-report method." *Journal of Research in Crime and Delinquency* 14:247–61 (1977).

Hindelang, Michael J. "Race and involvement in common law personal crimes." *American Sociological Review* 43:93–109 (1978).

Hindelang, Michael J., Travis Hirschi, and Joseph G. Weis. *Self-Reported Delinquency: Methods and Substance.* Proposal Submitted to the National Institute of Mental Health, Department of Health, Education, and Welfare, MH27778, 1975.

———. *Social Class, Sex, Race and the Discrepancy between Self-Reported and Official Delinquency.* Grant Number MH27778-03, Center for Studies of Crime and Delinquency, National Institute of Mental Health, Department of Health, Education, and Welfare, 1978.

Hirschi, Travis. *Causes of Delinquency.* Berkeley: University of California, 1969.

Hollingshead, August B. and Frederick C. Redlich. *Social Class and Mental Illness.* New York: Wiley, 1958.

Huizinga, David. *Description of the National Youth Sample.* Project Report Number 2. HEW Grant Number MH27552. *The Dynamics of Delinquent Behavior: A National Survey.* Boulder: Behavioral Research Institute, 1978.

Illinois Institute for Juvenile Research. *Juvenile Delinquency in Illinois.* Chicago: Illinois Department of Mental Health, 1973.

Krohn, Marvin, Gordon P. Waldo, and Theodore G. Chiricos. "Self-reported delinquency: a comparison of structured interviews and self-administered checklists." *Journal of Criminal Law and Criminology* 65:545–53 (1974).

Kulik, James A., Kenneth B. Stein, and Theodore R. Sarbin. "Disclosure of delinquent behavior under conditions of anonymity and nonanonymity." *Journal of Consulting and Clinical Psychology* 32:506–9 (1968).

Miller, Walter B. "Lower class culture as a generating milieu of gang delinquency." *Journal of Social Issues* 14:5–19 (1958).

———. "Violent crimes in city gangs." *Annals of the American Academy of Political and Social Science* 364:97–112 (1966).

Nettler, Gwynn. *Explaining Crime.* New York: McGraw-Hill, 1974.

Nye, F. Ivan and James F. Short, Jr. "Scaling delinquent behavior." *American Sociological Review* 22:326–31 (1956).

Quinney, Richard. *The Social Reality of Crime.* Boston: Little, Brown, 1970.

Short, James F., Jr., and F. Ivan Nye. "Reported behavior as a criterion of deviant behavior." *Social Problems* 5:207–13 (1957–1958).

Short, James F., Jr., and Fred L. Strodtbeck. *Group Process and Gang Delinquency.* Chicago: University of Chicago, 1965.

Taylor, Ian, Paul Walton, and Jock Young. *The New Criminology.* New York: Harper and Row, 1974.

Tittle, Charles R. and Wayne J. Villemez. "Social class and criminality." *Social Forces* 56:474–502 (1977).

Tittle, Charles R., Wayne J. Villemez, and Douglas A. Smith. "The myth of social class and criminality." *American Sociological Review* 43:643–56 (1978).

Turk, Austin. *Criminality and the Legal Order.* Chicago: Rand McNally, 1969.

U.S. Bureau of the Census. *Population Estimates and Projections.* Series P-25, No. 643, 1977.

West, D. J. *Who Becomes Delinquent?* London: Heinemann, 1973.

Wolfgang, Marvin, Robert Figlio, and Thorsten Sellin. *Delinquency in a Birth Cohort.* Chicago: University of Chicago, 1972.

Williams, Jay R. and Martin Gold. "From delinquent behavior to official delinquency." *Social Problems* 20:209–29 (1972).

Yablonsky, Lewis. *The Violent Gang.* New York: MacMillan, 1962.

Contemporary Trends in Female Delinquency: Stability or Change?

5

Ronald J. Berger

Prior to the 1970s, researchers treated females as marginal to the study of juvenile delinquency.[1] Moreover, while environmental factors were used to explain male delinquency, female delinquency was addressed in terms of stereotypical assumptions about females' inherent biological or psychological nature. For instance, Cowie et al. (1968) believed that female delinquents suffered from an excess number of male chromosomes. Vedder and Sommerville (1970:156) attributed female delinquency to "negative female narcissism," that is, to delinquents' lack of attractiveness, low self-image, or unsatisfying relationships with boys. Konopka (1966) emphasized factors such as emotional dependency, loneliness, insecurity, and the trauma associated with the onset of menstruation. Recently, premenstrual syndrome (PMS) was proposed as a cause of women's criminality, although no evidence existed to support this hypothesis (Binder, et al., 1988; Slade, 1984), and some criminologists reasserted their belief that biological factors (aggression) were at least partly responsible for different rates of male and female law-violation (Wilson and Herrnstein, 1985). In contrast, most contemporary sociological explanations of female crime and delinquency have used the concept of differential gender role socialization to explain patterns of male and female lawbreaking (see Note 1).

By the mid-1970s, studies began to indicate that female crime and delinquency were rising and that a new type of female offender had emerged who was more violent and aggressive than her predecessors (Adler, 1975; Bruck, 1975; Deming, 1977; Nettler, 1974; Rosenblatt and Greenland, 1974). Opponents of the women's movement proclaimed that women's liberation had contributed to an increase in female criminality (see Woodward and Malamud, 1975). A large volume of scholarly literature has developed that has attempted to measure and explain the alleged changes in the volume and character of female lawbreaking. Debate has centered around whether females have remained traditional and nonviolent in their patterns of crime and delinquency, whether the observed changes (if they exist at all) are real or the result of changing societal reactions to female misconduct, and whether female law-violators have been "masculinized" or in other ways influenced by the women's liberation movement or changing gender roles. In this article, I review this literature and argue that more attention needs to be given to understanding the "role strain" inherent in female delinquents' attempts to negotiate ambiguous or contradictory gender roles. As a background to this discussion, I first consider the basic premises of a gender role socialization theory of traditional patterns of female delinquency.

Gender Role Socialization and Female Delinquency

Gender roles involve socially expected behaviors that are learned from the sociocultural environment and that are rooted in the organization of social institutions, particularly the family and occupational structure. Traditional family arrangements have kept females, in comparison to males, dependent and cloistered, and females have been expected to provide support and nurturance to others. In the occupational world, these traditions have been reflected in and reinforced by "gender appropriate" occupations such as secretaries, waitresses, teachers, and social workers. As a result, girls have been more closely supervised by their parents than boys and have had less opportunity to commit delinquent acts. They have been more likely to accept general moral standards, blame themselves for their problems, feel shame about their misconduct, be taught to avoid risks, fear social disapproval, and be deterred by legal sanctions (Balkan and Berger, 1979; Giallombardo, 1980; Hagan et al., 1985; Mawby, 1980; Morash, 1983; Morris, 1965; Richards and Tittle, 1981).

Female gender role socialization has been reflected in official crime statistics. Table 5.1 presents arrest data from 1965

and 1975, and more recent data from 1987, which indicates that female juveniles, in comparison to males, accounted for a significantly lower percentage of total juvenile arrests for every crime except prostitution and running away from home, where females accounted for 67 to 75 percent and 48 to 57 percent of the arrests, respectively (FBI, 1988).[2] Following prostitution and running away, females were most likely, in comparison to males, to be arrested for non-violent crimes such as larceny-theft (27 percent of all juvenile arrests in 1987), forgery and counterfeiting (34 percent), fraud and embezzlement (26 percent), and liquor law violations (27 percent). These patterns, as has been suggested, reflect processes of gender role socialization. For instance, running away is typically a response to family problems (Roberts, 1981), and female prostitution is a function of women's role as sex objects in society (Balkan et al., 1980).[3] Similarly, shoplifting (larceny) and check forgery and fraud can be viewed as an extension of the female role as consumer (Hoffman-Bustamente, 1973; Messerschmidt, 1986).

On the other hand, the occupational sector of society has traditionally been the province of males, and males' identity, more than females', has been shaped by occupational roles. Male socialization has been more conducive to the development of independent, aggressive, and competitive behavioral characteristics, while at the same time mandating collective participation in such conventional pursuits as athletics, military service, and labor unions. Male gender role socialization has encouraged males to respond to conflict with aggressive behavior, blame others for their problems, channel frustration toward external targets (i.e., persons and property), and test their masculinity through a willingness to face danger. Males have been more likely to acquire a taste for risk-taking and have been less likely to be deterred by the threat of legal sanctions (Hagan et al., 1985). Male law-breaking, like conventional behavior, has also involved group participation such as in gangs and organized crime (Steffensmeier, 1983). Thus, male juveniles have been consistently more likely than females to be arrested for every crime category (except for running away and prostitution). For example, in 1987 male juveniles accounted for 89 percent of all juvenile arrests for "index" violent crimes (i.e., murder and nonnegligent manslaughter, forcible rape, robbery, aggravated assault) and 79 percent of all juvenile arrests for "index" property crimes

Table 5.1

Percentage of Juvenile Females Among Juveniles Arrested for Selected Crimes

	1965	1975	1987
Index Crimes			
Murder	7.1	10.1	8.7
Rape	0.0	1.4	2.3
Robbery	4.5	7.4	6.9
Aggravated Assault	12.6	15.9	15.4
Burglary	3.5	5.1	7.5
Larceny-theft	19.7	28.9	27.4
Motor Vehicle Theft	4.3	7.4	10.5
Arson	5.5	9.8	10.3
Non-Index Crimes			
Other Assaults	15.8	21.3	22.7
Forgery and Counterfeiting	20.5	29.4	33.7
Fraud and Embezzlement	17.2	26.7	26.2
Stolen Property	6.4	8.5	9.2
Vandalism	4.9	7.6	8.9
Weapons	3.2	6.3	1.3
Prostitution	73.1	75.1	67.2
Drug Abuse Violations	11.8	16.4	13.0
Drunkenness	10.1	13.6	16.0
Liquor Laws	13.8	20.6	26.8
Disorderly Conduct	14.7	16.7	18.7
Runaways	47.9	57.2	57.3

(i.e., burglary, larceny-theft, motor vehicle theft, arson), as well as 91 percent of arrests for vandalism and 81 percent of arrests for disorderly conduct (FBI, 1988).

To the extent that females have participated in more serious crimes, it has traditionally been as accomplices or auxiliaries to males, such as driving a getaway car or carrying weapons for male gang members,[4] or as a means of self defense, such as murdering an abusive "lover" or husband (Campbell, 1984; Jones, 1980; Miller, 1975; Quicker, 1983). When women have committed violent crimes, they have rarely used guns, more often relying on household implements such as kitchen knives (Ward et al., 1969; Wolfgang, 1958; but see Mann, 1988).

Data from victimization surveys generally supported the conclusion drawn from official arrest statistics—that male rates of delinquency were higher than female rates (Hindelang, 1979; Hindelang et al., 1981). Self-report studies told a similar story, although the differences were smaller than in the official data (Canter, 1982; Cernkovich and Giordano, 1979; Hindelang et al., 1981; Smith and Visher, 1980). While their frequency of involvement was generally lower, females appeared to be as varied or versatile in their delinquent activities as males; their law-violations were not more concentrated than boys in sex or "family problem" offenses such as prostitution or running away (Canter, 1982; Hindelang, 1971). Moreover, male-female differences were due primarily to a larger number of more serious and high frequency male offenders (Canter, 1982). Overall, the magnitudes of the observed sex differences were not that large, "suggesting that their statistical significance overstate[d] their practical importance" (p. 382). Some self report studies indicated that the rates of offending were minimal or essentially equal for minor thefts and use of marijuana and other drugs (Ageton and Elliott, 1978; Beschner and Treasure, 1979; Figueira-McDonough et al., 1981; Jessor and Jessor, 1977; Wechsler and McFadden, 1976). Some research on shoplifting suggested that juvenile females may have been even more involved in this crime than males (Sanders, 1981). Nevertheless, while alternative data sources qualify the findings of official statistics, the evidence is generally supportive of a gender role theory of female delinquency.

Have Rates of Female Crime and Delinquency Increased?

Freda Adler, in her book, *Sisters in Crime: The Rise of the New Female Offender* (1975:1, 14), stimulated much of the current debate about the changing nature of female law-breaking by provocatively claiming that:

> The phenonemon of female criminality is but one wave in . . . [the] rising tide of female assertiveness—a wave which has not yet crested and may even be seeking its level uncomfortably close to the high-water mark set by male violence . . . [Females are now] robbing banks singlehandedly, committing assorted armed robberies, muggings, loansharking operations, extortions, murders, and a wide variety of other aggressive, violence-oriented crimes.

To explain these trends Adler offered a "masculinity" theory of female misconduct. According to this theory, technological advances freeing females from unwanted pregnancies and home responsibilities, and the ideology of women's liberation, had "masculinized" female behavior, engendering an "imitative male maschismo competitiveness" (p. 98). As gender role expectations for males and

females have begun to converge, females have strived for equality in both the world of legitimate work and the world of crime.

Initial evaluations of Adler's claims questioned the accuracy of the view that female crime and delinquency had increased. Norland and Shover (1977:95), for instance, calculated the percentage of females (adult and juvenile) among all arrests for different offenses between 1966 and 1975 and did not observe any "clear-cut pattern of changes."[5] Similarly, Simon (1975) found little increase in female arrests for violent crimes and even reported a decrease in arrests for murder and aggravated assault between 1953 and 1974. She also observed that the significant increases that had occurred in female crime were in nonviolent property offenses such as larceny, fraud (e.g., welfare fraud, bad checks), and check forgery. She argued that these increases were not indicative of a change in the nature of female law-breaking. Rather, the rise in divorce rates, number of female heads of households, and females on welfare rolls or employed in low-paying jobs provided the incentive and/or opportunity for females to commit these non-violent offenses (see Balkan and Berger, 1979; Messerschmidt, 1986).

Most observers have looked to the work of Darrell Steffensmeier to draw conclusions about trends in female law-violation. In several studies, Steffensmeier (1978, 1980a; Steffensmeier and Cobb, 1981) confirmed Simon's findings that the major increases in female offenses (adult and juvenile, or adult only) between the early 1960s and the late 1970s had occurred in nonviolent property crimes, such as shoplifting and check forgery, that were consistent with traditional female gender role socialization. He believed these increases could be attributed to greater economic pressures facing women, to more opportunities for shoplifting created by the rise of self-service retail marketing, and to the expansion of consumer credit and governmental welfare which created new opportunities for credit card and welfare fraud. He also attributed increased female crime rates to merchants' greater willingness to prosecute law-violators and to growing concerns about welfare abuse (see Steffensmeier and Allan, 1988).

Steffensmeier et al. (1979), however, did challenge Simon's assumptions about a decline in female violence, finding the levels of female violence (adult and juvenile) to have risen between 1960 and 1977 (see Datesman and Scarpitti, 1980a). But contrary to Adler's assertions, Steffensmeier et al. emphasized that male violence had increased at an equal rate, that the increase in violence appeared to have leveled off by the early 1970s, that males continued to commit the overwhelming proportion of violent crimes, and that females had not reached parity (and would not in the future) with males in their violent offenses (see Giallombardo, 1980).

Thornton et al. (1987) supported Steffensmeier's conclusions, finding that rates of *juvenile* law-violation leveled off in the 1970s. In fact, violent and property crime rates (for index offenses) decreased for both male and female juveniles between 1975 and 1984, although the female decline was slower and even increased slightly for aggravated assault. They concluded that females "have not been that much more involved in serious crimes in the past ten years" (p. 55). On the other hand, Table 5.2 presents more recent data from 1978 to 1987 that cloud this picture by demonstrating that female juvenile crime increased at a faster rate than the male rate, or decreased at a slower rate, for most index and non-index offenses (FBI, 1988). Thus, it is difficult to draw conclusions based upon per-

centage increases from the mid-late 1970s to the mid-late 1980s. Moreover, analyses that rely on the percentage increase in crime from one time period to another can be misleading because low absolute rates of crime, such as those exhibited by females, can produce large percentage increases (Miller, 1986).

When Steffensmeir and Steffensmeir (1980) looked specifically at rates of male and female delinquency between 1965 and 1977, rather than adult criminality or overall rates, they also found a continued gap in the number of crimes committed by male and female juveniles. On the other hand, they did find a greater narrowing of arrest

Table 5.2

Percent Change in Juvenile Male and Female Arrests, 1978–1987

	Males Under 18	Females Under 18
Index Crimes		
Murder	+5.4	−46.4
Forcible Rape	+22.4	−38.6
Robbery	−27.7	+25.8
Aggravated Assault	+6.2	+21.1
Burglary	−43.5	−2.7
Larceny-theft	−5.7	+33.9
Motor Vehicle Theft	−14.0	+48.3
Arson	−22.9	+2.3
Non-Index Crimes		
Other Assaults	+25.0	+84.5
Forgery and Counterfeiting	−27.3	+115.8
Fraud	+139.8	+253.8
Embezzlement	−2.0	+352.2
Stolen Property	−9.1	+63.2
Vandalism	−20.1	+23.3
Weapons	+18.5	−.8
Prostitution	−50.2	+85.0
Drug Abuse Violations	−36.2	+6.0
Liquor Laws	+10.6	+230.9
Drunkenness	−51.4	−89.5
Disorderly Conduct	−22.1	+7.9
Runaways	−13.6	+22.7

trends between male and female adolescents than between male and female adults (see Giallombardo, 1980; Steffensmeier and Cobb, 1981). Balkan and Berger (1979) calculated the percentage of juvenile females among all juvenile arrests between 1960 and 1975, as Norland and Shover (1977) had done for the percentage of all females among all arrests, and found increases in the female contribution to both violent and property crimes. While more recent 1987 data indicated that the increase in the percentage of juvenile female arrests had tapered off for some crimes since the mid-1970s, the percentages were still generally higher than they were in the mid-1960s (FBI, 1988). Thus, although females still comprised a minority of adolescent arrests in absolute terms, some observers believed that meaningful changes had occurred in the level of female delinquency (see Datesman and Scarpitti, 1980a).

Furthermore, Austin (1982) challenged some of Steffensmeier's and Simon's most important findings. He pointed out that Steffensmeier (1978) ignored his own data which indicated that females' involvement in burglary and auto theft, two "male-oriented" crimes, was comparable to that of larceny-theft and fraud/embezzlement. Recalculating Simon's data, Austin also showed that increases for burglary were larger than those for larceny-theft and fraud/embezzlement. In his own statistical analysis, he found an accelerated increase in rates of both adult and juvenile female burglary and robbery between 1967 and 1976, a period following the rise of the contemporary women's movement, and an association between indicators of female emancipation (e.g., labor force participation, divorce) and female law-breaking. He suggested that other researchers, in their effort to defend the women's movement against those who wished to emphasize its

undesirable effects, had underestimated the increases that had occurred in female crime and delinquency.

All of the above studies that calculated changes in female rates of law-violation relied on official statistics. Self-report studies suggested that in the decade between 1967 and 1977 adolescent sex differences remained stable, and that increases in female delinquency occurred primarily in alcohol and drug use (particularly marijuana) and truancy (Ageton and Elliott, 1978; Canter, 1982; Gold and Reimer, 1974). For less serious offenses, however, the gender gap in self-reported delinquency had narrowed more rapidly than in official statistics (Smith and Visher, 1980), and as indicated above, the greatest sex differences were found in the larger number of more serious and high frequency male offenders (Canter, 1982). Finally, a comparison of two fifteen to seventeen year-old female cohorts in 1976 and 1980 found that the proportion of females (prevalence) engaged in theft was lower in 1980, but that the amount of theft in the cohort (incidence) was higher (Ageton, 1983). In other words, "while fewer fifteen to seventeen year-olds were stealing in 1980, the rate per cohort member [had] risen" (p. 575). Similar results were obtained with a general delinquency index, although the prevalence and incidence of assaultive behavior was lower for the 1980 cohort.[6]

While these self-report data indicated that traditional patterns have persisted to a considerable extent, they were also suggestive of a degree of change that was found in other studies. Giordano and Cernkovich (1979), for instance, surveyed females in two state institutions for delinquent girls and in three urban high schools. Contrary to the traditional view that females acted mainly as accomplices to male companions, about one-fifth of the institutionalized girls reported they were most likely to get into trouble alone, and about one-fifth of the institutionalized girls and one-fifth of the high school girls indicated they were most likely to get into trouble with other girls. For both groups of girls, the most significant pattern of delinquent involvement was with a mixed group of boys and girls. In these mixed-sex peer groups, the impetus for the crime did not seem to come just from the boys, as is suggested by girls' lack of agreement with the survey item: "It's usually the guy's idea and I just go along for the ride." As one girl explained, the group simply afforded the greatest opportunity for the successful execution of theft and that "the girls are as much or more into it as [the guys] are" (p. 475).

Similarly, interviews with juvenile probation officers and delinquent girls by Berger and Balkan (1983) revealed females taking an active role in planning and participating in serious criminal acts. A typical scenario involved a teenage girl hitchhiking a ride and giving a male driver the impression she was interested in "partying" with him. They would stop at a liquor store, he would go in leaving the keys in the car, and she would steal the car. Another common case involved a girl enticing a male to a secluded place where he would be jumped by female and male friends who would rob and beat him. Sometimes a girl only had to lean out of a car (with a low-cut blouse) and ask the time from a male passerby. As he moved closer to the car, friends hiding in the back seat would jump him and steal his money or jewelry. While these crimes showed females exploiting their sexuality for personal gain, the girls often initiated the plan and carried it out with or without male companions.

Victimization data from the 1970s also contradicted the notion that female offenders (adult and juvenile) acted merely as ac-complices to males, since females were more likely to act alone or with other females (Parisi, 1982). On the other hand, Laub and McDermott's (1985) analysis of victimization data for *juvenile* females (excluding mixed-sex and mixed-race groups of offenders) cautioned against exaggerated claims of increased female delinquency. They found that white female juveniles' rate of personal victimization remained stable between 1973 and 1981, and that black female juveniles' rate actually declined, though it remained higher than the rate for white females. Hindelang (1979:153) suggested, however, that victimization surveys may underestimate the degree of female law-violation because:

> it is possible that chivalrous or embarrassed respondents may fail to mention (to survey interviewers) victimizations involving female offenders, that they consciously lie about whether offenders are male or female, or even honestly but disproportionately perceive female offenders as men.

In sum, the picture one gets from examining official statistics, self-report surveys, and victimization data is somewhat mixed. Although the dominant view among researchers is that the nature of female law-violation (adult and juvenile) has not changed substantially over the years, conclusions are subject to subtleties of interpretation that may be slanted according to which studies one chooses to emphasize. With respect to female delinquency in particular, Empey (1982:115) may have been correct when he asserted that:

> while girls are not as delinquent as boys overall, they do report having committed a long list of illegal acts which historically have been viewed as "male" offenses . . . [E]xplanations are needed to account for . . . a picture of female behavior that is far differ-

ent from the one suggested by tradition (see Giordano et al., 1986).

Changing Societal Reactions to Female Offenders

Many criminologists attributed any observed increases in rates of female delinquency to changing societal reactions and increased official labeling of young female offenders. In the past, law enforcement and juvenile justice personnel, as well as researchers, tended to "sexualize" much female delinquency (Chesney-Lind, 1973; Cohn, 1970; Smith, 1978). In other words, female offenders were viewed primarily as sexually promiscuous, as prostitutes, or as runaways in need of parental supervision, irrespective of whether they were involved in other types of crimes. Thus, girls were more likely than boys to be arrested and processed in juvenile court for status offenses, although boys were treated more severely for criminal offenses (Chesney-Lind, 1977; Datesman and Scarpitti, 1980b; Hagan et al., 1979; Hasenfeld, 1976; Pawlack, 1977, Sarri, 1974).

Observers have suggested that the changing position of women in contemporary society, increased media attention to the "new female offender," concern with equality and the abolition of sex discrimination, and increased police professionalism have led authorities to take more seriously the nonsexual nature of female delinquency and reduce the disparities in official processing of female and male offenders (Box and Hale, 1984; Chesney-Lind, 1978; Smart, 1976; Steffensmeir and Cobb, 1981). Similarly, Curran (1984) attributed increased female rates in one juvenile court system in the late 1970s to a rising concern for "law and order." He also suggested that removal of status offenses from the

court's jurisdiction resulted in some classification as violent crime of delinquent conduct previously recorded as "uncontrollable behavior."

However, the overall evidence is somewhat mixed, and does not lead to the conclusion that changes in female crime rates can be attributed solely to changing societal reactions. Analysis of 1972-1976 victimization data on female offenders (adult and juvenile) found no greater propensity for victims to report female offenders to the police, though male victims were more likely than female victims to report female offenders to the police, and female victims were more likely to report male offenders to the police (Hindelang, 1979). Examining the research for adult criminal defendants, Steffensmeir (1980b) found little evidence that changing gender role definitions or the women's movement had affected sentencing outcomes. Chesney-Lind's (1987) review found evidence of lenient criminal justice treatment of adult women for serious but not less serious offenses, although Bernstein et al.'s (1979) study found that female violent offenders were treated more severely relative to males than were female property offenders. Kruttschnitt and Green's (1984) research did not find diminishing sentencing disparities over time between adult male and female defendants.

Some studies of female *juveniles* continued to find females treated more severely than males for status offenses but less severely for criminal offenses (Boisvert and Wells, 1980; Chesney-Lind, 1987; Datesman and Scarpitti, 1980b). Krohn et al. (1983) found diminished sex differences in the likelihood of police referral for adult felonies and adult and juvenile misdemeanors, but not for juvenile felonies or status offenses. Visher (1983) found that female property offenders in general were not treated more leniently by the police than male property offenders, but that lenient treatment for females was more likely to occur for those who displayed traditional gender role behaviors and characteristics. Older and white female suspects were less likely to be arrested than younger, black, or hostile suspects. Datesman and Scarpitti (1980b) found that black female juveniles relative to white female juveniles were given more severe court dispositions than black male juveniles relative to white male juveniles, perhaps because gender role expectations for black females and males were less differentiated than they were for whites (see Black, 1980; Smith and Visher, 1980).[7]

Finally, interviews with probation officers suggested that judges were still reluctant to believe that some girls were violent or dangerous (Berger and Balkan, 1983). For instance, one sixteen-year-old middle-class white female appeared before the juvenile court judge twelve times for burglary, robbery and assault before he ordered her incarcerated. She admitted that she consciously attempted to manipulate the judge through a polite and "little girl" demeanor. Girls from lower class neighborhoods, on the other hand, were reported to be treated more severely.

The Masculinity-Liberation Hypothesis

Irrespective of changes in the societal reaction to female delinquency, explanations are needed to account for the behavior of contemporary female delinquents. However, the *masculinity-liberation* hypothesis offered by Adler (1975) has not been particularly effective in explaining recent trends. Research found little or no consistent relationship between masculine personality traits or gender role expectations (e.g., leadership, aggressiveness, competitiveness, success orientation, fixing a car,

paying for expenses on a date) and self-reported female or male delinquency (Norland et al., 1981; Shover et al., 1979). While some research found a moderate association between masculinity and delinquency, males were more delinquent regardless of degree of masculinity (Cullen et al., 1979; Thornton and James, 1979).

Research has also not supported the hypothesis that female delinquency has been increased by attitudes favorable toward feminism or women's liberation. In fact, research indicated that feminist attitudes may actually inhibit female law-breaking. For instance, Giordano and Cernkovich (1979) found that liberated attitudes toward gender roles in the family and occupational sector were not related to self-reported delinquency, and that traditional beliefs about male and female personality traits and interpersonal relationships were associated with increased delinquency (see James and Thornton, 1980). These findings were compatible with research on adult female offenders who held traditional beliefs about motherhood and women's dependency upon men and who tended to reject the legitimacy of the women's movement (Glick and Neto 1977; Velimesis, 1972).

Changing Gender Roles and Role Strain

The masculinity-liberation explanation of contemporary female delinquency oversimplifies the manner in which changing gender roles have affected female delinquents. However, while preoccupation with masculinity and women's liberation has been misguided, it is insufficient to merely describe contemporary female gender roles and patterns of delinquency as "extensions of traditional role[s]" (Steffensmeier and Allan, 1988:70). In contrast, Giordano and Cernkovich (1979) suggested that contemporary females confront a much more complex, multidimensional, and often contradictory set of behavioral scripts that specify what is *"likely, possible, unlikely* and *impossible"* for them to do (Harris, 1977:11). Thus, I argue that there is considerable gender "role strain" inherent in females' attempts to negotiate contemporary expectations for themselves and others, and that the concept of role strain, the set of ambiguous or contradictory demands built into a single role (see Goode, 1960), offers a promising approach to understanding important aspects of contemporary female delinquency.[8]

Contemporary female adolescents are likely to have experienced gender role strain in the family and educational settings. For example, even parents who favor gender equality and who are concerned about sexism hesitate to deviate from traditional gender role socialization practices because of fear that their children might become "misfits" (Katz, 1979:24; see Block, 1978). Similarly, working mothers continue to serve as traditional role models for their daughters insofar as mothers are still expected to earn less than fathers, to be responsible for taking care of the home, to stay home with preschool children, and to compromise their careers for their family (Coverman, 1983; Herzog and Bachman, 1982; Komarovsky, 1981). In addition, although schools may no longer emphasize traditional feminine roles for girls (Sheley, 1985), and females are increasingly encouraged to participate in athletics and exert themselves physically (Searles and Berger, 1987), informal playground behavior among school children remains, for the most part, quite traditional—boys are still more likely to participate in team sports in the central play areas, while girls play hopscotch or jump rope in smaller groups (Best, 1983).

Given this social context of gender role strain, we should expect contemporary female delinquents to be capable of simultaneously identifying with traditional and nontraditional facets of contemporary gender roles. Indeed, Giordano and Cernkovich (1979) found that while delinquent girls maintained traditional gender role expectations in many aspects of their lives (e.g., work, family, interpersonal relationships), they did express nontraditional attitudes toward what they perceived as appropriate, acceptable, or possible for girls to do. For instance, female delinquents in their study indicated a high degree of agreement to the survey statement, "If a guy can do that, why can't I?" and they were more likely than nondelinquent girls to believe they had as much right as a guy to swear, to go into a bar alone, and so forth.

Similarly, Berger and Balkan (1983) found that while delinquent girls remained traditional in their concern for male approval to validate their self-worth, they also expressed a desire to receive the respect from others that they thought was generally reserved for males. As one seventeen-year-old Chicana said, "I want to prove to my father and my brothers that I'm worth something. I'm tough and not afraid of anything." She indicated that in her barrio (community) football games between neighborhoods (gangs) were considered very serious. The girls used to just watch the games, but now they wanted to play. At first the guys laughed, but now the girls have become part of the team. The games are still rough, often ending in a brawl with someone getting hurt. But according to this young woman, "we play mean and take the consequences. . . . The guys try to rip off . . . [our] . . . bras, so we just bought stronger ones" (p. 20). Another girl revealed other changes she had observed in how females were treated. "It used to be at a party the boys would show respect for the girls by taking a walk to get high or loaded. Now they stay in the room and the girls get high or loaded with them'' (p. 20). While girls were still typically introduced to drugs by male companions (see Gold and Reimer, 1974), these experiences suggested a greater desire of girls to be like the boys.

However, there is considerable gender role strain inherent in females' attempts to negotiate contemporary expectations for themselves and others. For example, current sexual norms encourage girls to be sexually active while also maintaining a traditional double standard. To be equal to boys requires girls to engage freely in sexual activity, but they still fear losing the respect of boys and are concerned about being labeled a ''whore.'' Thus, serial monogamy is the norm, and sex outside of a steady relationship is condemned. Delinquent girls avoid associating with ''loose' girls whose reputation might contaminate them by association'' (Campbell, 1987:452; Smith, 1978; Wilson, 1978). As a result, these girls seldom use birth control, even though they may be knowledgeable about it, because this would indicate that they planned their sexual involvements (they also may have heard that using birth control pills causes cancer). Sexual activity is thus engaged in ''spontaneously'' with pregnancy a very likely consequence. Abortions are rare for religious or economic reasons, because they want the baby, or believe only ''cowards'' get abortions. Moreover, motherhood releases females from their involvement in delinquency because they now have responsibility and purpose in their lives. For those who are members of extended family networks, having a baby means establishing themselves as ''somebody'' (a mother), and qualifying for welfare means they can make an economic contribution to the family (Berger and Balkan, 1983;

Campbell, 1987; Horowitz, 1983; Johnston, 1979; Williams and Kornblum, 1985).

Patterns of female involvement in gangs are also indicative of gender role strain. On the one hand, elements of traditionalism remain in that female gangs are largely auxiliaries to male gangs and female gang members mainly play a support role for males (Bowker and Klein, 1980, 1983; Campbell, 1984; Miller, 1975; Quicker, 1983). The names of female gangs are generally feminized versions of male gangs, and the males remain in control (Campbell, 1984). Yet, gang females take much pride in their claims of autonomy and reject ''any suggestion that they could be duped or conned by males'' (Campbell, 1987:460). Female gangs have their own leaders and make most of their routine decisions without males. Female members are proud of their ability to fight, and ''girls who are physically weak or unable to defend themselves . . . often will not be allowed to join'' (Quicker, 1983:15). But while females may occasionally participate in fights with males from rival gangs, most fighting is directed at other females and is often over a dispute about a male. Although gang males express pride over their females' willingness to fight, they are uncomfortable with female aggression (Campbell, 1987; Horowitz, 1983). As one gang female explained:

> I've asked my boyfriend and they all come up with the same answer: 'I don't think a girl should be in. It's all right for a guy, but she shouldn't be in the fights'. . . . They say it's right for a guy, but it's not right for the girls . . . . That's what they all say, yet they are happy to have their own girls. They're proud. They say our girls do this, our girls are bad. . . .[So] I don't know what they're talking about 'cause they get happy. If it wasn't for them we wouldn't be around 'cause the guys started . . .[the gang]. . . . The girls never start the gang; the guys do.

And girls that like them or back them up started it with their permission (Quicker, 1983:12).

Undoubtedly, some observers, as I indicated above, would prefer to characterize these patterns of female delinquency as "extensions of traditional role[s]" rather than as indications of an emancipated female role (Steffensmeier and Allan, 1988:70). But I suggest that the concept of gender role strain more accurately describes the contradictions or tensions that are inherent in contemporary gender roles.

Conclusion

Much of the female delinquency literature has focused on quantitative tests of the proposition that rates of female delinquency have increased in traditional and/or non-traditional female offense categories. The evidence is clear in finding considerable stability in traditional patterns. However, it is an oversimplification to suggest that what has occurred has been merely an extension of traditional roles. Refutations of these propositions oversimplify the complexity of contemporary gender roles, which are multifaceted and often contradictory. More attention in future research should be given to examining female delinquency as a consequence of gender role strain.[9]

Fortunately, female offenders are no longer residual subjects in contemporary delinquency research. It is becoming less acceptable to conduct studies "that either exclude female[s] or suggest that they will be considered in a future paper" (Chesney-Lind, 1988:17). But while the status of female delinquency research has been elevated, there has been a tendency to treat the female population as an undifferentiated group. More emphasis needs to be given to variations across social classes and racial and ethnic groups. For example, much evidence has indicated that lower-class and black females were more involved in some types of delinquent behavior, particularly violence, and that the delinquent conduct of black females was closer to that of black males than to white females (Ageton, 1983; Cernkovich and Giordano, 1979; Chilton and Datesman, 1987; Giordano et al., 1981; Laub and McDermott, 1985; Smith and Visher, 1980; Young 1986). These patterns have been attributed to greater similarity of economic and social roles among black males and females as compared to white males and females (see Freeman, 1973; Ladner, 1971; Schaffer, 1981; Treiman and Terrell, 1975). For example, Giordano (1978:132) attributed black girls' greater involvement in single-sex delinquent peer groups to black females' "longer tradition of independence and freedom of action"; black girls were less likely to need males to provide them with the techniques and motives to engage in delinquent activity.

On the other hand, Steffensmeier and Allan (1988) cautioned against hasty conclusions regarding the gender-race-delinquency relationship, noting studies that found similar sex disparities in crime rates for blacks and whites (Hindelang et al., 1981; Young, 1980). They argued that gender role convergence among black females and males has been inferred from black women's relative economic independence from men, but that black females are just as traditional in their gender role outlooks as whites (Canter and Ageton, 1984; Gackenbach, 1978). Steffensmeier and Allan (1988) did, however, underscore the need to examine the gender-delinquency relationship by different subgroups in the population and across different types of crime. Their analysis of arrest data indicated, for instance, that although female rates were lower than male rates of the same subgroup, they were often higher than the male rates of different subgroups. For some crimes the black female rate was higher than the white male rate, the urban female rate was similar to or exceeded the rural male rate, and the young female rate was higher than the older male rate. In addition, Steffensmeier and Allan (1988) urged researchers to move beyond theories that focus exclusively on gender roles to those that more accurately explain population subgroup variations in female crime and delinquency.

Notes

1. For reviews of this literature, see Balkan and Berger (1979), Heidensohn (1985), Klein (1973), Leonard (1982), Mann (1984), and Smart (1976).

2. The higher rates of male arrests in recent statistics does not preclude the possibility that changes have nevertheless occurred in the volume and character of female delinquency. Longitudinal trends and other data sources (e.g., self report and victimization surveys) need to be considered.

3. Sexual abuse in the family appears to be a significant factor in the decision of adolescent females to run away from home. These females then engage in prostitution and other crimes as a means of survival (Chesney-Lind, 1989; Janus et al., 1987).

4. Girls' presence at the site of gang activity even appears to have had a suppressing effect (Bowker and Klein, 1980).

5. Some studies analyzed female arrest data using the total arrests for adults and juveniles. Unless I specifically mention juveniles, delinquents, adolescents, or girls, or unless I mention adults only, my discussion of female offenders or law-violators refers to all females (i.e., adult and juvenile).

6. The rates of female law-violation also declined with age (Ageton, 1983), a pattern that has been observed with male delinquents (Greenberg, 1977).

7. Kruttschnitt (1982a, 1982b) argues that it is concern with enforcement of traditional gender roles rather than chivalry that accounts for differential treatment of females. She found that women who were economically dependent and "respectable" (e.g., no psychiatric care, history of drug or alcohol use, employee censorship, or peer deviance) were treated more leniently than women who were independent and less "respectable."

8. Role strain is similar to role conflict, the incompatibility or contradictory expectations between two different roles. In gender role research, the concept of role conflict has been used to analyze how college women, for example, experienced a conflict between the traditional role of "catching a husband" and the modern role of having a career (Komarovsky, 1946), or how married professional women experienced a conflict between their family role (wife and mother) and their occupational role (Polama and Garland, 1971). Insofar as data indicate that female delinquents do not identify with a "modern" or "career" role, I prefer the term role strain (as opposed to role conflict) to denote the tensions experienced by these girls.

9. Detailed ethnographic studies of the process of identify formation in delinquent girls would also be useful. For example, Campbell (1987) examined poor, Puerto Rican gang females' presentation of self in social talk to understand the role of gossip, "put-downs," and vilification of others in the construction of identity.

References

Adler, F. 1975. *Sisters in Crime: The Rise of the New Female Offender*. New York: McGraw Hill.

Ageton, S. 1983. "The dynamics of female delinquency, 1976-1980." *Criminology* 21:555-84.

Ageton, S. and D. S. Elliott. 1978. *The Incidence of Delinquent Behavior in a National Probability Sample of Adolescents*. Boulder. CO: University of Colorado, Behavioral Research Institute.

Austin, R. L. 1982. "Women's liberation and increases in minor, major, and occupational offenses." *Criminology* 20:407-30.

Balkan S. and R. J. Berger. 1979. "The changing nature of female delinquency. In C. Kopp (ed.), *Becoming Female: Perspectives on Development*. New York: Plenum.

Balkan S., R. J. Berger, and J. Schmidt. 1980. *Crime and Deviance in America: A Critical Approach*. Belmont, CA: Wadsworth.

Berger, R. J. and S. Balkan. 1983. "The violent female delinquent: Myth or reality?" Paper presented at the conference of the Academy of Criminal Justice Sciences, San Antonio.

Bernstein, I., J. Cardascia, and C. E. Ross. 1979. "Defendant's sex and criminal court decisions." In R. Alvarez et al. (eds.), *Discrimination in Organizations*, San Francisco: Josey-Bass.

Beschner, G. M. and K. G. Treasure. 1979. "Female adolescent drug use." In G. M. Beschner and A. S. Friedman (eds.), *Youth Drug Abuse: Problems, Issues, and Treatment*. Lexington, MA: Lexington Books.

Best, R. 1983. *We've All Got Scars: What Boys and Girls Learn in Elementary School*. Bloomington: Indiana University Press.

Binder, A., G. Geis, and D. Bruce. 1988. *Juvenile Delinquency: Historical, Cultural, Legal Perspectives*. New York: Macmillan.

Black, D. 1980. "Dispute settlement by the police." In D. Black (ed.). *The Manners and Customs of the Police*. New York: Academic Press.

Block, J. H. 1978. "Another look at sex differentiation in the socialization behaviors of mothers and fathers." In F. L. Denmark and J. Sherman (eds.), *Psychology of Women: Future Directions of Research*. New York: Psychological Dimensions.

Boisvert, M. J. and R. Wells, 1980. "Toward a national policy on status offenders." *Social Work* 25:230-4.

Bowker, L. H. and M. W. Klein, 1983. "The etiology of female juvenile delinquency and gang membership: A test of psychological and social structural explanations." *Adolescence* 18:739-51.

———. 1980. "Female participation in delinquent gang activities." *Adolescence* 15:509-19.

Box, S. and C. Hale. 1984. "Liberation/emancipation, economic marginalization, or less chivalry: The relevance of three theoretical arguments to female crime patterns in England and Wales. 1951-1980." *Criminology* 22:473-97.

Bruck, C. 1974. "Women against the law." *Human Behavior* 4:24-33.

Campbell, A. 1987. "Self definition by rejection: The case of gang girls." *Social Problems* 34:451-66.

———. 1984. *The Girls in the Gang*. New York: Basil Blackwell.

Canter, R. J. 1982. "Sex differences in self-report delinquency." *Criminology* 20:373-93,

Canter, R. J. and S. Ageton. 1984. "The epidemiology of adolescent sex-role attitudes." *Sex Roles* 11:657-76.

Cernkovich, S. A. and P. C. Giordano. 1979. "A comparative analysis of female delinquency." *Sociological Quarterly* 20:131-45.

Chesney-Lind, M. 1989. "Girls' crime and woman's place: Toward a feminist model of female delinquency." *Crime and Delinquency* 35:5-29.

———. 1988. "Doing feminist criminology." *The Criminologist* 13:1, 3, 16-17.

———. 1987. "Female offenders: Paternalism reexamined." In L. L. Crites and W. L. Hepperle (eds.), *Women, the Courts, and Equality*. Newbury Park, CA: Sage.

_____. 1978. "Young women in the arms of the law." In L. H. Bowker (ed.), *Women, Crime and the Criminal Justice System*. Lexington, MA: Lexington Books.

_____. 1977. "Judicial paternalism and the female status offender: Training women to know their place." *Crime and Delinquency* 23:121–30.

_____. 1973. "Judicial enforcement of the female sex role." *Issues in Criminology* 8:51–69.

Chilton, R. and S. K. Datesman. 1987. "Gender, race, and crime: An analysis of urban arrest trends, 1960–1980." *Gender and Society* 1:152–71.

Cohn, Y. 1970. "Criteria for the probation officer's recommendation to the juvenile court judge." In P. G. Garabedian and D. C. Gibbons (eds.). *Becoming Delinquent*. Chicago: Aldine.

Coverman, S. W. 1983. "Gender, domestic labor time, and wage inequality." *American Sociological Review* 49:487–93.

Cowie, J., V. Cowie, and E. Slater. 1968. *Delinquency in Girls*. London: Heineman.

Cullen, F. T., K. M. Golden, and J. B. Cullen. 1979. "Sex and delinquency: A partial test of the masculinity hypothesis." *Criminology* 17:301–10.

Curran, D. J. 1984. "The myth of the 'new' female delinquent." *Criminology* 30:386–99.

Datesman, S. K. and F. R. Scarpitti. 1980a. "The extent and nature of female crime." In S. K. Datesman and F. R. Scarpitti (eds.), *Women, Crime, and Justice*. New York: Oxford University Press.

_____. 1980b. "Unequal protection for males and females in juvenile court." In S. K. Datesman and F. R. Scarpitti (eds.) *Women, Crime, and Justice*. New York: Oxford University Press.

Deming, R. 1977. *Women: The New Criminals*. Nashville: Thomas Nelson.

Empey, L. T. 1982. *American Delinquency: Its Meaning and Construction*. Second edition. Homewood, IL: Dorsey Press.

Federal Bureau of Investigation. 1988. *Crime in the United States, 1987*. Washington, DC: U.S. Government Printing Office (July).

Figueira-McDonough, J., W. H. Barton, and R. C. Sarri. 1981. "Normal deviance: Gender similarities in adolescent subcultures." In M. Q. Warren (ed.), *Comparing Female and Male Offenders*. Beverly Hills, CA: Sage.

Freeman, R. 1973. "Changes in the labor market for black Americans." *Brookings Papers on Economic Activity*. Washington, DC: Brookings Institute.

Gackenbach, J. 1978. "The effects of race, sex, and career goal differences on sex role attitudes at home and at work." *Journal of Vocational Behavior* 12:93–101.

Giallombardo, R. 1980. "Female delinquency." In D. Shichor and D. H. Kelly (eds.), *Critical Issues in Juvenile Delinquency*. Lexington, MA: Lexington Books.

Giordano, P. C. 1978. "Girls, guys and gangs: The changing social context of female delinquency." *Journal of Criminal Law and Criminology* 69:126–32.

Giordano, P. C. and S. A. Cernkovich. 1979. "On complicating the relationship between liberation and delinquency." *Social Problems* 26:467–81.

Giordano, P. C., A. Kerbel, and S. Dudley. 1981. "The economics of female criminality: An analysis of police blotters. 1890-1976." In L. H. Bowker (ed.), *Women and Crime in America*. New York: Macmillan.

Glick, R. and V. Neto. 1977. *National Study of Women's Correctional Programs*. Washington, DC: U.S. Government Printing Office.

Gold, M. and D. J. Reimer, 1974. "Changing patterns of delinquent behavior among Americans 13 to 16 years old, 1967–1972." *Crime and /Delinquency Literature* 7:483–517.

Goode, W. J. 1960. "A theory of role strain." *American Sociological Review* 25:483–96.

Greenberg, D. F. 1977. "Delinquency and the age structure of society." *Contemporary Crises* 1:189–223.

Hagan, J., A. R. Gillis, and J. Simpson. 1985. "The class structure of gender and delinquency: Toward a power-control theory of common delinquent behavior.'' *American Journal of Sociology* 90:1151–78.

Hagan, J., J. Simpson, and A. R. Gillis. 1979. ''The sexual stratification of social control: A gender based perspective on crime and delinquency.'' *British Journal of Sociology* 30:25–38.

Harris, A. 1977. ''Sex and theories of deviance.'' *American Sociological Review* 42:3–16.

Hasenfeld, Y. 1976. ''Youth in the juvenile court: Input and output patterns.'' In R. Sarri and Y. Hasenfeld (eds.). *Brought to Justice? Juveniles, the Courts, and the Law.* Ann Arbor: University of Michigan, National Assessment of Juvenile Corrections.

Herzog, A. R. and J. Bachman. 1982. *Sex Role Attitudes Among High School Seniors: Views About Work and Family Roles.* Ann Arbor: University of Michigan, Institute for Social Research.

Heidensohn, F. M. 1985. *Women and Crime: The Life of the Female Offender.* New York: New York University Press.

Hindelang, M. J. 1979. ''Sex differences in criminal activity.'' *Social Problems* 27: 143–56.

————. 1971. ''Age, sex, and the versatility of delinquent involvement.'' *Social Problems* 18:527–35.

Hindelang, M. J., T. Hirschi, and J. G. Weis. 1981. *Measuring Delinquency.* Beverly Hills, CA: Sage.

Hoffman-Bustamente, D. 1973. ''The nature of female delinquency.'' *Issues in Criminology* 8:114–36.

Horowitz, R. 1983. *Honor and the American Dream.* Chicago: University of Chicago Press.

James, J. and W. E. Thornton. 1980. ''Women's liberation and the female delinquent.'' *Journal of Research in Crime and Delinquency* 17:230–44.

Janus, M., A. McCormack, A. W. Burgess, and C. Hartman. 1987. *Adolescent Runaways: Causes and Consequences.* Lexington, MA: Lexington Books.

Jessor, R. and S. L. Jessor. 1977. *Problem Behavior and Psychosocial Development.* New York: Academic Press.

Johnston, T. J. 1979. ''La vida loca.'' *New West* (January):38–45.

Jones, A. 1980. *Women Who Kill.* New York: Fawcett.

Katz, P. A. 1979. ''The development of female identity.'' In C. Kopp (ed.), *Becoming Female: Perspectives on Development.* New York: Plenum.

Klein, D. 1973. ''The etiology of female crime: A review of the literature.'' *Issues in Criminology* 8:3–30.

Komarovsky, M. 1981. ''College women and careers.'' *New York Times* (January):23.

————. 1946. ''Cultural contradictions and sex roles.'' *American Journal of Sociology* 52:184–9.

Konopka, G. 1966. *The Adolescent Girl in Conflict.* Englewood Cliffs, NJ: Prentice-Hall.

Krohn, M. D., J. P. Curry, and S. Nelson-Kilger, 1983. ''Is chivalry dead? An analysis of changes in police dispositions of males and females.'' *Criminology* 21:417–37.

Kruttschnitt, C. 1982a. ''Women, crime and dependency: An application of the theory of law.'' *Criminology* 19:495–513.

————. 1982b. ''Respectable women and the law.'' *Sociological Quarterly* 23:221–34.

Kruttschnitt, C. and D. Green. 1984. ''The sex-sanctioning issue: Is it history?'' *American Sociological Review* 49:541–51.

Ladner, J. 1971. *Tomorrow's Tomorrow: The Black Woman.* Garden City, NY: Doubleday.

Laub, J. H. and M. J. McDermott. 1985. ''An analysis of serious crime by young black women.'' *Criminology* 23:81–98.

Leonard, E. B. 1982. *Women, Crime, and Society: A Critique of Criminology Theory.* New York: Longman.

Mann, C. R. 1988. ''Getting even? Women who kill in domestic encounters.'' *Justice Quarterly* 5:33–51.

————. 1984. *Female Crime and Delinquency.* Birmingham: University of Alabama Press.

Mawby, R. 1980. ''Sex and crime: Results of a self-report study.'' *British Journal of Sociology* 31:526–43.

Messerschmidt, J. W. 1986. *Capitalism, Patriarchy, and Crime: Toward a Socialist Feminist Criminology.* Totowa, NJ: Rowman and Littlefield.

Miller, E. 1986. *Street Woman: The Illegal Work of Underclass Women.* Philadelphia: Temple University Press.

Miller, W. M. 1975. *Violence by Youth Gangs and Youth Groups as a Crime Problem in Major American Cities.* Washington, DC: U.S. Government Printing Office.

Morash, M. 1983. "An explanation of juvenile delinquency: The integration of moral reasoning theory and sociological knowledge." In W. S. Laufer and J. M. Day (eds.), *Personality Theory, Moral Development, and Criminal Behavior.* Lexington, MA: Lexington Books.

Morris, R. R., 1965. "Attitudes toward delinquency by delinquents, non-delinquents and their friends." *British Journal of Criminology* 5:249–65.

Nettler, G. 1974. *Explaining Crime.* New York: McGraw-Hill.

Norland, S. and N. Shover. 1977. "Gender roles and female criminality." *Criminology* 15:87–104.

Norland, S., R. C. Wessel, and N. Shover. 1981. "Masculinity and delinquency." *Criminology* 19:421–33.

Parisi, N. 1982. "Exploring female crime patterns: Problems and prospects." In N. H. Rafter and E. A. Stanko (eds.), *Judge, Lawyer, Victim, Thief: Women, Gender Roles, and Criminal Justice.* Stoughton, MA: Northeastern University Press.

Pawlack, E. J. 1977. "Differential selection of juveniles for detention." *Journal of Research in Crime and Delinquency* 14:1–12.

Polama, M. M. and T. N. Garland. 1971. "The married professional women: A study in the tolerance of domestication." *Journal of Marriage and the Family* 33:531–40.

Quicker, J. 1983. *Homegirls: Characterizing Chicana Gangs.* San Pedro, CA: International Universities Press.

Richards, P. and C. Tittle. 1981. "Gender and perceived chances of arrest." *Social Forces* 59:1182–99.

Roberts, A. R. 1981. *Runaways and Nonrunaways in an American Suburb.* New York: John Jay Press.

Rosenblatt, E. and C. Greenland. 1974. "Female crimes of violence." *Canadian Journal of Criminology and Corrections* 16:173–80.

Sanders, W. B. 1981. *Juvenile Delinquency: Causes, Patterns, and Reactions.* New York: Holt, Rinehart and Winston.

Sarri, R. C. 1974. *Under Lock and Key: Juveniles in Jails and Detention.* Ann Arbor: University of Michigan, National Assessment of Juvenile Corrections.

Schaffer, K. 1981. *Sex Roles and Human Behavior.* Cambridge, MA: Winthrop.

Searles, P. and R. J. Berger. 1987. "The feminist self-defense movement: A case study." *Gender and Society* 1:61–84.

Shover, N., S. Norland, J. James, and W. E. Thornton. 1979. "Gender roles and delinquency." *Social Forces* 58:162–75.

Simon, R. 1975. *Women and Crime.* Lexington, MA: D. C. Heath.

Slade, P. 1984. "Premenstrual emotional changes in normal women: Fact or fiction?" *Journal of Psychosomatic Research* 28:1–7.

Smart, C. 1976. *Women, Crime and Criminology: A Feminist Critique.* London: Routledge and Kegan Paul.

Smith, D. A. and C. A. Visher. 1980. "Sex and involvement in deviance/crime literature." *American Sociological Review* 45:691–701.

Smith, L. S. 1978. "Sexist assumptions and female delinquency: An empirical investigation." In C. Smart and B. Smart (eds.), *Women, Sexuality and Social Control.* London: Routledge and Kegan Paul.

Steffensmeier, D. J. 1983. "Organization properties and sex-segregation in the underworld: Building a sociological theory of sex differences in crime." *Social Forces* 61:1010–32.

————. 1980a. "Sex differences in patterns of adult crime, 1965–77: A review and assessment." *Social Forces* 58:1080–1108.

————. 1980b. "Assessing the impact of the women's movement on sex-based differences in the handling of adult criminal defendants." *Crime and Delinquency* 26:344–57.

_____. 1978. "Crime and the contemporary woman: An analysis of changing levels of female property crime, 1960–75." *Social Forces* 57:566–84.

Steffensmeier, D. J. and E. A. Allan. 1988. "Sex disparities in arrests by residence, race, and age: An assessment of the gender convergence/crime hypothesis." *Justice Quarterly* 5:53–80.

Steffensmeier, D. J. and M. J. Cobb. 1981. "Sex differences in urban arrest patterns, 1934–79." *Social Problems,* 29:37–50.

Steffensmeier, D. J. and R. H. Steffensmeier. 1980. "Trends in female delinquency: An examination of arrest, juvenile court, self-report, and field data." *Criminology* 18:62–85.

Steffensmeier, D. J., R. H. Steffensmeir, and A. Rosenthal. 1979. "Trends in female violence, 1960–1977." *Sociological Focus* 12:217–27.

Thornton, W. E. and J. James. 1979. "Masculinity and delinquency revisited." *British Journal of Criminology* 19:225–41.

Thornton, W. E., L. Voigt, and W. G. Doerner. 1987. *Delinquency and Justice.* Second edition. New York: Random House.

Treiman, P. and K. Terrell. 1975. "Sex and process of status attainment." *American Sociological Review* 40:174–201.

Vedder, C. and D. Somerville. 1970. *The Delinquent Girl.* Springfield, IL: Charles Thomas.

Velimesis, M. 1972. *Women in County Jails and Prisons.* Philadelphia: Pennsylvania Program for Women and Girl Offenders.

Visher, C. A. 1983. "Gender, police arrest decisions, and notions of chivalry." *Criminology* 21:5–28.

Ward, D. A., J. Jackson, and R. E. Ward. 1969. "Crimes of violence by women." In D. J. Mulvihill and M. M. Tumin (eds.), *Crimes of Violence.* Washington, D.C.: U.S. Government Printing Office.

Wechsler, J. and M. McFadden. 1976. "Sex differences in adolescent alcohol and drug use." *Journal of Studies on Alcohol* 37:1291–1301.

Williams, T. and W. Kornblum. 1985. *Growing Up Poor.* Lexington, MA: Lexington Books.

Wilson, D. 1978. "Sexual codes and conduct: A study of teenage girls." In C. Smart and B. Smart (eds.), *Women, Sexuality and Social Control.* London: Routledge and Kegan Paul.

Wilson, J. Q. and R. J. Herrnstein. 1985. *Crime and Human Nature.* New York: Simon and Schuster.

Wolfgang, M. 1958. *Patterns of Criminal Homicide.* New York: Wiley.

Woodward, K. and P. Malamud. 1975. "Now, the violent woman." *Newsweek* (October 6).

Young, V. D. 1986. "Gender expectations and their impact on black female offenders and victims." *Justice Quarterly* 3:305–27.

_____. 1980. "Women, race, and crime." *Criminology* 18:26–34.

PART 3

The Social Psychology of Delinquency

In Part 2 of this book, you were briefly introduced to some issues pertaining to the causes of delinquency in the course of examining social patterns related to the age, race, class, and gender distribution of delinquency. In Part 3 and Part 4, we focus more directly on casual explanations and consider various sociological theories that attempt to account for why delinquent behavior is more common among certain individuals and groups.

Before pursuing this line of inquiry, a few cautionary remarks are in order. Delinquency is a complex problem that undoubtedly requires multiple explanations, and no single theory can reasonably hope to explain all types of behaviors (Haskell and Yablonsky, 1988). Explanations of why a juvenile runs away from home may be considerably different from explanations of why another participates in a gang fight or robs a grocery store. Moreover, the difficulty of scientifically demonstrating the truth or falsity of a given theory has led some observers to "throw up their hands and virtually abandon the quest" (Binder et al., 1988:87) or simply resign us to the fact that "wicked people exist . . . and nothing avails except to set them apart from innocent people" (Wilson, 1975:235). Others have complained that much theory is overly deterministic, failing to understand the variability in human behavior that derives from individuals' ability to interpret ongoing life situations and choose particular courses of action for themselves (see Orcutt, 1983; Taylor et al., 1973).

In spite of such reservations, however, sound and carefully tested theory offers a better guide to delinquency prevention and control than does "a hit-or-miss or intuitive method" (Binder et al., 1988:87). All attempts to deal with the problem of delinquency explicitly or implicitly assume a particular explanation or set of causes underlying the phenomenon. If the theory associated with a particular intervention program is inaccurate, then the program will be likely to fail.

In Part 4 of this book, we will examine structural or institutional influences on delinquency that are related to the family, schooling, the economy, and the community. In this section (Part 3), we look at social psychological aspects of delinquency, that is, the ways in which social factors affect the psychological disposition and cognitive reasoning of individuals. In particular, we will consider the mechanisms of social learning that translate environmental factors into delinquent behavior. In contrast to more purely psychological explanations, which focus on "factors *within* the individual," social psychological explanations emphasize how human behavior develops through interpersonal interaction with others (Orcutt, 1983:151). Moreover, social psychological approaches typically address "general, normal psychological conditions that make all people responsive to variations in the social environment" rather than "psychological abnormalities or individual differences" (p. 152).

Before turning our attention to the social psychology of delinquency, we will first review biological and psychological approaches to the etiology of delinquency. Both biological and psychological theories view delinquency in terms of individuals who possess some flawed or defective trait, whether this trait is biological or psychological in origin. The general philosophy underlying these approaches, which is also shared by many sociological theories, is known as *positivism*, the idea that all actions or human behaviors are caused or determined by some prior event that can be discovered through the methods of scientific observation. In turn, scientific diagnosis of the cause of individuals' behaviors can lead to successful interventions to remedy the problem.

Biological Approaches

Researchers working in the biological tradition are generally credited with initiating the first attempts to study crime and delinquency scientifically. Early biological theories were especially influential in the field of criminology between the late nineteenth and early twentieth centuries. In general, these theories postulated that criminals were "born" and that hereditary rather than environmental factors lied at the root of human behavior. For instance, Lombroso (1911), an Italian physician, applied concepts from Darwin's theory of evolution and claimed that criminals were *atavists* or "throwbacks to more primitive species of man" and were easily recognizable on the basis of such physical features as "body type, skull shape, length of arms, hair texture, and facial characteristics" (Sheley, 1985:196).[1] Other criminologists in England and the United States followed in this tradition, with theories of criminal body types being influential as late as the 1950s (see Glueck and Glueck, 1956; Goring, 1913; Hooton, 1931; Sheldon, 1949). These researchers compared physical features of criminals and non-criminals (and delinquents and non-delinquents) and linked criminal behavior to a muscular and athletic body type that was associated with an aggressive temperant.

By the 1960s, biological explanations of crime began to turn inward. Rather than examining physical features, for instance, researchers began to look at individuals' chromosomal makeup. Researchers postulated that males suffering from the XYY syndrome (the normal male has one X and one Y chromosome) had a tendency to be taller, less intelligent, and more violent than the normal male. Early studies indicated that XYY males were disproportionately represented in prisons and mental institutions (e.g., Baker et al., 1970; Jacobs et al., 1965; Price and Whatmore, 1963). But while hundreds of books and articles have been written on the subject (Ellis, 1982), the consensus among criminologists is that research has *not* demonstrated a relationship between the XYY syndrome and violent behavior (Binder et al., 1988). Regardless, given the rarity of the trait,[2] the XYY syndrome could, at best, account for only a small percentage of criminal behavior (Sheley, 1985). In one of the most sophisticated studies to date, Theilgaard (1984:108) concluded that "there is no ground for anticipating that a person with a certain [chromosomal] status will demonstrate a preordained, inflexible and irremediable personality or pathology."

Following the XXY theory, other internal characteristics of the body were examined by biological researchers of crime and delinquency. For instance, some studies have indicated that various nutritional deficiencies associated with poor diet cause memory loss and brain dysfunctions, as well as depressive, restless, and aggressive behavior (Hippchen, 1981; Mednick and Volavka, 1980). However, environmental factors are implicated in the hypothesized nutrition-crime relationship since inadequate diet is inversely related to social class (see Dutton, 1986; Empey, 1982:170).

Another line of investigation has focused on deficiencies in the autonomic nervous system (ANS). Eysenck (1977) postulated that some ANS disorders make individuals less responsive to external stimulation and impede their ability to be socially conditioned. Similarly, Mednick (1977) hypothesized that chronic delinquent offenders may suffer from ANS malfunctioning (i.e., a sluggish nervous system) that makes them less able to dissipate fear and curb their aggressive impulses. He argued that juveniles whose fear toward external responses (e.g., a punishing adult) dissipates slowly will have more difficulty learning to inhibit their aggressive behavior. In support of this proposition, Mednick found that delinquents displayed significantly slower electrodermal responses (usually measured through sweat gland activity) than those of a non-delinquent control group (Mednick et al., 1982).

One of the most fascinating areas of biological research has involved studies of twins (see Ellis, 1982; Mednick et al., 1986; Rowe and Osgood, 1984). Several studies of criminal behavior in twins have found greater similarities or concordance between identical or monozygotic twins (one ovum that divided after fertilization by one sperm) than between fraternal or dizygotic twins (two ova fertilized by two separate sperms). These findings suggested a role of genetics in crime and delinquency since identical twins have the same biological makeup while fraternal twins do not. However, critics of these studies have noted that identical twins are more likely than fraternal twins to be treated similarly by others, and thus their common behavior patterns ''could just as easily be due to environmental influences'' (Bartol and Bartol, 1989:144). When controlling for such environmental factors, Dalgrad and Kringlen (1976) found negligible genetic effects on the behavior of twins.

Adoption studies also found higher concordance in criminal behavior between adoptees and their biological parents than would be expected by chance (see Ellis, 1982; Gabrielli and Mednick, 1983). This was especially true of chronic offenders (Mednick et al., 1986). However, since adoption agencies often attempt to match the biological and socioeconomic traits of adopted and natural parents, it becomes difficult to attribute the adoptee's behavior to genetic rather than environmental factors (Bartol and Bartol, 1989; Ellis, 1982).

Both the twin and adoption studies often beg the question of what precisely is being inherited that causes crime. Clearly, no one today seriously believes there is a ''crime gene'' that is comparable to a gene for hair or eye color. However, a genetic predisposition for alcoholism (Ellis, 1982; Mednick et al., 1982), or inheritance of particular temperant traits (Buss and Plomin, 1984; Scarr and McCartney, 1983), have been hypothesized as being related to delinquency.

Other areas of biological research have focused on the role of various brain disorders, as well as learning or intellectual deficiencies. While some types of brain dysfunctions, such as epilepsy, have long been discredited as causes of crime (Anderson, 1936; Hsu et al., 1985; Shaw and Roth, 1974), a relationship between learning disabilities and delinquency has been taken more seriously. Little is known about the actual causes of learning disabilities, but it is believed to have some organic basis. Children with learning disabilities have impaired language (verbal and written) and quantitative skills due to ''some nonobvious interference with the process of receiving information, utilizing it in cognitive process, or communicating the results of cognition'' (Keilitz et al., 1982:98). The link to juvenile delinquency has been explained in terms of either a ''susceptibility rationale'' or a ''school failure rationale'' (Murray, 1976). The former assumes that learning disabled (LD) children display personality characteristics such as impulsiveness and an inability to learn from experience and understand social cues. The latter, which has been favored by most observers, suggests that difficulty in school increases a child's negative self-image, negative attitude toward school, and association with delinquent peers. However, the established association between adjudicated (official) delinquents and learning disabilities also has been attributed to bias in the way the juvenile justice system treats LD children (Podboy and Mallory, 1978; Zimmerman et al., 1981). For instance, one self-report study of adjudicated delinquent and non-delinquent youth found that LD and non-LD youth "engage[d] in the same types and number of delinquent activities" (Keilitz et al., 1982:102).

IQ (intelligence quotient), as a measure of intelligence, has been found in numerous studies to be correlated with rates of official and self-reported delinquency (i.e., low IQ was related to high delinquency) (see Hirschi and Hindelang, 1977; Wilson and Herrnstein, 1985). However, the reasons for this association have provoked some controversy. Firstly, most social scientists reject the view that intelligence is largely inherited (see Jensen, 1979) rather than a product of social influences such as parents or teachers who encourage children to read and enjoy learning (Bartol and Bartol, 1989). Secondly, some question the adequacy of IQ as a measure of innate intelligence, since scores may change with the accumulation of experience. Thirdly, the view that the IQ-delinquency relationship can be attributed to "feeble-mindedness" or an individuals' inability to understand right and wrong has long been discredited (Bartol and Bartol, 1989; Binder et al., 1988; see Goddard, 1914). Rather, IQ is viewed as having an indirect casual relationship to delinquency (Hirschi and Hindelang, 1977). Since IQ does appear to measure the types of intellectual abilities that are related to academic success, individuals with low IQs are more likely to experience school failure. In turn, students who experience school failure are likely to develop negative attitudes toward teachers and school and consequently engage in more delinquent behavior. Others have emphasized that low IQ students' alienation from school is primarily a reaction to negative labeling by school authorities who deny youth "access to desirable social roles" (Menard and Morse, 1984:1349).

The effects on delinquency of intellectual deficiencies such as learning disabilities and IQ appear to be largely social rather than biological in nature. In any case, children with such deficiencies do need special educational services to help them with their academic difficulties.[3] On the other hand, the policy options derived from the other biological theories discussed above are more problematic and ethically questionable. During the early part of the twentieth century, theories of biological criminality were associated with the *eugenics* movement. Eugenics, which literally means "well-born," was a philosophy that favored social intervention to regulate the genetic composition of the population through methods such as forced sterilization and restrictions on marriages and immigration of undesirable (and allegedly biologically inferior) groups (Katz and Abel, 1984). More recently, biological theories of crime have led some to recommend testing of young children for genetic abnormalities to help identify and provide special treatment for *potentially* problem children. Sheley (1985:199) has raised a number of questions about such an approach:

> How do we treat children who *might* someday commit crimes? If we cannot predict perfectly accurately, do we proceed with treatment even if the target group includes

children who mistakenly have been identified as potential . . . offenders? Is the treatment physiological, psychological, or social? Is it voluntary? What stigma accompanies the label of potential deviants? How does it affect the child's future?

Other biological-oriented treatment remedies for delinquency that have been recommended include drug treatment and isolation or quarantine of suspect populations (Jeffery, 1978).

Perhaps the best that can be said of biological approaches is that such factors may affect individuals' responses to environmental conditions and that biological factors may be implicated in some unusual cases of chronic aggressive offending (Binder et al., 1988; Sheley, 1985). However, we should be extremely careful to avoid assuming that crime and delinquency in general result from such biological traits.

Psychological Approaches

Psychological approaches attribute crime and delinquency to a defect in the mental, emotional, or personality makeup of individuals. To a large extent, many of the biological theories discussed above postulate such psychological traits as intervening between biology and delinquency. And irrespective of their causes, individual traits such as intelligence are commonly considered in terms of a psychological theory of delinquency.[4]

The varieties of psychological approaches are as diverse as the biological ones. One of the most well known views is based on the *psychoanalytic* approach that was first developed by Sigmund Freud. In the late nineteenth and early twentieth centuries, Freud developed a theory of human behavior that was later adopted by a number of delinquency theorists (see Abrahamsen, 1944; Aichorn, 1935; Friedlander, 1947; Healy and Bronner, 1936). He argued that the human personality consisted of three interdependent yet often conflicting components: the id, ego, and superego. As Siegel and Senna (1988:97) summarize:

> The *id* is the unrestrained, primitive, pleasure-seeking component with which each child is born. The *ego* develops through the reality of living in the world and helps manage and restrain the id's need for immediate gratification. The *superego* develops through interactions with parents and other significant people and represents the development of conscience and the moral rules that are shared by most adults.

According to psychoanalytic theory, basic personality formation is completed in early childhood and thus early parental-child interaction is of paramount importance.[5] If parents are neglectful or abusive, or provide too little or too much socialization, imbalances may develop among the three personality components which create unconscious psychological conflicts within individuals. Delinquency in later life may represent a symbolic expression or acting out of such conflicts. For instance, if parental socialization is inadequate, the child's super- ego will be underdeveloped and the id will predominate the personality. Later-life delinquency may then result from the individual's general tendency to insist on the immediate gratification of needs, to feel a lack of compassion or sensitivity to others, or to behave aggressively and impulsively (Siegal and Senna, 1988). However, critics of psychoanalyic theory contend that it is too speculative. "The various components of the personality are neither observable nor measurable," requiring one to rely on a psychoanalyst's retrospective "interpretation of a pa- tient's interpretation of what is occurring in the subconscious" (Sheley, 1985:202). Moreover, the influence of early life events can be significantly di- minished if not eliminated by later experiences (Quay, 1983).

While other psychological theories reject some elements of psychoanalytic theory, they do postulate that crime and delinquency are caused by various per- sonality deficiencies or disorders. For instance, delinquents have been described as immature, insecure, aggressive, impulsive, emotionally unstable, egocentric, hostile, paranoid, lacking self-esteem, and so forth (see Sheley, 1985; Thornton et al., 1987). Among the most extreme personality types is the *psychopath* or *so- ciopath*. Such an individual is said to lack any internal self-control and appears incapable of experiencing feelings of guilt, responsibility, or obligation to others (Rabin, 1961).

Critics of personality disorder theory point to the ambiguity of psychologi- cal labeling. For instance, one study found that over two hundred terms were used to describe individuals with psychopathic or sociopathic symptoms (Carson, 1943). As Sanders (1983:81) noted, "[s]uch multiple definitions of a concept ren- der it so vague that it could mean almost anything." Moreover, personality inven- tory studies that have attempted to correlate various personality traits with rates of delinquency have not produced convincing results (Schuessler and Cressey, 1950; Waldo and Dinitz, 1967; Tennenbaum, 1977).

A major alternative to psychoanalytic and personality disorder theory is *be- haviorism*, sometimes referred to as *operant conditioning* or *learning- reinforcement theory*. Behaviorism is generally associated with the work of B.F. Skinner (1953) and is considered to be the predominant theory in psychology to- day (Vold and Bernard, 1986). Behaviorism focuses on observable behavior rather than on personality factors, and argues that "behavior is acquired or condi- tioned by the effects, outcomes, or *consequences* it has on a person's environ- ment" (Akers, 1985:43).[6] Behavior that is reinforced by a reward or positive re- action will persist, while behavior that is not rewarded or is punished will be discontinued. Children learn to favor particular courses of action depending on the types of rewards or punishments that have been attached to their behavior. Learning also takes place through the imitation or modeling of others' behavior.

Thus, the psychological mechanisms that produce criminal or delinquent behavior are the same as those that produce law-abiding behavior.

According to behaviorism, it is possible to modify behavior in a desired direction by controlling the rewards and punishments in an individual's environment (Bandura, 1969). For instance, in controlled institutional settings for delinquents, a juvenile's behavior may be modified through a "token economy" or point system whereby privileges are granted for good behavior and denied for bad behavior.[7] Such methods are generally considered more effective in producing immediate results than are other forms of psychotherapy or individual counseling that assume the individual is suffering from some personality disorder or emotional disturbance or that attempt to help juveniles gain insight into the reasons they behave as they do (see Braukmann et al., 1975; Gendreau and Ross, 1979; Romig, 1978; Ross and Gendreau, 1980).[8]

Social Psychological Approaches

While some versions of behaviorism have been criticized for being overly deterministic, *social learning theory* views individuals as active participants in their environment, rather than as passive recipients of external stimuli (Akers, 1985; Bandura, 1977). In addition to focusing on external behavior, social learning theory takes into account actors' "internal states," that is, individuals' cognitive processes, values, feelings, and choices (Akers, 1985:63).

Within sociology there have been important attempts to integrate aspects of behaviorism with *symbolic interaction* and *differential association theory* (Akers, 1985). Symbolic interactionism, which can be traced to the work of Charles Cooley (1902) and George Mead (1934), emphasizes the process by which individuals develop a concept of self and personal identity through the exchange of symbolic meanings that are communicated by language and gestures in face-to-face interaction. It views human beings as active organisms who are "subject to modification by social interaction" and who contribute "to change in the self conception and behaviors of others" (Empey, 1982:216). Thus, symbolic interactionism views individuals as exerting reciprocal influences on one another and as being capable of change "as the developmental process unfolds, life circumstances change, developmental milestones are met (or, for some, missed), new social roles are created, and new networks of attachments and commitments emerge" (Thornberry, 1987:881).

Edwin Sutherland's (1939) differential association theory has been considered to be both a type of symbolic interactionist and behaviorist or learning theory (Akers, 1985; Empey, 1982). According to Sutherland, criminal and delinquent behaviors are learned through interaction with others within intimate personal groups. Such groups, or differential associations, "vary in frequency, duration, priority, and intensity'' (cited in Akers, 1985:39–40). The learning of delinquent behaviors includes various ''techniques of committing crimes,'' as well as ''motives, drives, rationalizations, and attitudes.'' A person is likely to become delinquent when exposed to ''an excess of definitions favorable to violation of law over definitions unfavorable to violation of law.''

In ''Techniques of Neutralization: A Theory of Delinquency'' (Chapter 6), the first reading in this section of the book, Gresham Sykes and David Matza note that while Sutherland's initial formulation of differential association theory identified ''the process by which [delinquency] is learned,'' it had relatively little to say about ''the specific content of what is learned.'' Sykes and Matza also consider another influential view ''on the nature of this content, . . . the idea of a delinquent subculture.'' However, they are critical of the notion that delinquent subcultures can be characterized as consisting of an entirely deviant set of norms and values. Rather, they argue that delinquents have, in fact, internalized conventional values and must therefore neutralize their commitment to the law through various self-rationalizations, justifications, or *techniques of neutralization* before they can engage in delinquent behavior. Thus, Sykes and Matza view delinquents as relatively flexible in their moral commitments and able to easily ''drift'' between legal and illegal behaviors (Matza, 1964). While critics fault Sykes and Matza for failing to establish that techniques of neutralization actually precede rather than follow delinquent actions (Hamlin, 1988; Hirschi, 1969), they provide valuable insight into the social psychology of delinquency.[9]

In the second reading in this section (Chapter 7), ''Social Learning and Deviant Behavior: A Specific Test of a General Theory,'' Ronald Akers and associates apply a social learning approach to juvenile alcohol/drug use and abuse. This formulation of social learning theory involves an integration of behaviorism and differential association theory. Akers and associates use survey research methods to test the predictive value of their theory and measure the relative impact on alcohol/drug use and abuse of different aspects of the social learning process. Their study is part of a growing body of literature that lends empirical support to social learning theory, particular those elements of the theory that are related to differential association with peer groups that encourage violation of the law (see Akers, 1985; Akers and Cochran, 1985; Jackson et al., 1986; Marcos et al., 1986; Matsueda, 1982; Orcutt, 1987; Paternoster and Triplett, 1988; Tittle et al., 1986).

The social psychological approaches reviewed here (i.e., social learning, symbolic interaction, differential association, and neutralization theory) focus on the learning environments within which small groups of youth associate with one another. The policy implications of these approaches suggest utilization of such groups to change delinquents' behaviors. Various group methods are often referred to ''interchangeably . . . [as] group therapy, group counseling, group guidance, and guided group interaction'' (Trojanowicz and Morash, 1987:289).

These group-oriented interventions with juveniles in correctional settings are generally considered to be more effective than individual-oriented approaches (Feld, 1981; Shichor and Empey, 1974). The logic underlying these approaches is described by Trojanowicz and Morash (1987:289, 296–7):

> Because the delinquent often manifests behavior as part of a group or a gang, . . . the group therapy situation is the natural vehicle in which to view the way the youth reacts to the group and the group's influence on each member's behavior. . . . The group can either support or not support a member's reactions. . . . The . . . group member can find a great deal of reassurance from peers, thus facilitating the expression of feelings. . . . [Similarly], guided group interaction is . . . based on the assumption that through the group and its processes delinquents can solve their problems. . . . Guided group interaction assumes that delinquents will benefit from the freedom to discuss and analyze problems and their own roles and relationships within the group. . . . [It] operates most effectively in an informal atmosphere where most of the social controls evolve from the group itself and where meaningful interaction of group members can ultimately produce insight and new patterns of adaptation (see Empey and Erickson, 1972; McCorkle et al., 1958).

Rational-Choice and Deterrence

By the mid-1970s, a number of factors coincided that led to widespread criticism of various positivist approaches to crime and delinquency (including biological, psychological, and sociological theories). Crime rates had risen dramatically in previous years, reports of ineffective correctional treatment and the demise of rehabilitation were published, and conservatives were calling for tougher methods of crime control (see Martinson, 1974; Platt and Takagi, 1977; van den Haag, 1975; Wilson, 1975). Critics of positivism began questioning the emphasis in criminology on searching for the "root causes" of crime. Instead, they argued for a return to a view of the offender as a rationally calculating individual who chooses to commit crime and who may be deterred if the punishments for crime were increased to outweigh the benefits of crime.

This *rational-choice theory* of crime predates positivism and can be traced to the school of "classical criminology" that was developed by Cesare Becarria and Jeremy Bentham in the later half of the eighteenth century (see Bentham, 1962; Becarria, 1963). Also known as *utilitarianism,* because it considers the utility to individuals of particular courses of action, this view assumes that individuals have "free will," that is, that individuals make decisions and rational choices. People choose to violate the law because they believe that the positive gains or benefits from crime outweigh the negative costs or consequences. Thus, crime can be deterred if punishments are increased so that individuals believe that the costs of crime are greater than the benefits. Stated another way, individuals calculate "the expected utility or disutility of both illegal . . . and . . . legal actions," and they choose to commit crime if "the overall utility of illegal actions exceeds that [of] the legal alternatives" (Paternoster, 1989:289).

One contemporary application of the rational-choice or deterrence approach to delinquency control has been the popularly acclaimed "Scared Straight" program. "Scared Straight" attempts to make juveniles aware that "crime does not pay." In the third reading in this section (Chapter 8), Richard Lundman describes various "Scared Straight" programs and reviews evaluation studies of their effectiveness. He concludes that the "Scared Straight" approach has produced "mixed results" and "at best, scaring juveniles is not the panacea for the problem of delinquency" that proponents claimed it to be.

The less than impressive results of "Scared Straight" are not surprising in light of other deterrence research. Deterrence theorists, as Lundman notes, distinguish between *certainty of punishment* (the likelihood of apprehension) and *severity of punishment* (the harshness of sanctions). Several studies that have focused on juvenile's perceptions of punishment have found a modest deterrent effect for certainty of punishment and no consistent deterrent effect for severity of punishment.[10] Paternoster (1989) found a greater effect for perceived certainty of punishment on "the decision to continue offending once it has been initiated" (the frequency of offending) than on the initial "decision to participate in an offense" (the onset of offending) (Paternoster and Triplett, 1988:592). However, Piliavan et al., (1986) suggested that rational-choice models of deterrence focus too narrowly on punishment and have neglected to consider how persons' perceptions of legal alternatives influence their decisions to violate the law. Piliavin et al. found that while "risks of punishment [had] virtually no impact on criminal behavior . . . persons who perceive[d] greater opportunity to earn money illegally [were] more likely to violate the law" (p. 114). Thus, the relative availability of illegal and legal economic opportunities appeared to affect persons' decisions to commit crime and delinquency more than did the presence or absence of punishment risks. Other studies also suggested that social factors such as parental supervision and peer associations had greater effects on delinquency than did punishment-deterrence factors (see Akers et al. in this section; and Paternoster, 1989). These influences on delinquency will be considered in more detail in the next section of the book.

Notes

1. The reader will recall Platt's (Chapter 1) discussion of the influence of these ideas on the child-savers.

2. Dorus et al (1976) estimated that one out of every 236 males, and Jarvik et al., (1984) estimated that one or two per 1,000 males, have this biological trait.

3. Hyperactive children also fall into this category of children with special educational needs.

4. Since we have already discussed the IQ-delinquency controversy, we will not consider it further in this section.

5. Freud postulated that the personality develops through various psychosexual stages: oral, anal, phallic, latency and genital.

6. This discussion risks oversimplification, since behaviorism is a rather diverse and complex tradition in psychology (see Akers, 1985).

7. One form of behavior modification is known as aversion therapy or aversive conditioning, whereby the pleasure associated with a particular activity, such as alcohol drinking, becomes associated with a painful or negative response.

8. Behavior modification has been effective in inducing good behavior within juvenile correctional settings, though the effects do not appear to carry over after release.

9. Schwendinger and Schwendinger (1985) question the claim that delinquents subscribe to ''dominant moral norms.'' They believe that delinquent rationalizations are applied more to ''minimizing risks or other tactical considerations'' than to neutralizing moral commitment to the law (pp. 138–9).

10. See Paternoster (1987; 1989), Piliavin et al. (1986), and Williams and Hawkins (1986) for reviews.

References

Abrahamsen. 1944. *Crime and the Human Mind*. New York: Columbia University Press.

Aichorn, A. 1935. *Wayward Youth*. New York: Viking.

Akers, R.L. 1985. *Deviant Behavior: A Social Learning Approach*. Third edition. Belmont, CA: Wadsworth.

Akers, R.L. and J.K. Cochran. 1985. ''Adolescent marijuana use: A test of three theories of deviant behavior.'' *Deviant Behavior* 6:323–46.

Anderson, C.L. 1936. ''Epilepsy in the state of Michigan.'' *Mental Hygiene* 20:441–62.

Baker, D., M. Telfer, C. Richardson, and G. Clark. 1970. ''Chromosome errors in men with antisocial behavior.'' *Journal of the American Medical Association* 214:869–78.

Bandura, A. 1977. *Social Learning Theory*. Englewood Cliffs, NJ: Prentice-Hall.

———. 1969. *Principles of Behavior Modification*. New York: Holt, Rinehart and Winston.

Bartol, C.R. and A.M. Bartol. 1989. *Juvenile Delinquency: A Systems Approach*. Englewood Cliffs, NJ: Prentice-Hall.

Beccaria, C. 1963. *On Crimes and Punishments*. H. Paolucci (trans.). Indianapolis: Bobbs-Merrill.

Bentham, J. 1962. *The Works of Jeremy Bentham.* J. Bowring (ed.). New York: Russell and Russell.

Binder, A., G. Geis, and D. Bruce. 1988. *Juvenile Delinquency: Historical Cultural, Legal Perspectives.* New York: Macmillan.

Braukmann, C.J. et al., 1975. "Behavioral approaches to treatment in the crime and delinquency field." *Criminology* 13:299–331.

Buss, A.H. and R. Plomin, 1984. *Temperament: Early Developing Personality Traits.* Hillsdale, NY: Erlbaum.

Carson, H. 1943. "The psychopath and the psychopathic." *Journal of Criminal Psychopathology* 4:522–7.

Cooley, C.H. 1902. *Human Nature and the Social Order.* New York: Scribner.

Dalgaard, O.S. and E. Kringler, 1976. "A Norwegian twin study of criminality." *British Journal of Criminality* 16:213–32.

Dorus, E., W. Dorus, M.A. Telfer, S. Litwin, and C. E. Richardson, 1976. "Height and personality characteristics of 47 XYY males in a sample of tall, non-institutionalized males." *British Journal of Psychiatry* 129:564–73.

Dutton, D.B. 1986. "Social class, health, and illness." Pp. 31–62 in L. H. Aiken and D. Mechanic (eds.), *Applications of Social Science to Clinical Medicine and Health Policy.* New Brunswick, NJ: Rutgers University Press.

Ellis, L. "Genetics and criminal behavior: Evidence through the end of the 1970s." *Criminology* 20:43–66.

Empey, L.T. 1982. *American Delinquency: Its Meaning and Construction.* Second edition. Homewood, IL: Dorsey.

Empey, L.T. and M.L. Erickson, 1972. *The Provo Experiment: Evaluating Community Control of Delinquency.* Lexington, MA: D. C. Heath.

Eysenck, J.J. 1977. *Crime and Personality.* London: Routledge and Kegan Paul.

Feld, B.C. 1981. "A comparative analysis of organizational structure and inmate subcultures in institutions for juvenile offenders." *Crime and Delinquency* 27:336–63.

Friedlander, K. 1947. *The Psychoanalytic Approach to Juvenile Delinquency.* London: Routledge and Kegan Paul.

Gabrielli, W. and S.A. Mednick, 1983. "An adoption cohort study of genetics and criminality." *Behavior Genetics* 13:435.

Gendreau, P. and B. Ross. 1979. "Effective correctional treatment: Bibliotherapy for cynics." *Crime and Delinquency* 25:463–89.

Glueck, S. and E.T. Glueck. 1956. *Physique and Delinquency.* New York: Harper and Brothers.

Goddard, H.H. 1914. *Feeblemindedness: Its Causes and Consequences.* New York: Macmillan.

Goring, C.B. 1913. *The English Convict: A Statistical Study.* London: His Majesty's Stationery Office.

Hamlin, J.E. 1988. "The misplaced role of rational choice in neutralization theory." *Criminology* 26:425–38.

Healy, W. and A.F. Bronner, 1936. *New Light on Delinquency and Its Treatment.* New Haven, CT: Yale University Press.

Hippchen, L. 1981. "Some possible biochemical aspects of criminal behavior." *Journal of Behavioral Ecology* 2:1–6.

Hirschi, T. 1969. *Causes of Delinquency*. Berkeley, CA: University of California Press.

Hirschi, T. and M.J. Hindelang. 1977. "Intelligence and delinquency: A revisionist review." *American Sociological Review* 43:571–87.

Hooton, E.A. 1931. *Crime and the Man*. Cambridge: Harvard University Press.

Hsu, L.K., K. Wisner, E.T. Richey, and C. Goldstein, 1985. "Is juvenile delinquency related to an abnormal EEG?" *Journal of the American Academy of Child Psychiatry* 24:310–56.

Jackson, E., C. Tittle, and M.J. Burke, 1986. "Offense-specific models of the differential association process." *Social Problems* 33: 335–56.

Jeffery, C.R. 1978. "Criminology as an interdisciplinary science." *Criminology* 16:149–70.

Jacobs, P.A., M. Brunton, and M.M. Melville. 1965. "Aggressive behavior, mental abnormality and the XYY male." *Nature* 208:1351–2.

Jarvick, L.S., V. Klodin, and S.S. Matsuyama, 1984. "Human aggression and the extra Y chromosome: Fact or fantasy?" Pp. 74–89 in I. Jacks and S. G. Cox (eds.), *Psychological Approaches to Crime and its Correction: Theory, Research, Practice*. Chicago: Nelson-Hall.

Jensen, A. 1979. *Bias in Mental Testing*. New York: Free Press.

Katz, J. and C. F. Abel. 1984. "The medicalization of repression: Eugenics and crime." *Contemporary Crises* 8:227–41.

Keilitz, I., B.A. Zaremba, and P.K. Broder. 1982. "Learning disabilities and juvenile delinquency." Pp. 95–104 in L. D. Savitz and N. Johnston (eds.), *Contemporary Criminology*. New York: Wiley.

Lombroso, C. 1911. *Criminal Man*. New York: Putnam.

Marcos, A., S. Bahr, and R. Johnson. 1986. "Testing of a bonding/association theory of adolescent drug use." *Social Forces* 65:135–61.

Martinson, R. "What works? Questions and answers about prison reform." *Public Interest* 35:22–54.

Matsueda, R. 1982. "Testing control theory and differential association: A casual modeling approach." *American Sociological Review* 47:479–504.

Matza, D. 1964. *Delinquency and Drift*. New York: Wiley.

McCorkle, L.W., A. Elias, and F. L. Bixby. 1958. *The Highfields Story*. New York: Holt, Rinehart and Winston.

Mead, G.H. 1934. *Mind, Self and Society*. Chicago: University of Chicago Press.

Mednick, S.A. 1977. "A biosocial theory of the learning of law-abiding behavior." Pp. 1–8 in S. A. Mednick and K. Christiansen (eds.), *Biosocial Basis of Criminal Behavior*. New York: Gardner.

Mednick, S.A., T. Moffitt, W. Gabrielli, and B. Hutchings. 1986. "Genetic factors in criminal behavior: A review. Pp. 33–50 in D. Olweus, J. Block, and M. Radke-Yarrow (eds.), *Development of Antisocial and Prosocial Behavior*. Orlando, FL: Academic Press.

Mednick, S.A. and J. Volavka. 1980. "Biology and crime." Pp. 85–158 in N. Morris and M. Tonry (eds.), *Crime and Justice: An Annual Review of Research,* Vol. 2. Chicago: University of Chicago Press.

Mednick, S.A., V. Pollock, and J. Volavka. 1982. "Biology and violence." Pp. 85–158 in M. Wolfgang and N. Weiner (eds.), *Criminal Violence.* Beverly Hills, CA: Sage.

Menard, S. and B. J. Morse. 1984. "A structuralist critique of the IQ-delinquency hypothesis: Theory and evidence." *American Journal of Sociology* 89:1347–78.

Murray, C.A. 1976. *The Link Between Learning Disabilities and Juvenile Delinquency: Current Theory and Knowledge.* Washington, DC: U.S. Government Printing Office.

Orcutt, J.D. 1987. "Differential association and marijuana use: A closer look at Sutherland (with a little help from Becker)." *Criminology* 25:341–58.

_____. (ed.). 1983. *Analyzing Deviance.* Homewood, IL: Dorsey.

Paternoster, R. 1989. "Absolute and restrictive deterrence in a panel of youth: Explaining the onset, persistence/desistance, and frequency of delinquent offending." *Social Problems* 36:289–309.

_____. 1987. "The deterrent effect of the perceived certainty and severity of punishment: A review of the evidence and issues." *Justice Quarterly 4:* 173–217.

Paternoster, R. and R. Triplett. 1988. "Disaggregating self-reported delinquency and its implications for theory." *Criminology* 26:591–625.

Piliavin, I., R. Gartner, C. Thornton, and R.L. Matsueda. "Crime, deterrence, and rational choice." *American Sociological Review* 51:101–19.

Platt, T. and P. Takagi. 1977. "Intellectuals for law and order: A critique of the new 'realists'." *Crime and Social Justice* 8:1–16.

Podboy, J.W. and W.A. Mallory. 1978. "The diagnosis of specific learning disabilities in a juvenile delinquent population." *Juvenile and Family Court Journal* 30:11–13.

Price, W.H. and P.D. Whatmore. 1963. "Behavior disorders and patterns of crime among XYY males identified at a maximum security hospital." *British Medical Journal* 4:533–6.

Quay, H.C. 1983. "Crime causation: Psychological theories." Pp 330–42 in S. H. Kadish (ed.), *Encyclopedia of Crime and Justice.* New York: Free Press.

Rabin, A.I. 1961. "Psychopathic (sociopathic) personalities." Pp. 271–93 in H. Toch (ed.), *Legal and Criminal Psychology.* New York: Holt, Rinehart and Winston.

Romig, D.A. 1978. *Justice for Our Children: An Examination of Juvenile Delinquent Rehabilitation Programs.* Lexington, MA: Lexington Books.

Ross, R.R. and P. Gendreau (eds.). 1980. *Effective Correctional Treatment.* Toronto: Butterworths.

Rowe, D.C. and D.W. Osgood. 1984. "Heredity and sociological theories of delinquency: A reconsideration." *American Sociological Review* 49:526–40.

Sanders, W.B. 1983. *Criminology.* Reading, MA: Addison-Wesley.

Schuessler, K.F. and D.R. Cressey. 1950. "Personality characteristics of criminals." *American Journal of Sociology* 43:476–84.

Scarr, S. and K. McCartney. 1983. "How people make their own environments: A theory of genotype-environment effects." *Child Development* 54:424–35.

Schwendinger, H. and J.S. Schwendinger. 1985. *Adolescent Subcultures and Delinquency.* New York: Praeger.

Shaw, S. and L. Roth. 1974. "Biological and psychophysiological factors in criminality." Pp. 101–73 in D. Glaser (ed.), *Handbook of Criminology.* Chicago: Rand McNally.

Sheldon, W.H. 1949. *Varieties of Delinquent Youth.* New York: Harper.

Sheley, J.F. *America's "Crime Problem": An Introduction to Criminology.* Belmont, CA: Wadsworth.

Shichor, D. and L.T. Empey. 1974. "A typological analysis of correctional organizations." *Sociology and Social Research* 58:318–34.

Siegal, L.J. and J.J. Senna. 1988. *Juvenile Delinquency: Theory, Practice, and Law.* Third edition. St. Paul, MN: West.

Skinner, B. F. 1953. *Science and Human Behavior.* New York: Macmillan.

Sutherland, E.H. 1939. *Principles of Criminology.* Third edition. Philadelphia: Lippincott.

Taylor, I., P. Walton, and J. Young. 1973. *The New Criminology: For a Social Theory of Deviance.* New York: Harper and Row.

Tennenbaum, D. J. 1977. "Personality and criminality: A summary and implications of the literature." *Journal of Criminal Justice* 5:225–35.

Theilgaard, A. 1984. "A psychological study of the personalities of XYY- and XXY-men." *Acta Psychiatrica Scandinavia* 69:1–133.

Thornberry, T.R. 1987. "Toward an interactional theory of delinquency." *Criminology* 25:863–91.

Thornton, W.E., L.V. Voigt, and W.G. Doerner, 1987. *Delinquency and Justice.* Second edition. New York: Random House.

Tittle, C., M.J. Burke, and E. Jackson, 1986. "Modeling Sutherland's theory of differential association: Toward an empirical clarification." *Social Forces* 65:405–32.

Trojanowicz, R.C. and M. Morash. 1987. *Juvenile Delinquency: Concepts and Controls.* Fourth edition. Englewood Cliffs, NJ: Prentice-Hall.

van den Haag, E. 1975. *Punishing Criminals: Concerning a Very Old and Painful Question.* New York: Basic Books.

Vold, G.B. and T.J. Bernard. *Theoretical Criminology.* Third edition. New York: Oxford University Press.

Waldo, G.P. and S. Dinitz. 1967. "Personality attributes of the criminal: An analysis of research studies, 1950-65." *Journal of Research on Crime and Delinquency* 4:185–201.

Williams, K. and R. Hawkins. 1986. "Perceptual research on general deterrence: A critical review." *Law and Society Review* 20:211–36.

Wilson, J.Q. 1975. *Thinking About Crime.* New York: Vintage.

Wilson, J.Q. and. R.J. Herrnstein. 1985. *Crime and Human Nature: The Definitive Study of the Causes of Crime.* New York: Touchstone.

Yablonsky, L. and M.R. Haskell. 1988. *Juvenile Delinquency.* Fourth edition. New York: Harper and Row.

Zimmerman, J., W. Rich, I. Keilitz, and P. Broder. 1981. "Some observations on the link between learning disabilities and juvenile delinquency." *Journal of Criminal Justice* 9:9–17.

Techniques of Neutralization: A Theory of Delinquency

6

Gresham M. Sykes
David Matza

In attempting to uncover the roots of juvenile delinquency, the social scientist has long since ceased to search for devils in the mind or stigma of the body. It is now largely agreed that delinquent behavior, like most social behavior, is learned and that it is learned in the process of social interaction.

The classic statement of this position is found in Sutherland's theory of differential association, which asserts that criminal or delinquent behavior involves the learning of (a) techniques of committing crimes and (b) motives, drives, rationalizations, and attitudes favorable to the violation of law.[1] Unfortunately, the specific content of what is learned—as opposed to the process by which it is learned—has received relatively little attention in either theory or research. Perhaps the single strongest school of thought on the nature of this content has centered on the idea of a delinquent subculture. The basic characteristic of the delinquent subculture, it is argued, is a system of

From *American Sociological Review*, Vol. 22, No. 6, 1957, pp. 664–670.

values that represents an inversion of the values held by respectable, law-abiding society. The world of the delinquent is the world of the law-abiding turned upside down and its norms constitute a countervailing force directed against the conforming social order. Cohen[2] sees the process of developing a delinquent subculture as a matter of building, maintaining, and reinforcing a code for behavior which exists by opposition, which stands in point by point contradiction to dominant values, particularly those of the middle class. Cohen's portrayal of delinquency is executed with a good deal of sophistication, and he carefully avoids overly simple explanations such as those based on the principle of "follow the leader" or easy generalizations about "emotional disturbances." Furthermore, he does not accept the delinquent subculture as something given but instead systematically examines the function of delinquent values as a viable solution to the lower-class, male child's problems in the area of social status. Yet in spite of its virtues, this image of juvenile delinquency as a form of behavior based on competing or countervailing values and norms appears to suffer from a number of serious defects. It is the nature of these defects and a possible alternative or modified explanation for a large portion of juvenile delinquency with which this paper is concerned.

The difficulties in viewing delinquent behavior as springing from a set of deviant values and norms—as arising, that is to say, from a situation in which the delinquent defines his delinquency as "right"—are both empirical and theoretical. In the first place, if there existed in fact a delinquent subculture such that the delinquent viewed his illegal behavior as morally correct, we could reasonably suppose that he would exhibit no feelings of guilt or shame at detection or confinement. Instead, the major reaction would tend in the direction of indignation or a sense of martyrdom.[3] It is true that some delinquents do react in the latter fashion, although the sense of martyrdom often seems to be based on the fact that others "get away with it" and indignation appears to be directed against the chance events or lack of skill that led to apprehension. More important, however, is the fact that there *is* a good deal of evidence suggesting that many delinquents *do* experience a sense of guilt or shame, and its outward expression is not to be dismissed as a purely manipulative gesture to appease those in authority. Much of this evidence is, to be sure, of a clinical nature or in the form of impressionistic judgments of those who must deal first hand with the youthful offender. Assigning a weight to such evidence calls for caution, but it cannot be ignored if we are to avoid the gross stereotype of the juvenile delinquent as a hardened gangster in miniature.

In the second place, observers have noted that the juvenile delinquent frequently accords admiration and respect to law-abiding persons. The "really honest" person is often revered, and if the delinquent is sometimes overly keen to detect hypocrisy in those who conform, unquestioned probity is likely to win his approval. A fierce attachment to a humble, pious mother or a forgiving, upright priest (the former, according to many observers, is often encountered in both juvenile delinquents and adult criminals) might be dismissed as rank sentimentality, but at least it is clear that the delinquent does not necessarily regard those who abide by the legal rules as immoral. In a similar vein, it can be noted that the juvenile delinquent may exhibit great resentment if illegal behavior is imputed to "significant others" in his immediate social environment or to heroes in the world of sport and entertainment. In other words, if the delinquent does hold to a set of values and norms that stand in complete opposition to those of respectable society, his norm-holding is of a peculiar sort. While supposedly thoroughly committed to the deviant system of the delinquent subculture, he would appear to recognize the moral validity of the dominant normative system in many instances.[4]

In the third place, there is much evidence that juvenile delinquents often draw a sharp line between those who can be victimized and those who cannot. Certain social groups are not to be viewed as "fair game" in the performance of supposedly approved delinquent acts while others warrant a variety of attacks. In general, the potentiality for victimization would seem to be a function of the social distance between the juvenile delinquent and others and thus we find implicit maxims in the world of the delinquent such as "don't steal from friends" or "don't commit vandalism against a church of your own faith."[5] This is all rather obvious, but the implications have not received sufficient attention. The fact that supposedly valued behavior tends to be directed against disvalued social groups hints that the "wrongfulness" of such delinquent behavior is more widely recognized by delinquents than the literature has indicated. When the pool of victims is limited by considerations of kinship, friendship, ethnic group, social class, age, sex, etc., we have reason to suspect that the virtue of delinquency is far from unquestioned.

In the fourth place, it is doubtful if many juvenile delinquents are totally immune from the demands for conformity made by the dominant social order. There is a strong likelihood that the family of the delinquent will agree with respectable society that delinquency is wrong, even though the family may be engaged in a variety of illegal activities. That is, the parental posture conducive to delinquency is not apt to be a positive prodding. Whatever may be the influence of parental example, what might be called the "Fagin" pattern of socialization into delinquency is probably rare. Furthermore, as Redl has indicated, the idea that certain neighborhoods are completely delinquent, offering the child a model for delinquent behavior without reservations, is simply not supported by the data.[6]

The fact that a child is punished by parents, school officials, and agencies of the legal system for his delinquency may, as a number of observers have cynically noted, suggest to the child that he should be more careful not to get caught. There is an equal or greater probability, however, that the demands for conformity cannot be counteracted. In fact, as we shall see shortly, an understanding of how internal and external demands of conformity are neutralized may be crucial for understanding delinquent behavior. But it is to say that a complete denial of the validity of demands for conformity and the substitution of a new normative system is improbable, in light of the child's or adolescent's dependency on adults and encirclement by adults inherent in his status

in the social structure. No matter how deeply enmeshed in patterns of delinquency he may be and no matter how much this involvement may outweigh his associations with the law-abiding, he cannot escape the condemnation of his deviance. Somehow the demands for conformity must be met and answered; they cannot be ignored as part of an alien system of values and norms.

In short, the theoretical viewpoint that sees juvenile delinquency as a form of behavior based on the values and norms of a deviant subculture in precisely the same way as law-abiding behavior is based on the values and norms of the larger society is open to serious doubt. The fact that the world of the delinquent is embedded in the larger world of those who conform cannot be overlooked nor can the delinquent be equated with an adult throughly socialized into a alternative way of life. Instead, the juvenile delinquent would appear to be at least partially committed to the dominant social order in that he frequently exhibits guilt or shame when he violates its proscriptions, accords approval to certain conforming figures, and distinguishes between appropriate and inappropriate targets for his deviance. It is to an explanation for the apparently paradoxical fact of his delinquency that we now turn.

As Morris Cohen once said, one of the most fascinating problems about human behavior is why men violate the laws in which they believe. This is the problem that confronts us when we attempt to explain why delinquency occurs despite a greater or lesser commitment to the usages of conformity. A basic clue is offered by the fact that social rules or norms calling for valued behavior seldom if ever take the form of categorical imperatives. Rather, values or norms appear as *qualified* guides for action, limited in their applicability in terms of time, place, persons and social circumstances. The moral injunction against killing, for example, does not apply to the enemy during combat in time of war, although a captured enemy comes once again under the prohibition. Similarly, the taking and distributing of scarce goods in a time of acute social need is felt by many to be right, although under other circumstances private property is held inviolable. The normative system of a society, then, is marked by what Williams has termed *flexibility*; it does not consist of a body of rules held to be binding under all conditions.[7]

This flexibility is, in fact, an integral part of the criminal law in that measures for "defenses to crimes" are provided in pleas such as nonage, necessity, insanity, drunkenness, compulsion, self-defense, and so on. The individual can avoid moral culpability for his criminal action—and thus avoid the negative sanctions of society—if he can prove that criminal intent was lacking. *It is our argument that much delinquency is based on what is essentially an unrecognized extension of defenses to crimes, in the form of justifications for deviance that are seen as valid by the delinquent but not by the legal system or society at large.*

These justifications are commonly described as rationalizations. They are viewed as following deviant behavior and as protecting the individual from self-blame and the blame of others after the act. But there is also reason to believe that they precede deviant behavior and make deviant behavior possible. It is this possibility that Sutherland mentioned only in passing and that other writers have failed to exploit from the veiwpoint of sociological theory. Disapproval flowing from internalized norms and conforming others in the social environment is neutralized, turned back, or deflected in advance. Social controls that serve to check or inhibit deviant motivational patterns are rendered inoperative,

and the individual is freed to engage in delinquency without serious damage to his self image. In this sense, the delinquent both has his cake and eats it too, for he remains committed to the dominant normative system and yet so qualifies its imperatives that violations are "acceptable" if not "right." Thus the delinquent represents not a radical opposition to law-abiding society but something more like an apologetic failure, often more sinned against than sinning in his own eyes. We call these justifications of deviant behavior techniques of neutralization; and we believe these techniques make up a crucial component of Sutherland's "definitions favorable to the violation of law." It is by learning these techniques that the juvenile becomes delinquent, rather than by learning moral imperatives, values or attitudes standing in direct contradiction to those of the dominant society. In analyzing these techniques, we have found it convenient to divide them into five major types.

The Denial of Responsibility

In so far as the delinquent can define himself as lacking responsibility for his deviant actions, the disapproval of self or others is sharply reduced in effectiveness as a restraining influence. As Justice Holmes has said, even a dog distinguishes between being stumbled over and being kicked, and modern society is no less careful to draw a line between injuries that are unintentional, i.e., where responsibility is lacking, and those that are intentional. As a technique of neutralization, however, the denial of responsibility extends much further than the claim that deviant acts are an "accident" or some similar negation of personal accountability. It may also be asserted that delinquent acts are due to forces outside of the individual and beyond his control such as unloving parents, bad companions, or a slum neighborhood. In effect, the delinquent approaches a "billiard ball" conception of himself in which he sees himself as helplessly propelled into new situations. From a psychodynamic viewpoint, this orientation toward one's own actions may represent a profound alienation from self, but it is important to stress the fact that interpretations of responsibility are cultural constructs and not merely idiosyncratic beliefs. The similarity between this mode of justifying illegal behavior assumed by the delinquent and the implications of a "sociological" frame of reference or a "humane" jurisprudence is readily apparent.[8] It is not the validity of this orientation that concerns us here, but its function of deflecting blame attached to violations of social norms and its relative independence of a particular personality structure.[9] By learning to view himself as more acted upon than acting, the delinquent prepares the way for deviance from the dominant normative system without the necessity of a frontal assault on the norms themselves.

The Denial of Injury

A second major technique of neutralization centers on the injury or harm involved in the delinquent act. The criminal law has long made a distinction between crimes which are *mala in se* and *mala prohibita*—that is between acts that are wrong in themselves and acts that are illegal but not immoral—and the delinquent can make the same kind of distinction in evaluating the wrongfulness of his behavior. For the delinquent, however, wrongfulness may turn on the question of whether or not anyone has clearly been hurt by his deviance, and this matter is open to a variety of interpretations. Vandalism, for example, may be defined by the delinquent simply as

"mischief"—after all, it may be claimed, the persons whose property has been destroyed can well afford it. Similarly, auto theft may be viewed as "borrowing," and gang fighting may be seen as a private quarrel, an agreed upon duel between two willing parties, and thus of no concern to the community at large. We are not suggesting that this technique of neutralization, labelled the denial of injury, involves an explicit dialectic. Rather, we are arguing that the delinquent frequently, and in a hazy fashion, feels that his behavior does not really cause any great harm despite the fact that it runs counter to law. Just as the link between the individual and his acts may be broken by the denial of responsibility, so may the link between acts and their consequences be broken by the denial of injury, Since society sometimes agrees with the delinquent, e.g., in matters such as truancy, "pranks," and so on, it merely reaffirms the idea that the delinquent's neutralization of social controls by means of qualifying the norms is an extension of common practice rather than a gesture of complete opposition.

The Denial of the Victim

Even if the delinquent accepts the responsibility for his deviant actions and is willing to admit that his deviant actions involve an injury or hurt, the moral indignation of self and others may be neutralized by an insistence that the injury is not wrong in light of the circumstances. The injury, it may be claimed, is not really an injury; rather, it is a form of rightful retaliation or punishment. By a subtle alchemy the delinquent moves himself into the position of an avenger and the victim is transformed into a wrong-doer. Assaults on homosexuals or suspected homosexuals, attacks on members of minority groups who are said to have gotten "out of place," vandalism as revenge on an unfair teacher or school official, thefts from a "crooked" store owner—all may be hurts inflicted on a transgressor, in the eyes of the delinquent. As Orwell has pointed out, the type of criminal admired by the general public has probably changed over the course of years and Raffles no longer serves as a hero;[10] but Robin Hood, and his latter day derivatives such as the tough detective seeking justice outside the law, still capture the popular imagination, and the delinquent may view his acts as part of a similar role.

To deny the existence of the victim, then, by transforming him into a person deserving injury is an extreme form of a phenomenon we have mentioned before, namely, the delinquent's recognition of appropriate and inappropriate targets for his delinquent acts. In addition, however, the existence of the victim may be denied for the delinquent, in a somewhat different sense, by the circumstances of the delinquent act itself. Insofar as the victim is physically absent, unknown, or a vague abstraction (as is often the case in delinquent acts committed against property), the awareness of the victim's existence is weakened. Internalized norms and anticipations of the reactions of others must somehow be activated, if they are to serve as guides for behavior; and it is possible that a diminished awareness of the victim plays an important part in determining whether or not this process is set in motion.

The Condemnation of the Condemners

A fourth technique of neutralization would appear to involve a condemnation of the condemners or, as McCorkle and Korn have phrased it, a rejection of the rejectors.[11] The delinquent shifts the focus of attention from his own defiant acts to the mo-

tives and behavior of those who disapprove of his violations. His condemners, he may claim, are hypocrites, deviants in disguise, or impelled by personal spite. This orientation toward the conforming world may be of particular importance when it hardens into a bitter cynicism directed against those assigned the task of enforcing or expressing the norms of the dominant society. Police, it may be said, are corrupt, stupid, and brutal. Teachers always show favoritism and parents always "take it out" on their children. By a slight extension, the rewards of conformity—such as material success—become a matter of pull or luck, thus decreasing still further the stature of those who stand on the side of the law-abiding. The validity of this jaundiced viewpoint is not so important as its function in turning back or deflecting the negative sanctions attached to violations of the norms. The delinquent, in effect, has changed the subject of the conversation in the dialogue between his own deviant impulses and the reactions of others; and by attacking others, the wrongfulness of his own behavior is more easily repressed or lost to view.

The Appeal to Higher Loyalties

Fifth, and last, internal and external social controls may be neutralized by sacrificing the demands of the larger society for the demands of the smaller social groups to which the delinquent belongs such as the sibling pair, the gang, or the friendship clique. It is important to note that the delinquent does not necessarily repudiate the imperatives of the dominant normative system, despite his failure to follow them. Rather, the delinquent may see himself as caught up in a dilemma that must be resolved, unfortunately, at the cost of violating the law. One aspect of this situation has been studied by Stouffer and Toby in their research on the conflict between particularistic and universalistic demands, between the claims of friendship and general social obligations, and their results suggest that "it is possible to classify people according to a predisposition to select one or the other horn of a dilemma in role conflict.[12] For our purposes, however, the most important point is that deviation from certain norms may occur not because the norms are rejected but because other norms, held to be more pressing or involving a higher loyalty, are accorded precedence. Indeed, it is the fact that both sets of norms are believed in that gives meaning to our concepts of dilemma and role conflict.

The conflict between the claims of friendship and the claims of law, or a similar dilemma, has of course long been recognized by the social scientist (and the novelist) as a common human problem. If the juvenile delinquent frequently resolves his dilemma by insisting that he must "always help a buddy" or "never squeal on a friend," even when it throws him into serious difficulties with the dominant social order, his choice remains familiar to the supposedly law-abiding. The delinquent is unusual, perhaps, in the extent to which he is able to see the fact that he acts in behalf of the smaller social groups to which he belongs as a justification for violations of society's norms, but it is a matter of degree rather than of kind.

"I didn't mean it." "I didn't really hurt anybody." "They had it coming to them." "Everybody's picking on me." "I didn't do it for myself." These slogans or their variants, we hypothesize, prepare the juvenile for delinquent acts. These "definitions of the situation" represent tangential or glancing blows at the dominant normative system rather than the creation of an opposing ideology; and they are extensions of patterns of thought prevalent in society rather than something created *de novo*.

Techniques of neutralization may not be powerful enough to fully shield the individual from the force of his own internalized values and the reactions of conforming others, for as we have pointed out, juvenile delinquents often appear to suffer from feelings of guilt and shame when called into account for their deviant behavior. And some delinquents may be so isolated from the world of conformity that techniques of neutralization need not be called into play. Nonetheless, we would argue that techniques of neutralization are critical in lessening the effectiveness of social controls and that they lie behind a large share of delinquent behavior. Empirical research in this area is scattered and fragmentary at the present time, but the work of Redl,[13] Cressy,[14] and others has supplied a body of significant data that has done much to clarify the theoretical issues and enlarge the fund of supporting evidence. Two lines of investigation seem to be critical at this stage. First, there is need for more knowledge concerning the differential distribution of techniques of neutralization, as operative patterns of thought, by age, sex, social class, ethnic group, etc. On *a priori* grounds it might be assumed that these justifications for deviance will be more readily seized by segments of society for whom a discrepancy between common social ideals and social practice is most apparent. It is also possible, however, that the habit of "bending" the dominant normative system—if not "breaking" it—cuts across our cruder social categories and is to be traced primarily to patterns of social interaction within the familial circle. Second, there is need for a greater understanding of the internal structure of techniques of neutralization, as a system of beliefs and attitudes, and its relationship to various types of delinquent behavior. Certain techniques of neutralization would appear to be better adapted to particular deviant acts than to others, as we have suggested, for example, in the case of offenses against property and the denial of the victim. But the issue remains far from clear and stands in need of more information.

In any case, techniques of neutralization appear to offer a promising line of research in enlarging and systematizing the theoretical grasp of juvenile delinquency. As more information is uncovered concerning techniques of neutralization, their origins, and their consequences, both juvenile delinquency in particular, and deviation from normative systems in general may be illuminated.

Notes

1. E. H. Sutherland, *Principles of Criminology,* revised by D. R. Cressey, Chicago: Lippincott, 1955, pp. 77–80.

2. Albert K. Cohen, *Delinquent Boys,* Glencoe, Ill.: The Free Press, 1955.

3. This form of reaction among the adherents of a deviant subculture who fully believe in the "rightfulness" of their behavior and who are captured and punished by the agencies of the dominant social order can be illustrated, perhaps, by groups such as Jehovah's Witnesses, early Christian sects, nationalist movements in colonial areas, and conscientious objectors during World Wars I and II.

4. As Weber has pointed out, a thief may recognize the legitimacy of legal rules without accepting their moral validity. Cf. Max Weber, *The Theory of Social and Economic Organization* (translated by A. M. Henderson and Talcott Parsons), New York: Oxford University Press, 1947, p. 125. We are arguing here, however, that the juvenile delinquent frequently recognizes *both* the legitimacy of the dominant social order and its moral "rightness."

5. Thrasher's account of the "Itschkies"—a juvenile gang composed of Jewish boys—and the immunity from "rolling" enjoyed by Jewish drunkards is a good illustration. Cf. F. Thrasher, *The Gang,* Chicago: The University of Chicago Press, 1947, p. 315.

6. Cf. Solomon Kobrin, "The Conflict of Values in Delinquency Areas," *American Sociological Review,* 16 (October, 1951), pp. 653–661.

7. Cf. Robin Williams, Jr., *American Society,* New York: Knopf, 1951, p. 28.

8. A number of observers have wryly noted that many delinquents seem to show a surprising awareness of sociological and psychological explanations for their behavior and are quick to point out the causal role of their poor environment.

9. It is possible, of course, that certain personality structures can accept some techniques of neutralization more readily than others, but this question remains largely unexplored.

10. George Orwell, *Dickens, Dali, and Others,* New York: Reynal, 1946.

11. Lloyd W. McCorkle and Richard Korn, "Resocialization Within Walls," *The Annals of the American Academy of Political and Social Science,* 293, (May, 1954), pp. 88–98.

12. See Samuel A. Stouffer and Jackson Toby, "Role Conflict and Personality," in *Toward a General Theory of Action,* edited by Talcott Parsons and Edward A. Shils, Cambridge: Harvard University Press, 1951, p. 494.

13. See Fritz Redl and David Wineman, *Children Who Hate,* Glencoe: The Free Press, 1956.

14. See D. R. Cressey, *Other People's Money,* Glencoe: The Free Press, 1953.

Social Learning and Deviant Behavior: A Specific Test of a General Theory

7

Ronald L. Akers
Marvin D. Krohn
Lonn Lanza-Kaduce
Marcia Radosevich

Introduction

In the last decade we have seen a dramatic shift away from sociological explanations of deviant behavior toward developing theoretical perspectives on societal reactions to and definitions of deviance and crime. Labelling and conflict formulations have become major foci of sociological theorizing as well as the sounding boards for most of the controversy and discourse in the field of deviance. This shift in focus was deemed necessary to redress the previous imbalance of attention to the deviant behavior itself (Akers, 1968), and it clearly has had that effect. Unfortunately, it also has led to the neglect of theoretical developments in the etiology of deviant behavior. Neither labelling nor conflict perspectives has offered a general explanation of deviant behavior, although some conflict theorists

From *American Sociological Review*, Vol. 44, No. 4, 1979, pp. 636–655. Reprinted by permission of the American Sociological Association and the authors.

have offered preliminary but incomplete efforts in that direction (Taylor, et al., 1973; Spitzer, 1975). There have been other efforts directed toward explaining deviant behavior, but these have been fairly narrow in scope; they have usually been limited either to a specific type of deviant behavior or to a restricted range of substantive variables. For example, a good deal of attention has been paid to the modern resurrection of deterrence theory (Gibbs, 1975; 1977; Waldo and Chiricos, 1972; Tittle, 1975; Silberman, 1976; Erickson et al., 1977; Meier and Johnson, 1977; Geerken and Gove, 1977). The scope of deterrence theory has been changed little, however, since its statement by the classical criminologists two centuries ago and is limited to the actual or perceived certainty, severity, and celerity of formally administered legal sanctions for violations of the criminal law. Another example is Travis Hirschi's (1969) control (social bonding) theory which is a more general explanation of deviance than deterrence theory, but which is, in turn, primarily restricted to informal social control which comes from individuals being bonded to groups and institutions.

The most notable exception to the diminished attention to general explanations of deviant behavior is a form of social learning theory developed first by Robert L. Burgess and Ronald L. Akers as differential association-reinforcement theory (Burgess and Akers, 1966; Akers et al., 1968) and elaborated on later by Akers (1973; 1977). As the name which Burgess and Akers originally chose to apply to this theoretical perspective makes clear, it was constructed as a revision of Edwin H. Sutherland's differential association theory (Sutherland, 1947; Sutherland and Cressey, 1974) in terms of general behavioral reinforcement theory (Skinner, 1953; 1959; Bandura and Walters, 1963; Bandura, 1969; 1977; Staats, 1975).[1] Social learning theory as a general perspective in deviance is part of a larger move toward incorporation of modern behaviorism into sociological theory (Homans, 1961; Burgess and Bushell, 1969; Kunkel, 1975; Hamblin et al., 1971; Emerson, 1969; 1973; Kunkel and Nagasawa, 1973; Burgess and Nielsen, 1974; Chadwick-Jones, 1976; for reviews of the relevance of behavioral theory for sociology see Friedrichs, 1974; Tartar, 1973). As such it is a theoretical perspective which is compatible with the more specific forays into the explanation of deviant behavior. Indeed, the major features of such theories as deterrence and control theories (Hirschi, 1969) can be subsumed under the principles of social learning theory (Akers, 1977; Conger, 1976, 1977; Feldman, 1977). However, all too often the relevance for social learning theory of some of the deviance research has been ignored or unrecognized even when the authors employ central learning concepts such as reinforcement (Harris, 1975; 1977, Eaton,

1974; Meier and Johnson, 1977; Hirschi and Hindelang, 1977). This inattention is regrettable for, while other theories delineate the structural variables (class, race, anomic conditions, breakdown in social control, etc.) that yield differential rates of deviance, social learning stresses the behavioral mechanisms by which these variables produce the behavior comprising the rates. As such, social learning is complementary to other sociological theories and could be used to integrate extant formulations to achieve more comprehensive explanations of deviance (in this regard see Akers, 1977:63-8).

The basic learning principles on which this theory is based have received empirical support under laboratory and applied experimental conditions (see Skinner, 1953; Honig, 1966; Ullmann and Krasner, 1969; Bandura, 1969; 1977; McLaughlin, 1971; Staats, 1975). Also, prior research has been supportive of differential association theory (J. Ball, 1957; Short, 1957; Voss, 1964; R. Ball, 1968; Krohn, 1974; Jensen, 1972; Burkett and Jensen, 1975). However, there has been little direct research on learning principles as applied to deviant behavior in natural settings. Akers (1977) has organized a large body of existing research and theory on a wide range of deviant behavior supportive of or consistent with social learning, but his effort is a post hoc application of theoretical principles for he does not present research designed explicitly to test propositions from the theory (in this regard see also Feldman, 1977). The results of other studies are consistent with Akers's social learning approach (Jessor and Jessor, 1975; Thomas et al., 1975), and a couple of studies explicitly testing social learning using secondary data analysis have found support for it (Anderson, 1973; Conger, 1976). However, more crucial and conclusive tests await collecting the relevant primary data in the community. The present study does that. Our purpose here is to report a specific test of social learning theory using standard sociological techniques of data collection and data analysis.

Statement of Social Learning Theory

The social learning theory tested here is summarized frcm Akers (1977:39-68). The primary learning mechanism in social behavior is operant (instrumental) conditioning in which behavior is shaped by the stimuli which follow, or are consequences of the behavior. Social behavior is acquired both through direct conditioning and through *imitation* or modelling of others' behavior. Behavior is strengthened through reward (positive reinforcement) and avoidance of punishment (negative reinforcement) or weakened by aversive stimuli (positive punishment) and loss of reward (negative punishment). Whether deviant or conforming behavior is acquired and persists depends on past and present rewards or punishments for the behavior and the rewards and punishments attached to alternative behavior—*differential reinforcement.* In addition, people learn in interaction with significant groups in their lives evaluative *definitions* (norms, attitudes, orientations) of the behavior as good or bad. These definitions are themselves verbal and cognitive behavior which can be directly reinforced and also act as cue (discriminative) stimuli for other behavior. The more individuals define the behavior as good (positive definition) or at least justified (neutralizing definition) rather than as undesirable (negative definition), the more likely they are to engage in it.

The reinforcers can be nonsocial (as in the direct physiological effects of drugs) as well as social, but the theory posits that the principal behavioral effects come from interaction in or under the influence of those *groups which control individuals' major sources of reinforcement and punishment and expose them to behavioral models and normative definitions.* The most important of these groups with which one is in *differential association* are the *peer-friendship* groups and the *family* but they also include schools, churches, and other groups. Behavior (whether deviant or conforming) results from greater reinforcement, on balance, over punishing contingencies for the same behavior and the reinforcing-punishing contingencies on alternative behavior. The definitions are conducive to deviant behavior when, on balance, the positive and neutralizing definitions of the behavior offset negative definitions of it. Therefore, deviant behavior can be expected to the extent that it has been differentially reinforced over alternative behavior (conforming or other deviant behavior) and is defined as desirable or justified. Progression into more frequent or sustained use and into abuse is also determined by the extent to which a given pattern is sustained by the combination of the reinforcing effects of the substance with social reinforcement, exposure to models, definitions through association with using peers, and by the degree to which it is not deterred through bad effects of the substance and/or the negative sanctions from peers, parents, and the law.

The social learning theory proposes a process which orders and specifies the interrelationships among these variables. Differential association, which refers to interaction and identity with different groups occurs first. These groups provide the social environments in which exposure to definitions, imitation of models, and social reinforcement for use of or abstinence from any particular substance take place. The definitions are learned through imitation, and social reinforcement of them by members of the groups with whom one is associated, and once learned, these definitions serve as discriminative stimuli for use or abstinence. The definitions in interaction with imitation of using or abstinent models and the anticipated balance of reinforcement produces the initial use or continued abstinence. After the initial use, imitation becomes less important while the effects of definitions should continue (themselves affected by the experience of use). It is at this point in the process that the actual consequences (social and nonsocial reinforcers and punishers) of the specific behavior come into play to determine the probability that use will be continued and at what level. These consequences include the actual effects of the substance at first and subsequent use (the perception of which may, of course, be modified by what effects the person has previously learned to expect) and the actual reactions of others present at the time or who find out about it later, as well as the anticipated reactions of others not present or knowing about the use.

From this depiction of them as aspects of the same learning process, we expect the independent variables to be positively interrelated, and we examine the zero order relationships among them. Nonetheless, the major variables are conceptually distinct and our measures are empirically distinct enough that we do not expect their interrelationships to preclude separate independent effects. Thus, we also empirically order the independent variables in terms of how much variance is explained in the dependent variables. We test the general hypothesis from the theory that adolescent marijuana and alcohol use and abuse are related to each of the major sets of variables and to all of them combined.

Specifically, we expect that for both alcohol and drugs, the probability of abstinence decreases and the frequency of use increases when there is greater exposure to using rather than to abstinent models, when there is more association with using than with abstinent peers and adults, when use is differentially reinforced (more rewards, fewer punishers) over abstinence, and when there are more positive or neutralizing than negative definitions of use. Similarly, among users the probability of abuse increases with more exposure to abusing rather than moderate or abstinent models, more association with high frequency users or abusers, greater differential reinforcement for abuse over more moderate use, and with more positive and neutralizing rather than negative definitions of use.

Research on Adolescent Drug and Alcohol Behavior

Adolescent drug and drinking behavior is a particularly strategic area for the current effort for two reasons. First, the area is characterized by the narrow scope of current theories of deviant behavior outlined above. The research has been largely restricted to the prevalence and sociodemographic and social-psychological correlates of teenage drinking and drug use (Abelson et al., 1973; Johnston, 1973; Block et al., 1974; National Commission on Marijuana and Drug Abuse, 1972; Drug Abuse Council, 1975; Rachal et al., 1975; O'Donnell et al., 1976). Little has been done to develop and test explanations of the behavior drawn from general theories. (For a full and comprehensive review of the theory and research literature on adolescent drinking and drug use, see Radosevich et al., forthcoming.) One notable exception to this is the work of the Jessors (Jessor et al., 1968; 1970; 1973; Jessor and Jessor, 1975; 1977;

Jessor, 1976) who have built a social-psychological theory of "problem behavior" (deviance) which incorporates part of Rotter's (1954) learning theory (locus of control) and other personality and social variables. Their theory, which is also a version of social learning, consists of three categories of variables—personality, social, and behavioral. Their findings tend to support parts (primarily the social component) of the theory. The Jessors' findings point to the second reason why adolescent drug use and drinking promises to be a fruitful area in which to examine social learning theory; that is, the research on social psychological correlates of drug use and drinking lends support to the relevance of many of the variables in the social learning theory tested here. For instance, research consistently finds that those holding tolerant or positive attitudes toward a substance are much more likely to use it than those holding negative attitudes toward it (Fejer and Smart, 1973; Johnston, 1973; Jessor et al., 1973; Calhoun, 1974; Kendall, 1976). Also, peer and parental influence have been found to be important variables in teenage drug and drinking behavior. Users are more likely than abstainers to associate with peers who are also users and this relationship remains whether friends' use is measured by or independently of the individual's perception of friends' use. (For a review of this research on parental and peer influences see Akers, 1977; recent studies to see are Pearce and Garrett, 1970; Kandel, 1973; 1974; Jessor et al., 1972; O'Donnell et al., 1976; Tec, 1974a; 1974b; Krohn, 1974; Wechsler and Thum, 1973; Kendall, 1976; Lawrence and Velleman, 1974.) Further, the research findings seem to be consistent with the causal ordering of these variables proposed by social learning: the youngster associates with peers who are users, learns definitions favorable to use of the sub-

stance, and then uses (Jessor et al., 1973; Krohn, 1974).

Methodology

Sample and Procedure

Data were collected by administering a self-report questionnaire to 3,065 male and female adolescents attending grades 7 through 12 in seven communities in three midwestern states. A two-stage sample design was followed. First, we selected schools from within each participating school district which were representative in terms of school size and location within the district. In smaller districts this meant selecting all or most of the junior and senior high schools in the district. Secondly, we sampled two to three classrooms (depending on school and average class size) per grade level from among the required or general enrollment classes. Thus, although classrooms were sampled, each student has an approximately equal chance of being included in the sample.[2] The questionnaire (which was pretested in a district not included in the final sample) was administered to all students in attendance in the selected classes on the day of the survey who had obtained written parental permission. The attrition from this parental permission procedure combined with absenteeism on the day of the survey was not great and 67% of the total number of students enrolled (95% of those with parental permission) in the sampled classes completed the questionnaire.[3]

A small subsample, purposively sampled from among respondents who volunteered in five of the seven districts (n = 106, approximately 5% of the sample in these districts), was interviewed two to eight weeks after the administration of the questionnaire. The follow-up interview was intended to serve as a reliability and partial validity check on the questionnaire responses and to provide additional descriptive information. The interviews were conducted individually in private rooms at school during school hours.

Reliability and Validity

Prior research has consistently shown that the self-report questionnaire technique is reliable and valid in measuring adolescent delinquent, drug, and drinking behavior (Hardt and Peterson-Hardt, 1977; Groves, 1974; Block et al., 1974; Single et al., 1975; Whitehead and Smart, 1972). Our own checks in the present research confirm this. Internal consistency on interlocking questions was high (Gammas = .91 and higher). In addition, a comparison of the responses to the frequency and quantity of use questions on the questionnaire with responses to the same items given at the time of the interview demonstrated a high degree of reliability (Gammas = .89 and higher). Without exception the interview respondents reported that they believed the researchers assurances of confidentiality and that no one but the researchers would have access to identifiable answers; thus, all said that they felt secure in responding and answered questions both on the questionnaire and in the interview honestly.[4]

Measurement of Variables

Dependent variables
Abstinence-use of alcohol and marijuana is measured by a six-point frequency-of-use scale ranging from nearly every day to never. A quantity frequency (Q-F) scale was also computed but since there is a near perfect correlation between the Q-F scale and the frequency-of-use scale, the analysis here includes only the latter measure.[5]
Abuse among users is measured by

combining responses to the frequency questions with responses to a question asking the respondents to check whether or not they had experienced on more than one occasion any of a list of problems while or soon after using alcohol or marijuana.[6] This combination produced a four-point abuse scale ranging from heavy abuse to no abuse.

Independent variables
From the summary of social learning theory presented above it can be seen that the main concepts to be measured are *imitation, differential association, definitions, and differential reinforcement.* For the present analysis, we distinguish between differential reinforcement comprised of social reinforcement combined with nonsocial reinforcement (experienced or anticipated drug or alcohol effects) and that comprised only of social reinforcement. Each of the resulting five concepts are operationalized by a set of items measuring different aspects of each concept. (The Appendix provides a brief description of the way the five concepts are measured.) These five clusters of variables (a total of 15 variables in the abstinence-use analysis and 16 variables in the abuse analysis) constitute the independent variables in this analysis.[7]

Method of analysis
Although most of the measures yield ordinal-level data, we will use multiple regression techniques.* It has been demonstrated that regression can be confidently employed with ordinal data without introducing bias in the results (Labovitz, 1970; 1971; Kim, 1975). The use of regression techniques provides an overall summary of

---

*Editor's Note: See Appendix 2 for a brief discussion of "multiple regression."

the explanatory power of the model while also allowing us to examine the unique effects of the five subsets of variables and of each separate variable.

Presentation of Findings

Explaining Abstinence-Frequency of Use

The zero-order correlation** matrices for the alcohol and marijuana use variables are presented in Tables 7.1 and 7.2.[8] As expected, most of the independent variables are related in a positive direction with variability in the strength of the relationships. Of particular interest are the relatively weak relationships of the deterrence items to the other variables, especially within the matrix on alcohol behavior. Also, note the strength of the relationships of both alcohol and marijuana use to those variables of associations with and attitudes of peers, to reinforcement balance, and to reward-costs of use, and note the interrelationships among these variables. These zero-order relationships anticipate our findings in the multivariate analysis to which we now turn.

The results of the regression analyses show strong support for the social learning theory of adolescent alcohol and drug behavior.[9] When all the independent variables are incorporated into the full regression equation, the model explains 55% of the variance in drinking behavior (abstinence-frequency of use; Table 7.3) and 68% of the variance in marijuana behavior (abstinence-frequency of use; Table 7.4).[10]

The power of the full model including the five subsets of variables, therefore, is demonstrated. But, we are also interested

in determining the relative predictive values of the subsets and single variables to see if each part of the theory is supported. We do this in two ways. First, we regress the dependent variables on all variables and each subset of variables in separate regression equations. This provides a partial regression coefficient for each variable in each equation and estimates of the total amount of variance explained by each subset (Tables 7.3 and 7.4). Second, we compute the proportion of variance which the remaining subsets explain when each subset in turn is eliminated from the equation. By subtracting each of these values from the proportion of variance explained by the full equation, we have a measure of how much explained variance is lost when a given subset of variables is eliminated. The larger the proportion of explained variance lost (or the smaller the explained variance remaining) when a subset is eliminated, the greater its relative explanatory power (Table 7.5). By analyzing the data in this fashion, we also circumvent potential problems of multicollinearity among the variables within each subset since our primary concern is with the relative explanatory power of the different subsets of variables and not with the relative power of individual variables within subsets.

With the exception of imitation, each subset explains a substantial proportion of variance in both alcohol and marijuana use. The findings presented in Table 7.5 show that even when the most predictive subset of variables is eliminated the remaining variables are still able to explain 43% and 56% of the variance in alcohol and marijuana behavior, respectively. The fact that four of the five subsets of variables taken from social learning theory *each* explains a substantial proportion of the variance (and that the fifth is significantly related to the dependent variables in the expected direc-

---

**Editor's Note: A ''zero-order correlation'' is a measure of association between two variables. Its value may range from -1.0 (a negative association) to 1.0 (a positive association).

tion) demonstrates that the theory as a whole is supported; its power is not dependent on any single component.

However, the analyses also plainly show that some subsets of variables specified by the theory are more important than others. They are ranked in terms of relative effectiveness in explaining variance in alcohol and marijuana use as follows: (1) differential association, (2) definitions, (3) combined social/nonsocial differential reinforcement, (4) differential social reinforcement, and (5) imitation.[11] Not only does the differential association subset explain the highest proportion of variance, but the differential peer association vari-

able is the most important single variable. The definitions subset accounts for the second highest proportion of variance, and one's positive/negative definitions of the substances is the second most predictive single variable, while one's law-abiding/violating definitions rank third among the single variables. The differential reinforcements variables are next, followed by imitation variables which explain the least amount of variance in the dependent variables.

The fact of peer group influence on substance use comes as no surprise; it is documented by several previous studies. But, previous studies have not shown what the

Table 7.1

Zero-Order Correlation Matrix for Variables Included in Alcohol Use Analysis
(N = 2,414)*

Variables	1	2	3	4	5	6	7	8	9	10	11	12	13	14	15	16
1. Imitation	1.00															
2. Techniques of neutralization	.05	1.00														
3. Law abiding/violating definitions	.11	.40	1.00													
4. Positive/negative definitions	.19	.39	.39	1.00												
5. Adult norm qualities	.18	.08	.14	.35	1.00											
6. Peer norm qualities	.17	.32	.33	.58	.29	1.00										
7. Differential peer association	.22	.32	.44	.49	.18	.48	1.00									
8. Praise for not using	.09	.19	.22	.24	.16	.24	.29	1.00								
9. Friends' reaction	.16	.32	.32	.41	.17	.45	.46	.26	1.00							
10. Parents' reaction	.14	.11	.11	.29	.33	.19	.27	.24	.26	1.00						
11. Informal deterrence	.03	.19	.18	.19	−.01	.16	.17	.12	.18	.02	1.00					
12. Formal deterrence	.02	.07	.12	.09	.01	.08	.06	.10	.12	−.005	.43	1.00				
13. Interference with activities	.05	.20	.24	.24	.07	.19	.23	.14	.18	.10	.19	.14	1.00			
14. Rewards—costs of use	.14	.30	.31	.48	.18	.36	.42	.23	.41	.28	.21	.11	.23	1.00		
15. Reinforcement balance	.15	.36	.39	.47	.18	.37	.46	.21	.38	.23	.20	.09	.27	.44	1.00	
16. Alcohol use	.16	.34	.47	.52	.20	.40	.68	.28	.40	.29	.13	.04	.21	.44	.46	1.00

*In this and in all subsequent tables independent variables have been coded such that positive coefficients indicate the theoretically expected direction.

Table 7.2

Zero-Order Correlation Matrix for Variables Included in Marijuana Use Analysis
(N = 2,395)

Variables	1	2	3	4	5	6	7	8	9	10	11	12	13	14	15	16
1. Imitation	1.00															
2. Techniques of neutralization	.23	1.00														
3. Law abiding/violating definitions	.26	.23	1.00													
4. Positive/negative definitions	.39	.45	.53	1.00												
5. Adult norm qualities	.15	.16	.19	.28	1.00											
6. Peer norm qualities	.32	.38	.38	.63	.28	1.00										
7. Differential peer association	.38	.41	.47	.71	.24	.59	1.00									
8. Praise for not using	.15	.25	.24	.32	.13	.30	.32	1.00								
9. Friends' reaction	.32	.37	.39	.55	.18	.52	.59	.29	1.00							
10. Parents' reaction	.12	.10	.13	.20	.18	.13	.18	.09	.18	1.00						
11. Informal deterrence	.18	.24	.28	.38	.08	.31	.33	.18	.32	.11	1.00					
12. Formal deterrence	.11	.18	.22	.22	.01	.17	.18	.12	.20	.10	.49	1.00				
13. Interference with activities	.19	.27	.28	.39	.13	.30	.35	.20	.28	.13	.24	.17	1.00			
14. Rewards—costs of use	.33	.40	.43	.67	.17	.51	.56	.29	.52	.16	.39	.24	.35	1.00		
15. Reinforcement balance	.31	.41	.44	.61	.19	.47	.53	.25	.46	.18	.32	.18	.38	.59	1.00	
16. Marijuana use	.38	.48	.40	.72	.24	.50	.79	.29	.50	.18	.31	.15	.36	.15	.52	1.00

mechanisms are by which peer influence is exerted, and why, therefore, peer group association is so important. Our data show, as predicted by social learning theory, what these mechanisms are—friends provide social reinforcement or punishment for abstinence or use, provide normative definitions of use and abstinence, and, to a lesser extent, serve as admired models to imitate. This is indicated by the fact that these other variables, on their own, explain a substantial amount of the variance in marijuana and alcohol behavior when the effect of the differential peer association variable is removed. The fact that differential interaction explains more variance in the dependent variables than do the reinforcement, definitions, and imitation variables indicates that there may be additional vari-

ables at work in interaction beyond those identified by social learning theory, that there are additional effects of the mechanisms specified by our theory which are not captured by our measures of them, or that there are effects of other learning variables which we have not included (e.g., discriminative stimuli in the interactional setting in which reinforcement takes place).

Since social learning theory includes modelling as an important part of the process, the lower levels of variance explained by our imitation measures may seem surprising. However, the relatively weak effect of the imitation subset on our frequency of use and abuse measures was not unexpected. First, imitation refers to the narrowest empirical phenomenon among our measures (see footnote 7) and while, as

Table 7.3
Partial Regression Coefficients in Standard Form for Alcohol Use (N = 2,414)

Independent Variables	All Independent Variables	Imitation	Definitions	Differential Association	Differential Reinforcement: Social	Differential Reinforcement: Social/Nonsocial
1. Imitation	−.014	.161				
2. Techniques of neutralization	.040		.086			
3. Law abiding/violating definitions	.142		.288			
4. Positive/negative definitions	.160		.372			
5. Adult norm qualities	.002			.068		
6. Peer norm qualities	−.055			.071		
7. Differential peer association	.458			.629		
8. Praise for not using	.035				.141	
9. Friends' reaction	.008				.290	
10. Parents' reaction	.059				.168	
11. Informal deterrence	−.026				.060	
12. Formal deterrence	−.021				−.045	
13. Interference with activities	−.005				.119	
14. Rewards—costs of use	.067					.326
15. Reinforcement balance	.093					.301
R =	.738	.161	.598	.683	.483	.532
R^2 =	.545	.026	.357	.466	.233	.283

we have noted, multicollinearity is not a severe problem, the interrelationships specified in the theory would indicate that removing imitation has less effect because its impact is still reflected to some extent in the remaining broader measures. Second, and more important, as indicated in the process outlined in the statement of the theory above, imitation in social learning theory is considered to have its greatest effect in the first acquisition or initial stages of behavior while the associational, reinforcement, and definitional variables are more important in the maintenance of a behavioral pattern. We expect imitation to be more important in first starting to use than we find it to be in explaining frequency of use as analyzed

here (but still probably not more important than definitional and reinforcement variables). The analysis here which employs frequency of using as the dependent variable militates against finding a large effect for imitation variables. We would expect imitation to be even less important in accounting for maintenance of abusive patterns of use.

It is evident that social learning theory has been shown to be a powerful explanation of whether youngsters abstain from or are users of alcohol and marijuana. As predicted by the theory, the adolescents in our sample use drugs or alcohol to the extent that the behavior has been differentially reinforced through association in primary groups and defined as more desirable than, or at least as justified as, refraining from use. The next step in testing the validity of this perspective will be to examine how well these same variables account for levels of abuse of alcohol and drugs.

Explaining Abusive Patterns of Use

The results of the analyses of alcohol and marijuana abuse among adolescents are presented in Tables 7.6, 7.7 and 7.8. For these analyses, only users are included.

The results parallel those of the analyses of abstinence-frequency of use reported above. Both marijuana and alcohol abuse are strongly related to the social learning variables. The proportion of variance explained in use-abuse is well below the explained variance in abstinence-frequency of use but it is still substantial—32% and 39% of the variance in alcohol and marijuana abuse, respectively. The differential association subset again explains the greatest proportion of variance (Tables 7.6 and 7.7), but even without the differential association variables, the other variables in the model do well in accounting for the variance (22% and 30%; Table 7.8).

The variables are not ordered in terms of relative effectiveness in predicting abuse in the same way they were ranked in explaining abstinence-use. In the analysis of abstinence-use, definitions were the second

Table 7.4

Partial Regression Coefficients in Standard Form for Marijuana Use (N = 2,395)

Independent Variables	All Independent Variables	Imitation	Definitions	Differential Association	Differential Reinforcement: Social	Differential Reinforcement: Social/Nonsocial
1. Imitation	.033	.378				
2. Techniques of neutralization	.016		.070			
3. Law abiding/violating definitions	.054		.123			
4. Positive/negative definitions	.257		.619			
5. Adult norm qualities	.018			.057		
6. Peer norm qualities	− .080			.038		
7. Differential peer association	.550			.751		
8. Praise for not using	.001				.118	
9. Friends' reaction	− .016				.366	
10. Parents' reaction	.006				.063	
11. Informal deterrence	.007				.139	
12. Formal deterrence	− .035				− .044	
13. Interference with activities	.034				.196	
14. Rewards—costs of use	.016					.280
15. Reinforcement balance	.082					.410
R =	.826	.378	.728	.790	.579	.618
R² =	.683	.143	.530	.625	.335	.382

Table 7.5

Results from Regression Analysis Alternately Eliminating Subsets from the Full Equations for Alcohol and Marijuana Use

| | Alcohol Use (N = 2,414) | | Marijuana Use (N = 2,395) | |
| | When Subset Is Eliminated | | When Subset Is Eliminated | |
Subset Eliminated	R^2 Remaining =	Loss of Explained Variance =	R^2 Remaining =	Loss of Explained Variance =
Differential Association	.427	.118	.561	.122
Definitions	.510	.035	.657	.026
Imitation	.544	.001	.682	.001
Differential Reinforcement: Social	.539	.006	.681	.002
Differential Reinforcement: Social/Nonsocial	.535	.010	.679	.004
Full Equation R^2 =	.545		.683	

most effective subset, whereas this subset ranks fourth in accounting for use-abuse while the differential reinforcement variables are ranked higher. In substance abuse the user comes more and more to respond to direct reinforcement, especially from the drug effects themselves; definitions would be expected to play a less significant role. This is shown fairly clearly when we examine the effect of adding an alcohol and marijuana effects variable which was not included in the previous analysis of abstinence-frequency of use. This variable was measured by asking using respondents to report the effects which they usually obtained from smoking marijuana or drinking alcohol.[12] This variable has the largest beta weight among the single variables making up the social/nonsocial differential reinforcement subset and ranks second for marijuana abuse and third for alcohol abuse among the entire set of single variables.

The variable of parental reaction appears to be related to abuse in the direction opposite to that found in the analysis of use. For the latter a lower probability of use is found for those reporting the strongest or harshest parental punishment while for the

former a lower probability of abuse is found for those reporting lesser punishment or no parental response. A cross-tabular examination of these relationships reveals a curvilinear relationship between parental reaction and both adolescents' use and abuse of alcohol and marijuana. That is, higher frequency of use and abuse is found with parental response (actual or anticipated) at both the most lenient (encourage or do nothing) and the harshest end of the scale (take some drastic action such as kick the youngsters out of the house or turn them over to the police). The highest probability of abstinence and the lowest levels of use and abuse are found among adolescents who report that their parents have responded or would respond to their use with a moderate negative reaction such as a scolding. Out post hoc interpretation of these relationships is that anticipated parental punishment is a deterrent to use and sustains abstinence. Even after use has begun a reasonable amount of parental punishment holds down the chance of increasing frequency of use or moving into abuse. However, once adolescents have gotten into heavy use or abuse, parental reaction has lost its effect and the increasing abuse of the substances by their children may produce ever harsher reactions by parents in increasingly desperate attempts to do something about it.

While not contradictory to the theory, neither the difference between the amount of variance explained in abstinence-frequency of use and that explained in use-abuse for both alcohol and marijuana behavior nor the difference between the amount of variance explained in alcohol behavior and the amount explained in marijuana behavior was specifically anticipated. The lower level of explained variance in substance abuse than in substance use may be due simply to the fact that the variance in the abuse variables is restricted, thereby producing attenuation in the total variance explained. The differences in the explained variances in alcohol and marijuana behavior may be an artifact of our measurements, may indicate that the stimuli surrounding alcohol behavior are more uniform than those surrounding marijuana behavior, or may point to some real difference in the ability of the theory to account for the two kinds of substance use.

Summary and Conclusions

In the past decade sociological attention in the study of deviance has shifted to expla-

Table 7.6
Partial Regression Coefficients in Standard Form for Alcohol Abuse (N = 1,764)

Independent Variables	All Independent Variables	Imitation	Definitions	Differential Association	Differential Reinforcement: Social	Differential Reinforcement: Social/Nonsocial
1. Imitation	.046	.128				
2. Techniques of neutralization	−.005		.007			
3. Law abiding/violating definitions	.094		.220			
4. Positive/negative definitions	.077		.200			
5. Adult norm qualities	.050			.065		
6. Peer norm qualities	−.010			.040		
7. Differential peer association	.351			.474		
8. Praise for not using	.025				.115	
9. Friends' reaction	.042				.123	
10. Parents' reaction	−.130				−.195	
11. Informal deterrence	−.030				.010	
12. Formal deterrence	−.030				−.041	
13. Interference with activities	−.014				.057	
14. Rewards—costs of use	.039					.141
15. Reinforcement balance	−.036					−.047
16. Usual effects of alcohol	.144					.315
R =	.561	.128	.334	.500	.261	.366
R² =	.315	.016	.111	.250	.068	.134

nations of the control system and away from the equally important task of proposing and testing general explanations of deviant behavior. We have presented a social learning perspective on deviant behavior developed during this same time period which holds promise as a general theory of the process of coming to engage in deviant acts but which had not been tested with primary data collected in the community and subjected to multivariate analysis. We have tested it here on specific forms of adolescent deviance—drug and alcohol use and abuse.

The results of the tests support the theory. All of the dependent variables are strongly related to the social learning variables of dif-ferential association, definitions, differential reinforcement, and imitation. The most powerful of these independent variables is differential association. The other variables stand on their own, however, and explain substantial portions of variance even without the differential association measures (except for imitation which is the weakest of the variables for use and explains almost none of the variance in abuse).

The strength of empirical support for the theory suggests that the theory will have utility in explaining the use and abuse of other substances by adolescents. These findings also indicate that social learning theory will do well when tested with other

Table 7.7
Partial Regression Coefficients in Standard Form for Marijuana Abuse (N = 948)

Independent Variables	All Independent Variables	Imitation	Definitions	Differential Association	Differential Reinforcement: Social	Differential Reinforcement: Social/Nonsocial
1. Imitation	.032	.098				
2. Techniques of neutralization	.036		.106			
3. Law abiding/violating definitions	.098		.182			
4. Positive/negative definitions	.090		.298			
5. Adult norm qualities	.000			.047		
6. Peer norm qualities	−.061			.030		
7. Differential peer association	.384			.533		
8. Praise for not using	−.004				.080	
9. Friends' reaction	.057				.198	
10. Parents' reaction	−.130				−.195	
11. Informal deterrence	−.010				.024	
12. Formal deterrence	−.040				−.067	
13. Interference with activities	.070				.201	
14. Rewards—costs of use	.064					.228
15. Reinforcement balance	−.020					−.022
16. Usual effects of marijuana	.130					.260
R =	.623	.098	.440	.556	.381	.393
R^2 =	.389	.010	.194	.310	.146	.154

Table 7.8

Results from Regression Analysis Alternately Eliminating Subsets from the Full Equations for Alcohol and Marijuana Abuse

Subset Eliminated	Alcohol Abuse (N = 1,764)		Marijuana Abuse (N = 948)	
	When Subset Is Eliminated		When Subset Is Eliminated	
	R^2 Remaining =	Loss of Explained Variance =	R^2 Remaining =	Loss of Explained Variance =
Differential Association	.222	.093	.296	.093
Definitions	.302	.013	.372	.017
Imitation	.313	.002	.388	.001
Differential Reinforcement: Social	.292	.023	.364	.025
Differential Reinforcement: Social/Nonsocial	.297	.018	.371	.018
Full Equation R^2 =	.315		.389	

forms of deviant behavior in future research. Future research could test the general theory in any number of specific contexts. We believe that our study demonstrates that the central learning concepts are amenable to meaningful questionnaire measurement and that social learning theory can be adequately tested with survey data. This is important given the lack of survey data measuring social learning concepts, and the collection and analysis of cross-sectional data presented here is a necessary step, but a first step,

nonetheless. Therefore, the next steps in testing social learning theory not only should include analysis of the use and abuse of stronger and more severely disapproved substances than marijuana and alcohol (stimulants, depressants, psychedelics, and opiates), but also should include the collection of longitudinal data (Jessor and Jessor, 1977; Kandel, 1978). Longitudinal data will allow more adequate testing of the process of learning and temporal-ordering of variables in the theory.

Appendix

List of Social Learning Variables*

I. Imitation
   1. *Index of Imitation*
      Total of all the "admired" models (parents, friends, other adults, etc.) whom the respondent reports having observed using the substance.
II. Definitions Favorable or Unfavorable to Use
   2. *Techniques of Neutralization Scale*
      A scale of three items measuring Sykes and Matza's (1957) "techniques of neutralization" or

---

*The variable numbers in this list correspond to the variable numbers in the regression tables. For all items, questions were asked separately for alcohol and marijuana. Copies of the questionnaire and list of concepts measured by questionnaire items are available on request.

definitions justifying or excusing use by "denial of injury," "denial of responsibility," or "condemning the condemnors." Item to scale interrelation for the scale referring to alcohol range from .68 to .76; for marijuana the range is from .68 to .78.

3. *Scale of Law-Abiding or Law-Violating Definitions*
   A scale of items measuring obedient or violating attitudes toward the law in general and alcohol and drug laws in particular. Item to scale intercorrelations range from .53 to .76.

4. *Positive or Negative Definitions of Use*
   Respondents' own approval or disapproval of use.

III. Differential Association

5. *Significant Adults' Norm Qualities*
   Respondents' perception of the approving-disapproving attitudes toward use held by adults whose opinions they value.

6. *Significant Peers' Norm Qualities*
   Respondents' perception of the approving-disapproving attitudes toward use held by other teenagers whose opinions they value.

7. *Differential Peer Association Scale*
   A scale of three items measuring how many of respondents' best friends, friends with whom they associate most often, and friends whom they have known for the longest time use the substance. Item to scale intercorrelations of the alcohol scale range from .85 to .96; for marijuana the range is from .83 to .96.

IV. Differential Reinforcement: Social

8. *Praise for Not Using*
   Respondents' report as to whether or not friends, parents or both encouraged them *not* to use.

9. *Friends' Rewarding or Punishing Reactions*
   Respondents' report of anticipated or actual positive or negative sanctions of friends to respondents' use of the substance, ranging from encouraging their use to turning them in to the authorities.

10. *Parents' Rewarding or Punishing Reactions*
    Respondents' report of anticipated or actual positive or negative sanctions of parents for respondents' use of the substance, ranging from encouraging their use to turning them in to the authorities.

11. *Informal Parental Deterrence*
    Respondents' perceived probability that their parents would catch them if they used the substance.

12. *Formal Deterrence*
    Respondents' perceived probability that the police would catch them if they used the substance.

13. *Interference with Other Important Activities*
    Respondents' perception of the extent to which using the substance would interfere with their participation in activities (i.e., school work, athletics, etc.) important to them.

V. Differential Reinforcement: Combined Social/Nonsocial

14. *Index of Social/Nonsocial Rewards Minus Costs of Use*
    The total good things from a list of positive drug effects and social outcomes which the using respondent checked as having actually experienced and the nonusing respondents checked as what they perceived they would experience as a result of using the substance *minus* the total bad things checked (there is an equal number of good and bad possible consequences in the list).

15. *Overall Reinforcement Balance*
    Respondents' assessment of whether on balance mostly good things (such as "a good high or

get along better with others'') or mostly bad things (such as ''a bad high or get into trouble'') would (as perceived by nonusers if they were to use) or did (as reported by users when they used the substance) happen.

16. *Usual Effects Felt When Used*

Respondents' report of the effects the substance usually has on them (from no effect, to mostly good, to mostly bad effects). Asked only of those using more than once.

Notes

1. The label *social learning* has been applied to other theories based on reinforcement principles but the Burgess and Akers formulation is the first and only one which ties general learning theory to a long-standing sociological theory and is directed towards specific forms of deviant behavior (crime, delinquency, drug addiction, suicide, etc.). It is to this theory that social learning usually refers when used here. It will be clear from the context when this is not the case.

2. Our primary aim was to test an explanation of drug and drinking behavior and we had no plans to generalize about the prevalence or sociodemographic variations to a wider national or regional population. Therefore, there was no attempt to get a probability sample or to insure that the total sample was regionally or nationally representative. We did plan to report findings to the participating school districts and to generalize findings within each district. Also, we wanted to follow a design which would require the involvement of as few schools and school personnel as possible, which would minimize adjustments needed in the school routine, and which would facilitate administration of the questionnaire to groups of respondents. The sampling of a limited number of classrooms from within each selected school best served these purposes. We believe that being alert to the problem of minimizing interference of the survey into the school routine and proposing the sampling procedure which we followed was a significant element in gaining the approval and cooperation of the school officials. The resultant sample was sufficiently representative within each district that we could make reasonable generalizations about the drug and drinking problem in the district. Whether two or three classes per grade level were sampled from each school depended on the size of the classes. We tried to include enough classes to secure responses from at least 10% of the total school enrollment or a minimum of 100 respondents per school, whichever was greater, to help protect the confidentiality of respondents in the smaller schools.

3. Overall, 74% of the parental permission forms distributed were returned (the lowest percentage of return in a district was 62% and the highest return rate was 93%). The forms were first distributed by the researchers in the classrooms one week before the survey; then, one more visit was made to the classrooms to remind students to return the forms. For some classes, telephone calls were made to the parents of those students who had not returned the form. Without this call-back procedure, buttressed by telephone calls, the return rate would have been smaller. For the sample as a whole, 95% of those returning forms were granted parental permission to take part in the survey (we asked that the forms be returned whether permission was granted or denied). Ninety-five percent of those attended class and completed the questionnaire on the day of the survey.

4. Careful steps were taken to protect the rights of both questionnaire and interview respondents and of the school districts. The usual university procedures were followed regarding approval of the project's procedures for protection of the rights of research participants. At the time of the first visit to the classrooms, the students were informed of the survey and each one present was given an envelope containing a let-

ter explaining the purpose and content of the study to the parents and the parental consent form mentioned in fn. 3. The students were told that participation in the study was completely voluntary. It was made clear that no student had to participate as a condition for class credit or any other school requirement and that approval of the study by the district and school officials in no way made participation mandatory. All of the responses were and are held in strictest confidence. In five of the districts, respondents who were willing to be interviewed later were asked to indicate that willingness and to sign their questionnaires. Also, it was possible for anyone to place his or her name on the questionnaire even if not volunteering for an interview (and many did just that). To protect the confidentiality of those volunteering for an interview, all respondents, whether signing the name sheet or not, separated it from the rest of the questionnaire and deposited it in a separate box from the one in which the completed questionnaires were deposited. Only the research staff had and has access to the name lists which, when not in a locked drawer, were kept in a bank safety deposit box. All other respondents in these districts and all respondents in the other two districts where no interviews were conducted were anonymous. At the interview each respondent was again informed of the confidentiality of the information given. Upon completion of the interview, each respondent was paid the previously stipulated amount of $2.50 and signed a sheet acknowledging the voluntary nature of the interview and receipt of the payment. The list of interviewee's names was treated in the same way as the name sheets mentioned above. We also protected the identification of the school districts participating in the study. No community, school district, or school has been or will be identified by name in reports or disseminated findings.

5. Alcohol use was measured by responses to separate questions on beer, wine, and liquor. The highest percentage of use and most frequent use was reported for beer, and since there is a very high correlation between use of the three forms of alcohol, use of alcohol in this analysis is measured only by reported frequency of use of beer.

6. The problems included "had an accident," "couldn't remember later what I had done," "used more than I had planned." This is a fairly standard use of "problems associated with" as a nonclinical measure of abuse of some substance. It should not be confused with our measures of positive and negative consequences of use for the differential reinforcement variables. The questions used to measure abuse were asked separately from and never combined with the questions used to measure differential reinforcement.

7. The concepts are clearly not equal in the scope of concrete empirical phenomena to which each refers. Differential association with family, peer, and other groups exposes the adolescent to using and nonusing models and normative definitions of use. It is in interaction in these groups in which the reactions of others differentially reinforce substance use or abstinent behavior. It is in this sense, then, that the differential association could include empirical referents of each of the other concepts and a general measure of differential association (in addition to being a measure of with whom one interacts), could serve as a general, albeit indirect, index of the combined effects of social reinforcement, imitation, and exposure to normative definitions. But such an index could not distinguish among the specific mechanisms of taking on definitions, imitating, and reinforcing of behavior which occur within the groups with which one is differentially associated. The combined social/nonsocial reinforcement subset obviously includes a wider array of concrete reinforcers than the subset of only social reinforcers. But, while reinforcement is the most abstract concept, the concrete set of events to which our measures here refer makes neither the social/nonsocial reinforcement, nor the social reinforcement subset broader than the definitions subset. Since it refers specifically to observing the behavior of someone else without reference to attitudes toward or consequences of the behavior, the imitation subset represents the most limited range of phenomena.

8. The zero-order matrices for the abuse variables not presented here are similar to those for use.

9. The total N in the tables varies because of attrition due to listwise deletion of missing values. The respondents who were eliminated were not significantly different from those included on sociodemographic characteristics and on the dependent variable. We also computed the regression analysis employing pairwise deletion and obtained similar results.

10. This general level of explained variance and the relationships of the separate independent variables to the dependent variables held when we controlled for such variables as SES and sex (which were not related to the dependent variables) and when we controlled for such variables as grade in school and type of school district (which were related to the dependent variables).

11. It is possible that the relative explanatory power of each subset may be due in part to the different number of variables that are contained within each subset. To examine this possibility we selected the most predictive variable from each subset and entered those variables in a multiple regression equation. The result produced no change in the rank ordering of the concepts in either the alcohol or marijuana equation. This also allowed us to examine the possible effects of multicollinearity within subsets on the relative explanatory power of single variables. Again the results were similar to those obtained above, indicating small multicollinearity effects.

12. Since abstainers could only report anticipated effects, the question of actual physical effects usually obtained from using the substances could not be included in the analyses of abstinence-frequency of use. Only among users are we able to differentiate between social and nonsocial reinforcement.

References

Abelson, H. I., R. Cohen, D. Shrayer, and M. Rappeport. "Drug experience, attitudes and related behavior among adolescents and adults." Pp. 488–867 in *Drug Use in America: Problem in Perspective,* Vol. 1. Report prepared by the National Commission on Marijuana and Drug Abuse, 1973.

Akers, Ronald L. "Problems in the sociology of deviance: social definitions and behavior." *Social Forces* 46:455–65 (1968).

_____. *Deviant Behavior: A Social Learning Approach.* Belmont: Wadsworth, 1973.

_____. *Deviant Behavior: A Social Learning Approach.* 2nd ed. Belmont: Wadsworth, 1977.

Akers, Ronald L., Robert L. Burgess and Weldon Johnson. "Opiate use, addiction, and relapse." *Social Problems* 15:459–69 (1968).

Anderson, Linda S. "The impact of formal and informal sanctions on marijuana use: a test of social learning and deterrence." Master's thesis: Florida State University, 1973.

Ball, John C. "Delinquent and non-delinquent attitudes toward the prevalence of stealing." *Journal of Criminal Law, Criminology and Police Science* 48:259–74 (1957).

Ball, Richard A. "An empirical exploration of neutralization theory," Pp. 255–65 in Mark Lefton, James K. Skipper and Charles H. McCaghy (eds.) *Approaches to Deviance.* New York: Appleton-Century-Crofts, 1968.

Bandura, Albert. *Principles of Behavior Modification.* New York: Holt, Rinehart and Winston, 1969.

_____. *Social Learning Theory.* Englewood Cliffs: Prentice-Hall, 1977.

Bandura, Albert and Richard H. Walters. *Social Learning and Personality Development.* New York: Holt, Rinehart and Winston, 1963.

Block, J. R., N. Goodman, F. Ambellan and J. Revenson. "A self-administered high school study of drugs." Hempstead: Institute for Research and Evaluation, 1974.

Burgess, Robert L. and Ronald L. Akers. "A differential association-reinforcement theory of criminal behavior." *Social Problems* 14:128–47 (1966).

Burgess, Robert and Don Bushell (eds.). *Behavioral Sociology*. New York: Columbia University Press, 1969.

Burgess, Robert L. and Joyce McCarl Nielsen. "An experimental analysis of some structural determinants of equitable and inequitable exchange relations." *American Sociological Review* 39:427–43 (1974).

Burkett, Steven and Eric L. Jensen. "Conventional ties, peer influence, and the fear of apprehension: a study of adolescent marijuana use." *Sociological Quarterly* 16:522–33 (1975).

Calhoun, J. F. "Attitudes toward the sale and use of drugs: a cross-sectional analysis of those who use drugs." *Journal of Youth and Adolescence* 3:31–47 (1974).

Chadwick-Jones, J. K. *Social Exchange Theory: Its Structure and Influence in Social Psychology*. New York: Academic Press, 1976.

Conger, Rand D. "Social control and social learning models of delinquent behavior—a synthesis." *Criminology* 14:17–40 (1976).

_____. Rejoinder. *Criminology* 15:117–26 (1977).

Drug Abuse Council, Inc. *Students and Drugs: A Report of the Drug Abuse Council* (by Yankelovich, Skelly, and White, Inc.) Washington, D.C.: Drug Abuse Council, 1975.

Eaton, William W. "Mental hospitalization as a reinforcement process." *American Sociological Review* 39:252–60 (1974).

Emerson, Richard M. "Operant psychology and exchange theory." Pp. 379–405 in Robert L. Burgess and Don Bushell, Jr. (eds.). *Behavioral Sociology*. New York: Columbia University Press, 1969.

_____. "Exchange theory." Pp. 38–87 in Joseph Berger, Morris Zelditch, Jr. and Bo Anderson (eds.), *Sociological Theories in Progress*, Vol. 2. Boston: Houghton-Mifflin, 1973.

Erickson, Maynard L., Jack P. Gibbs and Gary F. Jensen. "The deterrence doctrine and the perceived certainty of legal punishment." *American Sociological Review* 42:305–17 (1977).

Fejer, Dianne and Reginald G. Smart. "The knowledge about drugs, attitudes toward them and drug use rates of high school students." *Journal of Drug Education* 3:377–88 (1973).

Feldman, M. P. *Criminal Behavior: A Psychological Analysis*. London: Wiley, 1977.

Friedrichs, Robert W. "The potential impact of B. F. Skinner upon American sociology." *The American Sociologist* 9:3–8 (1974).

Geerken, Michael and Walter R. Gove. "Deterrence, overload, and incapacitation: an empirical evaluation." *Social Forces* 56:424–47 (1977).

Gibbs, Jack P. *Crime, Punishment and Deterrence*. New York: Elsevier, 1975.

_____. "Social control, deterrence, and perspectives on social order." *Social Forces* 56:408–23 (1977).

Groves, W. Eugene. "Patterns of college student use and lifestyles." Pp. 241–75 in Eric Josephson and Eleanor E. Carrol (eds.), *Drug Use: Epidemiological and Sociological Approaches*. New York: Wiley, 1974.

Hamblin, Robert L., David Buckholdt, Daniel Ferritor, Martin Kozloff and Lois Blackwell. *The Humanization Process: A Social Behavioral Analysis of Children's Problems*. New York: Wiley, 1971.

Hardt, Robert H. and Sandra Peterson-Hardt. "On determining the quality of the delinquency self-report method." *Journal of Research in Crime and Delinquency* 14:247–61 (1977).

Harris, Anthony R. "Imprisonment and the expected value of criminal choice: a specification and test of aspects of the labeling perspective." *American Sociological Review* 40:71–87 (1975).

_____. "Sex and theories of deviance: toward a functional theory of deviant typescripts." *American Sociological Review* 42:3–16 (1977).

Hirschi, Travis. *Causes of Delinquency*. Berkeley and Los Angeles: University of California Press, 1969.

Hirschi, Travis and Michael J. Hindelang. "Intelligence and delinquency: a revisionist review." *American Sociological Review* 42:571–87 (1977).

Homans, George C. *Social Behavior: Its Elementary Forms.* New York: Harcourt Brace Jovanovich, 1961.

Honig, Werner. *Operant Behavior: Areas of Research and Application.* New York: Appleton-Century-Crofts, 1966.

Jensen, Gary F. "Parents, peers and delinquent action: a test of the differential association perspective." *American Journal of Sociology* 78:63-72 (1972).

Jessor, Richard. "Predicting time of onset of marijuana use: a developmental study of high school youth." *Journal of Consulting and Clinical Psychology* 44:125-34 (1976).

Jessor, R., M. I. Collins and S. L. Jessor. "On becoming a drinker: social-psychological aspects of an adolescent transition." *Annals of the New York Academy of Science* 197:199-213 (1972).

Jessor, R., T. D. Graves, R. C. Hanson and S. L. Jessor. *Society, Personality and Deviant Behavior: A Study of a Tri-Ethnic Community.* New York: Holt, Rinehart and Winston, 1968.

Jessor, R. and S. L. Jessor. "Adolescent development and the onset of drinking: a longitudinal study." *Journal of Studies on Alcohol* 36:27-51 (1975).

_____. *Problem Behavior and Psychosocial Development: A Longitudinal Study of Youth.* New York: Academic Press, 1977.

Jessor, Richard, Shirley L. Jessor and John Finney. "A social psychology of marijuana use: longitudinal studies of high school and college youth." *Journal of Personality and Social Psychology* 26:1-15 (1973).

Jessor, R., H. B. Young, E. B. Young and G. Tesi. "Perceived opportunity, alienation, and drinking behavior among Italian and American youth." *Journal of Personality and Social Psychology* 15:215-22 (1970).

Johnston, L. *Drugs and American Youth.* Ann Arbor: Institute for Social Research, 1973.

Kandel, Denise. "Adolescent marijuana use: role of parents and peers." *Science* 181:1067-70 (1973).

_____. "Interpersonal influences on adolescent illegal drug use." Pp. 207-40 in Eric Josephson and Eleanor E. Carrol (eds.), *Drug Use: Epidemiological and Sociological Approaches.* New York: Wiley, 1974.

_____. *Longitudinal Research on Drug Use.* Ed. by D. Kandel. New York: Halsted, 1978.

Kendall, Richard Fenwick. *The Context and Implications of Drinking and Drug Use among High School and College Students.* Ph.D. dissertation, Department of Psychology, New York University, 1976.

Kim, Jae-On. "Multivariate analysis of ordinal variables," *American Journal of Sociology* 81:261-98 (1975).

Krohn, Marvin D. "An investigation of the effect of parental and peer associations on marijuana use: an empirical test of differential association theory." Pp. 75-89 in Marc Reidel and Terrence P. Thornberry (eds.), *Crime and Delinquency: Dimensions of Deviance.* New York: Praeger, 1974.

Kunkel, John R. *Behavior, Social Problems, and Change: A Social Learning Approach.* Englewood Cliffs: Prentice-Hall, 1975.

Kunkel, John H. and Richard H. Nagasawa. "A behavioral model of man: propositions and implications." *American Sociological Review* 38:530-43 (1973).

Labovitz, Sanford. "The assignment of numbers to rank order categories." *American Sociological Review* 35:515-24 (1970).

_____. "In defense of assigning numbers to ranks." *American Sociological Review* 36:521-22 (1971).

Lawrence, T. S. and J. O. Velleman. "Correlates of student drug use in a suburban high school." *Psychiatry* 37:129-36 (1974).

McLaughlin, Barry. *Learning and Social Behavior.* New York: Free Press, 1971.

Meier, Robert F. and Weldon T. Johnson. "Deterrence as social control: the legal and extralegal production of conformity." *American Sociological Review* 42:292-304 (1977).

National Commission on Marijuana and Drug Abuse. *Marijuana: A Signal of Misunderstanding.* New York: New American Library, 1972.

O'Donnell, John, Harwin L. Voss, Richard R. Clayton, and Robin G. W. Room. *Young Men and Drugs—A Nationwide Survey.*

Rockville: National Institute on Drug Abuse, 1976.

Pearce, J. and D. H. Garrett. "A comparison of the drinking behavior of delinquent youth versus non-delinquent youth in the states of Idaho and Utah." *Journal of School Health* 40;131–5 (1970).

Rachal, J. V., J. R. Williams, M. L. Brehm, B. Cavanaugh, R. P. Moore, and W. C. Eckerman. *Adolescent Drinking Behavior, Attitudes and Correlates.* National Institute on Alcohol Abuse and Alcoholism: U.S. Department of Health, Education and Welfare, Contract No. HSM 42-73-80 (NIA), 1975.

Radosevich, Marcia, Lonn Lanza-Kaduce, Ronald L. Akers and Marvin D. Krohn. "The sociology of adolescent drug and drinking behavior: a review of the state of the field: part 1,2." *Deviant Behavior: An Interdisciplinary Journal* (Forthcoming).

Rotter, Julian. *Social Learning and Clinical Psychology.* Englewood Cliffs: Prentice-Hall, 1954.

Short, James F. "Differential association and delinquency." *Social Problems* 4:233–9 (1957).

Silberman, Matthew. "Toward a theory of criminal deterrence." *American Sociological Review* 41:442–61 (1976).

Single, Eric, Denise Kandel and Bruce D. Johnson. "The reliability and validity of drug use responses in a large scale longitudinal survey." *Journal of Drug Issues* 5:426–43 (1975).

Skinner, B. F. *Science and Human Behavior.* New York. Macmillan, 1953.

————. *Cumulative Record.* New York: Appleton-Century-Crofts, 1959.

Spitzer, Steven. "Toward a marxian theory of deviance." *Social Problems* 22:638–51 (1975).

Staats, Arthur. *Social Behaviorism.* Homewood: Dorsey Press, 1975.

Sutherland, Edwin H. *Principles of Criminology.* 4th ed. Philadelphia: Lippincott, 1947.

Sutherland, Edwin H. and Donald R. Cressey. *Criminology.* 9th ed. Philadelphia: Lippincott, 1974.

Tarter, Donald E. "Heeding Skinner's call: toward the development of a social technology." *The American Sociologist* 8:153–8 (1973).

Taylor, Ian, Paul Walton and Jack Young. *The New Criminology: For a Social Theory of Deviance.* New York: Harper and Row, 1973.

Tec, Nechama. *Grass Is Green in Suburbia: A Sociological Study of Adolescent Usage of Illicit Drugs.* Roslyn Heights: Libra, 1974a.

————. "Parent child drug abuse: generational continuity or adolescent deviancy?" *Adolescence* 9:351–64 (1974b).

Thomas, Charles W., David M. Petersen and Matthew T. Zingraff. "Student drug use: a re-examination of the hang-loose ethic hypothesis." *Journal of Health and Social Behavior* (16:63–73 (1975).

Tittle, Charles R. "Deterrents or labeling?" *Social Forces* 53:399–410 (1975).

Ullmann, Leonard P. and Leonard Krasner. *A Psychological Approach to Abnormal Behavior.* Englewood Cliffs: Prentice-Hall, 1969.

Voss, Harwin. "Differential association and reported delinquent behavior: a replication." *Social Problems* 12:78–85 (1964).

Waldo, Gordon P. and Theodore Chiricos. "Perceived penal sanction and self-reported criminality: a neglected approach to deterrence research." *Social Problems* 19:522–40 (1972).

Wechsler, Henry and Denise Thum. "Teenage drinking, drug use, and social correlates." *Quarterly Journal of Studies on Alcohol* 34:1220–7 (1973).

Whitehead, P. C. and R. G. Smart. "Validity and reliability of self-reported drug use." *Canadian Journal of Criminology and Corrections* 14:1–8 (1972).

Scared Straight

8

Richard J. Lundman

On November 2, 1978, an independent television station in Los Angeles presented a film documentary entitled *Scared Straight.*[1] This documentary was a partial record of an intensive confrontation session between adult inmates serving long or life sentences at New Jersey's Rahway State Prison and juveniles brought to the prison in an effort to control their involvement in delinquency. On March 5, 1979, *Scared Straight* was shown on national television, although some local stations initially refused to air it because of its frank language and graphic scenes.[2] In April 1979, *Scared Straight* won an Academy Award for best film documentary.

State legislators and prison administrators were quick to take notice of *Scared Straight.* California legislators introduced a bill requiring the busing of 15,000 juveniles to state prisons for Rahway-type confrontation sessions. Alabama juveniles attended confrontation sessions where one

From *Prevention and Control of Juvenile Delinquency* by Richard J. Lundman. Copyright © 1984 by Oxford University Press, Inc. Reprinted by permission.

inmate told of being gang raped while in prison.[3] In New York City, children of 11 and 12 years of age were taken on tours of city jails.[4]

What attracted the attention of legislators and prison administrators were the claims of success advanced in *Scared Straight.* Of the 17 frequently and seriously delinquent juveniles appearing in the documentary, 16 were said to be straight three months later. This was said to be common. Of the nearly 8,000 juveniles attending intensive confrontation sessions at Rahway State Prison through 1978, *Scared Straight* reported that approximately 90 percent had not experienced further trouble with the law, a success rate "unequalled by traditional rehabilitation methods."

This chapter examines prison-based efforts to scare juveniles straight. It begins by demonstrating that Rahway-type programs are grounded in the deterrence approach to the control of juvenile delinquency. Attention is then directed to Professor James O. Finckenauer's assessment of Rahway's Juvenile Awareness Project. Last, review of three replicative efforts to scare juveniles straight is undertaken.

149

Deterrence Theory[5]

Central to the deterrence argument is the rational juvenile. Deterrence theorists assume that juveniles pause to calculate the possible consequences of releasing delinquent actions. If their calculations suggest that perceived benefits will exceed possible costs, then rational juveniles release delinquent actions hoping to enjoy the anticipated rewards. However, if these calculations lead juveniles to conclude that costs will exceed rewards, then the rational course of action is to seek gratification in ways other than delinquency.

Deterrence theorists therefore argue that certain, swift, and severe punishment will stop juveniles from committing delinquent acts. Certainty of punishment refers to the probability of apprehension once a delinquent act has been committed. Swiftness of punishment refers to the amount of time between the commission of a delinquent act and punishment for that act. Severity of punishment refers to the harshness of the sanctions applied to offenders.

Certain, swift, and severe punishment is thought to deter youthful criminal offenders in at least two ways. Specific deterrence occurs when juveniles are punished by the state for their delinquent actions. The experience of being caught and punished alerts the offender to the painful consequences of continued involvement in delinquency and pushes the juvenile in the direction of law-abiding behavior. General deterrence occurs when others learn of the punishment of juvenile offenders and suppress involvement in delinquency out of fear that the same sanctions will be applied to them.

Efforts to scare juveniles straight are grounded in the deterrence approach to juvenile delinquency,[6] especially insofar as the severity of punishment argument is concerned. During intensive confrontation sessions, adult inmates worked to alter juveniles' perceptions of the severity of punishment by telling them vivid tales of sad men living dangerous lives inside the walls of maximum-security prisons. The message conveyed was that deprivation, assault, rape, and murder were part of the prison experience. The threat was that if the juveniles continued their delinquent ways they too would end up behind bars.

The Rahway State Prison Juvenile Awareness Project

The Juvenile Awareness Project at New Jersey's Rahway State Prison is easily the best known and most controversial of prison-based efforts to scare juveniles straight. In addition to the Academy Award winning documentary, Rahway's program has been the subject of debate in the popular[7] and social science literature[8] and the topic of two books,[9] including one by Rutgers University criminologist James O. Finckenauer. Table 8.1 summarizes the major features of Professor Finckenauer's assessment of the Juvenile Awareness Project and serves as a guide for the description and analysis that follow.

Description of the Project[10]

The Juvenile Awareness Project began at Rahway State Prison in September 1976. It continues to operate, although controversy over the effects of the intensive confrontation sessions has decreased the number of juveniles attending. Professor Finckenauer reports that the "number of sessions declined from ten a week to about two per week; participation from two-hundred juveniles a week to about twenty-five. In January 1980, for example, only 134 juveniles visited the prison as opposed to more than

Table 8.1
Description of the Juvenile Awareness Project

Project Name	The Juvenile Awareness Project
Location	Rahway State Prison, Rahway, New Jersey
Dates	September, 1976 to present
Subjects	Over 13,000 juveniles have attended intensive confrontation sessions at Rahway. Very little is known about them.
Type of treatment	Juveniles are given a taste of the prison experience by taking a brief tour of Rahway State Prison and attending an intensive confrontation session run by inmates serving long or life sentences. During the intensive confrontation session, the most negative aspects of prison life are emphasized. The primary methods for describing prison life are shouted taunts and threats of sexual assault.
Amount of treatment	The tour and intensive confrontation session last three hours, with most of the time devoted to the confrontation with the adult inmates.
Evaluative design	Quasi-experimental: Although efforts were made to randomly assign subjects to experimental and control groups, assignment was ''not purely random'' for all subjects.
Measures of results	Information on attitude changes was collected between one day and nine months after the experimental subjects visited Rahway. Recidivism data were collected six months after their visit.
Replication	The Juvenile Awareness Project has been replicated on several occasions.

Source: James O. Finckenauer, *Scared Straight! and the Panacea Phenomenon.* Englewood Cliffs, N.J.: Prentice-Hall, 1982.

eight-hundred a month during the project's heyday.''[11]

Through May 1979 over 13,000 juveniles had attended intensive confrontation sessions run by adult inmates serving long or life sentences. According to the documentary *Scared Straight,* juveniles attending these sessions were ''chronic . . . young offenders already desensitized and willing to continue their petty careers as muggers, rip off artists, pick pockets, and so forth.''[12] Actually, very little is known about the over 13,000 juveniles who have attended intensive confrontation sessions at Rahway. Moreover, what little is known suggests that many were straight even before they were scared.

In June 1979, Jerome Miller, president of the National Center on Institutions and Alternatives, appeared before a United States House of Representatives subcommittee holding hearings on Rahway's Juvenile Awareness Project.[13] Dr. Miller testified that the young people who appeared in *Scared Straight* lived in a small, middle-class New Jersey suburb, one without a serious delinquency problem. The juveniles congregated in a local park and had agreed to participate when asked to do so by a local police sergeant. Dr. Miller also testified that he had visited the high school attended by the juveniles appearing in the documentary. He learned that of the 1,200 middle-class students, 450 had already attended sessions at Rahway and that the typical method of recruitment was to make an announcement over the school's loud-

Figure 8.1:   The Juvenile Awareness Project's deterrence hypothesis in diagrammatic form

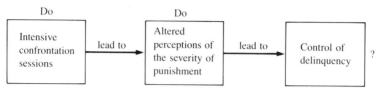

Source: The deterrence hypothesis is based on description of the Juvenile Awareness Project in James O. Finckenauer, *Scared Straight! and the Panacea Phenomenon*. Englewood Cliffs, N. J.: Prentice-Hall, 1982, pp. 29–44.

speaker. The apparent goal was to have all 1,200 students eventually attend sessions at Rahway.

Professor Finckenauer's data also challenge the image that juveniles attending Rahway sessions were seriously and frequently delinquent. As part of his assessment of the Juvenile Awareness Project, Professor Finckenauer found that 49 agencies had sent juveniles to Rahway in the three months ending in November 1977. He reported that most were counseling, educational, employment, and recreational organizations rather than agencies dealing exclusively with delinquent juveniles.[14] In addition, of the juveniles directly involved in his assessment of the project, 41.3 percent had no prior record of delinquency. Of those with a prior record, most had committed minor offenses.[15]

Type of Treatment

The Juvenile Awareness Project was designed to control delinquency by altering juveniles' perceptions of the severity of punishment for criminal acts.[16] It was hypothesized that attending intensive confrontation sessions would cause juveniles to refrain from delinquent acts out of fear that if they continued their delinquent ways they too could end up in a place like Rahway State Prison (see Figure 8.1).

The effort to alter juveniles' perceptions of the severity of punishment began with a brief tour of Rahway State Prison. The juveniles saw the crowded cells, heard the almost constant metal on metal sound of a maximum security institution, and listened to the verbal taunts of men who don't get to leave after only three hours. If the juveniles were attractive, inmates undoubtedly indicated what would happen to them in prison.

At the end of the brief tour, juveniles in groups of about 15 were taken to a room for an intensive confrontation session with about 20 adult inmates serving long or life sentences. During these sessions inmates attempted to "cover the full spectrum of crime and its nonrewards, . . . explain . . . about prison, crime and its ramifications, . . . show . . . young people that the stories about the big house . . . being the place of bad men is in all reality the place of sad men, . . . [and] prove the fact of what crime and its involvement is really all about."[17]

Explaining about crime and the reality of prison life involved shouting, swearing, and threats of physical abuse. What follows are some of the statements directed at the juveniles by the adult inmates:

I'm gonna hurt you.
You take something from me and I'll kill
     you.

You see them pretty blue eyes of yours?
 I'll take one out of your face and
 squish it in front of you.
Do you know what we see when we look
 at you—we see ourselves.
If someone had done this to me I wouldn't
 be here.
Who do you think we get? Young, tough
 mother fuckers like you. Get a pretty
 fat buck like you and stick a prick in
 your ass.[18]

However, confrontation sessions sometimes went beyond taunts and threats.
Jerome Miller testified that: "An earlier
study of the program sponsored by the New
Jersey Department of Corrections indicated that the Juvenile Awareness Program
had two primary techniques: (1) 'exaggera-
tion,' and (2) 'manhandling.' This latter
technique has probably led to certain incidents which have generally not been publicly known. We received allegations of
certain youngsters being culled about,
lifted by the head and shaken, 'goosed' or
pinched on their behind. We are also aware
of more serious allegations which we
would prefer to corroborate more completely before specifying."[19] Professor
Finckenauer reports much the same thing,
noting that some of the adolescent males attending sessions were "kissed and fon-
dled"[20] by inmates.

Evaluative Design

Professor Finckenauer's goal was to evaluate the Juvenile Awareness Project experimentally.[21] He secured the names of the 49
community agencies that had sent juveniles
to Rahway in the fall of 1977. He then selected a random sample of these agencies
(n = 28) and contacted them to determine
whether they would be willing to permit
random assignment of juveniles to an ex-

perimental and a control group. Of the
agencies contacted, 11 promised cooperation. However, only five of these agencies
actually abided by the random assignment
procedures. Of the other six agencies,
"two . . . took both experimental and controls to Rahway, . . . [t]wo other sponsors
failed to take the experimentals . . . as
scheduled, . . . [o]ne agency . . . twice
failed to show up at Rahway, . . . [and] one
other agency . . . backed out."[22]

These problems resulted in two important changes in Professor Finckenauer's
evaluation procedures. The projected sizes
of the comparison groups were reduced
from 50 each to 46 in the Rahway-visit
group and 35 in the control group. More
important, initial refusals by agencies to cooperate along with mistakes by cooperating
agencies in sending or failing to send experimental juveniles to Rahway resulted in a
quasi-experimental evaluative design.

Measures of Results

The extent to which attending intensive
confrontation sessions altered juveniles'
perceptions of the severity of punishment
was assessed by Professor Finckenauer using paper and pencil instruments. These instruments were designed to probe attitudes
toward prisons and punishment. Professor
Finckenauer found that attending intensive
confrontation sessions did not alter juveniles' perceptions of the severity of punishment.[23]

Attending intensive confrontation sessions also did not lead to control of juvenile
delinquency (see Table 8.2). Among juveniles visiting Rahway, 41.3 percent committed a new offense during the six months
following their visit. By comparison, only
11.4 percent of the juveniles in the control
group committed a new offense during that
same time period. The Juvenile Awareness

Table 8.2

Juvenile Awareness Project: Percent Experimental and Control Group Subjects Committing New Recorded Offense in the Six Months Following an Intensive Confrontation Session at Rahway State Prison

Group	New Recorded Offense	No New Recorded Offense	Totals
Experimental	41.3%	58.7%	100%
			($n = 46$)
Control	11.4	88.6	100
			($n = 35$)

Source: James O. Finckenauer, *Scared Straight! and the Panacea Phenomenon*. Englewood Cliffs, N.J.: Prentice-Hall, 1982, p. 135. Copyright © 1982 by Prentice-Hall, Inc. Reprinted by permission.

Project not only failed to control delinquency, but it apparently made things worse as well.

Replication

Although the Juvenile Awareness Project at Rahway State Prison is easily the best-known effort to scare juveniles straight, it was not the first such attempt. Some 15 years earlier a nearly identical project took place at the Michigan Reformatory with results strikingly similar to those reported by Professor Finckenauer. This section therefore stretches the meaning of replication by beginning with an examination of the Michigan Reformatory Visitation Program. Attention is then directed to two true replications of the Juvenile Awareness Project.

Michigan Reformatory Visitation Program[24]

Table 8.3 summarizes the major features of the Michigan Reformatory Visitation Program. When the program began in the early 1960s at the Michigan Reformatory in Ionia, Michigan, the institution was already 100 years old and showing its age. Surrounded by walls over 18 feet high, the Michigan Reformatory was overcrowded

and barely able to meet the needs of young male inmates who were serving "unusually long sentences, who . . . [were] . . . an escape risk or . . . who . . . [had] . . . been unresponsive to treatment programs in other facilities. . ."[25]

Very little is known about the juveniles who met with inmates at the Michigan Reformatory. Other than their residence in Ingham County some 40 miles southeast of the reformatory, all that is known is that they were male and had been adjudicated delinquent. The age, race, and social class of the juveniles as well as the types of offenses they had committed are all unknown.

However, it is possible to infer two of these characteristics: the severity of their offenses and their age. The juveniles involved were likely on probation since one purpose of the program was to act as a "catalyst to later counseling." It also is likely that the juveniles had not been previously incarcerated since it would make little sense to take them on a visit to the type of place they were already familiar with. Given their apparent probationary status and likely lack of previous institutionalization, it seems reasonable to assume that they were young and placed on probation for status or minor criminal offenses.

Little also is known about the nature of the treatment juveniles received at the Michigan Reformatory. The brief report describing the project indicates that they visited the reformatory and met with the young inmates serving long or life sentences. It is unlikely, however, that they were shouted at or physically threatened by the inmates. The report describing the program calls the trip to the reformatory a "visit," not an intensive confrontation session. Additionally, adults were not as worried about the delinquent actions of juveniles in the mid-1960s[26] and thus not as likely to permit inmates to verbally and physically threaten young offenders.

What does seem likely is that the juveniles toured the facility, talked with administrators and perhaps custodial personnel, and then met with the young adult inmates. They certainly saw the old and imposing reformatory grounds, witnessed the regimentation of life in an overcrowded institution, and listened to inmates' descriptions of the "pains of imprisonment."[27] It appears most

accurate to view the juveniles' visit as similar to a school field trip, albeit one to an odd location.

Other aspects of the Michigan Reformatory Visitation Program are certain, with two of prime importance. First, the visitation program was one of the first-known attempts to scare juveniles straight by showing young offenders "the ultimate consequences of delinquency."[28] Second, the project was experimentally evaluated. Members of the Ingham County juvenile court staff furnished Michigan Department of Corrections research personnel with the names of juveniles about to visit the Michigan Reformatory. Using a table of random numbers, research personnel assigned juveniles to the experimental visitation group or to a control group that did not visit the reformatory.

The results of the visitation program were assessed using juvenile court records obtained six months after the experimental group visited the reformatory. Among juveniles visiting the reformatory, 43 percent had a court petition or probation violation

Table 8.3
Description of the Michigan Reformatory Visitation Program

Project Name	The Michigan Reformatory Visitation Program
Location	Michigan Reformatory, Ionia, Michigan
Dates	Early 1960s to May 1967
Subjects	Males residing in Ingham County and sentenced to probation
Type of treatment	Juveniles visited the Michigan Reformatory and met with young inmates serving long or life sentences.
Amount of treatment	Likely a single-day field trip to the reformatory.
Evaluative design	Experimental: Juveniles about to visit the reformatory were randomly assigned either to make the trip or to a control group.
Measures of results	Juvenile court records were checked for the six months following the visit to the reformatory.

Source: Michigan Department of Corrections, Research Report #4, "A Six-Month Follow-up of Juvenile Delinquents Visiting the Ionia Reformatory," Program Bureau, Michigan Department of Corrections, Stevens T. Mason Building, Lansing, Mich. 48913, May 22, 1967. This report is reprinted in James O. Finckenauer, *Scare Straight! and the Panacea Phenomenon.* Englewood Cliffs, N.J.: Prentice-Hall, 1982, pp. 59–61.

Table 8.4
Michigan Reformatory Visitation Program: Percent Experimental and Control Group Subjects with Probation Violations or Court Petitions in the Six Months Following a Visit to the Michigan Reformatory

Group	Probation Violation or Court Petition	No Probation Violation or Court Petition	Totals
Experimental	43%	57%	100% (n = 28)
Control	17	83	100 (n = 30)

Source: Michigan Department of Corrections, ''A Six-Month Follow-up of Juvenile Delinquents Visiting the Ionia Reformatory,'' Program Bureau, Michigan Department of Corrections, Stevens T. Mason Building, Lansing, Mich. 48913, May 22, 1967, Research Report #4, p. 3. Reprinted by permission.

entered on their records as compared to only 17 percent of the juveniles in the control group (see Table 8.4). Clearly, visiting a reformatory did not control delinquency. On the contrary, visits to the Michigan Reformatory, as was true of intensive confrontation sessions at Rahway State Prison some 15 years later, increased involvement in delinquency.

Juvenile Offenders Learn Truth (JOLT)[29]

Prior to Professor Finckenauer's assessment of the effectiveness of Rahway's Juvenile Awareness Project, efforts to scare juveniles straight were fast becoming a major juvenile justice system fad.[30] Prompted by claims of success advanced in the film *Scared Straight* and elsewhere,[31] states created similar programs in their maximum security institutions involving thousands of juveniles. Attention is now directed to the results of two of these programs, starting with Michigan's Juvenile Offenders Learn Truth (JOLT).

Table 8.5 summarizes the major features of JOLT. JOLT was located at the State Prison of Southern Michigan, the world's largest walled prison.[32] It was begun by the Jaycee chapter at the prison in

the wake of initially positive reports of the effectiveness of Rahway's Juvenile Awareness Project. JOLT was then suspended in July 1979 following release of an initial evaluation of its effectiveness.

JOLT sessions were limited to adolescent males living in three contiguous Michigan counties—Wayne (which encompasses metropolitan Detroit), Washtenaw, and Jackson. Sessions were also limited to juveniles with a record of delinquency, as evidenced by a prior arrest or petition to juvenile court, and a parent or legal guardian willing to accompany them to the prison. Juveniles meeting these criteria during the time JOLT was evaluated averaged 15.45 years of age, and nearly one-half were black.

JOLT's purpose was to "deter juvenile delinquents from further criminal offenses."[33] Juveniles and their parent or guardian began their two-and-one-half-hour visit with a brief tour of the prison. Juveniles were then separated from the accompanying adults, searched and fingerprinted, and locked in an empty cell for a few minutes. While locked in the cell, juveniles were taunted and harassed by real inmates in nearby cells. Following this brief introduction to prison life, juveniles were taken to a small room for an intensive confrontation session with selected inmates. James C. Yarbo-rough, Chief of Research, Program Bureau, Michigan Department of Corrections, described a typical confrontation as "somewhat like the session depicted in the film documentary, *Scared Straight*, as far as format and structure are concerned. However, differences do exist which primarily involve language and tactics. For example, while 'street language' is used during JOLT sessions, it does not contain the extreme obscenities used in the New Jersey program. Gross verbal intimidation is also avoided. The message being delivered, however, is essentially the same: if you continue to engage in delinquent and criminal behavior, you may in time find yourself a prisoner confined in an institution like Jackson, and that the 'pains of imprisonment' and their consequences will then become a reality of considerable duration rather than a momentary pretense."[34]

JOLT was experimentally evaluated. When a county JOLT coordinator had assembled a list of juveniles eligible to make the visit to the prison, their identification numbers were reported to the Department of Correction's research office for random assignment to the experimental and control groups. The JOLT coordinator was then informed of the results of the random assignment procedure and arranged for the experimental juveniles to visit the prison.

Measures of involvement in delinquency were collected three and six months following the visit to the prison by the juveniles in the experimental group. Table 8.6 contains the six-month-follow-up data. Examination reveals virtually no differences between the two groups of juveniles in rates of recidivism: 30.8 percent of the juveniles who had visited the prison had one or more criminal charges filed against them as compared to

Table 8.5

Description of Juvenile Offenders Learn Truth (JOLT)

Project Name	JOLT
Location	State Prison of Southern Michigan, Jackson, Michigan
Dates	May 1978 to July 1979
Subjects	Juveniles residing in three Michigan counties: Wayne, Washtenaw, and Jackson. To be considered eligible, juveniles had to be male, have a prior record as evidenced by an arrest or court petition for a criminal offense, and be accompanied to the prison by a parent or legal guardian. Juveniles attending sessions averaged 15.45 years of age, and nearly one-half were black.
Type of treatment	The major part of the tour consisted of an "intensive confrontation session." Adult inmates used "street language" to describe prison life and to suggest what might happen to the juveniles if they continued their delinquent ways.
Amount of treatment	The tour and confrontation session together lasted two and one-half hours.
Evaluative design	Experimental: Juveniles about to visit the prison were randomly assigned either to make the trip or to a control group.
Measures of results	Criminal offenses charged in the six months following the visit to the prison by the juveniles in the experimental group were used to measure results.

Source: James C. Yarborough, "Evaluation of JOLT as a Deterrence Program," Program Bureau, Michigan Department of Corrections, Stevens T. Mason Building, Lansing, Mich. 48913, July 18, 1979. JOLT is briefly described in James O. Finckenauer, *Scared Straight! and the Panacea Phenomenon*. Englewood Cliffs, N.J.: Prentice-Hall, 1982, pp. 217–18.

28.9 percent of the juveniles in the control group.

The Insiders Juvenile Crime Prevention Program[35]

Table 8.7 summarizes the major features of The Insiders Juvenile Crime Prevention Program, a project that began at the Virginia State Penitentiary in Richmond in November 1978. Through June 1979, approximately 600 juveniles and young adults had attended "shock-confrontation lectures" at the penitentiary. All of those attending were between the ages of 13 and 20

Table 8.6

Juvenile Offenders Learn Truth (JOLT): Percent Experimental and Control Group Subjects Charged with Criminal Offense(s) in the Six Months Following an Intensive Confrontation Session at the State Prison of Southern Michigan

Group	One or More Criminal Charges	No Criminal Charges	Totals
Experimental	30.8%	69.2%	100% ($n = 39$)
Control	28.9	71.1	100 ($n = 45$)

Source: James C. Yarborough, "Evaluation of JOLT as a Deterrence Program," Program Bureau, Michigan Department of Corrections, Stevens T. Mason Building, Lansing, Mich. 48913, July 18, 1979, Table 26B. Reprinted by permission.

Table 8.7

Description of The Insiders Juvenile Crime Prevention Program

Project Name	The Insiders Juvenile Crime Prevention Program
Location	Virginia State Penitentiary, Richmond, Virginia
Dates	November 1978 to present
Subjects	As of June 1979, approximately 600 juveniles and young adults had attended "shock-confrontation lectures" at the penitentiary. All were between the ages of 13 and 20 and had been convicted of at least two criminal acts.
Type of treatment	Those visiting the penitentiary are given a taste of prison life by being searched, briefly locked in a prison cell, and exposed to a shock-confrontation lecture designed to "deter them from a life of crime and incarceration."
Amount of treatment	The visit takes approximately three hours, with two hours devoted to the shock-confrontation lecture.
Evaluative design	Experimental: Once court personnel had selected individuals to visit the penitentiary, subjects were randomly assigned to make the visit or to a control group.
Measures of results	Petitions to court 6, 9, and 12 months after the visit of the experimental subjects to the penitentiary were used to measure results.

Source: Stan Orchowsky and Keith Taylor, "The Insiders Juvenile Crime Prevention Program: An Assessment of a Juvenile Awareness Program." Research and Reporting Unit, Division of Program Development and Evaluation, Virginia Department of Corrections, August 1981. Report No. 79111.

Table 8.8

The Insiders Program: Percent of Experimental and Control Subjects to Court and Average Number of Court Intakes in the 6, 9, and 12 Months Following an Intensive Confrontation Session at the Virginia State Penitentiary

	6 Months		9 Months		12 Months	
Group	To Court	Average Number of Court Intakes[a]	To Court	Average Number of Court Intakes[a]	To Court	Average Number of Court Intakes[a]
Experimental	41% (16 of 39)	0.49	43% (10 of 23)[b]	0.48	47% (8 of 17)[d]	0.53
Control	39 (16 of 41)	0.61	67 (16 of 24)[c]	1.04	68 (13 of 19)[e]	1.27

a. Adjusted mean to "control for the small amout of variability . . . that could be accounted for by pre-insiders scores."
b. At the time the evaluation was undertaken only 23 experimental group juveniles had been out of treatment for 9 months.
c. At the time the evaluation was undertaken only 24 of the control group juveniles were available for analysis.
d. At the time the evaluation was undertaken only 17 experimental group juveniles had been out of treatment for 12 months.
e. At the time the evaluation was undertaken only 19 of the control group juveniles were available for analysis.
Source: Stan Orchowsky and Keith Taylor, "The Insiders Juvenile Crime Prevention Program: An Assessment of a Juvenile Awareness Program." Research and Reporting Unit, Division of Program Development and Evaluation, Virginia Department of Corrections, P.O. Box 26963, Richmond, Va. 23261, August 1981, pp. 23, 24, 27, 28, 31, and 32. Report No. 79111. Reprinted by permission.

and had been convicted of at least two criminal offenses.

The purpose of the Insiders Program is to "demonstrate the realities of prison life to hard-core youthful offenders in an effort to deter them from a life of crime and incarceration."[36] Juveniles and young adults visiting the penitentiary are searched, stripped of their personal possessions, and then briefly locked in a cell. The major part of their three-hour visit is devoted to a shock-confrontation lecture "full of very explicit, descriptive, and loud street language. . . . Inmates tell juveniles of murder, drugs, prison gangs, and homosexual rape that go on inside the prison, and are threatened that this will be part of their experience if they continue their life of crime."[37]

The Insiders Program was experimentally evaluated and court appearance measures were collected after 6, 9, and 12 months for both groups (see Table 8.8). After 6 months there were no important differences between experimental and control subjects. However 9 and 12 months after a visit to the penitentiary more control subjects had been to court at least once. In addition, control subjects had averaged more than twice as many court intakes. Although the data are incomplete 9 and 12 months following treatment, The Insiders Program apparently controlled delinquency.

Summary and Conclusions

This chapter examined prison-based efforts to scare juveniles straight. It began by showing that Rahway-type programs are grounded in the deterrence approach to the control of juvenile delinquency. Attention was then directed to Professor James O. Finckenauer's assessment of the Juvenile Awareness Project at New Jersey's Rahway State Prison. Last, review of three replicative efforts to scare juveniles straight was undertaken.

The results of these projects vary considerably. Rahway's Juvenile Awareness

Project and the Michigan Reformatory Visitation Program increased rather than decreased involvement in delinquency. JOLT at the State Prison of Southern Michigan had no effect on rates of involvement in delinquency. However, The Insiders Program at the Virginia State Penitentiary apparently controlled delinquency.

In addition to incomplete data,[38] the other important difference between the four projects examined in this chapter is the length of follow-up. The three projects that failed to control delinquency suspended follow-up measures after six months. The single project that apparently controlled delinquency extended follow-up to 9 and 12 months after treatment[39] and revealed a sleeper effect not apparent after 6 months.

What is unclear is why juveniles and young adults would be more scared 9 and 12 months after an intensive confrontation session than 6.[40]

Although new programs to scare juveniles straight continue to emerge . . ., the only conclusion that can be drawn is that such efforts produce mixed results. Intensive confrontation sessions sometimes increase involvement in delinquency. On other occasions they have no measurable impact. On still other occasions they apparently control delinquency. At best, scaring juveniles is not the panacea[41] for the problem of delinquency. At worst, scaring juveniles invites more rather than less delinquency.

Notes

1. Description of the film *Scared Straight* is based on notes I took when it was shown in Columbus, Ohio, on May 16, 1979. Other sources consulted include Aric Press and Donna Foote, "Does 'Scaring' Work?" *Newsweek,* May 14, 1979, p. 131; James O. Finchenauer, *Scared Straight! and the Panacea Phenomenon.* Englewood Cliffs, N.J.: Prentice-Hall, 1982, pp. 91–110; National Center on Institutions and Alternatives, *Scared Straight: A Second Look.* 1337 22nd Street, N.W., Washington, D.C. 20037, undated; James O. Finckenauer, "Juvenile Awareness Project: Evaluation Report No. 2," unpublished paper, Rutgers University School of Criminal Justice, April 18, 1979; and Testimony Before the Subcommittee on Human Resources, United States House of Representatives, by Jerome G. Miller and Herbert H. Hoelter, Hearings on Rahway State Prison "Juvenile Awareness Project" and the "Scared Straight" Film, June 4, 1979. The last source will hereafter be identified as Subcommittee, *Rahway State Prison.*

2. For example, *Scared Straight* was not shown in Columbus, Ohio, until May 16, 1979.

3. Press and Foote, "Does 'Scaring' Work?"

4. Subcommittee, *Rahway State Prison,* p.3. For a description of the very real possibilities of being raped while in prison, see Alan J. Davis, "Sexual Assaults in the Philadelphia Prison System," in David M. Petersen and Charles W. Thomas (eds.), *Corrections: Problems and Prospects,* Second Edition. Englewood Cliffs, N.J.: Prentice-Hall, 1980, pp. 102–13.

5. For an excellent description and analysis of deterrence theory, see Jack P. Gibbs, *Crime, Punishment, and Deterrence.* New York: Elsevier, 1975.

6. Finckenauer, *Scared Straight,* pp. 29–63.

7. Press and Foote, "Does 'Scaring' Work?"; and Eileen Keerdoja et al., "Prison Program Gets a New Boost," *Newsweek,* November 3, 1980, p. 16.

8. Finckenauer, *Scared Straight*, pp. 190–208.

9. Finckenauer, *Scared Straight*; and Sidney Langer, *Scared Straight? Fear in the Deterrence of Delinquency.* Washington, D.C.: University Press of America, 1982.

10. Description of Professor Finckenauer's evaluative efforts is based on Finckenauer, "Juvenile Awareness Project"; and Finckenauer, *Scared Straight.*

11. Finckenauer, *Scared Straight*, p. 196.

12. Notes taken during showing of *Scared Straight* in Columbus, Ohio, on May 16, 1979.

13. Subcommittee, *Rahway State Prison.*

14. Finckenauer, *Scared Straight*, p. 118. Also see National Center, *Scared Straight*, p. 7, where it is asserted that "40 to 60% of the juveniles who were visiting Rahway had never been inside an institution, gone to court, or even had a police record."

15. Finckenauer, "Juvenile Awareness Project," p. 7. Also see Finckenauer, *Scared Straight*, pp. 111–12.

16. Finckenauer, *Scared Straight*, pp. 29–44.

17. Cited in National Center, *Scared Straight*, p. 6.

18. From notes I took when *Scared Straight* was shown in Columbus, Ohio, on May 16, 1979.

19. Subcommittee, *Rahway State Prison,* pp. 14–15.

20. Finckenauer, *Scared Straight*, p. 85.

21. Finckenauer, *Scared Straight*, p. 111–31.

22. Finckenauer, *Scared Straight*, p. 121.

23. Finckenauer, *Scared Straight*, p. 156–70.

24. This section is based on Research Report #4, Michigan Department of Corrections, "A Six-Month Follow-up of Juvenile Delinquents Visiting the Ionia Reformatory," May 22, 1967. I thank James C. Yarborough, Chief of Research, Program Bureau, Department of Corrections, Stevens T. Mason Building, Lansing, Mich. 48913 for having the report retyped and sent along to me. The report has since been reprinted in Finckenauer, *Scared Straight*, pp. 59–61.

25. Michigan Department of Corrections, *Dimensions: A Report of the Michigan Department of Corrections.* Lansing, Mich.: Michigan Department of Corrections, Fall 1976, p. 44. I again thank James C. Yarborough for providing me with a copy of this report and for assuring me in a letter dated October 20, 1980, "that there has been little if any change" in the Michigan Reformatory since the mid-1960s, the time of the Michigan Reformatory Visitation Program.

26. Writing in 1973, Edwin M. Schur argued that the deterrence approach "does not at present exert a significant influence on delinquency policies." See Edwin M. Schur, *Radical Non-Intervention: Rethinking The Delinquency Problem.* Englewood Cliffs, N.J.: Prentice-Hall, 1973, p. 19.

27. For a discussion of the pains of imprisonment, see Gresham M. Sykes, *The Society of Captives: A Study of Maximum Security Prison.* Princeton, N.J.: Princeton University Press, 1958. Three more recent and equally useful descriptions and analyses of prison life are John Irwin, *Prisons in Turmoil,* Boston: Little, Brown, 1980; James B. Jacobs, *Stateville: The Penitentiary in Mass Society.* Chicago: The University of Chicago Press, 1977; and Hans Toch, *Living in Prison: The Ecology of Survival.* New York: Free Press, 1977.

28. Research Report, "A Six-Month Follow-Up," p. 1.

29. This section is based on James C. Yarborough, "Evaluation of JOLT as a Deterrence Program," Program Bureau, Michigan Department of Corrections, July 18, 1979, Stevens T. Mason Building, Lansing, Mich. 48913. I thank James C. Yarborough for sending me a copy of this paper.

30. For a discussion of the recurrent fads characteristic of efforts to control delinquency, see John R. Stratton and Robert M. Terry (eds.), *Prevention of Delinquency: Problems and Programs.* New York: Macmillan, 1968, pp. 2–3; James C. Hackler, *The Prevention of Youthful Crime: The Great Stumble Forward.* Toronto: Methuen, 1978, pp. 8–22; and Finckenauer, *Scared Straight*, pp. 3–6.

31. Numerous newspaper articles also con-

tained claims of success. See Finckenauer, *Scared Straight*, pp. 91–107 and 179–82.

32. Michigan Department of Corrections, *Dimensions,* pp. 35–39. The "world's largest prison" in terms of total walled acreage.

33. Yarborough, "Evaluation of JOLT," p. 1.

34. Yarborough, "Evaluation of JOLT," p. 3.

35. Description of the Insiders Program is based on Stan Orchowsky and Keith Taylor, "The Insiders Juvenile Crime Prevention Program: An Assessment of a Juvenile Awareness Program." Research and Reporting Unit, Division of Program Development and Evaluation, Virginia Department of Corrections, August, 1981, Report No. 79111. I thank Stan Orchowsky for sending me a copy of this report.

36. Orchowsky and Taylor, "The Insiders," p. 11.

37. Orchowsky and Taylor, "The Insiders," p. 11.

38. I called Mr. Orchowsky on March 10, 1983, to ask whether the incomplete data had been collected. He indicated that the data were still incomplete.

39. Langer, *Scared Straight*, conducted an evaluation of the Rahway program and found there were few important differences between comparison groups after six months. After 22 months, however, there were clear and important differences that favored the juveniles who attended an intensive confrontation session at Rahway. Evidence of delayed effects, then, is not limited to the Orchowsky and Taylor evaluation of the Insiders Program.

40. One possibility is that juveniles initially dismiss the possibility of being punished but with time and a larger number of brushes with the law they link their delinquent actions with what they saw and heard during their visit to a prison. Social psychologists call this phenomenon the "sleeper effect." For a brief discussion of the sleeper effect, see Carol H. Weiss, *Evaluation Research: Methods of Assessing Program Effectiveness.* Englewood Cliffs, N.J.: Prentice-Hall, 1972, p. 31.

41. Finckenauer. *Scared Straight*, pp. 3–28 and passim.

PART 4

Social Structural and Institutional Influences on Delinquency

In the previous section, we laid the foundation for a broader sociological theory of delinquency by examining social psychological aspects of delinquent behavior. In this section, we focus on social structural and institutional influences.

Sociologists are fond of the term *social structure*. The term is generally employed as a metaphor "for describing social interaction and relations that endure over time" (Turner, 1986:407). The concept conveys the idea that societies are organized to ensure their survival and provide their members with basic needs. Different societies do this more or less successfully. Members of a society are distributed, whether by birth (ascribed social status) or personal effort (achieved social status), into various social roles, groups, and classes. According to their position in the social structure, people have at their disposal different amounts of valued resources, as well as varying external constraints placed on their behavior. Thus, while people may, to some extent, be free to behave as they wish, they must do so under a particular set of social conditions which place limitations on the range of opportunities that are available to them (see Matza, 1964).

Social *institutions* are one of the most important aspects of social structure. Social institutions—such as the family, school, and economy—are designed to help societies meet one or more of their basic needs. When these institutions break down or fail to perform their basic functions, societies may have difficulty ensuring the cooperation of their members, and problems of crime and delinquency may develop.

Sociologists have developed various theories to help explain how social structures and institutions influence crime and delinquent behavior. The readings in this section have selected to convey an appreciation of these ideas. The articles focus on social influences related to the family, schooling, peer groups, the economy, and the community. They also include a consideration of major sociological theories such as social control theory, anomie-opportunity or strain theory, and others. All the readings imply, if not directly address, implications for the prevention of delinquency.

It becomes easy to get bogged down in a consideration of one theory after another, or one cause of delinquency after another, and surprisingly few attempts have been made to integrate theories into a coherent and comprehensive perspective (see Colvin and Pauly, 1983; Elliott et al., 1979; Gibbs, 1987; Thornberry, 1987). While different explanations compete with one another to satisfy standards of scientific (research) confirmation, it is also useful to view them as complementary, each being designed to illuminate one or more aspects of the complex problem of delinquency. For instance, social learning theory, as Akers et al. pointed out in the previous section (Chapter 7), may be viewed as "complementary to other sociological theories and could be used to integrate extant formulations to achieve more comprehensive explanations."

The first article in this section (Chapter 9) is Joseph Rankin and L. Edward Wells's "The Preventive Effects of the Family on Delinquency." Rankin and Wells focus on family problems related to "broken homes." They review research in this area, discuss different theoretical perspectives on the family's role in delinquency, and evaluate various preventive and treatment approaches.

Rankin and Wells distinguish between family "structure" (the number of parents in the home) and family "process" (the quality of family relationships or interaction), and find that the latter is far more important. Their interpretation of the evidence is consistent with the larger body of literature on the family and delinquency. While early studies using official statistics found children from non-traditional ("broken home")[1] families having higher rates of delinquency, self-report studies found that family structure was not the important family variable that influenced delinquency.[2] More important than family structure were factors related to family process or interaction, such as the degree of parental affection and supervision exercised toward children, the effectiveness of parental communication with children, the presence or absence of conflict in the home, and the marital adjustment of parents (Laub and Sampson, 1988; Rosen; 1985; Voorhis et al., 1988; Wells and Rankin, 1988). In fact, Cernkovich and Giordano (1987) found that several family process variables had similar effects on delinquency regardless of family structure.

On the other hand, elements of family structure may be indirectly related to delinquency as they are associated with other variables, such as social class (Rosen, 1985).[3] For instance, Sampson (1987) found that the percent of black households headed by females, as well as black crime rates, were influenced by the rate of black male joblessness. Similarly, while juveniles from large families were found to have higher rates of delinquency, these families were highly associated with low socioeconomic status, limited interaction and communication between parents and children, and less supervision by parents of each child (Hirschi, 1983: Rutter, 1980; Wadsworth, 1979).[4]

Family studies have also found inconsistent and overly permissive or harsh discipline to be related to delinquency (Patterson, 1982; Patterson and Stouthamer-Loeber, 1984). In addition, although the results have been mixed, several studies found that physical abuse of children by parents increased violence among some males, and that both male and female victims of abuse had higher rates of delinquency than non-abused youth (Kruttschnitt et al., 1986,; Widom, 1988). However, one recent study found that exposure to family violence was associated only with higher rates of delinquency among black male juveniles, but not white males (Kruttschnitt et al., 1986). Additionally, females appeared to respond to abuse (both physical and sexual) in less aggressive ways than males, being likely to run away from home and experience symptoms of psychological stress such as depression (Herman, 1981; Janus et al., 1987; Widom, 1988).[5]

Unfortunately, it has been difficult for researchers to disentangle the effects of abuse from other family problems and the relationship between abuse and delinquency is still not well understood. While there has been some support for a social learning explanation of the relationship between family violence and delinquency (through imitation and modeling, ''violence begets violence''), ''the pathway from childhood victimization to . . . criminal behavior is far from inevitable'' (Widom, 1988:266). However, exposure to family violence does appear to have a greater effect on juvenile violence than does exposure to media violence (Kruttschnitt et al., 1986).[6]

Many sociologists prefer to use Travis Hirschi's (1969) *social control theory*, also known as *social bond theory*, to explain the family's effects on delinquency, and Rankin and Wells (Chapter 9) discuss this theory in their article.[7] Hirschi bypasses the question of how individuals develop a motivation for delinquency. He assumes that ''human self-interest provides sufficient motivation to crime,'' so that it is conformity that needs to be explained (Paternoster and Triplett, 1988:596). Conformity arises if, through the socialization process, persons establish a ''bond'' with the conventional social order.

> The primary mechanisms that bind adolescents to the conventional world are attachment to parents, commitment to school, and belief in conventional values . . . Whenever [these] bonds . . . are substantially weakened, the individual is freed from moral constraints and is at risk . . . of . . . delinquency (Thornberry, 1987:873).

During early adolescence, parents are especially important agents of social control since ''the family is the most salient arena for social interaction and involvement'' at this stage of life (p. 873).

While Hirschi's theory has received considerable empirical support, the evidence appears most compelling as an explanation of minor delinquency rather than serious delinquency, of the onset of delinquency rather than the continuation of delinquency, and of delinquency in early rather than late adolescence (see Hirschi, 1969; Krohn and Massey, 1980; LaGrange and White, 1985; Wiatrowski et al., 1981). Moreover, as Thornberry (1987:874) notes:

> . . . attachment to parents is not . . . an immutable trait, impervious to the effects of other variables. Indeed, associating with delinquent peers, not being committed to school, and engaging in delinquent behavior are so contradictory to parental expectations that they tend to diminish the level of attachment between parent and child (see Liska and Reed, 1985).

Thus, although parental-family factors influence youths' commitment to school and susceptibility to delinquent peers, these later variables have dynamics of their own, and appear to be even more predictive of delinquency (see Agnew, 1985; Akers and Cochran, 1985; Cernkovich and Giordano, 1987; LaGrange and White, 1985; Krohn and Massey, 1980; Matsueda, 1982; Paternoster and Triplett, 1988; Wiatrowski et al., 1981).

In the second reading in this section (Chapter 10), David Greenberg's "Delinquency and the Age Structure of Society" brings together a wide range of sociological literature to analyze why crime rates peak during adolescence. Unlike Hirschi, Greenberg is concerned with understanding delinquent motivations. He reviews the contributions and limitations of *anomie-opportunity theory*, often referred to as *strain theory*, including its initial propositions as developed by Merton (1938) and its later application to delinquent subcultures as formulated by Cloward and Ohlin (1960) and Cohen (1955). Greenberg also reviews other literature that addresses problems associated with schooling, peer groups, and masculine anxiety. In addition, he draws upon a tradition of control theory that considers the potential costs to juveniles of being apprehended by the law. (To avoid confusion from overlapping terminology, the reader should note that Greenberg's use of control theory is more similar to the rational-choice/deterrence approach discussed in the previous section than it is to Hirschi's version of control theory.) Finally, Greenberg concludes by offering a Marxian-oriented analysis of juveniles' deteriorating labor market position in capitalist society.

Additional analysis of the school–delinquency relationship is presented in the third reading (Chapter 11). In their article on "The Effect of Dropping Out of High School on Subsequent Criminal Behavior," Terence Thornberry and associates note the divergent predictions made by strain and control theories regarding the crimonogenic effects of dropping out of school. They review previous research, which found that delinquency actually *decreased* following dropping out of school, and present the results of new research that attempts to resolve this question.

In the fourth selection (Chapter 12), Ronald Berger's "Organizing the Community for Delinquency Prevention" focuses on delinquency prevention programs that have attempted to mobilize the community to tackle problems of social disorganization, economic disadvantage, and lack of societal resources. He discusses and evaluates three models of community organization practice— locality development, social planning, and social action—through an appraisal of the Chicago Area Project (begun in the 1930s), the 1960s provision of opportunity programs, and the 1960s comprehensive community action projects such as Mobilization for Youth. Berger also considers more recent community prevention programs.

In the fifth article (Chapter 13), Clayton Hartjen's "Delinquency, Development, and Social Integration in India" offers the reader a comparative perspective by examining a society where serious problems of crime and delinquency are absent. Hartjen notes the importance of studying societies where delinquency is low in order to gain insights about the development and control of delinquent behavior. He analyzes the features of India's agrarian economy that promote family integration and that prevent the rise of an autonomous adolescent subculture. Hartjen's analysis suggests how the economic organization of a society has a significant impact on other social institutions such as the family.[8]

In the final reading in this section (Chapter 14), Ronald Berger returns to some issues first raised in Chapter 5 and reviews various sociological attempts at "Explaining Female Delinquency in the Emancipation Era." In particular, he considers the contributions of social control, power-control, strain, subcultural, and feminist theories.

Notes

1. The term "broken homes" has negative connotations, and it is perhaps preferable to use the term "non-traditional" or "alternative" family.

2. Johnson (1986:77) interprets the higher rates of official delinquency among children (especially females) from mother-only families as evidence of official bias: "It is very tempting to conclude that the official system is indeed responding differently to similar behavior by adolescents from different types of families."

3. Studies have found little effect on delinquency of mothers' employment, provided that adequate supervision for children was arranged (see Hirschi, 1983; Wells and Rankin, 1988).

4. There is evidence that intermediate children have higher rates of delinquency than first-born or later-born children (Ernst and Angst, 1983: Rehav, 1980;Viles and

Challinger, 1981), although the reasons for this are unclear. Perhaps middle children suffer in overcrowded households "because they are the most likely to be home when large numbers of sibling are present" (presumably older children are more likely to have left the home before younger siblings are born) (Siegal and Senna, 1988:249). Or perhaps middle children "get 'lost' in the childrearing process, . . . are not . . given the responsibility and meaningful roles assigned to the oldest, . . . [and] are not granted the tolerance and freedom from responsibilities" allowed to younger children (Bynum and Thompson, 1989:229).

    5. Females are more likely than males to experience sexual abuse (Janus et al., 1987; Russell, 1984).

    6. While there is much experimental evidence that suggests exposure to media violence increases aggression in laboratory settings (see Goldstein, 1986), "no study has been able to directly link exposure to mass media violence with behavior that is criminally violent" (Kruttschnitt et al., 1986:236). Surveys that attempt to correlate youths' exposure to media violence with aggressive behavior and violent delinquency have yielded inconsistent results (compare Eron et al., 1972, and Hartnagel et al., 1975). Aggregate analysis actually finds that official violent crime rates are inversely related to the population's exposure to violent television programming, perhaps because "high levels of television viewing imply that residents are spending large amounts of time within the relatively safe confines of the household," reducing their exposure to delinquent peers and criminal subcultures (Messner, 1986:230).

    7. See Reiss (1951), Nye (1958), and Reckless (1961) for general theories of social control that consider personal and social controls, internal and external controls, and inner and outer containments.

    8. In a similar vein, Colvin and Pauly's (1983) "integrated structural-Marxist" theory analyses how authority relations in the capitalist workplace are reproduced within the working-class family. At work, adults are required to conform to the demands of an external and often coercive authority. Parents transfer these authority relations on to their children, creating a family control structure that weakens parent-child bonds and deprives youth of close family ties. Once placed in a similar control structure at school, youth associate with similarly alienated peers who are attracted to delinquent modes of conduct.

References

Agnew, R. 1985. "Social control theory and delinquency: A longitudinal test." *Criminology* 23:47–61.

Akers, R.L. and J.K. Cochran. 1985. "Adolescent marijuana use: A test of three theories of deviant behavior." *Deviant Behavior* 6:323–46.

Bynum, J.E. and W.E. Thompson. 1989. *Juvenile Delinquency: A Sociological Approach*. Boston: Allyn and Bacon.

Cernkovich, S.A. and P.C. Giordano. 1987. "Family relationships and delinquency." *Criminology* 25:295–321.

Cloward, R.A. and L.E. Ohlin. 1960. *Delinquency and Opportunity: A Theory of Delinquent Gangs*. New York: Free Press.

Cohen, A.K. 1955. *Delinquent Boys: The Culture of the Gang*. Glencoe, IL: Free Press.

Colvin, M. and J. Pauly. 1983. "A critique of criminology: Toward an integrated structural-Marxist theory of delinquency production." *American Journal of Sociology* 89:513–51.

Elliott, D.S., S.S. Ageton, and R.J. Canter. 1979. "An integrated theoretical perspective on delinquent behavior." *Journal of Research in Crime and Delinquency* 16:3–37.

Ernst, C. and J. Angst. 1983. *Birth Order: Its Influence on Personality*. Berlin: Springer-Verlag.

Eron, L.D., L.R. Huesmann, M.M. Lefkowitz, and L.O. Walder. 1972. "Does television violence cause aggression?" *American Psychologist* 27:253–63.

Gibbs, J.P. 1987. "The state of criminological theory." *Criminology* 25:821–40.

Goldstein, J.H. 1986. *Aggression and Crimes of Violence*. Second edition. New York: Oxford University Press.

Hartnagel, T.F., J.J. Teevan, and J.J. McIntyre. 1975. "Television violence and violent behavior." *Social Forces* 54:341–51.

Herman, J. 1981. *Father-Daughter Incest*. Cambridge, MA: Harvard University Press.

Hirschi, T. 1983. "Crime and the Family." Pp. 53–68 in J.Q. Wilson (ed.), *Crime and Public Policy*. San Francisco: ICS Press.

————. 1969. *Causes of Delinquency*. Berkeley, CA: University of California Press.

Janus, M., A. McCormack, A.W. Burgess, and C. Hartman. 1987. *Adolescent Runaways: Causes and Consequences*. Lexington, MA: D.C. Heath.

Johnson, R.E. 1986. "Family structure and delinquency: General patterns and gender differences." *Criminology* 24:65–80.

Krohn, M.D. and J.L. Massey. 1980. "Social control and delinquent behavior: An examination of the elements of the social bond." *Sociological Quarterly* 21:529–43.

Kruttschnitt, C., L. Heath, and D.A. Ward. 1986. "Family violence, television viewing habits, and other adolescent experiences related to violent criminal behavior." *Criminology* 24:235–66.

LaGrange, R.L. and H.R. White. 1985. "Age differences in delinquency: A test of theory." *Criminology* 23:19–42.

Laub, J.H. and R.J. Sampson. 1988. "Unraveling families and delinquency: A reanalysis of the Gluecks' data." *Criminology* 26:355–80.

Liska, A. and M. Reed. 1985. "Ties to conventional institutions and delinquency." *American Sociological Review* 50:547–60.

Matsueda, Ross. 1984. "Testing control theory and differential association: A causal modeling approach." *American Sociological Review* 50:547–60.

Matza, D. 1964. *Delinquency and Drift*. New York: Wiley.

Merton, R.K. 1938. "Social structure and anomie." *American Sociological Review* 3:672–82.

Messner, S.F. 1988. "Television violence and violent crime: An aggregate analysis." *Social Problems* 33:218–35.

Nye, I. 1958. *Family Relations and Delinquent Behavior.* New York: Wiley.

Paternoster, R. and R. Triplett. "Disaggregating self-reported delinquency and its implications for theory." *Criminology* 26:591–625.

Patterson, G.R. and M. Stouthamer-Loeber. 1984. "The correlation of family management practices and delinquency." *Child Development* 55:1299–1307.

Patterson, G.R. 1982. *A Social Learning Approach: Coercive Family Process.* Volume 3. Eugene, OR: Castalia.

Rahav, G. 1980. "Birth order and delinquency." *British Journal of Criminology* 20:385–95.

Reckless, W.C. 1961. *The Crime Problem.* New York: Appleton-Century-Crofts.

Reiss, A.J. 1951. "Delinquency as the failure of personal and social controls." *American Sociological Review* 16:196–207.

Rosen, L. 1985. "Family and delinquency: Structure or function?" *Criminology* 23:553–73.

Russell, D.E.H. 1984. *Sexual Exploitation: Rape, Child Sexual Abuse, and Workplace Harassment.* Beverly Hills, CA: Sage.

Rutter, M. 1980. *Changing Youth in a Changing Society: Patterns of Adolescent Development and Disorder.* Cambridge, MA: Harvard University Press.

Sampson, R.J. 1987. "Urban black violence: The effect of male joblessness and family disruption." *American Journal of Sociology* 93:348–82.

Thornberry, T.P. 1987. "Toward an interactional theory of delinquency." *Criminology* 25:863–91.

Turner, J.H. 1986. *The Structure of Sociological Theory.* Fourth edition. Chicago, IL: Dorsey.

Viles, D. and D. Challinger. 1981. "Family size and birth order of young offenders." *International Journal of Offender Therapy and Comparative Criminology* 25:60–6.

Voorhis, P.A., F.T. Cullen, R.A. Mathers, and C.C. Garner. 1988. "The impact of family structure and quality on delinquency: A comparative assessment of structural and functional factors." *Criminology* 26:235–61.

Wadsworth, M.E.J. 1979. *Roots of Delinquency: Infancy, Adolescence and Crime.* Oxford: Martin Robinson.

Wells, L.E. and J.H. Rankin. 1988. "Direct parental controls and delinquency." *Criminology* 26:263–85.

Wiatrowski, M.D., D.B. Griswold, and M.K. Roberts. 1981. "Social control and delinquency." *American Sociological Review* 46:525–41.

Widom, C.S. "Child abuse, neglect, and violent criminal behavior." *Criminology* 27:251–71.

The Preventive Effects of the Family on Delinquency

9

Joseph H. Rankin
L. Edward Wells

Because the family plays a critical role in the socialization of children, parents presumably also play a critical role in determining whether or not their children misbehave.[1] This common assumption has had considerable impact in the research on the place of the family in both the etiology and prevention of juvenile delinquency. Children from broken families and families-in-conflict are thought to be psychologically at "risk" and liable to a greater incidence of undesirable behaviors and attitudes—including acute psychiatric disturbances, poor school achievement, poor sex-role identification, negative evaluations of parents, low self-esteem, lack of peer friendships, anxiety, immaturity, and depression, plus a number of behavioral problems such as juvenile delinquency.[2] Although studies in this area encompass a number of academic disciplines (e.g., psychology,

psychiatry, and sociology), they share a common theme: children whose families have been disrupted by divorce, separation, or death display a greater degree of maladaptive attitudes and behaviors.

The findings from this substantial body of research are equivocal, however; they do *not* permit the general conclusion that a change in family structure (such as divorce) has any definite negative impact on children. In fact, several studies have concluded that this general psychological damage (if present) is much less than has been previously assumed or asserted. Such a conclusion has broad implications for delinquency prevention. If the specific impact of family structure on delinquency is unknown, how can we expect family-based intervention strategies (which are theoretically based) to have a preventive effect on delinquency? This suggests that the effects of family variables must be further explored before we can realistically expect positive results from family-based prevention strategies.

This chapter examines the possible etiological impact of "broken homes" and familial relations on one type of undesirable

171

behavior—juvenile delinquency. Assuming that such a relation exists, we next explore how family variables might prevent delinquency, examining a variety of family-based intervention strategies. We conclude by arguing that existing programs are essentially inadequate for preventing serious kinds of delinquent behaviors.

The Family as a Cause of Delinquency

Questions regarding the causal impact of the family on delinquency are not merely academic. Rates of divorce increased dramatically during the 1960s and 1970s, prompting some researchers to estimate that by the year 2000 more than half of all children under eighteen years of age will spend some time in a single-parent family.[3] As divorce rates increase and a greater number of children are raised in single-parent (especially father-absent) households, social scientists have only recently begun to discover its debilitating effect on children's behaviors.

After half a century of opinions, however, findings and interpretations remain contradictory. According to some researchers, the family is the single most important determinant of delinquent behavior.[4] For example:

> All in all, the stability and continuity of family life stands out as a most important factor in the development of the child. . . . The relationship is [so] strong that, if ways could be found to do it, a strengthening and preserving of family life, among the groups which need it most, could probably accomplish more in the amelioration and prevention of delinquency and other problems than any other single program yet devised.[5]

However, other researchers discount the etiological primacy of the family, arguing that:

> . . . virtually none of the studies relating family variables—particularly structural ones—to delinquency produces very strong relationships. . . . It may well be that such family variables are not in fact very significant indicators of delinquent behavior. As other socializing agents, such as the peer group and mass media, become more powerful in our society, this explanation seems increasingly likely.[6]

Despite these divergent opinions, most researchers have found at least small (and statistically significant) associations between some dimension of family context and delinquency. In fact, a considerable body of research evidence exists that delinquency is related to various indicators of problematic family characteristics, either structural or relational in nature.

Family Structure

Substantial disagreement exists on the empirical significance of the broken home as an etiological factor in delinquency. Many practitioners and researchers consider it to be a strong factor,[7] while others argue that its effects are spurious or negligible.[8] Although statistically significant relations between broken homes and delinquency have frequently been found, the numerical strength of this relationship is generally small.[9]

A number of factors could possibly account for the ostensibly weak relationship between broken homes and delinquency. For example, broken homes may simply be less important than school or peer factors in the etiology of delinquency, especially for adolescents. Or broken homes may not be a significant antecedent for all *types* of delinquency. Whereas Robert Dentler and Lawrence Monroe[10] and Roy L. Austin[11] found no relation between broken homes and theft, F. Ivan Nye,[12] Karen Wilkinson,[13] and Joseph H. Rankin[14] found the highest percentage of broken homes among adolescents committing "ungovernable conduct" (e.g., truancy and running away from home). Thus, broken homes may be positively related to some delinquent acts and unrelated to others. The study of delinquency as a general concept could suppress any significantly large association between specific types of delinquent behavior and broken homes.

Not only may family breakup be differentially related to specific types of juvenile misconduct, but it may also differentially affect certain categories of juveniles. For example, the effects of broken homes may be felt more strongly by juveniles of a certain race or socioeconomic status. Roland Chilton and Gerald Markle found that broken homes may have a greater effect on the delinquency of whites than blacks and on adolescents from high-income families than from low-income families.[15] Similarly, John Johnstone's results indicate that the effect of broken homes on delinquency varies directly with the neighborhood's socioeconomic status.[16] He argues that in low-income, deteriorated areas of the city the effect of broken homes is outweighed by the negative influences of ubiquitous poverty. Only in the more affluent and stable neighborhoods will family disruption have negative behavioral effects on children. Thus, it is probably not accurate to assume that all children are equally affected by broken homes. In addition, divorce (or separation), poverty, and race are highly interrelated.[17] Until the effects of such variables are statistically controlled, we will not be able to accurately assess the effect of broken homes on delinquency.

Another problem concerns the conceptual ambiguity of the term "broken home." The most widely used definition is the absence of at least one natural (biological) parent. However, this taxonomy reduces the family structure variable to a simple dichotomy: a home is either "broken" or "intact." As Lawrence Rosen[18] and Jona M. Rosenfeld and Eliezar Rosenstein[19] have noted, this is a gross oversimplification of a rather complicated family condition. Various precipitating causes for the break (e.g., divorce, death, disability, military service), the longevity of the break (temporary or permanent), the absence of one or both parents (mother, father, or both), the presence of a stepparent, and the frequency, duration, and quality of the contact between the child and absent parent can all affect (either positively or negatively) both the psychological and behavioral risk of the child. Thus, the most common definition of a broken home—loss of at least one biological parent—conceals the fact that the difficulty in raising a child might not be the same for all types of breaks. Only recently have researchers been examining empirically the impact of different kinds and degrees of parent-absence on the child's behavior.

This brief overview of the literature on the broken home indicates its limited contribution to an understanding of what it is about parent-absence that affects the child negatively. Most research has emphasized the loss of a father as being directly detrimental to the child's development without considering other variables that may occur simultaneously with parental absence. One major exception is the research by Cynthia Longfellow, who examined the reorganization process that occurs after divorce.[20] Problems in child care, lack of a social life, apprehension in regard to visitation rights, and especially financial problems all plague the single parent. In this context, the departure of a parent is just one of many circumstances to which the child must adjust. The effect of broken homes on delinquency can be more accurately assessed only when we know more about the strains that are placed on the family as a result of a parent's departure.

Thus, it is not enough to focus only on family structure variables. The departure of the father or mother from the family unit is often characterized by a strained relationship between the parents before, during, and after the separation/divorce. Thus, a final reason for the apparently weak effect of broken homes on delinquency is that this relationship is mediated by relational variables (e.g., the *quality* of the marital or parent-child relationship). In other words, the effect of broken homes on delinquency is indirect.

Intervening Processes

Instead of a simple direct effect of family structure on the likelihood of juvenile misbehaviors, a three-step causal process is usually proposed in which structural conditions (e.g., broken homes) precipitate certain interactions or relational patterns (e.g., parent-child relationships) which in turn affect the probability of delinquency. Because this intermediate step remains implicit in most research on broken homes, its specific contribution to the causal sequence between family structure and delinquency remains implicit and ambiguous. In clarifying these intervening processes, we note that various theoretical frameworks are possible, each identifying a different set of intervening variables and providing a different interpretation of the causal process. Four general theoretical perspectives can be identified, each distinguishing a different causal dynamic between family structure and delinquency: (1) socialization, (2) social control, (3) family crisis, and (4) social structure.

The *socialization* perspective identifies the family as the primary agency for the socialization of children into cultural roles and normal adult personalities. Because socialization is a developmental process, this perspective focuses on the effects of family structure as extending over a period of years—particularly the years when children are fairly young (i.e., pre-adolescence). Structural changes in the family do not necessarily have an immediate effect on children's behaviors. Instead, the causal effects of family structure are likely to be delayed and cumulative, affecting long-term changes in behavior. Thus, the focus of this perspective is on family structure during the early, formative years of childhood which eventually precipitates unwanted behavioral changes in later adolescence.

According to this reasoning, family structural changes may differentially affect behaviors, depending on the developmental age of the child at the time of the break. This conclusion has several consequences for social policy. First, the effects of prevention strategies may be more valuable and immediate for younger children whose parents have separated/divorced in the recent past. Because the behavioral effects will be delayed and cumulative, the shorter the time frame between parental departure and preventive intervention, the less the likelihood of faulty learning of deviant behaviors, values, and concepts. Simply put, less "resocialization" will be necessary. By implication, such intervention strategies would not be expected to produce immediate, positive results for older children whose parents had separated/divorced in the distant past. Within the relatively brief time frame of most prevention programs (and evaluation research), there is a high probability that few corrective behavioral changes will be noted in these children.

A second consequence of the "cumulative'' nature of this perspective is that (everything else being equal) parental breaks that occur late in the child's adolescence may have fewer developmental effects on the child. Much of the child's socialization will already have occurred by this stage. In addition, many delinquency theorists assume that by later adolescence juveniles are more strongly influenced by their peers and school than by parents. Thus, prevention strategies based on the family socialization perspective may have little effect on older children. Rather, school- and peer-oriented prevention strategies should be utilized at this stage of the child's development. The problem, of course, is that this relationship is variable; some parents may retain a great deal of influence over children at later stages of adolescence. To the degree that a child's peer and school networks contain persons that are also part of the family network, parents will remain effective in their socialization efforts throughout adolescence. Thus, age (maturation) is only one of many possible variables that make children differentially susceptible to parental influence.

As a basic proposition, the literature on the broken home generally presumes that a family structure that deviates from the Western ''norm'' (i.e., a nuclear family in which both biological parents are present) will retard the normal learning of proper social roles; concomitantly, broken homes will facilitate the development of behavioral problems such as delinquency. Even though they presently make up a significant proportion of family households, separated families are commonly assumed to be deviant and pathological, as exemplified in the terms by which they are commonly described—''broken,'' ''disorganized,'' ''disintegrated.'' Equation of child rearing by a single parent with a greater likelihood of delinquency is consistent with a rather

''functional'' view that the presence of both biological parents is the necessary minimum requirement for normal child development.[21] Because fathers generally average significantly less time per week in childcare activities relative to mothers, this functional argument may seem highly suspect.[22] Indeed, recent versions of the socialization perspective may recognize that appropriate social habits can be learned in the context of a relationship with any individual who fulfills the parenting function in a stable relationship (e.g., foster parent, guardian, grandparent, stepparent, even a single parent). The negative effects of broken homes may be neutralized if substitute structures for socialization (especially substitute role models) are provided.

A *social control* framework provides a different interpretation of the intervening causal process between family structure and delinquency. In contrast to the developmental approach, this perspective views family structure more as a synchronous cause than as a lagged, developmental cause of delinquency. Because the negative effects of family structure should be relatively immediate rather than delayed and cumulative, the social control perspective gives a potentially more optimistic view of the short-run impact of delinquency prevention. Intervention strategies should obtain relatively quick, positive results regardless of the child's current age and/or age at the point of parental breakup.

According to the social control perspective, the conventional (intact) family provides a source of basic ''ties'' or ''bonds'' to conventional social order and involvement in conventional activities and institutions. The intact family acts as a control (buffer) against deviant influences by providing a source of motivations (termed ''stakes in conformity'' or ''attachments'') to conform to social norms and rules. Thus, the properly functioning family helps to control deviant impulses, limiting the likelihood of delinquent behaviors. In this sense, social control is really a perspective on conformity rather than deviance. When the family structure breaks down, the family can lose its ability to supervise and control the behaviors of its children, thereby increasing the likelihood of delinquency.

Among the various social control perspectives, Travis Hirschi provides the most elaborated and explicit theory.[23] A central focus of his perspective is the inverse relationship between the child's bond or attachment to parents and delinquency. The greater the sensitivity to parents' wishes and concerns, the more likely the child is to consider those concerns when contemplating the commission of a delinquent act. Family bonds inhibit or control delinquency because the child does not want to jeopardize positive relationships with his or her parents. On the other hand, lack of family support is conducive to delinquency. A weak bond minimizes one's sensitivity to the opinions of parents, "freeing" the child to deviate in response to situational demands and peer encouragements. This bond between parent and child can be strengthened along three dimensions: (1) parental supervision over their child's behavior; (2) identification with or closeness to parents; and (3) intimacy of communication.

In contrast to other social control perspectives,[24] Hirschi suggests that (a) attachment to one parent can be as effective in preventing delinquency as attachment to both parents; and (b) the difference between the mother's and father's impact on a child's delinquency is negligible.[25] The implications of this suggestion are twofold. First, a broken home may have little facilitating effect on delinquency as long as the child is strongly attached to the remaining parent. Since the important consideration is whether or not *one* parent is psychologically present (providing "indirect control") when delinquent opportunities arise, it is not necessary for both parents to be present to act as a buffer against delinquency. Thus, broken homes should be associated with delinquency only when the quality of the relationship (attachment) between the child and remaining parent is poor. This reasoning contrasts with other social control approaches which suggest that the ability to supervise, punish, and generally restrain a child's behavior (providing "direct control") is substantially attenuated in a single-parent family.[26]

A second implication of Hirschi's perspective is that it does not matter to which of the parents (mother or father) the child is attached as long as the strength of this bond is high. The strength of the relation between parental attachment and delinquency is not contingent on the gender of the parent or the child. A boy raised only by his mother ought to be no more at risk than a girl raised by her mother. Hirschi's view is in contrast to some versions of the socialization perspective (especially clinical models or sex-role identification models) which have assumed that father absence has graver behavioral and psychological consequences for sons than for daughters; conversely, mother absence should have a greater adverse effect on daughters. Although research findings consistent with this latter assumption have been reported, the available evidence is very sketchy and inconclusive.[27] In fact, Joseph Rankin found no evidence to support this claim.[28] This remains an open theoretical and empirical question. Even within the socialization perspective, numerous researchers recognize that there are many others (besides biological parents) from whom gender-linked roles can be learned (e.g., peers, extended kinship relations, and step-fathers, as well as the media).

The *family crisis* perspective also views the relationship between family structure and delinquency as synchronous. Disruptions in family structure lead to temporary disturbances which must be resolved to re-establish some semblance of the pre-crisis family order and routine. In contrast to the social control perspective which emphasizes the nonmotivational, psychological aspect of parental "attachment" and the family's inability to control delinquent impulses, this approach views a change in family structure as a motivational cause of delinquency—the crisis actually "pushes" a juvenile toward misbehaving. Basically, the loss of a parent produces stress and conflict that are expressed in acting out behaviors such as parental defiance, running away from home, truancy, or general ungovernability. Thus, this approach predicts less serious, maladaptive juvenile misbehaviors (rather than serious, hard-core delinquency) that are likely to be directed against the parents themselves. Moreover, these misbehaviors are likely to be a temporary rather than a long-lasting problem, being resolved as the broken family adapts to its new conditions. By contrast, the socialization perspective and certain social control perspectives suggest that delinquency is likely to be less transient and more serious in content than the family crisis perspective suggests.

A family crisis approach does not provide a determinate model of delinquency, recognizing that several extraordinary events may be increased by the family separation—some negative, some positive.[29] The crisis could have prosocial rather than antisocial effects on the children. Conceivably, the loss of a parent could pull the remaining family closer together in a fashion similar to how relatives and friends "pitch in" to help one another after natural disasters. In a similar fashion, some children may help in the crisis by taking over the roles and responsibilities of the missing parent in such tasks as child rearing, earning an additional household income, or housekeeping. Delinquency is only one of many behavioral responses that can result from a family crisis. Future research must specify and clarify under what conditions delinquency is the most likely response.

Thus, the family crisis perspective does not necessarily imply that a change in family structure will lead to delinquency or that delinquency affects only broken homes. The quality of the relation between parent and child is not necessarily good in intact homes nor poor in broken homes. Indeed, homes that are physically intact but in a state of marital conflict may present more of a crisis than homes in which parental relationships are severed. Separation or divorce could end parental conflict and restore peace to what was already a "socially" or "psychologically" broken home.[30] Moreover, parental breakups are only one type of crisis that could initiate juvenile misbehaviors. Parental abuse (e.g., physical beatings and sexual assaults) can also motivate a child toward some type of "acting out" or "striking back" behaviors (e.g., defying parents or running away from home).[31]

The intervening causal processes discussed thus far have centered on either the characteristics of the delinquents themselves (socialization perspective) or the juvenile's family (social control and family crisis perspectives). A *social structure* perspective follows a still different approach, viewing the relationship between family structure and delinquency within the context of the larger social structure or organization of society. Broken homes affect the likelihood of delinquency by altering conditions "external" to the family. Hence, questions germane to this perspective include: What are the external characteristics of the structure or situation in which delinquent behaviors occur? Do delinquency rates vary as these situations vary?

According to this perspective, the broken home constitutes a socially and economically disadvantaged unit. Not only are the parents of lower income families more likely to divorce or separate, but many middle-income families are likely to suffer downward economic mobility as a result of a parent's departure from the family unit.[32] Less income means not only a reduction in economic and material consumption; it may also necessitate a move to poor housing accommodations in lower class neighborhoods. A low income translates into fewer educational opportunities as well as more frequent associations with delinquent values and behaviors in lower class schools and neighborhoods. Thus, legitimate opportunities for success and goal-achievement are more likely to be limited for children from broken homes.

The social structure perspective has several distinct implications for social policy. First, this approach suggests that the social forces that cause delinquency begin to affect children when they are relatively young and then continue to influence behaviors and attitudes throughout the child's life. In this sense, the social structure approach is similar to the socialization perspective. The sooner that intervention takes place after parental breakup, the more effective will be the treatment. However, there is a large difference in treatment strategies between these two approaches. Instead of focusing on the resocialization of the individual or family, the social structure approach suggests that larger scale changes must take place which attempt to reduce the

socioeconomic disadvantages of the broken home (e.g., the reduction of economic discrimination against the poor or single mothers).

Second, most social structure perspectives view lower class delinquency as more violent and destructive than middleclass delinquency. Rather than assuming that delinquency is a rather mild form of "acting out" behaviors against parents (the family crisis approach), this perspective views the delinquent behavior of children from broken homes as much more serious in nature. Because the structural effects of low income are cumulative, delinquent behaviors are likely to become more serious as the child grows older.

Family-Based Prevention

One basic test of a theoretical perspective is its ability to predict delinquency; another equally important test is its ability to translate into practicable prevention programs. Equally predictive causal variables do not always lend themselves equally well to manipulation in actual programs of prevention.[33] Prevention strategies invariably are directed toward the intervening causal processes rather than toward the family structure per se, which is more difficult to manipulate or reform. Indeed, intervention strategies that attempt to reduce or prevent delinquency by keeping families physically intact (e.g., through modification in the economic reward structure or through welfare requirements) are probably doomed to failure.[34] Even if such programs were successful in keeping the family physically intact, all the problems associated with a conflicted, socially, or psychologically broken home (e.g., family crises, poor marital or parent-child relationships, child abuse) would remain unsolved.

Conceptualizing theoretical perspectives on the family dynamics of delinquency is an important first step toward the development and evaluation of family-based prevention strategies. However, the search for causes must be paralleled with a search for programs that can control the causal factors. Ostensibly, the perspectives outlined above may be used by criminologists and practitioners alike to assess family dynamics and the extent to which certain programs may or may not work in preventing delinquency.

Assessing the Problems

Probably the first task of the practitioner is a diagnostic assessment of families "at risk" and the causal problems associated with a child's delinquent behavior. As outlined earlier, there are at least four different causal perspectives on the relationship between home and delinquency, each with fairly unique implications for social policy. Differing perspectives describe different problems and prescribe different remedies. An assessment of the originating cause(s) of delinquency is necessary before "treatment" (whether preventive or corrective) can be prescribed. For example, delinquent behavior that is produced by social structural factors (such as economic discrimination and disadvantage) will not be responsive to programs that prescribe foster parents for children with behavior problems. Economic discrimination illustrates a "social structural" explanation whereas reliance on foster parents is consistent with the "family crisis" orientation. In addition, the assessment aims of the two approaches will be quite different. One will be concerned only with categorically identifying families "at risk" (for eligibility to supplementary services or resources designed to reduce structural disadvantage), while the other will be concerned mainly with assessing the causal structure of each family's crisis. In the latter, the purpose of an initial diagnostic analysis is to assess the nature of the problem and thus the forms of intervention most likely to benefit a particular child in a particular family.

To systematize this initial diagnosis, objective measures may be used to identify key factors in the family situation, thus reducing the reliance on simple value judgment. Rudolf H. Moos and Bernice S. Moos have developed the Family Environment Scale (FES), which may be used to assess the "social climate" of families.[35] "Social climate" refers to the interpersonal relations among family members, the direction of personal growth emphasized within the family, and the family's basic organizational structure. Moos' FES items are grouped into ten subscales: "three assess Relationship dimensions (cohesion, expressiveness, conflict), five assess Personal Growth or Personal Development dimensions (achievement orientation, intellectual-cultural orientation, active recreational orientation, moral-religious emphasis), and the other two assess System Maintenance dimensions (Organization and Control)."[36] Among other things, their scale can be used for detailed descriptions of family social environments and for the longitudinal assessment of changes in family environments.

Where and by whom is the family assessment made? In present programs (scattered and mostly experimental), heaviest reliance is placed on the courts (particularly "family courts" responsible for mediating and resolving domestic disputes) as well as on social service agencies connected with the courts.[37] As an alternative strategy making possible wider and earlier coverage, some approaches suggest the schools as an additional point of identification and intervention.[38]

In developing intervention strategies for children from broken homes, Christine Burns and Marla Brassard argue that the school psychologist can assess the strengths of the child's environment (the school as well as the home), suggesting use of an adaptation of Kelly and Wallerstein's Divorce Specific Assessment.[39] This developmental assessment scale includes information from both the parent and school as well as direct observation of the child over a period of time. Based on the results of such an assessment, Burns and Brassard conclude that the type of intervention strategy most suitable for the child can be chosen.

Assuming that some diagnostic assessment is administered, the next step is to choose the prevention strategy best suited to the child's needs. In general, such strategies can be classified as residential, nonresidential, or family support services.

Residential Treatment

In some instances, it may be beneficial to treat the child outside the context of the family when that environment is momentarily inadequate or threatening. For example, situations of "family crisis" may dictate the temporary removal of the child from the home (for reasons of physical safety) until the crisis is resolved. Residential programs allow children to be placed outside the home without the more destructive and stigmatizing outcome of institutionalization. Generally, placements are brief because the goal is to return the children to their families as soon as possible after a period of intensive supervision.

Even though the prospect of severing family ties can be frightening, *foster family care* can serve as a temporary shelter or haven for youths (e.g., runaways, truants, ungovernables) who may need protection as well as individualized care and affection in

an atmosphere that simulates a home-like environment. A number of foster homes may even work together in clusters to better develop the sense of a caring community of which the child can feel a part.[40] To insure even greater supervision and individual treatment, "intensive" foster care such as at Kaleidoscope Inc. in Chicago, Ill., usually requires that no more than two children be housed with any married couple.[41]

Temporary foster care is liable to have few positive, long-lasting effects on the child, however, unless the whole family's patterns of interaction can be changed. Parents must also learn to cope with pressures and crises. At the Baltimore Family Life Center, staff members assigned to each of the foster homes hold weekly therapeutic meetings with all family members.[42] In addition, staff members may initiate referrals to needed community services for the child and his or her parents as well as arrange recreational and social activities involving the child's family. The program's philosophy "is that a youth's natural family, his or her foster care family, and BFLC staff members are all part of the extended family and all participate in caring for the youngster."[43]

A second form of residential treatment for delinquents and "disturbed" children is the *group home,* in which approximately six to twelve children live together with houseparents. As with foster care, the purpose of the group home is to temporarily neutralize negative parental influences by placing the child in the care of adults who become temporary substitute parents in a kind of quasi-family setting.[44] During the day, the youths either attend school, hold jobs, or make use of other community resources.

Because many centers now view treatment of a child apart from his or her family as artificial or unnatural, many group homes have implemented some form of family counseling or psychotherapy as part of the treatment strategy. The purposes of such a family-oriented approach are three-fold. First, parental involvement helps parents to identify the agency as being therapeutically valuable for the child.[45] Ostensibly, this may increase parent-staff cooperation which, in turn, could benefit the child's treatment. Second, it is hoped that greater contact with agency staff will make the parents themselves more responsive, empathetic, and caring. Only within the total family context can a critical understanding of the child's problems he obtained. Finally, the family's involvement in the treatment process may make the child's return to home much faster and his or her reintegration into the family and community much easier.

Nonresidential Treatment

Juvenile delinquents living in their own homes can benefit from programs developed specifically as alternatives to residential treatment or incarceration. For example, parental involvement in treatment is more likely to he realized when the treatment setting is the home rather than an office or other facility located away from the family's residence. Although residential treatment may provide short-term benefits in situations of "family crisis," since the 1960s many practitioners have believed that residential intervention strategies provide an artificial or unnatural environment in which to trcat children. Because a child's behavior can be influenced by the novelty of the treatment setting, it cannot he determined whether deviant behaviors are, in fact, "normal" or an artifact of the unfamiliar treatment surroundings. Reinforcers (both positive and negative) may, for ex-

ample, produce new and unwanted deviant behaviors unique to the treatment setting.

Behavior therapy applies social learning or behavior modification principles to family prevention strategies in familiar treatment surroundings—the child's own home. In this manner, the reinforcers in the child's natural environment which maintain the deviant behaviors can be directly observed and later extinguished. Whereas most traditional therapies tend to emphasize the treatment of the child only, in behavior therapy the parents are an integral part of the mechanism for change. Parents themselves are trained in noncoercive methods (e.g., positive reinforcement and negotiating skills) for recording and changing the child's deviant behaviors.[46]

Baseline observations of the child's disobedient and aggressive behaviors are taken in the period prior to therapy. This serves both as a base from which to measure changes in family interaction patterns as well as a gauge of the effect of behavior therapy on a child's behavior. Generally, the therapy itself focuses on three different aspects of parent-child interaction: stimulus control, consequation, and shaping. Parental directives (verbal and behavioral) cue the child's responses and channel behaviors. "Stimulus control" refers to changing these cues so that the child clearly understands what is expected of him or her. These cues provide clear expectations for behavior through the consistent use of appropriate verbal and behavioral reactions (termed "consequation"). The development of consistent discipline coupled with positive reinforcement for prosocial behaviors is essential. Finally, because learning is usually a gradual and incremental process, the concept of "shaping" or successive approximation is used to slowly change negative family behavioral patterns toward more positive interactions.[47]

A series of articles by Gerald R. Patterson and his colleagues illustrates the use of behavior therapy for the elimination of juvenile "conduct disorders" (i.e., "noxious" but not necessarily delinquent behaviors such as fighting, teasing, whining, and yelling).[48] Parents were trained in behavior modification principles to alter the deviant behaviors of problem children. Observational data of the children's behaviors were collected in the homes before, during, and after therapy. Their results indicated statistically significant reductions in problem behaviors from the baseline data. Moreover, follow-up data indicated that these family intervention effects persisted twelve months after termination of treatment. Gerald R. Patterson and M. T. Fleischman also reviewed data from comparison studies which showed that social learning procedures were more effective in reducing problem behaviors than no treatment, client-centered treatment, and traditional treatment.[49]

Unlike much of the psychoanalytic and social work literature which relies on impressionistic data to evaluate the effectiveness of delinquency prevention strategies, Patterson's conclusions were based on observable behavioral changes in both the parents and the children prior to, during, and following treatment. Nevertheless, at least two questions remain concerning the effectiveness of behavior therapy: (1) Can behavior therapy effectively reduce the frequency of more serious forms of delinquency which are committed outside the home environment? (2) Do these effects really persist after treatment is terminated?

Patterson has shown that behavior therapy seems to work well in reducing relatively mild, socially aggressive behaviors (e.g., temper tantrums, hitting, yelling)

that can be identified and treated within the context of the home. However, it has yet to be shown that such a strategy can help reduce more serious delinquencies such as theft and burglary which occur outside the relatively "closed" setting of the home. J. B. Reid and A. R. Hendricks, for example, found that 57 percent of the more seriously delinquent children (e.g., those who stole, set fires, and ran away from home) were classified as failures of behavior therapy, compared to only 18 percent of the less serious, socially aggressive children.[50] It may be that behavior therapy will have its most pronounced effect on those noxious but not necessarily delinquent behaviors that tend to occur within a relatively "closed" setting, such as the home or school, where parents and teachers can closely and consistently observe and modify unwanted behaviors.

With regard to the second question, a number of authors have debated the post-termination persistence effects of behavior therapy. For example, close reexamination of Patterson's research has revealed inadequacies in the study design and data analysis. Upon reanalysis of these data, Ronald Kent argued that Patterson's conclusion regarding the persistence of treatment effects was unwarranted.[51] Other studies lend support to Kent's conclusion: there is no unequivocal evidence of post-treatment persistence effects.[52] Patterson and Fleischman have responded to this criticism by arguing that the persistence of effects is not a function of the treatment per se, but of how significant others (especially parents) react to the positive changes in the child.[53] Unless the parents continue to consistently use noncoercive means of maintaining the child's prosocial level of behavior, in the long run the child may return to baseline levels of noxious behaviors. That is, not only must treatment extinguish the coercive system of punishment, but it must also leave the family in a state where these punishments are unlikely to reassert themselves.

Difficulties experienced by single-parent families both during and following divorce/separation vary as to their frequency, duration, and magnitude. A variety of *family therapy* programs has developed as a response to these differing needs. In general, the specific counseling/casework strategies are as divergent as the number of implemented programs. For example, goal-directed counseling attempts to identify specific divorce-related problems (e.g., visitation controversies, financial planning, homemaking assistance) and fashions programs to modify these specific problems. Other strategies teach children how to deal successfully with crisis situations and cope with feelings associated with parental divorce, separation, and death. Intensive one- or two-day workshops are another family counseling strategy, the goals of which include learning to cope with feelings about marriage and divorce and developing communication skills for handling difficult situations. Trained caseworkers can also provide services in the child's home, including crisis intervention and counseling.

Although a great amount of expenditure and effort has gone into such varied and multifaceted programs, as yet little evaluative effort has been directed toward those strategies specifically involved in preventing delinquency. One exception is the study by Dennis Romig who reviewed and evaluated twelve studies of over 2,180 youth who participated in various types of family therapy prevention programs, including family crisis counseling, family communication skills programs, family casework, behavior modification, family recreation, family discussion groups, and psycho-

dynamic family therapy.[54] He concluded that such strategies can be effective in reducing juvenile deviance when they focus specifically on teaching parents skills in communication, problem solving, and discipline. Although these counseling skills may be helpful in reducing deviance among predelinquents and status offenders, Romig cautions that this conclusion cannot be generalized to delinquents involved in more serious criminal behaviors.

Family Support Services

As an alternative to intervention programs that operate after the family situation has reached crisis proportions (thus reaching public attention and mediation), family support services aim at making basic family resources available to families in disadvantaged circumstances (generally single-parent families). Concerned with families "at risk" or "in need" rather than "in crisis," they aim at reducing the structural disadvantages attached to families rather than mediating internal family dynamics. These include a variety of volunteer or public organizations for providing a basic array of services to families, including: child care, legal assistance, informational services (on schools, other educational programs, nutrition), socio-emotional services (counseling, cooperative support groups, recreational programs), referral services (for employment, public facilities, medical care), and material assistance (emergency aid, housing supplements).

The general rationale for such programs is a structural one. Certain family structures or situations predispose to delinquency because of the socioeconomic disabilities that attach to them. Thus, reduction in this disadvantage means reduction in delinquency risks. This approach seems more clearly preventive than the treatment programs outlined earlier which are often more remedial or corrective (of extant problems) than preventive. However, at present such programs are at most experimental and suggestive. The theoretical logic of the programs, while persuasive, remains unexplicated and untested—at least with respect to delinquency prevention.

Discussion and Conclusions

Our knowledge of prevention is not very fully developed at this point, probably because we have less than complete knowledge about the causes of juvenile delinquency. It surely would be a mistake to pin all hopes on the family as a corrective or preventive instrument in delinquency. No one would regard the family as the sole determinant of delinquency. Indeed, prior research has shown that delinquency is a complex problem, consisting of a variety of different behaviors and caused by a variety of interacting factors. Even if family context caused initial delinquent behavior, other factors (e.g., peer influence) may help to maintain the delinquency, even to supplant family factors as the effective maintenance variable. Causal explanations of the origin of delinquency may not explain its persistence.[55] Thus, to be successful a program may need to offer a variety of services, only some of which may pertain directly to the family.

Because of our lack of knowledge concerning the causes of various types of delinquency, it is not surprising that its prevention and correction should prove so difficult to systematically practice and document. To date there is little existing evaluative research on the effectiveness of family-based prevention strategies, although there is no shortage of those claiming to have the solu-

tion. Unfortunately, those programs that appear to be the most successful are those that either have not been carefully evaluated or have never been implemented (i.e., recommendations set forth as "model" prevention programs). Thus, it is nearly impossible to give prevention recommendations based on known "facts" (since the latter consist of opinions and beliefs rather than verifiable data).

This chapter does suggest, however, that the broken home may not be the primary cause of serious forms of delinquency and that family-oriented prevention strategies are probably not the choice treatment for serious delinquents. Family variables generally appear to be most highly associated with less serious forms of family-related deviance (i.e., noxious but not necessarily delinquent behaviors such as general ungovernability, running away from home, and temper tantrums); concomitantly, family-oriented prevention strategies seem to be most effective in reducing family-related status offenses and "acting out" types of behaviors. Thus, prior research on both the etiology and prevention of delinquency suggests a case for specificity of family treatment. The problem of juvenile delinquency may require a host of partial solutions rather than a single, overall resolution. Shotgun approaches that treat all youth alike will probably not be as successful as those that individualize treatment.

This conclusion may he premature and should not be considered the definitive word on the viability of the family in the cause and prevention of delinquency. Little has been mentioned in this chapter about family prevention in relation to delinquency per se because, to date, little has been done in this area. To reiterate, knowledge and practice in the field of delinquency causation and prevention are not fully developed. In addition to our inability to be able to predict delinquency with any accuracy, there has been little in the way of evaluative efforts to support a claim of success for any delinquency prevention program. "Family treatment" is a jumbled mixture of conceptual models and techniques,[56] only a handful of which focus specifically on delinquency prevention. Even fewer programs have been systematically evaluated. Thus, there is a need for further consideration of the role of the family in prevention of delinquency before we can come to any firm conclusions.

Notes

1. Walter R. Gove and Robert D. Crutchfield, "The Family and Juvenile Delinquency," *Sociological Quarterly* 23 (Summer 1982): 301–319.

2. Michael Rutter, "Parent-Child Separation: Psychological Effects on the Children," *Journal of Child Psychology and Psychiatry* 12 (1971): 233–260; Elizabeth Herzog and Cecelia Sudia, "Children in Fatherless Families," in B. Caldwell and H. Ricciuti, eds., *Review of Child Development Research,* Vol. 3 (Chicago: University of Chicago Press, 1973), pp. 141–232; Marybeth Shinn, "Father Absence and Children's Cognitive Development," *Psychological Bulletin* 85, no.2 (1978): 295–324; E. Mavis Hetherington, Martha Cox, and Roger Cox, "The Development of Children in Mother-Headed Families," in D. Reiss and H. Hoffman, eds., *The American Family: Dying or Developing* (New York: Plenum, 1979), pp. 117–145; Elaine A. Blechman, "Are Children with One Parent at Psychological Risk? A Methodological Review," *Journal of Marriage and the Family* 44 (February 1982): 179–195.

3. Richard S. Benedek and Elissa P. Benedek, "Children of Divorce: Can We Meet Their Needs?" *Journal of Social Issues* 35, no. 4 (1979): 155–169; Christine W. Bums and Marla R. Brassard, "A Look at the Single Parent Family: Implications for the School Psychologist," *Psychology in the Schools* 19, no. 4 (1982): 487–494.

4. Thomas Monahan, "Family Status and the Delinquent Child: A Reappraisal and Some New Findings," *Social Forces* 35 (March 1957): 251–258; Gove and Crutchfield, "The Family and Juvenile Delinquency."

5. Monahan, "Family Status and the Delinquent Child," p. 258.

6. David Schulz and Robert Wilson, "Some Traditional Family Variables and Their Correlations with Drug Use Among High School Students," *Journal of Marriage and the Family* 35 (November 1973): 638.

7. Monahan, "Family Status and the Delinquent Child," Roland Chilton and Gerald Markle, "Family Disruption, Delinquent Conduct and the Effect of Subclassification," *American Sociological Review* 37 (February 1972): 93–99.

8. Michael Hennessy, Pamela Richards, and Richard Berk, "Broken Homes and Middle-Class Delinquency: A Reassessment," *Criminology* 15 (February 1978): 505–527.

9. Lawrence Rosen and Kathleen Neilson, "Broken Homes," in Leonard Savitz and Norman Johnston, eds., *Contemporary Criminology* (New York: John Wiley, 1982), pp. 126–135.

10. Robert Dentler and Lawrence Monroe, "Social Correlates of Early Adolescent Theft," *American Sociological Review* 26 (October 1961): 733–743.

11. Roy L. Austin, "Race, Father-Absence, and Female Delinquency," *Criminology* 15 (February 1978): 487–504.

12. F. Ivan Nye, *Family Relationships and Delinquent Behavior* (New York: John Wiley, 1958).

13. Karen Wilkinson, "The Broken Home

and Delinquent Behavior: An Alternative Interpretation of Contradictory Findings,'' in Travis Hirschi and Michael Gottfredson, eds., *Understanding Crime: Current Theory and Research* (Beverly Hills, Calif.: Sage Publications, 1980).

14. Joseph H. Rankin, ''The Family Context of Delinquency,'' *Social Problems* 30 (April 1983): 466–479.

15. Chilton and Markle, ''Family Disruption, Delinquent Conduct and the Effect of Subclassification,'' pp. 96–98.

16. John W. C. Johnstone, ''Juvenile Delinquency and the Family: A Contextual Interpretation,'' *Youth and Society* 9 (March 1978): 299–313.

17. Ruth A. Brandwein, Carol A. Brown, and Elizabeth Maury Fox, ''Women and Children Last: The Social Situation of Divorced Mothers and Their Families,'' *Journal of Marriage and the Family* 36 (August 1974): 498–514.

18. Lawrence Rosen, ''The Broken Home and Male Delinquency,'' in Marvin Wolfgang, Leonard Savitz, and Norman Johnston, eds., *The Sociology of Crime and Delinquency* (New York: John Wiley, 1970).

19. Jona M. Rosenfeld and Eliezer Rosenstein, ''Towards a Conceptual Framework for the Study of Parent-Absent Families,'' *Journal of Marriage and the Family* 35 (February 1973): 131–135.

20. Cynthia Longfellow, ''Divorce in Context: Its Impact on Children,'' in George Levinger and Oliver C. Moles, eds., *Divorce and Separation* (New York: Basic, 1979).

21. Blechman, ''Are Children with One Parent at Psychological Risk?,'' pp. 179–180.

22. Richard Berk and Sarah Berk, *Labor and Leisure at Home: Content and Organization of the Household Day* (Beverly Hills, Calif.: Sage, 1979); Joann Vanek, ''Household Work, Wage Work, and Sexual Equality,'' in Sarah F. Berk, ed., *Women and Household Labor* (Beverly Hills, Calif.: Sage, 1980); Heidi I. Hartman, ''The Family as the Laws of Gender, Class and Political Struggle: The Example of Housework,'' *Signs* 6 (Spring 1981): 366–394.

23. Travis Hirschi, *Causes of Delinquency* (Berkeley, Calif.: University of California Press, 1969).

24. E.g., Nye, *Family Relationships and Delinquent Behavior;* Walter C. Reckless, ''A New Theory of Delinquency and Crime,'' *Federal Probation* 25 (December 1961): 42–46.

25. Hirschi, *Causes of Delinquency,* pp. 100–107.

26. Nye, *Family Relationships and Delinquent Behavior,* pp. 41–52.

27. John W. Santrock and Richard Warshak, ''Father Custody and Social Development in Boys and Girls,'' *Journal of Social Issues* 35, no. 4 (1979): 112–125.

28. Rankin, ''The Family Context of Delinquency,'' pp. 474–475.

29. Joseph Weis, *Jurisdiction and the Elusive Status Offender: A Comparison of Involvement in Delinquent Behavior and Status Offenses,* Report of the National Juvenile Justice Assessment Centers (Washington, D.C.: U.S. Government Printing Office, 1979).

30. Cf. Rankin, ''The Family Context of Delinquency.''

31. Dorothy Miller, Donald Miller, Fred Hoffman, and Robert Duggan, *Runaways— Illegal Aliens in Their Own Land* (New York: Praeger, 1980).

32. Brandwein et al., ''Women and Children Last,'' pp. 500–502.

33. Hyman Rodman and Paul Grams, ''Juvenile Delinquency and the Family: A Review and Discussion,'' in the President's Commission on Law Enforcement and Administration of Justice, *Task Force Report: Juvenile Delinquency and Youth Crime* (Washington, D.C.: U.S. Government Printing Office, 1967), pp. 188–221.

34. Blechman, ''Are Children with One Parent at Psychological Risk?'' p. 180.

35. Rudolf H. Moos and Bernice S. Moos, ''Families,'' in Rudolf H. Moos, ed., *Evaluating Correctional and Community Settings* (New York: John Wiley, 1975), pp. 263–287.

36. Ibid., p. 274.

37. Benedek and Benedek, ''Children of Divorce,'' pp. 161–163.

38. Bums and Brassard, ''A Look at the Single Parent Family,'' Jan McCarthy, ''Prevent-

ing Juvenile Delinquency Through Provision of Family-Support Services,'' in F. Dutile, C. Foust, and D. R. Webster, eds., *Early Childhood Intervention and Juvenile Delinquency* (Lexington, Mass.: Lexington Books, 1982).

39. Burns and Brassard, ''A Look at the Single Parent Family,'' pp. 488–490.

40. Yitzak Bakal and Howard W. Polsky, *Reforming Corrections for Juvenile Offenders* (Lexington, Mass.: D. C. Heath, 1979).

41. Margaret L. Woods, *Alternatives to Imprisoning Young Offenders: Noteworthy Programs* (Hackensack, N.J.: National Council on Crime and Delinquency, 1982).

42. Ibid.

43. Ibid., p. 23.

44. Morris F. Mayer, ''The Parental Figures in Residential Treatment,'' *Social Service Review* 34 (September 1960): 273–285.

45. Alvin E. Winder, Lindo Ferrini, and George E. Gaby, ''Group Therapy with Parents of Children in a Residential Treatment Center,'' *Child Welfare* 44 (May 1965): 266–271.

46. N. A. Wiltz, ''Behavioral Therapy Techniques in Treatment of Emotionally Disturbed Children and Their Families,'' *Child Welfare* 52 (October 1973): 483–492; Gerald R. Patterson, ''Interventions for Boys with Conduct Problems: Multiple Settings, Treatments, and Criteria,'' *Journal of Consulting and Clinical Psychology* 42, no. 4 (1974): 471–481.

47. Wiltz, ''Behavioral Therapy Techniques,'' pp. 483–491.

48. Patterson, ''Intervention for Boys''; Gerald R. Patterson and M. J. Fleischman,

''Maintenance of Treatment Effects: Some Considerations Concerning Family Systems and Follow-up Data,'' *Behavior Therapy* 10 (March 1979): 168–185; Gerald R. Patterson, Patricia Chamberlain, and John B. Reid, ''A Comparative Evaluation of a Parent-Training Program,'' *Behavior Therapy* 13 (November 1982): 638–650.

49. Patterson and Fleischman, ''Maintenance of Treatment Effects,'' pp. 172–181.

50. J. B. Reid and A. R. Hendricks, ''A Preliminary Analysis of the Effectiveness of Direct Home Intervention of Pre-Delinquency Boys Who Steal,'' in L. A. Hamerlynck, L. C. Handy, and E. J. Mash, eds., *Behavior Therapy: Methodology, Concepts, and Practice* (Champaign, Ill.: Research Press, 1973).

51. Ronald Kent, ''A Methodological Critique of 'Interventions for Boys with Conduct Problems,' '' *Journal of Consulting and Clinical Psychology* 44, no. 2 (1976): 297–302.

52. See Patterson and Fleischman, ''Maintenance of Treatment Effects,'' pp. 183–185.

53. Ibid.

54. Dennis Romig, *Justice for Our Children* (Lexington, Mass.: D. C. Heath, 1978), pp. 87–95.

55. For an example, see McCarthy, ''Presenting Juvenile Delinquency,'' pp. 143–148.

56. Joan M. Druckman, ''A Family-Oriented Policy and Treatment Program for Female Juvenile Status Offenders,'' *Journal of Marriage and the Family* 41, no. 3 (1979): 627–636.

Delinquency and the Age Structure of Society

10

David F. Greenberg

An extraordinary amount of crime in America is the accomplishment of young people, . . . [although] delinquents commonly abandon crime in late adolescence, . . . [and] arrest rates for vandalism and [nonviolent] property crimes . . . decline with age . . . [more] rapidly . . . than . . . arrest rates for narcotics violations and [violent] offenses . . .[1] This pattern is a fairly recent development. The peak ages for involvement in crime seem to have been higher in nineteenth-century America than they are today. Other industrialized capitalist nations, such as England, seem to have undergone a similar shift in the age distribution of involvement in crime. By contrast, comparatively few crimes are committed by young people in the less industrialized nations of the modern world.[2]

From David F. Greenberg (ed.), *Crime and Capitalism: Readings in Marxist Criminology,* Mayfield Publishing Company, 1981, pp. 118–139. This version was adapted from David F. Greenberg, "Delinquency and the Age Structure of Society," *Contemporary Crises: Crime, Law and Social Policy* Vol. 1, 1977, pp. 189–223. Reprinted by permission of Kluwer Academic Publishers.

The increasingly disproportionate involvement of juveniles in major crime categories is not readily explained by current sociological theories of delinquency, but it can be readily understood as a consequence of the historically changing position of juveniles in industrial societies. This changing position has its origin, at least in Europe and the United States, in the long-term tendencies of a capitalist economic system.

Delinquency Theory and the Age Distribution of Crime

Since neither the very young nor the very old have the prowess and agility required for some types of crime, we might expect crime rates to rise and then fall with age. But the sharp decline in involvement in late adolescence cannot be explained in these terms alone. If age is relevant to criminality, the link should lie primarily in its social significance. Yet contemporary sociological theories of delinquency shed little light on the relationship between crime and age. If, for example, lower class male gang delinquency is simply a manifestation of a lower class subculture, as Miller (1958) has maintained, it would be mysterious why 21-year-olds act in conformity with the norms of their subculture so much *less* often than their siblings just a few years younger—unless the norms themselves were age-specific. While age-specific expectations may contribute to desistance from some forms of delinquent play, such as vandalism and throwing snowballs at cars, as Clark and Haurek (1966) suggest, there is no social class in which felony theft and violence receive general *approval* for persons of any age. Moreover, adult residents of high crime areas often live in fear of being attacked by teenagers, suggesting that if delinquency is subcultural, community does not form the basis of the subculture.

The difficulty of accounting for "maturational reform" within the framework of the motivational theories of Cloward and Ohlin (1960) and Cohen (1955) has already been noted by Matza (1964:24–27). In both theories, male delinquents cope with the problems arising from lower class status by entering into and internalizing the norms of a subculture which repudiates conventional rules of conduct and *requires* participation in crime. As with other subcultural theories, it is not at all clear why most subculture carriers abandon activities that are so highly prized within the subculture with such haste.

This desistance is especially perplexing in anomie or opportunity theories (Merton, 1957; Cloward and Ohlin, 1960) because the problem assumed to cause delinquency, namely the anticipation of failure in achieving socially inculcated success goals through legitimate means, does not disappear at the end of adolescence. At the onset of adulthood, few lower and working class youths are close to conventionally defined "success," and their realization that opportunities for upward mobility are drasti-

cally limited can only be more acute. Students can perhaps entertain fantasies about their future prospects, but graduates or dropouts must come to terms with their chances.

Cloward and Ohlin do note that many delinquents desist, but explain this in ad hoc terms unrelated to the main body of their theory. Writing of neighborhoods where violence is common, they assert:

> As adolescents near adulthood, excellence in the manipulation of violence no longer brings status. Quite the contrary, it generally evokes extremely negative sanctions. What was defined as permissible or tolerable behavior during adolescence tends to be sharply proscribed in adulthood. New expectations are imposed, expectations of "growing up," of taking on adult responsibilities in the economic, familial, and community spheres. The effectiveness with which these definitions are imposed is attested by the tendency among fighting gangs to decide that conflict is, in the final analysis, simply "kid stuff." . . . In other words, powerful community expectations emerge which have the consequence of closing off access to previously useful means of overcoming status deprivation (Cloward and Ohlin, 1960:185).

In view of Cloward and Ohlin's characterization of neighborhoods where gang violence is prevalent as so disorganized that no informal social controls limiting violence can be exercised (1960:174–75), one can only wonder whose age-specific expectations are being described. Cloward and Ohlin do not say. This explanation, for which Cloward and Ohlin produce no supporting evidence, is inconsistent with their own larger theory of delinquent subcultures. In addition, it seems inconsistent with the *slowness* of the decline in the violence offense categories.

In a departure from the emphasis placed on social class membership in most motivational theories of delinquency, Bloch and Niederhoffer (1958) interpret such forms of delinquency as adolescent drinking, sexual experimentation, and "wild automobile rides" as responses to the age status problems of adolescence. Denied the prerogatives of adulthood, but encouraged to aspire to adulthood and told to "act like adults," teenagers find in these activities a symbolic substitute which presumably is abandoned as soon as the genuine article is available. As an explanation for joy-riding and some status offenses, this explanation has manifest plausibility. For other categories it is more problematic, since it assumes that delinquents interpret activities engaged in largely by adolescents as evidence of adult stature. When Bloch and Niederhoffer turn to more serious teenage crime, their explanations are vague and difficult to interpret, but in any event seem to depend less on the structural position of the juvenile.

In *Delinquency and Drift*, Matza (1964) provides an alternative approach to the explanation of desistance. His assumption that many delinquents fully embrace neither delinquent nor conventional norms and values, but instead allow themselves to be easily influenced without deep commitment, makes desistance possible when the delinquent discovers that his companions are no more committed to delinquency than he is. This discovery is facilitated by a reduction in masculinity anxiety that accompanies the attainment of adulthood. There are valuable insights in this account, but unresolved questions as well. Insofar as the discovery of a shared misunderstanding depends on chance events, as Matza suggests (1964:54–58), *systematic* differences in desistance remain unexplained. Why does desistance from violence offenses occur later and more slowly than for theft offenses?

Why are some juveniles so much more extensively involved in delinquency than others? Matza's remarkable presentation of the subjective elements in delinquency must be supplemented by an analysis of the objective, structural elements in causation, if such questions are to be answered.

That is the approach I will take. I will present an analysis of the position of juveniles in American society and elaborate the implications of that position for juvenile involvement in crime. The explanation of high levels of juvenile involvement in crime will have two major components. The first, a theory of motivation, locates sources of motivation toward criminal involvement in the structural position of juveniles in American society. The second, derived from control theory, suggests that the willingness to act on the basis of criminal motivation is distributed unequally among age groups because the cost of being apprehended are different for persons of different ages. Although some of the theoretical ideas (e.g. control theory) on which I will be drawing have already appeared in the delinquency literature, each by itself is inadequate as a full theory of delinquency. When put together with some new ideas, however, a very plausible account of age and other systematic sources of variation in delinquent involvement emerges.

Anomie and the Juvenile Labor Market

Robert Merton's discussion of anomie has provided a framework for a large volume of research on the etiology of crime. Although Merton observed that a disjunction between socially inculcated goals and legitimate means for attaining them would produce a strain toward deviance, *whatever the goal* (Merton, 1957:166), specific application of the perspective to delinquency has been restricted to an assessment of the contribution to delinquency causation of the one cultural goal Merton considered in depth, namely occupational success. Cloward and Ohlin for example, attribute lower class male delinquency to the anticipation of failure in achieving occupational goals as adults. These youths' involvement in theft is interpreted as a strategy for gaining admission to professional theft and organized crime circles, that is, a way of obtaining the tutelage and organizational affiliations necessary for the successful pursuit of *career* crime, rather than for immediate financial return. Crime is thus seen as a means toward the attainment of *future* goals rather than *present* goals.

The assumption that delinquency is instrumentally related to the attainment of adult goals is plausible only for limited categories of delinquency, however; e.g. students who cheat on exams in the face of keen competition for admission to college or graduate school, and youths who save what they earn as pimps or drug merchants to capitalize investment in conventional business enterprises. For other forms of delinquency this assumption is less tenable. Delinquents would have to be stupid indeed to suppose that shoplifting, joy-riding, burglary, robbery or drug use could bring the prestige or pecuniary rewards associated with high status lawful occupation. Nor is there evidence that most delinquents seek careers in professional theft or organized crime. In the face of Cohen's characterization of delinquents as short-run hedonists (1955:25), and the difficulty parents and teachers encounter in attempting to engage delinquent youths in activities which could improve chances of occupational success (like school homework), the future orientation assumed in opportunity theory is especially farfetched.

The potential explanatory power of ano-

mie theory, is, however, not exhausted by Cloward and Ohlin's formulation, because delinquency can be a response to a discrepancy between aspirations and expectations for the attainment of goals other than occupational ones. Most people have a multiplicity of goals, and only some of them are occupational. As the salience of different life goals can vary with stages of the life cycle, our understanding of delinquency may be advanced more by examining those goals given a high priority by adolescents than by considering the importance attached to different goals in American culture generally.

The transition from childhood to adolescence is marked by a heightened sensitivity to the expectations of peers and a reduced concern with fulfilling parental expectations (Blos, 1941; Bowerman and Kinch, 1959; Tuma and Livson, 1960; Conger, 1973:286–92). Popularity with peers becomes highly valued, and exclusion from the most popular cliques leads to acute psychological distress.

Adolescent peer groups and orientation to the expectations of peers are found in many societies (Eisenstadt, 1956; Bloch and Neiderhoffer, 1958); but the natural tendency of those who share common experiences and problems to prefer one another's company is accentuated in American society by the importance that parents and school attach to popularity and to developing social skills assumed to be necessary for later occupational success (Mussen et al., 1969). In addition, the exclusion of young people from adult work and leisure activity forces adolescents into virtually exclusive association with one another, cutting them off from alternative sources of validation for the self (as well as reducing the degree of adult supervision). A long-run trend toward increased age segregation created by changing patterns of work and education has increased the vulnerability of teenagers to the expectations and evaluations of their peers (Panel on Youth, 1974).

This dependence on peers for approval is not itself criminogenic. In many tribal societies, age-homogeneous bands of youths are functionally integrated into the economic and social life of the tribe and are not considered deviant (Mead, 1939; Eisenstadt, 1956:56–92). In America, too, many teenage clubs and cliques are not delinquent. Participation in teenage social life, however, requires resources. In addition to personal assets and skills (having an attractive appearance and "good personality," being a skilled conversationalist, being able to memorize song lyrics and learn dance steps, and in some circles, being able to fight), money is needed for buying clothes, cosmetics, cigarettes, alcoholic beverages, narcotics, phonograph records, transistor radios, gasoline for cars and motorcycles, tickets to films and concerts, meals in restaurants, and for gambling. The progressive detachment of teenage social life from that of the family and the emergence of advertising directed toward a teenage market (this being a creation of post-war affluence and the "baby boom") have increased the importance of these goods to teenagers and hence have inflated the costs of their social activities.

When parents are unable or unwilling to subsidize their children's social life at the level required by local convention, when children want to prevent their parents from learning of their expenditures, or when they are reluctant to incur the obligations created by taking money from their parents, alternative sources of funds must be sought. Full or part-time employment once constituted such an alternative, but the long-run, persistent decline in teenage employment and labor force participation has progressively eliminated this alternative.

During the period from 1870 to 1920, many states passed laws restricting child labor and establishing compulsory education. Therefore, despite a quadrupling of the "gainfully employed" population from 1870 to 1930, the number of gainfully employed workers in the 10- to 15-year-old age bracket *declined*. The Great Depression resulted in a further contraction of the teenage labor force and increased the school-leaving age (Panel on Youth, 1974:36–38). In 1940 the U.S. government finally stopped counting all persons over the age of 10 as part of the labor force (Tomson and Fiedler, 1975)!

In recent years, teenage labor market deterioration has been experienced mainly by black teenagers. From 1950 to 1973, black teenage labor force participation declined from 67.8% to 34.7%, while white teenage labor force participation remained stable at about 63%. The current recession has increased teenage unemployment in the 16- to 19-year-old age bracket to about 20%, with the rate for black teenagers being twice as high.

This process has left teenagers less and less capable of financing an increasingly costly social life whose importance is enhanced as the age segregation of society grows. Adolescent theft then occurs as a response to the disjunction between the desire to participate in social activities with peers and the absence of legitimate sources of funds needed to finance this participation.

Qualitative evidence supporting this explanation of adolescent theft is found in those delinquency studies that describe the social life of delinquent groups. Sherif and Sherif noted in their study of adolescent groups that theft was often instrumentally related to the group's leisure-time social activities:

> In several groups . . . stealing was not the incidental activity that it was in others. It was

regarded as an acceptable and necessary means of getting needed possessions, or, more usually, cash. Members of the afore-mentioned groups frequently engaged in theft when they were broke, usually selling articles other than clothing, and *often using the money for group entertainment and treats* (1964:174).

Similarly, Werthman (1967) reports that among San Francisco delinquents,

shoplifting . . . was viewed as a more instru-mental activity, as was the practice of steal-ing coin changers from temporarily evacu-ated buses parked in a nearby public depot. In the case of shoplifting, most of the boys wanted and wore the various items of cloth-ing they stole; and when buses were robbed, either the money was divided among the boys, or it was used to buy supplies for a party being given by the club.

Studies of urban delinquent gangs or indi-viduals in England (Fyvel, 1962; Parker, 1974), Israel and Sweden (Toby, 1967), Taiwan (Lin, 1959), Holland (Bauer, 1964), and Argentina (DeFleur, 1970) present the same uniform picture: unem-ployed or employed-but-poorly-paid male youths steal to support their leisure-time, group-centered social activities. Only to a very limited extent are the proceeds of theft used for biological survival (e.g., food).

Where parents subsidize their children adequately, the incentive to steal is obvi-ously reduced. Because the cost of social life can increase with class position, a strong correlation between social class membership and involvement in theft is not necessarily predicted. Insofar as self-reporting studies suggest that the correla-tion between participation in nonviolent forms of property acquisition and parental socioeconomic status is not very high, this may be a strong point for my theory. By

contrast, the theories of Cohen, Miller, and Cloward and Ohlin all clash with the self-reporting studies.

In view of recent suggestions that in-creases in female crime and delinquency are linked with changing gender roles (of which the women's liberation movement is taken either as a cause or a manifestation), it is of interest to note that the explanation of adolescent theft presented here is appli-cable to boys and girls, and in particular, al-lows for female delinquency in support of *traditional* gender roles related to peer in-volvement in crime. The recent increases in female crime have occurred largely in those forms of theft where female involvement has traditionally been high, such as larceny (Simon, 1975), and are thus more plausibly attributed to the same deteriorating eco-nomic position that males confront than to changes in gender role.

As teenagers get older, their vulnerabil-ity to the expectations of peers is reduced by institutional involvements that provide alternative sources of self-esteem; more-over, opportunities for acquiring money le-gitimately expand. Both processes reduce the motivation to engage in acquisitive forms of delinquent behavior. Conse-quently, involvement in theft should fall off rapidly with age, and it does.

Delinquency and the School

To explain juvenile theft in terms of struc-tural obstacles to legitimate sources of money at a time when peer-oriented leisure activities require it is implicitly to assume that money and goods are stolen because they are useful. Acts of vandalism, thefts in which stolen objects are abandoned or de-stroyed, and interpersonal violence not necessary to accomplish a theft cannot be explained in this way. These are the activi-ties that led Albert Cohen to maintain that much delinquency is "malicious" and "non-utilitarian" (1955:25) and to argue that the content of the delinquent subculture arose in the lower class male's reaction to failure in schools run according to middle class standards.

Although Cohen can be criticized for not indicating the criteria used for assessing rationality—indeed, for failure to find out from delinquents themselves what they perceived the goals of their destructive acts to be—and though details of Cohen's theory (to be noted below) appear to be inaccurate, his observation that delinquency may be a response to school problems need not be abandoned. Indeed, the literature proposing a connection between one or another aspect of school and delinquency is voluminous (see for example, Polk and Schafer, 1972). I believe that two features of the school experience, its denial of student autonomy, and its subjection of some students to the embarrassment of public degradation, are especially important in causing "non-utilitarian" delinquency.

In all spheres of life outside the school, and particularly within the family, children more or less steadily acquire larger measures of personal autonomy as they mature. Over time, the "democratization" of the family has reduced the age at which given levels of autonomy are acquired. The gradual extension of freedom that normally takes place in the family (not without struggle!) is not accompanied by parallel deregulation at school. Authoritarian styles of teaching, and rules concerning such matters as smoking, hair styles, manner of dress, going to the bathroom, and attendance, come into conflict with expectations students derive from the relaxation of controls in the family.[3] The delegitimation of hierarchical authority structures brought about by the radical movements of the 1960s has sharpened student awareness of this contradiction.

The symbolic significance attached to autonomy exacerbates the inherently onerous burden of school restrictions. Parents and other adults invest age-specific rights and expectations with moral significance by disapproving "childish" behavior and by using privileges to reward behavior they label "mature." Because of this association, the deprivation of autonomy is experienced as "being treated like a baby," that is, as a member of a disvalued age-status.

All students are exposed to these restrictions, and to some degree, all probably resent them. For students who are at least moderately successful at their schoolwork, who excel at sports, participate in extracurricular school activities, or are members of popular cliques, this resentment is likely to be more than compensated for by rewards associated with school attendance. These students tend to conform to school regulations most of the time, rarely collide with school officials, and are unlikely to feel overtly hostile to school or teachers. Students who are unpopular, and whose academic record, whether from inability or disinterest, is poor, receive no comparable compensation. For them, school can only be a frustrating experience: it brings no current gratification and no promise of future payoff. Why then should they put up with these restrictions? These students often get into trouble, and feel intense hostility to the school.

Social class differences must of course be taken into account. Preadolescent and early adolescent middle and upper class children are supervised more closely than their working class counterparts, and thus come to expect and accept adult authority, while working class youths, who enter an unsupervised street life among peers at an early age, have more autonomy to protect, and guard their prerogatives jealously (Psathas, 1957; Kobrin, 1962; Werthman,

1967; Rainwater, 1970:211–34; Ladner, 1971;61–63). To the extent that they see in the school's denial of their autonomy, preparation for a future in occupations that also deny autonomy, and see in their parents' lives the psychic costs of that denial, they may be more prone to rebel than middle class students, who can generally anticipate entering jobs that allow more discretion and autonomy.

Middle class youths also have more to gain by accepting adult authority than their working class counterparts. Comparatively affluent parents can control their children better because they have more resources they can withhold and are in a better position to secure advantages for their children. Children who believe that their future chances depend on school success are likely to conform even if they resent the school's attempt to regulate their lives. On the other hand, where returns on school success are reduced by class or racial discrimination (or the belief that these will be obstacles, even if the belief is counter to fact), the school loses this source of social control. For similar reasons, it loses control over upper class children, since their inherited class position frees them from the necessity of doing well in school to guarantee their future economic status.

Only a few decades ago, few working class youths—or school failures with middle class family backgrounds—would have been exposed to a contradiction between their expectations of autonomy and the school's attempts to control them, because a high proportion of students, especially working class students, left school at an early age. However, compulsory school attendance, low wages and high unemployment rates for teenagers, along with increased educational requirements for entry-level jobs, have greatly reduced dropout rates. Thus in 1920, 16.8% of the 17-year-old population were high school graduates; and in 1956, 62.3% (Toby, 1967). In consequence, a greater proportion of students, especially those who benefit least from school, is exposed to this contradiction.[4]

Common psychological responses to the irritation of the school's denial of autonomy range from affective disengagement ("tuning out" the teacher) to smouldering resentment, and at the behavioral level responses range from truancy to self-assertion through the flouting of rules. Such activities as getting drunk, using drugs, joy riding, truanting, and adopting eccentric styles of dress, apart from any intrinsic gratification these activities may provide, can be seen as forms of what Gouldner has called "conflictual validation of the self" (1970:221–22). By helping students establish independence from authority (school, parents, etc.), these activities contribute to self-regard. Their attraction lies in their being forbidden.

As a status system, the school makes further contributions to the causation of delinquency. Almost by definition, status systems embody invidious distinctions. Where standards of evaluation are shared, and position is believed to reflect personal merit, occupants of lower statuses are likely to suffer blows to their self-esteem (Cohen, 1955:112–13; Sennett and Cobb, 1972). The problem is somewhat alleviated by a strong tendency to restrict intimate association to persons of similar status. If one's associates are at roughly the same level as oneself, they provide the standards for self-evaluation (Hyman, 1968). In addition, "democratic" norms of modesty discourage the flaunting of success and boasting of personal merit, thereby insulating the less successful from an implied attribution of their failures to their own deficiencies. These niceties are not, however, universal in applicability. In our society, certification as a full-fledged social member is provided those whose commitment to the value of work and family is documented by spouse, home, car and job (for women, children have traditionally substituted for job). Institutional affiliations are thus taken as a mark of virtue, or positive stigma. Those who meet these social criteria are accorded standards of respect in face-to-face interaction not similarly accorded members of unworthy or suspect categories (e.g., prison and psychiatric hospital inmates, skid row bums, the mentally retarded). In particular, these full-fledged members of society are permitted to sustain self-presentations as dignified, worthy persons, regardless of what may be thought or said of them in private.

Students, especially failing students, and those with lower class or minority origins, are accorded no comparable degree of respect. As they lack the appropriate institutional affiliations, their moral commitment to the dominant institutions of society is suspect. In this sense, they are social strangers; we don't quite know what we can expect from them. They are, moreover, relatively powerless. In consequence, they are exposed to evaluations from which adults are ordinarily shielded. School personnel continuously communicate their evaluations of students through grades, honor rolls, track positions, privileges, and praise for academic achievement and proper deportment. On occasion, the negative evaluation of students conveyed by the school's ranking systems is supplemented by explicit criticism and denunciation on the part of teachers who act as if the academic performance of failing students could be elevated by telling them they are stupid, or lazy, or both. Only the most extreme failures in the adult world are subjected to degradation ceremonies of this kind.

Cohen (1955) has argued that working class youths faced with this situation protect their self-esteem by rejecting conventional norms and values. Seeking out one another for mutual support, they create a delinquent subculture of opposition to middle class norms in which they can achieve status. This subculture is seen as supporting the non-utilitarian acts of destructiveness that alleviate frustration. There is little difficulty in finding evidence of adolescent destructiveness, but the choice of target may be more rational (or less non-utilitarian) than Cohen allows. If the school is a major source of the juvenile's frustration, then the large and growing volume of school vandalism and assaults on teachers may, in the perpetrator's own frame of reference, not be irrational at all, even though it may be targeted on those who themselves are not necessarily to blame for what the school does. Other targets may be chosen because of their symbolic value, such as members of a despised racial group or class stratum, or adults, who represent repressive authority. Even random violence, though comparatively rare, can be a way of experiencing the potency and autonomy that institutions—the school among them—fail to provide (Silberman, 1978).

Self-reporting studies of delinquency indicate the association between class and most forms of delinquency to be weaker than Cohen supposed. School failure, though class-linked, is not the monopoly of any class, and the self-esteem problems of middle class youths who fail are not necessarily any less than those of working class schoolmates; indeed since parental expectation for academic achievement may be higher in middle class families, and since school failure may augur downward mobility, their problems could conceivably be worse. If delinquency restores self-esteem lost through school failure, it may serve this function for students of all class backgrounds.

The impact of school degradation ceremonies is not limited to their effect on students' self-esteem. When a student is humiliated by a teacher the student's attempt to present a favorable self to schoolmates is undercut. Even students whose prior psychological disengagement from the value system of the school leaves their self-esteem untouched by a teacher's disparagement may react with anger at being embarrassed before peers. It is the situation of being in the company of others whose approval is needed for self-esteem that makes it difficult for teenagers to ignore humiliation that older individuals, with alternative sources of self-esteem, could readily ignore.

Visible displays of independence from, or rejections of, authority can be understood as attempts to reestablish moral character in the face of affronts. This can be accomplished by direct attacks on teachers or school, or through daring illegal performances elsewhere. These responses may or may not reflect anger at treatment perceived to be unjust, may or may not defend the student against threats to self-esteem, may or may not reflect a repudiation of conventional conduct norms. What is crucial is that these activities *demonstrate* retaliation for injury and the rejection of official values to an audience of peers whose own resentment of constituted authority causes it to be appreciative of rebels whom it would not necessarily dare to imitate. Secret delinquency and acts that entailed no risk would not serve this function.

Field research on the interaction between teachers and delinquent students (Werthman, 1967), and the responses of delinquent youths to challenges to their honor (Short and Strodtbeck, 1965; Horowitz and Schwartz, 1974), support this dramaturgical interpretation of delinquency. Most gang violence seems not to erupt spontaneously out of anger, but is chosen and manipulated for its ability to impress others. Non-utilitarian forms of theft, property destruction and violence may well be understood as quite utilitarian if their purpose is the establishment or preservation of the claim to be a certain sort of person, rather than the acquisition of property.

Goffman (1974) has called attention to the common features of other, mainly noncriminal activities in which participants establish moral character through risk-taking. Such activities as dueling, bull fighting, sky diving, mountain climbing, big game hunting, and gambling for high stakes are undertaken for the opportunity they provide to carve out a valued social identity by exhibiting courage, daring, pluck and composure.

These qualities are those the industrial system (factory and school) tend to disvalue or ignore: the concept of seeking out risks and "showing off" is antithetical to the traditional ethos of capitalism, where the emphasis has been placed on minimizing risk, using time productively, and suppressing the self to demonstrate moral character. Consequently, those who seek prestige through risk-taking traditionally come from classes not subject to the discipline and self-denial of industrial production, e.g. the European nobility, bohemian populations, and the unemployed poor.

More recently, as production has come to require less sacrifice and self-denial from large sectors of the work force, and to require the steady expansion of stimulated consumption for its growth, the more affluent sectors of the labor force are increasingly encouraged to seek an escape from the routine of daily life through mild forms of risk-taking (e.g., gambling and skiing) as well as through the leisure use of drugs and sex.

The similarity between the subculture of delinquency and that of the leisurely affluent, noted by Matza and Sykes (1961), makes sense in view of the position of the delinquent vis à vis the school. Like the factory, the school frequently requires monotonous and meaningless work. Regimentation is the rule. Expressions of originality and spontaneity are not only discouraged, but may be punished. Sociability among students is prohibited by the discipline of the classroom. Students who reap no present rewards from their schoolwork or who anticipate only the most limited occupational returns as a compensation for their adherence to the onerousness of school discipline are free to cultivate the self-expressive traits which the school fails to reward, because they will lose nothing that is important to them by doing so. As Downes (1966) points out, they may come to regard adults who work as defeated and lifeless because of their subordination to a routine that necessitates self-suppression, and hence try to avoid work because of the cost in self-alienation.

Traditionally this has been especially true of students with lower class backgrounds; however, when the political and economic institutions of sectors of society lose their legitimacy, students of other classes may find the prospect of entering conventional careers in those sectors so repugnant that they lose the motivation to achieve in school, and also cultivate lifestyles based on self-expression or politically motivated risk-taking. The bright hippies and radicals from white middle class backgrounds in the late 1960s are a case in point.

The similarity between delinquent and non-criminal recreational risk-taking warns us that the pursuit of status through risk-taking does not *necessarily* arise from problems in self-esteem. Once a status system rewarding delinquent activity exists, students may act with reference to it in order to *increase* prestige in the group, not only to prevent prestige from falling. Thus teachers may be provoked (Werthman, 1967), gang rivals taunted, and daring thefts and assaults perpetrated, even in the absence of humiliation.

When students drop out or graduate from high school, they enter a world that, while sometimes inhospitable, does not restrict their autonomy and assault their dignity in the same way the school does. The need to engage in crime to establish a sense of an autonomous self and to preserve moral character through risk-taking is thus reduced. In addition, the sympathetic audience of other students of the same age is taken away. Thus school-leaving eliminates major sources of motivation toward delinquency. Indeed, American studies indicate that the self-esteem of dropouts rises after they leave school (Bachman et al., 1972) and that dropping out produces an immediate decline in delinquency involvement (Mukherjee, 1971; Elliot and Voss, 1974). In England, when the school-leaving age was raised by one year, the peak age for delinquency rose simultaneously by one year (McClean and Wood, 1969). These findings are especially ironic, in that nineteenth-century reformers touted the extension of public schooling as a way of reducing delinquency; and present-day delinquency prevention programs have involved campaigns to keep delinquents in school.[5]

Masculine Status Anxiety and Delinquency

Many observers have remarked on the disproportionate involvement of males in delinquency, and the exaggerated masculine posturing that characterizes their involvement, particularly where violence offenses are concerned. This behavior pattern has been explained as a "masculine protest" against maternal domination and identification, especially in the female-based households of the lower class (Parsons, 1947; Cohen, 1955:162–69; Miller, 1958). In such households, the argument goes, boys will tend to identify with the mother, and hence will experience uncertainty and anxiety in later years in connection with their identification as a male. To allay this anxiety, they reject the "good" values of the mother and engage in "masculine" forms of delinquency.

Application of the theory to delinquency in the United States has not been entirely successful. Male delinquency does appear to be associated with what has been interpreted as anxiety over masculinity, but it is independent of whether the household in which the child is raised lacks an adult male (Monahan, 1957; Tennyson, 1967; Rosen, 1969). This finding points to the need for a revision in the argument.

Hannerz (1969) has pointed out that children raised in homes without fathers may still have alternative male role models. Indeed, children raised in a community where adult male unemployment rates are high may spend more of their time in the company of adult males who could serve as role models than their middle class peers. Males who are not in doubt about their identity as males may nevertheless feel anxiety in connection with anticipated or actual inability to fulfill traditional sex role expectations concerning work and support of family. This masculine *status* anxiety can be generated by a father who is present but ineffectual, and by living in a neighborhood where, for social-structural reasons, many men are unemployed—regardless of whether one's own father is present in the household.

Men who experience such anxiety because they are prevented from fulfilling conventional male role expectations may attempt to alleviate their anxiety by exaggerating those traditionally male traits that *can* be expressed. Attempts to dominate women (including rape) and patterns of interpersonal violence can be seen in these terms. In other words, crime can be a response to masculine status anxiety no less than to anxiety over male identity; it can provide a sense of potency that is expected and desired but not achieved in other spheres of life.

In this interpretation, a compulsive concern with toughness and masculinity arises not from a hermetically sealed lower-class subculture "with an integrity of its own" nor from the psychodynamics of a female-headed household (Miller, 1958), but as a response to a contradiction between structural economic-political constraints on male status attainment and the cultural expectations for men that permeate American society. The role of the subculture Miller describes is to make available the behavioral adaptations that previous generations have developed in response to this contradiction.

If I am correct in assuming that delinquents in the last years of elementary school and early years of high school are not excessively preoccupied with their occupational prospects, but become more concerned with their futures toward the end of high school, then masculine anxiety during these early years must stem from other sources. One plausible source lies in the contradiction between the school's expectations of docility and submission to authority, and more widely communicated social expectations of masculinity. While the school represses both boys and girls, the message that girls get is consistent with society's message; the message boys receive is contradictory. This difference would help to explain sex differences in delinquency in early adolescence. Most of the male behavior that can be explained plausibly in this way—smoking, sexual conquests, joy-riding, vandalism, fighting—is fairly trivial, and either becomes legal in mid to late adolescence or abates rapidly. Anxiety over inability to fulfill traditional male occupational roles would be expected to show up late in adolescence.

One would expect masculine status anxiety to appear with greatest intensity and to decline most slowly in those segments of the population in which adult male unemployment is exceptionally high. This conforms to the general pattern of arrests for violent offenses such as homicide, forcible rape and assaults—offenses often unconnected with the pursuit of material gain, and hence most plausibly interpreted as a response to masculine status anxiety. Rates of arrest for these offenses peak in the immediate post–high school age brackets (several years later than for the property offenses) and the decline is slower than for property offenses. Moreover, blacks are overrepresented in violence offense arrests to a much greater degree than in arrests for property offenses.

Costs of Delinquency

So far, some possible sources of age-linked variation in motivation to participate in criminal activity have been identified, but this is only half the story, for one may wish to engage in some form of behavior but nevertheless decide not to do so because its potential costs are deemed unacceptably high. Costs can be a consequence of delinquency, and must be taken into account. Control theorists have begun to do so (Briar and Piliavin, 1965; Hirschi, 1969; Piliavin et al. 1969).

In early adolescence the potential costs of all but the most serious forms of delinquency are relatively slight. Parents and teachers are generally willing to write off a certain amount of misbehavior as "childish mischief," while enormous caseloads have forced juvenile courts in large cities to adopt a policy that comes very close to what Schur (1973) has called "radical nonintervention." Given the slight risk of apprehension for any single delinquent act, the prevalence of motivations to violate the law, and the low cost of lesser violations, we should expect minor infractions to be common among juveniles, and the self-reporting studies generally suggest that they are. As teenagers get older, the potential costs of apprehension increase: victims may be more prone to file a complaint, and police to make an arrest. Juvenile court judges are more likely to take a serious view of an older offender, especially one with a prior record. Older offenders risk prosecution in criminal court, where penalties tend to be harsher, and where an official record will have more serious consequences for later job opportunities.

Delinquents are acutely sensitive to these considerations. According to several youthful offenders testifying before the New York State Select Committee at a hearing on assault and robbery against the elderly, "If you're 15 and under you won't go to jail. . . . That's why when we do a 'Rush and Crib'—which means you rush the victim and push him or her into their apartment, you let the youngest member do any beatings. See, we know if they arrest him, he'll be back on the street in no time" (Williams, 1976). Thus the leniency of the juvenile court contributes to high levels of juvenile crime.

Just as the costs of crime are escalating, new opportunities in the form of jobs, marriage, or enlistment in the armed forces create stakes in conformity and, as Matza points out (1964:55), may also relieve problems of masculine status anxiety. Toward the end of high school, when student concern about the future increases, the anticipation of new opportunities is manifested in desistance from delinquency and avoidance of those who do not similarly desist. Consistent with this interpretation is the fact that in both England and the United States, the peak year for delinquent involvement is the year *before* school-leaving.

Those whose opportunities for lucrative employment are limited by obstacles associated with racial and/or class membership, however, will have far less reason to desist from illegal activity than those whose careers are not similarly blocked. The jobs available to young members of the lower strata of the working class tend to be limited, tedious, and low paying. Marriage may appear less appealing to young men whose limited prospects promise inability to fulfill traditional male expectations as breadwinner. Even an army career may be precluded by an arrest record, low intelligence test scores, physical disability, or illiteracy. Thus the legitimate opportunity structure, even if relatively useless for understanding entrance into delinquency, may still be helpful in understanding patterns of desistance.

The same may be said of the illegal opportunity structure. Those few delinquents who are recruited into organized crime or professional theft face larger rewards and less risk of serious penalty than those not so recruited, and their personal relationships with partners may be more satisfying. They should be less likely to desist from crime, but their offense patterns can be expected to change.

This reasoning suggests that the association between criminal involvement on the one hand and race and class on the other should be stronger for adults than for juveniles. If this is so, arrest rates in a given offense category should decline more rapidly for whites and youths with middle class backgrounds than for blacks and youths with working class and lower class backgrounds, and they do (Wolfgang et al., 1972).

Delinquency and the Social Construction of the Juvenile

Among the structural sources of adolescent crime identified here, the exclusion of juveniles from the world of adult work plays a crucial role. It is this exclusion that simultaneously exaggerates teenagers' dependence on peers for approval and eliminates the possibility of their obtaining funds to support their intensive, leisure-time social activities. The disrespectful treatment students receive in school depends on their low social status, which in turn reflects their lack of employment and income. In late adolescence and early adulthood, their fear that this lack of employment will persist into adulthood evokes anxiety over achievement of traditional male gender role expectations, especially among males in the lower levels of the working class, thus contributing to a high level of violence.

Institutionalized leniency to juvenile offenders, which reduces the potential costs of delinquency, stems from the belief that teenagers are not as responsible for their actions as adults. The conception of juveniles as impulsive and irresponsible gained currency around the turn of the century, when organized labor and Progressive reformers campaigned for child labor laws to save jobs for adults, a goal given high priority after the Depression of 1893. This conception was, in a sense, self-fulfilling. Freed from ties to conventional institutions, teenagers *have* become more impulsive and irresponsible.

The exclusion of teenagers from serious work is not characteristic of all societies. Peasant and tribal societies could not afford to keep their young idle as long as we do. In such societies, juvenile crime rates were low. Under feudalism, too, children participated in farming and handicraft production as part of the family unit beginning at a very early age.

In depriving masses of serfs and tenant farmers of access to the means of production (land), European capitalism in its early stages of development generated a great deal of crime, but in a manner that cut across age boundaries. Little of the literature on crime in Elizabethan and Tudor England singles out juveniles as a special category.

The industrial revolution in the first half of the nineteenth century similarly brought with it a great deal of misery, but its effect on crime was not restricted to juveniles. Children of the working class in that period held jobs at an early age and in some sectors of the economy were given preference. Only middle and upper class children were exempt from the need to work, and they were supervised much more closely than they are nowadays. As far as can be judged, juvenile crime in that period was a much smaller fraction of the total than at present, and was more confined to the lower classes than it is now.

In modern capitalist societies, children of all classes share, for a limited period, a common relationship to the means of production (namely exclusion) which is distinct from that of most adults, and they respond to their common structural position in fairly similar ways. Although there are class differences in the extent and nature of delinquency, especially violent delinquency, they are less pronounced than for adults, for whom occupational differentiation is much sharper.

The deteriorating position of juveniles in the labor market in recent years has been as-

cribed to a variety of causes, among them the inclusion of juveniles under minimum wage laws; changes in the structure of the economy (less farm employment); teenage preference for part-time work (to permit longer periods of education), which makes teenage labor less attractive to employers; and the explosion in the teenage labor supply, created by the baby boom, at a time when women were entering the labor market in substantial numbers (Kalacheck, 1973). Whatever contribution these circumstances may have made to shifting teenage employment patterns in the short run, the exclusion of juveniles from the labor market has been going on for more than a century, and may more plausibly be explained in terms of the failure of the oligopoly-capitalist economy to generate sufficient demand for labor than to these recent developments (Carson, 1972; Bowers, 1975).[6]

In both the United States and England, the prolongation of education has historically been associated with the contraction of the labor market, casting doubt on the view that more education is something that the general population has wanted for its own sake. Had this been true, the school-leaving age would have jumped upward in periods of prosperity, when a larger proportion of the population could afford more education, not during depressions. Moreover, the functionalist argument that increased education is necessary as technology becomes more complex would apply at best to a small minority of students, and rests on the dubious assumption that full-time schooling is pedagogically superior to alternative modes of organizing the education of adolescents.

The present social organization of education, which I have argued contributes to delinquency, has also been plausibly attributed to the functional requirement of a capitalist economy for a docile, disciplined and stratified labor force, as well as to the need to keep juveniles out of the labor market. Thus the high and increasing level of juvenile crime we are seeing in present-day United States and in other Western countries originates in the structural position of juveniles in an advanced capitalist economy.

Delinquency is not, however, a problem of capitalism alone. Although there are many differences between crime patterns in the United States and the Soviet Union, the limited information available indicates that delinquency in the Soviet Union is often associated with leisure-time consumption activities on the part of youths who are academic failures, and who either are not working or studying, or are working at or preparing for unrewarding jobs (Connor, 1970; Polk, 1972). This suggests that some of the processes described here may be at work in the Soviet Union. Since Soviet society is based on hierarchical domination and requires a docile, disciplined and stratified labor force, this parallel is not surprising. Yet it must not be forgotten that the parallel is only partial. The Soviet economy, for example, does not generate unemployment the way the capitalist economies of the West do. Insofar as can be learned from Soviet sources, juvenile delinquency has declined in recent decades, whereas it has increased rapidly in most of the capitalist nations.

Discussion

For decades, criminologists have proposed such reforms as eliminating poverty and racial discrimination to solve the crime problem (see Silberman, 1978, for the latest of this genre). None of them seriously addresses how the serious obstacles to achieving this task are to be overcome within the framework of a capitalist society. To suppose that the writing of an article or a book calling for an end to poverty and racism will actually contribute to ending poverty and racism is to betray a whimsical bit of utopianism. Marxist theorists tend to see these problems as largely produced by a class society, and insoluble within it. Efforts to tackle these problems may certainly be worthwhile, but not because they can be expected to achieve full success.

My analysis of delinquency suggests that most proposed "solutions" to the delinquency problem would have limited impact. Thoroughly integrating teenagers into the labor force, on at least a part-time basis, would go far toward reducing delinquency. But the jobs for adolescents are not there; and the drastic restructuring of education that would be required is hardly to be expected in the forseeable future.

If young people had a good understanding of the structural sources of their frustration and oppression, their response might well be different. Instead of individualistic and predatory adaptations, we might see collective, politicized, and non-predatory challenges to their exclusion. It seems unlikely that such a radical transformation in consciousness would develop spontaneously, but in the context of a mass socialist movement, it could well occur.

Notes

1. Arrest rates broken down by age can be found in any recent edition of the FBI's *Uniform Crime Reports*.

2. See, for example, Christiansen (1960), Toby (1967), DeFleur (1970), and Christie (1978).

3. These expectations are derived from young peoples' knowledge of family arrangements in our society generally, not from their own family circumstances alone. When controls in their own family are not relaxed, this can provide an additional source of conflict.

4. The emphasis given to school problems as a cause of delinquency in the criminological literature of the 1950s and 1960s was probably due at least in part to there being more delinquents *in* school then than in earlier decades.

5. Although this evidence confirms that the school does contribute to delinquency, it is hardly necessary. In Argentina, patterns of delinquency are fairly similar to those in the U.S., even though the school-leaving age for working class children is 10, and delinquents report favorable attitudes toward school (DeFleur, 1970). In the United States, unsatisfactory school experiences simply add to the economic motivations created by the exclusion of juveniles from the labor market.

6. The theory of supply and demand in economics demonstrates that with a given demand for a product, profits will be maximized at a lower level of production if the producing firm is a monopoly than if it is faced with competition. Thus the demand for labor has declined relative to the volume of production as American business has become more concentrated in a small number of giant corporations. The replacement of workers by machinery further reduces employment. Monopolization speeds up this process because large firms can more easily afford large investments in machinery. Large corporations can also relocate in other parts of the country or overseas to reduce costs of production, generating unemployment where disinvestment occurs. Since the labor market is not fully competitive, wages do not fall to a level that would permit full employment; such factors as minimum wage laws, labor unions, welfare for the unemployed, and illegal income all help to maintain wages above the competitive level.

References

Bachman, J.G., S. Green and I. Wirtanen (1972). *Dropping Out: Problem or Symptom*. Ann Arbor: Institute for Social Research.

Bauer, E.J. (1964). "The Trend of Juvenile Offenses in the Netherlands and the United States." *Journal of Criminal Law, Criminology and Police Science* 55:359–69.

Bloch, H.A., and A. Niederhoffer (1958). *The Gang*. New York: Philosophical Society.

Blos, P. (1941). *The Adolescent Personality: A Study of Individual Behavior*. New York: Appleton.

Bowerman, C.E., and J.W. Kinch (1959). "Changes in Family and Peer Orientation of Children between the Fourth and Tenth Grades." *Social Forces* 37:206.

Bowers, N. (1975). "Youth and the Crisis of Monopoly Capitalism." In *Radical Perspectives on the Economic Crisis in Monopoly Capitalism*. New York: Union of Radical Political Economics.

Briar, S., and I. Piliavin (1965). "Delinquency, Situational Inducements, and Commitment to Conformity." *Social Problems* 13:35–45.

Carson, R.B. (1972). "Youthful Labor Surplus in Disaccumulationist Capitalism." *Socialist Revolution* 9:15–44.

Christiansen, K. (1960). "Industrialization and Urbanization in Relation to Crime and Juvenile Delinquency." *International Review of Criminal Policy* 16:3.

Christie, N. (1978). "Youth as a Crime-Generating Phenomenon." In Barry Krisberg and James Austin (eds.), *The Children of Ishmael*. Palo Alto, Calif.: Mayfield.

Clark, J.P., and E.W. Haurek (1966). "Age and Sex Roles of Adolescents and Their Involvement in Misconduct: A Reappraisal." *Sociology and Social Research* 50:495–503.

Cloward, R., and L. Ohlin (1960). *Delinquency and Opportunity*. New York: Free Press.

Cohen, A. (1955). *Delinquent Boys*. New York: Free Press.

Conger, J.J. (1973). "A World They Never Knew: The Family and Social Change." *Daedalus* 100:1105–38.

Connor, W. (1970). *Deviance in Soviet Society*. New York: Columbia University Press.

DeFleur, L. (1970). *Delinquency in Argentina*. Pullman: Washington State University Press.

Downes, D.M. (1966). *The Delinquent Solution: A Study in Subcultural Theory*. New York: Free Press.

Eisenstadt, S.N. (1956). *From Generation to Generation: Age Groups and Social Structures*. New York: Free Press.

Elliott, D.S., and H.L. Voss (1974). *Delinquency and Dropout*. Lexington: D.C. Heath.

Fyvel, T.R. (1962). *Troublemakers*. New York: Schocken Books.

Goffman, E. (1974). "Where the Action Is." In *Interaction Ritual*. Garden City: Anchor Books.

Gouldner, A. (1970). *The Coming Crisis in Western Sociology*. New York: Basic Books.

Hannerz, U. (1969). *Soulside: Inquiries into Ghetto Culture*. New York: Columbia University Press.

Hirschi, T. (1969). *The Causes of Delinquency*. Berkeley: University of California Press.

Horowitz, R., and G. Schwartz (1974). "Honor, Normative Ambiguity and Gang Violence." *American Sociological Review* 39:238–51.

Hyman, H.H. (1968). "The Psychology of Status." In H.H. Hyman and E. Singer (eds.), *Readings in Reference Group Theory and Research*. New York: Free Press.

Kalacheck, E. (1973). "The Changing Economic Status of the Young." *Journal of Youth and Adolescence* 2:125–32.

Kobrin, S. (1962). "The Impact of Cultural Factors in Selected Problems of Adolescent Development in the Middle and Lower Class." *American Journal of Orthopsychiatry* 33:387–90.

Ladner, J. (1971). *Tomorrow's Tomorrow: The Black Woman*. Garden City: Doubleday.

Lin, T. (1959). "Two Types of Delinquent Youth in Chinese Society." In Martin K. Opler (ed.), *Culture and Mental Health*. New York: Macmillan.

McClean, J.D., and J.C. Wood (1969). *Criminal Justice and the Treatment of Offenders*. London: Sweet and Maxwell.

Matza, D. (1964). *Delinquency and Drift*. New York: Wiley.

———— and G. Sykes (1961). "Juvenile Delinquency and Subterranean Values." *American Sociological Review* 26:712–19.

Mead, M. (1939). *From the South Seas: Part III. Sex and Temperament in Three Primitive Societies*. New York: Morrow.

Merton, R.K. (1957). *Social Theory and Social Structure*, rev. ed. New York: Free Press.

Miller, W.B. (1958). "Lower Class Subculture as a Generating Milieu of Gang Delinquency." *Journal of Social Issues* 14:5–19.

Monahan, T.P. (1957). "Family Status and the Delinquent Child: A Reappraisal and Some New Findings." *Social Forces* 35:251–58.

Mukherjee, S.K. (1971). *A Typological Study of School Status and Delinquency*. Ann Arbor, Mich.: University Microfilms.

Mussen, P.H., J.J. Conger and J. Kagan (1969). *Child Development and Personality*. New York: Harper and Row.

Panel on Youth of the President's Science Advisory Committee (1974). *Youth: Transition to Adulthood*. Chicago: University of Chicago Press.

Parker, H.H. (1974). *View from the Boys*. North Pomfret, Vt.: David and Charles.

Parsons, T. (1947). "Certain Primary Sources

and Patterns of Aggression in the Social Structure of the Western World." *Psychiatry* 10:167–81.

Piliavin, I.M., A.C. Vadum and J.A. Hardyck (1969). "Delinquency, Personal Costs and Parental Treatment: A Test of a Reward-Cost Model of Juvenile Criminality." *Journal of Criminal Law, Criminology and Police Science* 60:165–72.

Polk, K. (1972). "Social Class and the Bureaucratic Response to Youthful Deviance." Paper presented to the American Sociological Association.

Polk, K., and W.E. Schafer (1972). *Schools and Delinquency*. Englewood Cliffs, N.J.: Prentice-Hall.

Psathas, G. (1957). "Ethnicity, Social Class, and Adolescent Independence from Parental Control." *American Sociological Review* 22:415–23.

Rainwater, L. (1970). *Behind Ghetto Walls*. Chicago: Aldine.

Rosen, L. (1969). "Matriarchy and Lower Class Negro Male Delinquency." *Social Problems* 17:175–89.

Schur, E.M. (1973). *Radical Non-Intervention: Rethinking the Delinquency Problem*. Englewood Cliffs, N.J.: Prentice-Hall.

Sennett, R., and J. Cobb (1972). *The Hidden Injuries of Class*. New York: Alfred A. Knopf.

Sherif, M., and C.W. Sherif (1964). *Reference Groups: Exploration into Conformity and Deviation of Adolescents*. New York: Harper and Row.

Short, J.F., and F.L. Strodtbeck (1965). *Group Process and Gang Delinquency*. Chicago: University of Chicago Press.

Silberman, C. (1978). *Criminal Violence, Criminal Justice*. New York: Random House.

Simon, R.J. (1975). *Women and Crime*. Lexington, Mass.: Lexington Books.

Tennyson, R.A. (1967). "Family Structure and Delinquent Behavior." In M.W. Klein (ed.), *Juvenile Gangs in Context*. Englewood Cliffs, N.J.: Prentice-Hall.

Toby, J. (1967). "Affluence and Adolescent Crime." In *Task Force Report: Juvenile Delinquency and Youth Crime*, pp. 132–44. Washington, D.C.: Government Printing Office.

Tomson, B., and E.R. Fiedler (1975). "Gangs: A Response to the Urban World," Part II. In D.S. Cartwright, Barbara Tomson, and Herschey Schwartz (eds.), *Gang Delinquency*. Monterey, Calif.: Brooks/Cole.

Tuma, E., and N. Livson (1960). "Family Socioeconomic Status and Attitudes toward Authority." *Child Development* 31.

Werthman, C. (1967). "The Function of Social Definitions in the Development of Delinquent Careers," pp.155–70. In *Task Force Report: Juvenile Delinquency*. Washington, D.C.: Government Printing Office.

Williams, L. (1976). "Three Youths Call Mugging the Elderly Profitable and Safe." *New York Times*, December 8, p. B2.

Wolfgang, M.E., R.M. Figlio and T. Sellin (1972). *Delinquency in a Birth Cohort*. Chicago: University of Chicago Press.

The Effect of Dropping Out of High School on Subsequent Criminal Behavior

11

Terence P. Thornberry
Melanie Moore
R. L. Christenson

The relationship between school failure and criminal behavior is a recurrent theme in theories of delinquency. Eventual dropouts have been found to have considerably higher rates of delinquency during high school than do graduates (e.g., Elliott and Voss, 1974; Polk, Adler, Bazemore, Blake, Cordray, Coventry, Galvin, and Temple, 1981), a finding consistent both with conventional wisdom and most theories of delinquency. However, what is not clear either theoretically or empirically is the effect that dropping out of high school has on subsequent criminal behavior. Indeed, for this relationship two basic models of delinquency, strain theory and social control theory, offer rather divergent predictions.

In strain theory (Cohen, 1955; Cloward and Ohlin, 1960), the middle class environment of the school is viewed as a major source of frustration and alienation for

lower class youth. To alleviate their frustration, these students withdraw legitimacy from middle class norms and turn to delinquency as a source of success, status, and approval. Thus, for lower class students strain theory views school and its attendant failure as a major cause of criminal activity. On the other hand, in his formulation of social control theory, Hirschi (1969) posits that delinquency arises when the person's bond to conventional society is weakened. Individuals who are attached to conventional others and committed to conventional institutions are strongly bonded to society and hence are unlikely candidates for crime. Since school is " . . . an eminently conventional institution" (Hirschi, 1969: 110), social control theory views it as a major source of bonding which should reduce delinquent activity.

Strain and control theories, therefore, offer divergent assessments of the relationship between school and delinquency, especially for lower class youths.[1] In the former school is a source of failure and frustration which increases delinquent con-

From *Criminology*, Vol. 23, No. 1, 1985, pp. 3-18. Reprinted by permission of the American Society of Criminology and the authors.

duct; in the latter it is a source of social control which decreases delinquent conduct.

Based on these divergent viewpoints, strain and control theory present contradictory predictions concerning the effect of dropping out of high school on subsequent criminal involvement. According to strain theory, because dropping out eliminates the source of frustration brought about by failure in the school, criminal conduct should decline sharply following dropout. According to control theory, however, because dropping out reduces institutional control, criminal behavior should increase.

Dropouts and Later Criminality

Although these theories offer contradictory predictions about the relationship between dropping out and delinquency, both enjoy some degree of empirical support. The most influential investigation of the relationship between dropping out and delinquency, Elliott and Voss's panel study (1974), is clearly supportive of strain theory. Elliott and Voss followed 2,617 subjects from the ninth grade until "the usual date for graduation from high school" (Elliott, 1978: 457) and hypothesized that " . . . the act of leaving school should reduce school-related frustrations and alienation and thereby lower the motivational stimulus for delinquency" (Elliott, 1978: 454). To test this hypothesis they compared rates of official delinquency for high school graduates and dropouts. The rates for dropouts were both higher and increased more rapidly than those for graduates throughout the high school years. Indeed, for the dropout group delinquency was highest just before leaving school and then, regardless of the age at which the student dropped out, declined sharply. Thus, dropping out of school was followed by a clear reduction in delinquent activity. Elliott and Voss conclude that these results ". . . support the basic proposition that the school is the critical social context for the generation of delinquent behavior" (Elliott and Voss, 1974: 124).

Other researchers examining the relationship between dropping out and subsequent criminal activity have produced similar results. In a pilot study to the one just described, Elliott (1966) also found that delinquency declined after students dropped out of high school. Mukherjee (1971), using data from the Philadelphia birth cohort of 1945, replicated the basic finding of Elliott and Voss. He found delinquency rates to be higher while subjects were in school as compared to the postschool period. But for high school dropouts, over two-thirds of those who had juvenile arrest records were no longer delinquent once they dropped out, and only 7% of the delinquent dropouts committed their first offense after dropping out (Mukherjee, 1971: 87). Finally, LeBlanc, Biron, and Pronovost (1979) also report that delinquency declined for dropouts once they left high school.

Although these results support strain theory's hypothesis, the strength of that support is limited by two methodological considerations. First, the observations in all four studies were completed by the time the subjects were nineteen years of age, an exceedingly short follow-up period. Thus these studies only demonstrate the short-term effects of dropping out and cannot determine if dropping out has a dampening effect on criminal behavior in the long term.

Second, the relationship between dropping out and delinquent behavior observed in these studies could be severely contaminated by the influence of the age distribution of crime. Following a steady upward trend during the early teenage years, criminal behavior exhibits a precipitous drop after age sixteen or seventeen (see for example Wolfgang, Thornberry, and Figlio, in press, chapter 4). Since most dropouts leave school at these same ages, the ensuing reduction in criminal activity coincides quite closely with a reduction expected from the age distribution alone. Therefore, in assessing the relationship between these variables, it is essential to control explicitly for the influence of age.

Despite the importance of Elliott and Voss's research in this area, these methodological limitations suggest that it is premature to conclude that there is overwhelming support for a strain theory interpretation. In addition, other studies which extend the follow-up period until subjects are in their mid-twenties report findings more consistent with a social control perspective. Polk et al. (1981: 300–301) report that during the early twenties dropouts have consistently higher rates of criminality than do graduates. Indeed, it is not until the mid-twenties that the rates for the two groups converge. Hathaway, Reynolds, and Monachesi (1969) also followed dropouts and graduates into the mid-twenties and report consistently higher rates of criminal involvement for dropouts. Finally, Bachman and O'Malley (1978) examined this relationship for a nationally representative sample of adolescents. Through the early twenties they find higher rates of criminal activity for the high school dropouts than any other educational group (Bachman and O'Malley, 1978: 176–178).

Although results from these three studies are consistent with control theory's hypothesis that dropping out is positively associated with subsequent criminal behavior, they focus on the long-term effects of dropping out rather than the more immediate consequences that were investigated by Elliott and Voss. Polk et al., for example, indicate that " . . . measures regarding the

timing of the dropout are not as finely tuned as those used by Elliott and Voss, so that we do not observe these young persons in that crucial period immediately after withdrawal'' (1981: 300). Nor do the other two studies.

In general, therefore, while these two sets of empirical studies report contradictory results, they also emphasize different consequences of dropping out. Elliott and Voss report that dropping out has a rather immediate dampening effect on delinquency (see also Elliott, 1966; Mukherjee, 1971; LeBlanc et al., 1979), while Polk et al. report that in the long run dropping out has an enhancing effect on criminal involvement (see also Hathaway et al., 1969; Bachman et al., 1978.) Thus, empirical evidence on the relationship between dropping out and later criminal behavior is equivocal and does not provide clear support for either strain or control theory.

Research Problem

The present study reevaluates the relationship between these variables to provide a clearer assessment of the divergent predictions that can be derived from strain and control theories. The design replicates that of Elliott and Voss as closely as possible and at the same time attempts to remedy methodological problems of previous studies. Three methodological factors are considered:

1. The observation period is extended to cover the early adult years as well as the period immediately following the act of dropping out. Thus, both short-term and long-term effects of dropping out of high school are examined.
2. In light of the massive dampening effect that age has on criminal conduct after age sixteen, the association between dropping out of high school and later crime is assessed in relativistic terms. Specifically, analysis poses the

question of whether dropping out of high school alters (i.e., whether it increases or decreases) the general downward trend in criminal involvement expected at these ages. The anticipated answers to this question from strain and control perspectives are as follows:

Strain Theory: since dropping out alleviates the frustration arising from school failure, dropping out should reduce the motivation to delinquency and should increase the downward trend in criminal behavior observed at these ages. The criminal behavior of dropouts should decline *more sharply* than that of graduates after departure from school and the rates for dropouts should converge rather quickly with those of graduates.

Control Theory: since dropping out represents a reduction in social control, dropping out should increase the likelihood of criminal and delinquent behavior and the general downward trend in criminal involvement should be slowed down or decreased. Thus, rates of criminal involvement will decline *gradually* for dropouts and will not converge with those of graduates.

3. Finally, the relationship between dropout status and subsequent criminality is tested within major demographic subgroups and when the influence of postschool experiences are controlled. For the former, race and social status or origin are introduced into the analysis. For the latter, Elliott and Voss's design is again followed and marital status and employment status are held constant to see how postschool experiences mediate the effect of dropping out on subsequent crime.

Methodology

The present study reevaluates the association between dropout status and later criminal involvement, examining both short-term and long-term effects and controlling for the influence of both age and postschool experiences. To do so, it utilizes longitudi-

nal data from a 10% sample of the Philadelphia birth cohort of 1945. The cohort consists of all males (n = 9,945) born in that year who resided in Philadelphia from at least the age of ten to the age of eighteen (Wolfgang, Figlio, and Sellin, 1972). The members of the 10% sample were the focus of a follow-up study that extended the observation period to age twenty-five. For the entire sample (n = 975) complete arrest histories are available and, in addition, attempts were made to interview all members of the sample. Successful interviews were conducted with 567, or 62%. Given this response rate the necessity of weighting the data for nonresponse was carefully assessed and the effect of nonresponse was found to be negligible on correlational analyses and on the estimation of significance levels (Wolfgang et al., in press; Singer, 1977). Thus, while the attrition rate is fairly substantial, its consequences on drawing inferences from these data appear to be relatively minor. Moreover, the disadvantages of attrition are clearly offset by the fact that the cohort design traces the criminal careers of dropouts and graduates from the beginning of high school until the age of twenty-five.

Variables for analysis

The measure of the independent variable, dropout status, is based on responses to interview items in which each subject reported his educational attainment. Subjects are divided into high school dropouts, those who report completing less than twelve years of schooling, and high school graduates, those who report completing twelve or more years.[2] For most analyses dropouts are further divided into groups based on the age at which they left high school.

The dependent variable, criminal involvement, is measured by the number of times each subject was arrested. These data are arrayed in annual intervals so that criminal involvement both before and after dropout can be compared.

For reasons mentioned above, four additional variables are included in analysis. Race is a dichotomous variable with the sample divided into white and black subjects. Social status of origin is also a dichotomy in which subjects are divided into white- and blue-collar categories based on the U.S. Census classification scheme. The occupation for this classification is that of the subject's father while the subject was in high school. Marital status is based on responses to interview items in which each subject described his marital history. Finally, unemployment is based on an interview item in which each subject traced his employment history from high school until the time of the interview. Unemployment is defined as any period of time the person was not employed, a full-time student, or in the armed services. Due to incomplete unemployment or educational histories, analyses including these variables are based on a sample size of 555.[3]

Results

The mean number of arrests at each age, from ages thirteen to twenty-five, are presented in Table 11.1 and Figure 11.1. These annual rates are displayed for all high school dropouts, three subgroups based on the age at dropout,[4] and for comparative purposes all high school graduates and graduates who did not continue on to college.

In general, the age distribution of criminality is similar for all groups, rising during the teenage years, peaking at sixteen or seventeen, and then declining throughout the early twenties. The central theoretical question, however, is whether dropping out of high school produces an additional

Table 11.1
Mean Number of Arrests at Each Age for Graduates and Dropouts by Age of Dropping Out

| | Age | | | | | | | | | | | | | N |
	13	14	15	16	17	18	19	20	21	22	23	24	25	
All Graduates	.02	.04	.06	.13	.11	.05	.04	.06	.04	.04	.04	.04	.05	433
Graduates with No College	.02	.06	.10	.20	.19	.05	.08	.08	.05	.04	.07	.08	.08	201
All Dropouts	.13	.24	.36	.49	.48	.37	.35	.32	.25	.19	.22	.17	.18	127
Dropouts at:														
Age 16	.14	.66	.34	.55	.59	.34	.38	.38	.38	.45	.41	.31	.07	29
Age 17	.11	.16	.36	.52	.50	.39	.29	.27	.16	.09	.14	.14	.12	56
Age 18	.16	.06	.39	.39	.35	.35	.45	.36	.29	.13	.16	.10	.39	31

effect on subsequent crime rates over and above the basic downward trend produced by maturation.

Little support is found for the strain hypothesis that dropping out of school has a short-term dampening effect on criminal behavior. For two of the age-at-dropout groups, those who dropped out at sixteen and at eighteen, the mean number of arrests are higher in the year following dropout than in the preceding year. For those who dropped out at age seventeen the percentage decrease in arrests from seventeen to eighteen, 22%, is less than the comparable percentage decrease for all graduates, 55%, and for graduates who did not attend college, 74%. While this analysis closely replicates Elliott and Voss's study, which ended the follow-up period at age nineteen, it does not produce comparable results. There does not appear to be an immediate reduction in criminal involvement following dropping out.

When analysis addresses the long-term impact of dropping out, results indicate that dropping out of high school is positively related to adult criminal involvement. For high school graduates arrest rates drop sharply from age sixteen to age eighteen and reach a point of stability at approximately nineteen years of age. Indeed, after age eighteen the rates do not exceed .06 for all graduates or .08 for graduates who did not attend college. For dropouts, however, these rates do not exhibit the same precipitous drop in the late teenage years. They decline rather gradually throughout the early twenties and it is not until age twenty-two or twenty-three that the rates converge with those of the graduates and reach a point of stability. Even at these ages, however, dropouts are arrested more frequently than are graduates. Thus, rather than reducing criminal involvement, dropping out of high school tends to be related to high rates of crime throughout the early twenties.

Although dropping out appears to have a long-term enhancing effect on later criminal involvement, the data in Figure 11.1 indicate that for all groups criminal behavior

Figure 11.1: Annual Arrest Rates by Dropout Status

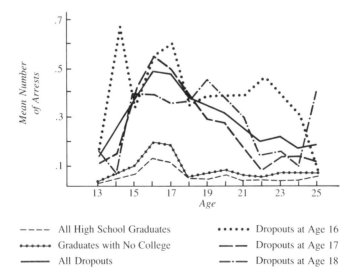

Table 11.2
Regression of Offense Rates by Age on Dropout Status and Age

	All Dropouts	Dropouts at 16	Dropouts at 17	Dropouts at 18
Intercept	.58*	.37*	.71*	.55*
Age	−.03*	−.02*	−.03*	−.02*
	(−.44)	(−.21)	(−.55)	(−.44)
Dropout	.25*	.36*	.22*	.23*
	(.84)	(.94)	(.70)	(.79)
R^2	.90*	.92*	.79*	.82*

Standardized regression coefficients are in parentheses.
*p < .05

declines substantially throughout the early twenties. It is necessary, therefore, to determine if dropout status has a significant effect once the dampening influence of age is controlled. To do so, annual arrest rates, from age sixteen, the peak age of delinquency, to age twenty-four,[5] are regressed on age and a dummy variable representing dropout status.* High school dropouts are coded 1.[6] The term of primary interest is that of dropout status; if control theory is accurate, as the previous descriptive results suggest, this term should be positive and significant. Results are presented for all dropouts as well as the three age-at-dropout groups. In all cases, dropouts are contrasted with all high school graduates.

In the model comparing all dropouts with all graduates (Table 11.2), the coefficient of determination is .90 and both terms are significant.** Age has a negative effect on criminal involvement as expected. Con-

*Editor's Note: See Appendix 1 for a brief discussion of "multiple regression."

**Editor's Note: A "coefficient of determination" (R^2) is a measure of the percentage of variance in the dependent variable explained by the independent variables used in the multiple regression analysis. A value of .90 indicates that age and dropout status explain 90% of the variance in the offense rate.

trolling for the influence of age, dropout status has a significant positive effect on crime rates throughout these years. Moreover, the standardized regression coefficients suggest that dropout status has a stronger impact on the frequency of arrest than does age. Thus, dropping out is positively related to criminal involvement even when the general decline produced by the age distribution is held constant.

When this model is estimated separately for the three age-at-dropout groups (Table 11.2), the basic results are replicated. Age has a significant negative impact on criminal involvement, and when the effect of age is held constant dropout status is seen to exert a significant positive effect on arrest rates. Thus, regardless of the age of dropout, dropouts have significantly higher rates of subsequent criminal involvement than do graduates.

In general, therefore, results of this analysis offer little support for a strain model interpretation of the association between dropping out of high school and subsequent criminal involvement; dropouts exhibit neither a short-term nor long-term reduction in criminal activity. These results are, however, quite consistent with a control perspective which suggests that criminal behavior should remain high following the reduction in social control represented by dropping out of school. Even controlling for the influence of age, dropout status is found to be positively related to later criminal behavior.

Controlling for Social Status and Race

To this point the results appear more consistent with a social control perspective than a strain perspective. Since strain theory's prediction is made specifically for lower class students, however, it is necessary to hold social status of origin constant in assessing its prediction. In addition, given the high correlation between social status and minority group status, race is also held constant. When this is done the number of subjects in each age-at-dropout group becomes quite small so data are only presented for the total group and those who dropped out at age seventeen, the modal age at dropout.

Social status

In general, the pattern of results observed for the total sample is replicated when social status of origin is held constant (Figure 11.2).[7] For subjects from blue-collar homes, the group of particular interest in strain theory, there is no evidence of a sharp drop in delinquent activity following departure from school. Comparing their postschool crime rates to those of blue-collar graduates, one sees that they are considerably higher and that they exhibit only a gradual decline following the time of dropout. Indeed, it is not until age twenty-three that the arrest rates for these groups begin to converge.

Results for dropouts from white-collar backgrounds are more difficult to interpret since there are only twenty-two subjects in this category and only twelve dropped out at age seventeen. Dropouts have higher crime rates than do graduates, but the rates for the two groups converge at an early

Figure 11.2:   Annual Arrest Rates by Dropout Status and Social Status

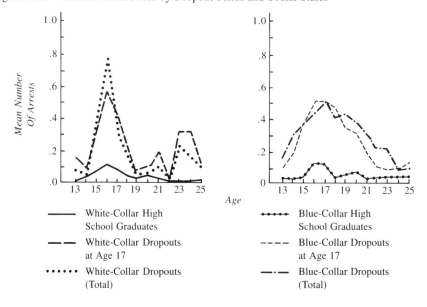

————— White-Collar High
           School Graduates

— — White-Collar Dropouts
           at Age 17

• • • • • • White-Collar Dropouts
           (Total)

••••• Blue-Collar High
           School Graduates

— — — — Blue-Collar Dropouts
           at Age 17

—•— Blue-Collar Dropouts
           (Total)

point (age nineteen) after which they remain relatively low. Thus, for these subjects dropping out is less frequent and tends to have a small impact on subsequent crime.

Regression analyses confirm this interpretation (Table 11.3). For subjects from white-collar homes the coefficient of determination is relatively low (.38) and only the regression coefficient for dropout status is significant. For those from blue-collar

backgrounds, however, both dropout status and age are significant, with a coefficient of determination of .89.

Race

When race is held constant the general pattern is again replicated (Figure 11.3). For white graduates arrest rates are low and show remarkably little variation throughout the study period; at no time does the rate exceed .10 arrests per year. For white

Figure 11.3:   Annual Arrest Rates by Dropout Status and Race

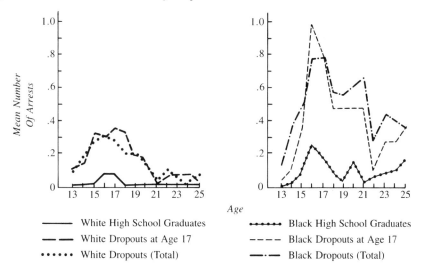

———— White High School Graduates   •••••• Black High School Graduates

— — White Dropouts at Age 17   — — — — Black Dropouts at Age 17

•••••• White Dropouts (Total)   —•— Black Dropouts (Total)

Table 11.3

Regression of Offense Rates by Age on Dropout Status and Age, Controlling for Race and Social Status

	Social Status		Race	
	White-Collar	Blue-Collar	White	Black
Intercept	.63*	.57*	.51*	.79*
Age	−.03	−.03*	−.02*	−.03*
	(−.43)	(−.40)	(−.60)	(−.33)
Dropout	.16*	.28*	.13*	.46*
	(.44)	(.86)	(.62)	(.88)
R²	.38*	.89*	.75*	.88*

Standardized regression coefficients are in parentheses.
*p < .05

dropouts, however, the rates peak at sixteen and seventeen and then begin a gradual decline until age twenty-one. From that point on they are comparable to rates for white graduates.

For black subjects major differences are again observed between dropouts and graduates. At all ages the dropouts exhibit considerably higher rates of criminal involvement than do graduates. Indeed, for black subjects rates for dropouts and graduates do not converge even by age twenty-five. Criminal involvement for black dropouts declines at age twenty-two but then increases and remains moderately high until age twenty-five.

Results of regression analyses also indicate the strong influence of dropout status on later criminal behavior for both blacks and whites (Table 11.3). In both cases, regression coefficients for dropout status and age are significant and in the expected direction.

Summary

Holding constant social status of origin and race does not alter the basic finding of this analysis. At all ages, both before and after dropping out, high school dropouts have higher rates of criminal involvement than do graduates. Of particular interest, given strain theory's class-specific predictions, are the results for blue-collar subjects and blacks. In both cases, analysis indicates that dropping out is not followed by a substantial reduction in criminal involvement. On the contrary, dropping out is positively related to later crime for these subjects.

Postschool Experiences

Overall, these results are quite consistent with a social control model. For all subjects and all subgroups examined, dropout status has a positive effect on subsequent crime.

The final analysis examines the postschool experiences of these subjects to see if dropping out has an independent effect on later crime or if the effect is primarily due to different experiences of dropouts and graduates. Following Elliott and Voss's design, the influences of marital status and unemployment status are examined.

Since each subject's status on these two variables can vary from year to year, analysis is conducted separately at each age from twenty-one to twenty-four.[8] Marital status is a dummy variable, with subjects classified as married (coded as 1) if they reported being married at any time during the year of interest.[9] Unemployment is an interval measure reflecting the proportion of time during the year that the subject was unemployed. Finally, the dependent variable is the number of times the subject was arrested during the same year.

Results of this analysis indicate that, at all four ages, high levels of unemployment are positively associated with criminal behavior (Table 11.4). For marital status, however, the regression coefficients are close to zero and do not attain statistical significance at any age. Finally, dropout status exerts the expected positive effect on adult crime, even when the influence of marriage and employment are held constant. From ages twenty-one to twenty-three, the regression coefficients for dropout status are positive and significant while at the last age studied, twenty-four, the coefficient is not significantly different from zero. The latter finding is consistent with earlier results which indicate that arrest rates for dropouts and graduates converge by the mid-twenties. Overall, therefore, these results indicate that dropout status does have a positive impact on criminal involvement, especially during the early twenties, even when appropriate postschool experiences are held constant.

Table 11.4
Regression of Annual Arrest Rates on Dropout, Marital and Unemployment Statuses by Age

	Age			
	21	22	23	24
Intercept	− .01	.01	.04	.01
Dropout	.16*	.08*	.11*	− .02
Status	(.15)	(.11)	(.15)	(−.03)
Marital	.04	.01	− .02	.01
Status	(.05)	(.02)	(−.02)	(.00)
Unemployment	.62*	.28*	.19*	− 1.03*
Status	(.22)	(.18)	(.10)	(.40)
R^2	.09*	.05*	.04*	.15*

Standardized regression coefficients are in parentheses.
*$p < .05$

Conclusion

Criminological research has yet to provide a clear understanding of the relationship between dropping out of high school and subsequent criminal activity. Indeed contradictory assertions, both theoretical and empirical, can be found concerning the direction of this association. According to strain theory dropping out should be *negatively* related to the level of criminal involvement, a prediction that has received some empirical support (e.g., Elliott and Voss, 1974). On the other hand, social control theory predicts that dropping out should be *positively* related to later criminal behavior, and that prediction has also received some support (e.g., Polk et al., 1981).

Because of these contradictory findings, we reexamined the direction of the association between dropping out of high school and subsequent criminal behavior. In doing so we attempted to reduce the confounding influence of some methodological shortcomings of previous studies. Specifically, we examined both short-term and long-term effects of dropping out and explicitly considered the influence of age on this relationship.

Regardless of how the analysis was conducted, one ineluctable conclusion emerged: dropping out of high school is positively associated with later criminal activity. Unlike Elliott and Voss, we do not find an immediate dampening effect of dropping out on criminal involvement. Indeed, for two of the three age-at-dropout groups, criminal behavior increased in the year following departure from school. Moreover, dropping out of high school was also found to have a positive long-term effect on criminal behavior. Throughout the early twenties dropouts have consistently higher rates of arrests than do graduates and it is not until the mid-twenties that the rates for the two groups begin to converge. These findings are also observed for minority group subjects and those from blue-collar backgrounds, the groups of particular interest to strain theory. Finally, dropout status was also found to have a significant positive effect on crime when the postschool experiences of marriage and employment are controlled. In general, therefore, results of this analysis are quite consistent with the theoretical expectations of social control theory; dropping out has a positive effect on subsequent arrest even when age and postschool experiences are controlled.

Although control theory appears to be more accurate than strain theory in assessing the role that dropping out of school plays in the genesis of delinquency, these results cannot be interpreted as providing general support for a control perspective versus a strain perspective. The present analysis has focused exclusively on one behavioral area—dropping out of school—while the theories are concerned with a much wider array of behavioral issues—family, peers, beliefs, and so forth. Nevertheless, with respect to dropping out of school, where the theories do offer contradictory predictions, the evidence from this study is quite clear: dropping out is significantly and positively related to subsequent criminal involvement as predicted by social control theory.

Notes

1. Because the expected relationship between school and crime varies by social class in strain theory and is invariant in control theory, the remainder of this discussion will focus on lower class youth where the contrast between the theories is clearest. Social class of origin will be held constant in the analysis so that the more specific prediction offered by strain theory can be tested.

2. It is possible that some subjects who report completing twelve years of schooling did not actually graduate, but the available data do not allow distinguishing between these subjects and actual graduates. An examination of available records suggests, however, that this is not a large group.

3. The basic difference between this study and Mukherjee's (1971), which also uses the Philadelphia cohort of 1945, is that his analysis is based on the original study that relied solely on official data and which completed data collection when the subjects were 18. The present analysis is based on the follow-up study which collected interview data and which extended the study to age 25. Hence the differences in design and results.

4. There were also dropouts at ages 14 (n = 2), 15 (n = 8), and 19 (n = 1), but these frequencies are too small to permit age-specific analysis.

5. The arrest rates at age twenty-five exhibit large and unpatterned changes for some of the age-at-dropout groups (see Figure 11.1) and have been eliminated from the analysis. Their inclusion reduced the coefficient of determination somewhat but did not affect the pattern of the results. Also, the models presented in Table 11.2 were estimated using the logarithm of the annual arrest rates as the dependent variable with no appreciable improvement in the fit of the model. Thus, the simpler linear models are presented.

6. A regression model including a term representing the interaction of age and drop-out status was also considered, but severe problems of collinearity between dropout status and the interaction term precluded its estimation.

7. Tables that present the mean values for these groups are available upon request.

8. Prior to age twenty-one the number of subjects who were married is too small for analysis.

9. A more precise measure, such as the proportion of time each year that the subject was married, is not available in these data.

References

Bachman, Jerald G. and Patrick M. O'Malley. Youth in Transition Volume VI: Adolescence to Adulthood: Change and Stability in the Lives of Young Men. Ann Arbor: University of Michigan Press, 1978.

Cloward, Richard A. and Lloyd E. Ohlin. Delinquency and Opportunity: A Theory of Delinquent Gangs. Glencoe, IL: Free Press, 1960.

Cohen, Albert K. Delinquent Boys. New York: Free Press, 1955.

Elliott, Delbert S. and Harwin Voss. Delinquency and Dropout. Lexington, MA: Lexington, 1974.

Elliott, Delbert S. "Delinquency, school attendance, and school dropout." Social Problems 13: 307–14 (1966).

————. "Delinquency and school dropout." In Leonard D. Savitz and Norman Johnston (eds.), Crime in Society. New York: Wiley, 1978.

Hathaway, Starke R., Phillis C. Reynolds, and Elio D. Monachesi. "Follow-up of the later careers and lives of 1,000 boys who dropped out of high school." Journal of Consulting and Clinical Psychology 33: 370–80 (1969).

Hirschi, Travis. Causes of Delinquency. Berkeley: University of California Press, 1969.

LeBlanc, Marc, Louise Biron, and Louison Pronovost. "Psycho-social development and delinquency evolution." Mimeograph, University of Montreal, 1979.

Mukherjee, S.K. A Typological Study of School Status and Delinquency. Unpublished doctoral dissertation. Philadelphia: University of Pennsylvania, 1971.

Phillips, John C. and Delos H. Kelly. "School failure and delinquency: Which causes which?" Criminology 17: 194-207 (1979).

Polk, Kenneth, Christine Adler, Gordon Bazemore, Gerald Blake, Sheila Cordray, Garry Coventry, James Galvin, and Mark Temple. Becoming Adult: An Analysis of Maturational Development from Age 16 to 30 of a Cohort of Young Men. Final Report of the Marion County Youth Study. Eugene: University of Oregon, 1981.

Polk, Kenneth. "Schools and the delinquency experience." Criminal Justice and Behavior 2: 315–38 (1975).

Singer, Simon I. "The effect of non-response on the birth cohort follow-up survey." Unpublished. Center for Studies in Criminology and Criminal Law. Philadelphia: University of Pennsylvania, 1977.

Wolfgang, Marvin E., Robert M. Figlio, and Thorsten Sellin. Delinquency in a Birth Cohort. Chicago: University of Chicago Press, 1972.

Wolfgang, Marvin E., Terence P. Thornberry, and Robert M. Figlio. From Boy to Man—From Delinquency to Crime: Followup to the 1945 Philadelphia Birth Cohort (In press).

Organizing the Community for Delinquency Prevention

12

Ronald J. Berger

Juvenile delinquency prevention encompasses a wide range of practices, and there is little consensus on what the term "prevention" means (Johnson, 1987; Wright and Dixon, 1977). In general, three preventive orientations can be identified: primary prevention, secondary prevention, and tertiary prevention. Primary prevention attempts to keep delinquent behavior from arising in the first place; it involves strategies directed at the entire community and not just at individuals who are "the casualties seeking treatment" (Klein and Goldston, 1977:vii). Secondary prevention focuses on early diagnoses and treatment of vulnerable children, and tertiary prevention aims to avoid recidivist behavior after delinquent acts have already occurred. Some observers argue that it would be preferable to limit the use of the term prevention to primary prevention, while rehabilitation would be a more appropriate label for

secondary and tertiary prevention (Gilbert, 1982; Klein and Goldston, 1977).

The purpose of this paper is to critically examine approaches to delinquency prevention that embody the notion of primary prevention. These efforts involve large-scale intervention and social change strategies that attempt to provide opportunities to disadvantaged youth, develop community resources, implement institutional reform, and organize and mobilize target-area residents for collective action.[1] A typology of community organization practice, as developed by Jack Rothman (1979a; Cox et al., 1979), will be used to analyze the assumptions, objectives, and methods underlying programs of this nature. While there is controversy as to whether there exists a coherent body of community organization *theory* (Schwartz, 1977), there are clearly delineated models of community organization practice. In this article, three models of community organization—locality development, social planning, and social action—are used to evaluate three exemplary delinquency prevention programs: the Chicago Area Project (begun in the 1930s), the 1960s provision of opportunity

Parts of this article, which are reprinted with permission, appeared as "Community Organization Approaches to the Prevention of Juvenile Delinquency" in the *Journal of Sociology and Social Welfare*, Vol. 12, No. 1, 1985, pp. 129–53.

programs, and the 1960s comprehensive community action projects such as Mobilization for Youth. These programs spanned a range of local and federal efforts that emphasized alteration of neighborhood, institutional, and economic conditions that were believed to cause delinquency.

After outlining the assumptions underlying the three models of community organization practice and evaluating the delinquency prevention programs, I also consider their implications for contemporary efforts at crime prevention. In the 1970s and 1980s prevention strategies shifted away from a "social problems" or "root causes" approach that focused on the behavior and motivation of potential offenders toward an "opportunity reduction" approach that focused on the behavior of potential victims (Lewis and Salem, 1981; Rosenbaum, 1988).[2] Moreover, criticism of this shift has led to a renewed interest in traditional offender-oriented approaches (Curtis, 1987a). Since the assumptions underlying the more recent victim-oriented and offender-oriented programs are rooted in earlier efforts, it is imperative that these strategies take into account the advantages and limitations of past practices.

Models of Community Organization Practice

Community organization is defined as "intervention at the community level oriented towards improving or changing community institutions and solving community problems" (Cox et al., 1979:3). For analytic purposes, Rothman (1979a) delineates three different models of community organization practice: locality development, social planning, and social action.[3] Each of these has its own assumptions, utilities, and limitations. Locality development and social planning more readily lend themselves

to a consensus view of society and the maintenance of social stability. Social action is oriented toward a conflict view of society and the promotion of institutional social change. However, these approaches need not be applied in a mutually exclusive manner and can be either mixed or phased in their application to specific community problems.

According to Rothman, the central assumption of *locality development* is that community change is best brought about by enlisting the broadest range of people at the local level to collectively identify needs, goals, and solutions to problems. The basic themes include "democratic procedures, voluntary cooperation, self-help, development of indigenous leadership, and educational objectives" (Rothman, 1979a:27). Process goals are accorded the highest priority; that is, the primary goal is to establish cooperative working relationships and widespread interest and participation in community affairs. Consensus tactics are used by the community organizer to bring various interest groups, social classes, and ethnic groups together to identify their common concerns. It is assumed that these groups have interests that are basically reconcilable and amenable to rational problem-solving. However, it is the process of bringing the community together, rather than the accomplishment of particular tasks, that is central to locality development.

In the *social planning* approach, emphasis is placed on the design and application of controlled rational change by "experts" who possess specialized skills and knowledge. The emphasis is on task goals, that is, the completion of a specified task related to the solution of a tangible problem. Community members are viewed as customers or beneficiaries of services and are not involved in the planning or delivery process.

Social change tends to be gradual, maintenance-oriented, removed from politics, and regulated and controlled by professionals who are not themselves members of the client population. The organizer often acts as a mediator between conflicting interests and attempts to tone down more radical demands.

Finally, in the *social action* approach, the community organizer seeks to mobilize the economically and politically disadvantaged members of the community to make effective demands for the redistribution of resources and alteration of institutional policies. This approach may involve both task and process goals. Conflict tactics are frequently engaged in as the organizer attempts to build a large constituency capable of obtaining and utilizing power to promote its own interests. Dominant political and economic groups and institutions are often the targets of change and considered to be part of the community's problems. The organizer is a partisan and advocate of the disenfranchised and not a mediator of conflicting community interests.

As ideal types, locality development, social planning, and social action identify the basic assumptions underlying various large-scale delinquency prevention programs. In the following sections, I use these community organization models to evaluate the Chicago Area Project, the provision of opportunity programs, and the comprehensive community action projects. While these efforts were not pure applications of any single model of community organization practice, each contained different emphases that can be illuminated by applying community organization concepts.

The Chicago Area Project

The Chicago Area Project (CAP) is considered to be the classic illustration of locality

development as applied to juvenile delinquency, as well as the foundation for most contemporary prevention efforts (Mech, 1975; Reiss, 1986). Originated by sociologist Clifford Shaw in 1934, it was "the first systematic challenge to the dominance of psychology and psychiatry in public and private programs for the prevention and treatment of . . . delinquency" (Schlossman et al., 1984:2). The CAP was rooted in the social disorganization theory of Shaw and Henry McKay who examined the ecological distribution of delinquency and found it related to the environmental conditions associated with urban slums (Shaw et al., 1929: Shaw and McKay, 1942). But unlike the anomie-opportunity or strain theory that formed the basis of later programs (Cloward and Ohlin, 1960; Merton, 1938), Shaw and McKay did not consider employment or economic issues to be the central problems.[4] Rather, the social disorganization of these communities was indicative of a breakdown in adults' abilities to supervise and exert informal social control over youth and to socialize them (through family, education, and religious institutions) to law-abiding values (Bursik, 1988; Simcha-Fagan and Schwartz, 1986).

The underlying philosophy of the CAP was that only through the mobilization and active participation of the entire community was it possible to impact significantly upon the problem of delinquency (Dixon and Wright, 1974; Spergel, 1969). While the CAP was overseen by a board of directors that raised and distributed money and assisted community groups in obtaining grants to match local government funds, the various community committees that were formed operated as independent, self-governing organizations with their own names and charters (Krisberg, 1978).

Thus, self-help and democratic procedures were major themes. Project staff workers functioned in an advisory role, but decisions about policies and programs were made by community members, independent of the approval or disapproval of the project staff. The task for community organizers was to convince local residents to assume responsibility for the prevention of delinquency, to help them exercise more influence over their children, and to facilitate cooperation and joint problem-solving among the residents, the churches, the schools, the courts, the police, and other significant community groups. The focus was on building community cohesion and pride and on developing residents' confidence in their ability to change their lives (Empey, 1982; Schlossman and Sedlak, 1983; Schlossman et al., 1984).

The CAP engaged people in a variety of activities intended to achieve its goals. The development of recreation and camping programs, as well as boys' clubs, hobby groups, and rap groups were central features. These efforts aimed to provide youth with structured, supervised alternatives to crime, and they served as springboards for bringing people together, counseling delinquent youth, and providing minimal employment for youth leaders. The CAP also pioneered the use of detached workers to provide "curbstone counseling" for juveniles and identify indigenous gang leaders who might be encouraged to adopt the legitimate community's values. Such counseling was less social work *per se* and more an "aggressive, omnipresent caring and monitoring of 'youth at risk' in their natural, criminogenic habitats" (Schlossman et al., 1984:15).

Efforts to intercede in matters related to the schools and juvenile justice system foreshadowed more contemporary efforts at child advocacy and diversion. School mediation involved attempts to modify inappropriate curricula, to transfer students to schools with more suitable programs or personnel, to mainstream students who were incorrectly placed in classes for deficient or incorrigible youth (or conversely, to place students who required special treatment into appropriate programs), and to reinstate students who had been expelled for minor delinquencies. Juvenile justice mediation involved efforts to divert youth to appropriate community agencies, to reform the jails and prisons, and to assist parolees in adjusting to community life (Schlossman et al., 1984).

The CAP applied the model of locality development in a purist fashion and utilized consensus tactics. The accommodative spirit was illustrated by the community's willingness to accept responsibility for the city's dilapidated physical appearance and by its decision not to indict the city's service departments. On the other hand, the assumption of consensus and cooperative problem-solving that underlies locality development was often lacking. It was difficult to find common ground between local residents and representatives of the business community, schools, churches, and the criminal justice system. For instance, attempts to enlist the help of the business community in expanding the employment opportunities for delinquent youths were not always successful. The project was also criticized for its heavy reliance on the voluntary services of the Polish Catholic Church, which was accused of using the recreational programs to proselytize potential converts, even though the Church was effective in galvanizing community support (Schlossman et al., 1984). In addition, programs in some neighborhoods were criticized for interfering with those sponsored by other groups. Even the professional staff of organizers was sometimes annoyed and upset about its loss of control over the project, suggesting a preference for a social planning approach to community organizing (Schlossman and Sedlak, 1983).

One of the strongest criticisms was leveled by Saul Alinsky, the CAP's most aggressive detached worker. Although the CAP attempted to increase community empowerment by training indigenous leadership and intervening in institutional affairs, Alinsky argued that it was inadequate to achieve significant economic change. He advocated confrontational tactics indicative of a social action approach to community organizing in order to force more fundamental political and economic concessions from the power structure. Alinsky's frustration undoubtedly derived from a basic dilemma of locality development strategies—how to sustain community interest following mobilization when process goals are given priority over task goals (Schlossman and Sedlak, 1983).

In spite of some statistical evidence (particularly regarding the parolee assistance program) that delinquency was slightly reduced by the CAP in the first decade of its operation, Shaw himself was aware of the difficulty of demonstrating conclusively the effectiveness of the project (Krisberg, 1978; Schlossman et al., 1984). As he observed, trends in delinquency rates were influenced by variations in the official definition of delinquency, changes in population composition, and variations in the administrative procedures employed by law enforcement agencies (cited in Witmer and Tufts, 1954). Nevertheless, Shaw was decidedly optimistic about the success of the CAP (Schlossman and Sedlak, 1983), and perhaps, as Kobrin (1959) argued, the case for the CAP ultimately rests on logical and analytic grounds. Shaw was mainly interested in demonstrating the possibility of operationalizing his analysis of social problems through particular organizational mechanisms. He believed that: (1) delin-

quency was symptomatic of underlying social processes; (2) simply responding on a one-to-one basis with individual youths was ineffective; and (3) the entire community must and could be organized effectively to solve its own problems.

However, according to some observers, by the late 1950s the "vibrant and successful" CAP was being transformed into a rather rigid bureaucratic organization as its staff positions were absorbed by the Illinois State Division of Youth Services (Krisberg, 1978:33). Similarly, Schlossman et al. (1984) noted how external funding agencies have influenced the goals and priorities of CAP community groups. Thus, the CAP has lost some of the autonomy characteristic of a locality development approach to community organization. Nevertheless, Schlossman et al., in their preliminary evaluation of the "modern-day" CAP, concluded that the evidence suggests that the CAP has been effective in reducing delinquency. As they observed, "to rediscover the CAP is to be reminded" that disadvantaged communities "still retain a remarkable capacity for pride, civility, and the exercise of a modicum of self-governance" (p. 47).

The 1960s Provision of Opportunity Programs

Many observers view the delinquency prevention programs of the 1960s as direct descendants of the CAP (Empey, 1982; Freeman et al., 1979; Ohlin, 1983). However, there are significant differences that can be highlighted by applying Rothman's community organization typology. The various programs associated with the 1960s period and the "War on Poverty" were predicated on the anomie-opportunity or strain theory of Robert Merton (1938) and Richard Cloward and Lloyd Ohlin (1960). Essentially, the theory postulated that delinquent behavior develops because of a discrepancy between the aspirations of disadvantaged youth for culturally approved goals (i.e., success, money, material goods) and their opportunities to achieve these goals through legitimate means (i.e., education, employment). In general, the prescribed remedy involved significant improvement in the economic and educational opportunities of low-income and minority youth.

The 1960s programs included two major orientations—the "provision of opportunity" programs and the "comprehensive community action" projects. The former utilized a social planning model of community organization, while the latter employed a social action model mixed with locality development and social planning. Because the provision of opportunity programs relied on a single model, I will discuss them first and consider the comprehensive community action projects in the following section.

The provision of opportunity programs attempted to increase low-income and minority youths' access to socially approved means of obtaining success. The Economic Opportunity Act of 1964 authorized the Department of Labor to become involved in delinquency prevention through the Neighborhood Youth Corps and the Job Corps. The Neighborhood Youth Corps included an in-school program to provide jobs and training on a part-time basis to youths who were enrolled, a summer work program for students who needed summer jobs to remain in school, and an out-of-school program for youths who were both unemployed and unenrolled in school. The Job Corps was designed to take low-income urban youths out of their delinquency-prone environments and place them in residential centers for job-training. These residential centers were frequently located in

rural areas where participants were taught forest conservation skills (Griffen and Griffen, 1978).

During the same decade, the Department of Health, Education and Welfare and the Department of Housing and Urban Development also developed a broad range of delinquency prevention programs. For instance, HEW's Upward Bound program was designed to facilitate educational achievement by increasing the motivation and skills of disadvantaged youth. Similarly, HUD's Model Cities programs provided youth in deteriorated urban areas with college scholarships, job placements, college prep programs and health career projects. They also included direct social services such as counseling, drug abuse treatment, assistance for unwed mothers, recreation, and teen clubs (Griffen and Griffen, 1978).

The provision of opportunity programs were the outcome of a straightforward social planning approach. Professional planners with specialized skills and knowledge designed a program of controlled rational change to solve the delinquency problem. The planners, working for the government, created programs considered to be in the public interest, but the recipients of these services had a minimal role or no role in the determination of program policies or goals. Community workers tended to operate as agents of the state, helping to regulate the poor and phase out social action oriented projects and confrontational tactics (Piven and Cloward, 1971).

Rooted in liberal ideology, the social planning approach to providing opportunities sought only to establish conditions of equal opportunity for individuals to compete for society's scarce economic rewards. While these programs did help to secure a fragile black middle class, equality of result has not been achieved for the intransigent underclass that contributes disproportionately to the serious crime and delinquency problem in urban areas (Wilson, 1978). While ignoring locality development strategies (e.g., community involvement, self-help, and use of indigenous community resources and leadership), the social planning model lent itself to an expensive, bureaucratic welfare apparatus that administered "prevention" to clients but which created as much "opportunity" for social welfare professionals as it did for the target population. Moreover, the programs "undercut autonomous behavior by the poor, fostering dependency on institutions that were out of the poor's control" (McGahey, 1986:255; see Murry, 1984; Piven and Cloward, 1971). To some extent, the social planning programs were not community-focused *per se*, for their objective was to serve high-risk youth rather than to mobilize all residents for collective action (see Rosenbaum, 1988).

As was the case with the CAP, few of the provision of opportunity programs were subjected to systematic program evaluation (Dixon and Wright, 1974). Rather than reaching hard-core delinquent or delinquent-prone youth, the programs may have only helped those who were more motivated and upwardly mobile to begin with (Grosser, 1976; Spergel, 1969). Though the Job Corps appeared to have some short-term success in reducing delinquency, because youth were "physically and socially removed from their high-crime neighborhoods and crime-prone peer groups" (McGahey, 1986:257), one must question a social planning approach that emphasized rural-type employment training for urban youth returning to the city to search for jobs. Similarly, the Neighborhood Youth Corps merely offered job training without guaranteeing employment upon completion of training. Thus, most of the opportu-

nity training programs produced few demonstrable positive results on the labor market status or recidivism of participants (McGahey, 1986).[5]

Conservative critics have pointed to the rise in crime rates that occurred during the 1960s, suggesting that the provision of opportunity programs were based on a naive liberal optimism and a blind "throwing money" approach to solving social problems (Wilson, 1975). I will have more to say about the limitations of these programs after discussing the social action component of the 1960s efforts. It suffices here to say that anomie-opportunity or strain theory in its original form no longer guides delinquency prevention strategies in the United States.

Comprehensive Community Action Projects

Like the provision of opportunity programs, the comprehensive community action projects (CCAP) of the 1960s attempted to prevent delinquency through alteration of social conditions believed to cause delinquency.[6] However, promoters of CCAP attempted to utilize and integrate all three models of community organization: locality development, social planning, and social action.

CCAPs began in the early 1960s through the auspices of the President's Committee on Juvenile Delinquency and Youth Crime and continued under the Office of Economic Opportunity. These large-scale, multi-dimensional social welfare programs were established under federal control and funded with government money, but rooted in the local neighborhood. CCAP placed a great deal of emphasis on locality development strategies of community organization. As in the CAP, residents were involved in autonomous, community-controlled organizations. The projects focused on increasing the ability of communities to develop the services and conditions necessary to enable both adults and youths to participate in and have influence upon community affairs (Freeman et al., 1979; Grosser, 1976). In 1964, a demonstration review panel summed up the basic assumption of CCAP:

> The panel is unanimous in its opinion that major involvement on the part of community residents to improve their own situation is the *sine qua non* of a successful comprehensive program to combat delinquency in disadvantaged and demoralized communities (Grosser, 1976:24).

One year later, Title II of the Economic Opportunity Act translated this recommendation into a mandate for "maximum feasible participation." This mandate generated much controversy and criticism when coupled with the social action components of these projects (Moynihan, 1969).

Mobilization for Youth (MFY) is viewed as the blueprint for comprehensive community-based delinquency prevention strategies (Empey, 1982). Developed by Cloward and Ohlin working with the Henry Street Settlement on the Lower East Side in New York, MFY utilized a combination of the three community organization strategies to achieve a broad range of objectives, including: (1) the improvement of educational opportunities through teacher training, the development of relevant curricula and teaching methods, increased parent-school contacts, and pre-school programs; (2) the creation of job opportunities through work subsidies, vocational training, and career guidance; (3) the organization of the low-income community through the formation of neighborhood councils and the mobilization of residents for social action; (4)

the provision of specialized services to youth through detached gang workers, recreation, and rap groups; and (5) the provision of specialized services to families through Neighborhood Service Centers offering child care, counseling, and assistance in applying for public social services. As such, MFY was conceived not merely as a social service program, but as a "social experiment" (Empey, 1982:241; Marris and Rein, 1973; Moynihan, 1969; Short, 1975).

Inspired by MFY, the President's Committee sponsored additional legislation and invited other communities to submit proposals and demonstrate how they would set up a comprehensive, large-scale program aimed at achieving institutional and social change. The federal government offered funding and assistance in planning, but the communities had to utilize their own resources and involve residents of the target area in the planning and implementation (Empey, 1982). The central features shared by these diverse projects, which expanded to more than a thousand by 1966 (McGahey, 1986), were: (1) the development and promotion of community involvement and self-help capabilities; (2) the organization of formal structures for indigenous leadership and decision-making, such as neighborhood councils, policy boards, and committees; (3) the maintenance of local autonomy; and (4) the involvement of both adults and youth in social action activities designed to increase the responsiveness of social institutions to the needs of the target population and redress specific grievances in areas such as housing, health care, and employment discrimination (Grosser, 1976; Mech, 1975).

The social action component of CCAP generated a great deal of criticism, debate, and withdrawal of support. In MFY, for instance, the residents were encouraged to participate in strikes, protests, and confrontations with public institutions. The intended goal was to make political leaders aware that the community was an organized interest group that demanded their response. Frequently, the community's grievances concerned the same institutions (e.g., schools, welfare, juvenile justice system) that the prevention program attempted to bring together in a cooperative alliance. The consequence was that local, federal, and private sponsors became the targets of social action strategies (Grosser, 1976). It was a classic case of "biting the hand that feeds you," a dilemma created by attempting to mix the consensus tactics of locality development with the confrontational tactics of social action. This built-in contradiction pitted the goals of political leaders and funding agencies against community organizers and local residents. Whereas the politicians and funding agencies desired to achieve community stability by getting youths involved in legitimate activities, the community attempted to challenge the power structure and change the political process that distributed inequitable social opportunities and resources in the first place. By the mid-1960s, MFY was overrun by accusations of communist sympathies and misuse of government funds, and organizers who favored social action were eventually purged (Krisberg, 1975; Moynihan, 1969).

Other CCAPs experienced similar difficulties. Local interest groups and institutions such as landlords, police, school officials, and the news media, mounted counter-offensive propaganda that encouraged curtailment of funds. The escalating Vietnam military budget also reduced funds, and remaining program resources had to be devoted to organizational survival rather than to the original social change objectives. Confrontational tactics and innovative programs were toned down or altered to conform to a social planning model of social service delivery that was more attractive to funding sponsors. Many were transformed into predominately counseling-treatment programs or ones that stressed vocational education or legal assistance (Burkhardt, 1973; McGahey, 1986).

Some observers question whether there was ever full political support for the radical changes implied by anomie-opportunity or strain theory and CCAP (Marris and Rein, 1973). Many staff in community agencies did not believe that such large-scale changes could be justified merely to prevent delinquency (Ohlin, 1983). Bureaucratic funding policies, administrative demands, and a preoccupation with accountability, efficiency, and cost-benefit analysis took precedence over innovation and experimentation. Many projects were only granted short-term funding with no commitment for continued, long-term support. Evaluation efforts assessing the impact of programs were unimpressive (see Braithwaite, 1979; Grosser, 1976; McGahey, 1986; Rosenbaum, 1988). It was difficult to demonstrate that the interventions of a specific program with particular methods brought about specific changes. It was not possible to designate control and experimental groups since services were not selectively provided, and it was difficult to isolate or disentangle the problem of delinquency from the wider range of community problems (see Fagan, 1987). Finally, the explicit focus on delinquency tended to get lost in the escalation of the larger "War on Poverty."

The various approaches that were implemented in the 1960s failed to bring about the anticipated social changes and reductions in delinquency. Ohlin (1983) argued that programs proliferated too rapidly and exceeded the talent and knowledge available to achieve tangible results. Wilson (1975:24) believed "it was the failure to appreciate the importance of community and gravity of the threats to it that led to some mistaken views during the 1960s of the true nature of the 'urban crisis.' " While Ohlin's observations appear correct, Wilson's criticisms ignore the explicit focus on community that was at the heart of CCAP. In contrast, a more reasonable critique of CCAP's ineffectiveness would emphasize: (1) the lack of full political support and the counter-offensive efforts waged by vested interest groups; (2) the limitations imposed by bureaucratic funding policies, administrative concerns, and competition for scarce resources; (3) the provisions for job training without a concomitant effort to increase the supply of available jobs; and (4) the contradictions inherent in attempting to integrate different models of community organization practice, particularly, the conflict between social action strategies and those of locality development and social planning. Publicly funded projects that organize residents for social action can expect to have great difficulties achieving consensus among diverse elements of the community, as well as establishing and perpetuating their autonomy and original objectives. Priority from funding agencies will inevitably be given to programs attempting to implement gradual, controlled reform through a social planning approach rather than through programs involving community action against established institutions.

Opportunity Reduction and Victim Prevention

As I indicated at the outset, in the 1970s and 1980s crime prevention strategies shifted away from approaches that focused on the behavior and motivation of potential of-fenders toward an "opportunity reduction" approach that focused on the behavior of potential victims (Lewis and Salem, 1981; Rosenbaum, 1988).[7] Like earlier offender-oriented programs, these efforts aimed to increase the capacity of the community to respond collectively to social problems (Lewis and Salem, 1981). Boostrom and Henderson (1983) classified these victim-oriented approaches as : (1) mobilization of the community to increase the effectiveness of individual security; and (2) crime prevention through environmental design. The individual security strategy includes both personal and household protection measures such as firearms, self-defense, and risk-avoidance training; property marking and improved security systems (e.g., locks, alarms, window bars); neighborhood watch groups, citizen patrols, and whistlestop programs; and use of citizen-band radios. Environmental design involves urban planning and architectural modifications to create a "defensible space" where like-minded residents share a common territory, public areas are highly visible, paths of movement are clearly delineated, and particular areas are designated for legitimate users and activities and delegitimated for others (LeBeau, 1987; Murray, 1983; Newman, 1972). Both the individual security and environmental design models are based on one or more of the community organization models discussed in this paper.

The individual security strategy is indicative of a locality development approach to community organization insofar as it attempts to mobilize residents to take responsibility for crime control in their neighborhood. However, political officials and law enforcement agencies have preferred a social planning emphasis. Though citizen involvement has been favored as a way to reduce reliance on expensive, bureaucratic methods of crime control, police desire to maintain their role as experts who possess the skills and knowledge necessary to "define the nature of the problem, gather the information necessary to implement the . . . preventative measures, and . . . oversee, supervise, and regulate" the community's activities (Boostrom and Henderson, 1983:26). The police view their involvement in victim prevention programs as a form of public relations or as an extension of their own outreach efforts, and they are often not interested in responding to residents' suggestions regarding changes in police policies (Fagan, 1987). The conflict between locality development and social planning approaches to victim prevention is illustrated by police opposition to autonomous, citizen-initiated efforts such as the Guardian Angels (Michalowski, 1983). In addition, the social planning orientation favored by the police becomes especially problematic when their prevention activities favor middle class communities and thus reinforce existing neighborhood patterns of victimization (Batten, 1984).[8]

Boostrom and Henderson (1983) view environmental design as more conducive to the maintenance of the citizen autonomy that is characteristic of locality development. Because environmental design requires the skills of urban planners and architects, not police officers, it contains no inherent mandate for expanded police resources or control. The themes of self-help and self-reliance are stressed over the surrender of "responsibilities to any formal authority" (Newman, 1972:14). Residents are encouraged to develop a stake in protecting their neighborhood spaces and to define the norms of legitimate activity within these spaces (Boostrom and Henderson, 1983).

Nevertheless, the locality development emphasis in victim-oriented crime preven-

tion, as in offender-oriented prevention, is not without its inherent contradictions and dilemmas. On the one hand, locality development is predicated on a consensus approach to solving problems whereby different interest groups come together to identify common concerns and objectives. On the other hand, victim crime prevention may become a means by which residents attempt to defend the purity of their neighborhoods and prevent "undesirables" and "outsiders" from using their streets. This orientation can lead to incidents such as the one that occurred in the Howard Beach district in Queens, New York, where black "outsiders" were attacked (leading to one fatality) by white neighborhood youths (Curtis, 1987b). Thus, victim prevention has the potential to create territorial conflicts between diverse classes and races that are attempting to establish their neighborhood boundaries (Boostrom and Henderson, 1983). Moreover, victim prevention carries the potential for conflict over what behaviors will be tolerated in the community. For instance, although research on crime seriousness suggests an absence of consensus on less serious offenses (Bursik, 1988; Rossi et.al, 1974), participants in victim prevention programs appear to be as much concerned about various "incivilities" (e.g., teenagers hanging around, illegal drug use) as they are about more serious crimes of violence and theft (Lewis and Maxfield, 1980).

At the same time, evaluations of victim prevention programs indicate that such efforts have been "oversold as a stand-alone strategy" for reducing crime (Rosenbaum, 1986:363; see Murray, 1983; Rosenbaum, 1987).[9] The best results have been obtained with measures of success that focus on "fear reduction" rather than on the reduction in crime *per se* (see Police Foundation, 1986; Rosenbaum, 1988). However, Curtis (1987b:76) has suggested that the "institutionalization of fear as an accepted measure of success" has been used by "agencies running opportunity-reduction programs . . . [as] a public relations vehicle" for the "stand-alone" approach. Such an approach has obvious limitations for those residents who live in neighborhoods where fear of crime is a realistic assessment of reality. Thus, opportunity-reduction strategies may be more appropriate for low crime neighborhoods than high crime neighborhoods (see Rosenbaum, 1988). The primary problem in these latter communities is that they are economically disadvantaged compared to other areas and are "consistently underserved" by social service agencies (Fagan, 1987:68). Surveys indicate that residents, particularly in low income communities, continue to view the "social problems" approach as an effective means of preventing crime (Bennett and Lavrakas, 1988; Podelefsky, 1983; Podelefsky and DuBow, 1981).

Back to Basics: Recent Offender-Oriented Programs

Criticism of the "stand-alone" approach to opportunity reduction has led to renewed interest in traditional offender-oriented approaches to delinquency prevention (Curtis, 1987a). Preliminary evaluations of two recent programs are reported in a publication on "Policies to Prevent Crime: Neighborhood, Family, and Employment Strategies" (Curtis, 1987a). These are the Violent Juvenile Offender Research and Development Program (Fagan, 1987) and the Neighborhood Anti-Crime Self-Help Program (Curtis, 1987b). These projects have attempted to replicate "models of success" delinquency reduction programs that utilized strategies reminiscent of the Chicago Area Project and the 1960s compre-

hensive prevention programs (see Fattah, 1987; Ferre, 1987; Shonholtz, 1987; Sturz and Taylor, 1987). These "models of success" strategies included: (1) extended-family environments that addressed the emotional and self-esteem needs of youth; (2) day care, early childhood education, and parental training; (3) foster grandparent programs and neighborhood assistance in family problems; (4) community health programs and drug treatment; (5) educational and vocational training; and (6) neighborhood mediation of community conflicts. In these various programs, one finds the themes of locality development: self-help, volunteerism, and educating the community to become aware and take advantage of its own resources.

The Violent Juvenile Offender Research and Development Program (VJORDP) was a federally sponsored research and development project implemented between 1981 and 1986 through neighborhood organizations in seven different communities around the country (Fagan, 1987). Drawing upon social control and social learning theories (see Akers et al., 1979; Hirschi, 1969), the VJORDP attempted to increase youths' attachment or bonds to family and school, increase their commitment to conventional behavior and values, and reduce their attraction to peer group and neighborhood norms that encouraged delinquency. Project staff assisted neighborhood volunteers in developing "resident mobilization councils" consisting of neighborhood leaders. Each council attempted to recruit other residents, including delinquent and nondelinquent youth. The councils in the different sites formulated intervention strategies in four areas: violent crime intervention, institutional mediation, family support networks, and youth skills development.

Recruiting neighborhood leadership was one of the most difficult problems experienced by the resident councils. "Volunteerism was difficult to sustain," in part, because residents felt that their neighborhood's real problems (e.g., economic disadvantage, underservice by social service agencies) could not be addressed (Fagan, 1987:64). While youth who participated on the councils demonstrated improved decision-making, planning, and analytic skills, attempts to develop self-help businesses (e.g., automobile repair, housing rehabilitation) were unsuccessful.

The police and juvenile courts were generally cooperative, viewing the resident councils as complementary to their own efforts, and were willing to provide assistance and grant access to data. However, several other institutions (i.e., schools, child protective services, juvenile probation, and district attorney offices) remained resistant to outside scrutiny. According to Fagan (1987:69), the challenge in the future is for community organizations to gain entry to and open up these "relatively closed institutions," although such efforts may require confrontational strategies more indicative of a social action approach than the locality development approach used by the VJORDP.

As with earlier offender-oriented efforts, the overall impact of the VJORDP on reducing delinquency in the different project sites was unimpressive, although the short period of the projects "did not afford sufficient time to determine if the underlying crime-supporting conditions were altered" (Fagan, 1987:66). Nevertheless, Fagan believed the VJORDP demonstrated "the natural strength of informal networks" of residents as a means of reweaving the social fabric of communities to control the delinquency problem (p. 70). Moreover, one resident council was able to attract additional outside funds to continue its drug program, and four of the councils

were successful in getting the city or county to incorporate several of their intervention strategies into local government-sponsored efforts.

In 1982, the Eisenhower Foundation began another locality development demonstration project, the Neighborhood Anti-Crime Self-Help Program (NASP), in ten different communities around the country. Funds were provided by the government, private foundations, and businesses to help local community organizations carry out their programs and to provide them with technical assistance and consultants for an initial six months of planning and an additional two years of implementation. Community organizations applied for support if they could raise matching funds, "demonstrate that [they] had . . . a good management track record, a competent staff and board, and experience in organizing," and develop a prevention program that combined some form of opportunity reduction with initiatives that addressed the "causes of crime" (Curtis, 1987b:77–8). In addition to reducing crime, one of the key goals of the NASP was to help community organizations become financially self-sufficient.

Curtis (1987b) reviewed the preliminary results for eight of the ten locality development projects. Although the evidence was insufficient to convince skeptics (see Rosenbaum, 1988), positive outcomes were obtained in at least some areas of evaluation in six of the eight sites. For instance, five of the programs reported some reductions in crime and/or community fear. However, the "most successful single component" of the NASP was in the area of financial self-sufficiency (Curtis, 1987b: 87). All eight sites were able "to raise additional resources and carry on in one form or another after the original" funding period (p. 87). Overall, the projects generated over one million dollars in additional revenues. One community developed several business enterprises, including a promising weatherization business, that employed high-risk youths and ex-offenders. This community also reported improved math, budgeting, and tool use skills among project participants. Moreover, the NASP appeared to be less expensive and more effective in reducing crime than police-directed programs that did not integrate victim-oriented and offender-oriented approaches to prevention (see Police Foundation, 1986). Curtis (1987b:88) concluded:

> We have demonstrated that modestly funded initiatives (under two million dollars) that begin to address the causes of crime can be mixed with opportunity reduction with considerable, if guarded, success in our most deteriorated inner cities. We have shown that such progress is possible with inner-city community organizations, rather than police, in the lead, even though police can and should play an important role.

Conclusion

Large-scale approaches to the prevention of juvenile delinquency began with the 1930s Chicago Area Project and emerged full bloom in the 1960s provision of opportunity programs and comprehensive community action projects. All of these strategies shared a view of delinquency as symptomatic of underlying social conditions that could not be prevented or remedied by responding to individuals on a one-to-one basis. However, the programs applied the models of community organization practice in different ways. The Chicago Area Project pioneered the use of locality development in delinquency prevention, along with specific innovations such as recreation, detached workers, mediation, and diversion. The social planning

model employed in the provision of opportunity programs has left its legacy on current efforts at economic and vocational training, equal opportunity programs, and affirmative action. And the social action emphasis of the comprehensive community action projects has now been transmuted in the form of increased citizen involvement in grass-roots, neighborhood organizations (Rothman, 1979b).

Future efforts to implement primary delinquency prevention strategies must avoid replicating the problems encountered in earlier programs and avoid "merely trying to win back liberal ground lost to neoconservative policy makers" (Michalowski, 1983:13). However, in a period of budget deficits and declining state resources, it is not clear whether the constraints placed on community organization strategies can be overcome. The often-praised emphasis on process goals in locality development has serious pitfalls. Expectations may be raised without providing concrete gains. This may lead to increased anger, frustration, apathy, and sense of relative deprivation. Local organizing efforts are ineffectual if they are not linked to legislation and policy at higher governmental levels. However, the experience of programs such as the Job Corps and Neighborhood Youth Corps demonstrates that social planning to equip youths with job skills is limited if the economy has no room for them. Similarly, social action strategies that confront public institutions with demands for better services are useless if legislators are endorsing significant cutbacks.

Many observers believe that prevention strategies that ignore the need for economic policies leading to full employment and income redistribution are likely to fail (Chester, 1977; Conyers, 1979). Michalowski (1983) suggests that publicly run nonprofit corporations might need to be established, along with increased taxation on corporate profits and restrictions on plant closures. Perhaps partnerships between the public sector and private businesses (such as in the Job Training Partnership Act), which include tax incentives for businesses, may provide a realistic means of financing job-creation efforts that provide youth employment and training (Kohlberg, 1987; Williams and Kornblum, 1985). Certainly the minimum wage will need to be increased (Williams and Kornblum, 1985). Jobs will also need to be attractive enough, with opportunities for advancement, to motivate individuals to undertake adequate training. These jobs will need to include a literacy component to help youth develop basic skills, as well as offer youth the opportunity to interact with positive adult role mentors (McGahey, 1986; Williams and Kornblum, 1985).[10] Otherwise, job and training programs merely become "another temporary step in the dead-end urban labor market and . . . another erratic source of low income along with regular ill-paying jobs, transfer payments, and crime" (McGahey, 1986:257). Some of these economic policies would undoubtedly require community organization for social action to create pressure for change, but these actions in themselves could lead to short-term reductions in delinquency, as the experience of communities in protest have shown.[11]

In addition to social planning for economic reform, the principle of community control that is central to locality development should be maintained. Residents need to be involved in the planning and implementation process. This involvement helps to minimize the sense of alienation that people can experience when services are "dispensed" to them by social welfare professionals. Residents must have a sense that the program "belongs" to them and that they are capable of succeeding on their own given a fair chance (Walker, 1984).

More projects, such as the Neighborhood Anti-Crime Self-Help Program, that combine offender-oriented strategies with victim prevention should also be developed. Community mobilization for victim prevention can help reduce the need for an expensive, bureaucratic law enforcement apparatus and thus make funds available for neighborhood improvements and social services. In addition, youths' involvement in protective community patrols might reduce alienation and divert interest from destructive community activities (Michalowski, 1983). Programs to assist juvenile victims of crime would also reinforce conventional standards of behavior (Alcabes and Jones, 1980).

A major caveat of such a comprehensive approach to delinquency prevention is the difficulty of designing a method of quantitative program evaluation. Klein and Goldston (1977) argued that primary prevention strategies should not be expected "to prove that an individual who did not become the victim of a condition would without question have incurred the condition except for the preventive intervention" (1977:vii). Spergel (1969), on the other hand, believed that primary prevention programs can be evaluated through the designation of experimental and control groups. However, such a design would offset the premise of a comprehensive community-based project—that the entire community be involved and that the provisions of the program be multifaceted. Moreover, the goal of primary prevention should not merely be decreased delinquency, but improvement in the quality of life for the entire community. Bureaucratic funding policies that require short-term demonstrations of delinquency reduction need to be re-evaluated if primary prevention is to receive more long-term support. Primary prevention strategies cannot be expected to produce instantaneous results because the social, economic, and political patterns that underlie the delinquency problem are deeply ingrained.

Realistically, it is unlikely that our society has the genuine commitment to the widespread social changes required for an effective primary prevention approach to delinquency (see Curtis, 1987b). Preference will inevitably be given to secondary and tertiary prevention strategies that are more limited in scope and more accurately characterized as rehabilitative rather than preventive in nature (Gilbert, 1982; Klein and Goldston, 1977). Even most professionals working within community-based agencies prefer a counseling and treatment approach to the delinquency problem (Selke, 1982).

In spite of the difficulties confronting future primary prevention efforts, the projects I have reviewed indicate it is possible to design and implement an effective strategy that mobilizes the entire community to address the delinquency problem. Typically, however, assessments of past successes and failures have been made in terms of the "scientific adequacy" of the particular theory underlying the program (Empey, 1982), rather than the organizational mechanisms through which the theory was implemented. But while the popularity of various theories may change, the organizational principles underlying their application to large-scale prevention will continue to be predicated on the community organization models discussed in this article. The current debate over the future direction of delinquency prevention should not be limited to considerations of theoretical adequacy. Greater attention needs to be given to the potentialities and limitations inherent in utilizing the locality development, social planning, and social action models of community organization practice.

Notes

1. I will only address other forms of delinquency prevention (e.g., recreation, detached workers, community-based treatment) insofar as they are related to or are included within large-scale programs.

2. It is interesting that criminologists now use the concept of "opportunity" to refer to victim-oriented approaches (see Cohen et al., 1981) rather than to programs that provide offenders with economic opportunities (see Cloward and Ohlin, 1960).

3. Using a similar typology, Spergel (1969) identifies four community organization strategies: development, maintenance, contest, and conflict. Essentially, development is the same as Rothman's locality development, maintenance is similar to social planning, and contest and conflict are aspects of social action. Spergel also identifies four corresponding practitioner roles: developer, enabler, advocate, and organizer.

4. McGahey (1986) suggests that this was perhaps because Shaw and McKay believed that these problems were outside of the local community's control.

5. While initial evaluations of 1960s preschool programs such as Head Start were unimpressive, more recent studies found such programs to increase employment and lower delinquency among participants (Berrueta-Clement et al., 1984; McGahey, 1986).

6. These programs are usually abbreviated with the acronym CAP (Community Action Programs). I use the acronym CCAP for "comprehensive community action projects" to avoid confusion with the Chicago Area Project.

7. Victim prevention strategies are also re-

ferred to as "situational crime prevention" or "target hardening" (Bell and Bell, 1987; Rosenbaum, 1988; Weiss, 1987).

8. See Rosenbaum (1986, 1988) for discussions of police-directed crime prevention programs.

9. This might have been expected given studies that found social and demographic variables more related to crime than features of the physical environment (Byrne and Sampson, 1986; Merry, 1981; Taylor et al., 1984).

10. Of course, youth should always be encouraged to remain in school, and part-time jobs linked to continued school attendance would be preferable (McGahey, 1986). Early childhood education and enrichment programs, curriculum reform, and alternative educational strategies will also need to be explored (Hawkins and Lishner, 1987).

11. In a study of a Chicano community during the late 1960s and early 1970s, community members reported that gang activity subsided when the community was mobilized in protest activities (Erlanger, 1979).

References

Akers, R. L., M. D. Krohn, L. Lonza-Kaduce, and M. Radosevich. 1979. "Social learning and deviant behavior: A specific test of a general theory." *American Sociological Review* 44:635–55.

Alcabes, A. and J. A. Jones. 1980. "Juvenile victim assistance programs: A proposal." *Crime and Delinquency* 26:202–5.

Batten, D. 1984. "The established and the outsiders: The stratification of community crime control." Paper presented at the conference of the American Society of Criminology, Cincinnati.

Bell, M. M. and M. M. Bell. 1987. "Crime control: Deterrence and target hardening." Pp. 45–68 in E. H. Johnson (ed.), *Handbook on Crime and Delinquency Prevention*. New York: Greenwood.

Bennett, S. F. and P. J. Lavrakas. 1988. *Evaluation of the Planning and Implementation of the Neighborhood Program. Final Process Report to the Eisenhower Foundation*. Evanston, IL: Northwestern University, Center for Urban Affairs and Policy Research.

Berrueta-Clement, J. R., L. J. Schweinhart, W. S. Barnett, A. S. Epstein, and D. P. Weikart. 1984. *Changed Lives: The Effects of the Perry Preschool Program on Youth through Age 19*. Ypsilanti, MI: High/Scope.

Boostrom, R. L. and J. H. Henderson. 1983. "Community action and crime prevention: Some unresolved issues." *Crime and Social Justice* 19:24–30.

Burkhardt, W. R. 1973. *The Application of Opportunity Theory to Delinquency Prevention: Evaluation of a Case Study and Critique of the Literature*. Ann Arbor, MI: University Microfilms.

Bursik, R. J. 1988. "Social disorganization and theories of crime and delinquency: Problems and prospects." *Criminology* 26:519–51.

Braithwaite, J. 1979. *Inequality, Crime, and Public Policy*. London: Routledge and Kegan Paul.

Byrne, J. and R. Sampson (eds.). 1986. *The Social Ecology of Crime*. New York: Springer-Verlag.

Chester, C. R. 1977. "The effects of a redistribution of wealth on property crime." *Crime and Delinquency* 23:272–89.

Cloward, R. A. and L. E. Ohlin, 1960. *Delinquency and Opportunity: A Theory of Delinquent Gangs*. Glencoe, IL: Free Press.

Cohen, L. E., J. R. Kluegel, and K. C. Land. 1981. "Social inequality and predatory criminal victimization: An exposition and test of a formal theory." *American Sociological Review* 46:505–24.

Conyers, J. 1979. "Criminology, economics, and public policy." *Crime and Delinquency* 25:137–44.

Cox, F. M., J. L. Erlich, and J. Rothman (eds.).

1979. *Strategies in Community Organization.* Itasca, IL: Peacock.

Curtis, L. A. (ed.). 1987a. *Policies to Prevent Crime: Neighborhood, Family, and Employment Strategies. (Annals of the Academy of Political and Social Science* 494.)

_____. 1987b. ''The retreat of folly: Some modest replications of inner-city success.'' *Annals of the Academy of Political and Social Science* 494:71–89.

Dixon, M. D. and W. E. Wright. 1974. *Juvenile Delinquency Prevention Programs: An Evaluation of Policy-Related Research on the Effectiveness of Prevention Programs.* Washington, DC: National Science Foundation.

Empey, L. T. 1982. *American Delinquency: Its Meaning and Construction.* Second edition. Homewood, IL: Dorsey.

Erlanger, H. S. 1979. ''Machismo and gang violence.'' *Social Science Quarterly* 60:235–48.

Fagin, J. 1987. ''Neighborhood education, mobilization, and organization for juvenile crime prevention.'' *Annals of the Academy of Political and Social Science* 494:54–70.

Fattah, D. ''The house of Umoja as a case study for social change.'' *Annals of the Academy of Political and Social Science* 494:37–41.

Ferre, M. I. ''Prevention and control of violence through community revitalization, individual dignity, and personal self-confidence.'' *Annals of the Academy of Political and Social Science* 494:27–36.

Freeman, H. E., W. C. Jones, and L. G. Zucker. 1979. *Social Problems: A Policy Perspective.* Chicago: Rand McNally.

Gilbert, N. 1981. ''Policy issues in primary prevention.'' *Social Work* 27:293–7.

Griffen, B. S. and C. T. Griffen. 1978. *Juvenile Delinquency in Perspective.* New York: Harper and Row.

Grosser, C. F. 1976. *New Directions in Community Organization: From Enabling to Advocacy.* New York: Praeger.

Hawkins, J. D. and D. M. Lishner, 1987. ''Schooling and delinquency.'' Pp. 179–221 in E. H. Johnson (ed.), *Handbook on Crime and Delinquency Prevention.* New York: Greenwood.

Hirschi, T. 1969. *Causes of Delinquency.* Berkeley: University of California Press.

Johnson, E. H. (ed.). 1987. *Handbook on Crime and Delinquency Prevention.* New York: Greenwood.

Klein, D. and S. E. Goldston (eds.). 1977. *Primary Prevention: An Idea Whose Time Has Come.* Rockville, MD: National Institute of Mental Health.

Kobrin, S. 1959. ''The Chicago Area Project—a 25 year assessment.'' *Annals of the American Academy of Political and Social Science* 322:1–29.

Kolberg, W. H. ''Employment, the private sector, and at-risk youth.'' *Annals of the Academy of Political and Social Science* 494:94–100.

Krisberg, B. A. (ed.). 1978. *The Children of Ishmael: Critical Perspectives on Juvenile Justice.* Palo Alto, CA: Mayfield.

_____. 1975. *The Gang and the Community.* San Francisco: R and E Research Associates.

LeBeau, J. L. ''Environmental design as a rationale for prevention.'' Pp. 69–85 in E. H. Johnson (eds.), *Handbook on Crime and Delinquency Prevention.* New York: Greenwood.

Lewis, D. A. and M. G. Maxfield. 1980. ''Fear in the neighborhood: An investigation of the impact of crime.'' *Journal of Research in Crime and Delinquency* 17:160–89.

Lewis, D. A. and G. Salem. 1981. ''Community crime prevention: An analysis of a developing strategy.'' *Crime and Delinquency* 27:405–21.

Marris, P. and M. Rein. 1973. *Dilemmas of Social Reform.* Chicago: Adline.

McGahey, R. M. 1986. ''Economic conditions, neighborhood organization, and urban crime.'' Pp. 231–70 in A. J. Reiss and M. Tonry (eds.), *Communities and Crime.* Chicago: University of Chicago Press.

Mech, E. V. 1975. *Delinquency Prevention: A Program of Intervention Approaches.* Portland, OR: Regional Research Institute for Human Services, Portland State University.

Merry, S. E. 1981. *Urban Danger: Life in a Neighborhood of Strangers.* Springfield, IL: Mombiosse.

Merton, R. K. 1938. "Social structure and anomie." *American Sociological Review* 3:672–82.

Michalowski, R. J. 1983. "Crime control in the 1980's: A progressive agenda." *Crime and Social Justice* 19:13–23.

Moynihan, D. P. 1969. *Maximum Feasible Misunderstanding: Community Action in the War on Poverty.* New York: Free Press.

Murray, C. A. 1984. *Losing Ground: American Social Policy, 1950–1980.* New York: Basic Books.

————. 1983. "The physical environment and community control of crime." Pp. 107–22 in J. Q. Wilson (ed.), *Crime and Public Policy.* San Francisco: ICS Press.

Newman, O. 1972. *Defensible Space: Crime Prevention Through Urban Design.* New York: Macmillan.

Ohlin, L. E. 1983. "The future of juvenile justice policy and research." *Crime and Delinquency* 29:463–72.

Piven, F. F. and R. A. Cloward. 1971. *Regulating the Poor: The Functions of Public Welfare.* New York: Vintage.

Podelefsky, A. M. 1983. *Case Studies in Community Crime Prevention.* Springfield, IL: Thomas.

Podelefsky, A. M. and F. DuBow. 1981. *Strategies for Community Crime Prevention: Collective Responses to Crime in Urban America.* Evanston, IL: Center for Urban Affairs.

Police Foundation. 1986. *Reducing Fear of Crime in Houston and Newark: A Summary Report.* Washington, DC: U.S. Department of Justice.

Reiss, A. J. "Why are communities important in understanding crime?" Pp. 1–33 in A. J. Reiss and M. Tonry (eds.), *Communities and Crime.* Chicago: University of Chicago Press.

Rosenbaum, D. P. 1988. "Community crime prevention: A review and synthesis of the literature." *Justice Quarterly* 5:323–95.

————. (ed). 1986. *Community Crime Prevention: Does It Work?* Newbury Park, CA: Sage.

Rossi, P. H., E. Waite, C. E. Bose, and R. E. Berk. 1974. "The seriousness of crime:

Normative structure and individual differences." *American Sociological Review* 39:224–37.

Rothman, J. 1979a. "Three models of community organization practice: Their mixing and phasing." Pp. 25–45 in F. M. Cox et al. (eds.), *Strategies in Community Organization.* Itasca, IL: Peacock.

————. 1979b. "Macro social work in a tightening economy." *Social Work* 24:274–81.

Schlossman, S. and M. Sedlak. 1983. "The Chicago Area Project revisited." *Crime and Delinquency,* 29:398–462.

Schlossman, S., G. Zellman, R. Shavelson, M. Selak, and J. Cobb. 1984. *Delinquency Prevention in South Chicago: A Fifty-Year Assessment of the Chicago Area Project.* Santa Monica, CA: Rand Corporation.

Selke, W. L. 1982. "Diversion and crime prevention." *Criminology* 20:395–406.

Schwartz, E. E. 1977. "Macro social work: A practice in search of some theory." *Social Service Review* 51:207–27.

Shaw, C. R. and H. D. McKay. 1942. *Juvenile Delinquency and Urban Areas.* Chicago: University of Chicago Press.

Shaw, C. R., F. M. Zorbaugh, H. D. McKay, and L. S. Cottrell. 1929. *Delinquency Areas.* Chicago: University of Chicago Press.

Shonholtz, R. 1987. "The citizen's role in justice: Building a primary justice system at the neighborhood level." *Annals of the Academy of Political and Social Science* 494:42–53.

Short, J. F. 1975. "The natural history of an applied theory: Differential opportunity and Mobilization for Youth." Pp. 193–210 in N.J. Demarath et al. (eds.), *Social Policy and Sociology.* New York: Academic Press.

Simcha-Fagan, O. and J. E. Schwartz. 1986. "Neighborhood and delinquency: An assessment of contextual effects." *Criminology* 24: 667–703.

Spergel, I. A. 1969. *Community Problem Solving: The Delinquency Example.* Chicago: University of Chicago Press.

Sturz, E. L. and M. Taylor. 1987. "Inventing

and reinventing Argus: What makes one community organization work.'' *Annals of the Academy of Political and Social Science* 494:19–26.

Taylor, R. B., S. Gottfredson, and S. A. Shumaker. 1984. *Neighborhood Responses to Disorder. Final report.* Baltimore: Johns Hopkins University: Center for Metropolitan Planning and Research.

Walker, S. 1984. *Sense and Nonsense About Crime: A Policy Guide.* Monterey, CA: Brooks/Cole.

Weiss, R. P. 1987. ''The community and prevention.'' Pp. 113–36 in E. H. Johnson (eds.), *Handbook on Crime and Delinquency Prevention.* New York: Greenwood.

Williams, T. and W. Kornblum. 1985. *Growing Up Poor.* Lexington, MA: D.C. Heath.

Wilson, J. Q. 1975. *Thinking About Crime.* New York: Random House.

Wilson, W. J. 1978. *The Declining Significance of Race: Blacks and Changing American Institutions.* Chicago: University of Chicago Press.

Witmer, H. and E. Tufts. 1954. *The Effectiveness of Delinquency Prevention Programs.* Washington, DC: U.S. Government Printing Office.

Wright, W. E. and M. C. Dixon. 1977. ''Community prevention and treatment of juvenile delinquency.'' *Journal of Research in Crime and Delinquency* 14:35–67.

Delinquency, Development, and Social Integration in India

13

Clayton A. Hartjen

A body of cross-national and comparative research indicates that rates of crime and delinquency are closely linked to economic development, in that the more developed a country becomes, the higher its crime and delinquency rates (Cavan and Cavan, 1968; Clinard and Abbott, 1973; Friday, 1980; Friday and Hage, 1976; Shelley, 1981; Toby, 1979). This finding reflects Durkheim's (1947; 1951) speculations that differences in rates of delinquency (or deviance in general) between societies might be the result of differences in their structural characteristics. In the case of delinquency, these characteristics could serve to disenfranchise the young (and others) in economically developed countries, but have the opposite effect in developing countries. A number of writers have argued that it is the disintegrative characteristics of economically developed nations, characteristics that are generic to the industrialization and urbanization that economic develop-

ment necessitates, that are responsible for the higher rates of delinquency (and crime) typically found in those countries (Chambliss, 1978; Clinard and Abbott, 1973; Friday, 1980; Friday and Hage, 1976; Greenberg, 1978; Martin, 1973; Pepinsky, 1976; Quinney, 1977; Shelley, 1981; Tifft, 1979).

While the argument that high delinquency rates are a product of political and economic development is plausible, little effort has been made to delineate those integrative features that may retard the development of a "delinquency problem" in developing countries. Nor is it known to what extent these integrative or disintegrative features are unique to specific societies or characteristic of types of societies that can be classified on the basis of economic development.

This paper seeks to cast some light on these issues by trying to account for some findings of a multi-faceted study I conducted with S. Priyadarsini of delinquent behavior and its control in the southeastern Indian state of Tamil Nadu (Hartjen and Priyadarsini, forthcoming; Priyadarsini and Hartjen, 1981).[1] Specifically, this pa-

Reprinted from *Social Problems*, Vol. 29, No. 5, 1982, pp. 464–73, by permission of the Society for the Study of Social Problems, and the author. Copyright © by the Society for the Study of Social Problems.

per identifies some of the integrative features of Indian society which (1) impede the development of an adolescent subculture and the socially objectionable conduct such subcultures are believed to stimulate; and (2) reduce the frequency with which formal mechanisms of social control are employed to deal with young people engaged in that conduct.

The Research and Its Findings

Our research was designed to investigate: (1) the types, relative amounts, and distribution of delinquent behavior among Indian youth; (2) the perceptions and reactions of Indian adults toward delinquency laws and youths who violate these laws; and (3) the judicial and correctional treatment of young offenders. Although we interviewed people throughout India, the research focused on the state of Tamil Nadu, its major city of Madras, and a representative village named Thamaraikulam. Besides observing juvenile courts and several correctional facilities in the state, the research employed four major data sources. (1) We constructed a self-reported delinquency questionnaire and administered it to samples of urban and rural high school boys of varying socio-economic backgrounds (N=517) and boys institutionalized in four correctional facilities (N=306). The questionnaire was modeled after several used in research in the United States and consisted of 16 offense items, as well as biographical and judicial contact questions, ranging in severity from status offenses (e.g., truancy) to personal offenses (e.g., assault, gang fighting).[2] (2) To tap public sentiments toward delinquency laws and juvenile misconduct, we surveyed adult Tamilians from Madras (N=603) and Thamaraikulam (N=200). The questionnaire consisted of 25 scenarios depicting a wide range of delinquent conduct engaged in by individuals of varying socio-economic characteristics. (3) We analyzed the crime/delinquency news in three major, local daily newspapers over two three-month periods to gauge the extent to which delinquency is treated as a social problem by the media and the image of delinquency it disseminates to the public. (4) We studied national crime statistics, similar to the Uniform Crime Reports used in studies of the United States, and other statistics on the economy and population of India. The basic findings derived from these sources are:

1. There is less delinquent behavior, and crime in general, in India than in the United States and many countries in Western Europe.[3]
2. The type of delinquent behavior found in India, and such variables as the residence and social class of delinquents, correspond roughly to that found in developed countries.[4]
3. Adult perceptions of and reactions to delinquency are generally mild and non-punitive. Indians feel that the family, rather than officials, should deal with delinquents through the use of extra-legal and informal sanctions.[5]
4. Judicial and correctional officials express a tolerant view of delinquency.[6]
5. Delinquency is rarely discussed in the media in India.[7]

The explanatory problem posed by these findings is: Why is delinquency in India, a large, heterogeneous, and impoverished country, not a social problem either in terms of the frequency with which delinquent behavior occurs or the severity or frequency of societal reaction to it?

Delinquency in Post Industrial Society

Crime has become a major problem in countries that are economically advanced, affluent, industrialized, and urbanized.

Moreover, rates of delinquency are increasing in those societies attaining a post-industrial stage of development and in others faced with rapid modernization.[8] A few economically developed nations, such as Japan (Clifford, 1976) and Switzerland (Clinard, 1978), have low rates of delinquency, and there is considerable variation in the dimension and character of the "youth problem" of these societies. But the fact that increased rates of delinquency are linked to modernization seems inescapable. On the other hand, the distribution of delinquent behavior within specific societies is similar: rates tend to be highest in urban areas and among the more impoverished or socially and economically disenfranchised segments of the population.[9] Thus, while possibly important variations within a society do exist, the fundamental explanatory issue concerning cross-national analyses of delinquency is the persistent differences in delinquency rates (both in terms of behavior and/or the frequency of official reaction) between developed and developing countries.

Several writers have suggested that high rates of delinquency in post-industrial societies may be the result of certain economic requirements of post-industrial development (Christie, 1978; Friday, 1980; Friday and Hage, 1976; Greenberg, 1978; Toby, 1963). They particularly indicate that the elimination of a need for a large pool of unskilled labor has led to a lengthening of the period of adolescence and the exclusion of young people from the labor market. Entrance into the adult work-world is delayed, so that young people are isolated from many work-related role relationships which integrate people into the dominant social system. Consequently, the commitment of young people to the norms of the dominant system decreases: they become isolated from adult society and create an ad-

olescent subculture that is often perceived by adults to be at variance with their own. Although not all youths are affected in the same way or to the same extent by the social isolation generated by their economic irrelevance, the alienations of youth attributed to the necessities of postindustrial development increases the probability that large numbers of them will act in ways that violate the law (Larkin, 1979).

Christie (1978) and Martin (1973) suggest that the same economic forces that have created the youth subculture ensure that young people and their behavior will be perceived by adults as troublesome and reacted to as a problem. First, since youth are a marginal group, if not complete outcasts, their behavior is more likely to be perceived as threatening and, therefore, worthy of repressive reaction. Second, since youth lack a place in the production system, they lack the resources and power to ward off official control or to alter the conditions of their exclusion. Third, as post-industrial economy requires the delineation of distinct work roles separate from and antithetical to the role relationships of family and community, it also provides the affluence necessary for employing a class of service workers to control the behavior of others in the society. The scope and reliance upon formal, rather than informal, agents of control increases. The police and the courts, rather than the family or community, become the agencies to contend with misbehaving youth.

The social requirements attributed to economic development promote the separation and alienation of youth, and therefore increase the likelihood of their being involved in acts considered inappropriate or illegal. They also promote the growth of formal means of social control. In both ways, post-industrial economic development could stimulate a delinquency problem. Where the characteristics of post-industrial development are absent, the consequences which follow from the role relationships this economic form generates should also be absent. India appears to be a case in point.

Indian Agrarian Economy

India is an impoverished, rural society. Eighty percent of the Indian population live in 560,000 villages around the countryside. Less than 15 percent of the country's gross national product is derived from manufacturing. While the gross national product was substantial at the time of this research (over 42 billion rupees in 1978), per capita income was low (about 600 rupees). Less than 10 percent of the labor force in India is engaged in industrial production or manufacturing, and of these, approximately 40 percent are employed in household or "cottage" industries such as hand loom weaving. About 60 percent of India's industrial workers (equal to six percent of the labor force) are engaged in industrial production outside the home; most are employed in small factories employing 30 workers or less. Seventy-two percent of India's workers are engaged in agricultural-related pursuits. Of these, about 25 percent are landless laborers (*Europa Year Book,* 1978; Ministry of Information, 1975; Nyrop *et al.,* 1975).

Within regions, Indian society is stratified on the basis of religion, subcaste (*jati*), and, to a lesser extent, social class (Beals, 1980; Beteille, 1974; Maddison, 1971). Throughout the countryside, the ownership or control of land still influences power relationships, patterns of deference and respect, and interpersonal relationships among village residents. But land ownership, as well as labor-force participation itself, is determined by other factors, such as *jati* member-

ship, which profoundly affect social integration and interpersonal relationships. This is a point to which I return below.

The economic facts of Indian society do not alone explain the lack of a delinquency problem: that is, India does not necessarily have low delinquency rates simply because it has an agrarian economy. Rather, these facts help explain the network of interpersonal relationships found in India (which may also exist in some other form in other agrarian societies). This network in turn may be related to the amount of delinquent behavior and its control found in Indian society. Specifically, to the extent that the exclusion of young people from meaningful economic and social activity promotes the development of a youth subculture, thereby increasing delinquency rates and necessitating formal mechanisms of social control, the low delinquency rates in India and the tendency to treat delinquent behavior in an informal, nonpunitive manner, may stem from a number of integrative features of Indian society.[10]

Integration and Delinquent Behavior

Indians are immersed in a network of role relationships that involve a variety of obligations toward kin, *jati*, and community (Beteille, 1974; Mandelbaum, 1970). The social system is organized around these ties and the personal loyalties and interdependency they demand. In India, people are expected to care for other members of the family, including distant relatives. The *jati* and family remain the main criteria for marriage, dietary patterns, social contacts, and economic opportunities. Regardless of one's place in the village, an attack on a fellow villager by some outsider is likely to bring reprisals from the village as a whole (Beals, 1980; Gough, 1955; Srinivas, 1955).

Although in India, as elsewhere, work-role relationships are significant in themselves, they are intertwined with those of family, *jati*, and community. Interpersonal relationships are largely determined by family, *jati,* and community membership, not by one's work or occupational position. While access to the means of livelihood is an important factor in determining one's life chances, that access alone does not dictate the other spheres of social life; rather, it is in part dictated by them. For example, class membership (based, for instance, on the ownership of land) is largely influenced by family and *jati* membership and the meaning these have in the village community (Gough, 1955). One's place in the class structure, in short, is to a considerable extent a function of family and *jati* rather than monetary earnings alone. As such, the essence of one's existence is dictated by ascribed rather than achieved attributes. Regardless of one's place or participation in the economy, a set of ready-made, alternate role relationships and their corresponding rights and obligations exist for the individual. While these are partly influenced by one's work-role, they also determine the economic or work relationships an individual may achieve. Being excluded from the labor force does not have the same meaning for young people in India that it seems to have for youth in post-industrial societies.

This is as true for urban as it is for rural dwellers. Although urban-industrial production separates work from other roles, family, *jati*, and community identity remain central to the urban Indian (Beteille, 1974). Rural and urban Indians are immersed in a network of role relationships apart from the labor market. While participation in the work force is important, it is not the essence of one's existence nor necessarily the major criterion for self- and social identification. This may be one reason why a youth subculture has not emerged in India and why, as a consequence, India has relatively low rates of delinquent behavior.

Even in circumstances conducive to separating youth from adult society, the mediating forces of family, *jati*, and community ties impede the development of a youth subculture. For example, most Indian children attend school, if not always regularly, and are placed in classes according to age. (Most schools are segregated by sex.) But schools in India do not seem to have the same impact Christie (1978) suggests they have in post-industrial societies. They do not appear to foster a distinctive, youth-oriented subculture. In part this may be a consequence of the tendency of Indian youth to form associational and play groups with siblings and other relatives rather than school peers. Moreover, there is little opportunity for Indian children to engage in activities apart from, or out of view of, some adult.

Distinct adolescent subgroups are also not likely to emerge from the work-related pursuits of young people in India. Although they are normally given the most menial tasks to perform, the tasks themselves and the situations in which they are performed are typically closely tied with, and form an integral part of, the work activities of adult coworkers.

Besides having alternate self- and social-identity resources available to them, even in situations that could enhance a sense of group separateness and identity, little opportunity appears to exist for Indian youth to develop a distinctive subculture based on age. Those youths who do engage in group misconduct or criminality are just as likely to be associated with adults, or working under their direction (e.g., carrying illegal alcohol), as to be involved with a group of peers.

Role Relationships and Social Control

The apparent reluctance of Indian adults and legal authorities to control juvenile misconduct by formal, legal means is also partially explained by the network of role relationships. As Beteille (1974) points out, in agrarian, as opposed to industrial societies, social life is governed more by persons than by abstract rules or laws. Because social life occurs within the domains of family and locality, norm violations and interpersonal disputes are perceived as family, *jati*, or village concerns. Agencies of the state have minimal contact with, and are insignificant for, ordinary matters of social control. Informal mechanisms are commonly relied upon. For example, since an Indian's prestige is to a considerable extent gained from family or *jati* status within a village or community, a "bad name" reflects upon all members (Beals, 1980; Gough, 1955: Srinivas, 1955). And since Indians are dependent upon other members of the family, *jati*, or community for almost all aspects of economic and social life, the opinions of others are crucial. Gossip, scolding, or the withholding of rewards are strong inducements to conformity. Also, the expectations regarding the economic and other contributions of young people, particularly to their parents or relatives, act as a strong moral force for children and a positive inducement to conform.

Deviance by or disputes among family members that cannot be otherwise controlled may be referred to family elders. Prestigious *jati* elders may be called upon to mediate intra-*jati* disputes, and village elders asked to deal with inter-*jati* problems or matters that cannot be handled by the family or *jati*. Although without formal power to sanction, the interdependency of Indians and the norms of deference, respect, and obedience accepted in Indian society give these elders considerable power to control the behavior of others.[11]

This reluctance to make the misbehavior of young people (and others) a public or official matter may explain the relatively low rates of "official delinquency" found in India.[12] In this way, delinquency is not a problem either in the social-reaction or the behavioral sense.

Children, Work, and Family

The economic scarcity and labor-intensive nature of work in agrarian societies such as India necessitate that, for large segments of the population, all members of the family contribute financially. In contrast to post-industrial societies where unskilled labor is economically irrelevant, India's economy depends upon large numbers of unskilled workers. Children provide a ready source of such labor: in spite of laws prohibiting or limiting child labor, they are employed in some capacity in practically every realm of the nation's economy.[13] Even in major industries, young children work as "apprentices."

The small cottage or family industries found throughout India routinely employ large numbers of children. In the countryside, children are essential to the family's financial survival, especially among the more deprived. The one or two rupees or bowl of rice a child might earn each day for helping in the fields, herding cattle, or carrying water, may be all that keeps the family from starvation. Even in non-agricultural commercial enterprises, children are working: filling tires with air, packing groceries in the tiny shops along the streets, or working with their parents on construction and highway crews. Throughout India, the typical economic activity operates on a family scale, whether a farm, manufacturing industry, or commerce.

Most such pursuits are the principal source of employment for relatives and *jati* members, and children are an integral part of the enterprise.[14]

Sometimes the "work" activities of children are the very things that get them into trouble with the law. A majority of the children that judicial and correctional officials deal with are either involved in activities such as begging or carrying illegal alcohol, or have turned to petty crime because they lost family relationships and were thus severed from economic support. Petty theft, hustling train tickets (scalping), and similar conduct become their only means of livelihood.

Even when children are not directly involved in the productive realm, their labor is essential to the daily life of the household. Lacking the capacity to purchase or produce many of the labor-saving devices found in more affluent societies, innumerable tasks must be performed by household members to sustain its operation. Many of these tasks are performed by children. Collecting cow dung or wood for the fire, cleaning rice, grinding grain, keeping watch over younger siblings, and fetching water not only contribute to the operation of the household, they also make the child an essential part of it (Beals, 1980).

Although exploited in terms of wages, and low on the universal pecking order, children in India are regarded as economic assets, both in terms of their immediate and future contributions. In a society where there is little separation between work and home, Indian children are included in almost all forms of social activity. The kind of "adults only" party found in countries like the United States is rare in India. Adolescent hangouts are practically nonexistent. Children and adults are found together almost everywhere.

This inclusion of children in social and economic activities impedes the development of a delinquency problem in India, both by reducing the pressures to deviate and the likelihood that adults will find it necessary to take formal-legal action against their children. Being a part of the social and economic system, Indian youth develop a stake in the *status quo*. They have little reason to establish the kind of subcultural values and patterns of behavior found among adolescents in countries such as the United States. Nor are Indian children likely to be placed in the kind of "outgroup" status that has been ascribed to children in many post-industrial nations. Therefore, Indian children and their behavior are less likely to be perceived as deviant and in need of official control.

Conclusions

To explain variations in the delinquency rates among countries of differing socioeconomic development, and to explain the extent and nature of these countries' reactions to delinquency, sociologists must identify and elucidate the socio-economic conditions that promote or block social integration. If one's proclivity to deviate is influenced by one's commitment to the larger socio-normative order (Hirschi, 1969), and if one's degree of commitment is shaped by the degree to which individuals are integrated into and made a meaningful part of the dominant society, then the delinquency rate is a function of the socio-economic forces that affect the society's capacity to integrate young people. Within India, three features of the society seem to be most salient in this regard:

1. Because the economy of India is marked by scarcity and labor-intensive work, an adolescent subculture separate and distinct from adult society has had no room or need to develop. As a

result, the delinquency-promoting effects believed to emanate from such a subculture are absent.

2. In spite of the pressures on India to industrialize and modernize, the traditional role relationships of family, *jati*, and community have remained largely intact. These traditional role relationships provide an alternative, integrative mechanism, apart from labor force participation. Regardless of one's position in the economic structure, therefore, one still belongs to the larger social system in terms of family, *jati,* and community membership. An Indian may be low on the membership hierarchy, but he or she is still a member.

3. Since the social sphere of family, *jati*, and community interconnects with the economic sphere of labor-force participation, self-identity is not solely linked to labor force participation. Rather, one's place in the economic sphere is in part determined by one's location in the social sphere. In other words, *who one is* rather than *what one does* is an important determinant of an Indian's place in the social order.

The integrative features of Indian society identified in this paper may, of course, be unique to India. But it is also possible that some such mechanisms are to be found in other societies with little delinquency or crime. Although the relationship between economic development and crime/delinquency rates has been documented by research, albeit limited, just why economic development leads to increased criminality has yet to be fully explored. Our understanding of this phenomenon can only be advanced by analyzing societies with differing socio-economic forms. Thus, if it is true that post-industrial development generates disintegrative structures which alienate youth (and others), thereby stimulating the formation of a delinquency problem, the study of societies not exhibiting these characteristics may enhance our understanding of the relationships between socio-economic forms and the forces that affect rates of delinquent behavior and orientations toward its control. This paper suggests two general areas of inquiry in this regard: (1) the investigation of integrative mechanisms and their relationship to delinquent or criminal behavior as well as social reactions to such conduct; and (2) the exploration of the link, if any, between these mechanisms and economic development.

Notes

1. Our research was supported by the Indo-U.S. Subcommission on Education and Culture and the Indo-American Fellowship Foundation. Additional funds were received from the National Science Foundation and the Research Council of Rutgers University.

2. Except for the fact that "status offenses" are not specifically listed, "delinquency" laws in India are modeled after British law and are similar to those found in the United States and Europe.

3. Of the 3,800,000 offenses reported in the 1974 edition of *Crime in India* (Bureau of Police Research and Development, 1977), only 102,000 were attributed to juveniles. About half the population of India is under 21, yet the official offense and arrest rates of Indians under 21 is only three percent of the adult rate, which is itself lower than that of the United States. Thus, the juvenile crime rate in India is quite low, and this is true also of Tamil Nadu. Similarly, the self-reported delinquency findings indicate that although about 80 percent of the respondents did admit to at least one offense, most admitted to either status violations or petty theft. Of the total sample, 38 percent admitted to the four status offenses, 26 percent to

petty theft, 12 percent to assault or gang fighting, and fewer than 10 percent to the two substance-abuse offenses (alcohol or marijuana use) or the more serious property crimes.

4. Official delinquency rates are higher in urban than rural areas of India, although no significant differences were found in the self-reported delinquency of Madras and Thamaraikulam boys. Similarly, minority groups and lower socio-economic status groups are over-represented in official arrest statistics. But, with the exception of socio-economic status, this was not true of self-report respondents. Institutionalized boys, who are generally lower in socio-economic status than are high school boys, have higher rates of self-reported delinquency. Among high school boys, however, the relationship between socio-economic status and delinquency appears to vary with the type of behavior.

5. Less than 10 percent of adult Tamilians felt that status-offense delinquent behavior should be reported to a formal agent of control such as the police. Although most felt that formal agents should be called in for most criminal offenses, in several instances (alcohol use, vandalism, and petty theft) most respondents said they would not report the offender to the authorities. Even in serious criminal cases, respondents frequently stated that some informal agent (such as the family) should deal with the matter. Surprisingly, even when informal agents were preferred, many respondents felt that some official sanction (fine or incarceration) should be imposed; but even then the percentage of respondents wanting informal sanctions were often equal to or greater than those preferring formal sanctions. Considerable variation in these sentiments existed between rural and urban respondents: higher-status, urban respondents expressed harsher attitudes than rural respondents. Interestingly, although urban respondents were more willing to impose punitive sanctions, they were no more willing than villagers to report offenders to the authorities.

6. Practically all the correctional and judicial officials interviewed stated they did not feel young offenders were "bad" and deserved punishment, or "disturbed" and in need of therapy.

Instead, they felt delinquents were deprived or exploited children who had not been properly cared for by parents, and preferred to provide these children with the necessary support and training to sustain them in adult life, rather than punish them. In fact, few delinquents are actually incarcerated and over one-half of the delinquency cases processed by Tamil Nadu courts are released with or without supervision (Central Bureau of Correctional Services, 1977).

7. At the time of this research, most crime news in Tamil Nadu consisted of reports on riots and demonstrations or "political" crimes. Almost no stories or reports appeared on delinquency or youth crime.

8. I use the term modernization in the same sense that Lerner (1958) employed it.

9. This appears to be true also of India, at least with regard to arrests and judicial/correctional processing (Bureau of Police Research and Development, 1977).

10. Hinduism and the caste system are unique to India, and may, therefore, make it a somewhat atypical example of an agrarian or developing country. But the apparent consistency in the relatively low delinquency rates found in developing countries suggests that integrative mechanisms that may, perhaps, take various forms are generic to these societies (but see De-Fleur, 1969, for a discussion of the extent to which a single theory can be applied across cultures). On the other hand, as Clinard (1978) found in Switzerland, integrative mechanisms may also exist in industrial-urban societies as well. It is not so much that India is typical of agrarian societies that makes it suitable for analysis, but the example it offers for investigating the proposition that delinquency is less of a social problem in societies that provide its youth with integrative social structures and higher in those which do not.

11. This can, of course, mean that children (and adults) from dominant *jatis* or families "get away" with things less powerful segments of the population are sanctioned for. However, the interdependence of groups within the village or community may reduce the chances of this occurring. The frequent clashes that take place between religious and *jati* groups throughout India

suggest that a tenuous balance exists between the interests of various groups and the mediating influence of elders and community leaders.

12. Other possible explanations may be the lack of resources available in India to spend on the police and correctional programs (there are, for example, about one-half as many police per 1,000 population in India than in the United States) and the fact that people in India are generally suspicious of and hostile to the police (Bayley, 1969; Shane, 1980).

13. These laws are largely intended to reduce the exploitation of children, not to prevent them from working. But since most enterprises using child labor are small and/or family businesses in which children work seasonally or sporadically, enforcing these laws would not only be difficult but impose a severe hardship on the family.

14. That child labor is recognized in the community is suggested by the reluctance of school officials to enforce mandatory education laws. Imposing a fine on parents when the child is needed to help in the shop or fields would cause an unwarranted hardship. Extralegal measures, such as scolding or shaming the parents, are relied upon instead.

References

Bayley, David H. The Police and Political Development in India. Princeton: Princeton University Press, 1969.

Beals, Alan R. Gopalpur: A South Indian Village. New York: Holt, Rinehart and Winston, 1980.

Beteille, André. Studies in Agrarian Social Structure. Delhi: Oxford University Press, 1974.

Bureau of Police Research and Development. Crime in India, 1974. New Delhi: Ministry of Home Affairs, Government of India, 1977.

Cavan, Ruth S., and Jordan T. Cavan. Delinquency and Crime: Cross-Cultural Perspectives. Philadelphia: Lippincott, 1968.

Central Bureau of Correction Services. Social Defense: A Statistical Year Book. New Delhi: Department of Social Welfare, Government of India, 1977.

Chambliss, William J. "Toward a political economy of crime." Pp. 191–212 in Charles E. Reasons and Robert M. Rich (eds.), The Sociology of Law: A Conflict Perspective. Toronto: Butterworth, 1978.

Christie, Nils. "Youth as a crime-generating phenomenon." Pp. 221–230 in Barry Krisberg and James Austin (eds.), The Children of Ishmael: Critical Perspectives on Juvenile Justice. Palo Alto, Calif.: Mayfield, 1978.

Clifford, William. Crime Control in Japan. Lexington, Mass.: Lexington, 1976.

Clinard, Marshall B. Cities with Little Crime. New York: Cambridge University Press, 1978.

Clinard, Marshall B., and Daniel J. Abbott. Crime in Developing Countries. New York: Wiley, 1973.

DeFleur, Lois B. "Alternative strategies for the development of delinquency theories applicable in other countries." Social Problems 17:30–39 (1969).

Durkheim, Emile. The Division of Labor in Society. Translated by George Simpson. New York: The Free Press of Glencoe, 1947.

_____. Suicide. Translated by John A. Spaulding and George Simpson. New York: The Free Press of Glencoe, 1951.

Europa Year Book. Europa Year Book: A World Survey, vol. 2. London: Europa Publications, Ltd., 1978.

Friday, Paul C. "International review of youth crime and delinquency." Pp. 100–129 in Graeme R. Newman (ed.)., Crime and Deviance: A Comparative Perspective. Beverly Hills, Calif.: Sage, 1980.

Friday, Paul C. and Jerald Hage. "Youth crime in post-industrial societies: An integrated perspective." Criminology 14:347–368 (1976).

Gough, Kathleen E. "The social structure of a Tanjore village." Pp. 36–52 in McKim Marriott (ed.), Village India: Studies in the Little Community. Chicago: University of Chicago Press, 1955.

Greenberg, David F. "Delinquency and the age structure of society." Pp. 66–86 in Peter Wickman and Phillip Whitten (eds.), Readings in Criminology. Lexington, Mass.: D.C. Heath, 1978.

Hartjen, Clayton A., and S. Priyadarsini. Delinquency in India: A Comparative Analysis. New Brunswick, N.J.: Rutgers University Press (forthcoming).

Hirschi, Travis. Causes of Delinquency. Berkeley: University of California Press, 1969.

Larkin, Ralph W. Suburban Youth in Cultural Crises. New York: Oxford University Press, 1979.

Lerner, Daniel. The Passing of Traditional Society: Modernizing the Middle East. New York: The Free Press, 1958.

Maddison, Angus. Class Structure and Economic Growth: India and Pakistan Since the Moguls. New York: W. W. Warton, 1971.

Mandelbaum, David. "Family, jati, village." Pp. 29–50 in Milton Singer and Bernard S. Cohn (eds.), Structure and Change in Indian Society. Viking Fund Publication in Anthropology #47 (1970).

Martin, John M. "Toward a political definition of juvenile delinquency." Pp. 345–360 in R. Serge Denisoff and Charles H. McCaghy (eds.), Deviance, Conflict, and Criminality. Chicago: Rand McNally, 1973.

Ministry of Information and Broadcasting. India: A Reference Annual. New Delhi: Research and Reference Division, Government of India, 1975.

Nyrop, Richard F., Beryl Lieff Benderly, William W. Cover, Milissa J. Cutter, and Newton B. Parker. Area Handbook for India. Washington, D.C.: U.S. Government Printing Office, 1975.

Pepinsky, Harold. Crime and Conflict. New York: Academic Press, 1976.

Priyadarsini, S., and Clayton A. Hartjen. "Delinquency and corrections in India." Pp. 109–123 in Gary F. Jensen (ed.), Sociology of Delinquency: Current Issues. Beverly Hills, Calif.: Sage, 1981.

Quinney, Richard. Class, State, and Crime. New York: Longman, 1977.

Shane, Paul G. Police and People: A Comparison of Five Countries. St. Louis: C. V. Mosby, 1980.

Shelley, Louise I. Crime and Modernization: The Impact of Industrialization and Urbanization on Crime. Carbondale, Ill.: Southern Illinois University Press, 1981.

Srinivas, M. N. "The social structure of a Mysore village." Pp. 1–35 in McKim Marriott (ed.), Village India: Studies in the Little Community. Chicago: University of Chicago Press, 1955.

Tifft, Larry. "The coming redefinition of crime: An anarchist perspective." Social Problems 26:392–402 (1979).

Toby, Jackson. "The prospects for reducing delinquency rates in industrial societies." Federal Probation 27:23–25 (1963).

————. "Delinquency in cross-cultural perspective." Pp. 105–149 in LaMar T. Empey (ed.), Juvenile Justice: The Progressive Legacy and Current Reforms. Charlottesville: University Press of Virginia, 1979.

Explaining Female Delinquency in the Emancipation Era

14

Ronald J. Berger

In Chapter 5, "Contemporary Trends in Female Delinquency: Stability or Change?," I discussed issues related to a gender role socialization theory of delinquency and the apparent increase in rates of female law-violation. I suggested that the evidence did not support the masculinity-liberation explanation of contemporary female delinquency, but that the concept of gender role strain offered a promising explanation of the contradictions or tensions inherent in female delinquents' attempts to negotiate contemporary role expectations for themselves and others.

In this chapter, I review more general sociological theories that attempt to account for contemporary patterns of female delinquency. Specifically, I consider social control, power-control, strain, and subcultural theories. I also discuss the contributions of feminist theory to the analysis of female delinquency.

Social Control and Power-Control Theory

Smith (1979) and Steffensmeier and Allan (1988) argued that much female law-

violation can be explained by the same variables that have been used to analyze male law-violation.[1] Indeed, applications of *social control* theory to female delinquency have proven more fruitful than the masculinity-liberation hypothesis. In general, social control theory predicts that individuals who exhibit strong bonds or ties to social institutions such as the family or school, and who are more controlled or regulated by these institutions, will have lower rates of law-violation (Hirschi, 1969; Reiss, 1951). Although some studies found that males exhibited higher rates of delinquency regardless of level of social control (Cernkovich and Giordano, 1987; Jensen and Eve, 1976), indicators of social control (e.g., attachment to conventional others, belief in the legitimacy of rules) were better predictors of female and male delinquency than indicators of masculinity (Shover et al., 1979). Cernkovich and Giordano (1987) found that lower rates of female delinquency were partly explained by the greater degree of parental supervision and intimate communication between daughters and parents (but see Canter, 1982).

To the extent that traditional families exhibit greater social control and supervision over daughters than sons, we should also expect females in non-traditional families to exhibit higher rates of delinquency. Hagan and associates (1987) have developed a *power-control* theory of gender variations in common forms of delinquency (e.g., theft, fighting) to explain how authority relations between husbands and wives are transferred to children. For instance, in traditional patriarchal families consisting of a dominant father and subordinate mother who does not work outside the home, mothers have less power relative to fathers and daughters are more controlled than sons. In egalitarian families, on the other hand, where both parents are employed in authority positions, mothers and fathers have relatively equal power and daughters and sons are subjected to similar levels of control. Daughters in patriarchal families are taught to avoid risk, whereas daughters in egalitarian families are encouraged to take risks in order to prepare themselves for nontraditional occupational roles. Hagan et al. also suggested that gender patterns of delinquency in mother-only families are similar to those in egalitarian families.

In their research, Hagan et al. found rates of female self-reported delinquency to be lower in patriarchal families than in either egalitarian or mother-only families, and rates of female and male delinquency to be more similar in these latter families. Insofar as egalitarian families are more common as one moves up the class hierarchy, and insofar as mother-only families are more common as one moves down the class hierarchy, power-control theory explains how both circumstances of women's equality *and* financial deprivation are related to increased rates of female delinquency— female juveniles in both egalitarian and deprived families are relatively free from male domination (see Hagan et al., 1985;

Hill and Atkinson, 1988; Singer and Levine, 1988).

Though power-control theory has received empirical support, Chesney-Lind (1989) has been concerned that it has become another, albeit more sophisticated, version of the liberation theory of female delinquency—now, *mothers'* liberation is blamed for daughters' misconduct. She also has objected to the way Hagan et al. (1987) equated "female-headed households" with "upper-status 'egalitarian' families where both parents work," and to their failure to include status offense items in their delinquency index (p. 20). Female involvement in status offenses, she argued, is essential to understanding female delinquency (see below).

Strain and Subcultural Theory

Conventional theories of male delinquency have often relied on *anomie-opportunity* or *strain* theory to explain males' involvement in delinquency (Cloward and Ohlin, 1960). Strain theory postulated that delinquency would arise when individuals' aspirations for material success were frustrated because of limited employment opportunities or lack of educational attainment. Applying this to females, we could hypothesize that: (1) if women's entrance in the labor force has increased females' aspirations for economic success (Figueira-McDonough, 1980); (2) and if economic goals for females are becoming increasingly important vis-a-vis domestic goals (Harry and Sengstock, 1978), especially if the schools have been encouraging females to develop occupational ambitions (Sheley, 1985); (3) and if the actual opportunities for females, especially lower and working class females, have not kept pace with rising aspirations or economic need;[2] or if females have been experiencing the strain of school failure (Empey, 1982); (4) it follows that female rates of crime and delinquency would rise (Empey, 1982; Figueira-McDonough, 1980).

Some research is available to help evaluate this hypothesis for female delinquency. Datesman et al. (1975) found that female delinquents were more likely than nondelinquents to see themselves as having fewer opportunities. Cernkovich and Giordano (1979) found that the most delinquent girls believed they would not finish school or find satisfactory employment, though they were not more likely than nondelinquents to believe that females experienced discrimination in the job market. Rankin (1980) found that negative school attitudes and poor academic performance were even stronger predictors of delinquency among females than among males.

Traditional extensions of strain theory as applied to delinquent boys also postulated that frustrated youth rebelled against established authority by developing a *subculture* that substituted delinquent values for conventional ones (Cloward and Ohlin, 1960; Cohen, 1955). In delinquent subcultures, juveniles are influenced by associations who define law-violation favorably and who transmit rationalizations or justifications for delinquent conduct (Sutherland and Cressey, 1974; Sykes and Matza, 1957). While some observers cite "the relative absence of subcultural support for female delinquency" (Datesman et al., 1975:112) as a limitation of strain theory's applicability to females (Empey, 1982), Akers et al. (1979) found that differential association and other social learning variables were effective predictors of alcohol and drug use among both male and female adolescents.[3] Similarly, Giordano (1978) found that involvement in mixed-sex peer groups was central to females' acquisition of attitudes favorable toward delinquent conduct, and that girls were not involved in

these groups in passive ways, as mere accomplices to boys. Rather, females' participation in mixed-sex peer groups simply afforded them the greatest opportunities to learn and engage in delinquent acts (see Giordano and Cernkovich, 1979). Giordano et al. (1986) also found that females were just as likely as males to indicate that they got drugs or alcohol from friends or that they hung out at friends' houses when parents were away. Although females were not as delinquent as males, their responses pointed to a greater participation than is typically assumed "by girls and their friends in . . . 'hedonistic/youth culture' activities" (p. 1188). Contrary to the traditional view of females as cloistered by their families, Giordano et al. (1986:1194) noted that:

> Females spend as much . . . time in the company of their friends as do males . . . [Those] who . . . become involved in delinquent acts . . . adopt both a set of attitudes in which they [see] delinquency as appropriate, possible, or desirable . . . and a friendship style in which they . . . encourage each other as a group to act on these orientations (see Morash, 1986).

Additional support for the importance of peer group subcultural influences on the development of female delinquency was found in a recent extension of power-control theory (Singer and Levine, 1988). While earlier studies found that girls from patriarchal households (unbalanced authority relations between parents) were less delinquent than girls from egalitarian households (balanced authority relations between parents) (Hagan et al., 1987), Singer and Levine (1988) found that peer group relations, as measured by respondents' taste for risk-taking in groups, mediated the effect of parental control on females. They found that girls in patriarchal families tended to rebel against paternal authority and were more likely than boys in these families "to follow peers in group-related risk taking" (p. 643). On the other hand, boys in egalitarian families tended to rebel against maternal authority and were more likely than girls in these families to follow peers.

Feminist Theory

Feminist theory attempts to illuminate how the position of women in male-dominated (patriarchal) societies affects the lives of contemporary females.[4] Feminists view traditional gender roles as integral to the maintenance of gender inequality and the ways in which women's sexuality and procreative capacities are appropriated by males to their advantage (Chesney-Lind, 1989; Klein, 1981). They are critical of the "double standard" society uses to evaluate male and female behavior, particularly in the area of sexuality. Behavior considered "normal" for boys ("sowing wild oats") is considered deviant for girls. Consequently, girls have been more likely than boys to be arrested and processed in juvenile court for status offenses, even though many of their status offense "crimes" have involved running away from a sexually abusive family situation (Chesney-Lind, 1977, 1989; Janus et al., 1987).

Chesney-Lind (1989:23) has analyzed "girls' victimization and their response to that victimization" in terms of the "gender and sexual scripts found in patriarchal families."

Men, particularly men with traditional attitudes toward women, are likely to define their daughters or stepdaughters as their sexual property. In a society that idealizes inequality in male/female relationships and venerates youth in women, girls are easily

defined as sexually attractive by older men. In addition, girls' vulnerability to . . . abuse is heightened by norms that require that they stay at home where their victimizers have access to them (p. 24; see Bell, 1984; Finkelhor, 1982).

Thus, girls are much more likely than boys to be victimized by sexual abuse. Girls' abuse also tends to begin earlier and last longer than boys' abuse. The trauma of sexual victimization has both "dramatic short- and long-term term effects . . . [which] . . . move from . . . fear, anxiety, depression, anger and hostility, and inappropriate sexual behavior . . . to . . . running away from home, difficulties in school, truancy, and early marriage" (Chesney-Lind, 1989:21–22; see Adams-Tucker, 1982; Browne and Finkelhor, 1986; DeJong et al., 1983; Finkelhor and Baron, 1986; Herman, 1981).

Chesney-Lind also noted that girls who run away from home are "forced further into crime in order to survive" (p. 22). Moreover, it "is no accident that [they] . . . get involved in criminal activities that exploit their sexual object status, . . . [for they] have little else of value to trade" (p. 24). Nevertheless, these girls "do not have a lot of attachment to their delinquent activities. In fact, they are angry about being labeled as delinquent [even though they] engaged in illegal acts" (p. 22). Girls, however, are powerless in relation to their victimizers who:

have the ability to invoke official agencies of social control in their efforts to keep young women at home and vulnerable. That is, . . . abusers have traditionally been able to utilize the uncritical commitment of the juvenile justice system toward parental authority to force girls to obey them. Girls' complaints about abuse were, until recently, routinely ignored (p. 24).

Thus, statutes that were originally designed to protect girls have ended up criminalizing their strategies of survival.

Conclusion

In order to supplement explanations of delinquency that focus on gender role socialization, masculinity-liberation, and role strain (see Chap. 5), this chapter reviewed applications to female delinquency of social control, power-control, strain, subcultural, and feminist theories. As I indicated in the earlier chapter, female delinquency is no longer a marginal topic in delinquency research, although much work remains to be done. Perhaps efforts to develop an "integrated" theory of female delinquency (see Elliott et al., 1979) utilizing the perspectives reviewed in this and the earlier article would prove fruitful. Certainly, more attention needs to be given, as feminists have suggested, toward understanding female delinquency in its patriarchal context. Feminist theory poses a significant challenge to those who have sug-

gested that theories used to explain male delinquency are sufficient to explain female delinquency (see Smith, 1979; Steffensmeier and Allan, 1988). It also suggests that the phenomenon of female delinquency cannot be adequately addressed without modifying the social conditions that maintain gender inequality. Contrary to the claim that women's emancipation has led to an increase in female law-breaking, studies suggest that "liberated" females may actually be less delinquent (see Giordano and Cernkovich, 1979). In fact, Balkan and Berger (1979: 224) have argued that "liberated" attitudes and involvement in the women's movement may increase females' ability "to express their grievances against oppressive economic, political, and social conditions in constructive ways." Female delinquents would benefit from efforts by women's movement adherents to provide "girls with alternative role models and concrete programs that emphasize the need for structural change instead of adjustment to existing values and roles" (p. 224).

Notes

1. Steffensmeier and Allan (1988) found that male crime rates for particular subgroups were highly predictive of female crime rates for these groups. They used the male rate as a proxy variable for general structural conditions that affected law-violations of both sexes, leaving relatively little variance to be explained by conditions unique to females.

2. The "feminization of poverty" indicates that this is indeed the case for many women (see Balkan and Berger, 1979; Messerschmidt, 1986; Miller, 1986; Steffensmeier and Cobb, 1981).

3. The reader will recall that Akers et al.'s "social learning" theory (see Chap. 7) integrates differential association theory into a more general behavioral reinforcement theoretical framework. Social learning theory emphasizes the social psychological (behavioral) mechanisms that translate strain, subcultural, and other social variables into delinquent conduct.

4. There is no single feminist perspective, but rather a variety of views that make "different assumptions about the causes of gender inequality" (Daley and Chesney-Lind, 1988:501; see Jaggar, 1983; Messerschmidt, 1986).

References

Adams-Tucker, C. 1982. "Proximate effects of sexual abuse in childhood." *American Journal of Psychiatry* 193:1252–6.

Akers, R. L., M. D. Krohn, L. Lanza-Kaduce, and M. Radosevich. 1979. "Social learning and deviant behavior: A specific test of a general theory." *American Sociological Review* 44:636–55.

Balkan, S. and R. J. Berger. 1979. "The changing nature of female delinquency." Pp. 207–27 in C. Kopp (ed.), *Becoming Female: Perspectives on Development*. New York: Plenum.

Browne, A. and D. F. 1986. "Impact of child sexual abuse: A review of research." *Psychological Bulletin* 99:66–77.

Canter, R.J. 1982. "Family correlates of male and female delinquency." *Criminology* 20:149–67.

Cernkovich, S.A. and P.C. Giordano. 1987. "Family relationships and Delinquency." *Criminology* 25:295–321.

———. 1979. "Delinquency, opportunity, and gender." *Journal of Criminal Law and Criminology* 70:145–51.

Chesney-Lind, M. 1989. "Girl's crime and woman's place: Toward a feminist model of female delinquency." *Crime and Delinquency* 35:5–29.

———. 1977. "Judicial paternalism and the female status offender: Training women to know their place." *Crime and Delinquency* 23:121–30.

Cloward, R.A. and L.E. Ohlin. 1960. *Delinquency and Opportunity: A Theory of Delinquent Gangs*. New York: Free Press.

Cohen, A.K. 1955. *Delinquent Boys: The Culture of the Gang*. New York: Free Press.

Daley, K. and M. Chesney-Lind. 1988. "Feminism and criminology." *Justice Quarterly* 5:497–538.

Datesman, S. K., F. R. Scarpitti, and R. M. Stephenson. 1975. "Female delinquency: An application of self and opportunity theories." *Journal of Research in Crime and Delinquency* 12:107–23.

DeJong, A. R., A. R. Hervada, and G. A. Emmett. 1983. "Epidemiologic variations in childhood sexual abuse." *Child Abuse and Neglect* 7:155–62.

Elliott, D. S., S. S. Ageton, and R. J. Canter. 1979. "An integrated theoretical perspective on delinquent behavior." *Journal of Research in Crime and Delinquency* 16:3–27.

Empey, L. T. 1982. *American Delinquency: Its Meaning and Construction*. Second edition. Homewood, IL: Dorsey Press.

Figueira-McDonough, J. 1980. "A reformulation of the 'equal opportunity' explanation of female delinquency." *Crime and Delinquency* 26:333–43.

Finkelhor, D. 1982. "Sexual abuse: A sociological perspective." *Child Abuse and Neglect* 6:95–102.

Finkelhor, D. and L. Baron. 1986. "Risk factors in child sexual abuse." *Journal of Interpersonal Violence* 1:43–71.

Giordano, P.C. 1978. "Girls, guys and gangs: The changing social context of female delinquency." *Journal of Criminal Law and Criminology* 69:126–32.

Giordano, P.C. and S.A. Cernkovich. 1979. "On complicating the relationship between liberation and delinquency." *Social Problems* 26:467–81.

Giordano, P.C., S.A. Cernkovich, and M.D. Pugh. 1986. "Friendships and delinquency." *American Journal of Sociology* 91:1170–1202.

Hagan, J., A.R. Gillis, and J. Simpson. 1985. "The class structure of gender and delinquency: Toward a power-control theory of common delinquent behavior." *American Journal of Sociology* 90:1151–78.

Hagan, J., J. Simpson, and A.R. Gillis. 1987. "Class in the household: A power-control theory of gender and delinquency." *American Journal of Sociology* 92:788–816.

Harry, J. and M.C. Sengstock. 1978. "Attribution, goals, and deviance." *American Sociological Review* 43:278–80.

Herman, J.L. 1981. *Father-Daughter Incest.* Cambridge, MA: Harvard University Press.

Hill, G.D. and M.P. Atkinson. 1988. "Gender, familial control, and delinquency." *Criminology* 26:127–47.

Hirschi, T. 1969. *Causes of Delinquency.* Berkeley: University of California Press.

Jaggar, A. 1983. *Feminist Politics and Human Nature.* Totowa, NJ: Rowman and Allanheld.

Janus, M., A. McCormack, A. W. Burgess, and C. Hartman. 1987. *Adolescent Runaways: Causes and Consequences.* Lexington, MA: Lexington Books.

Jensen, G.F. and R. Eve. 1976. "Sex differences in delinquency: An examination of popular sociological explanations." *Criminology* 12:427–48.

Klein, D. 1981. "Violence against women: Some considerations regarding its causes and elimination." *Crime and Delinquency* 27:64–80.

Messerschmidt, J.W. 1986. *Capitalism, Patriarchy, and Crime: Toward a Socialist Feminist Criminology.* Totowa, NJ: Rowman and Littlefield.

Miller, E. 1986. *Street Woman: The Illegal Work of Underclass Women.* Philadelphia: Temple University Press.

Morash, M. 1986. "Gender, peer group experiences, and seriousness of delinquency." *Journal of Research in Crime and Delinquency* 23:43–67.

Rankin, J.H. 1980. "School factors and delinquency: Interaction by age and sex." *Sociology and Social Research* 64:420–34.

Reiss, A.J. 1951. "Delinquency as the failure of personal and social controls." *American Sociological Review* 16:196–207.

Sheley, J. 1985. *America's 'Crime Problem': An Introduction to Criminology.* Belmont, CA: Wadsworth.

Shover, N., S. Norland, J. James, and W.E. Thornton. 1979. "Gender roles and delinquency." *Social Forces* 58:162–75.

Singer, S.I. and M. Levine. 1988. "Power-control theory, gender, and delinquency: A partial replication with additional evidence on the effects of peers." *Criminology* 26:627–47.

Smith, D.A. 1979. "Sex and deviance: An assessment of major sociological variables." *Sociological Quarterly* 20:183–95.

Steffensmeier, D.J. and E.A. Allan. 1988. "Sex disparities in arrests by residence, race, and age: An assessment of the gender convergence/crime hypothesis." *Justice Quarterly* 5:53–80.

Steffensmeier, D.J. and M.J. Cobb. 1981. "Sex differences in urban arrest patterns, 1934–79." *Social Problems* 29:37–50.

Sutherland, E.H. and D.R. Cressey. 1974. *Criminology.* Ninth edition. Philadelphia: Lippincott.

Sykes, G. and D. Matza. 1957. "Techniques of neutralization: A theory of delinquency." *American Sociological Review* 22:664–70.

PART 5

The Delinquent Experience: Girls, Guys, and Gangs

The articles in this section of the book all reflect the theme of the delinquent experience, especially as it is perceived by youths themselves. The selections include journalistic accounts and ethnographic research that highlight the feelings and perceptions of female and male delinquents, that sensitize the reader to the day-to-day life experiences of delinquent youth, and that offer a portrait of the varieties of delinquent behaviors.

The first selection in this section (Chapter 15) is an article on runaways, ''No Place to Hide,'' by journalist Dotson Rader. This moving account is based on interviews with female and male runaways who describe their abusive treatment at home and how they manage to survive on the streets through prostitution and theft.

The next reading (Chapter 16), ''Players and Ho's,'' is a chapter from Terry Williams and William Kornblum's ethnography, *Growing Up Poor*. This selection offers readers a generous sampling of interviews with youths who describe their lives in prostitution as players or pimps and as whores. The article also includes accounts of the early childhood life experiences of these youth.

The third article (Chapter 17), ''Adolescent Perspectives on Drugs/Alcohol and Crime,'' is another ethnographic study taken from a book on *Kids, Drugs, and Crime* by Cheryl Carpenter and associates. This piece presents youths' own views of the relationship between drug/alcohol use and other criminal activities.

The fourth reading (Chapter 18) is Ronald Berger's ''Adolescent Subcultures, Social Type Metaphors, and Group Delinquency.'' In this article, Berger reviews previous research on adolescent subcultures and common varieties of delinquency, focusing on the social type names or metaphors (such as Jocks, Dirtballs, and Freaks) used by youth to communicate with one another about the relative status of various adolescent groups in their high school community. He also presents results of new research on social type metaphors and adolescent subcultures.

The last three readings in this section focus on inner-city street gangs. In "La Vida Loca—The Crazy Life" (Chapter 19), journalist Tracy Johnston describes gang life, drugs, and violence from the point of view of Chicana females. Similarly, Glenn Weisfeld and Roger Feldman's "A Former Street Gang Leader Reinterviewed Eight Years Later" (Chapter 20) describes gang experiences from the perspective of a former male gang leader, including his views on different theories of crime causation. Finally, Joan Moore and associates' "Residence and Territoriality in Chicano Gangs" (Chapter 21) challenges traditional views regarding the territorial basis of gangs and considers sources of gang solidarity and non-resident gang membership. The article also includes a number of quotes from their interviews with gang members.

No Place to Hide: A Story of Runaways

15

Dotson Rader

Ann is a very pretty girl, with a round, child-like face, lovely smile and large brown eyes. She dresses colorfully and delights in collecting stuffed animals, bunnies mostly. When she moves from one cheap hotel to another, as she frequently does, she piles her toys into two enormous plastic garbage bags and drags them with her.

Ann is 15. Like hundreds of other runaways, she hangs out around First and Post Streets in Seattle, a derelict in an area of porn shops, saloons, and fleabag hotels. She sleeps late, spending her nights wandering the streets or sitting in the Donut Shop. While it's an unpleasant place, runaways feel welcome there, safe from the johns, pushers, and pimps outside, and from the cops. For many, the Donut Shop is the only place they have to go.

Like Ann, all the children in this story are real. While their names have been changed, their stories are true. What they say here is typical of what hundreds of other kids told

From *Parade,* February 7, 1982. Reprinted by permission of Parade Publications, Inc. and the author, copyright © 1982.

me across America, from Key West to Boston, and New York to Los Angeles.

This article centers on the runaways in Seattle and San Diego, cities chosen because they anchor the ends of U.S. I-5, the main road for kids on the run in the West. Also, they are representative places, largely middle class. These children could be from your town, from next door.

I sat opposite Ann at one of the long Formica tables, under harsh fluorescent lights. I asked her about why she didn't go home to her family.

"Everytime I try to go home to live, my Dad starts hitting me," she said. "Now I only go home on Christmas, Thanksgiving and on my birthday. I owe them that. I'd like to live at home again, but I know it would start all over again, Daddy drinking and beating me up. That's why I left. The first time I ran away, I was 11. When I was 12, I was gone for good. I got a job at the Exotic Body Exercise Club downtown near the Donut Shop.

"After I lost that job, I met this old man on the street. He said he needed a babysitter. I'd get paid well. He lived in a hotel in Chinatown. He had a prostitute there, and she had a baby I took care of. After a while, the old man made me a prostitute. I was 13 years old, and I had no place to go.

"The old man knew all these Japanese guys who'd come to the hotel for sex. Two or three times a week I'd turn tricks, usually five or six a night. They each paid the old man $40 for sex with me. He was good to me. Sometimes he gave me $7 to go to the disco, and $10 to spend. But I left him after nine months."

Ann glanced around the Donut Shop at the other kids. Then she leaned forward, lowering her voice, not wanting the other children to hear. Her modesty was touching and sad.

"My parents never spoke to me about sex. What I knew about it I learned at the movies," she confided. "When I first did it, I'd drink before the sex happened, and then I'd pretend it wasn't happening to me. I'd think about *pretty* things, like I wasn't even there. The first time, I was scared because I didn't know what was going to happen. Then I didn't care anymore. I really only like sex with someone I love. Other times I'm indifferent. I'm very lucky. I haven't been hurt by a trick. A lot of kids have."

"After I left the pimp," she continued, "I started mud wrestling on weekends all over the country. I was 14."

Ann told me about the mud show circuit, how she was auctioned off after each match to the highest bidder, who then had the right to bathe her down. She added that her life was okay. Anyway, what choice did she have? Nobody since she first ran away had ever tried to help her. Nobody.

We left the Donut Shop. Kids were huddled in doorways or walking back and forth to keep warm, some as young as 10, waiting around in the cold for someone to stop and buy their bodies for a few dollars or a meal or a warm place to stay. Police cars cruised

by, as did johns peering through closed car windows, looking for kids to pick up.

Up to one million children in the United States run away from home each year, according to the federal Health and Human Services Administration. And most, after a few weeks, turn to prostitution and theft for survival. The average age of a runaway child is 15.

Forty-seven percent of runaways are girls, the agency says.* More than half leave home because of child abuse. One-third are sexually abused. Of these children, 83 percent come from white families. The majority are never even reported as missing by their parents. Knowing all that, it was still disheartening to see in Seattle so many kids with nowhere to go.

As we walked, Ann introduced me to other street children, two of whom I asked to interview. Most of the runaways I met were unusually bright, attractive, lonely, and hungry for adult regard and affection.

There were also johns who came up, trying to solicit Ann.

These men who have sex with children are almost entirely middle-class, usually married, and most often they have children at home about the same age as the child they violate, according to social workers. They are rarely arrested. When the police act, it is always against the children.

Before I left Ann, I asked how she envisioned her future. It was now after midnight. She stood near the entrance of a smut parlor, her small hands shoved in her jacket pockets, looking weak and defenseless. "Oh, I don't plan to be a prostitute for the rest of my life," she declared. "In Seattle, most of the runaway girls on the street end up in prostitution. It's do or die. The same with the boys. Do you know how hard it is for a kid to

---

*Editor's Note: This figure was 57% in 1987.

get a job in Seattle?'' She shook her head. ''If I had my life to do over again, I wouldn't live like this. I would have stayed home. I'd rather be abused at home than this. Seriously, I would.''

She paused.

''But it's too late now.''

The following day I found Ann waiting in my hotel lobby with two of her friends, Daniel and Melanie.

Daniel, who just turned 15, is tall, handsome and unusually articulate. He told me about running away from home at 12, of being raped a week later by a middle-aged man in the back of a van and being too frightened to tell anybody. In almost deferential tones, he outlined his brief life—hitchhiking up and down the West Coast. His was an account of sexual abuse, drugs, desperation and an aching need to belong somewhere, to somebody. Now he was working as a busboy. He wants to be a radio announcer. Someone told him he had the voice for it.

After speaking with Daniel, I talked with Melanie. She spoke rapidly, chainsmoking. There was a bravado in her manner, belied by her sorrowful gray eyes. She was five feet and underfed.

She told me about her parents' divorce and the death of her grandmother, whom she loved deeply. At 13 she became pregnant. She didn't know how pregnancies happened, she said. She left home when her mother forced her to abort the child. Melanie has been on the run since.

''I ran away on Christmas night, about two months after the abortion,'' she said. ''I hated Mom after that. One night I went to downtown Seattle. I met a guy named Jim. He was 18, and he'd been a runaway since he was 14. We got an apartment together. It was really a hotel for bums. I started tricking [prostitution] to get money for us because Jim was having a hard time of it. The johns wanted younger boys, 14, 15, and Jim was

too old. When I first started tricking, I didn't let Jim know. I wanted him to think I was an innocent little girl. Now it doesn't bother him.''

Melanie sat by the window in my room. It was an overcast day, but you could still see past the skyscrapers to the lake beyond and, farther still, the hills of the neighborhood where she had been reared.

''I used to live over there,'' she remarked. ''It was a nice house.''

Now she lived with Jim, who was a bum dealing drugs, drinking and hanging out. She loved him, but she hated prostitution, all her years lost to the streets. She felt trapped.

''I'm so tired of sex,'' Melanie said wearily. ''It doesn't do me any good, sex with anybody, even Jim. I don't enjoy it anymore.'' She is 16 now.

I suggested that she return home. If she told her parents what she had been through, they would help.

She laughed. *''My parents know I'm a prostitute,''* she said. ''All my father says is, don't get arrested. He doesn't want it in the newspapers.''

Before I left for San Diego, I took Daniel and Ann to the restaurant at the hotel. They ate a lot and talked as children will about all they are going to do in life and what shining futures awaited them, but I knew they didn't believe a word of it.

''I'm flying to California on Tuesday to go on the roller-coaster and see a guy down there named Walt,'' Ann boasted. ''He's a television producer.''

''I've been to Disneyland!'' said Daniel. *''Twice!''*

She ignored him. ''I met Walt at an amusement park last year in Santa Cruz. I went to his ranch and rode horses and drank lemonade. He likes little girls. He likes me.''

I asked how old he was, this man who likes little girls.

"Sixty-five," Ann said.

When they finished eating, they said they had to go to the bathroom. As I waited for them to return, I grew wary and began to suspect they were conspiring to hit me for money.

When they returned, each had a small gift for me they had bought at the hotel's gift shop. A bottle of aftershave and a souvenir mug.

For three days in San Diego, a runaway named Patrick took me to places where children on the lam gather. They're not hard to find. They sleep in the bus depot, or in the parks, particularly the area near the zoo. You find them in abandoned cars or empty houses or grouped around fires on beaches. They are everywhere.

Of the hundreds of children I met, Patrick was the most private. He was wounded inside, and the pain bred distrust and silence. He was 17, although he looked much younger. Blond, with blue-green eyes, he was small but athletic, liking gymnastics. Quiet, shy, suspicious. But despite that, he had a natural winsomeness, a ready smile and easy laugh joined by an insistent vulnerability that made him at once likeable and sad. He elicited in me, as did the others, a desire to protect. But he was different, possessed by an almost palpable rage. When I first asked about his life, he angrily refused to reply. So I let it go by.

On my second day, we drove to Chula Vista Park, where many runaways live. They survive by doing odd jobs, stealing, helping each other out.

We came to the park two days after the police had raided it, and we saw children with bruised faces and cuts on their heads. The police don't like children living in the parks.

Among the runaways I interviewed there was Steven, 15, from Ocean Beach, Califor-

nia. He ran away when he was 13, he said. Like most runaways, his chief concern was getting enough food and a dry place to sleep. He comes from a good family, but he can't go home again.

"It's frightening to be a runaway," Steven said, "because you don't know about tomorrow. You wonder where you're going to eat or live. Am I going to be all right? Will I be able to sleep somewhere other than in the park? You got nothing to grab onto because all that you own is what's on your back. Nothing is mine. When I want something to eat, I steal it.

"When you run away, you meet a lot of kids who got no place," he added.

"Why don't kids want to go home?" I asked.

"Some of them get beat up so bad," he said. "But the streets are bad too. The cops hassle you. Sometimes they beat you up. I don't want to go home because I really hate my mother. When I was 13, she kicked me out.

"If I had a child who ran away, I'd find him. I'd do my best. I'd sit down and ask him what was on his mind. What's troubling you, kid? And after we talked, I'd try to change the things he didn't like. We'd compromise. I want to go back home, but I can't. I see how small I am. *I'm nothing.* God, I can't live on my own. It's mad out there. It's crazy! Whew! It's scary! I can't pay my own way. And I know it."

The day I was to leave San Diego, Patrick and I went to Ocean Beach to interview more runaways. I talked to a girl and a boy who lived in a broken-down car. And to a girl of 15 with a year-old baby, and her friend of 13. They had been traveling together for two years and could not see beyond tomorrow. Also, there were young runaways spaced out on drugs or staggering about on cheap booze; children obviously undernourished, unhealthy, unwanted. America's children.

As the sun began to set, Patrick and I sat on the pier watching the light fade.

"I've had a pretty hard life," Patrick suddenly said, staring at the ocean.

I replied that I knew, although I didn't.

"I don't want to tell all of it," he said. "I was always made to feel less." He sipped a beer as he sat hunched on the pier, his feet dangling above the water. "My mom hated me," he went on, "because I reminded her of my dad. I always knew she was bad, from the first day I can remember, like when I was two years old. She was always doing weird things, like wanting me and my little brother to take a bath with her." He stopped. I said nothing, for I sensed Patrick was trying to tell me what he had never told any other adult.

"She tried to do sexual stuff with us, too," he began again, staring out to sea as if he were addressing the ocean and not me. "To go to bed with her. All through my growing up, she was always trying something with me, and my little brother too. She was dating a guy, and she had a girlfriend at the same time, and they were all sleeping in the same bed, running around naked all the time. It makes me sick. My own mother. I've blocked it all out. That's the only way I've survived.

"Then when I was 13, I was sent to live with my grandparents," he said.

"They cheated and lied. When I was 15, they sold me to a lady for $500. I ran away. So I never had a real family. I never saw my real father. I was always lonely . . . I feel like there must be something wrong with me. How come no one ever loved me? I must be bad. I feel like I don't exist because nobody ever *loved* me.

"My mom used to beat me with boards," he continued. "You wouldn't believe some of the stuff she whipped me with. Hot Wheel tracks. And my stepfather? He whipped me 25 times on the back

of the legs with a rubber hose. I tried to block it, and I got hit on the hands. I counted every swat. Twenty-five times he hit me. And now he beats my little brother. How can I get even? I *can't* get even. But I'll remember it, believe me."

I asked Patrick if that was why he ran away, because of the beatings. He looked at me, full of anger, and then he threw his beer can into the sea. He stood. We walked on the pier.

"I didn't want to be a runaway," he said. "I had no place to go. I didn't want to starve. I didn't want to steal. I had nowhere to go."

He stopped and grabbed my arm.

"No one ever helped me! Teach me. Help me! I need help. *Seriously!*"

"I know." I pulled my arm free.

"There's a lot of things I don't know, and I'd like to learn. I want to learn to survive legally," he went on. "I don't have my ID, and I don't know how to get it. I'm willing to learn. I don't want to be a dummy all my life. I don't want to be a bum, because I'm better than that. Do you understand where I'm coming from? I need to know things to survive! I don't know anything. I can barely *read,* to tell the honest truth. My mom never helped me with my schoolwork. They didn't care about me."

I looked at him, his eyes expressing beseechment, pain and deep humiliation. *I can barely read.*

"Patrick," I began, and gave up. I had no answer to give him.

We walked toward the fence separating the parking lot from the beach.

"Don't you think loving is hard?" he asked.

I said nothing.

He glanced at me, and then he declared manfully, *"I never cry!"*

With that, Patrick rushed to the fence, climbed it, and like a circus acrobat ran along the top of it quickly—away from me.

Players and Ho's

16

I don't exactly fill out a W2 form after I turn a trick.
—*Margo Sharp*

Terry Williams
William Kornblum

Cooksey's, D's Inferno, Club 437, Mc-Donald's, and the mall are familiar hangouts for teenagers in Louisville. The mall is located in downtown Louisville; although it is integrated, it is a meeting place for black youth from all over the city. Many of the teenagers hustle in the pool rooms and discos, peddling marijuana and sex.

For the young women, hustling is synonymous with prostitution. Indeed, in all the cities we studied, prostitution is the main occupation for girls in the underground economy—girls like Donna White, who hustles in Louisville's mall area.

> I am 19 years old. About two years ago my parents moved to a little town called Madisonville, Kentucky. I hated that place. But I

stayed long enough to finish school at Norman Hopkins [High School]. I wanted to go places and see different things and not stay in that damn place. I wanted to make something out of myself so I left and came here to Louisville. I couldn't find no job for nine months here so I met up with some friends who told me I could hustle and make some money. They said they would show me how. All I had to do was learn.

So I first started hustling in the pool rooms and pushing a few petty drugs. My boyfriend and/or his friend would stand in the pool room or out in the hall and wait till they saw some men, soldiers, businessmen, or whatever, and ask them if they wanted to have some sex. If they said yes, he would steer them over to the pool room and then tell me where to go meet them.

In the Hough district of Cleveland, dilapidated, burned-out structures from the 1960s riots are still visible. The housing consists mainly of single-family units. It is odd to see so many old houses, many in the

Reprinted by permission of the publisher from pp. 61–72 of *Growing Up Poor* by Terry Williams and William Kornblum (Lexington, Mass.: Lexington Books, D. C. Heath and Company, Copyright © 1985, D. C. Heath and Company).

grand style, decaying, unpainted, and broken. Hough is the ghetto of Cleveland. Its citizens, black and white alike, seem helpless to change it. The community is bankrupt economically, politically, and socially. Many feel that Hough is being punished for the "sins" it committed in the 1960s.

Pearl Varnedoe has worked as a prostitute in the Hough area and downtown near the University of Cleveland since she was fourteen. Pearl left home in order to "make money and live free." She says hustling came easily to her because "my parents had a club that always had pimps, whores, and gamblers in it."

My mother was always beating me. My father tried to make her stop but he couldn't. My mother was always drunk and she couldn't stop that either. My father ran this after-hours club and when I left home I met up with some of them from his joint and they turned me out [set me up as a prostitute]. I always had real big titties and a nice body. As a matter of fact, the vice squad know me on sight and arrest me sometimes just to have something to do. I've been arrested about 21 times. They never knew I was a minor during all the time I spent there. When I went home to check on my father, I found out my mother had been beating my brothers and sisters too. Our neighbor had called in a child-abuse worker to talk to her, she told me she knew about my being on the street and filed a delinquency report with the juvenile authorities.

In Meridian, Mississippi, a large naval base on the outskirts of town has created a thriving market for drugs and sex. Thus the young people in Meridian perceive numerous opportunities in the illegal economy. The young men between the ages of 16 and 20 are the players or pimps, and the young women between the ages of 13 and 20 are the prostitutes—making prostitution the main

source of illegal income for youths. Teenagers like Curly and his girls make up the "supply side" of prostitution in Meridian.

Curly is eighteen years old. His hustle is young women. He's a "player" and they are "ho's" or "tricks." (In Meridian "trick" refers to the prostitute or seller of sex; in New York the converse is true— "trick" refers to the buyer of sex.)

I have one or two girls on the street. I still got a couple of them doing things for me. You know I gotta have that paper [money]. The only rule I have is that my main lady don't go out there. The others I have them boosting, tricking, whatever, as long as they keep giving up the money. See, baby, you do what you have to do to survive in this world now. The more money they have, the more I have. They do what they want to to get it. And when I ask them for it, I get it. Sometimes I'll help out if I get hip to someone who wants to make a buy. I'll let them know. But it depends on how much they get and how much I need. But I don't take all of their money. I usually leave them a little. And I don't feel I'm responsible for putting no ho on the street. Look, they are out there trying to be grown. They put themselves out there. If I didn't take their money, they would give it to someone else. Them tricks ain't gonna be nothing but whores. All I did was fuck them a couple of times and they started giving me money. See, a woman doesn't have to sell her body for a man to pimp her. There are plenty of women that are smart and pretty with good jobs and taking care of men. That's pimping.

Among Curly's "tricks" are Maylee Jones, Clara Thompson, and Dorothea Caddy, aged sixteen, sixteen, and seventeen, respectively. Here's what they have to say about "the life":

Maylee: There ain't no jobs around here. Besides I can make more money doing this. Sometimes I make one hundred or two, sometimes more, sometimes less. If I had a job, I wouldn't make that much. If I could make as much money in a job as I do hustling, I would work. The Navy boys they spend a lot of money. All these old white men do too. Anyway around here they give all the good jobs to the white people.

The most important thing in my life right now is surviving. That's all I believe in. Well, I believe in God but not preachers 'cause all the preachers do is ride around in Cadillacs and wear silk suits.

Clara: I have four boyfriends who give me $15 a week to go to bed with them. I only go out with one of them. The money I get I just spend it on clothes and stuff to get high with. I don't like to do it too much. I think it might do something to me. All the men are young, in their 20s. I give them a bit here and there but they give me the money on time. I like to show my legs and breast. It fascinates me to watch men cream.

Dorothea: I started tricking because I didn't know what time it was. I was at a friend's house getting high and they said, hey, you want to turn a trick for someone? And I said, it depends on the cash, what time, and who. At that time, I needed the money, you know. My boyfriend was there and I didn't know he was no pimp. But he kept encouraging me to do it. Anyway, after that I set my own thing up with one of my girlfriends. I have them [johns] call her. I used to have them call my pimp till I got rid of him. He got mad, but he knew I could fight him if he tried some shit like hitting on me. I didn't need him anymore, you know. I only had him for protection and the first time I went to jail for fighting, the man was out of town. I would make $150 or so and put $75 back and show him the rest, and he would give me $25 of that plus what I had, you know. He didn't know what time it was.

Dorothea dropped out of school in the ninth grade. At seventeen she organized a group of teenage prostitutes and set up a brothel in a fashionable black section of town.

Young women in each of these cities—and in New York as well—are shocked and depressed by the bleakness of their situation. Many do not believe they have a choice between getting a job and hustling. Hustling—meaning prostitution—is the only choice. (Theft and prostitution are often combined, but prostitution is by far the easiest, most convenient, and most profitable form of illegal activity for these teenagers.)

Most girls are recruited into prostitution, but some are tricked, coerced, or charmed into the life. The latter are talked into believing that it is an exciting life complete with fine cars and endless amounts of money. There is a note of self-delusion in some of their comments, like "A lot of the men are lonely and I feel I can help them" or "Most of the time the tricks don't know what time it is, so you can get their money."

While there are adult role models and community institutions that try to steer teenagers away from the life, many find the incentives too strong. Margo Sharp's life as a prostitute in Harlem illustrates the careers young women pursue in the underground economy.

Margo's parents separated when she was four years old. Her mother remarried, and during the ensuing years her father made sporadic appearances. When Margo was twelve or thirteen her mother became embroiled in domestic problems with her stepfather. Arguments and fights were common. Margo's mother began to have relationships with other men, including some of her husband's friends. One of those men had a traumatic impact on Margo.

My mother had an affair with this man who was later to become my stepfather. Well, he had this friend, best friend no less, who was this little horny Dominican motherfucker. I was 12 years old then and I knew about sex and all of that, although I had never had sex. He would come around the house all the time and even though my mother was seeing my stepfather, this guy would come over sometimes and they would laugh and drink and my stepfather would leave them alone sometimes because he trusted his friend so much. Well, my mother and this little Dominican started to have a thing behind my stepfather's back. And this little motherfucker was so horny, he wound up fucking my mother's best friend too.

Anyhow, one day I was upstairs doing my homework and he comes into my room and tells me he wants to talk to me. I don't remember if anybody was home or not that day, but I assumed he was gonna talk about my mother and their little thing, you know. So he told me to sit on the bed next to him. And I did. Still not thinking anything about it. Well the next thing I know he's taking my blouse off. And all the time he's asking me if I feel anything. Well I don't know why I didn't scream or anything but I just sat there. After he had taken off my panties, the only thought I had in my mind was not to panic. Not to scream because I had read all about how men had killed women and kids molesting them or something, and I wasn't about to say a thing. So he took off my panties and the only thing that stood out in my mind was how big he was. It seemed like he was as big as a tree trunk, I swear to God, I was hurting so bad, I was so sore. I felt, my God, what did he do to me? Well, when it was over, he helped me put back on my clothes and I sat on the bed for a long time just thinking.

I never told my mother anything for two years. And when I did her reaction was typical of women in love. She slapped me. She thought I was lying for years after I told her this. She didn't believe nothing I told her. One day two years later this little bastard drove up to my house to see my mother. Well my mother told me to come out and say hello to him. But I was not too excited about seeing the little fucker ever again. So I refused. But she insisted so I went out to say hello. But when I saw his face I just got angry. The window of the car door was down. And he reached his face out to kiss me and I spat in it. My mother jerked me away and slapped me. But I grabbed her arm and told her I was no kid any more. I was 14 years old and that she had no reason to protect a man who had not only cheated on her by fucking her friend but had cheated on her by fucking her daughter. She didn't believe me. Like I said, she thought I was lying. She was so in love with this faggot that she didn't believe her own daughter. I hated him for that more than his act against me because it made my relationship with my mother a stormy one for years to come.

Margo was fourteen then. Her mother was unwilling to assume responsibility for her wayward daughter, so she sent Margo to a social worker at the Children's Aid Society. After a series of bad experiences in a variety of schools, Margo finally dropped out. Considered gifted by her teachers, she could not make herself sit still long enough to complete her studies. Instead, she was habitually absent. Her lateness and absenteeism eventually resulted in expulsion.

Margo's attitudes about men were formed early. She was more game than most men could handle. Standing tall and shapely with big eyes and a warm, inquisitive intelligence, she was no child and knew it. After leaving school, she refused to work but always seemed to have money. Her mother occasionally asked her how she was able to get along without working, but Margo always had an explanation.

I would have $200, $300, $400 and my mother knew nothing about it. I wouldn't tell her where I had been. So half the time she didn't know. I didn't buy a lot of stuff or give her money because I was afraid she would ask me where I got it from. I tried to explain it to her one day. I told her a friend of hers,

Mr. George, who was about 50 years old had hinted he wanted to have sex with me. So I jokingly told my mom that if he wanted it, it would cost him a hundred bucks. Well, she laughed and said, ''Yeah, that's better than giving it to him for free.'' So in a way, I guess, she didn't really object to what I was doing.

By the time Margo was fifteen she was involved in casual prostitution, averaging two hundred dollars per customer. She was in the life as an ''outlaw,'' that is, without benefit of a pimp. Her method was a bit unorthodox. When a man approached her, she would take the money from the transaction and give it to one of her male friends.

Sometimes my friend would look at me funny when I told him to hold the cash. It would be a few hundred dollars. And that I would be back later. I would go to a hotel and after it was over I'd go back to pick up my money. If a guy approached me and said I was beautiful and asked how much would it cost him to have me, I would tell him whatever came to my mind. If he looked well dressed and clean I would say $200, $300, $400. It depended on my mood. If I was real horny, I would react quicker but that didn't mean the price went down. I would just choose someone who I thought was good looking. Someone who I thought would be pleasant to fuck. Sometimes I would get off with these guys but most of the time I would pretend.

At least some liked it enough to pay high prices for it. It started out with offers of $100 or more for an hour or two. When they first started asking me I would decline, and then decided to stop being such a fool. I started accepting, not only money, but gifts, trips, etc. It was sort of like getting your cake and eating it too. I was not only compensated for time, but I was spent time with as well. The sexual acts were sexual acts. But if they brought on a smile, a kiss or hug the morning after, it was worthwhile. I felt not only

wanted but needed. At the same time, a lot of lonely hearts were warmed. Call it what you will, I see my actions in a benevolent light. I enjoyed the money, spending highly, indulging in things I wouldn't normally have. The gifts were sweet. They showed a touch more of consideration. The men were usually much older than myself. I, in some cases, portrayed a prized china doll that they flaunted.

Yes, I did get tired of the life at times, but it was an experience, and I learned a lot. I met some very interesting people. I always tried to establish a good rapport with my friends. One never knows who one may need some day. But only as friends. My intimate relationships were always kept separate and never came about from a trick night. It was difficult at times having both a main man and my pastime, but I managed. In some cases, where I felt the person I was dealing with was due more respect, I would cool off my friendly encounters and devote myself to that one person.

For young women like Margo, prostitution becomes a distinctive lifestyle, known as ''the life.'' But for the pimps or players, hustling sex isn't very different from any other kind of hustle. The young man usually has tried a variety of ways of earning money, finally settling on pimping as involving the least effort for the greatest reward. Ray-Ray Southern is typical.

I came to Meridian when I was 11 years old. I went to Oakland Heights Elementary School in the fifth grade. I got along very well with the teachers. We caught the city bus every day to school. I got out of school one day by playing sick and stole a bicycle. I had to go by the babysitter's house to pick up my little sister and brother. They were very happy to see me. My momma came home by the babysitter's house and found out about the bicycle. She asked me where it was and I told her somewhere else, but I didn't know where. Momma took me home and whipped me. The police came and talked to me and we got over that.

About three weeks later our house caught on fire. My sister was smoking a cigarette and threw the butt on the floor. After the fire, we changed schools and I met the wrong type of friends. I had a fight the first day of school. Later on, I stole another bicycle and I didn't get caught. I began to turn out with this girl I was running with. We would do things like stealing, smoking, drinking, and breaking out people's windows.

Everything was happening to me then. My girlfriend and I got caught in the act of love making. My mother was very upset. She wanted to whip me but my dad talked her out of it. She was upset because she didn't know I knew too much about sex. My mother talked to us about it but I wasn't listening. I liked what I was doing. After a few more incidents, we broke up because of her mother. So I met another girl. I was going over there every day. I was going to school but I would play hooky with her. We didn't stay together because all she wanted was sex. The first day of the next term I was kissing this girl and they said I had to go. This happened too many times. So I left because there was too many rules anyhow. You couldn't hold hands, you couldn't talk to white girls, etc.

I got into trouble again and this time they sent me to Columbia Training School. I was there for four months and two weeks. Three months later I was in more trouble—breaking and entering. I got some items out and sold them to the wrong person. I had to go back to the juvenile center. I was out one day and the next one I was in.

I got a job when I got out working at Morrison's [Restaurant] as a cook. But at $1.95 an hour, that's bullshit. At Morrison's they thought they had a real nigger working 'cause I really tried to keep that job. But that damn man [boss] was crazy. He started bitching with me. Now he knows a cook don't wash no damn dishes. I wouldn't do that shuffling routine, so I quit. I started stealing hams and making some money. I would take my girlfriend with me to the su-

permarket and I'd have a box underneath the cart. We'd walk around filling the box with steaks, pork chops, hams, chickens, all kinds of shit. I'd have tape in my pocket and some stamps with rope. This is so it would look like a package. That don't never fail to work. I'd steal about $1,500 worth of meat and sell it for $800. Sometimes I buy a little weed to sell. I pay $45 for an ounce or $150 for a pound and make more than $300 every three or four days. All I want is a Cadillac, two tons of weed, five pounds of crystal T, a nice house, and be financially well off. I would much rather work than hustle because working is steady. When you work you know where the money is coming from.

We did not find any consistent pattern in the backgrounds of young men who become pimps. Husbands, boyfriends, and transient players all play the role. Young boys sometimes identify with the player image—New York players set standards of dress and lifestyle that are widely imitated—but in most cases the motivation is economic necessity. Frances H., a close observer of the street scene in Meridian, described the situation of teenage pimps in this southern town as follows:

It's not that all these kids want to be players or hustlers. The first thing you think is they don't want to work. That's misleading. Most of them, and I mean the major portion of them, have tried at one time or another to get a job. They have beat down the doors of the unemployment offices. They have been in these stores, dealing with all these crackers who constantly make wisecracks and comments about how dumb they are and stuff like that. And they, rightly so, get tired of it. Then they come back out here on the street and say, "Fuck it. I'll make it any way I can. I'll be a player. I'll be a hustler. I'll be cool. I'll be clean." They want to have that paper. Just like everybody else does. You can't tell 'em they don't know what time it is because they think they do. So it ain't like they ain't tried. It's just that they got tired of all the bullshit. A lot of what this is about is discrimination. It's prejudice against these kids. Them young white boys can go to daddy and say, "I need a job" or "I need money" and get it. But these black kids have to kiss ass and then be told, "Ain't no jobs for you, nigger boy." So you know it ain't about not wanting to work.

The experiences of young people in other regions of the country reveal few differences in lifestyle and some basic similarities in values and outlook toward their immediate future. Most teenagers in the underground economy, regardless of region, maintain the traditional values of work, money, and success. Although these are limited commodities, the youths are as desperate in their search as anyone else.

One thing is clear—teenagers like Ray-Ray will more often than not find illegal opportunities more attractive than legal ones. Those who have had negative experiences in the work place, no matter how brief, will move on to the underground economy and try to forge an identity there. Ray-Ray, however, is the first to admit that he is not going to get rich stealing meat, selling marijuana, or even pimping.

Some teenage hustlers do manage to find jobs. But often they leave within a few months because the demands of the job appear to be too great, especially when hustling seems to offer an easier life. Here's what Margo has to say about her brief career in the nine-to-five world:

If you're the type that can never be without a job, not having one may cause a problem. I'm not that type. I can live with or without one. I've never been one to worry about work. Occasionally I might find myself in a jam, but I believe things work themselves out and they usually do. Not working doesn't

bother me so much as having to do that regular nine to five. I hate straight hours, time clocks and suspicious bosses. I enjoy not having to deal with the same environment and people within that structure on a daily basis. That type of contact, being constant, tires me. I love to free-lance. I enjoy change in work situations. I'm trying other ways to make money, not necessarily legal ways, and I'm open to ideas.

Not working steadily, I will admit, causes problems for me. Because the cash flow isn't there all the time. Naturally I will find other ways to make up for this lack of money, but the market isn't always open to me. When I say this, I'm speaking of the people I may be with at that particular time in my life, or my access to the street. Making illegal money is a whole different scene. It's part of what I categorized before as free-lancing. Some examples of free-lancing would be anything from hocking your personal property or someone else's, to dealing drugs or selling yourself, borrowing, mediating, touting, you know. If you can do any of these and hold down a tax-paying job, you're alright. But if you can keep this life up and survive from it alone, you're doing better.

One thing about prostitution, it's a tax-free job. The risk is the thrill. I feel one has to be adventurous, daring, and mischievious to a point. The first thing one has to keep in mind is that you're going to get caught. Not by the authorities, no! That's the last thing in my mind. When I say get caught, I mean by the street. If you're dealing in anything against the law, you always have heavy competition. If your game is good, people want to tear it down. It's a constant battle in the streets for survival. There is a lot of planning, scheming, lying, cheating, and a little bit of fear out there. The fear has to be natural or you're doomed. You have to love danger.

I hate what society considers normal. So I find other ways of living within this world, without letting it bother me. If it bothers others, that's their problem. Every man for himself. When it comes to money you will find very few are going to help you make it. And if you're the type that helps others, you'll find yourself taken for a sucker. So you resign to helping yourself. The advantages of this street business, hustling, it's on you. You wake up, eat, sleep, you don't punch no clocks, you don't conform to no rules and regulations or courtesy to co-workers, customers, bosses, clients, patients, staff, etc. Best of all, you don't pay taxes either.

Margo's work history includes both legitimate and illegitimate roles. Although she possesses the skills to work in a mainstream occupation, she has not developed the discipline to remain in a job very long. This is partly a result of immaturity. However, it is a well-known fact that few teenagers maintain jobs for more than a few months at a time. It is Margo's street and family values that have kept her at odds with the straight world. Her forays into the regular workaday routine are always of short duration because there is more money to be made on the streets. There is always an available market of older men who will buy her services, yet she sees the weakness of her own game. She knows that a prostitute's life—even a high-class call girl's life—is a short one. She knows she won't always have a youthful face and body. And when things get tough—for instance, after a brutal trick—she looks for work in a regular job. Margo sees no discernible difference between her straightout prostitution and what other women do as secretaries or as wives at home.

Margo's views are not shared by the parents and friends of most of the teenage prostitutes we met. There appears to be a double standard operating in this area: the pimps/players are seen as smooth, slick, and smart, the girls as stupid and dirty. Feelings of revulsion and pity were expressed by some of the parents, while others did not seem to know or care what their children were doing. Many of the girls turned to prostitution after becoming pregnant and being rejected by their boyfriends and parents.

Once a girl enters the life, ties with family and friends are usually broken. It is common practice for a pimp to insist that his girls sever all such relationships. Independent prostitutes like Margo may maintain contact with their friends but tend not to explain to them what they do for a living.

In addition to the availability of prostitution as an option and the perceived disadvantages of straight jobs, certain experiences during childhood and adolescence can lead to a career in prostitution. Rose M. of Hough is a case in point.

Things were okay at home until I turned 13. I moved out when I turned 13 and quit school. My stepfather and I couldn't get along any more. I kept moving in and out until I was 15. My mother didn't mind because I always let her know where I was and went by to see her when my stepfather was at work. I didn't have to worry about supporting myself then. When I was 14 I got put on probation for not going to school. At 15, when my mother died, my stepfather sent my sister and myself down south to stay with our real father. I didn't like my father so I came back to Cleveland to stay with a friend. I was getting a social security check from my father so I had money.

The girl I was staying with worked the streets. She was only 16. I didn't have to but I started working with her. It was scary but it was a living. I grew up very fast in the streets. I shot dope but I never got hooked. At 16 I got pregnant and left my man. I went to the Safe Space Station, a runaway shelter. The people were really nice. They tried to help, but I was used to being on my own. So I went back to my man and worked until I was seven months. I also shot dope while I was pregnant. The dope only made my baby small.

We moved from place to place after that. Then my stepfather had me put in D.H. and tried to take my baby. I stayed there for ten days, then went to a child-care center for three weeks. I turned 17 in there. The court placed me in the custody of the county. My social worker took me down and got me on welfare. Before that I was still turning tricks. I still worked some even though I was on welfare and got social security because I wasn't used to getting money once a month. I still moved from place to place. My son has never had a stable home until now, and he'll be two next month.

Now I'm 18 and I'm three months pregnant. One thing I promised myself, with this baby I'm not going to go through the things I went through with the first. I feel I have an advantage over most people my age and older because I know and have experienced things they'll never know. The only disadvantage is I don't have as much interest in men like I had. My pimp beat me up and tried to make me have an abortion. But I ran away from him because I was tired of the streets and let myself get pregnant on purpose. I know I wasn't forced to get into the life. Because I used to do it a lot with my girlfriends after school to get money to buy extra clothes. When my mother would ask me where I got the clothes from I would tell her I exchanged them with friends. After my mom died and I wasn't going to my stepfather's anymore, I lived with the rest of the girls at my pimp's stable.

For some teenage girls, incestuous relationships with their fathers and encounters with pimps at school may have started them on the road to prostitution. Kate Strolls is a seventeen-year-old dropout who moved away from home after a series of incidents with her father.

I dropped out of school in the ninth grade. At this point I have no interest in going back. I used to live in the Woodland Projects apartments. It was ugly as hell. It had all these empty houses, old buildings, and winos everywhere. I first hooked up with this pimp

at school. I started turning tricks in the afternoon and bringing some of the money home to my mother. She took the money and never asked me where I got it from. She just told me not to get myself killed.

My father moved away after we, my sister and me, got together and told my mother that he had been having sex with both of us and then threatening to kill us if we told anybody. I feel okay about the whole thing but my sister turned real mean and won't talk to nobody. She has no friends and stays at home with my brother even though she is old enough to be on her own. I don't feel that way about men. I just don't develop feelings for them when I'm working. And I prefer to be with women anyhow.

I had this woman stop me one night down on Prospect and give me $100 to go with her. I was scared but, shit, I figured I could outfight the broad if it got too crazy. She had this nice place to stay and all this nice furniture and a man. She turned me out that night.

For many young women, a crucial factor is the lifestyles of the adult women who are closest to them. This was the case for Margo. Her adult role models were her mother, her aunt, and a very close friend of her mother who was active in civil rights, all of whom were rebels and fought private battles at home or public battles against society. Unlike many of the other girls in our study, Margo had a relatively stable home and social environment. She had opportunities to travel, to attend school and do well. But the examples set by her family, her early experiences, and the complexities of her own personality led her to choose the fast life. There is no doubt that young women like Margo could lead successful lives in a professional career were it not for one or two incidents that shaped their life patterns. As she herself explains:

As a baby, not from what I recall, but only hearsay, I was alert, smart, too fast for my britches, and loved to party and drink. One might say that I haven't changed a bit. I was walking at the age of six months, but didn't let go of my bottle till around four years. I was a year old and one still couldn't tell whether I was a girl or a boy, since I still had not grown hair. There was no way to add ribbons, bows or clips to my scalp. So I spent my first year as a child with an undefined sexuality. At eight months my mom was fed up with me, so I say. She claims that it was in my best interest for her to have sent me to my grandparents in South America. This was for a period of three years. I've been told that as a toddler, I spoke too much, knew too much, ate too much, and never liked going to bed on time. I was spoiled, having been the first granddaughter, and yet was very charming and lovable.

At 3¹/₂, I was sent back home to my mother, who by this time I'd forgotten. This, of course, was after having traveled throughout South America and the Virgin Islands. I wish they would have saved those trips now. I arrived at Kennedy International Airport via Avianca Airlines, escorted by my aunt, and was received by everyone from a to z that was a member of my family or knew someone in it.

My room was filled with an accumulation of toys over the past three years. Most of them I still have. One that I loved in particular was a teddy bear named Moy-Moy. He used to be white and fluffy, nowadays he is skinned of all his hair, dyed and ripped. One of the dolls I used to have was four feet tall. Now I was a tiny 3¹/₂-year-old, so you can imagine in comparison to me this thing was a giant. Sometimes I honestly feel that parents are not practical. An example is that by the time I was five, my father, whom I rarely saw, had given me a collection of dolls from all different nations. By the time I was seven, the collection was destroyed. To this day, my mother still curses me out over it and calls me irresponsible.

I may sound ungrateful, but I'm really not. I really can't complain about my childhood. It's my teen years that I hated the most. I knew my real father as the man who came to give me money, or to take me shopping to buy things. He was very well off and he proved it to me. But I didn't want his fucking money. He deprived me of his presence. He deprived me of his love. What is money to try and replace that? I'll tell ya, it ain't shit. So I threw all of that in his face. I guess that's why he's been so reluctant to contact me now. He knows I hate what he did. All my life I've had negative feelings about my father due to the fact that in my eyes his time was too precious to spend with me. All these years I've denied ever having needed him, loved him, missed him, or wanting him. Now I wonder. I remember when I was real small. He would come in, pick me up, and put me on his shoulders. You see, my father was real tall and skinny and when he would lift me up, it seemed like—oh God—it was to the ceiling. It seemed so high to me. But I would hold my breath and close my eyes and in a few seconds I was on top of the world.

Teenage prostitutes, and the men who exploit them, have developed a negative self-image and considerable hostility toward members of the opposite sex. They are at risk of remaining in the criminal subculture as adults, and if they do not find better role models and opportunities that is the most likely prognosis. But these teenagers, street wise and cynical as they are, are not "lost" or "fallen," even though they may think of themselves in such terms. Timely intervention by caring adults could counteract the experiences that led them into prostitution and could guide them onto more constructive paths to maturity.

Adolescents' Perspectives on the Relationship between Drugs/Alcohol and Crime

17

Cheryl Carpenter
Barry Glassner
Bruce D. Johnson
Julia Loughlin

Quantitative research has systematically documented that users of drugs other than marijuana and alcohol are quite likely to engage in serious crime. Conversely, most persons who commit felony crimes (most of whom also commit many minor crimes) are among the most routine users of drugs and alcohol (Huizinga and Elliott, 1981; Johnson, Wish, and Huizinga, 1986; Johnston, O'Malley, and Eveland, 1976, 1978; Inciardi, 1980; Gandossy, Williams, Cohen, and Harwood, 1980). A relatively small proportion (probably 5 percent or less) of all youths appear to engage in a life-style that includes routine drug and alcohol use and frequent commission of crimes. Similar associations are evident among [our] subjects. This statistical association between drug use and crime, however, tells us nothing about

the meaning of this relationship. The youths' own perspectives on drug–crime links offer some insight into this association.

The youths in this study have a rich repertoire of commonsense theories about the association between drugs and crime. Some were derived from broad cultural beliefs, but most were drawn from their own experiences and observations. This chapter examines adolescents' theories and how they differentiate along lines of youth experience and involvement in drug use and crime.

The Respondents and Their Responses

The respondents in this section are 84 subjects who answered a direct question about the relationship between drugs/alcohol and crime. The interview schedule included the following basic question about this topic:

Q: We've talked about a lot of things having to do with your involvement in alcohol, drugs, and crime. Basically, we've dealt with each as a separate behavior. One of the main things we are trying to study is how these

Reprinted by permission of the publisher from pp. 27–37 of *Kids, Drugs, and Crime,* by Cheryl Carpenter, Barry Glassner, Bruce D. Johnson, and Julia Loughlin (Lexington, Mass.: Lexington Books, D. C. Heath and Company, Copyright © 1988, D. C. Health and Company.

things are interrelated. That is, are these somehow related to each other? And if so, how?

In many instances, subjects had already addressed this topic at length earlier in the interview. These earlier discussions have been used to supplement the responses to the direct question.

In general, subjects' responses can be divided into three categories based on the extent of their involvement in drug/alcohol use and crime. First, those respondents with little personal involvement in, or knowledge of, the focal behaviors gave brief, conventional answers. They perceived crime as irrational, inexplicable behavior or saw drugs and alcohol as related to crime because of a need for money for drugs.

A second group was able to comment more thoughtfully on the relationship between drugs and crime. These were youths with more experience—those who had reported observing others using drugs, who knew about crimes in their neighborhoods, or who had experimented with alcohol and drugs and had been involved in minor criminal behavior. They estimated that a substantial proportion of crimes were committed by those using drugs or alcohol. They emphasized a broad range of "causes" of crime, including poverty, insanity, a desire for attention, and the rational choice of crime as a source of income.

The third group, those with extensive involvement in drugs/alcohol use and crime, offered several explanations of how drugs and alcohol may affect the criminal behavior of others, as well as several interpretations of why their own behavior was *not* affected by drugs or alcohol. Relevant sections of the interview transcripts are quoted hereafter to elaborate on these differing perspectives.

Noninvolved Youths

About three-quarters of the random sample* consisted of youths who engaged in no or very minor delinquent activity and who were non-users or only experimental users of alcohol or marijuana. Such youths typically had difficulty articulating what the relationship between drugs and crime might be, even after relatively extensive discussions of similar issues earlier in the interview. Typically, they would agree that there could be a relationship, because all were illegal activities, but they had trouble thinking of examples, other than violations of motor vehicle laws. A 15-year-old girl in the random sample who had experimented with alcohol and marijuana, but who reported no criminal involvement, explained:

Q: Do you think these issues are related—alcohol, drugs, and crime?
A: They could be.
Q: In what way?
A: I guess that, uh, if you drink alcohol, I guess it's an easy risk for crime, especially if you're driving, I guess. And the same thing for drugs, I guess.

Other relatively inexperienced respondents drew on the social stereotype of the drug addict's need for money to explain a relationship between substance abuse and crime. Addiction was also perceived as the cause of unpredictable, uncontrolled, "crazy" behavior. A 13-year-old boy in the random sample whose only experience of the focal behaviors was experimentation

*Editor's Note: Youths for this study came from a "random sample" (subjects selected randomly from school enrollment lists), a "purposive sample" (subjects observed by researchers to be using drugs routinely or believed to be active in delinquency), and a "detained sample" (subjects residing in the local detention facility or group home).

with alcohol described this model and referred to the media as confirmation.

Q: Do you think that getting into using drugs and drinking heavily will lead people to other kinds of illegal or criminal kinds of things, or do you think it's separate?
A: Yeah, I think, I think that it would probably be connected because, like, they, they've either done it because they don't like their life anymore and drugs has certain effects on them and it may persuade them, in a way, to do a type of crime like rob something, try to kill someone, and do all sorts of crazy things like that and try to kill themselves. And stuff like that. And I see movies, I saw a movie like that in school one time.

A similar response was given by a 17-year-old girl from the random sample. The respondent had been involved in minor theft in the past and had tried alcohol and marijuana:

A: The crime and the drugs. Let me see. Well, as you become addicted and you want to feel, need to get money, you might hold up a bank or something, hold up somebody, snatch gold, snatching purses, or mugging people 'cause you're angry at somebody but you can't hit that person. So, you might as well mug somebody. Or maybe it's some psychopath out there that's mad at his grandmother so he goes mugging little old ladies.

Other respondents who perceived addiction as an important cause of crime often mentioned insanity or mental instability as a related cause.

In sum, relatively inexperienced youths generally invoked conventional explanations for drug–crime links. But they did not compare these beliefs with their observations of others whom they knew or believed to be using drugs and/or to be involved in criminal activities.

Relatively Experienced Youths

An important finding to emerge from secondary analyses of the National Youth Survey data is that virtually all youths, regardless of how heavily involved with drugs or delinquency, deny that their self-reported delinquent acts were committed in order to obtain money to purchase drugs (Johnson and Wish, 1986). This same denial was evident among [our] subjects, who observed that others—but not themselves or their peers—committed crimes to purchase drugs. They employed a variety of explanations to bridge this apparent discrepancy between their observations about others and their self-perceptions. Without invoking addiction as an explanation, relatively experienced youths spontaneously noted that many drug and alcohol users were involved in theft, and they mentioned incidents they had heard about or observed. For them, drugs and alcohol might be defined by those who used them as "necessities," much like clothing and records, and drug/alcohol users might steal for money to obtain any of these goods if they had no other source of money or if they were "someone who just steals."

A 19-year-old girl in the purposive sample, for instance, emphasized that she did not steal, although she had used cocaine and amphetamines, as well as alcohol and marijuana, and had been involved in vandalism and fighting. She contrasted her behavior with that of her friend, who stole not only for drugs but as a regular source of money and other goods:

Q: Is that true of most people you know that they steal so they can buy drugs?
A: Uh huh, Aster steal, 'cause she wants some money to get herb, or, to buy the baby some Pampers, or something . . . or she just want money to have in her pocket, just to be spending it.

The subjects were also explicit about other motives for theft. These imputed motives included: poor people's lack of alternatives, old people's (adults') need to "pay the rent," and kids' bids for attention (mentioned primarily by subjects with no actual personal criminal experience). Some relatively experienced youths also defined criminal activity, such as theft, as "fun" and "exciting"; this, and not gaining money for drugs, was their professed motive for stealing.

Seriously Involved Youths

The seriously involved youths not only had had varied and continuing experience with the use of alcohol and drugs but also had been involved in the commission of serious crimes—that is, index crimes or persistent and systematic minor crime, such as property destruction and shoplifting. These youths used their own experience as a reference point: although they sometimes referred to more general social beliefs or their observations of others' behavior, for them the final authority was their own behavior. Few accepted a simple drugs-cause-crime explanation of anyone's behavior.

Drugs lead directly to crime

Only a few of the heavily involved youths asserted that there was a strong and important relationship between drug use and crime, both in general and their own behavior. Two were boys who had been in serious trouble and had reformed—that is, were no longer involved in drugs or crime and insisted that their lives had changed. One of the boys, a 16-year-old who was in detention and had been involved in assault, joyriding, and serious shoplifting, affirmed:

A: Um, there's always a relationship between drugs and crime. 'Cause drugs distorts peo-

ple values, their morals, their state of mind at the time, it always distorts that, you know, no matter what drug you do, I mean, a drug is a distortion, you know.

He modifies that position quickly, however:

Q: Do you think there are many kids who do crime who do not do any drugs or drinking?
A: Oh, I know there are a few, there are definitely a few people who do that. You know, it's just, you can't really, you can't blame it on one or the other, you know, you can't blame it on the drugs, you know, because I know a lot of people who do drugs and never think of rippin' anybody off, you know.

The other boy . . . age 20, had completed a drug rehabilitation program. He asserted that both for him and for others the need for drugs led to theft:

Q: What makes the use of drugs different from just wanting clothes or wanting other kinds of possessions?
A: What make the difference?
Q: Hmm-mmm.
A: 'Cause there's a real psychological need, it's like I got to have this, or I won't be happy, all bummed out, and you know. So a lot of kids believe that the only way you can be happy is to be high. And things like that; they're looking for the instant payoff. It's not of no interest to them . . . what they're doing to their minds or their bodies, or to the people that love them.

A 15-year-old boy in the purposive sample who was involved in serious criminal behavior (including assault, joyriding, and shoplifting), as well as using various drugs, defined theft as an available means of obtaining money to buy what was "needed." Since drugs are relatively expensive and are not provided by parents, he argued, people may steal to obtain them; in fact, he thought he might do so if he moved on from the marijuana he could now afford to more expensive cocaine. The interviewer followed up on his statement that there was a connection between drugs and crime:

Q: Do you think the kids who get high, drink, are the same kids who are going to do crime?
A: Yup, yup, yup, yup.
Q: Why? What's the connection?
A: Because, because they, they'll be needing money if they wanna get high. Something like that, but, I guarantee most everybody get high still.
Q: Do you think any straight kids commit crimes?
A: Yeah, but not heavy crimes, not burglary; they do that light stuff, may steal a candy bar, or somethin', bubble gum, no serious money, they don't need money. What they gonna do with money? Their mom's gettin' 'em everything else, clothes, house; they ain't gonna buy no marijuana, if ya don't smoke, ya don't need it.

Drugs and alcohol have psychological effects

Both experienced and inexperienced subjects commented on this topic. They agreed that alcohol and marijuana (or "drugs" in general) affected responses in social settings, but they did not always agree about the likely direction. Several saw violence or aggression as more likely; others perceived some substances as having pacifying effects. The following comments were typical.

A: 'Cause, um, when you have alcohol, when you get drunk you might not know what you are doing and start beating up on somebody you know. Or with drugs, if you can't get the drugs you want then, you know, you might beat up somebody too, or you might try to hurt somebody because you can't have some more drugs or some more alcohol or something like that, you know, have physical con-

tact because you don't get what you want, you know.

A 17-year-old from the purposive sample recognized that he was more aggressive and dangerous when he was stoned:

A: Yeah. My temper gets faster, you know, it's faster. 'Cause you fuck with me when I am stoned, and I'm liable to kill you or something. You know, I'm a little bit crazier when I don't have a clear head, you know. I'll just beat the shit out of you if I ain't got a clear head. If I'm stoned, I'll shoot you in a minute. You know, that's why I usually try not to carry my gun when I'm stoned. But if you fuck with me when I'm stoned, I'll shoot you.

An 18-year-old girl in the random sample who had been involved in minor crimes and polydrug use drew on her own observations in describing how "alcohol and drugs make you commit crimes":

A: Yeah, in some instances it has occurred, like these guys I know that used to be in gang fights up in my neighborhood, you know, they would get drunk, go stand by the corner store, buy quarts of beer and get drunk and then go fight.

Another 18-year-old girl with similar experience agreed that alcohol use was related to violence, but asserted that marijuana was not:

A: Herb don't make you do that, it just make you, be up in the morning for everything.

A 15-year-old boy from the random sample, on the other hand, seemed more willing to link drugs to crime than to view alcohol as criminogenic:

A: Um, oh, probably when they're drunk or stoned or something, from what I know they don't really know what they're doing. Well, they might commit a crime . . . or I thought—it seems to me that if someone is getting drunk they're doing it for fun unless they're a real heavy alcoholic, um, they wouldn't be thinking about doing any crimes or anything, just having a good time.

Without ever using the term, these respondents frequently referred to drugs and alcohol as *disinhibitors*. Room and Collins (1983:v) discuss disinhibition:

Drunkenness not only makes one more clumsy, but also removes social constraints, making us, for instance, aggressive or affectionate, maudlin or mean, in a way that we would not be if we were sober. In recent years, evidence . . . suggests that the link between alcohol and disinhibition is a matter of cultural belief rather than of pharmacological action.

Although this model of disinhibition may be far more elaborate than described here, our youths were clearly drawing from several elements of this model to explain drug–crime linkages. Alcohol or drugs may impulsively bring about illegal acts that might not have occurred otherwise. An example is given by an 18-year-old boy in the purposive sample who had engaged in assault and minor shoplifting:

A: I think because—if you, when you start drinking or doing drugs, you know, you start losing, losing [sense] or, you know, losing touch with reality, and then you start—like you lose control. It ain't you. You the person you know. Some—something else takes over, and make you do that stuff. And, I don't know, it's just, you, you, your brains or your mind ain't, at its full, you know, you wouldn't do it, you ain't doing stuff, that you know, you do straight.

A 15-year-old boy from the random sample who had experimented only with alcohol

commented more directly on the element of impulse:

A: 'Cause I think if people, you know, when they go off and smoke marijuana or something and get high. And someone all of a sudden says, hey man, let's go rob the liquor store or something. So the other people I think are just plain crazy.

A 15-year-old boy from the detained sample, who had experience with auto theft and other grand larceny, said:

A: I think that, ah, that if you take the drugs, that you might be pushed easily into doing something that you probably wouldn't do if you weren't on the drugs.
Q: What about with alcohol?
A: I think it's probably just about the same as drugs.

Most of the seriously involved youths were quite clear in denying, however, that such explanations invoking disinhibition applied to themselves. Though reporting crimes in which drugs and alcohol were used beforehand, during, or afterward, they denied that their drug or alcohol use had an important role in the occurrence or course of their crime. They always had their criminal behavior, as well as their drug and alcohol use, under control. Rather, they suggested a variety of other explanations for why their drug/alcohol use was essentially irrelevant to the conduct of their crimes. Discussion of several such explanations follows.

Drugs and alcohol make life, including crime, more fun

Drugs and alcohol are widely used to have fun, for socialization, and to combat boredom (Glassner and Loughlin, 1987). Seriously involved youths were frequently having "fun" while being high or drunk;

criminal opportunities subsequently presented themselves or were sought out.

A 16-year-old detained youth who had
used a variety of drugs and engaged in burglary and robbery said he was usually high
during criminal events. When asked, ''Why
do you think people your age do crime?'' he
answered in terms of his own experience:

A: Ah, ah, a lot of us do it 'cause they need
somethin' more, do it just to do it, man. Now
me I used to do it just to do it, it was fun, you
know. I ain't never really need nothin', man,
I just do it for the hell of it, man, just bust out
somethin' or rob somebody for their property, just to see the reactions on their faces in
the mornin'. Somethin' like that, just be fun.

Another detained youth, 13 years old,
who had used hallucinogens and amphetamines as well as alcohol and marijuana, reviewed with the interviewer the crimes they
had discussed and the frequency with which
drug use was associated with those criminal
events. He was asked:

Q: Why do you commit crime?
A: For the money. And for the fun of it, sometimes.
Q: Uh-huh. Which is which, when do you do it
for fun and when do you do it for money?
A: When I need the money I do it for money.
When I just don't need any I just do it for the
fun of it, see if I can break in and not get
caught.

*My drug and alcohol use is incidental to
my crime*

In several instances, seriously involved
youths reported using drugs or alcohol
shortly before or during criminal events.
They would be drinking and getting high—
their normal state during the day. For various reasons, an opportunity for crime would
present itself, or the group would decide to

do some crime. But they denied that the alcohol or drug use contributed in a significant
way to the probability that they would commit a crime or to the severity of a crime.
Rather, they saw their drug or alcohol use as
incidental and not a cause of their crimes.

For example, a 16-year-old boy in the
random sample who had been involved in
burglary, assault, theft, and arson described
a burglary:

Q: So you don't think that people break into
houses to steal things, to get money to buy
drugs?
A: Yeah, I know they do. But, if, I still think
people would break into the house for that
money, if even, if even, even, if it wasn't for
drugs, for, you know.

Although this boy had used a variety of
drugs and had been involved in a series of
crimes, including burglary, grand larceny,
and drug sales, he was unable to give an example of something he had done while under
the influence of drugs that he would not have
done ''straight.'' He responded:

A: I . . . don't know if I did it because I was
drunk, or I did it because I just wanted to do
it. I don't know the reason why I did it.

*My motivation for crime did not include
drug use*

In general, the youths involved in serious crime tended to agree that people may
do things under the influence of drugs or alcohol that they would not otherwise do, and
they identified minor events in which their
own behavior was so influenced. They
maintained, however, that their drug or alcohol use was not relevant to their decision
to engage in criminal activity. They had
other reasons for doing crimes. A 13-year-
old boy in the detained sample, who had

taken hallucinogens, amphetamines, alcohol, and marijuana, had been involved in auto theft, burglary, and shoplifting in addition to more minor offenses. He associated drugs and crime with impulsivity for others, but he denied that he engaged in behavior that might get him into trouble when he was high: "I just never want to get in trouble when we're high." A 16-year-old boy from the purposive sample who had been involved in grand larceny and major property destruction agreed. He rejected the notion of a general drug–crime relationship:

Q: Do you think that there's any relationship between people who do smoke reefer, or do drugs and do crime?

A: Naw, I don't think there is no "relishlationship."

Q: No? Why not, how come?

A: They jus' get high wit' one another 'n' leave again, they don't give a fuck about you.

Q: You don't think people that are doing crime are usually doing drugs too?

A: Nope.

I choose to use drugs before some crimes; I avoid drugs before other crimes

Seriously involved youths were very clear about making choices to use or not to use drugs or alcohol before committing some crimes they plan. They discussed the avoidance of drugs or alcohol prior to some crimes to ensure their safety and to improve their skill. At other times, they may consume sizable amounts of alcohol or drugs to achieve desired levels of courage or increase the fun of the crime. But there was no agreement on which substances to use or avoid.

A 15-year-old detained youth with experience in burglary explained why he would not engage in crime if he had been drinking:

A: How would you, you're laughin' when you're drunk so how would you walk in there, "Aaah, give me your money, or I'll blow your head off," you know; they'd just think of you're doin' a practical joke, that's all. And I'd go, they'd probably get smart, you know, "Get out of here," you know, and then you'd probably lose your temper still laughin' and start pullin' the trigger.

A 16-year-old boy from the random sample reviewed his involvement in stealing "fuzz-busters," a daylight burglary, and a gang fight. Although he reported relatively high drug use, including alcohol, marijuana, amphetamines, and barbiturates in the month preceding the interview, he insisted that in each instance he was not using drugs. He observed, "You get high when it's time." But if you don't want to get caught engaging in crime, you avoid drugs: "You got to be mellow for that shit."

This choice of using drugs or alcohol before crime to achieve certain desired psychological effects (for example, to "get courage") is as close as seriously involved youths come to attributing their own behavior to disinhibition. In the process, however, they turn such disinhibition explanations inside out. Rather than consuming large amounts of alcohol or drugs and subsequently losing control of their behavior and doing crimes they would not otherwise commit, these youths begin with plans to commit a crime and only then seek to suppress their fears. They claim to control their consumption to a desired level so as to be better able to commit the crime effectively. Yet they also recognize that intoxicated states are not appropriate to every specific type of crime. This rhetoric of explanation, however, is a continued assumption of their ability to maintain their own self-control over the important physical and psychological effects of heavy drug and alcohol consumption.

Summary and Conclusions

In this chapter we delineated how adolescents themselves view the relationship between drugs, alcohol, and crime. Substantial differences appear to exist between youths who are themselves involved in these activities and those who are not.

Noninvolved youths talked about the drug/alcohol–crime relationship in the most conventional or stereotypic terms—emphasizing the irrationality that results from drug use and the criminogenic aspects of drug addiction. These respondents did not offer lengthy or complicated responses.

More involved youths drew on their own experiences in order to make sense of the drug/alcohol–crime connection. For some, this was restricted simply to statements they had heard—that, for example, drug users steal, or that persons steal because they need something they could not otherwise acquire. These respondents disagreed about the influence of alcohol and drug use on crimes of violence (some described violence as more likely, others as less likely) where drugs or alcohol are involved. Quite consistently, however, the respondents viewed drug and alcohol use as resulting in *impulsive* behavior, including theft or vandalism, and thus as indirectly contributing to crime.

The most criminally involved subjects did not differ from the other respondents in these conclusions—they concur that drug use indirectly leads to crime under certain circumstances—but they often deny such a connection in *their own* cases, and few accept a simple drugs-cause-crime explanation of anyone's behavior. About themselves, they report behaving impulsively at times when under the influence of alcohol or drugs, but say they were never out of control. Rather, they maintain that they choose when and how to use alcohol and drugs; under some conditions these substances are ingested because they enhance the activity, at other times they are avoided because they interfere with skillful performance.

These different views on the relationship between drugs/alcohol and crime reflect varying experiences available to categories of adolescents and reveal the views of those most experienced in drug use and criminal involvement as being most different from adult understandings of delinquent behavior.

References

Gandossy, R. P., J. R. Williams, J. Cohen, and H. J. Harwood. 1980. *Drugs and Crime: A Survey and Analysis of the Literature.* Washington, DC: National Institute of Justice.

Glassner, B. and J. Loughlin. 1987. *Drugs in Adolescent Worlds.* New York: St. Martin's.

Huizinga, D. and D. S. Elliott. 1981. *A Longitudinal Study of Drug Use and Delinquency in a National Sample of Youth: An Assessment of Causal Order.* Project Report No. 16. Boulder, CO: Behavioral Research Institute.

Inciardi, J. A. 1980. "Youth, drugs, and street crime." Pp. 175–204 in F. Scarpitti and S. K. Datesman (eds.), *Drugs and the Youth Culture.* Beverly Hills, CA: Sage.

Johnson, B. D., E. Wish, and D. Huizinga. 1986. "The concentration of delinquent offending: The contribution of serious drug involvement in high rate delinquency." Pp. 106–43 in B. D. Johnson and E. Wish (eds.), *Crime Rates Among Drug Abusing Offenders.* New York: Interdisciplinary Research Center.

Johnston, L., P. O'Malley, and L. K. Eveland. 1978. "Nonaddictive drug use and delinquency: A longitudinal analysis. Pp.137–56 in D. B. Kandel (ed.), *Longitudinal Research on Drug Use: Empirical Findings and Methodological Issues.* New York: Wiley.
_____. 1976. "Nonaddictive drug use and delinquency: A longitudinal analysis. Pp.

325–50 in R. Shellow (ed.), *Drug Use and Crime: Report on the Panel on Drug Use and Criminal Behavior.* Washington, DC: National Technical Information Service.
Room, R. and G. Collins (eds.). 1983. *Alcohol and Disinhibition: Nature and Meaning of the Link.* Rockville, MD: National Institute on Alcohol Abuse and Alcoholism.

Adolescent Subcultures, Social Type Metaphors, and Group Delinquency

18

Ronald J. Berger

Few types of juvenile delinquency have generated more interest among criminologists than gangs (Stafford, 1984). Klein (1971:13) defined a "gang" as an adolescent group consisting of youth who consider themselves a distinct group (usually with a group name), who are generally perceived as a distinct group by others in the community, and who have "been involved in a sufficient number of delinquent incidents to call forth a consistent negative response from neighborhood residents and/or law enforcement agencies." The third element in Klein's definition—a consistent negative response from the community—would exclude as "gangs" many groups of adolescents who engage in delinquent acts but who have avoided societal labeling. The reader will recall Chambliss' (1973) description of "The Saints and the Roughnecks" (see Chapter 3). Because of differential selection and perception, the Roughnecks, who were "visible, poor, nonmobile, outspoken, undiplomatic 'tough' kids," were more likely to bring forth a negative response from authorities. The

Saints, on the other hand, who had "established a reputation for being bright (even though under-achieving), disciplined and involved in respectable activities," and who were "mobile and monied," remained essentially invisible and immune from official sanctioning even when they engaged in violations of the law. Thus, Chambliss found that many delinquent youths were not societal outcasts, but were rather well-integrated into the "respectable" society both during and following adolescence.

Chambliss' study made clear that while most delinquent acts are committed in group contexts (Empey, 1982; Erickson and Jensen, 1977; Giordano et al., 1986), group delinquency should not be considered synonymous with gang delinquency (Stafford, 1984). Indeed, Miller (1980) found far more delinquent groups and group members than delinquent gangs or gang members in his study of several large urban cities. Thus, Miller suggested that "law-violating youth group" may be a more appropriate term for the preponderance of delinquent offenses committed in groups. He defined a law-violating youth group as "an association of three or more youths whose members engage recurrently in illegal activities with the cooperation and/or moral support of their companions" (p. 118).

More recently, Schwendinger and Schwendinger (1985) suggested that the phenomenon of juvenile delinquency might be addressed in terms of a broader theory of adolescent subcultures.[1] In advanced capitalist societies such as the United States, adolescents are differentiated from adults and segregated for ever-increasing numbers of years in institutions of education (Bloch and Niederhoffer, 1958; Eisenstadt, 1956; Greenberg, 1981). Thus, it is the school, rather than the neighborhood per se, that is the physical site of much adolescent subcultural formation (see Polk and Schafer, 1972).[2] The segregation of adolescents in schools increases the frequency and intensity of interaction among peers who turn to one another for social approval and personal validation. Although much youthful behavior involves emulation of the larger adult culture, adolescents display distinctive subcultural patterns of social activities, beliefs, values, argot, and material objects (e.g., clothes). In Schwartz and Merten's (1967:453) terms, adolescent subcultures are "relatively self-contained" insofar as "peer-group interaction is guided by expectations which do not govern the behavior of other members of the community."

In this article, I review the Schwendingers' (1985) work on adolescent subcultures, particularly their research on the social type names or metaphors used by youth to communicate with one another about the relative status of various groups of adolescents. I then discuss my own research, based on data derived from student papers written for my courses on Juvenile Delinquency, on adolescent subcultures in Wisconsin.

Adolescent Status and Social Type Metaphors

According to the Schwendingers (1985), adolescent subcultures reflect, yet are relatively independent of, social class background. Like social classes, networks of adolescent groups are stratified in terms of social status and prestige. While the higher status groups invariably recruit from the middle and upper classes, and the lower status groups from the working and lower classes, youths often disagree about the relative worth or status of the different groups. Moreover, regardless of one's social class position, personal attributes such as athletic ability, physical attractiveness, personality, and interpersonal skills may allow movement up or down the status hierarchy of peer relations. Nevertheless, as Schwartz and Merten (1967:461) noted, the "dominant values institutionalized in the status system of the . . . high school are those held by the majority of the upper-middle class segment of [the] youthful population."

Initial indications of status differentiation among children can be seen as early as elementary school, when small cliques of boys and girls set themselves apart from others by displaying inordinate attention to hair grooming and clothing styles (Schwendinger and Schwendinger, 1985). By the end of elementary school, their preoccupation with impressing peers, rather than parents or teachers, becomes increasingly noticeable. In urban areas in particular, where youth are concentrated in large numbers, the transition from childhood to adolescence is accompanied by a consolidation of independent peer group formations consisting of youth who are extremely self-centered, who compete intensively with one another for status recognition, and who are especially insensitive to lower status youth.

In elementary school, students refer to peers who are distinguishable from others as "football and baseball types," the "gang of boys," the "crowd of sixth-grade girls," and the like (p. 68). By junior high, various linguistic categories or metaphors that denote social regularities in personal behavior, attitude, and appearance, begin to be used to identify particular crowds or cliques. For instance, members of the "in" crowd are perceived as being "cool," while outsiders are "square." These metaphors "bestow either negative or positive esteem on those who manifest or exemplify [particular] personal characteristics" (Merten and Schwartz, 1967:454).

While adolescent subcultures consist of a diversity of loosely knit, interlocking peer groups, crowds, or cliques, the Schwendingers (1985) identified three of the most persistent social types: *streetcorner*, *socialite*, and *intellectual* youth. Streetcorner groups recruit from the economically marginal sector of the adolescent population. These are the groups, like Chambliss' (1973) Roughnecks, that are more likely to be perceived and labeled as delinquent by authorities in the community. These youth are at a competitive disadvantage, economically and culturally, when they begin formal schooling, and their position relative to more privileged youth often deteriorates further as time goes on. Moreover, unlike privileged youth who fail to achieve in school, streetcorner youth do not have the family resources to provide them with the extra tutoring, counseling, cultural experiences (e.g., travel), etc., that might help them recover from initial setbacks. Nor do they have the financial backing of their families which allows them a "second chance" in life by financing their way through college after a mediocre educational career (Schwendinger and Schwendinger, 1985).

The socialite groups are akin to Chambliss' Saints. They are generally the elite group of adolescents who are, for the most part, college-bound regardless of academic achievement. These youth are better able to finance the material commodities necessary for full participation in adolescent subcultural activities—e.g., fashionable clothes, cars, rock concerts, records and tapes, alcohol, and drugs. While these youths "are less likely to be involved in the most serious violent and economic forms of delinquency, . . . the socialites are frequently equivalent to streetcorner youth, or not far behind, . . . with regard to vehicle violations, vandalism, drinking, gambling, petty theft, truancy, sexual promiscuity, and other garden varieties of delinquent behavior" (Schwendinger and Schwendinger, 1985:56). When their delinquencies are discovered by the authorities, they are likely to be "treated as 'pranks,' lapses of judgment, or expressions of 'bad taste,'" and are typically ignored or covered up (p. 54). Though socialite youth are unlikely to get into trouble with the law, when they do they are better able than streetcorner youth to finance fees for an attorney to help them avoid any serious consequences of their misconduct.

The third group of adolescents discussed by the Schwendingers is the intellectuals. These youth are high academic achievers who are sometimes "overspecialized" in their academic or technical interests (e.g., computers, electronics, mathematics, physics). They are the adolescents who spend "a greater amount of time after school doing homework, helping in household activities, or participating in adult-directed youth organizations" (p. 67). They are less interested in fashion and are the least delinquent (if at all) of the three adolescent groups. Ironically, the youth who are most committed to legitimate academic activities are perceived negatively by other youth and have low status in the adolescent social hierarchy.[3]

The Schwendingers studied these three social types in various southern California communities between 1959 and 1967. The adolescents they interviewed used various names or metaphors, which varied over time and location, to communicate with another about the relative status of various groups of adolescents. These metaphors served as shorthand linguistic devices that helped establish the boundaries of appropriate interaction within and between different groups.

The youths interviewed by the Schwendingers referred to various streetcorner groups as *Greasers*, *Hoods*, *Eses*, *Rowdies*, *Jo-Bads*, and *Dudes*. These youth shared particular stylistic characteristics. In the late 1950s, for instance, both the *Greasers* (who were Anglo) and the *Eses* (who were Chicano) wore "blue denims" or "khakis." *Greaser* boys typically wore "Sir Guy shirts" and combed their hair straight back at the sides, had pompadours at the front that flopped forward in a "jelly roll," and had "ducktails" at the back. *Greaser* girls wore short skintight skirts, tight sweaters over pointy brassieres, and long earrings, and had high-combed "ratted" hair. The *Socialites* or *Socs*, as they were called, dressed in an "Ivy League" or "continental" style, wearing cashmere sweaters with white tennis shoes. Boys cut their hair short and often had "crew cuts." Girls had hairstyles known as "bubbles" and "guiches." The intellectual types were known as *Brains*, *Bookworms*, *Pencil Necks*, or *Egg Heads*. They appeared conservative or undistinguished in their dress.

Along with the three most stable social types, the Schwendingers found a variety of complementary, interrelated, or intermediary crowds. For instance, the *Athletes*

and *Surfers* or *Gremmies* often interpenetrated or overlapped with other groups. These youth held relatively high status because of their athletic ability. While the *Surfers* were eventually absorbed by more enduring social types, the *Athletes* (usually called *Jocks* today) have remained relatively distinct. *Athletes*, particularly those in the aggressive, fast-paced spectator sports such as football and basketball, continue to symbolize the "ideal" male who is all-powerful and aggressive; and physically attractive athletes are especially desired by adolescent females (Larkin, 1979; Schwartz and Merten, 1967; Weisfeld and Feldman, 1982). In his study of a New Jersey suburban high school in the late 1970s, Larkin (1979) found that the leading crowd, the *Jocks* and *Rah-rahs*, consisted of male athletes and their friends, female cheerleaders, and other females who gained status through the achievements of their athlete boyfriends, their personal appearance, or their vivacious personality (see Schwartz and Merten, 1967). The *Jocks* and *Rah-rahs* were known for being the core of "school spirit" and for their frequent dating, partying, and drinking.

During the late 1960s to early 1970s, the *Hippies* (also known as *Freaks* or *Flower Children*) emerged as a relatively distinct social type. Drawing especially from middle-class social strata, the *Hippies* were known for their drug use and "free love" attitude toward sex. They also introduced more "feminized" hair and clothing fashion for males (e.g., long hair, necklaces and earrings, colorful clothing). The Schwendingers noted that the *Hippies* did not alter fundamentally the more enduring socialite and streetcorner subcultures. Drug use, which had already been firmly established among streetcorner groups, merely became more acceptable among socialite crowds. Moreover, the "pseudo Hippies" studied by Weis (1973) in an upper-middle-class northern California community, merely coopted Hippie appearances, which had already been commercialized by the fashion industry, without adopting the anti-competitive or anti-materialistic ideology associated with the Hippie counterculture. Similarly, the *Freaks* studied by Larkin (1979) expressed less interest in the Hippies' utopian idealism, and more interest in achieving status through a "macho" competitiveness over sexual achievements and drug consumption.[4]

In addition to the above-mentioned social types, the Schwendingers identified students who were referred to as the *In-betweens*. This non-derogatory metaphor was used to identify adolescents who occupied an intermediary status position between socialite and streetcorner youths such as the *Socs* and *Greasers*. These "in-between" youth were sometimes called *Neutralites* or *Regulars*. Some adolescents, however, preferred this group over the *Socs* because they were "less snobbish, less exclusive, and more friendly" (Schwendinger and Schwendinger, 1985:114). Larkin (1979) described them as the "silent majority" to indicate how common this less distinguishable group of adolescents was. The "silent majority" was subdivided into smaller groups according to particular interests.

Finally, the Schwendingers found a number of derogatory metaphors used by youth who ridiculed peers as a means of establishing their own superior status. These metaphors included *Square*, *Spaz* or *Spastic*, *Clod*, *Misfit*, *Lame*, *Nerd*, *Weirdo*, and *Wimp*. Their common usage, particularly during the formative years of peer group development, typifies the insensitivity and cruelness toward others that is often part of adolescent social interaction.

When the Schwendingers returned to southern California in the early 1980s they found new metaphors in use. For instance, *Preps* and *Preppies* had replaced *Socs* and *Socialites*. *Punkers* or *Punk Rockers* and *Heavy Metalers* were apparent among older white streetcorner youth. At teen clubs, the Schwendingers observed a variety of fashion and grooming styles, including "'new wave,' 'mod,' 'flash dance,' 'punker,' 1920s and 1950s styles" (p. 62). On the other hand, black and Hispanic streetcorner youth, such as *Homeboys* and *Ese Vatos*, who lacked the buying power of white youth, appeared less affected by these changes.

Adolescent Subcultures in Wisconsin

The linguistic metaphors used by adolescents to identify status differences among various social types provide a "window" through which the characteristics of adolescent subcultures are revealed. It is unfortunate that criminologists have been preoccupied with gang delinquency to the neglect of these more common adolescent groups. Most studies of this nature were conducted in the 1960s and had drugs as their primary focus.[5] The research that has been conducted finds remarkable similarity in metaphors or social types that exist in communities across the country. At the same time, some metaphors or social types appear to be unique to particular areas and may be virtually unknown by youth in other parts of the same city (Schwendinger and Schwendinger, 1985).

In the remainder of this article, I identify and discuss a variety of adolescent subcultures that can be found in various communities in Wisconsin. The data were derived from papers written by forty-two undergraduate students in my courses on Juvenile Delinquency between 1983 and 1988. In these papers, I asked students to reflect upon their adolescent years and write about the youth groups that congregated around their high school. The papers were generally part of a broader assignment involving an autobiographical analysis of students' delinquent (or non-delinquent) histories and the impact of the larger community on their adolescent experiences. While the data are limited by students' personal knowledge and recall ability, they indicate a fascinating variety of adolescent groupings.

Table 18.1 presents the social type names or metaphors used by students to refer to the constellations of adolescents in their high school. Twenty-six different Wisconsin cities or towns of different population sizes are identified, along with three unknown Wisconsin communities. In addition, Table 18.1 includes social types reported by students who attended out-of-state high schools in Illinois (4) and California (2). Both metropolitan and rural areas are represented.[6] In two cities, students reported on different high schools in the same city (i.e., five from Milwaukee and two from Watertown). In two other communities (i.e., Burlington and Lake Mills), two students who attended the same high school at different times identified different groups.

The degree of social differentiation among adolescents in these various communities varied from one place to another, although there was no correlation between the size of the high school and the number of groups identified by the students. While the same social type metaphors were often found in different communities, there were also types and names that were unique to particular areas. Similar social types in different communities were also identified by different metaphors. Occasionally, within one community more than one metaphor was used to refer to the same social type. In

the case of one metaphor, the same name, *Space-Cadets*, was used to identify different types.[7] In some instances, the metaphors were used to refer to males only or females only, and in other cases to both males and females. Occasionally students identified male and female versions of the same name, such as *Jocks* and *Jockettes*, or groups of males and females, such as *Jocks* and *Cheerleaders* or *Rah-rahs*, that hung out together.

The most prevalent divisions within the high schools paralleled Chambliss' (1973) Saints and Roughnecks or the Schwendingers' (1985) socialite and streetcorner types. *Jocks* was the most common metaphor used to identify the Saints or socialite groups. While the *Jocks* were involved in a considerable amount of "garden variety" delinquent activities, they were perceived by the community to be basically "good" kids. Depending on the city or town, the behavior patterns of the *Jocks* may have been similar to what students in other areas observed in the *Collegiates*, *Clique*, *Elite*, *Preppies*, *Partyers*, *Populars*, and *Sportos*. On the other hand, *Freaks* and *Dirtballs* were the most common names for the Roughnecks or streetcorner types. These groups were perceived by the community to be basically "bad" kids, although their delinquent behavior overall was not necessarily greater than the *Jocks*. In some areas, these "bad" kids may have been called *Burnouts*, *Druggies*, *Greasers*, *Heads*, *Hoods*, or *Junkies*.

The *Jocks*' name denoted members' involvement in school athletics. Female *Jocks*, *Jockettes*, or *Rah-rahs* were either involved in athletics themselves,[8] were cheerleaders, or merely associated with male *Jocks*. The *Jocks* were generally from the relatively higher class families in the community and were among the most popular students. One student referred to them

Table 18.1
Adolescent Student Groups[a,b]

		Wisconsin Communities		

Boscobel
(2,687)
Geeks and Nerds[c]
High Class
Jocks
Losers, Scodes,
  and Druggies[c]
Studs
	Brookfield
	(33,324)
	Freaks
	Populars
	In-Betweens
		Burlington
		(8,464)
		Cheerleaders
		Jocks
		Geeks
			Burlington
			(8,464)
			Band Jocks and
			  Band Buddies[c]
			Burnouts
			Future Farmers
			  of America
			Jocks
			Student Council
				Edgerton
				(4,302)
				Band Jocks
				Dirtballs
				The Clique

Franklin (19,430) Bandos Brains Computer Geeks Freaks Frocks Pets The Clique	*Green Bay* (93,942) Brains Freaks Jocks	*Janesville*[d] (52,202) Eggheads Goody-Two-Shoes Greasers Hippies Hoods Jocks	*Johnson Creek* (1,227) College Preps Dirtballs Jocks Nerds Partyers	*Kenosha* (76,173) Black Gangster Disciples Burnouts Jocks Nerds Preppies Sluts Serious Girls Studs Virgins Wimps

Lake Mills
(3,722)
Dirtballs
Greaseballs
Jocks
The Clique
	Lake Mills[d]
	(3,722)
	Clique
	Floaters
	Heads
	Hoods
	Nerds
		Madison
		(175,664)
		Dirtballs
		  and B-Wingers[c]
		Jocks and
		  Jockettes
		Radicals (Punkers)
		Theater Geeks
			Manitowoc
			(32,482)
			Dirtballs
			Jocks
			Preppie Faggots
				Milwaukee
				(608,443)
				Blacks
				Freaks
				Greasers
				Jocks

Milwaukee (608,443) Dirtballs Jocks Zoners	*Milwaukee* (608,443) Brains Floaters Freaks Nerds Preppies	*Milwaukee* (608,443) Blacks Freaks Greasers Jocks Nobodies	*Milwaukee* (608,443) Ball Players Brains Breakers Burnouts Freaks Geeks Jocks Latin Kings Preps Rah-Rahs Spanish Cobras Trackettes 2-7s, 2-6s, 2-4s, and 1-9s	*Monroe* (10,458) Band Members Druggies Elite Jocks Loners "Normal" Crowd

(continued on next page)

a. Numbers in parentheses indicate population size of city or town. Figures for Wisconsin are from *State of Wisconsin Blue Book*, Wisconsin Legislative Reference Bureau, Madison, WI 1987–88. Figures for Illinois and California are from *General Population Characteristics, Census of the Population*, U.S. Department of Commerce, Bureau of Census, 1982.

b. Wisconsin students who attended high schools in Illinois and California are also included in this Table.

Table 18.1 *(continued)*

		Wisconsin Communities *(continued)*		
Pewaukee	*Poynette*	*Racine*	*Ripon*	*Sharon*
(9,238)	(1,529)	(81,635)	(7,241)	(1,288)
Brains	Fruits	Blacks	Eggheads	Jocks
Freaks	Jocks	Freaks	FFARMs [Future	Fontana Fags and
Jocks	No-Minds	In-Betweens	Farmers (Fuckers)	Poloheads[c]
Preps		Jocks and	of America Rural	Puterheads
		Jockettes	Manure]	Sharon Greasers
		Mexicans	Jocks and Jockettes	Walworth Preppies
		Think-Tanks	Mafia	
			Space-Cadets	
Stoughton	*Two Rivers*	*Waterford*	*Watertown*	*Watertown[e]*
(8,456)	(13,208)	(2,141)	(18,846)	(18,846)
Hoods	Band Buddies	Freaks	Clicky-Preps	Bible-bangers
Jocks	Freaks	Jocks	Hoods	Missionary Kids
In-Betweens	Jocks		Nerds	Preachers Kids
Retards				Reps (Reprobates)
				Stickers
				Tumbleweeds
				Zoobies

Waukesha	*Wauwatosa*	*Williams Bay[d]*	*Unidentified Wisconsin Communities*		
(52,723)	(50,070)	(1,868)	*(small towns)*		
Brains	Floaters	Collegiates	Brains	Dirtballs	Jocks
Freaks	Freaks	Dupors	Druggies	Freaks	Hoods
In-Betweens	Jocks	Greasers	Jocks	Goodies	Rednecks
Jocks	Nerds	Hippies	Losers	Hoods	
Preppies	Preps			Jocks	
				Preppies	

	Illinois Communities		
Naperville	*Rockford*	*Unidentified*	*Unidentified*
(42,330)	(139,712)	(Chicago Suburb)	(Chicago Suburb)
Freaks	A Team	Freaks	Freaks
Frocks	Academy Fags	Geeks	Sportos
Jocks	and Bitches	Jocks	
Preppies	Bad Boys	Preps	
	Disciples	Rahs	
	Jocks	Space-Cadets	
	Junkies		
	Vegetables		
	Vicelords		
	Zulus		

	California Communities		
Fairfield		*Hayward[e]*	
(58,099)		(94,167)	
Band Members	Jocks	In-Betweens	Low-Riders
Cheerleaders	Rockers and	Intellectuals	Trouble-Makers
Drama Crowd	Burnouts[c]	Jocks and	
Intellectual		Girlfriends	
Bookworms			

c. These names were used interchangeably.
d. These groups were identified by a returning (older) student.
e. These groups were identified by a student who attended a parochial high school.

as "your basic student," in part because they maintained a "B" or "C" average in school. (Only one student referred to the *Jocks* as "dumb.") Some *Jocks* were known for "brown-nosing" teachers who typically gave them the "benefit of the doubt" and accepted their excuses for missing class. In addition, athletic coaches were known to intervene on *Jocks'* behalf to get them out of trouble and help them maintain their eligibility for school sports.

The *Jocks* tended to dress neatly and to keep their hair short and were considered "stylish." According to one student, they dressed "casual, but with taste, the Sporty look." Sometimes they wore expensive designer clothes, but more often they would wear athletic sweaters, lettermen jackets, Levis, t-shirts, and "brand name" tennis shoes, frequently high tops. While the *Jocks* generally behaved themselves within school grounds, they were frequently truant and engaged in drinking, using and selling drugs (especially marijuana), driving under the influence, and vandalism. But because they were more likely to have cars that enabled them to conduct their delinquencies outside of the area, or because they had access to homes when parents were vacationing or out for the evening, much of the *Jocks'* activities remained invisible to the community.

The *Jocks* were especially known for their heavy drinking. One student remarked that the boys on the football team probably drank "more than the entire school combined." Another student indicated that the *Jocks'* parents seemed to have "accepted the fact that their children went out, partied, and got drunk," and that their main concern was that "their child did not get caught doing it." Still another described weekly parties on Friday and Saturday nights, which would be held at a house selected according to whose parents were

not present. At these parties, they "drank to get drunk," and one was considered a "loser" and would not be invited again if he or she did not drink. Being seen at these parties increased one's popularity and prestige among peers so that one "could then date all the right people or join all of the popular clubs in school" (quotes from student papers).

Unlike the *Jocks*, the *Freaks* and *Dirtballs* were more likely to come from the lower or working class families in the community. They had a distinct dress that differed from the *Jocks*. They wore torn and faded jeans, town, rock and roll or concert t-shirts, blue jean jackets, flannel shirts, and hiking boots (one student mentioned "black suede G.A.S.S. shoes from Kinneys"). They were also more likely than the *Jocks* to have long hair and beards. The *Freaks* and *Dirtballs* were generally unable to participate in school athletics because of their poor academic records, although one student identified a group called the *Frocks* who were "freaks who played sports" (quote from student paper).

Some students indicated that the *Freaks* and *Dirtballs* used more drugs and engaged in more petty thievery than the *Jocks*, but others believed that they were actually less delinquent. Regardless of their actual rates of delinquency, the *Freaks* and *Dirtballs* had reputations for being overly specialized, preoccupied, or "burned out" with drugs (especially marijuana). They were generally held in low esteem by other students and ranked toward the bottom of the adolescent social hierarchy. The same was true of other streetcorner drug-using groups such as the *Burnouts*, *Druggies*, *Heads*, *Hippies*, *Junkies*, *No-Minds*, and *Zoners*. These groups were also associated with smoking cigarettes in specific locations such as parking lots, school bathrooms, a corner of the auto shop, or between two high school buildings. These places were sometimes referred to by names such as the "smoking lounge" or "cancer corner." One group of *Dirtballs* was also known as the *B-Wingers* because members hung out in the B-wing of a school building. In another case, *Freaks* often smoked cigarettes (and even marijuana) in a building known as "Freak Hall." At this school, they were also observed occasionally snorting cocaine behind a raised book in the classroom. This practice was called "sneak-a-toke."

Some of the streetcorner type groups were also known to be involved with cars or motorcycles and were similar to the *Greasers*. The *Greasers* is a term carried over from the 1950s and there were still groups in the 1980s that were identified by this metaphor because of their tendency to grease down their hair and wear black leather jackets (the same was true of the *Greaseballs* and the *Hoods*). In one community, a similar group, who were Hispanic, were labeled *Low-riders* because they drove cars that were "jacked up" in the back and low in the front. The males in this group dressed in "Ben Grey trousers," while the females dressed in "red pants and painted their faces with as much makeup as possible" (quote from student paper).

As the Schwendingers (1985) found, the Wisconsin students also identified a number of complementary or interrelated social types. For instance, the *Disco Broads*, known for hanging out in bars when they were underage, got along well with the *Rah-rahs*. In a couple of high schools, some *Jocks* overlapped with the *Studs* when they were known for both their athletic and sexual prowess.[9] *Jocks* from affluent families may have also overlapped with other affluent students such as the *Preppies*, *Collegiates*, or *The Clique*.

On the other hand, when affluent students like the *Preppies* were not involved in sports, they were clearly differentiated from the *Jocks*. *Preppies* could be identified by a distinct dress (e.g., polo shirts, baggies, docksider shoes or penny loafers, with or without argyle socks), and in some cases, they were viewed in decidedly negative terms such as *Preppie Faggots* or *Fontana Fags*. These derogatory metaphors were used by students who resented the *Preppies'* affluence and social privilege.

The *Preppies* were also viewed negatively when they were perceived to be "A" students. Indeed, some *Preppie* students overlapped with other intellectual social types who were labeled with derogatory metaphors such as *Academy Fags and Bitches*, *Bookworms*, *Brains*, *Eggheads*, *Geeks*, *Puterheads*, *Nerds*, *Pets*, or *Think-Tanks*. These students were seen as "teacher's pets," "brown-nosers," "study bugs," or "goody-two-shoes." They were "smart kids who didn't have any social life" and who had an overly "strict attitude" toward school (quotes from student papers). One student described the *Brains* as "the ones who scuttle down the hallway, carrying more books than they can handle, while pushing their glasses up onto their noses as they walk." Such intellectual social types dressed conservatively or wore "out of date clothes that the *Preps* just got rid of" (quote from student paper). They were also described as "immature," often making "noises like robots or computers." Not surprisingly, the intellectuals were the least likely to engage in delinquency.

Some of the intellectuals were highly specialized. The *Computer Geeks*, for instance, were "totally engrossed with computers," had "absolutely no social life outside of their computers," and had personalities "like wet fishes" (quotes from student paper). The *Pets* were seen as more well-rounded academically (though still of low status) since they were good in subjects other than science and math. Other specialized groups that were described as either of low or middle status were those who were involved in music or the arts, such as *Band Jocks*, *Bandos*, and *Theater Geeks* (which included a few "punkers" called *Radicals*).

The relatively low status of the intellectual social types was further indicated by the fact that a metaphor such as *Nerds* could be used to describe students who were "either very bright or very dumb" (quote from student paper). Similarly, students with learning or physical disabilities were identified with derogatory metaphors such as *Retards* or *Vegetables*. Students who were from farm families and who were involved in Future Farmers of America [or *Future Farmers (Fuckers) of America Rural Manure*] were also viewed negatively and seen "as not amounting to much except for farmers or their wives" (quote from student paper). Other farm kids, the *Rednecks*, fared somewhat better, being seen as "swaying" between the "outside borders of the Jocks and Hoods" (quote from student paper).

Also, as the Schwendingers (1985) found, the Wisconsin students identified groups of adolescents who were referred to by nonderogatory metaphors such as *In-Betweens* and who occupied an intermediary status position between the socialite and streetcorner crowds. Generally lacking the specialization that was characteristic of the *Jocks*, *Freaks*, or *Brains*, this social type may not have been labeled with any particular metaphor. In some cases, however, a group like the *Frocks* would be considered "in-between" because they got along with both the *Freaks* and the *Jocks*. Similarly, the *Floaters* were a group of youth who "floated from group to group without committing to just one," and the *Mafia* was a

group that was a "combination of all the other groups" (quotes from student papers).[10] In some instances, "in-between" youth were viewed positively as "flexible" and "able to interact [with] and . . . belong to more than one group at a time," although one "in-between" group, the *Fruits*, was viewed negatively because its members did "not fit into any group" (quotes from student papers).

Most of the students who provided the data presented in Table 18.1 were white. Some of them identified groups of students that they referred to as the *Blacks* or *Mexicans*. With the exception of an occasional confrontation with whites, these groups generally kept to themselves. These groups were described as coming from the inner city and/or lower class areas (sometimes through bussing) and as having some members who were particularly prone to thievery or violence. Black females were also believed to be more likely to get pregnant. One group of black students, the *Breakers*, were known for their break-dancing. In three cities (Milwaukee and Kenosha, Wisconsin, and Rockford, Illinois), students were identified who associated with black street gangs such as the *Vicelords*, *Black Gangster Disciples*, *Zulus*, *Bad Boys*, *A Team*, *2-7s*, *2-4s*, and *1-9s*.[11] Hispanic street gangs such as the *Latin Kings* and *Spanish Cobras* were also mentioned.

Finally, Table 18.1 includes youth groups that were found in two parochial high schools. The metaphors used to describe the groups in one of these schools (Hayward, California) were similar to those found in public high schools. However, the metaphors in another (Watertown, Wisconsin) were unique. What is fascinating about this high school is the degree to which students managed to create a differentiated adolescent subculture in spite of authorities' attempts to induce rigid conformity among students. In this school, authorities' tolerance for deviation was low. Minor variations on dress or hair length, listening to rock and roll music, and conversing with members of the opposite sex were viewed as indications of delinquent tendencies. The group of students known as the *Reps* (for Reprobates) were the most likely to engage in such activities. Included in this group was a subgroup known as the *Tumbleweeds* who were the heavy drinkers and more likely to use marijuana, occasionally steal, be sexually active, and get pregnant. The *Zoobies* were described as students with emotional problems that were curiously connected to their religious beliefs.[12] The conformists, on the other hand, included the *Bible-Bangers* who were like the *Brains* or *Eggheads* of the school; they felt "a definite 'call' from God" to be attending the school, collected "Biblical notes and books much as a chipmunk gathers nuts," and had visiting preachers sign their Bible (quotes from student paper). This group was further divided among the *Missionary* and *Preachers Kids*, those whose parents were missionaries or preachers, and the *Stickers*, those whose "holier than thou" attitude led them to continuously report other students' transgressions to the school authorities (quote from student paper).

Conclusion

I began this article by suggesting that the phenomenon of gang delinquency should be expanded in terms of a broader conceptualization of adolescent subcultures. After reviewing the Schwendingers' research, I presented data on the social type names or metaphors used by adolescents in Wisconsin to delineate the status hierarchy of adolescent social relations. An examination of this element of adolescents' "semantic domain" reveals "an internally consistent system" of values and norms that establishes the boundaries of appropriate behavior within and between different groups (Schwartz and Merten, 1967:455).

While accumulation of similar data on adolescent groups in other communities would be valuable, the discussion of Wisconsin groups as presented in this article remains largely descriptive. Additional research is needed to investigate community perceptions of these social types and how these perceptions influence the community's reaction to its delinquency "problem." Further investigation into the post-adolescent "careers" of adolescents in different groups would also be useful. As Chambliss (1973) noted in "The Saints and the Roughnecks," upon leaving adolescence, youths like the Saints can be expected to "follow the expected path, settling into the ways of the middle class, remembering fondly the delinquent but unnoticed fling of their youth." On the other hand, youths like the Roughnecks, might "turn around," but more likely their "noticeable deviance will have been so reinforced by the police and community that their lives will be effectively channeled into careers consistent with their adolescent background." Research along these lines would contribute to a greater understanding of the role of stratified adolescent networks in reproducing the larger community social structure and in mediating the relationship between macro-level processes (especially socioeconomic) and particular patterns of delinquent behavior.

Notes

1. In this article, the concept of adolescent subcultures refers to adolescents in general, and is not restricted to the delinquent subcultures that are typically associated with strain theory (see Cloward and Ohlin, 1960; Cohen, 1955).

2. Even school-age youth who do not attend classes regularly generally go to school to meet their friends and to "congregate with others around the building" (U.S. Subcommittee, 1977:22).

3. Wiatrowski et al. (1981) found that the least delinquent youth were those who were most involved in academic activities (see Hirschi, 1969).

4. Larkin also noted the influence of the 1960s student protest movement on the *Politicos* (who were also considered intellectuals), the liberals in student government who expressed an affinity for the anarchist, anti-elitist ideologies of the 1960s.

5. In addition to research cited above, see Blumer et al. (1967), Friedman (1969), Gitchoff (1969), Poveda (1970), Riggle (1965), and Weis (1969).

6. In rural communities, two forms of automobile-related delinquency included "road tripping," the practice of driving around on rural roads while drinking, and "mailbox baseball," the practice of driving by roadside mailboxes and vandalizing them with baseball bats.

7. In one community the *Space-Cadets* were like *Greasers* who were "spaced-out" on drugs, while in another they were girls who "did terrible in school, . . . acted like they had no idea of what was going on, . . . [and] spent most of their time worrying about their hair and makeup" (quote from student paper).

8. In one instance, female athletes in particular sports were referred to by specialized names such as *Ball Players* (softball) or *Trackettes*.

9. While the *Studs* were males who "had been with a lot of girls," the *Wimps* were males who "hadn't been with anybody." In addition, females were classified as *Sluts*, *Virgins*, and *Serious Girls*. The *Sluts* "hopped around from one guy to the next in a short period of time," the *Virgins* "didn't go out with any guys and kept up their studies," and the *Serious Girls* "stayed with one guy for a long period of time" (quotes from student paper).

10. A returning (older) student described the *Dupors* in her high school as "middle-of-the-roaders," who dressed like the *Collegiates*, though less expensively and more casually, and who hung out at the local coffee shop drinking a lot of coffee.

11. Some of these Milwaukee gangs (e.g., 2-7s, 2-4s) took their name from the street corners where they congregated. See Hagedorn (1988) for a discussion of these Milwaukee gangs and their relationship to gangs in Illinois.

12. One student saved bottles of water under his bed because of the Book of Revelation prediction that the "rivers will turn to blood."

References

Bloch, H.A. and A. Niederhoffer. 1958. *The Gang: A Study in Adolescent Behavior.* New York: Philosophical Library.

Blumer, H., A. Sutter, S. Ahmen, and R. Smith. 1967. *The World of the Youthful Drug User.* ADD Center Final Report, School of Criminology, University of California, Berkeley.

Chambliss, W.J. 1973. "The saints and the roughnecks." *Society* 11:24–31.

Cloward, R.A. and L.E. Ohlin. 1960. *Delinqency and Opportunity: A Theory of Delinquent Gangs.* Glencoe, IL: Free Press.

Cohen, A.K. 1955. *Delinquent Boys: The Culture of the Gang.* Glencoe, IL: Free Press.

Eisenstadt, S.N. 1956. *From Generation to*

Generation: Age Groups and Social Structures. New York: Free Press.

Empey, L.T. 1982. *American Delinquency: Its Meaning and Construction*. Second edition. Homewood IL: Dorsey Press.

Erickson, M.L. and G.F. Jensen. 1977. "Delinquency is still group behavior: Toward revitalizing the group premise in the sociology of deviance." *Journal of Criminal Law and Criminology* 68:388–95.

Friedman, S.D. 1969. *A Typology of Adolescent Drug Users*. Unpublished master's thesis, University of California, Berkeley.

Giordano, P.C., S.A. Cernkovich, and M.D. Pugh. 1986. "Friendships and delinquency." *American Journal of Sociology* 91:1170–1202.

Gitchoff, G.T. 1969. *Kids, Cops and Kilos: A Study of Contemporary Urban Youth*. San Diego: Malter-Westerfield.

Greenberg, D.F. 1981. "Delinquency and the age structure of society." Pp. 118–39 in D. Greenberg (ed.), *Crime and Capitalism: Readings in Marxist Criminology*. Palo Alto, CA: Mayfield.

Hagedorn, J. 1988. *People and Folks: Gangs, Crime, and the Underclass in a Rustbelt City*. Chicago: Lake View Press.

Hirschi, T. 1969. *Causes of Delinquency*. Berkeley, CA: University of California Press.

Klien, M.W. 1971. *Street Gangs and Street Workers*. Englewood Cliffs, NJ: Prentice-Hall.

Larkin, R.W. 1979. *Suburban Youth in Cultural Crisis*. New York: Oxford University Press.

Miller, W.B. 1980. "Gangs, groups, and serious youth crime." Pp. 115–38 in D. Shichor and D. Kelly (eds.). *Critical Issues in Juvenile Delinquency*. Lexington, MA: Lexington Books.

Polk, K. and W.E. Schafer (eds.). 1972. *Schools and Delinquency*. Englewood Cliffs, NJ: Prentice-Hall.

Poveda, A. 1970. *Drug Use Among the Major Social Types in High School*. Unpublished doctoral dissertation, University of California, Berkeley.

Riggle, W. 1965. *The White, the Black, and the Gray: A Study of Student Subcultures in a Suburban California High School*. Unpublished doctoral dissertation, University of California, Berkeley.

Schwartz, G. and D. Merten. 1967. "The language of adolescence: An anthropological approach to the youth culture." *American Journal of Sociology* 72:453–68.

Schwendinger H. and J.S. Schwendinger. 1985. *Adolescent Subcultures and Delinquency*. New York: Praeger.

Stafford, M. 1984. "Gang delinquency." Pp. 167–90 in R. F. Meier (ed.), *Major Forms of Crime*. Beverly Hills, CA: Sage.

U.S. Senate Subcommittee on Delinquency. 1977. *Challenge for the Third Century: Education in a Safe Environment*. Washington, DC: U.S. Government Printing Office.

Weis, J.G. 1973. *Delinquency Among the Well To Do*. Unpublished doctoral dissertation, University of California, Berkeley.

_____. 1969. *A Social Typology of Adolescent Drug Use*. Unpublished master's thesis, University of California, Berkeley.

Weisfeld, G.E. and R. Feldman. 1982. "A former street gang leader reinterviewed ten years later." *Crime and Delinquency* 28:567–81.

Wiatrowski, M.D., D.B. Griswold, and M.K. Roberts. 1981. "Social control and delinquency." *American Sociological Review* 46:525–41.

La Vida Loca— The Crazy Life

19

Tracy J. Johnston

Spider had his melancholy expression, the one that always made Loca forgive him. His sable brown eyes looked so sympathetic and sad—like those of a wounded dog giving soundless cries for help—that she forgot about the ways he treated her bad, the times he messed up on her with other girls or went out shooting with his home boys while she stayed at home. She was feeling sorry for him even before he had the hallucinations. He was a *vato loco*, a crazy guy, in the barrios of East Los Angeles, but it was because he didn't give a fuck about life. When he was thirteen and got busted by the cops he found out that the person he loved as his mother was actually his grandmother. His birth certificate said that his mother was his oldest sister, Marianna, the sister who had looked after him when she had the inclination and the time.

They were sitting on the back porch of his grandmother's house, tripping out on angel dust, when it happened. It was a

From "La Vida Loca," *New West Magazine*, January 29, 1979, pp. 38–45. Reprinted by permission of *New West Magazine* and the author. Names and locations have been changed in this story.

warm night in December and Loca felt good. She liked getting dusted with Spider because it made her feel as if she could do anything; as if she were better than everyone else even though she was only a *chola* in the barrios. Angel dust made her feel like the guys. When she was dusted she wanted to get into a fight and go shooting with them. She knew they would never let her, but just the thought of it was exciting. Sometimes, when she and Spider were dusted, they would get wrapped up in each other's trips. He would make her feel things; he would say something funny to make her laugh and then he'd suddenly act all mean, and make her cry. She would look at his eyes and they would have that melancholy look and then she'd start thinking about her problems and they would just sit there for a long time, sharing their sadness. Spider sometimes hit her, but she didn't mind. She always did something to deserve it. She knew he loved her, because she had broken up with him twice, and each time he was the one who came back to her, crying.

"Hey, Spider!" Loca said suddenly. "Spider?"

Something was wrong.

Loca can't quite remember the exact sequence of things because, after all, she was loaded on PCP, an animal tranquilizer, but she remembers clearly how Spider's eyes looked when he turned and stared at her—as if he had just seen a bright red devil with horns and a pitchfork. He leaped to his feet, grabbed Loca's arm, and tried to twist it behind her back. When she yelled out, "Spider, it's me!" he looked at her with an expression that made her stomach go into a knot, turned, and ran inside the house.

Loca felt confused and sick to her stomach. For a couple of seconds she let herself trip out all alone on the porch, looking up at the stars, feeling how they twinkled in time with her heartbeat; but then she made herself go into the house.

Loca went to the glass cabinet in the dining room and found a rosary next to the collection of porcelain saints and plastic animals. Although she never went to church she believed in its symbols. She took out the rosary and prayed for about five minutes, with her eyes closed, then went back to Spider's room and peeked inside. Thank God, he seemed to have calmed down—he had ripped the medallion of Saint Christopher that she had given him off his neck and was holding it in both hands.

Later that night Loca held Spider in her arms for a long time, feeling his thin body tremble. He was so wild and impulsive and crazy most of the time, and his reputation as a soldier for their barrio was so great, that she felt blessed by this submission. Before she went home they both knelt down and prayed to God for forgiveness. They would settle down and give up *la vida loca*, "the crazy life" of getting loaded and fighting for their gang. They would get married in June.

Spider's promises lasted for one day. The next morning when Loca met him in the park he acted as if it had all been a joke—just too much angel dust or maybe dust poisoned by an enemy gang. Three days after that, on New Year's Eve, all the home girls and home boys in their barrio got together at Pedro's place in back of the park and had the best party of their entire lives. At about three in the morning the girls went outside and yelled out, PEREZ MARAVILLA RIFA" ("Perez Maravilla Barrio Rules"), until the guys came out and told them to shut up. They said they were mad because the screaming might attract the cops, but Loca knew they were proud that Perez was all together and acting crazy. They had to respect the home girls because they were leading *la vida loca* too.

Two weeks after the party Loca got a call from the East Los Angeles sheriff's office. Spider got on the phone and said that he had been busted with some of the home boys for carrying a gun. They had been set up, he said; it wasn't his gun. Loca started crying and had to hang up. She put on her sweater and went to the park with the intention of drinking some Thunderbird and finding someone to fight.

Fighting was one thing she knew how to do well. She was big for a Chicana, and unless other girls jumped in, she never lost. It was sunset when she went out, and the colors in the small, quiet streets of her neighborhood were as intense as the picture postcards her grandmother sent her from Mexico. Before she found the girls, however, she heard the voices of her home boys. They were sitting on the grass waiting to play soccer, and when she was still several yards away she started screaming. She was tired of the barrio. It was supposed to mean that you had a lot of friends to back you up in a fight, or take you in if you needed a home, but where did it get anyone? In prison, she thought. Or dead.

"You call yourself home boys!" she yelled. "You *knew* that Spider is on probation and that if he got busted he couldn't get out, and you took him along shooting anyway. You don't care about Spider, do you? He's your home boy and you don't even *care*."

When Loca stopped yelling, Spider's best friend, Payaso, got up and walked over to her. He put his arm around her shoulders, turned her away from the other guys, and said, "You know there's no way anyone can tell Spider what he can or cannot do. Come on, let's go home." Loca knew it was true.

"He'll be in jail for *at least* eight months," she wailed.

"Spider loves you," Payaso said. "Last night in the car, just before we got busted, he said that before anything happened to him he wanted you and him to get married."

"If he loves me so much, why did he go shooting?"

"That's his business, not yours," Payaso said sternly. "Your business is to wait for Spider until he gets out. If we see you with anyone else we'll shoot him."

When Loca tells me this tale of tragedy and dime-store sentimentality, her voice has an edge of envy. Those were the days when no one could tell her what to do; when being Spider's woman made her special in the only world she knew. Now everything has changed, and it will never be the same. Loca is married to Spider and has two babies.

Loca and Spider live with their sons, Fernando, two, and Michael, one, and Spider's mother in an apartment in the dirtiest and poorest of the East Los Angeles projects. The apartments look like army barracks: long, two-story-high wooden rectangles, interspersed with strips of grass. In the tiny living room where Loca and I sit and Fernando crawls about on the floor,

there are none of the touches that grace almost every other barrio home—no plastic flowers, dolls in frilly dresses, crimson-and-gold shrines to the Virgin of Guadalupe. The television and stereo are big and functional, and the other two pieces of furniture—a chair and couch—are ragged and ugly.

Loca never leaves this room during the day. She dosen't like to take the babies on a bus, and Spider won't buy her a car. She watches soap operas, listens to her 45 collection and plays with the children, and at night when Spider comes home from his job working for his uncle, they go upstairs to their bedroom and spend the rest of the evening watching cops-and-robbers shows on television. At least once and usually twice a week Spider presses his khaki pants, puts on his small-brimmed felt hat, and goes out to spend the night partying with his home boys.

The move from virgin to mother is made quickly for girls in the barrios, and the change is absolute.

"Maybe I should have known that I'd be like all the rest," Loca says, sadly, "but I thought Spider was different. He's good to me in some ways—he provides for me and the babies. I think it's his mother that puts a lot of shit into his head. I didn't really know much about her until Spider said we'd have to live here because she needs the money to pay the rent. I don't like her—she goes out to bars and comes home with guys that are just as young as Spider. When Spider started going out on me at night, I got mad. But whenever I argued with him, his mother would tell him not to listen to me, right in front of my face. 'You're a man,' she says, 'and you can do whatever you want. The women are supposed to listen to you; you don't have to listen to them.' I tell her what I think, now; I argue back. I'm ashamed because I don't show her no respect, but I don't care anymore. I tell her, 'You're thinking about centuries ago; man, that stuff is *dead*. We don't live that way no more.' ''

Loca sighs. "I guess with his mother talking bad about me and him being out all the time, I lost my love for Spider. I'm just happy I had the babies because they got me off drugs. Spider and I, we don't have no relationship no more. I just huddle over on my side of the bed. Sometimes we talk about it and he says he thinks he was too young to get married. I say, 'Why didn't you think about that before? You're 25, I'm only 19. Why am I the one who has already become an old lady?' ''

Negra, Chica, and Shorty are just like Loca was, four years ago. They are fifteen and have, as they say, "seen a lot." They have seen their mothers grow hysterical with too many children and not enough support; their fathers and brothers get mean and violent on drugs and booze; their relatives bloody each other up with broken bottles and fists. Now, for the first time in their lives, they are proud. They give superficial signs of respect, still, to their parents—both Chica and Negra, for instance, don't smoke at home—but their family is now the barrio; the home boys and home girls of Segundo Flats.

When I arrive for a scheduled interview, they are sitting on Shorty's front porch, drinking beer and in no mood to talk about their future. Just before I arrived they sneaked into Shorty's brother's room, put paper bags over their heads and sniffed his spray paint. And before that they were out on Brooklyn Avenue kicking ass with two girls from Lorca Street.

Shorty is the "baddest" looking of the three girls. She is big, fat, has tattoos on her arms and shoulders, and still wears an enormous amount of makeup even though the style is on its way out. The makeup, called *máscaras* (mask), seems to be, like tattoos, graffiti and murals, a peculiarly Chicano style of self-expression. All the girls pluck out their eyebrows, pencil in thin new ones that rise like arches high on their foreheads, and paste on long black eyelashes that give their toughness an odd, feminine touch. Shorty, however, paints a white mask around her eyes, from the top of her cheekbones up to her eyebrows and all the way out to her hairline. The effect is best described as "Raccoon."

Shorty seems unfazed by my presence and comfortable with herself, as well as tough. I've heard her story from Negra. She has an older brother in Segundo Flats who is a crazy, a wildman *vato loco* who does a lot of shooting and is a hero to younger boys. Her mother is trying to keep the other six kids out of the gang wars, but it's an impossible task for a woman. Since her husband left her eight years ago, her eldest son, the *vato*, has taken over as head of the household. When I ask Shorty later about her brother, she tells me something that leaves me too dumbfounded to ask her to explain.

"My brother is a monster," she says, "but he is also my king."

Negra is the prettiest of the three girls. She has red cheeks, clear ivory skin, and dark, almost black eyes. She looks like the dolls that Chicana women buy and prop up on the mantles over their fireplaces. Negra's mother abandoned her and Li'l Man, her brother, when Negra was four. Now she lives with her aunt and uncle, grandmother and grandfather in a two-bedroom house so relentlessly clean that the furniture and lampshades are all covered in clear plastic. Negra doesn't know much about this family. Her grandparents lived in Mexico, but she doesn't know from which town or even which state. Her uncle has a well-paying job in a factory, but she doesn't know what he does or what the factory makes.

"I mind my own business," she told me. "I don't ask questions."

Chica is the least *chola* looking of the three girls, and also the smartest and most likely to "straighten up." She is the only *chola* I've met who gets better than Cs and Ds in school.

Chica's father is a former *vato loco* in Segundo Flats who survived all the warfare, but just barely. Although he's always had a $300-a-week factory job, he's been addicted to heroin for most of his life. Chica says she keeps telling her mother to throw him out of the house, but the two times her mother actually has done it, he has come back crying, pleading with her to take him back.

"A few months ago I tried to have it out with him," Chica confided. "He was all— like that—you know, and I ran away from home. I stayed at my boyfriend's house for a few days. I guess I wanted my father to straighten up and come and get me, but he didn't. Finally I gave up and went home by myself, but it was awful. He called me a tramp for staying at my boyfriend's, and when I told him I didn't do nothing and slept in another bedroom he didn't believe me. He called me a whore and got out a knife. I was crying and crying and I felt like leaving again. After that was over, he went into this thing where he said he was tired of life and was going to kill himself, and I felt real bad because I thought it was because of me. But my mother told me not to feel guilty. 'He's been tired of life since he was fifteen,' she said. 'Don't think it's you.'

"I would say I hate my father because he's mean to me and he don't trust me. But inside I know I love him because I'm going to do what he told me already: finish high school, don't get pregnant, don't be like I am. You might call me a *veterana* someday because I gangbang [fight] and all, but I'm not going to be like a lot of them. I know how it is. You get pregnant and then you have to get married. And your husband goes out on you, and when you want to go someplace you have to borrow a car. My boyfriend wants me to marry him after I finish high school, but I say, 'I'm not going to finish school for a while. I want to be a counselor and that takes some college.' He says, 'But I can support you.' and I say, 'On $200 a week?' He says, 'Yeah,' and I say, 'Uh-uh. That's not enough.' "

As I sit with Shorty, Negra and Chica on the porch this afternoon I am ignored but tolerated with good humor. They tell the story of their fight over and over again to themselves and each time their roles get more heroic. Although the fight was broken up by a security guard from the projects soon after it started, they all agree that they were down on the ground by that time, getting dirty and kicking and stomping ass. As I listen to them talk, laugh, and giggle with delight the way I did when I was fifteen and something made me feel big and important, I remember my conversation the night before with Rachel Ruiz. Rachel is a Chicana community organizer who took me into the heart of the barrios. She grew up in them and still lives in East Los Angeles, devoting most of her time to working with teenage girls. She had warned me that they would try and make their life seem glamorous.

"Don't let them tell you that their life is exciting," she said. "These girls have absolutely nothing to do. They fight for one day and hang around for twenty. The girls are mothers, the guys are fighters, and that's it. The girls have no models of women doing anything interesting or positive. If they have any ambition they want to be probation officers, policewomen or counselors. That's all they know. People don't grow up here. It's an adolescent culture—full of petty jealousies, paranoia, macho bravado. It's a defeated culture, really. The men think they are shit, and the women are even lower than the men.''

Rachel doesn't want me to glamorize the barrios, and yet she stays to work with the girls and finds it warm, comfortable, and even fun to hang out and talk with them, just as I do.

Right now, Negra, whose eyes are slightly out of focus, is flying:

"That girl with the big old tattoo on her neck that says Lorca Street? When I asked her *de dónde* [Where are you from?] she says, 'Nowhere.' *Fuck.* Who does she think we are, man? When she's with her *sister* she's from Lorca Street. I saw her sister and her in a fight once and she was kicking ass.''

"I hate every one of those guys from Lorca Street,'' says Shorty. "They ain't even in their own neighborhood and they think they're big shit. We gotta tell the guys to take care of business. They come in here and think they can go anywhere they want. Dopey said she saw a guy from Lorca Street right down there by the gym and no one did nothing to him.''

"He's probably on his way to see Yo,'' says Chica.

"YO!'' Shorty cries out. "T-s-s-s-s-s!''

"Guys from Lorca Street can't get it anywhere else,'' says Chica, laughing.

Both Chica and Shorty are laughing now, and Negra has to shout to make herself heard.

"Hey, wait a minute, WAIT A MINUTE! WHO'S YO? HEY. STOP IT, COME ON! What the fuck does Yo *do*?''

"What do you think, Negra?'' "She give 'em everything.''

"Hey,'' says Chica, playing the dummy. "What's everything?'' She puts her face right up next to Shorty's and teases her: "What's everything, ple-e-ese tell me.''

Shorty puffs up her cheeks, sits up very straight, and then spits out the next word right into Chica's face:

"BLOW JOBS.'' (Screeches of laughter from everyone.)

"SCREW IT IN HER EAR.'' (Shorty, Negra, and Chica grab their stomachs and roll around on the ground.)

"Hey, man,'' says Negra after a while. "Like, ah, I don't want to be dumb or anything, but what's a blow job?''

"*Una mamada*, dummy.''

"E-e-e-e-e YUK!'' says Negra and makes a vomiting motion. (Everyone laughs.)

"Yo *wants* it,'' says Shorty. "My brother says there's girls like that. They get raped when they're real young and they learn to like it and they can't get enough of it.''

"Ain't no one gonna rape me,'' says Chica.

"What you gonna do about it?'' says Negra, looking at her. "You get all loaded some night and he's got you alone and your home boys don't care?''

Chica sits up. "I say, 'Sure, man, come on. I'm on the rag.' '' (Yowls of laughter.)

"You say, 'I always wanted a blow job, honey. Here, first take out this.' '' (Shorty holds up an imaginary Tampax and everyone goes, "E-e-e-e'' and "Ah-h-h-h-h'' and bursts into more laughter.)

"You say, 'I'm glad you're the type who don't care about VD because I got it.' ''

By this time I'm caught up in the sheer energy of the girls' dirty talk and the intense edge the drugs have given it.

"Hey,'' I say, joining them for the first

time. "How much do you girls really know about sex?"

They stop laughing and look embarrassed.

"We know everything," says Shorty. "We know it all."

"Do you know," I ask, "about orgasms?"

Silence.

"What?" says Chica.

"An orgasm. A climax."

"What is it?" says Chica. Negra and Shorty look down at the ground. Somehow I'm stuck with explaining orgasms to girls who think sex is for getting pregnant.

"My sister," says Shorty, "says she doesn't feel nothing."

"I'm scared of sex," says Chica. "I ain't gonna do it until I get married."

"I know all about sex that I have to know," says Negra, suddenly turning cold.

"What's that?"

"What happens when it's over, man."

"What's that?"

"You feel like you want to throw up."

For most travelers to the City of the Angels, the intersection just east of the Civic Center where five freeways come together is a terrifying swirl of speed and concrete, lanes and arrows that lead to fantasy destinations: Hollywood, Pasadena, Santa Monica, Long Beach. The San Gabriel Mountains rise up to the north; the beach is 40 minutes west; Disneyland is less than a half hour away, and the tall buildings of the old city center are practically close enough to touch.

For the people who live in the small wooden two-bedroom houses that lie low around the intersections, however, the freeways are no more than scars across the land that they call home. Despite the speed and movement that surround them, the Mexican-American barrios of East Los Angeles have remained relatively unchanged. Except for increasing news reports on gang violence, they are also unseen and unheard. These barrios are the mecca for Mexicans coming to California from the northern high deserts of Mexico, and they are also the place where, since the 1930s, a violent and unique subculture, based on continuing gang warfare, has thrived amidst poverty and dislocation. It is a subculture that is lower-class Mexican, rural, and macho; isolated even from the rest of Los Angeles Chicano culture in the barrios and at least twenty years behind Mexican-American culture in general. The men in it are warriors in a battle that, at best, will celebrate their annihilation; the women, virgins and mothers who rarely venture outside the confines of their family homes.

In each barrio, which may have anywhere from 100 to 2,000 families living within its boundaries, there are only about 30 to 50 men of fighting age (11 to 30) who define the barrio territory and keep the warfare going. Called *pachucos* in the 1940s, they are now called *cholos*. They call themselves *vatos locos*, crazy guys.

The *vatos locos* live out their lives much the way their forefathers did when they first came to Los Angeles from Mexico via Arizona and Texas. They are overwhelmed by the wealth that surrounds them, and by the poverty and sorrow that seem to be their fate. Rather than shuffle around in disgrace, they choose to lead *la vida loca*, the crazy life, where they can at least be defiant and macho and say "What the fuck"; where they can get a reputation for risking their lives without flinching and taking drugs without caution; where they can die the most glorious death of all—the death of a soldier fighting for his country, or, in this case, his barrio. The cost is high. There were 24 deaths from gang warfare in this seven-and-a-half square-mile area last year.

In their own fantasies, the *vatos locos* are Homeric heroes: soldiers of an ancient battle, whose origin is unknown; fighting wild men who are willing to settle their own problems with guns and sacrifice themselves for altruistic codes of loyalty, honor, and revenge. The sociological reality is that these are ghetto boys who live in the worst pocket of poverty, unemployment, drug abuse, and family disintegration in the West. Supported first by their families, then by relatives or the welfare checks of the women who have their babies, the hardcore *vatos* spend their days hanging out, talking to each other, living in the past, alternately protecting and bullying their sisters, mothers and girl friends, fighting and reliving their fights in endless detail, and always, always, getting high.

I have emphasized the men in explaining gang warfare because they do the killing; they make up the rules. But there are women in the barrios who also believe in holding up the tattered remnants of this distorted pride. As mothers, they bring up their sons to think they must get ''a reputation'' in order to be a man. As sisters and girlfriends, they support the *vatos* with the bad reps by forming girl gangs that are like women's auxiliaries. The girls active in the barrio gang have no say about the fighting between guys, but they do fist-fight *cholas* from other gangs who either walk into their territory or give them a ''look.'' The ''look'' is created by making one's expression as sullen as possible, slouching with one hand on a hip, and staring directly up and down the body of an enemy girl. Some girls, like Loca, join a girl gang, even though their brothers are ''straight,'' because their own families have collapsed and they need to feel that someone will accept

and take care of them no matter what. They often go through a period, from age eleven to thirteen, of trying to act like the guys—painting their faces and tattooing their bodies to look ''bad.'' Some even go through a stage of dressing *cholo*—starched khaki pants, white T-shirt, Pendleton shirt worn as a jacket, and a headband worn just over the eyes.

As with Loca, however, this stage is short-lived. Very soon they fall in love with a home boy who tells them that he wants to get married. After that, they have his baby (only whores use the Pill and only cowards have abortions). For a while they bask in the rewards of pregnancy—people treat them with respect, their mothers don't hate them anymore, guys don't try to hit up on them or give them drugs. Then they start to worry about the rest of their lives.

The girls like Loca were not hard to find. Many of them were angry—disgusted with the *vatos* and eager to get an education, a job, and a day-care center to take care of their kids. But there are also girls at the dead center of the gang culture—girls who can't see how the fighting can be stopped just as fish can't see how anything can exist out of water, girls who know no way of life other than being mothers to the men and children of their barrio and are fearful of the world outside their traditionally Mexican turf. After they have their babies they become Penelopes—they wait for their heroes to return victorious from the battle, wait for them to satiate themselves with glory, wait for them to care enough about their babies to straighten up and settle down. They are often good mothers and close to their families, who give them a lot of love and support. They are proud of their husbands or boyfriends, if only for their ''bad reps.'' When they think about their future, however, they begin to weep passively. They clean and polish their tiny houses, fill them with babies, hand their welfare checks over to their husbands, and with a needle and ink tattoo teardrops just below their eyes.

Rachel Ruiz said she would introduce me to a girl in Yellow Rock barrio, one of maybe four or five barrios in East L.A. that are small, isolated from the rest of the world, and closed to outsiders. Jeanette, she said, is "stone barrio." Although the world is changing around her, she cannot see it, and does not dream of a future that will be in any way different from the past. She was born into a family of gang warriors and from the age of three she started hating the world outside her neighborhood for killing her brothers and cousins. I was shocked when I first saw Jeanette. I had expected her to look "badder," even, than Shorty, but instead, she looked like a college girl. She is pretty, feminine, and not dumb.

Jeanette, Rachel Ruiz and I meet in the basement of Jeanette's house—a spacious, windowless room that was, for many years, a Yellow Rock hangout. Now that most of Jeanette's brothers and cousins are either dead, in prison, born-again Christians or simply too old for fighting, the basement is no longer the center of shooting-strategy sessions. There are no parties there anymore, and joints of angel dust and marijuana are forbidden. Nevertheless, it is still bustling. When we take a break from talking, the basement fills up with children, who turn on the radio, bring in ice cream cones from the neighborhood store, and sit around on the old couches and mattresses laughing and talking. When toddlers and young children wander in and out, they are hugged and played with affectionately by both the girls and the boys. Clearly no one in Yellow Rock grew up lonely or uncared for, like Negra, Shorty and Chica. And no one grew up bored.

Jeanette tells me that she thinks the girls in Yellow Rock are different from the girls in other barrios. They don't have nicknames, they don't call themselves home girls, and they don't dress or make themselves up to look bad.

"We have respect," she says with pride. "The guys listen to us, they really do."

"Why is that?"

"We've grown up with them since we were little. We fought them and beat them up. They know we can take care of business."

"I heard that the girls from Yellow Rock are pretty," I say.

"I know that's what they say. If you can handle your stuff you don't need to look bad. We just laugh at the *cholas* who try and act like the guys. To me, they look dumb. All that makeup and their eyebrows plucked out."

Jeanette, herself, is delicate and slim. She smokes her cigarette like Lauren Bacall.

"Do you think you'll get married?" I ask. "You're twenty years old; isn't that time to be settling down?"

"I am settled down," she says. "There aren't many guys left to choose from."

"Guys in Yellow Rock?"

"Most of them are either married, dead, in jail or all scarred up. Some of them are dusted every day."

"Do you have to marry a guy from Yellow Rock?"

"No."

"Would the guys let you marry someone from another barrio?"

"They couldn't stop me."

"Would you do it?"

"No."

"Why not?"

"It's too much trouble. The guys would kill him if he came to live here, and if I moved into his neighborhood no one would talk to me. I know how it is because I've seen the way we treat the girls from other neighborhoods who move in here. Some of the guys have married girls who aren't from around here, and they just sit in their houses all day. No one will talk to them. One of them came up to me last week and asked me to tell her husband to stop fighting. She said, 'He listens to you more than me,' and it's true. I've known him since he was three.''

''What will you do if you don't get married?''

''Stay here.''

''For the next 50 years?''

She shrugs.

''Don't you think this fighting has gotten out of hand?''

''Yeah, it has. We tell the guys to slow down, but they get loaded and who gives a fuck?''

''Would you shoot the guy who killed your brother?''

''I guess I have enough hate in me to do it.''

''What about the guys who killed your cousins next door?''

''Them too.''

It's early evening now, some of the *vatos* are coming into the basement and I know I'm not wanted. Yellow Rock got into a fight two days ago and tonight everyone expects a retaliation.

When Rachel and I finally leave the basement, I notice again the bullet holes scarring the shingles—at least four different blasts of buckshot. Both of us quicken our steps. It is dusk, but all the little houses lined up in rows down the street, including Jeanette's, are absolutely dark, as if no one were home. The shades are drawn, there are no lights on inside, and an eerie stillness fills the growing darkness; even the crickets seem to have gone into hiding.

''Everyone's inside,'' whispers Rachel as we hurry to our car. ''They're all in back. They know about the fight and they know there may be some shooting.''

From a block away, a car door slams, and we both give an involuntary start.

I was vaguely afraid during much of the time that I spent in the barrios. Sometimes I worried about getting caught in random crossfire, but mostly I worried that some of the *vatos* would hear about my comments on independence and orgasms and, in a macho fury, spurred on by dust and booze, decide I was a threat. One of the girls I spoke with said she had to do a lot of talking to convince her home boys not to go after a *Los Angeles Times* reporter who wrote that his gang was ''trying to make peace.'' I would not say that any of the *vatos* I knew were trying to make peace, but I might say that the barrios were a sad place to grow up, that the men were pitiful heroes and the women, silly martyrs. I might also talk about the courage of the girls like Chica who are going to try to make it in an alien world, without any money or friends, all alone.

I think the last word, however, should be that of the boy who was pitching a baseball in a neighborhood game when I was walking down Entrada Street on my way to an afternoon appointment at Negra's house. The batter stood poised and ready for the pitch, but the pitcher turned around to look at me.

''Hey,'' he said, tugging on his hat. ''This ain't where you belong.'' He pressed the ball into the pocket of his glove, made the pitch, and the batter hit a foul, off to the left.

The pitcher turned to look at me again as if I were a small child. I kept my eyes fixed on the sidewalk. ''This is *Mexican* territory,'' he said. ''*Todo se paga.*'' [All is avenged.]

A Former Street Gang Leader Reinterviewed Eight Years Later

20

Glenn E. Weisfeld
Roger Feldman

In 1973 we published an article on crime, based largely on an interview with a white twenty-four-year-old Chicago street gang leader.[1] Our informant discussed various theories of criminal behavior and evaluated them by drawing upon his experience with numerous young criminals. Basically, he supported the economic interpretation of crime pioneered by Becker,[2] although he invoked other motives as well, especially the influence of fellow gang members and the desire for the prestige of being a successful thief. Our informant maintained, however, that a more positive value system also operated among his friends. A man who holds a legitimate, decent-paying job, lives with his family, and is loyal to his friends is, he claimed, respected too. By interviewing him again on the same subject, we wished to see whether his views on

street crime had changed, and to learn the fate of his fellow gang members.

Our informant, whom we shall call Tom Nichols, has lived up to the legitimate value system quite successfully in the intervening years. Now thirty-four years old, he operates his own business, has moved out of his former neighborhood to a more desirable one, still lives with his wife and child, and remains respected by his friends. Nichols has been accepted by community leaders also, and is sometimes asked to speak to civic groups and law school classes.

His current life is a far cry from his earlier years. Nichols was born to a Protestant family in Northern Ireland and came to Chicago at an early age. He dropped out of school, lived on the streets, and learned to fight while in jail. Eventually he became president of one of the prominent gangs in the area, and was well known among delinquent youths of the entire city. He was shot, stabbed, and otherwise scarred numerous times. When we met him he was getting ar-

From *Crime and Delinquency*, Vol. 30, No. 4, 1982, pp. 567–581. Reprinted by permission of Sage Publications, Inc., and the authors.

rested about once a week on various charges.

Our research team worked with Nichols on a participant-observation, community organizing project in 1969–71.[3] The project began with several postgraduation students' efforts at counseling street gang members, whom we initially contacted at a local pool hall. We offered legal counseling, job counseling, and suggestions on dealing with a wide range of personal problems, including drug use, marital relations, and the military draft. The project received some foundation support but was otherwise unaffiliated with any institution. We intervened on the youths' behalf with local bodies such as the police, employers, and parents' organizations. We acted as mediators during a racial dispute at a local high school, and made it a policy to discuss the issue of racism with the youths.

We attempted to help establish a permanent youth organization so that the young people could defend their own interests independently. With Tom as the obvious choice as leader, an organization that embraced several gangs began to emerge. A bail fund and other programs were established. As solidarity developed, however, the youth organization began to be perceived as a political threat by the local police precinct, and pressure was brought to bear on the organization. When the youths' clubhouse was burned down, the project began to disintegrate. Tom was sentenced to jail shortly thereafter on a manslaughter conviction after an accidental shooting, and the project was effectively over.

The organizing project took place in a predominantly white, working-class neighborhood of 100,000 people on Chicago's near Northwest Side. Once the fashionable residence of many of the city's business and professional leaders, the area saw its economic base nearly vanish in the postwar suburban flight. The broad boulevards still remained, but they stood in sharp contrast to the decline of public and private services. For example, there were no hospitals at all in the area. The population was largely of eastern (i.e., Polish) and southern European extraction. Two miles to the south lay the city's West Side ghetto, and a strip of Puerto Rican and Chicano streets, which has since expanded steadily northward, acted as a buffer zone between whites and blacks. Median family income was under $8,000. Most of the men were nonunion factory or construction laborers. The women were clerks, beauticians, factory workers, and the like. The high school dropout rate was high, and almost no one attended college. The community had shown a remarkable degree of residential stability, with only 1.4 percent of the population leaving from 1960 to 1966. During the past ten years the area has undergone an increase in its Latino population, and many whites have moved away. Some important factories have relocated out of the area. The neighborhood is regarded by the police as one of the most dangerous in the city.

The gang members with whom we worked had generally dropped out of school at age fourteen or fifteen. Many worked intermittently at factory jobs paying about $100 a week before deductions, but burglary and drug selling were perhaps the most common sources of income. Most of the younger adolescents lived with their parents or other relatives. The older unmarried boys lived in bleak, sparsely furnished apartments in groups of from two to five. The girls usually lived at home until marriage. Rates of illegitimacy, teenage marriage, and divorce were high.

We have maintained contact with Nichols since the organizing project. Recently the first author taped an interview with him in which he again discussed crime with reference to his acquaintances. We were interested primarily in his current views of the causes of street gang–related crime; in what had happened to his friends who had persisted in criminal activity, to compare their experiences with his own; and in his recommendations for crime prevention. We were curious about his comments on crime prevention because he has served as an advisor on this subject to community groups and has given it careful thought. We shall again follow our previous format of quoting him directly, interspersing his remarks with our own commentary as deemed necessary. Names have been changed to protect the privacy of people mentioned.

The Role of Street Gangs

In the 1973 article Nichols estimated that peer pressure emanating from fellow gang members accounted for 10 percent of crimes, especially car theft and wanton assaults. Most of the boys in the area joined a gang, or "club," at thirteen or fourteen; most disaffiliated in their early twenties. Gang members provided the security of a group identity and acceptance, as well as mutual protection and a modicum of economic security through sharing of resources. Many girls belonged to gangs, each girls' gang operating as a sort of ladies' auxiliary to a particular boys' gang. The girls' gangs sometimes fought each other but were less likely than the boys to use guns, knives, and other weapons. Fights between individual gang members usually were precipitated by sexual jealousy, theft of personal property, an insult, betrayal to the police, or the suspicion of one of these acts. When the participants belonged to rival gangs, the fight might escalate to involve all the members of the two gangs and even allied gangs. Fighting between gangs also occurred when ethnic ri-

valries were intense, as when a neighborhood was in racial transition, or when one gang member ventured into another's turf. Some gang rivalries persisted for years. Fights between members of the same gang were relatively rare. They usually involved disputes over a girl or constituted a "dominance struggle" for leadership. Roughhousing, or fighting for amusement, was rare among the senior gang members (ages eighteen to about twenty-eight), fairly frequent among the junior boys (ages sixteen to eighteen), and common among the peewees (ages thirteen to sixteen). Each age grade within a gang had its own leadership structure. Although elected, the leader invariably was the best fighter. Often a leadership contest ensued when the president returned to the streets from jail and was challenged by the acting president.

Gang members often cooperated in committing crimes. There was little stigma attached to being a thief among the neighborhood youths, who, if they pondered the ethical issue at all, were convinced that wealthy people were just as dishonest as they, and more profitably so. When neighborhood burglars preyed upon the suburbs, however, it was due not to class consciousness but to greater availability of goods, less chance of being recognized, and less intense police surveillance.[4]

The present interview began with a discussion of Nichols's observation that many of his criminal friends had died. This soon led to the subject of gangs and how prevalent they are.

Weisfeld: You were talking about how so many guys have died around here. How did they die?

Nichols: Like the Kelly brothers. Four of them were shot. One got shot the day before yesterday.

W: Was it in a gang fight?

N: Yeah, it was one of the Lords. The Lord shot Kelly because he was one of the peewee Saints.

The interview was then interrupted by a telephone call for Nichols, who then reported on its content.

N: That was a guy who got stabbed last Monday night. The kid was coming home and some guys were robbing a grocery store and they thought he was going to break in on them. He wasn't going to do nothing. He walked past and they jumped out of the store window and stabbed him in the arm, through the muscle. He's getting okay, though.

W: Now, what happened with the Kelly brothers?

N: It all started about three or four years ago. Do you remember the old Gateway Restaurant? Well, a Puerto Rican guy bought the Gateway and they were in there and got in an argument with him. Well, he went crazy behind the counter and pulled out a big butcher knife, and commenced to cutting two of them, Neil Kelly and Ike Kelly. And he left them for dead in the back of the Gateway. One of them was still alive. He crawled out to the street and stopped a pedestrian and got the cops to come. When the cops came they found the other Kelly brother behind the counter, dead. Well, when the one Kelly brother got better, he came back to the Gateway to ask him why he did it, why he killed his brother. And the restaurant owner took out a .45 and shot him in the head twice, and twice in the chest. Well, it just so happened me and Mike the cop was up there at the Gateway that night, at the tavern drinking. And we walked in the Gateway and me and Mike found him, lying on the floor. Nobody else was there. So now, about a year later—that's two Kelly boys dead—Steve got killed, he drowned himself down at the lake.

W: Was it suicide?

N: That's what they say. And then, two nights ago, the Lords, again, killed Irv Kelly, the fourth brother. Shot him in the chest.

W: Do you know what the fight was about?

N: It was the old Saint thing, when they used to fight each other in the old days, back when I was growing up. The vendetta never stops.

W: Now, these gangs have been around for eight, ten years.

N: Oh, more than that. The Saints have been around since 1950. The Lords, since 1965 or 1966. They were just another part of the Latin Squares. Then you got different clubs. The kids grow up, but there's always more kids to take their place.

W: Now, what happens to these guys? How did the Kelly brothers make a living?

N: Ripping off, dealing, . . . same old thing that I was doing. They make their living any way they can.

W: Do you think anything has changed?

N: No, nothing's changed. Like I said, we get older, that's all. The older guys drop out of circulation, but there's another kid to take their place right away. I guess as long as there's a ghetto, there's going to be gangs.

W: Obviously the police haven't been very successful in doing anything about gangbanging. Is there anything they can do except sit on the sidelines and watch it all happen?

N: They sit on the sidelines and watch it all happen because they have to. I mean, let's face facts. There's 2,300, 2,600 police officers in the city of Chicago. There are thousands of club members. There's 14 clubs in my old district. There's 26 districts in Chicago.

W: And how many in each club?

N: At one time the Saints had 400 members, when you guys first came around. We were going strong. We ran a turf over a hell of a big area. And in Elmwood High School alone there was maybe 30 percent of the school was Saints.

W: What percentage of the boys in a school would be in some gang or other?

N: Eighty percent. In Elmwood, or Grover, or Harper, 70 to 80 percent.

W: And what about the guys who are not in a club?

N: There's a few that are still trying to be straight. I don't see nothing wrong with them now that I'm grown. But when I was younger I didn't think much of them. They couldn't handle themselves.

W: So they might not even have been accepted in a club.

N: No, I doubt it. We had a few of them in the Saints that was—how do I put it?—was simps. They weren't shit but we took them in anyway because they had money, they had a little bit of something to offer us. There's all kinds of different guys in a club anyway. There's followers and there's leaders. Eighty percent of the club is followers, just guys that want something to look up to, want something to belong to.

W: Do you think there's any kind of activity that could be organized that would take the place of these clubs? Suppose there were some organized sports activities?

N: We tried that once. The Saints in reality was a baseball club, back in the early 50s. . . . We belonged to the Off-the-Street Club. Well, you're born, you're raised in a ghetto-type neighborhood and here you got 10 guys together to play baseball. All of a sudden you've got a little power, you've got 10 or 15 guys together, you've got strength. So they go from being a baseball club to a club, you know, a gang.[5] People call them gangs. I never did myself, I always called them a club. I was talking to a guy today, a Jewish kid from Philadelphia. He told me when he was in high school he tried to have power. He used to run around trying to be tough. And he asked me the difference between his middle-class type thing and our neighborhood. And I says middle-class kids, they steal for a prank. When a ghetto kid steals, he steals to survive. If he whips somebody, he whips him for the power of it. If he carries a gun to shoot somebody, he wants the reputation of it, of being a macho man, a guy what doesn't take no shit from nobody—"Don't mess with Joe, he'll blow you away."

Here Nichols has reiterated his earlier view of the principal reason for engaging in property crime in his neighborhood: finan-

cial gain available on more favorable terms than those inherent in legitimate employment. He viewed as secondary factors the prestige of being a successful thief, the need to belong to a street gang and share in its activities which included crime, and the example of crimes portrayed in the mass media. He largely discounted sociological or psychological theories of personality deviance. Next we asked Nichols why boys joined street gangs, how this might lead to criminal activity, and what had happened to his former fellow gang members.

W: What can a guy do, coming from the kind of neighborhood that you came from?

N: It's hard to say, man, because if you don't belong to a club you're in trouble as it is. Take Dexter and Indiana—that's Aces turf. Take Edwards and Harlow, that's Lords. Mercer and Shepherd—Latin Squares. You've got 14 clubs in one neighborhood, and you don't belong to none of them. You're bound to get hurt on one of them corners. But when you belong to a club, people kind of bypass you. It's either belong or get hurt.

W: Once you're in a club, how does that change your life?

N: Well, it gives you something to swing with, something to hang with, people to call family. Like the Saints, when there was seven of us—that's how many there was at the beginning—and we were all like brothers, and we could count on each other.

W: Do you get involved in crime together?

N: Yes.

W: Suppose that some guy stayed out of all of it. Wouldn't they worry that he'd rat on them?

N: Not if he was one of us.

W: Were there any guys who stayed out of it like that, just because they didn't want to get involved?

N: Yeah, two, . . . three.

W: Okay, what happened to those guys?

N: Nothing ever happened to them. Everybody liked them. But the funny thing about it is, we grew out of it and they grew into it. They became the toughies in Cicero, Illinois. Everybody in their own time wants to get a little power. Thompson grew into a big guy—six foot six, 245. He started bopping heads, he got to like it. So that's what he does now. And now he's the big toughie in the neighborhood, in Cicero. And he's 30 years old.

W: What has happened to guys you've known? You say a lot of guys have been killed.

N: I think out of the original seven Saints, two of them are in the penitentiary, a couple of them are dead, and one of them escaped, that's me. The rest of them were drug addicts. Only one of the seven didn't shoot dope, that was me. The other six were all drug addicts, at the end. They didn't realize that you grow up, that time passes. Frank, Dick—they're always looking back. Dick's 33 now, Frank's 31, Paulson is 30, he's running around the penitentiary yelling "Saint love." He's president of the Saints up there. Frank, he thinks he's back in '67. He still thinks he's Macho Man.

W: Did Dick get involved in drugs, too?

N: Yeah, he was a junkie for a while, and he still deals today. Wally Isabel is doing seven years, . . . murder.

W: How about Steve?

N: Steve Isabel went crazy, he went nutty. Bob Hammerschmidt, he's still on the streets, he's got a job. Dick's a dealer, Frank's a drunk, Paulson's doing six years in the penitentiary.

Lower-Class Value System

We then discussed the prestige value of lucrative criminal activity and of being tough. Nichols had mentioned both values briefly in the earlier interview, and he returned to the issue of retaining these gang-related values in the beginning of this interview, above. Here he elaborates.

W: When the younger kids see all this happening around them, don't they figure they ought to get involved in something else? How can they look up to these guys who come out of the pen?

N: They think it's cool. They want to be a Wild Bill or a Jack Paulson or a tough Dick. They see guys like Dick standing around on a corner, showing their money and everything, and not working. Well, they don't know that Dick's had the same dollar bill in his pocket for years. He takes it out, it cries, it hasn't seen sunlight in so long. When they see this money and they see the power that this guy Bill had, they think it's cool, they think it's worth doing a few years in jail to have this much "prestige." My idol when I was a kid, 11 or 12 years old, was the president of the Saints. He was tough. Got anything he wanted in the neighborhood. The chicks all liked him.

W: Do they still look up to gang leaders?

N: Yeah. I guess they'll always do that.

The preceding passage, with its emphasis on the value of toughness, suggests that these youths are delayed in progressing to other criteria of respect from peers. They remain at the stage of respecting physical prowess. Research indicates that, from preschool to early adolescence, boys in various cultures seem to evaluate each other primarily on the basis of physical prowess such as toughness, attractiveness, and athletic ability.[6] In middle-class late adolescence, however, intelligence and other skills of economic benefit begin to supersede physical traits as the main determinants of males' status with peers of both sexes.[7] Crime-prone adolescents in the United States, then, appear to remain committed to the stage of respecting physical prowess—roughly, machismo. However, it is difficult to act macho as a closely supervised laborer. Therefore, most youths in this economic environment who want to be macho can gain money only by resorting to crime. Jobs offering an opportunity for personal autonomy are seldom available to them.[8]

Nichols's comments on the kind of boys that girls find attractive were of particular interest to us. Our research on middle-class girls[9] indicates that they are attracted to good-looking athletes throughout high school, but that in college they take intelligence and expected earning power into account also. In Nichols's neighborhood few young men are able to parlay their intelligence into steady, substantial financial support of a wife and children. Perhaps as a consequence, the young women remain primarily concerned with a young man's physical characteristics. Their preferences presumably act as powerful factors in shaping the behavior of the young men.

Another well-known side of this subculture is drug use, which we then discussed. Earlier, Nichols had stated that drugs (including alcohol) had played a role in his friends' remaining in the gang way of life. When we returned to the subject, he could name only two or three addicts who had permanently quit using opiates. He then alluded to the prestige value of drugs.

N: A lot of people think that drugs are cool. They all got the same thing, with the pimp walk and their actions. They're always trying to show off in front of each other—"Look at me, man, I done so much a day." It's the same with alcoholics, or the same with a gang member. They all think they're cool, they're super boss, super mellow. I've seen them go up to 40 years like this, 45 years old.

W: Do the girls get involved in drugs too?

N: Oh, yeah, very heavy. $150, $200 a day.

W: What do they do for money?

N: They rip off. Prostitution, boosting, pulling flops, . . . anything they can.

In summary, those youths who engage in crime, according to Nichols, are com-mitted to the street gang value system of violence, drugs, and easy money. Belonging to a gang and engaging in crime in the teen years may be a statistically normal and rational response to the existing incentives and penalties. Available jobs are unappealing to them and, perhaps most important, conflict with the ideal of the independent, carefree tough guy. When these individuals enter adulthood, however, the costs of criminal activity may increase. Criminal sentences become more likely and longer, especially for repeat offenders. Criminal habits presumably become more ingrained. If the individual is married, he usually suffers disproportionately more from imprisonment than does a single man, according to Becker. If he is still single, his macho behavior may be less appealing to women of his age. If he has continued to use opiates, alcohol, or barbiturates, he is liable to become addicted eventually. Thus, behavior that in adolescence is statistically normal and even rational perhaps becomes maladaptive but continues out of habit and out of ignorance of changing costs and benefits.

Nichols's Subsequent History

We then tried to understand why Nichols had succeeded in escaping from a life of crime and associated values.

W: What's happened to you since your gang days?

N: I just finally realized it wasn't where it was at. Being a wild man was played out. I was taking downfalls, I was getting stabbed and shot at. So I figured it was time to quit. I got myself a job and learned an occupation what I can relate to, what I can dig.

W: What job did you get?

N: Roofing.

W: Did you go to work for somebody?

N: Yeah, Jones Roofing Company, on Franklin Avenue.

W: And they hired you even though they knew you had a record?

N: Yeah.

W: Was it hard to get that? Did you know this guy?

N: No, he just hired me as a flunky, a laborer. He just thought I was another guy that would be around for a week or two. Only I started working and I liked it. I got a weird thing in my mind that when you're working in a factory it's like jail. The foremen are guards. They tell you when you can use the bathroom, tell you when you can have a cigarette, tell you when you can sit down. And roofing isn't. Roofing is like you're on your own. No one tells you what to do. You've got your own job, you do it. Might be one foreman for 16, 17 men.

W: How long did you work for this company?

N: A year.

W: Then what happened?

N: I went to work for another company. And then I just took over my own thing, doing little jobs here and there, till I started doing bigger jobs, buying a truck. Bought two trucks. Just kept on.

W: And you hired guys then.

N: Eighty percent of my help was Saints. So in a way I guess I was still president. Here's one of the gang members grew up and hires a bunch of them.

Later in the interview Nichols returned to the theme of macho values. He described an abrupt change in his own value system, whereas most of his former friends remained committed to the macho value system, associated in Nichols's mind with the 1960s.

W: Whatever happened to Ralph?

N: He's a junkie. Stealing stuff. Every one of them are living in the past of 1966. And I was, too, until two years ago. Everything I listened to on television was the Fonz, the old days, *American Graffiti,* the old music, old everything. It was driving my friends nuts. And then one day something changed.

What happened was Ted Sawyer and Frank came to my house. And you know me and them guys was always tight. I was really glad to see them. And Ted came in there and seen my long-haired friends. And right away that was a turn-off to him. He said, "Man, I didn't think you'd ever change." I said, "I haven't changed." He said, "Well, what are you hanging with these guys for?" "They're my friends, that's why." Five minutes after he was there, he showed power. Told Frank to get him some whiskey. Frank said, "What kind do you want?" He said vodka. He said, "Have you got any money for it?" He said, "For that, buy me two bottles and you pay for it." And I just seen that we were no longer alike any more. He was still living back in the 60s and I wasn't. He was still giving the orders, still the big bullshitter, the big he-man. And here he was 30 years old already.

W: What is important to you now?

N: My family, my nieces. They're important to me. . . . I married my wife when she was 16. We've been together ever since. That's another thing that was different between me and the guys. They're all divorced, I'm not. I still love my wife as much as I ever did. . . . Surviving, the honest way. That's important to me. I'd like to work a lot more with kids. Some day in the future, maybe. Every day I see a lot of kids who are still like me. They're still at the same place I was. It never changes. Same people, different faces.

In the earlier interview, Nichols recognized that he never would be able to work for an employer because, as a former convict, he would be the first fired in the event of a layoff. He vowed then to "do my own kind of thing," a remark that also suggests the operation of the lower-class value of autonomy, or "freedom." He has indeed started his own business, a modest but stable one. On the advice of one of the organizers on our research team, he hired an accountant to do his taxes. The fact that most of his workers are former members of his gang suggests that they are not averse to hard work so long as they perceive their supervision to be benign. Recently Nichols, who was virtually illiterate in the old days, began preparing for his high school equivalency test. He also has overcome a serious drinking problem.

We would ascribe Nichols's escape from criminal activities to a combination of factors. He married early and has always been exceptionally devoted to his wife and child. Unlike most of his peers, he had someone to live for. As an unusually intelligent individual, he was able to formulate and to execute a viable financial strategy for himself. He realized that his prison record closed off most opportunities, and that he was temperamentally unsuited for factory work and its close supervision; that is, being autonomous was important to him. By owning his own business, he solved this problem. His leadership qualities enabled him to command the respect of his employees, who were accustomed to regarding him as their superior. Furthermore, for unknown reasons he was able to avoid opiate use and to overcome a drinking problem. Nichols has always been ambitious. Just as he once aspired to be a gang leader, he has now become a respected community spokesman. His self-confidence probably also was instrumental in the development of his economic aspirations and their fulfillment.

Crime Prevention

Nichols had made it clear that he did not believe that prison rehabilitates offenders. We pursued this subject.

W: I take it you don't think too much of putting people in jail and expecting them to come out clean.

N: No. When you went to high school you learned something, otherwise you wouldn't have made it through high school. You learned enough to get you into college and then onward. Well, it's the same thing as a jail. St. Charles Reformatory was grammar school, the county jail was high school, and Stateville is college. Every place you go to you learn something. You might learn how to steal here, and how to burglarize here. You might learn how to stick up here. As you go up, as you go to bigger places, you're going to learn more.

W: And once you've got those tools it seems a short step to try them out.

N: Right. It's natural. You never once think that the guy what taught me this is in Stateville.

W: He's an older guy. . . .

N: Right, you think he knows more than you do, because he got busted at a late age. He's 30 years old and you're 17. He made it all the way to 30. He never told you he'd been busted 10 times before that.

Nichols recalled that as a teenager he had been subjected to *Scared Straight* tactics by the first judge before whom he appeared. Nichols believes that this approach is no panacea. He suggests a more low-key alternative.

W: What about the court system? Do they treat you fairly?

N: Judge Saul Epton was one of the best people I ever met in my life. He was one of the honestest and one of the outspokenest judges I ever met. The rest of them can all be bought, just the same as any lawyer can be hired. You don't think for one minute that when these lawyers go in there and beat crimes like a murder beef where the guy is stone-out guilty with three witnesses against him, somebody's got to be paid someplace.

W: Let's talk about Epton a little bit. I think you said he was pretty strict.

N: Well, if you were guilty he'd let you know about it. But if you were innocent he'd let you know about it, too. I remember he used to sentence guys to one day. One day behind his chair. He would let you listen to all the bullshit he listened to all day long, every day of the year. During a one-day stay behind his chair, you would hear every lie there ever was. You'd find out what everybody had to say, what kind of bullshit story they were telling. And he used to turn around and look at you and say, ''Think he's telling the truth?'' And you didn't know what to say because you might meet this guy in jail some day, so you say, ''Sure.'' And he'd say, ''Bullshit.'' He'd say it just like that: ''Bullshit.'' He'd say, ''He's lying through his teeth.'' Then he had another thing he used to give you, say if you were a new kid, your first time up. He done this to me and my mother. My mother was with me. He says, ''Tom, this is serious. I can't let this bypass. I've got to give you some kind of time.'' Well, I was 15 years old, my heart was beating through my chest. I didn't know what was going on. He gave me a year. He sent me for a year to the county jail. Well, I was 15, I didn't know they couldn't send me to the county jail, that you had to be 17. He had the bailiff take me to the lock-up. I went back there with 50 black guys. He let you sit there, all the way to four o'clock. Then I come back and he says, ''Well, if I let you go right now, think you could change your ways a little bit?'' ''Yeah, yeah, I'll change my ways.'' ''Go on home with your mother.'' After he had me locked up, of course he told my mom, ''Nah, he's not going nowhere. Here, wait in my chambers, give Mrs. Nichols some coffee.'' A lot of kids it helped. Me it didn't.

W: They're trying that approach now.

N: *Scared Straight.* Well, if it helps two kids out of a hundred it's worth it. The inmates are trying to do something for a change, instead of just sitting up letting their time pass.

Nichols then contended that, although having good intentions, the inmates of the state prison in Rahway, New Jersey who tried to frighten young offenders with the realities of prison life could not be succeeding in deterring young offenders from continuing in crime. He said that, once the program had been shown on television, future participants would know that they would not be harmed while visiting the prison and therefore would not be frightened. He also felt that most criminals are not deterred from committing crimes because they do not expect to be apprehended. Nichols offered an alternative approach: a low-key recounting, with photographs, of his own friends' lives and fates.

N: I'd like to get a room and take kids as they come through the police department and say, ''Look, I'm not going to jive you. I'm not here to scare you to death. I want to show you something. If you don't want to listen, take a walk. I'm going to show you kids what was just like you, what never got busted, was never 'scared straight.' I'm going to show you what happened to these kids. Here's kids that never did no big time. But look at them. One died of an O.D. One died in a shooting. One died of this, one died of that.'' And I think they'd relate more to this. Because they're hearing it from somebody what's been through it, and they're seeing it in front of their own eyes. They see he's not trying to scare me, he's not trying to bullshit me, he's giving it to me like it is. It's right here, black and white. Jack Haller, died of an O.D., which he did. He got away with it so long, then he took a fall. These people on TV, I'm not saying they're doing wrong, but I think if you showed them in this way, you'd get a lot more response to it than you would be trying to scare the shit out of them. If you took a kid and just sat down and rapped to him: . . . ''Look, this was my friend and I loved him like a brother but he's dead. This was my friend. He's dead. This is me. This is what I done. This is my record. This is when I quit. And this is what I got now, and this is what I had then.'' I don't think a social worker could do it, I don't think a police officer could do it, I don't think a reverend could do it. A punk like me, what I was, I think I could. What I'm trying to do now is work with the youth as much as I can. I don't give a shit where they come from. If you give them an even break, they'll do you right. That kid that you just seen walk in my house, he's been around me since he was 11. All his friends wound up in the penitentiary. Not Hal. Hal's been around me and listened to a few things I said. He listened because I've been there before, I know what's happening.

Nichols's recommendation, then, is for men such as himself with criminal backgrounds, and hence having credibility with similar young people, to present the alternatives in simple, stark fashion, avoiding recrimination.[10] He is convinced that, in the long run, crime doesn't pay. He was not convinced until he saw friend after friend die or turn into a hopeless addict or alcoholic. He proved to himself, and is proving to his employees and some of the neighborhood youths, that it is possible to escape the criminal life style.

In the earlier interview he maintained that another set of values—perhaps subterranean in these neighborhoods—also exists, one that includes holding a decent job, staying with one's family, and being loyal to friends and community. This is the value system to which Nichols has aspired for at least ten years and which he is now fulfilling. He views crime as a bad bargain in the long run, and believes that few young people are so sociologically or psychologically impaired that they cannot go straight, if they can be made to learn and accept the facts regarding costs and benefits. But he stresses that dismal jobs offering no hope of advancement are not sufficient inducements to avoid crime. He remains convinced, as he stated in the earlier interview, that the existing jobs are unacceptable. He

favors making attractive jobs available and believes they would sell themselves.

W: What about getting people to take straight jobs? Do you think there's a way?

N: Yes, if they're not thrown on them. You remember Artie? He used to be the social worker type. He's a junkie now. He was always telling us we got to get a job. He never once showed us a damned thing. He took us to a job at $1.75 an hour, what he wouldn't touch for nothing. But he expected us to. He expected guys like Ralph to work 40 hours a week and bring home less than $70 and feed his family on it. But he wouldn't do it. And Ralph has the same amount of kids he had.

Nichols's dim view of available employment opportunities agrees with prevailing opinion in his former neighborhood at the time of the organizing project. Youths frequently complained of the poor wages, boredom, hazards, and close supervision of factory jobs.

Conclusion

Nichols's analysis is that the employment opportunities available to youths in many urban areas are insufficiently appealing to compete effectively with the attractions of street crime and its associated value system. In the long run, the criminal life style is usually disastrous, but it does not appear that way initially to the many young people who adopt it. They are impressed with the fast buck, and perceive the available jobs to be boring, dangerous, low paying, humiliating, and dead-end. Nichols believes that young people will respond to reasonable alternatives, that they do not engage in crime out of some personality defect that would be refractory to counseling efforts. Therefore, if the employment opportunities of young people were noticeably improved, fewer individuals would embark on criminal activities, and more would abandon crime at younger ages. In other words, if the differential opportunity structure were altered appropriately, the appeal of legitimate employment would be stronger and that of crime correspondingly weaker.

Nichols's own life provides an encouraging example of the possibility of change. However, he is a very unusual individual. The vast majority of his friends failed to make the transition from the macho, street gang value system and criminal activities to a constructive alternative. Judging from the fates of his friends, the present system of incentives needs correction. That counseling efforts alone are basically ineffectual is suggested by Nichols's dim view of available jobs and by the generally poor record of rehabilitative programs.[11]

Notes

1. Roger Feldman and Glenn Weisfeld, "An Interdisciplinary Study of Crime," *Crime and Delinquency,* April 1973, pp. 150–62.

2. Gary S. Becker, "Crime and Punishment: An Economic Approach," *Journal of Political Economy,* March–April 1968, pp. 169–217. See also Richard Cloward and Lloyd E. Ohlin, *Delinquency and Opportunity* (Glencoe, Ill.: Free Press, 1960), on differential opportunity.

3. Glenn Weisfeld, "An Inside Look at Outside Agitating: Street Gang Organizing in Chicago" (University of Wisconsin, 1972). The organizing project followed the Alinsky model in attempting to work with the indigenous leadership, address concrete grievances rather than stress ideology, and operate on a basis of equality and shared responsibility with community members.

4. One of the better accounts of street gangs, at least insofar as it agreed with most of our own observations, is Lewis Yablonsky's *The Violent Gang* (New York: Macmillan, 1962).

5. Ethel Shanas, *Recreation and Delinquency*, Chicago Recreation Commission (1942), reported a *positive* relation between participation in recreational programs and delinquency among boys in five areas of Chicago.

6. Donald R. Omark, Fred F. Strayer, and Daniel G. Freedman, eds., *Dominance Relations: An Ethological View of Human Conflict and Social Interaction* (New York: Garland,

1980); Glenn E. Weisfeld et al., "Development of Dominance in Boys: Stability, Determinants, Expressions, and Prerogatives of Rank" (in prep.).

7. Ibid.; Ritch C. Savin-Williams, "Dominance Hierarchies in Groups of Middle to Late Adolescent Males," *Journal of Youth and Adolescence,* vol. 9 (1980), pp. 75–85.

8. Walter B. Miller, "Lower Class Culture as a Generating Milieu of Gang Delinquency," *Journal of Social Issues,* vol. 14, no. 3 (1958), pp. 5–19, discusses lower-class values, including toughness and autonomy, as criteria for determining status. Miller's and Nichols's assessments agree very closely.

9. Weisfeld et al., "Development of Dominance in Boys."

10. Henry D. McKay, "The Neighborhood and Child Conduct," *Annals of the American Academy of Political and Social Science,* January 1949, pp. 32–41, made the same recommendation thirty years ago.

11. John J. Conger, *Adolescence and Youth: Psychological Development in a Changing World* (New York: Harper & Row, 1977), p. 586. Henry D. McKay, "Social Influence on Adolescent Behaviors," *Journal of the American Medical Association,* Nov. 10, 1962, pp. 643–49, refers to lack of employment opportunities as the Achilles' heel of existing street work programs making use of the indigenous leadership.

Residence and Territoriality in Chicano Gangs

21

Joan Moore
Diego Vigil
Robert Garcia

Youth gangs are a serious problem in many U.S. cities. Many young Mexican Americans and blacks, in particular, are attracted by the street life and companionship of belonging to a gang, especially in cities with large minority populations. The resulting drug use, minor and serious crime, and friction with schools and law enforcement have stimulated sensational press and television coverage of the problem. In Los Angeles where more than a million Mexican Americans live, Chicano gangs have been isolated from the non-Mexican world for generations.

Although street warfare and gang influence in schools have been a public issue for many years, there is little sociological research on gangs. Members are suspicious and difficult to interview in their natural environments. Furthermore, much of

Reprinted from *Social Problems*, Vol. 31, No. 2, 1983, pp. 182–194, by permission of the Society for the Study of Social Problems and the authors. Copyright © by the Society for the Study of Social Problems.

what public agencies define as "research" is in fact designed to police the streets more effectively or to serve the needs of correctional institutions. The major body of sociological theory about gangs was developed from a world now long vanished—the Chicago of the 1920s. In this paper we show that a key premise of this older work—that gang members all live in the turf they defend—is not true. In Los Angeles, boys from other neighborhoods join Chicano gangs through practices which offer insight into the structure and meaning of the gangs in Mexican American neighborhoods.

In this paper we first discuss this outmoded premise, which is a product of the settlement and assimilation pattern of European ethnics of the early 20th century, and contrast these patterns with those of the Chicano gangs of Los Angeles. Then we discuss our approach to the study of these gangs, fashioned over the course of several research projects. Our findings are concerned with two general issues: how gangs reach outside their neighborhoods to incorporate non-resident members, and how this institutionalized pattern of "fictive residence" affects individual gang members and gang behavior in general. We conclude with a more general discussion of the Chicago ecological model and argue that further insight is needed into the strains of adolescence in the large, stable black and Hispanic slums of modern U.S. cities, which have generated most of the youth gang activity since the Second World War.

Changing Gangs, Unchanging Assumptions

Research on gangs in U.S. cities began with the work of Frederick Thrasher (1927), who studied the Chicago gangs of the 1920s. Two key principles of the so-called Chicago school of sociology were of particular importance for Thrasher, and are especially questionable today. The first was ecological: the Chicago gangs were one aspect of the general "social disorganization" of the central business district and the edge of the Black Belt. Ethnicity was the second principle. "Gangland" was largely an area of first settlement for European immigrants, and the gangs were "one symptom of a type of disorganization that goes along with the breaking up of the immigrant's traditional social system without adequate assimilation to the new" (1927: 217). Thrasher was applying the concepts developed by Thomas and Znaniecki (1959), and when he looked at ethnic gang traditions that had been transplanted from the old country he was applying the concepts developed by Park and Miller (1921). But by far the most important feature of ethnicity for Thrasher was ecological succession, whereby one nationality and its gangs succeeded another, inevitably involving fights between gangs of different ethnicity

(1927:199). Ethnic invasion and succession were, of course, prime concepts of the Chicago school of human ecology.

Both ecology and ethnicity meant that the residence of gang members was not an issue. The gang was a transitory phenomenon: it characterized neighborhoods in transition both residentially and socially, and it was "a manifestation of the period of readjustment between childhood and maturity" (1927:37), or, in other words, it was a feature of adolescence. Thus, the gang disintegrated easily, and "those which endure over a period of years are relatively rare" (1927:37). If the gang is unstable and transitory, then it is not likely to have nonresident members: the gang disintegrates because its ethnic base moves away.

In addition, Thrasher overlooked residence for another reason: emphasis on warring ethnic groups as a source of ganging invariably makes the question of individual residence uninteresting. It is ethnic, rather than territorial, solidarity that prompts a Jewish gang to fight a Polish gang.

Chicano gangs in Los Angeles do not fit these patterns for four reasons:

1. The gangs are long-lasting, not transitory phenomena. They are based in neighborhoods that are scattered all over the metropolitan area, where Chicanos have lived for generations.

2. The gangs are Mexican-American. Unlike European ethnics they have not, as a group, assimilated or faded into the larger U.S. population. Many individuals have assimilated, of course, especially those who lived in the Southwest before the region was annexed by the United States. But many others have not, and retain their ancestral language and features of their culture. Furthermore, immigration from Mexico has never stopped. Chicano neighborhoods have continuously experienced waves of newcomers (Vigil, 1983). With few exceptions, the Chicano communi-

ties of Los Angeles never have been invaded by another ethnic group, nor has another ethnic group succeeded them,[1] nor has there been total cultural disintegration. Instead, there has been more or less continuous immigration of yet more Mexicans, with a reinforcement of some of the traditional culture.

3. Some Chicanos remain members of gangs until middle age.

4. The Chicano settlements of Los Angeles cover such a vast area that fights between neighborhoods generally mean Chicano versus Chicano. Most of the increasingly lethal conflict involves *only* Chicano gangs (Frias, 1982).

Chicano gangs are graded by age, somewhat like some tribal societies described by anthropologists and somewhat like the U.S. school structure. That is, every few years a new *klika,* or cohort, forms in the gang as young, would-be members find themselves rejected by older, existing members, and decide to form their own *klika.* (*Klika* is a slang Spanish word meaning "clique" and we use it to refer to these cohorts throughout this paper.) Each *klika* has a name and a distinct identity, because members of different *klikas* have distinct experiences: when the gangs fight each other, for example, it is actually members of the named *klikas* who are involved. The fight becomes part of the *klika's* special history. Occasionally a member from an older *klika* will help out, but that is rare in street life, though common in adult and youth detention and incarceration settings. Members of each *klika* usually are no more than a few years apart in age. The *klika* is the more intimate membership group. The gang is the larger membership group, but the *klika* is not a separate organization any more than the Yale "Class of '86" is separate from Yale University.

The two gangs we studied, White Fence (WF) and Hoyo Maravilla (HM), are known in the communities as "heavy" gangs with long-established reputations for all the values that Mexican youth gangs are supposed to embody.[2] Both gangs are based in East Los Angeles, which includes pieces of the city of Los Angeles, county areas, and overgrown small towns. In more traditional eastern U.S. cityscapes, East Los Angeles would be the "inner city." Both gangs are surrounded by rival gangs and are among the oldest and most established. Members feel that the two gangs are very different: Hoyo Maravilla is more traditionally Mexican and White Fence is more urbane.[3]

Territory in the Chicano Gangs

Territoriality is generally considered a defining characteristic of youth gangs (Miller, 1975:9). The term implies: (1) that the gang's activities (playing, hanging-out, partying) are concentrated within a "turf"; (2) that the turf is relatively clearly bounded; (3) that the turf is defended against invaders and that fights with other gangs center on intentional invasions of territory; and (4) that members and their families live inside the territory.

Chicano gangs are especially interesting for the study of residence because the gang subculture strongly emphasizes territoriality (Klein, 1968: Moore *et al.*, 1978; Stumphauzer *et al.*, 1977; Torres, 1979). Gang terminology associates membership with residence in the turf. Gang members call each other "homeboys," and the Spanish word for neighborhood (*barrio*) is regularly used to mean "gang." The interchangeability of these terms is important in the gang subculture: a boy is a member of a gang, of a neighborhood, and of a *barrio.* We use this terminology throughout this paper, as in "He belongs to my neighborhood."

But what does territoriality actually mean? Gang members are supposed to be "all for their *barrio*," and this includes the squares (conventional non-gang residents). Gang members feel accepted by the neighborhood: the gang claims to help the elderly and to advise the younger members against taking dangerous drugs or acting excessively "crazy" (Moore *et al.*, 1979).

However, only rarely is the territory of the gang clear. Usually there is a gray area around the heartland or "home base."

> Many of the guys from my clique lived in or around the edges of the *barrio*, from our interpretation of the *barrio*. . . . These boundaries have gray areas, areas claimed by other gangs. For example, the guys from First and Indiana would dispute that we controlled the area around First Street and Lorena. However, we had at least eight guys that lived fairly close to that street corner and it was no matter for dispute with us. . . . Where nothing overlaps in White Fence is the heart of the *barrio*. When a carload of guys comes in *there*, they're looking for a fight. But in the gray areas there were no territory fights, just personal fights (WF Veterano).

This is a behavioral borderland. It is far more ambiguous than is implied by the usual tactic followed, by researchers and by police, of mapping gang territories. This emerged clearly when our respondents named the streets forming the boundaries. In general, respondents agreed, although there were often minor disagreements, even among members of the same *klika*. One member expressed this by distinguishing between behavioral and "official" border streets:

Q: What were the boundaries?
A: Of the neighborhood?
Q: Yeah.

A: Third, Sunol, Atlantic—what boundaries? We used to go all over the place.
Q: Officially?
A: It would be Floral to Third and from Eastern to Rowan, I guess. That was home base and anything after that (HM Santo).

In these Chicano gangs, social and cultural processes expanded the meaning of territory well beyond simple geography. Neighborhood boys share something by virtue of living near one another. But once in the gang, they share something that transcends feelings based on proximity. This obscures the fact that some members live outside the area claimed by their gang. Membership is not based merely on residence, but is seen by active members as permanent and lifelong. It doesn't matter where you live; it's how you act and feel: "Your barrio is in your heart."

> This guy was a hope-to-die, viva White Fence type of person, and I asked about the boundaries, and he said wherever the guys from White Fence live, that's White Fence. I said, "What do you mean?" He said he was living in Maravilla right now and that's White Fence now. And I said, "No wonder you guys from White Fence fight with all of Los Angeles, with that attitude" (Staff member).

Gang members often gave different answers to two related questions. Asked "Where are you from?" they responded with the name of their *barrio* gang. Asked "Where do you live?" they gave their address.[4] They saw this inconsistency as unimportant.

Research Methods and Sources of Data

The authors are a sociologist (Moore), an anthropologist (Vigil), and a former member of the White Fence gang (Garcia). The paper is based on participant observation, extensive field work, and, in particular, a series of funded interview studies which began in 1974 and continued through 1981. Much of the data reported here is drawn from a 1979 study (Moore, 1979) in which we interviewed at least two members of each of the *klikas* of the White Fence (WF) and Hoyo Maravilla (HM) gangs. (The first of these klikas was formed in the late 1930s and the last in the early 1970s, and all are listed in Figure 21.1.) The interviews during the funded project were conducted by hired researchers drawn from older *klikas* of the two gangs studied. This work was done in a research corporation in which community researchers collaborated with an academic staff to focus the research design, determine interview schedules, conduct interviews, and interpret the findings (Moore, 1977).

A side goal of our studies was to develop histories of the two gangs. To that end, we collected a variety of statistics about each *klika*. But not until late in the project did we discover that residence was an issue. After a series of intra-staff discussions, we conducted some limited focused interviewing in 1982 with gang members about the topic. Quotes in the paper are largely from the original interviews in 1979 and are attributed to gang and *klika*, thus: WF Veterano. Other quotations are from members of the project staff and attributed only if relevant.

The relative strengths and weaknesses of our data on residence reflect both its structure and our accidental discovery of it. On the institutional practices that incorporate non-residents into the gang (fictive residence) we have substantial information, just as in any ethnographic study of a well-institutionalized arrangement. But on the second topic of this paper, residential inconsistency, there is less information. Core *barrio* values deny any difference in the be-

havior of residents and non-residents. When we began to pursue this topic with younger gang members in active *klikas*, we rapidly exhausted their capacity to violate their own normal modes of thinking about their homeboys: they *couldn't* answer the questions, because they *didn't* think about people that way. Police and youth-serving agency statistics are useless because gang members habitually lie about personal details, including residence. These are gangs that are continually harassed by police, and *all* members conceal their home addresses. A non-resident, known only by his nickname, easily evades the police by lying.

How Gangs Reach Outside for Members

Klikas vary considerably in their proportion of non-residents (Figure 21.1). But almost every *klika* has some fictive residents and occasionally a majority of the members live outside the *barrio*. There are three reasons for this variation: (1) There are differences in the extent to which the *klika* uses one or another institutionalized tradition of extension of membership. (2) Residents sometimes move away, either because their family moves or, occasionally, they are displaced by ecological changes. (3) There are factional struggles within some *klikas*.

Institutionalized Extension of Membership

Four general traditions guide the admission of non-residents into gangs: kinship; alliance in fights; extension of *barrio* boundaries; and forming branches. The first two are the most important and are gang versions of more general Mexican traditions. The latter two are specific to gangs. We discuss each in turn.

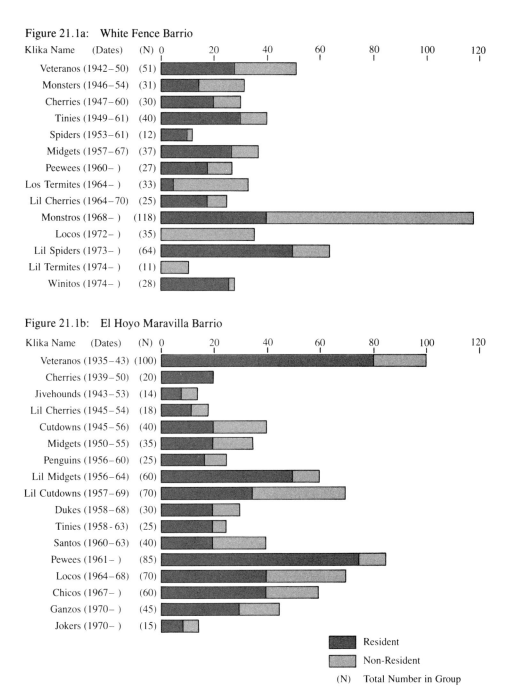

Figure 21.1a: White Fence Barrio

Klika Name	(Dates)	(N)
Veteranos	(1942–50)	(51)
Monsters	(1946–54)	(31)
Cherries	(1947–60)	(30)
Tinies	(1949–61)	(40)
Spiders	(1953–61)	(12)
Midgets	(1957–67)	(37)
Peewees	(1960–)	(27)
Los Termites	(1964–)	(33)
Lil Cherries	(1964–70)	(25)
Monstros	(1968–)	(118)
Locos	(1972–)	(35)
Lil Spiders	(1973–)	(64)
Lil Termites	(1974–)	(11)
Winitos	(1974–)	(28)

Figure 21.1b: El Hoyo Maravilla Barrio

Klika Name	(Dates)	(N)
Veteranos	(1935–43)	(100)
Cherries	(1939–50)	(20)
Jivehounds	(1943–53)	(14)
Lil Cherries	(1945–54)	(18)
Cutdowns	(1945–56)	(40)
Midgets	(1950–55)	(35)
Penguins	(1956–60)	(25)
Lil Midgets	(1956–64)	(60)
Lil Cutdowns	(1957–69)	(70)
Dukes	(1958–68)	(30)
Tinies	(1958-63)	(25)
Santos	(1960–63)	(40)
Pewees	(1961–)	(85)
Locos	(1964–68)	(70)
Chicos	(1967–)	(60)
Ganzos	(1970–)	(45)
Jokers	(1970–)	(15)

Resident

Non-Resident

(N)   Total Number in Group

327

1. *Kinship*: Gang membership is extended easily to relatives who live outside the *barrio*. Following an important Mexican cultural norm, the gang takes on kinlike characteristics, with kinlike norms of mutual obligation among fellow gang members and their families. Many gang members are related. For all gang boys, a "homeboy" (fellow gang member) is the equivalent of a "*carnal*" (or blood brother). When this equation is read backwards (*carnal* = homeboy), the non-resident relatives of the gang members can easily be included if they meet other criteria for membership, especially fighting ability.

Extension through kinship probably is the most common form of fictive residence. This is not surprising because kinship is important for most Chicanos. Large families live in close proximity to cousins and other relatives. When a *barrio* Chicano moves from childhood to adolescence or from adolescence to adulthood his relationships with blood relatives are usually maintained. In addition, the kinlike relationships often are formally and informally extended to non-relatives. [The best-known type of formal extension is the much-described institution of *compadrazgo*. This involves calling a friend to become a *compadre* or *comadre* (coparent) in life events important enough to be marked in religious ceremonies, such as baptism, first communion, and marriage.]

2. *Alliance*: Gangs may also extend membership through alliance. The most common activities of the *barrio* gangs are the same as those of many adolescent friendship groups—partying, hanging around, and getting high on drugs and alcohol—but their defining activities involve fighting, usually with another gang. In essence, the gang is a group of boys who are allied in fights, and boys from other communities may be pressed into service.

Boys from other communities may seek to join a gang because of its behavior or reputation. One non-resident member of the first *klika* of White Fence was "always getting into fights," and found his first gangs to be ineffectual in "backing him up." He was impressed by White Fence. Talking to a resident member of the same *klika* he said, "I used to see you guys walking to pick the guys up. A big, long line of dudes walking up the street. . . . Bobby and Kiki asked me to go down to the neighborhood," and he joined willingly. He had already proved himself in fights, and his reputation led to this invitation.

In a later *klika* of White Fence (the Peewees) procedures had changed, and fighting initiations ("being jumped in") now were graded by the degree of residential association.[5] That is, the *barrio*-born had the mildest initiation, followed by non-residents, and, finally, by members of rival gangs who wanted to switch:

A: The original Peewees, we all lived in the *barrio*. We were originally the kids from the *barrio*.

Q: How about initiation, in order to join White Fence?

A: Different kinds of initiation.

Q: Like what kinds?

A: Like in my case it was a free-for-all. . . .

Q: Is that mostly true with everybody, that's the way they did it?

A: Yeah . . . especially you coming from another *barrio*. Like there was a lot of dudes that were from Marianna and from Varrio Nuevo. Now those were the ones that had problems getting into the neighborhood. Curly 62, we called him 62 because he got in in 1962, that guy got into the neighborhood. They stabbed him and they threw him into the bushes. He wanted to get into the neighborhood but he came from another *barrio*. The dudes that got him in were loaded and they were *muy locos* [crazy], and he kept getting up and he kept saying he was from the neighborhood. They kept getting him in and getting him out and finally they just stabbed him. He got bandaged up, and he came back and he's still from the neighborhood (WF Peewee).

The cultural equivalency assumes that the "original" homeboys, who live in the neighborhood, *can* be relied on to back one another up. An ally, once tested, is by extension also a trustworthy homeboy, even if he doesn't live in the neighborhood. Thus the equation "homeboy = ally" can be read backwards ("ally = homeboy") by decision of the group and after testing.

Klikas normally start with a group of residents, and then extend membership as the boys get into increasingly serious fights in junior and senior high school. Then allies become necessary. Adolescence is a time of social expansion as boys leave the neighborhood elementary school to attend remote junior high schools. For a middle-class boy, the neighborhood and the family decline in importance as the boy finds relationships with peers from new environments. Friendships are based on personal and achieved concerns rather than anchored in ascribed statuses. For a Chicano gang member, however, the kinlike neighborhood increases in importance. The move to junior high school is likely to confirm academic failure for most boys, who leave school as soon as they reach the legal age of 16. These boys develop a "counter-school" subculture, the *barrio*-based gang, which organizes activities that break the "flow of meanings which are unsatisfactory, imposed from above, or limited by circumstances" (Willis, 1981:34). This counter-school subculture is a true alternative culture with its own long-standing traditions and norms. Erlanger (1979:237) argues that this gang subculture grows from the estrangement experienced by Chicano youth, which "fosters a strong identity with the peer group in the immediate neighborhood (*barrio*) because the peer group is the most readily available source of identity. The consequence is a strong consciousness of turf, which in turn greatly increases the potential for conflict and thus for violence."

The principle of alliance in fights is evident. For Chicanos, the adolescent expansion also means moving into potential conflict. Junior high school brings boys into contact with new gangs, each with its own homeboys. A new pecking order is established in sports and other activities. Most Chicano boys evade the gang scene altogether and try to avoid conflicts. Others anticipate the challenge because they are socialized to fight, both by male members of their families and by the older gang boys. In junior high school their psychological well-being depends on their ability to accept challenges or confrontations. Physical survival often means depending on the homeboys.

The equation "ally = homeboy" also explains recruitment in juvenile hall, forestry camps, jails, prisons, and other incarceration settings. A long-established, prestigious gang usually has a few members in any given juvenile facility who depend on each other and on allied gangs for emotional and material support, as well as backup in fights. Boys from neighborhoods without gangs are at a serious disadvantage and form alliances. Gangs in adult prisons profit from an additional member, and sometimes the decision may simply confirm a budding friendship. Such members may or may not reside in the *barrio* when they come out. One of our respondents lived in the neighborhood before prison, but did not join the gang until he was in jail. He lived elsewhere when he came out and "went down to the neighborhood" when he was released because that was the center of his social life with fellow gang members and he considered it his home. As the following quotation shows, the Huero's fate was different, because he was never out of prison long enough to form ties on the street:

> Like Huero from Sotelo [a Chicano neighborhood], I was telling you I got him in, me and Turtle. We beat the shit out of him up there but he was a good dude and he liked it so we got him in. This happened in 1971 when we were in Soledad [prison]. He hasn't been out more than a month since that time, everytime he gets out he goes back in, so nobody knows him out here and he only knows people who are *torcido* [locked up]. . . . All he knows is what we told him. He's from the neighborhood (WF Peewee).

3. *Expansion of boundaries*: The borders of a gang territory may be claimed by several *barrios*, at least in part because members of several gangs live in these disputed areas. Typically, expansion works as follows: as White Fence recruits one or two boys who live a block or so outside one of its boundaries, it becomes more difficult for a rival gang to defend that area. Thus White Fence begins to claim the area as its own. Eventually the rival gang ceases to claim the area and White Fence's boundaries have expanded.

Gangs vary in their expansion possibilities. El Hoyo Maravilla is much more ecologically confined than is White Fence (Moore *et al.*, 1978). The neighborhood is located in a broad *arroyo* (dry river bed). (The word *hoyo* means "hole".) This physical setting means that the Hoyo Maravilla neighborhood is close-knit socially. The gang did not expand beyond the ecological boundaries. Instead, adjacent

small neighborhoods saw new gangs spring up. The generic Maravilla name grew to include some dozen Maravilla gangs, including Arizona Maravilla, Ford Maravilla, Kern Maravilla, and Marianna Maravilla. Mostly these were named after streets, and each territory was quite small, reflecting *barrios* packed tightly, one next to the other. Although there also is a narrow "hole" in the heart of the White Fence neighborhood where gang members often congregate, White Fence has fewer natural boundaries. The gang's territory expanded rapidly to incorporate at least four small neighboring gangs. Expansion feeds on itself. Extension through kinship and alliance enhances the feelings of mutual attachment and the fighting strength of the gang and lets it prosper, thus legitimating more non-residents and further expansion of territory.

4. *Forming branches*: Gangs also extend themselves far from the home *barrio* by forming branches. The branch gang represents a total departure from residence in the *barrio* as a criterion of membership. Both El Hoyo Maravilla and White Fence developed such branches as Chicanos from East Los Angeles moved into new areas, developing parallel forms of organization to those of the old *barrio*. The Locos of White Fence actually live in El Monte, some 15 miles to the east of the White Fence *barrio*. A White Fence Termite was visiting his relatives:

> It was in 1970: I went to my aunt's house in El Monte. I went with my cousin Kiki—he's a Termite too. He's four years older than I am; he lived there [in El Monte]. The guys from El Monte were kind of straight. And then they saw us, it was like a different thing. . . . When they saw us they liked our ways. The *gavacho* [Anglo people] was always pushing them around; we made the *gavachos*

run from us. After hanging around with us they wanted to get into White Fence. Finally, they couldn't be from the Termites and the Monsters[6] . . . so we started a different clique—the Locos. We jumped them: they were the Locos (WF Termite).

Like the Westside White Fence, a similar group, the Locos commute to the "old *barrio*" for many activities. This poses some problems for the resident members:

The Locos, they come to the *barrio*, and there's a lot of them because they come in three or four car loads. . . . We don't even know half of them but they all say they're from the neighborhood, and they all got White Fence [tattoos] on their hands and arms. They all got a big White Fence, but they got Locos on the bottom (WF Peewee).

Barrio tatoos mark many gang members. In the above example, the addition of "Locos" beneath the White Fence tattoo marks a *klika* that is existentially but not spatially part of the White Fence *barrio*.

Noninstitutionalized Extension of Membership

Three other processes increase the proportion of non-residents in any gang *klika*. They are less important as *barrio* institutions but they may seriously tip the composition of the membership. These are: moves out of the *barrio* for family reasons; moves to make way for public improvements; and factional struggles within the *klikas* themselves.

1. *Family moves*: East Los Angeles is an area of poor families. Because few residents own their own homes, families move frequently. When a gang member moves he has, realistically, only two options: to retain membership in his original gang and

rely on his friends to protect him from the gang in his new residence, or to quit the old and join the new gang. There may be good reason to do the latter: a new neighborhood may pose problems for the entire family, not only for the gang member.

Well, the girls are up for grabs because the guys don't respect the son. And it also might jeopardize the younger sons, who might join the new neighborhood and get involved in fights, and it makes it harder to get a job from the locals if somebody in the family is from a different *barrio* (WF Veterano).

That is, the sisters of the gang boy moving into a hostile neighborhood are vulnerable, as are his brothers because of hostility from the gang in the neighborhood. Many boys decide to stay with the old gang, rather than join a new one.

A: In order to get out of the *barrio*, either you get out with broken bones or stab wounds, because you're not just going to walk out of the *barrio*.
Q: Why?
A: Because if you go to another *barrio* and say, "*Sabes que* I was from White Fence and *sabes que* they didn't fix shit; I got out of White Fence, they didn't do me *madre*," you know, *pero* we're going to leave them some scars to remember the *barrio*. It's not just a name, White Fence. It's something to be proud of (WF Lil Termite).

2. *Ecological displacements*: Historical events alter the basic ecology of a neighborhood and push many families out of the *barrios*. Five freeways have cut through the *barrios* of East Los Angeles since the early 1940s, in each case displacing large numbers of families. Renovations and neighborhood improvements also displace families: in the mid-1960s several blocks in the heart of Hoyo Maravilla were elimi-

nated in order to build a park and a county service center. Moves for these reasons may account for lower proportions of resident members in some of the *klikas* active in the 1960s:

> At that time that we're talking about, from 1960 to 1963, the park wasn't there at the time. . . . The Long Beach Freeway wasn't built either. . . . In about 1966 or 1967, a lot of the homeboys' families were moving out (HM Santo).

3. *Factional struggles*: Special circumstances may greatly affect the membership of a *klika*. Two extreme cases appeared in our data: there are two *klikas* in White Fence (Los Termites and the Lil Termites) with few or no members of the *klikas* actually living in the *barrio*.

Los Termites broke up after two of their leaders had a fight. About half went to the Peewees, and the rest started a new gang, Lil Inez. This presented a problem to the rest of the neighborhood:

> [The Peewees] told them to think about it, that they had to get into the neighborhood or break up and not be from anywhere. But there couldn't be any other *barrio* in our *barrio* but White Fence. So they said OK, but . . . we're going to start our own clique. . . . So they decided to call themselves the Lil Cherries after the Big Cherries. So that was when the Lil Cherries started. . . . [Los Termites started up again] in 1966 or 1967. The Termites, Jesse Termite and them, started up the Termites from White Fence again, and that's still going to now, 1979 (WF Peewee).

There was substantial flux in the largest *klika* of White Fence (the Monstros) and the Lil Termites were carved out of the Monstros when:

Joker and them decided that they were badder than some of the Monstros and they started their own clique. They chose their own *vatos* [guys] to start into the Lil Termites (WF Winito).

Thus, both Los Termites and the Lil Termites were secessionist *klikas*. Members were recruited by individualistic and more violent ("badder") leaders. In view of our hypotheses about nonresidence and conflict, it is not surprising that these two *klikas* include more nonresidents.

Fictive Residence: Strains and Consequences

Fictive residence is an institutionalized pattern in Chicano gangs, and is firmly grounded in general features of Mexican American culture. But the pattern creates serious strains, both for the individual nonresident member and for the gang as a whole. This section deals with these individual strains, which we call residential inconsistency, following the lead of sociologists who have explored the effects of other kinds of status inconsistency, such as blue-collar workers with college educations. In tracing these ideas, we are combining observations with hypotheses, and we are primarily concerned with the increase in violence.

We have observed that gangs will admit non-residents who are good fighters, and—at least in theory and according to the group norms—will then treat them like any other homeboy. But gang theory and gang norms do not overcome the fact that, to the resident members, the non-resident remains an outsider to some extent. Paradoxically, any resident of the *barrio* who can fight can get into the gang, but only an *exceptional* non-resident can do so. If he is a relative of one of the members, the non-resident may be able to offset this handicap by claiming a legitimate right to membership, but the boy without relatives must be both an exceptionally good fighter and also exceptionally committed to the fighting ideal.

Once admitted to the gang, the nonresident is more subject to question than the resident; as a result, the nonresident overcompensates (Short and Strodtbeck, 1963). He must continue to prove that he is reliable. He is tested in normal *barrio* fights and he is also routinely tested verbally, in joking fashion:

> A friend of ours moved from our neighborhood [Kern Maravilla] to Ford [another Maravilla gang]. It was just a couple of blocks away, but he had to be backed up, walked home. He was not accepted by Ford—he can't get in even if he wants to. But in Kern, we're capping on him, we're teasing him for being "from Ford," acting like one of them (Member of Kern Mara).

He is made to feel less of a member, and behavioral consequences follow:

> That makes him mad, and more than ever determined to prove he's from Kern. He becomes more boisterous, starts fights on the playground, at dances (Member of Kern Mara).

At times a resident sponsor may be called upon again. When (as a non-resident member of White Fence reported) "people talked about throwing me out," his fighting achievements permitted resident members to act as his advocates.

Chicano gangs are too aggressive to permit members to withdraw as a way of coping with the strain of living in one gang neighborhood and allying oneself with another. Boys who leave the gang are typically "jumped out" (exit fight, counterpart of initiation fight). There is, however, a special status which permits gang members to move relatively freely between neighborhoods: *Tecatos* (addicts) are exempted from fights because they are considered unreliable. This may be a fringe benefit of heroin use, which is considered by social theorists to be a form of general retreat from all social reality.

There are five reasons why overcompensating boys value their membership more highly than do residents:

1. The kinlike quality of the gang may be particularly attractive to boys from troubled families who are looking for a family-like supportive network. Analysis of data on 83 men who had been members of White Fence and Hoyo Maravilla showed that non-residents were no more likely to have lived in a broken family than residents. But family breakup is not the only family trouble; less extreme disruptions included a family member going to prison. Many gang members reported that their families moved frequently, sometimes more than once a year. Such instability disturbs children, even without other troubles.
2. The nonresident gang member knows that he is to some extent exceptional; it is what he has done, rather than a simple matter of residence, that has allowed his membership. This may enhance his self-esteem: he is special to at least one group of people that matter to him.
3. Because the nonresident member is continually tested, he also must continually question his desire to belong. Resident members have fewer occasions to question their membership.
4. When a nonresident boy goes "down to the neighborhood" he is happy to be back and often in the mood to recreate the peak experiences that form the basis of his memories of the *barrio*, especially parties and fights. He avoids the boring and routine aspects of daily *barrio* life.
5. He is also freer than the resident boy to recreate those peak experiences. His parents are not nearby. The police don't know where he lives. Thus, the temptation to do what he wants is increased.

This has three consequences for the gang as a whole:

1. A *klika* with a high proportion of nonresident members may engage in more conflicts. Even if a *klika* tries to keep conflict down and control the nonresident members, widespread residential inconsistency weakens the territory-based clarity of the distinction between members and nonmembers. The blurring of the social boundary may lead the group to re-establish its boundaries through conflicts with other groups (Coser, 1956; Simmel, 1955). Boundary maintenance is, of course, one of the functions of conflict.
2. Nonresident members may generate conflict. Several men mentioned that nonresident members are escorted back to their homes to see if the boy is jumped. This can be interpreted as provocation for a fight.
3. Nonresident members can avoid gang retaliations. The Lil Termites of White Fence seceded from the Monsters because "they thought they were badder." None of those boys lived in White Fence. If in fact they were "badder," they would surely have brought new troubles to the White Fence neighborhood. If Arizona Maravilla nonresident boys raided Lote Maravilla, the act called for revenge. But the Lote boys don't know how to find the actual raiders so they "go down to the neighborhood" and take vengeance on whoever they happen to find there. In late 1982, this led to the shooting of four Arizona boys who were not even members of the gang. The Arizona nonresidents escaped.

Issues in Research on Minority Gangs

Residence was not an issue in gangs of the 1920s because of the nature of ethnicity and of Chicago and other eastern and midwestern cities. Ethnicity and the city have changed since then. The gangs have changed, too. At the beginning of our research we followed the usual assumption that residence was not an issue; questions on residence were almost an afterthought. When we found that many members lived outside the *barrio* we realized that minority urban ghettoes and *barrios* have changed drastically in recent decades, and that modern gangs are overwhelmingly minority (Miller, 1975). When a "Jew from Twelfth Street" (a Thrasher gang of Chicago) moved in the 1920s, his family was likely to move west a few miles to Lawndale to "escape the ghetto" (Wirth, 1928:127). "Escaping the ghetto" usually meant escaping the gang scene. But a Chicano from White Fence now usually moves to another neighborhood in the large segregated Chicano area of Los Angeles, where there is another long-standing gang. It is not easy to "drop out" of the gang scene altogether.[7] The Los Angeles Chicano gangs form a system—they are old and well-established features of stable slums; and they are very much aware of one another.[8] This system is an aspect of the institutionalization of the gangs and institutionalization can develop only when there are long-standing stable slums.

A territorial home allows the alternative culture of the gang a place for symbolic elaborations. Gang territory is the scene of conflicts and competition, and the locus of the gang's mythology. A child inevitably becomes aware of the neighborhood gang. Its alternative subculture is highly visible. Territoriality also has implications in terms of class analysis. Poor Chicanos have far less personal space at home than middle-class boys. Homes are smaller and more crowded. Often there is little or no private space, and the Los Angeles climate permits year-round outdoor activity. Public space for small or large groups becomes "owned" or "their (collective) property" (Malmberg, 1981:83). Ownership is a strong principle in U.S. society, and particularly valued among

Chicanos. The gang's "ownership" of the nearby playground provides a symbolic participation in a value from which they may otherwise be excluded.

Residential inconsistency is widespread among Chicano gangs and, perhaps, among all minority youth gangs in large urban ghettos. Institutional management of residential inconsistencies adds up to what we call fictive residence. These arrangements, in turn, permit the gangs to function more effectively in painful status passages during adolescence and adulthood.[9] Nonetheless, institutional management does not eliminate the strains of residential inconsistency. The strains occur on both the individual and group level and may be related to the accelerating levels of violence.

These patterns are rooted in cultural norms that are distinctly Chicano and relate to some special features of Los Angeles's ecology. Urban gangs of other ethnic backgrounds may draw on different cultural practices to manage these tensions, and the particular features of a city's climate and minority ecology may be important. The long efforts of gang researchers to delineate general, universal features of youth gangs has been fruitful, but our analyses show that new efforts to understand the ecological and minority-subcultural context of variations are long overdue.

Notes

1. The rare exceptions to this general rule in Los Angeles tend to be in areas like Watts. Here blacks displaced Chicanos, ending all Chicano gangs.

2. These are the actual names of the gangs. Members were opposed to disguising the names, and followed the findings of our studies with great interest. See Moore (1979) on the importance of feedback to research respondents.

3. See Moore et al. (1978) for a discussion of the dimensions of variation in gangs and on the representativeness of these two.

4. Alfredo Gonzales, June 2, 1982: personal communication.

5. We have no way of telling how widespread this "graded initiation" was. In at least one instance, the remnants of a defeated gang were incorporated with no initiation.

6. That is, according to the norms of the gang, they could not join either of the active White Fence klikas.

7. When Suttles (1968) examined residence as a criterion for membership in adolescent street-corner groups, he correctly pointed out its precariousness compared with other criteria. His Addams community in Chicago was much like Thrasher's gangland, and a family move usually meant that the boy quit the group. Interestingly, the only group whose members were largely non-residents of the hangout area was also the most combative, and the only one among the groups which referred to its hangout as "turf." But Suttles' boys were not typical of gang members surveyed by Miller (1975): they were not living in segregated ghettoes.

8. Cloward and Ohlin (1960) ignored the ecological aspect of the minority community and its implications for juvenile delinquency. While they note that "the experience of the Negroes may not directly parallel that of other groups before them" (1960:202), they do not develop the point. Their predictions might have been different if they had not ignored ecological factors altogether.

9. Moore et al. (1978) and Horowitz (1982) are among the few researchers to look at the functions of neighborhood gangs in adulthood.

References

Cloward, Richard A., and Lloyd Ohlin. Delinquency and Opportunity: A Theory of Delinquent Gangs. New York: The Free Press, 1960.

Coser, Lewis. The Functions of Social Conflict. New York: The Free Press, 1956.

Erlanger, Howard. "Estrangement, machismo, and gang violence." Social Science Quarterly 60(2):235–248 (1979).

Frias, Gus. Barrio Warriors: Homeboys of Peace. Los Angeles: Diaz Publications, 1982.

Horowitz, Ruth. Honor and the American Dream. New Brunswick, New Jersey: Rutgers University Press, 1982.

Klein, Malcom W. Street Gangs and Street Workers. Englewood Cliffs, New Jersey: Prentice-Hall, 1968.

Malmberg, Torsten. Human Territoriality. The Hague: Mouton Publishers, 1980.

Miller, Walter B. Violence by Youth Gangs and Youth Groups as a Crime Problem in Major American Cities. Washington, D.C.: U.S. Department of Justice, National Institute for Juvenile Justice and Delinquency Prevention, 1975.

Moore, Joan W. "The Chicano Pinto Research Project: A case study in collaboration." Journal of Social Issues 33(2):144–158 (1977).

_____."Feedback of research results." Paper presented at the Conference on Ethics and Fieldwork, Coolfont, Virginia, October 13, 1979.

Moore, Joan W., et al. Homeboys: Gangs, Drugs, and Prison in the Barrios of Los Angeles. Philadelphia: Temple University Press, 1978.

_____.A Model for Chicano Drug Use and for Effective Utilization of Employment and Training Resources by Barrio Addicts and Ex-Offenders. Los Angeles: Chicano Pinto Research Project, 1979.

Park, Robert E., and Herbert Miller. Old World Traits Transplanted. New York: Harper, 1921.

Short, James F., and Fred L. Strodtbeck. "The response of gang leaders to status threats: An observation on group process and delinquent behavior." The American Journal of Sociology 68(5):571–579 (1963).

Simmel, Georg. Conflict and the Web of Group Affiliations. New York: The Free Press, 1955.

Stumphauzer, Jerome S., Thomas W. Aiken, and Esteban V. Veloz. "East Side Story: Behavioral analysis of high juvenile crime community." Behavioral Disorders 2(3):76–84 (1977).

Suttles, Gerald. The Social Order of the Slum. Chicago: University of Chicago Press, 1968.

Thomas, William I., and Florian Znaniecki. The Polish Peasant in Europe and America. Volume 2. New York: Dover, 1959 [1918–20].

Thrasher, Frederic M. The Gang. Chicago: University of Chicago Press, 1927.

Torres, Dorothy M. "Chicano gangs in the East L.A. barrio." California Youth Authority Quarterly 32(3):207–222 (1979).

Vigil, James D. "Chicano gangs: One response to Mexican urban adaptation." Urban Anthropology (forthcoming).

Willis, Paul. Learning to Labor. New York: Columbia University Press, 1981.

Wirth, Louis. The Ghetto. Chicago: The University of Chicago Press, 1956 [1928].

PART 6

The Juvenile Justice System

Every state in the United States has a juvenile code and specialized court structure that deals with the problems of children and youth in trouble with the law. However, there are more than three thousand juvenile court jurisdictions around the country (Krisberg et al., 1984), and these systems are not standardized or uniform, but vary from one place to another. Moreover,

> delinquency and status offense cases represent only a portion of the total workload of juvenile courts. Most juvenile courts also handle a variety of matters pertaining to the welfare of children. Cases involving dependency and neglect (where parents or guardians have failed to provide adequate care for children) as well as cases of suspected child abuse generally are handled in juvenile courts. In addition, the legal activities involved in adoptions, in setting and enforcing child support orders which result from divorce, and in hearing requests for the termination of parental rights are generally the responsibility of juvenile courts (Waegel, 1989:153–4).

The Stages of Juvenile Justice

In spite of this diversity, it is possible to make some generalizations regarding the stages of the system through which juveniles are processed. While juveniles may be referred to the juvenile court from parents, school authorities, and other sources, most (more than 70 percent) are referred by the police (Snyder et al., 1985).[1] However, at every stage, including the police stage, juveniles are screened out of the system and are either released outright or diverted to some alternative agency for assistance. Figure P6.1 illustrates some of the options available to the police. About one-third of the cases handled by the police do not result in referral to the juvenile court (Waegel, 1989).

Following police or other referral to the juvenile court, a youth goes through the *intake* stage. At intake, a juvenile is screened by an intake officer who deter-

Figure P6.1 The Juvenile Justice System

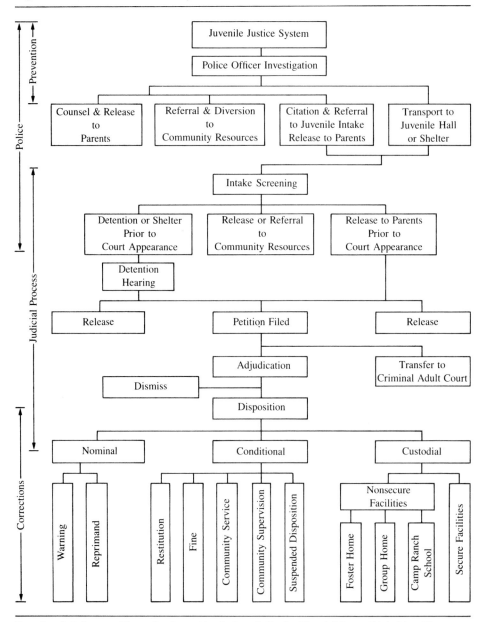

From *Juvenile Delinquency: Theory, Practice, and Law* by Larry J. Siegel and Joseph J. Senna, Third edition, West Publishing Company, 1988, p. 335. Reprinted by permission of West Publishing Company.

mines whether the youth should be released, handled through alternative or informal means, or required to appear at a formal hearing before a juvenile court judge. Over one-half of all juveniles who are referred to intake are processed without the filing of a formal petition that would require court appearance. However, many of these youths must admit to the charges and agree in writing to meet the conditions of an *informal disposition*, such as a requirement to receive counseling, or a formal petition will be filed at a later date (Creekmore, 1976). Juveniles may also be released at the intake stage if there is insufficient evidence or legal criteria to maintain court jurisdiction.[2] For those youths who remain under the jurisdiction of the court, most are released into the custody of their parents while waiting to appear before a judge, but about 20 percent of youth processed at intake are held in *detention* or preventive custody (Snyder et al., 1985). In most jurisdictions, decisions to detain youth must be reviewed by a judge at a detention hearing. Figure P6.1 illustrates some of the alternatives available at the intake stage of juvenile court screening.

After a petition is filed, the juvenile appears before a judge for an *adjudication* hearing. At the beginning of the hearing, the judge asks the juvenile if he or she admits or denies the petition—in essence, if he or she pleads guilty or not guilty. In most cases, the juvenile admits to the charges in order to make a favorable impression on the judge (Emerson, 1969; Fox, 1977). Nearly two-thirds of youth who appear before a judge are adjudicated "delinquent" or found to be "in need of supervision." Some cases are dismissed because of insufficient evidence. Others are held in abeyance pending completion of an informal disposition ordered by the judge. If a juvenile does not meet the terms of the informal disposition, the youth will be brought back before the judge to be formally adjudicated.

Juvenile justice statutes in most states also contain provisions whereby serious juvenile offenders (usually fourteen years of age or older) can be transferred to an adult criminal court for prosecution.[3] As a result of the U.S. Supreme Court decision of *Kent v. U.S.* (383 U.S. 541, 1966), youth are entitled to be represented by an attorney at a *waiver* hearing where the presiding judge must provide justification for waiving juvenile court jurisdiction.

After a youth is adjudicated delinquent or found to be "in need of supervision," the judge must make a determination as to the *disposition* or sentence. Typically, a probation officer makes a recommendation based on criteria such as the youth's prior record, family situation, and school performance. At an ensuing disposition hearing, the judge generally follows the probation officer's recommendations (Ariessohn, 1972). Figure P6.1 illustrates some of the dispositional alternatives available to the court that vary in degrees of seriousness. Nominal dispositions are limited to a warning or official reprimand, conditional dispositions involve some type of community supervision (such as probation) or participation in a community-based program, and custodial dispositions may occur in nonsecure or secure settings.

Due Process Rights for Juveniles

In the first section of the book, we noted that the philosophy of informality (*parens patriae*) associated with the early juvenile courts was a means by which the state expanded its jurisdiction over an increasing number of juveniles without providing them with constitutional due process protections against unfair governmental intrusion into their lives. The problems associated with this system came to a head in the 1960s following a number of United States Supreme Court decisions that expanded the rights of adult criminal defendants.[4]

The landmark U.S. Supreme Court decision regarding the rights of juveniles came in the 1967 case of *In re Gault* (387 U.S. 1). Binder et al. (1988:250–1) summarize the case:

> Fifteen-year-old Gerald Gault and a friend were arrested by a deputy sheriff in Gila County, Arizona, on the basis of a complaint by a neighbor . . . about a telephone call that involved lewd and indecent remarks. . . . When arrested for the call, Gault was under probation as a result of . . . having been in the company of another boy who had stolen a wallet. After his arrest, Gault was taken to a detention home where he was kept for several days. His parents were not notified of the arrest, of his custody in the home, or of a petition filed with the juvenile court for an initial hearing. In a subsequent adjudicatory hearing, Gault and his parents were not formally notified of the charges against him, there was no right to counsel, there was no right to confrontation and cross-examination (the offended woman never even appeared at the hearing), there was no privilege against self-incrimination (Gault's admissions of guilt were accepted with an absence of procedural safeguards), and there was no right either to a transcript of the proceedings or to appeal to a higher court in Arizona. As a result of the . . . hearing, Gault was committed to an institution for six years.

Binder et al., note that the maximum penalty for an adult committing a similar offense was a fine of $50 or a jail term of not more than two months.

Gault and his parents appealed the case, which eventually reached the U.S. Supreme Court. In its decision, the Court ruled that the Due Process Clause of the Fourteenth Amendment applied to delinquency proceedings that could result in institutional commitment. In particular, the Court ruled that under such circumstances juveniles should be granted:

> the right to an adequate notice of charges, the right to counsel, the right to confront and cross-examine witnesses, the right against self-incrimination, the right to a

transcript of the proceedings, and the right to appellate review (Thornton et al., 1987:313).

Although the Court in subsequent decisions was willing to expand the rights of juveniles in other areas of law (see Appendix 2), it did not desire to abolish entirely the *parens patriae* philosophy of the juvenile court. In its 1971 decision of *McKiever v. Pennsylvania* (403 U.S. 528), the Court ruled that juveniles did not have a constitutional right to a trial by jury (although individual states could grant this right if they so desired). In its decision, the Court argued that a jury trial was not necessary for a fair and equitable hearing and that granting juveniles this right ''would transform the juvenile court system into an adversary process and spell the end of the *parens patriae* doctrine'' (Thornton et al., 1987:314).

While Gault and other decisions have made juvenile justice professionals more cognizant of due process issues (Binder and Binder, 1982), most observers question its impact on providing juveniles with equal protection under the law. For instance, Lefstein et al. (1969) found that juveniles and their parents were often discouraged from exercising their right to an attorney and were not informed of their right to a court-appointed attorney if they could not afford one. Juveniles were also not informed of their privilege against self-incrimination, and judges often did not dismiss cases when key witnesses failed to appear. More recent studies found that juveniles generally waived their right against self-incrimination (Grisso, 1981), and that less than 50 percent were represented by counsel (Bortner, 1982; Clarke and Koch, 1980; Feld, 1984). Feld (1988) found that large, urban states were much more successful than midwestern states in providing juveniles with the right to counsel, and that within states there was considerable county-by-county variation in legal representation, with ranges from over 90 percent to less than 10 percent (Feld, 1984). He considered several possible explanations for the frequently low representation by attorneys:

> parental reluctance to retain an attorney; a judicial encouragement of and readiness to find waivers of the right to counsel in order to ease administrative burdens on the courts; a continuing judicial hostility to an advocacy role [for attorneys] in a traditional, treatment-oriented court; or a judicial predetermination of dispositions with nonappointment of counsel where probation is the anticipated outcome (p.395).

Discretion and Intervention

At each point in the juvenile justice process, beginning with referral by the police, through intake, adjudication, and disposition, authorities make discretionary decisions and choose among a variety of alternatives. Such discretion is inevitable when decision-makers apply general rules pertaining to juvenile law (both substantive and procedural) to specific, concrete cases. Juvenile justice officials are not "decision-making automatons . . . with little latitude for subjective judgments" (Waegel, 1989:130).

One of the most important issues in the sociology of juvenile justice involves the question of how these discretionary decisions are made. Are they made largely on the basis of legal variables such as the seriousness of the offense and the prior record of the juvenile? Or are they based on social variables or extra-legal factors such as race, class, gender, or other criteria?

In the first reading in this section, Ronald Berger (Chapter 22) provides a succinct review of research that has examined the role of "Legal and Extra-Legal Factors in Police and Court Processing of Juveniles." In the next article, Carl Werthman and Irving Piliavin's ethnographic study of "Gang Members and the Police" (Chapter 23) discusses in more detail the phenomenon of police discretion and juveniles' perception of this discretion. In the third selection, Robert Emerson's ethnography, "Judging Delinquents" (Chapter 24), considers how court personnel attempt to distinguish cases of genuine "trouble" that require official intervention from cases that do not require "doing something" with the juvenile. Emerson discusses how denunciations and defenses of youths' moral character become important in the determination of juvenile court decisions.

Next, Lee Ann Osbun and Peter Rode's "Prosecuting Juveniles as Adults: The Quest for 'Objective' Decisions" (Chapter 25) examines the decision-making process in a study of juveniles who were waived to adult court. They review the rationale, history, and trends of the waiver procedure, and present the results of research that illustrates the difficulty of developing objective criteria upon which to transfer juveniles to adult court. Their study raises questions about whether the waiver procedure is producing its intended effects, that is, removing from juvenile court jurisdiction the most serious and dangerous offenders who are beyond the rehabilitative capabilities of the court (see Bortner, 1986; Bishop et al., 1989).

The last two articles in this section focus on the disposition of juveniles in institutional and community settings. Berry Feld's "A Comparative Analysis of Organizational Structure and Inmate Subcultures in Institutions for Juvenile Offenders" (Chapter 26) evaluates different organizational structures and treatment modalities that are used in juvenile correctional institutions and their effect on both the staff and inmates. In particular, Feld demonstrates that correctional institutions which emphasize treatment over custody, especially those which utilize group-oriented strategies, are better able to reduce the violence that occurs in the inmate subculture.

In "Juvenile Diversion: A Look at the Record" (Chapter 27), Kenneth Polk examines the effects of community-based *diversion* alternatives to official juvenile court processing. As originally used, diversion had two meanings: diversion *away* from the official justice system and diversion *to* an alternative community treatment program (Billington et al., 1978). However, Siegal and Senna (1988:441–2) suggest that the concept of diversion "implies more than simply screening out" individuals from the juvenile justice system.

> *Screening* involves abandoning efforts to apply any coercive measures to a defendant . . . [whereas] *diversion* encourages an individual to participate in some specific program or activity by express or implied threat of further prosecution (see Nejelski, 1976).

The shift away from diversion and toward community alternatives began in the late 1960s as a result of growing criticism of secure juvenile correctional facilities (Lerman, 1984). For instance, the President's Commission on Law Enforcement and the Administration of Justice (1967:7) noted that:

> Institutionalization too often means storage—isolation from the outside world—in an overcrowded, understaffed, high-security institution with little education, little vocational training, little counseling or job placement or other guidance upon release.

Moreover, a number of exposés of so-called juvenile reformatories and training schools (i.e., juvenile prisons) found deplorable physical conditions and abusive treatment of inmates by staff (NBC, 1971; Sorrentino, 1975; Teeters, 1950; Wooden, 1976). These included overutilization of solitary confinement, physical punishment and psychological intimidation of inmates by staff, and unhealthy living conditions. In addition, as Feld discusses in his article (Chapter 26), weaker inmates were exploited and victimized by stronger inmates (see Bartollas and Sieverdes, 1981). These criticisms were coupled with the arguments of labeling theorists that official intervention in the lives of juveniles made matters worse by negatively labeling or stigmatizing youth, facilitating the development of a delinquent self-image, and exposing less serious juvenile offenders to more hardened criminals (see Lemert, 1951, 1971; Mahoney, 1974; Schur, 1971, 1973).

Encouraged by monetary incentives provided through the federal Juvenile Justice and Delinquency Prevention Act of 1974, state and local governments increased their commitment to funding community-based diversion alternatives to secure correctional institutions for juveniles (Binder et al., 1988). In his article (Chapter 27), Polk reviews arguments made by contemporary proponents of community diversion programs, and presents his own critique of the way diversion has been generally practiced in the U.S. Polk is concerned that many diversion programs have been ineffective in reducing delinquency, that diversion has "widened the net" of social control over juveniles who might otherwise have been released, and that juveniles have been coerced into participation without adequate due process protections.

Notes

1. These and subsequent figures are averages derived from aggregate U.S. data (see Snyder et al., 1985; Waegel, 1989).

2 Prosecutors in some jurisdictions are becoming more involved in the intake process to provide for early legal review of cases in the event that youths intend to deny the charges when they appear before a judge (Rubin, 1980).

3. See Hamperian et al. (1982) or Siegal and Senna (1988) for the minimum age of waiver in the 50 states.

4. "The court ruled, among other things, that the Constitution protected adult citizens from unreasonable search and seizure (*Mapp v. Ohio*, 1961), afforded accused persons the right to an attorney (*Escobedo v. Illinois*, 1964; *Gideon v. Wainwright*, 1963), prohibited cruel and unusual punishment (*Robinson v. California*, 1962), allowed citizens the privilege against self-incrimination *(Wong Sun v. U.S.*, 1963), set down guidelines concerning pretrial identification (*Gilbert v. California*, 1967; *U.S. v. Wade*, 1967), specified stop-and-frisk practices (*Terry v. Ohio*, 1968), and established proper warnings to be given prior to a custodial investigation (*Miranda v. Arizona*, 1966)" (Thornton et al., 1987:311).

References

Ariesohhn, R.M. 1972, "Offense v. offender in juvenile court." *Juvenile Justice* 23:17–22.

Bartollas, C. and C.M. Sieverdes. 1981. "The victimized white in a juvenile correctional system." *Crime and Delinquency* 27:534–43.

Billington, B., J. Sprowls, D. Katkin, and M. Phillips. 1978. "A critique of diversionary juvenile justice." *Crime and Delinquency* 24:59–71.

Binder, A. and V.L. Binder. 1982. "Juvenile diversion and the constitution."*Journal of Criminal Justice* 10:1–24.

Binder, A., G. Geis, and D. Bruce. 1988. *Juvenile Delinquency: Historical, Cultural, Legal Perspectives.* New York: Macmillan.

Bishop, D.M., C.E. Frazier, and J.C. Henretta. 1989. "Prosecutorial waiver: Case study of a questionable reform." *Crime and Delinquency* 35:179–201.

Bortner, M.A. 1986. "Traditional rhetoric, organizational realities: Remand of juveniles to adult court." *Crime and Delinquency* 32:53–73.

————. 1982. *Inside a Juvenile Court: The Tarnished Ideal of Individualized Justice.* New York: New York University Press.

Clarke, S.H. and G.G. Koch. 1980. "Juvenile court: Therapy or crime control, and do lawyers make a difference?" *Law and Society Review* 14:263–308.

Creekmore, M. 1976. "Case processing: Intake, adjudication and disposition." Pp. 119–50 in R. Sarri and Y. Hasenfeld (eds.), *Brought to Justice? Juveniles, the Courts, and the Law.* Ann Arbor, MI: National Assessment of Juvenile Corrections, University of Michigan.

Emerson, R.M. 1969. *Judging Delinquents.* Chicago: Aldine.

Feld, B.C. 1988. "*In re Gault* revisited: A cross-state comparison of the right to counsel." *Crime and Delinquency* 34:393–424.

_____. 1984. "Criminalizing juvenile justice: Rules of procedure for juvenile court." *Minnesota Law Review* 69:141–276.

Fox, S.J. 1977. *The Law of Juvenile Court in a Nutshell.* Second edition. St. Paul, MN: West.

Grisso, T. *Juveniles' Waiver of Rights: Legal and Psychological Competence.* New York: Plenum.

Hamperian, D., et al., 1982. *Youth in Adult Courts.* Washington, DC: U.S. Government Printing Office.

Krisberg, B., P. Litsky, and I. Schwartz. 1984. "Youth in confinement: Justice by geography." *Journal of Research in Crime and Delinquency* 21:153–81.

Lefstein, N., V. Stapleton, and L. Teitelbaum. 1969. "In search of juvenile justice: *Gault* and its implementation." *Law and Society Review* 3:491–62.

Lemert, E. 1971. *Instead of Court: Diversion in Juvenile Justice.* Washington, DC: U.S. Government Printing Office.

_____. 1951. *Social Pathology.* New York: McGraw-Hill.

Lerman, P. 1094. "Child welfare, the private sector, and community-based corrections." *Crime and Delinquency* 26:281–98.

Mahoney, A.R. 1974. "The effect of labeling upon youths in the juvenile justice system: A review of the evidence." *Law and Society Review* 8:583–614.

NBC. 1971. *This Child is Rated X* (film documentary).

Nejelski, P. 1976. "Diversion: The promise and the danger." *Crime and Delinquency* 22:393–410.

President's Commission on Law Enforcement and Administration of Justice. 1967. *Task Force Report: Juvenile Delinquency and Youth Crime.* Washington, DC: U.S. Government Printing Office.

Rubin, H.T. 1980. "The emerging prosecutor dominance of the juvenile intake court process." *Crime and Delinquency* 26:299–318.

Schur, E.M. 1973. *Radical Non-Intervention: Rethinking the Delinquency Problem.* Englewood Cliffs, NJ: Prentice-Hall.

_____. 1971. *Labeling Deviant Behavior: Its Sociological Implications.* New York: Harper and Row.

Siegal, L.J. and J.L. Senna. 1988. *Juvenile Delinquency: Theory, Practice, and Law.* Third edition. St. Paul, MN: West.

Snyder, H.N., J.L. Hutzler, and T.A. Finnegan. 1985. *Delinquency in the United States—1982.* Pittsburgh: National Center for Juvenile Justice.

Sorrentino, J.H. 1975. *The Concrete Cradle.* Los Angeles, Wollstonecraft.

Teeters, N.K. 1950. "Institutional treatment of juvenile delinquents." *Nebraska Law Review* 29:577–604.

Thornton, W.E., L. Voight, and W.G. Doerner. 1987. *Delinquency and Justice.* Second Edition. New York: Random House.

Waegel, W.R. 1989. *Delinquency and Juvenile Control: A Sociological Perspective.* Englewood Cliffs, NJ: Prentice-Hall.

Wooden, K. 1976. *Weeping in the Playtime of Others: America's Incarcerated Children.* New York: McGraw-Hall.

Legal and Extra-Legal Factors in Police and Court Processing of Juveniles

22

Ronald J. Berger

In the introduction to this section of the book, I noted that authorities make discretionary decisions at every stage in the juvenile justice system, and that one of the central areas of sociological research on juvenile justice involves the question of how these discretionary decisions are made. Are these decisions made on the basis of legal variables such as the seriousness of the offense and the prior record of the juvenile? Or are they based on social variables or extra-legal factors such as race, class, gender, or other criteria?

In this chapter, I review research that has examined the impact of legal and extra-legal factors on police and court processing of juveniles. Much of the research, particularly studies regarding bias against individuals of certain race or class backgrounds, has produced inconsistent results, making it difficult to develop generalizations that apply to different jurisdictions around the country. Most observers would probably agree that the seemingly contradictory findings reflect actual differences among different departments in different jurisdictions

(see Binder et al., 1988; Dannefer and Schutt, 1982; Empey, 1982; Smith et al., 1980; Stapleton et al., 1982; Thornton et al., 1987; Waegel, 1989). Juvenile justice systems are not standardized or uniform, but vary from one place to another. Moreover, the inconsistent research findings may also stem, in part, from differing time frames of studies (e.g., pre-*Gault* vs. post-*Gault* era), as well as from various methodological issues related to how variables are operationalized, what variables (if any) are used as statistical controls, and what types of statistical analyses are employed (Dannefer and Schutt, 1982; McCarthy and Smith, 1986).

The Police

Much of the research on juveniles and the police has focused on the criteria used by police to make decisions regarding whether or not to arrest or release with only a reprimand or warning juveniles who are suspected of violating the law. Research has indicated that most juvenile encounters with the police (excluding traffic offenses) were initiated in response to a citizen complaint. Most of these encounters involved less serious offenses, with only 5 to 10 percent involving felonies. While arrest was "virtually automatic" with felonies, "informal resolution" was the norm in the remaining cases (Waegel, 1989:132; see Black and Reis, 1970; Empey, 1982; Lundman et al., 1978).

As indicated above, the evidence regarding race and class bias in police decisions to arrest juveniles has been mixed. While black juveniles have been more likely than whites to be arrested, most observers explain this in terms of black youths' greater involvement in serious crime and prior arrest records (see Black and Reiss, 1970; Elliott and Ageton, 1980; Hindelang, 1978; Lundman et al., 1978; Terry 1967a; Weiner and Willie, 1971). In an oft-cited study, Lundman et al. (1978:88) also attributed "the higher arrest rate of black juveniles to the more frequent presence of black complainants who lobby for formal police action" (see Black and Reiss, 1970; Hohenstein, 1969; Smith and Visher, 1981). Thus, the conventional sociological wisdom suggests that evidence regarding discrimination by police toward black youth is weak (Griswold, 1978; Lundman et al., 1978; Waegel, 1989).

On the other hand, a number of studies have pointed to a racial bias in arrest decisions in some jurisdictions while taking into account the seriousness of offending and prior record of black and white youths (Dannefer and Schutt, 1982; Ferdinand and Luchterhand, 1970; Piliavin and Briar, 1964; Sampson, 1986; Smith and Visher, 1981; Thornberry, 1973).[1] Dannefer and Schutt (1982) found racial bias related to the proportion of the population that belonged to a minority group. They argued that as a minority group's presence increased, police may have greater fear of residents "getting out of their place" (p. 1115; see Groves and Rossi, 1971). However, Binder et al. (1988:283) concluded that "while there does seem to be differential disposition of youths on the basis of race in some departments, there is no evidence that it is a common or widespread phenomenon."

Like the evidence on race, the research on social class bias in police processing of juveniles has been inconsistent (see Polk et al., 1974; Shannon, 1963; Terry, 1967b; Williams and Gold, 1972). However, in an important study, Sampson (1986:876) found that social class, as measured by neighborhood socioeconomic status, had an "inverse effect on police contacts independent of actual law-violative behavior as measured by self-reported delinquency." Moreover, this relationship persisted while controlling for "prevalence, frequency and type of delinquency, race, family structure, delinquent peers, and gang membership."

Sampson argued that the police do, in fact, behaviorally orient themselves to patrolling in lower class communities, and officers view youth in lower class areas as more prone to delinquency than youth in higher class areas (see Garrett and Short, 1975; Irwin, 1985; Werthman and Pilivan, 1968). However, Sampson (1986:877–8) emphasized that:

a large part of any effect of individual SES on arrests is spurious and reflects an ecological bias in police perceptions rather than a bias directed solely at lower-class juveniles in actual police encounters. . . . The police may be equally likely to arrest juveniles given an encounter for a particular offense, but are more likely to detect offenses and initiate encounters in contexts where youths are more heavily scrutinized (see Morash, 1984).

In addition, lower-class areas have a more active street life than middle-class communities, largely because residents have less access to private space (Irwin, 1985; Stinchcombe, 1963).[2] "Since the regulation of public places is a central task of policing, . . . people in lower-class areas are subjected to greater surveillance" (Sampson, 1986:878). These processes ultimately translate into a greater likelihood of lower-class youth to accumulate a prior record of offending. Thus, research which finds that prior record predicts likelihood of subsequent arrest ignores the possibility that earlier biases may affect later outcomes whether or not bias is present in these later situations (see Dannefer and Schutt, 1982; Farrell and Swigert, 1978; Liska and Tausig, 1979).

Gender is another social variable that has been examined in studies of police decision-making. There is some evidence that girls have been the beneficiaries of police "chivalry" when they displayed traditional gender role characteristics, appeared to "know their place," and were "apologetic, submissive, and deferential" to the police (Waegel, 1989:137). These females were more likely to receive preferential treatment than females who were less traditional in their demeanor (Visher, 1983; see Kruttschnitt, 1982). On the other hand, while some females were treated more leniently than males for criminal offenses, they were treated more severely for status offenses (Chesney-Lind, 1987; McFachern and Bauzer, 1967; Teilmann and Landry, 1981). In these circumstances, police may have felt that further intervention was necessary to "help the girl" and prevent her from getting into further trouble (Waegel, 1989:137). Girls were also victims of a "double standard" insofar as boys were expected to "sow their wild oats" while

girls were expected to show restraint, particularly with regard to sexual matters (Chesney-Lind, 1977, 1989). Moreover, police arrest of female status offenders appears to have reflected parental preferences for legal assistance in controlling daughters more than sons.

In addition to social factors related to race, class, and gender, studies have also shown that a youth's demeanor plays an important role in police decisions, especially in the absence of clear-cut evidence linking a youth to the offense in question (Lundman et al., 1978).[3] The conventional sociological wisdom suggests that youths who are overly disrespectful or unusually respectful have a greater probability of being arrested. The higher arrest probability for the unusually respectful (the "Eddie Haskel syndrome") is best explained by the suspicion aroused in police who perceive the insincerity of this display of deference (Cicourel, 1968; Lundman et al., 1978; Piliavan and Briar, 1964; Smith and Visher, 1981; Werthman and Piliavan, 1967).

One reason for variation in police practices from one jurisdiction to the next is that few police departments have written guidelines for the handling of juveniles (Klein et al., 1975; Wilbanks, 1975). This heightens "the influence of informal intradepartmental and personal forces on decision making" (Binder et al., 1988:275). Departments vary by different "operating codes" or "organizational styles" of policing (Wilson, 1968). For instance, departments that operate according to a "legalistic style" adopt a more professional or "by the book" approach that results in higher arrest rates but which minimizes discretion and bias. On the other hand, "watchman style" departments emphasize the maintenance of order that can often be accomplished without resort to arrest, but which also gives officers more discretionary authority that results in greater bias or discriminatory treatment of certain groups of juveniles.[4]

The Juvenile Court

In addition to research on the police, numerous studies have examined discretionary decisions at the intake and disposition stages of the juvenile justice system. At the intake stage, the intake officer must decide whether to release a juvenile, refer him or her to another agency, or file a petition for formal court processing. Over one-half of the cases handled at intake are resolved without filing of a formal petition (Snyder et al., 1985). At the disposition stage, the judge, who takes into account a probation officer's recommendation, must decide whether to grant an adjudicated youth probation or other community supervision, or send the youth to a secure correctional facility. Over 60 percent of adjudicated youth are released on probation (Snyder et al., 1985).

Studies of legal and extra-legal influences on intake and disposition decisions have produced results parallel to those of police processing of juveniles. For instance, research findings have been inconsistent regarding the effect of race and class, with no "predominant pattern of discrimination" (Binder et al., 1988:300; Smith et al., 1980). Some studies found evidence of racial bias against minorities (Arnold, 1971; Bell and Lange, 1985; Fagen et al., 1987; Frazier and Bishop, 1985; Liska and Tausig, 1979; Reed, 1984; Thomas and Cage, 1977; Thornberry, 1973; Thornberry and Christenson, 1984), while others did not (Bailey and Peterson, 1981; Carter, 1979; Chused, 1979; Cohen and Kluegal, 1978; Ferdinand and Luchterhand, 1970; Horwitz and Wasserman, 1980a, 1980b; Kowalski and Rickicki,

1982; Meade, 1974; Phillips and Dinitz, 1982; Terry 1967a, 1967b).[5] Scarpitti and Stephenson (1971:148) actually found harsher court dispositions for whites because "black boys had to exhibit a much greater degree of delinquency commitment before the most punitive alternative was selected." Dannefer and Schutt (1982) found evidence of racial bias, but much less so than at the police stage. They suggested that racial bias may decrease at the later stages of juvenile justice processing as police "bias may be compensated for, to some extent, by the courts" (p. 1113). Palazzari (1982) found such compensation at intake, where black youths were more likely than whites to be released. However, for those who remained in the system, blacks received harsher treatment at the disposition stage. Other studies also found black youths more disadvantaged at the later stages of the system, suggesting that as the cohort of processed offenders becomes more homogeneous with respect to legal criteria, the influence of extra-legal factors increases (Bishop and Frazier, 1988; Fagan et al., 1987; McCarthy and Smith, 1986).

Similarly, some studies found lower-class youth receiving harsher treatment at the intake and disposition stages (Carter, 1979; Sampson, 1986; Scarpitti and Stephenson, 1971; Thomas and Cage, 1977; Thornberry, 1973), while others did not (Clark and Koch, 1980; Cohen and Kluegel, 1978; Horwitz and Wasserman, 1980a, 1980b; Meade, 1974; Phillips and Dinitz, 1982). Carter and Clelland (1979) found evidence of class bias only for less serious offenders. Findings were also inconsistent over whether class bias increased or diminished at later stages in the system (see Palazzari, 1982; McCarthy and Smith, 1986).

The findings on gender and juvenile court processing have been similar to those on gender and the police.[6] Although several studies did not find gender a significant factor in intake and dispositions decisions (Bortner et al., 1985; Carter, 1979; Dannefer and Schutt, 1982; Horwitz and Wasserman, 1980a, 1980b), others suggested that girls were treated more severely than males for status offenses but less severely for criminal offenses (Boisvert and Wells, 1980; Chesney-Lind, 1977, 1987; Datesman and Scarpitti, 1977, Empey, 1982).[7] One study did find that black females were given more severe court dispositions than white females (Datesman and Scarpitti, 1977).

With regard to legal factors, the most consistent finding across all jurisdictions has involved the influence of a juvenile's prior record on intake and court decisions (Smith et al., 1980).[8] On the other hand, offense seriousness has appeared to be less related because of variations across jurisdictions over how various offenses are treated (Smith et al., 1980). For instance, in some jurisdictions, status offenders have had a high probability of being retained because of their adverse family situations (see Binder et al., 1988; Smith et al., 1980; Waegel, 1989).[9]

Just as different organizational styles influence police processing of juveniles, varying juvenile court philosophies affect the relative influence of legal and extra-legal factors on intake and court dispositions. Juvenile court philosophies range from a more informal *parens patriae* or treatment orientation to a more formal or legalistic one (Stapleton et al., 1982). The former may emphasize social criteria (e.g., family background, school achievement) in evaluating a youth's behavior, while the latter may focus on legal issues (e.g., prior offenses, whether there is sufficient evidence to convict). Some studies have found that variables related to a juvenile's family life and school and employment record were used by officials to decide whether an offense was "a direct manifestation of a delinquent character and thus a sign of future trouble, or simply incidental to a juvenile's character and thus unlikely to occur again" (Liska and Tausig, 1979:203; see Arnold, 1971; Carter, 1979; Clarke and Koch, 1980; Cohen and Kluegel, 1978; Horwitz and Wasserman, 1980a, 1980b; Needleman, 1981; Scarpitti and Stephenson, 1971; Smith et al., 1980).

In addition, Hasenfeld and Cheung (1985) identified a number of other factors that influenced juvenile court decisions. At intake, for instance, the likelihood that juveniles would be held for formal court processing was increased if there was pressure from the referral agency (e.g., police, school). On the other hand, the likelihood of formal processing was decreased if the juvenile court was part of a "court of general jurisdiction rather than a court of limited jurisdiction" (p. 806). Because they have appellate review, courts of general jurisdiction tend to adopt a more legalistic orientation. Such courts are:

> less likely to process formally cases lacking legal merit and more inclined to process them nonjudicially, thus freeing themselves of . . . [appellate] review. Moreover, courts of general jurisdiction encounter more diverse cases and must establish priorities and are more likely, therefore, to use nonjudicial handling to screen out 'minor' cases (pp. 806-7).

Hasenfeld and Cheung also found that the likelihood of formal processing was less in communities with greater economic resources, higher volumes of referrals, and more available youth services. As for judges' dispositional decisions, juveniles received harsher sentences from judges who were elected (as opposed to appointed) and lighter sentences from judges who focused on "due process" issues. Presumably, elected judges were more sensitive to public demand to "crack down" on juvenile crime, while due process judges were concerned with protecting the rights of juveniles.

Finally, a number of studies on the representation of juveniles by attorneys in the post-*Gault* era found that juveniles represented by counsel actually received more severe dispositions than juveniles who were not represented (see Feld, 1988, for a review). Feld considered several possible explanations for these findings:

> Attorneys in juvenile court . . . [may be] incompetent and prejudice their clients' case . . . Public defender offices . . . [may] in many jurisdictions assign their least capable lawyers or newest staff attorneys to juvenile courts to get trial experience. . . . Court-appointed counsel may be beholden to the judges who select them and more concerned with maintaining an ongoing relationship with the court than vigorously protecting the interests of their clients. . . . It may be that presence of lawyers antagonizes traditional court judges. . . . It may be that early in a proceeding, a juvenile court judge's greater familiarity with a case may alert him or her to the eventual disposition that will be imposed and counsel may be appointed . . . [only in cases] of more severe consequences. . . . [Or] judges may treat more formally juveniles who appear with counsel . . . [and] may feel less constrained when sentencing a youth who is represented (pp. 405, 419–20).

Conclusion

The interaction between legal and extralegal variables is complex and it is difficult to tease out their relative effects at different points in the police and court processing of juveniles. Moreover, the complexity of the interdependence may be lost by focusing on one only decision point at a time, as has been the case with many studies (McCarthy and Smith, 1986).[10] Analyses of the juvenile justice process become particularly difficult if one is trying to pinpoint whether bias or discrimination occurs at particular stages and for particular types of offenses (Fagan et al., 1987). For instance, Feyerherm and Pope (1988:5) suggest some different possibilities:

1. When discrimination exists, it may be present at any decision-making point in the juvenile justice system. It may exist at one point in some jurisdictions and [at] a wholly different point in other jurisdictions.
2. Discrimination may be accomplished by either large differences in processing at . . . one stage in the system, or (more likely) by . . . accumulations of relatively small differences in processing, with a net effect which is relatively large.
3. Because each jurisdiction may specify many of its own rules and practices, the search for discrimination may require identifying possible jurisdictions for more intense scrutiny. Each locality in essence has its own version of the juvenile justice system and they [each] behave differently.

In any case, it is clear that legal factors alone cannot explain how youths are processed through the juvenile justice system. Analyses that take into account the extralegal or social factors that influence the discretionary decisions of juvenile justice authorities are necessary if one really wants to understand how the system operates.

Notes

1. Fagan et al. (1987) found that police were more likely to arrest minorities, except for crimes of violence.

2. Juveniles were especially likely to be arrested when they were found associating with delinquent peers (Morash, 1984).

3. Younger offenders were also found to be treated more leniently than older offenders (Goldman, 1963; Williams and Gold, 1972).

4. Wilson also identified "service style" departments that may be found in middle-class communities. The relative absence of serious crime in these areas reduces police reliance on arrest as a means to resolve problems and increases their service, social welfare, or guidance function.

5. Most studies, with the exception of Bortner and Reed (1985) and Frazier and Cochran (1986), did not find racial bias in decisions to detain youth prior to adjudication (Coates et al., 1975; Cohen and Kluegel, 1979; Dungworth, 1977; Fenwick, 1982; McCarthy, 1985; Pawlak, 1977).

6. Studies of the influence of age on intake and dispositional decisions have produced mixed results (see Carter, 1979; Chused, 1973; Cohen, 1975; Ferster and Courtless, 1971; Terry 1967a, 1967b).

7. Girls were also more likely than boys to be placed in detention for status offenses (Chesney-Lind, 1977; Cohen and Kluegel, 1979; Pappenport and Young, 1977; Pawlak, 1977; Sarri, 1974).

8. In addition to the race and class studies cited above, which also examined prior record, see Dungworth (1977), Fenwick (1982), Needleman (1981), and Rosen and Carl (1974). For reviews, see Binder et al., (1988), Smith et al., (1980), and Waegel (1989). Prior record also appears to have been important in decisions to place juveniles in detention (Bailey, 1981; Cohen, 1975; Pawlak, 1977; Summer, 1971).

9. Seriousness of the offense was also not related to detention decisions (Pawlak, 1977; Sumner, 1971).

10. For instance, detained youth received more severe dispositions than nondetained youth (Bailey and Peterson, 1981; Chused, 1973; Clarke and Koch, 1980).

References

Arnold, W. R. 1971. "Race and ethnicity relative to other factors in juvenile court dispositions." *American Journal of Sociology* 77: 211-7.

Bailey, W. C. 1981. "Preadjudicatory detention in a large metropolitan juvenile court." *Law and Human Behavior* 5:19-43.

Bailey, W. C. and R. D. Peterson. 1981. "Legal versus extra-legal determinants of juvenile court dispositions." *Juvenile and Family Court Journal* 32:41-59.

Bell, D. and K. Lang. 1985. "The intake disposition of juvenile offenders." *Journal of Research in Crime and Delinquency* 22:309-28.

Binder, A., G. Geis, and D. Bruce. 1988. *Juvenile Delinquency: Historical, Cultural, Legal Perspectives.* New York: Macmillan.

Bishop, D. M. and C. S. Frazier. 1988. "The influence of race in juvenile justice processing." *Journal of Research in Crime and Delinquency* 25:242-63.

Black, D. J. and A. J. Reiss, 1970. "Police control of juveniles." *American Sociological Review* 35:63-77.

Bortner, M. A. and W. L. Reed. 1985. "The preeminence of process: An example of refocused justice research." *Social Science Quarterly* 66:413-25.

Carter, T. J. 1979. "Juvenile court dispositions." *Criminology* 17:341-59.

Carter, T. J. and D. Clelland. 1979. "A neo-

Marxian critique, formulation and test of juvenile dispositions as a function of social class." *Social Problems* 27:96–108.

Chesney-Lind, M. 1989. "Girls' crime and woman's place: Toward a feminist model of female delinquency." *Crime and Delinquency* 35:5–29.

_____. 1987. "Female offenders: Paternalism reexamined." Pp. 114-39 in L. L. Crites and W. L. Hepperle (eds.), *Women, the Courts, and Equality.* Newbury Park, CA: Sage.

_____. 1977. "Judicial paternalism and the female status offender: Training women to know their place." *Crime and Delinquency* 23:121–30.

Chused, R. 1973. "The juvenile court process: A study of three New Jersey counties." *Rutgers Law Review* 26:488–615.

Cicourel, A. V. 1968. *The Social Organization of Juvenile Justice.* New York: Wiley.

Clarke, S. H. and G. G. Koch. 1980. "Juvenile court: Therapy or crime control, and do lawyers make a difference?" *Law and Society Review* 14:263–308.

Coates, R. B., A. D. Miller, L. E. Ohlin. 1975. *Juvenile Detention and Its Consequences.* Cambridge, MA: Center for Criminal Justice, Harvard University School of Law.

Cohen, L. E. 1975. *Delinquency Dispositions: An Empirical Analysis of Processing in Three Juvenile Courts.* Washington, DC: U.S. Government Printing Office.

Cohen, L. E. and J. R. Kluegel. 1979. "The detention decision: A study of the impact of social characteristics and legal factors in two metropolitan juvenile courts." *Social Forces* 58:146–61.

_____. 1978. "Determinants of juvenile court dispositions: Ascriptive and achieved factors in two metropolitan courts." *American Sociological Review* 43:162–76.

Dannefer, D. and R. K. Schutt. 1982. "Race and juvenile justice processing in court and police agencies." *American Journal of Sociology* 87:1113–32.

Datesman, S. K. and F. R. Scarpitti. 1977. "Unequal protection for males and females in the juvenile court." Pp. 59-77 in T. N.

Ferdinand (ed.), *Juvenile Delinquency: Little Brother Grows Up.* Beverly Hills, CA: Sage.

Dungworth, T. 1977. "Discretion in the juvenile justice system: The impact of case characteristics on prehearing detention." Pp. 19–43 in T. N. Ferdinand (ed.), *Juvenile Delinquency: Little Brother Grows Up.* Beverly Hills, CA: Sage.

Elliott, D. S. and S. S. Ageton. 1980. "Reconciling race and class differences in self-reported and official estimates of delinquency." *American Sociological Review* 45:95–110.

Empey, L. T. 1982. *American Delinquency: Its Meaning and Construction.* Second edition. Homewood, IL: Dorsey.

Fagin, J., E. Slaughter, and E. Hartsone. 1987. "Blind justice? The impact of race on the juvenile process." *Crime and Delinquency* 33:224–58.

Farrell, R. A. and V. L. Swigert. 1978. "Prior offense record as a self-fulfilling prophecy." *Law and Society Review* 12:437–53.

Feld, B. C. 1988. "*In re Gault* revisited: A cross-state comparison of the right to counsel." *Crime and Delinquency* 34:393–424.

Fenwick, C. R. 1982. "Juvenile court intake decision-making: The importance of family affiliation." *Journal of Criminal Justice* 10:443–52.

Ferdinand, T. and E. Luchterhand. 1970. "Inner-city youth, the police, the juvenile court, and justice." *Social Problems* 17:510–27.

Ferster, E. Z. and T. F. Courtless. 1971. "The intake process in the affluent county juvenile court." *Hastings Law Journal* 22:1127–53.

Feyerherm, W. and C. E. Pope. 1988. "Minority youth and the juvenile justice system: A critical review of the evidence." Paper presented at the conference of the American Society of Criminology, Chicago.

Frazier, C. E. and D. M. Bishop. 1985. "The pretrial detention of juveniles and its impact on case dispositions." *Journal of Criminal Law and Criminology* 76:1132–52.

Frazier, C. E. and J. C. Cochran. 1986. "Detention of juveniles: Its effects on subsequent juvenile court processing decisions." *Youth and Society* 17:286-305.

Garrett, M. and J. F. Short. 1975. "Social class and delinquency: Predictions and outcomes of police-juvenile encounters." *Social Problems* 22:368-83.

Goldman, N. *The Differential Selection of Juvenile Offenders for Court Appearance.* New York: National Research and Information Center, National Council on Crime and Delinquency.

Griswold, D. 1978. "Police discrimination: An elusive question." *Journal of Police Science and Administration* 6:65-6.

Groves, W. E. and P. H. Ross. 1971. "Police perceptions of a hostile ghetto." Pp. 175-91 in H. Hahn (ed.), *Police in Urban Society.* Beverly Hills, CA: Sage.

Hasenfeld, Y. and P. P. L. Cheung. 1985. "The juvenile court as a people-processing organization: A political economy perspective." *American Journal of Sociology* 90:801-24.

Hindelang, M. J. 1978. "Race and involvement in common law personal crimes." *American Sociological Review* 43:93-109.

Hohenstein, W. F. 1969. "Factors influencing the police disposition of juvenile offenders." Pp. 138-49 in T. Sellin and M. E. Wolfgang (eds.), *Delinquency: Selected Studies.* New York: Wiley.

Horwitz, A. and M. Wasserman. 1980a. "Formal rationality, substantive justice, and discrimination." *Law and Human Behavior* 4:103-15.

————. 1980b. "Some misleading conceptions in sentencing research." *Criminology* 18:411-24.

Irwin, J. 1985. *The Jail: Managing the Underclass.* Berkeley, CA: University of California Press.

Klein, M. W., S. L. Rosenzweig, and R. Bates. 1975. "The ambiguous juvenile arrest." *Criminology* 1:78-89.

Kowalski, G. S. and J. P. Rickicki. 1982. "Determinants of postadjudication dispositions." *Journal of Research in Crime and Delinquency* 19:66-83.

Kruttschnitt, C. 1982. "Women, crime and de-

pendency: An application of the theory of law." *Criminology* 21:417-37.

Liska, A. F. and M. Tausig. 1979. "Theoretical interpretations of social class and racial differentials in legal decision-making for juveniles." *Sociological Quarterly* 20:197-207.

Lundman, R. L., R. E. Sykes, and J. P. Clark. 1978. "Police control of juveniles: A replication." *Journal of Research in Crime and Delinquency* 15:74-91.

McCarthy, B. R. 1985. "An analysis of detention." *Juvenile and Family Court Journal* 36:49-50.

McCarthy, B. R. and B. L. Smith. 1986. "The conceptualization of discrimination in the juvenile justice process: The impact of administrative factors and screening decisions on juvenile court dispositions." *Criminology* 24:41-64.

McEachern, A. W. and R. Bauzer. 1967. "Factors related to disposition in juvenile police contacts." Pp. 148-60 in M. W. Klein and B. G. Myerhoff (eds.) *Juvenile Gangs in Context: Theory, Research and Action.* Englewood Cliffs, NJ: Prentice-Hall.

Meade, A. 1974. "Seriousness of delinquency, the adjudicative decision, and recidivism—A longitudinal configuration analysis." *Journal of Criminal Law and Criminology* 64:478-85.

Morash, M. 1984. "Establishment of a juvenile record: The influence of individual and peer group characteristics." *Criminology* 22:97-112.

Needleman, C. "Discrepant assumptions in empirical research: The case of juvenile court screening." *Social Problems* 28:247-62.

Palazzari, T. A. 1982. *The Impact of Race and Socioeconomic Status on Juvenile Court Dispositions.* Unpublished master's thesis, University of Wisconsin, Milwaukee.

Pappenfort, D. M. and T. M. Young. 1977. *Use of Secure Detention for Juveniles and Alternatives to Its Use.* Washington, DC: Law Enforcement Assistance Administration, Office of Juvenile Justice and Delinquency Prevention.

Pawlak, E. J. 1977. "Differential selection of juveniles for detention." *Journal of Re-*

search in Crime and Delinquency 14:152–65.

Phillips, C. D. and S. Dinitz. 1982. "Labeling and juvenile court dispositions: Official responses to a cohort of violent juveniles." *Sociological Quarterly* 23:267–79.

Piliavin, I. and S. Briar. 1964. "Police encounters with juveniles." *American Journal of Sociology* 70:206–14.

Polk, K., D. Frease, and L. Richmond. 1974. "Social class, school experience, and delinquency." *Criminology* 12:84–96.

Reed, W. L. 1984. *Racial Differentials in Juvenile Court Decision-Making: Final Report*. Washington, DC: U.S. Department of Justice, National Institute for Juvenile Justice and Delinquency Prevention.

Rosen, L. and C. Arlene. 1974. "The decision to refer to juvenile court for a judicial hearing." Pp. 154–66 in M. Reidel and T. Thornberry (eds.), *Crime and Delinquency: Dimensions of Deviance*. New York: Praeger.

Sampson, R. J. 1986. "Effects of socioeconomic context on official reaction to delinquency." *American Sociological Review* 51:876–85.

Sarri, R. C. 1974. *Under Lock and Key: Juveniles in Jails and Detention*. Ann Arbor, MI: National Assessment of Juvenile Corrections, University of Michigan.

Scarpitti, F. R. and R. M. Stephenson, 1971. "Juvenile court dispositions: Factors in the decision-making process." *Crime and Delinquency* 17:142–51.

Shannon, L. W. 1963. "Types and patterns of delinquency referral in a middle-sized city." *British Journal of Criminology* 10:206–14.

Smith, C. P., T. E. Black, and A. W. Weir. 1980. *Reports of the National Juvenile Justice Assessment Centers. A National assessment of Case Disposition and Classification in the Juvenile Justice System: Inconsistent Labeling. Volume II: Results of a Literature Search*. Washington, DC: U.S. Government Printing Office.

Smith, D. and C. Visher. 1981. "Street-level justice: Situational determinants of police ar-

rest decisions." *Social Problems* 29:167–77.

Snyder, H. N., J. L. Hutzler, and T. A. Finnegan. 1985. *Delinquency in the United States—1982*. Pittsburgh: National Center for Juvenile Justice.

Stapleton, V., D. Aday, and J. Ito. 1982. "An empirical typology of American metropolitan juvenile courts." *American Journal of Sociology* 88:549–65.

Stinchcombe, A. 1963. "Institutions of privacy in the determination of police administrative policy." *American Journal of Sociology* 69:150–60.

Sumner, H. 1971. "Locking them up." *Crime and Delinquency* 17:168–79.

Teilman, K. S. and P. H. Landry. 1981. "Gender bias in juvenile justice." *Journal of Research in Crime and Delinquency* 18:47–80.

Terry, R. M. 1967a. "Discrimination in the handling of juvenile offenders by social-control agencies." *Journal of Research in Crime and Delinquency* 4:218–30.

_____. 1967b. "The screening of juvenile offenders." *Journal of Criminal Law, Criminology and Police Science* 58:173–81.

Thomas, C. W. and R. Cage. 1977. "The effect of social characteristics on juvenile court dispositions." *Sociological Quarterly* 18:237–52.

Thornberry, T. R. 1973. "Race, socioeconomic status, and sentencing in the juvenile justice system." *Criminology* 64:90–8.

Thornberry, T. R. and R. L. Christenson, 1984. "Juvenile justice decision-making as a longitudinal process." *Social Forces* 63:433–44.

Thornton, W. E., L. Voigt, and W. G. Doerner. *Delinquency and Justice*. Second edition. New York: Random House.

Visher, C. A. 1983. "Gender, police arrest decisions, and notions of chivalry." *Criminology* 21:5–28.

Waegel, W. B. 1989. *Delinquency and Juvenile Control: A Sociological Perspective*. Englewood Cliffs, NJ: Prentice-Hall.

Weiner, N. L. and C. V. Willie. 1971. "Decisions by juvenile officers." *American Journal of Sociology* 77:199–210.

Werthman, C. and I. Piliavin. 1967. "Gang

members and the police." Pp. 72–94 in D. Bordua (ed.), *The Police: Six Sociological Essays*. New York: Wiley.

Wilbanks, W. L. 1975. *The Insertion/Diversion Decision at the Police Level.* Unpublished Ph.D. dissertation, State University of New York, Albany.

Williams, J. R. and M. Gold. 1972. "From delinquent behavior to official delinquency." *Social Problems* 20:209–28.

Wilson, J. Q. 1968. *Varieties of Police Behavior.* Cambridge, MA: Harvard University Press.

Gang Members and the Police

23

Carl Werthman
Irving Piliavin

The juvenile officer exercises a good deal of discretion in deciding how to process offenders, a discretion that far transcends the measure of ambiguity ordinarily involved in legal assessments of motivation and intent. Although a truant may not be responsible for his behavior, he may be a touch rebellious, or he may be acting in complete and willful disregard for law, the nature and intent of this crime is not as important to a juvenile officer as what he learns about the attitude of the offender towards the idea of the law itself. For example, if an officer decides he is dealing with a boy who is "guilty but essentially good" or "guilty but sometimes weak," the probability is high that he will decide to let the boy go with a warning about the consequences of committing this crime again. He might feel that contact with the unsavory clientele of a juvenile hall would damage an otherwise positive attitude towards the law or that moral contamination in the eyes of parents and teachers as a result of

being sent to jail might weaken an otherwise firm commitment to conventional behavior. On the other hand, if the officer decides that the offender is a "punk," a "persistent troublemaker," or some other version of a thoroughly bad boy, he may well decide to make an arrest.[1]

A "delinquent" is therefore not a juvenile who happens to have committed an illegal act. He is a young person whose moral character has been negatively assessed. And this fact has led some observers to conclude that the transformation of young people into official "delinquents" is best looked at as an organizational rather than a legal process since policemen, probation officers, and juvenile court judges often base their dispositions on a host of criteria that are virtually unrelated to the nature of the specific offense.[2]

The *magnitude of an offense*, of course, can become a factor in dispositions. One responsibly planned and willfully executed robbery, rape, or assault can ruin the moral status of a juvenile indefinitely. Since 90% of the crimes committed by juveniles are minor offenses, however, this criterion is only rarely used.

Abridged from David Bordua (ed.), *The Police: Six Sociological Essays*, pp. 72–81 and 90–94. Copyright © 1967, John Wiley and Sons, Inc. Reprinted by permission of John Wiley and Sons, Inc.

The number of *previous contacts with police* has a more important effect on dispositions. These contacts are typically recorded on easily accessible files, and these files contain everything from arrests and convictions to contacts made on the flimsiest of contingent grounds. If a boy confesses to a crime and is not known to the police, he is often released. If he is caught for a third or fourth time, however, the sum total of previous contacts may be enough to affect a judgment about his moral character adversely, regardless of the nature or magnitude of the present offense and regardless of the reasons he was previously contacted. For example:

Like last night, man, me and Willy got busted for curfew. I mean I got busted for curfew. We was walkin' up the hill towards home, and these cops pull up. It was a Friday night, man, so we didn't want no trouble. When the cops ask us what we was doing and what about our names we was all nice. So then the cop gets on that radio and checks us out. There was a whole bunch of noise comin' over that box. I couldn't hear what they was sayin'. But then the cop comes out and says to Willy, "O.K., you can go." And I say, "What about me?" And the cop says, "You been in trouble before. We don't want you walkin' the streets at night. We going to take you down to the station for curfew." Then I got real mad. I almost ran. Lucky thing I didn't though. I woulda been in real trouble then.

There is even some evidence to suggest that assessments about the type and quality of *parental control* are even more important factors in dispositions than *any* of the offense-related criteria. One of the main concerns of a juvenile officer is the likelihood of future offense, and this determination is often made largely on the basis of "the kinds of parents" a boy happens to possess. Thus, the moral character of parents also passes under review; and if a house appears messy, a parent is missing, or a mother is on welfare, the probability of arrest increases. Similarly, a boy with a father and two older brothers in jail is considered a different sort of person from a boy whose immediate family is not known to the police. As Cicourel points out, these judgments about family life are particularly subject to bias by attitudes related to class.[3]

See, like if you and maybe one of your brothers, say both of you, been to Y.A.,[4] or your sister, every time they see you they get on your back. They know all your family. If they ever pick you up and look at your records, they automatically take you in. They see where your sister been to jail, your brother, or if you ever went to jail. And they start saying, "Your whole family is rotten. Your whole family is jailbirds." Shit like that. And this is what really make you mad, when they tell you your mother don't know how to read!

Although the family situation of a boy and his record of prior police contacts both enter into dispositions, the most important factor affecting the decision of juvenile officers is the *attitude* displayed by the offender, both during and after the confession itself. Cicourel, for example, found that juvenile officers were strongly influenced by the style and speed with which the offender confessed.[5] If a boy blurts out his misdeeds immediately, this behavior is taken as a sign that the boy "trusts" authority and is therefore "under control." If the boy proves to be a "tough nut to crack," however, he is viewed with suspicion. As soon as a juvenile is defined as "hardened," he is considered no less dangerous to society than the adult criminal.

Similarly, the boys who appear frightened, humble, penitent, and ashamed are also more likely to go free. They are often defined as "weak, troubled, and the victim of circumstances" but basically "good boys," an assessment of moral character that may win them a release.

On the other hand, if a boy shows no signs of being spiritually moved by his offense, the police deal harshly with him. Not only has he sinned against a legal rule, but he has also symbolically rejected the normative basis for conforming to it in the first place; and it is this double deviation that has fateful consequences for the way he is treated by the police. Once he gets himself defined as "the kind of person who doesn't respect the law," he becomes a perfect candidate for arrest, detention, and eventual incarceration. Most of the juvenile officers we interviewed felt that the attitude of the offender was the major determinant of dispositions in 50% of their cases, and Nathan Goldman reports that "defiance on the part of a boy will lead to juvenile court quicker than anything else."[6]

It is hardly necessary to describe the way most gang boys feel about the equity of these dispositions. One only needs to imagine the look on a boy's face when he is told that he is about to spend a year in jail for an offense committed with a friend who was sent home when he promptly confessed.

The Situation of Suspicion

. . . Policemen develop indicators of suspicion by a method of pragmatic induction. Past experience leads them to conclude that more crimes are committed in the poorer sections of town than in the wealthier areas, that blacks are more likely to cause public disturbances than whites, and that adolescents in certain areas are a greater source of trouble than other categories of the citizenry. On the basis of these conclusions, the police divide the population and physical territory under surveillance into a variety of categories, make some initial assumptions about the moral character of the people and places in these categories, and then focus attention on those categories of persons and places felt to have the shadiest moral characteristics. As one patrolman states:

> If you know that the bulk of your delinquency problem comes from kids who, say, are from 12 to 14 years of age, when you're out on patrol you are much more likely to be sensitive to the activities of juveniles in this age bracket than older or younger youth. This would be good law enforcement practice. The logic in our case is the same except that our delinquency problem is largely found in the black community and it is these youth toward whom we are sensitized.[7]

According to both gang members and patrolmen, residence in a *neighborhood* is the most general indicator used by the police to select a sample of potential law violators. Many local patrolmen tend to consider *all residents* of "bad" neighborhoods rather weakly committed to whatever moral order they make it their business to enforce, and this transforms most of the people who use the streets in these neighborhoods into good candidates for suspicion. . . .

Although many patrolmen believe that some entire neighborhoods are morally inferior to others, they do not enforce their standards with the same severity in all parts of "poor" neighborhoods. According to gang members, the "territory" contains both *safe spots* and *danger spots*. The danger spots tend to be public places of business, such as outdoor drive-in hamburger stands or pool halls, where a great many young people in the neighborhood often congregate and where fights and arguments frequently break out. The probability of being defined as suspicious by the police in these places is quite high, and thus physical presence is more of a risk than in other spots. . . .

Although the police seem to create a few "safe spots" within "bad neighborhoods," gang members report that the *boundaries of neighborhoods* are patrolled with great seriousness and severity. The police are seen as very hard on "suspicious looking" adolescents who have strayed from home territory.

> (Do you guys stay mostly at Hunters Point or do you travel into other districts?) If we go someplace, they tell us to go on home. Because every time we go somewhere we mostly go in big groups and they don't want us. One time we was walking on Steiner Street. So a cop drove up and he say, "Hey! Hanky and Panky! Come here!" And he say, "You all out of bounds, get back on the other side of Steiner Street." Steiner Street is supposed to be out of bounds. (What's on the other side of Steiner?) Nothin' but houses.

Gang members interpret the policy of trying to stop them from traveling into other lower-class neighborhoods as a tactic to stop gang wars, and our research on the police suggests that the boys are right. The police do tend to see all sojourns into neighboring territories as potential attacks on rival gangs. . . .

In addition to preventing gang members from traveling into neighborhoods of the same class and ethnic status as their own, the police are equally as stringent about preventing the boys from crossing boundaries into neighborhoods of a higher status or a different color. Although the policy of the police is the same in both cases, they attribute different motives to the boys for wanting to enter higher-status areas. When gang members visit other lower-class neighborhoods, the

police suspect them of instigating war; when they are found in middle- or upper-class neighborhoods, the police suspect them of intentions to commit robbery or rape.

> Me and a friend of mine, we went to a girl's house name of, ah, no, I ain't gonna say her name. You might know her. She was stayin' in a white district. So when we was up there, I guess they saw we was colored. You know, not mostly colored people stay up there. It was about ten o'clock 'cause we was leaving the girl's flat. Just walked out the door. Comin' out the door, and here's the curb. We right there by the curb. Gonna go down the block. Cops come around the corner with an orange light. I believe they just sitting there waiting to nab us. They probably seen us go in there. They come and pull us out. Shake us down. *All* the way down, too, man. They shake us all the way down. And ask us what we doing over here. We tell them we came out to this girls' house. He say, "Where'd you stay?" I say, "Well, you just saw us come out the house 'cause I saw you right around the corner." He say, "Well, she's colored." So they say, "Some girl got raped up here." Or something like that. Some old lie. Then he say, "Where you live?" I say, "Hunters Point." He say, "I'm gonna give you about ten or fifteen minutes to catch the bus, and if you're not off this corner, if I see you over here, I'll bust you." Just like that. If the police catch you walkin' with a white girl, boy, you in big trouble."

Race thus becomes a particularly salient indicator of "suspiciousness" when blacks or Hispanics are found in white neighborhoods. Being a black per se (or being a black in a black neighborhood) is apparently not as important a criterion of suspiciousness as being a black who is "out of place."

> If boys from Hunters Point or Fillmore (black neighborhoods in San Francisco) go

in all white districts, the police will stop you and ask you where you from. If you say Fillmore or Hunters Point, they'll take you down to the station, and run checks on you. Any burglaries, any purse snatchings, anything. . . .

In addition to the variety of *places* used to draw samples, however, the police also seem to rely on a number of physical or material *individual attributes*. Certain kinds of clothing, hair, and walking styles seem instrinsically to trigger suspicion. The general description of these styles had best be left to the boys themselves.

(Why do you think the cops pick you up all the time?) Why do they pick us up? They don't pick everybody up. They just pick up the ones with the hats on and trench coats and conks.[8] If you got long hair and hats on, something like this one, you gonna get picked up. Especially a conk. And the way you dress. Sometimes, like if you've got on black pants, better not have on no black pants or bends[9] or Levi's. They think you going to rob somebody. And don't have a head scarf on your head. They'll bust you for having a head scarf.[10] (All right, so they bust you for clothes. That's one thing. Is there anything else?) The way you walk sometimes. If you walk pimp. Don't try to walk pimp. Don't try to be cool. You know. They'll bust you for that. (Could you tell me how you walk pimp?) You know. You just walk cool like. Like you got a boss high.[11] Like you got a fix or something. Last night a cop picked me up for that. He told me I had a bad walk. He say, "You think you're bad." You know.

Finally, the police also use *themselves* as an instrument for locating suspicious people. Every time an officer makes visible contact with a citizen, the citizen is forced to confront his status in the eyes of the law, and the police soon learn to rely on hostile *looks* and furtive *glances* as signs of possi-

ble guilt. A policeman's uniform is a potent symbolic device. It sometimes has the power to turn a patrolman into a walking test of moral identity.

It should not be construed from the above discussion that the process of locating a population of potential offenders always proceeds on such slim grounds. There are a variety of "scenes" that constitute much more obvious bases for investigation. However, since policemen rarely stumble on armed men standing over dead bodies, much of their activity involves a subtle and exceedingly tenuous reading of both appearances and events. For example, when dealing with people who possess the ecological and personal indicators of suspiciousness outlined above, patrolmen may turn a screwdriver into a "deadly weapon" and a scratch on the neck into evidence of rape.

Like you be walking. Just come from working on the car or something. And if you've got a screwdriver or something in your back pocket, hell, they may beat the shit outa you. They talk about you got a burglary tool or you got a deadly weapon on you. Remember the time when we was getting ready to go up to the gym? We came home from school one day. He had some scratches on his neck, and the cop pull over and say, "Turn around!" The cop grabbed him. I didn't say nothing. I was walking. I got to the top of the stairs, and the cop holler "Turn around" at me too. So I turn around. And the cop look at my neck and he say, "Yeah. You too. You got scratches on your neck too." So he took us down to the police station. It seems like some girl way over in another district got raped. And the girl say, "I think they live over at Hunters Point and I scratched one of them on the neck." Some stuff like that.

Gang members are very much aware of their moral status in the eyes of the police.

On most occasions, they are likely to know that the police have singled them out for interrogation because of the neighborhood they live in, because of their hair styles, or perhaps because they are temporarily "out of place." They know how the police operate, and they are particularly aware of the role played by judgments about moral character in this methodology. . . .

Outcomes

If a juvenile being interrogated in the situation of suspicion refuses to proffer the expected politeness or to use the words that typically denote respect and if no offense has been discovered, a patrolman finds himself in a very awkward position. He cannot arrest the boy for insolence or defiance, since for obvious reasons no charges of this nature exist. The patrolman is thus faced with the choice of three rather unpleasant alternatives.

First, he can back down, thereby allowing his authority to evaporate. If a patrolman allows his authority to escape, however, there is no guarantee that it can be recaptured the next day or any day thereafter. Since patrolmen are structurally locked into the authority role over long periods of uninterrupted time, any fleeting defeat at the hands of a gang member has the prospect of becoming permanent. In a certain sense, then, gang members have a great deal of power. With the mere hint of impiety they can sometimes manage to strip a patrolman symbolically of his authority.

For these reasons, if a patrolman does decide to back down, he must be careful to retreat strategically by withdrawing from the encounter without a public loss of face. This is usually done by communicating to the juvenile that his innocence is fortuitous, that he is the kind of person who *could* have committed an offense, and that he owes his

release to the grouchy good graces of the interrogating officer. If executed artfully, comments such as "keep your nose clean or we'll run you in next time" can pave the way out of a potentially damaging encounter. From the point of view of the boys, of course, this technique simply constitutes an additional insult to moral character.

If a patrolman chooses to press his claims to authority, however, he has only two sanctions available with which to make these claims good. On the one hand, he can attempt an arrest.

> One day we were standing on the corner about three blocks from school and this juvenile officer comes up. He say, "Hey, you boys! Come here!" So everybody else walked over there. But this one stud made like he didn't hear him. So the cop say, "Hey punk! Come here!" So the stud sorta look up like he hear him and start walking over. But he walking over real slow. So the cop walk over there and grab him by the collar and throw him down and put the handcuffs on him, saying, "When I call you next time, come see what I want!" So everybody was standing by the car, and he say, "All right you black mother fuckers! Get your ass home!" Just like that. And he hand-cuffed the stud and took him to juvenile hall for nothing. Just for standing there looking at him.

On the other hand, there are a variety of curfew, vagrancy, and loitering laws that can also be used to formally or officially prosecute the informal violation of norms governing deportment in the situation of suspicion.

> I got arrested once when we were just riding around in a car. There was a bunch of us in the car. A police car stopped us, and it was about ten after ten when they stopped us. They started asking us our names and wanted to see our identification. Then they called in

on us. So they got through calling in on us, and they just sit in the car and wait 'til the call came through. Then they'd bring back your I.D. and take another one. One at a time. They held me and another boy till last. And when they got to us it was five minutes to eleven. They told everybody they could go home, but they told us it didn't make no sense for us to go home because we was just riding around and we'd never make it home in five minutes. So they busted us both for curfew.

In addition to these laws, a boy can also be charged with "suspicion" of practically anything. When the police use suspicion as a charge, however, they usually try to make the specific offense as serious as possible. This is why the criminal records of many gang boys are often heavily laced with such charges as "suspicion of robbery" and "suspicion of rape."

(Could you tell me some of the things you have been busted for?) Man, I been charged with everything from suspicion of murder to having suspicious friends. I think they call it "associates!" (laughter) They got me on all kinda trash, man, and they only make but one thing stick. (What's that?) A couple of years ago they caught me stone cold sittin' behind the wheel of a '60 Pontiac. I said it belong to my uncle, but it turn out that the name of the registration was O'Shaunessee or O'Something, some old fat name like that. The cop knew there wasn't no bloods [blacks] named things like that.

Gang boys are aware that the police have a very difficult time making these illusory charges stick. They can always succeed in sending a boy to jail for a few hours or a few days, but most of these charges are dismissed at a preliminary hearing on recommendations from probation officers. Moreover, gang members also understand the power of probation officers, and by behaving better in front of these officials they can

often embarrass the local authority of patrolmen by having decisions to arrest reversed over their heads. As far as the patrolmen are concerned, then, the boys can make a mockery of false charges as a sanction against impertinence in the situation of suspicion.

Perhaps more important, however, a patrolman's sergeant also knows that most trivial or trumped up charges are likely to be dropped, and thus the police department itself puts a premium on ability to command authority without invoking the sanction of arrest. Unlike the juvenile officer who is judged by his skills at interrogation, a patrolman's capacity to gain respect is his greatest source of pride as well as his area of greatest vulnerability. If he is forced to make too many "weak" arrests, he stands to lose prestige among his peers and superiors on the police force and to suffer humiliation at the hands of his permanent audience of tormentors on the beat.

It is largely for these reasons that many patrolmen prefer to settle a challenge to authority on the spot, an alternative that necessarily poses the prospect of violence. As William Westley has pointed out, in the last analysis the police can always try to "coerce respect."[12]

They don't never beat you in the car. They wait until they get you to the station. And then they beat you when the first shift comes on and they beat you when the second shift comes on. I've seen it happen. I was right there in the next cell. They had a boy. His name was Stan, and they had beat him already as soon as they brought him in. And then when they was changing shifts, you know, the detective came and looked on the paper that say what he was booked for, I think it was robbery or something like that, and they started beating on him again. See, the police are smart. They don't leave no bruises. They'll beat you somewhere where it don't show. That's the main places where they look to hit you at. And if it did show, your word wouldn't be as good as theirs. They can lie too, you know. All they have to say is that you was resisting and that's the only reason they need for doing what they do.

Resisting arrest is the one charge involving violence that seems uniquely designed to deal with improper deportment in the situation of suspicion. A policeman interviewed by Westley suggests that when the challenge to authority is not sufficiently serious to warrant this charge, the police may continue to provoke the suspect until the level of belligerence reaches proportions that legitimate invoking this category of offense.

For example, when you stop a fellow for a routine questioning, say a wise guy, and he starts talking back to you and telling you that you are no good and that sort of thing. You know you can take a man in on a disorderly conduct charge, but you can practically never make it stick. So what you do in a case like this is to egg the guy on until he makes a remark where you can justifiably slap him, and then if he fights back, you can call it resisting arrest.[13]

And from a gang member's point of view:

Another reason why they beat up on you is because they always have the advantage over you. The cop might say, "You done this." And you might say, "I didn't!" And he'll say, "Don't talk back to me or I'll go upside your head!" You know, and then they say they had a right to hit you or arrest you because you were talking back to an officer or resisting arrest, and you were merely trying to explain or tell him that you hadn't done what he said you'd done. One of those kinds of things. Well, that means you in the wrong when you get downtown anyway. You're always in the wrong.

Unlike encounters between gang members and patrolmen, the confrontations between gang members and juvenile officers rarely end in violence. This is because the ability to command respect is not as crucial to a juvenile officer as it is to a patrolman. A juvenile officer is not judged by his capacity to command authority on a beat, and he can therefore leave a situation in which his authority has been challenged without having to face the challenger again the next day. Since he is evaluated largely by his skill at interrogation, he rarely finds himself structurally predisposed to "coerce respect."

Notes

1. For a more complete discussion of police discretion in dealing with juveniles, see Irving Piliavin and Scott Briar, "Police Encounters with Juveniles." *The American Journal of Sociology*, Vol. LXX, No.2 (Sept. 1964), pp. 209-211.

2. The problem of discretion has been formulated and studied by Aaron Cicourel in these terms. See Aaron V. Circourel, *The Social Organization of Juvenile Justice*. New York: Wiley (1968).

3. Aaron Cicourel, "Social Class, Family

Structure and the Administration of Juvenile Justice,'' Center for the Study of Law and Society, University of California at Berkeley, Working Paper, MS.

4. ''The detention facilities administered by the California Youth Authority.

5. Cicourel, *The Social Organization of Juvenile Justice, Loc. cit.*

6. Nathan Goldman, *The Differential Selection of Juvenile Offenders for Court Appearances*, National Council on Crime and Delinquency (1963), p. 106.

7. Irving Piliavin and Scott Briar, *op. cit.*, p. 212.

8. A ''conk'' is a hair straightening process used by blacks that is similar in concept to the permanent wave.

9. ''Bends'' are a form of the bell-bottom trouser which, when worn effectively, all but obscure the shoe from the vision, thus creating the impression that the wearer is moving down the street with an alarmingly irresponsible shuffle.

10. Head scarves (sometimes called ''mammy rags'') are worn by blacks around the forehead to keep ''conk jobs'' in place.

11. ''Boss'' is a synonym for ''good.''

12. The above analysis of why policemen retaliate when the legitimacy of their authority is challenged differs somewhat from Westley's analysis of why a large percentage of the policemen he studied ''believed that it was legitimate to use violence to coerce respect.'' Westley argues that disrespectful behavior constitutes a threat to the already low ''occupational status'' of policemen and therefore comes as a blow to their self-esteem. Westley's hypothesis would suggest, however, that those policemen who *accepted* their low occupational status would therefore allow their authority to be challenged. Although Westley's variables no doubt affect the behavior of patrolmen, there also seems to be more at stake than status as a workman when claims to authority are ignored. In a sense the patrolman whose authority has been successfully called into question has already abdicated a sizable chunk of his honor as well as his job. See William A. Westley, ''Violence and the Police.'' *American Journal of Sociology*, Vol. LIX (July 1953).

13. *Ibid.*, p. 30.

Judging Delinquents

24

Robert M. Emerson

"Trouble"

[Y]ouths brought before the juvenile court generally represent "trouble" for some caretaking or control institution. In this sense every delinquent is "trouble" for someone, . . . [and] every delinquency complaint represents a plea that the court "do something" to remedy or alleviate that "trouble." Hence, one fundamental set of problems and demands confronting the juvenile court arises from the pressures and expectations of those initiating court action that "something be done." In this sense the court must work out practical solutions to cases that satisfy, or at least take some cognizance of, the concerns of complainants.

But not all cases represent "trouble" in the eyes of the court; the court does not automatically accept the contentions of complainants. Rather the court makes an independent assessment of "trouble" and of the necessity of "doing something," an assessment that reflects its own organization-

al priorities and "problem relevances" (Schutz, 1964, p. 235).

These distinctive problem relevances turn on two fundamental features of the court situation. First, the time, personnel, and resources available for dealing with delinquency cases are severely limited. Consequently, court operations are subject to strict economy in the uses of resources and personnel. Second, court personnel have a higher tolerance of "delinquency" than most complainants. Routinely encountering a wide range of youthful misconduct, the court develops a relatively narrow definition of delinquency. This definition generally requires quite frequent and serious manifestations of disturbing conduct before a youth will be categorized as "really delinquent." As a result, court workers often feel that complainants' "troubles" are exaggerated and that the kinds of official responses they seek are inappropriately drastic.

The court thus comes to follow a principle of conservatism in case management. This in turn requires it to separate "serious" cases where there is "real" trouble, from those where the "trouble" is "mild" or "normal," requiring little attention.[1]

Abridged from *Judging Delinquents* (Chicago: Aldine, 1969), pp. 83–86, 89–90, 137–141, and 155–164. Reprinted by permission of the author.

The search for "real" trouble emerges as a recurring theme throughout court staff's explanations of their work. For example, the judge described his orientation toward the conduct of formal hearings in the following terms:

> We look for tip-offs that *something is really wrong.* We get some tip-offs just from the face-sheet; truancy, school attendance, conduct, and effort marks. . . . *If you get something wrong there, you know there's trouble.* When you get truancy or bad conduct plus delinquency, there's definitely something wrong. [Emphasis added.]

Similarly, a woman probation officer in talking about girl shoplifting cases said:

> Shoplifters are the simplest and most promising kind of girls I have. Often they come from good families. But there may also be *"a very serious problem"* involved. Sometimes while taking the face sheet you can see how "serious" it is. But usually these cases are continued without a finding in order to determine if there is any "serious problem." . . . Then again, some are dealt with more severely, "depending on the girl's attitude." For some of the cases are more *"severe"* and have to be dealt with accordingly.

By this sifting process the court begins to allocate its time, efforts, and resources among delinquency cases. On the one hand, the court locates cases where "something has to be done," where special handling is required; on the other hand, it finds cases which can be "let go." The great majority of the court's cases are of the latter sort—"untroubled"—and require staff to devote only a minimum of time and effort to overseeing and changing the life circumstances of the delinquent. A woman probation officer, for example, commented on the unserious nature of girl shoplifters by

noting: "I don't see them any more [after their hearing]." On the other hand, in cases where "trouble" is found, where "something wrong" is noted, the court more actively intervenes, concentrating its efforts and resources for change. Extraordinary measures are taken in managing these cases, and much effort is devoted to working out some adequate remedy.

In general, a case brought to juvenile court under a definition of "trouble" has three possible outcomes. First, complainant and court definitions of trouble may more or less coincide; the court then seeks some satisfactory remedy for the case. Second, complainant and court definitions of trouble may diverge. Usually this disparity reflects a judgment of a lesser degree of trouble by the court, for the reasons discussed previously. In this situation the court initially tries to convince the complainant that it has no power to do anything or that nothing need be done. This may require special efforts to satisfy the complainant, to persuade him not to press for special action, or to induce him to accept some less drastic solution than he originally envisioned.[2]

Finally, the court may feel there is no trouble, but be unable to "cool out" the complainant. In this situation the court may be moved to "do something" even though it feels such action is not really necessary. A course of events leading to such an outcome occurred in the following case:

> A 16-year-old black boy was brought to court for assaulting a fire chief. The previous night the boy's best friend had been knifed during a fight and a fire department "ambulet" called to the scene. When the fire chief directing the operation had refused to let the defendant accompany his critically wounded friend to the hospital in the ambulance, the youth had punched him. As a result, the chief

had insisted that the police take out the assault complaint.

In court, a social-worker sponsor of the youth reported that the police had expected the case to be settled with an apology by the boy, but that the chief had refused to drop his complaint. The police officer acting as prosecutor outlined the alleged facts briefly, requested a two-week continuance before the hearing, and concluded by stating, "the boy came here on his own volition this morning," suggesting that bail would not be required. Outside the courtroom, in discussing this continuance with me, the police officer noted: "We let it cool. Let the chief cool off."

When the hearing was finally held, the judge placed the youth on a suspended sentence after finding him delinquent on the assault complaint. At the same time, the judge complemented this relatively severe judgment with special efforts to soothe the fire chief's indignation.

As this case suggests, the strength of a complainant's demands to "do something" may constitute a crucial factor in the court's identification of "trouble." Strong demands create a presumption that "something has to be done" and demonstrate the existence of behavior intolerable to someone with responsibility for controlling the delinquent. . . .

The Relevance of Moral Character

In seeking practical solutions to cases felt to involve "trouble," the juvenile court is largely guided by its judgments and inferences regarding the nature of the delinquent actor involved. That is, the solution to the problem—what can and what must we do with this case?—generally depends on the answer to: what kind of youth are we dealing with here? This involves a process of inquiry into the youth's *moral character*. . . .

If the court decides that there is no trouble in a case, it assumes that the delinquent

involved is *normal* in character. If trouble is located, however, character is rendered *problematic*. This initiates more intensive court involvement with the case, as well as more intensive concern with accounting for the youth's behavior. Upon examination, it may be felt that the delinquent is really possessed of normal character despite indications of trouble. As a result, assessments of normal character may occur at either initial or subsequent stages of the court sorting process.

Similarly, damaged character may not be identified on first contact but begin to "emerge" in subsequent encounters. For example, a case may be treated as routine until the delinquent appears in court for a second or third time within a period of several months. Such reappearances cast doubt on the previously assumed normality of character. Initial judgments may fall before a variety of factors. At almost any point in a court career, doubts cast on character may be minimized or dismissed or, alternatively, confirmed and explained as expressions of some discredited kind of moral character. The court builds up experience with an individual delinquent and accumulates a biographical file on him so that its assessments of his character become stable. Yet this view is nearly always open to some modification: while an assessment of poor character is not easily removed, it may at least be reinterpreted as of a different kind. . . .

A Note on Total Denunciation

Consideration of the structural features of total denunciation provides additional insight into the processes of establishing moral character in the juvenile court. For a successful total denunciation must transcend routine denunciation by *foreclosing* all possible defenses and by *neutralizing* all possible sources of support.

Foreclosure of defenses available to the delinquent . . . has two related elements. First, in order to discredit moral character totally, it must be clearly demonstrated that the denounced delinquent has been given a great many "breaks" or "chances" which he has, however, rejected and spoiled. Such a demonstration is necessary to prove that the case is "hopeless," that the delinquent youth's character is so ruined as to preclude any possiblity of reform. The role of the disregarded "chance" is clearly seen in the following case, where a probation officer convinces both judge and public defender to go along with his punitive recommendation by proving that the youth has received chances not even officially reported:

> Two escapees from reform school were brought into court on a series of new complaints taken out by the police. Public defender argued that these complaints should be dismissed and the boys simply returned to the school. The probation officer, however, argued strongly that the boys should be found delinquent on the new complaints (this would require reconsideration of their cases by the Youth Correction Authority, perhaps leading to an extension of their commitment). The probation officer described how one of his colleagues had worked hard on one of these cases earlier, giving the boy a great many chances, none of which did any good. The judge accepted the probation officer's recommendation.
>
> After the hearing, the public defender admitted that he felt the probation officer had been right, acknowledging the validity of his picture of the character of this boy: "I did not realize he was such a bastard. . . . Apparently one of the probation officers had given him a lot of breaks. He had him on so many cases that he should be shot."

Second, it must be made to appear that the delinquent himself "messed up" the

chances that he had been given. It should be established not only that the youth misbehaved on numerous occasions, but also that he did so in full knowledge of the possible consequences and with no valid excuse or extenuating circumstances. In this way, responsibility or "fault" for the imminent incarceration must fall completely on the denounced delinquent. Any official contribution to the youth's "messing up" (e.g., an official's intolerance) must be glossed over so that the delinquent bears total blame.

Court probation is in fact constructed so that responsibility for "messing up," should it occur, unavoidably falls on the delinquent. . . . Probationers are constantly warned that they will be committed if there is any further misconduct, and they are given a number of "breaks" on this condition. As one probation officer commented about a youth who had been "given a break" by the judge: "This way, if he gets committed, he knows he has it coming." Furthermore, the constant warnings and lectures against getting into trouble that occur throughout probation tend to undermine in advance the possibility of defending subsequent misbehavior. For example, it is difficult for a youth to excuse a new offense as the product of peer group influence when he has continually been warned to stay away from "bad friends."

A second key element in a successful total denunciation is the neutralization of all possible sources of support. There are several components in this neutralization. First, the assessment of discredited and "hopeless" character must be made to appear as a general consensus among all those concerned in the case. A delinquent without a spokesman—with no one to put in a good word for him—stands in a fundamentally discredited position.

Here the stance taken by the delinquent's lawyer, normally a public defender, becomes crucial. A vigorous defense and pitch by a lawyer often might dispel the appearance of consensus and weaken the denunciation. This occurs very rarely, however, because of court cooptation of the public defender. Working closely with the probation staff, the public defender comes to share their values and indexes of success and failure in delinquency cases. Consequently, he will generally concur with the court's highly negative assessments of delinquent moral character. As a public defender noted in response to a question about how he usually handled his cases in the juvenile court:

Generally I would find the probation officer handling the case and ask him: "What do you have on this kid? How bad is he?" He'll say: "Oh, he's bad!" Then he opens the probation folder to me, and I'll see he's got quite a record. Then I'll ask him, "What are you going to recommend?" He'll say, "Give him another chance. Or probation. Or we've got to put him away."

But probation officers don't make this last recommendation lightly. Generally they will try to find a parent in the home, "someone who can keep him under control, someone who can watch him." But if the probation officer has given the kid a number of chances, it is a different story: "He's giving the kid chances and he keeps screwing up. . . . [Commitment will then be recommended.] And I say the kid deserves it. Before a kid goes away he's really got to be obnoxious—he will deserve it."

Adoption of probation standards for assessing delinquent character becomes crucial in total denunciation. The public defender is then in the position of arguing on behalf of a youth whose moral character has been totally discredited in his eyes and who he feels should indeed be committed.

His courtroom defense will generally reflect this assessment. He will make only the most perfunctory motions of arguing that the delinquent be let off, and he will do so in a way that communicates an utter lack of conviction that this is a desirable course of action. Or, as in the following case, he will not even go through the motions of making a defense but will explicitly concur with the recommended incarceration and the grounds on which it rests:

A policeman told of finding an 11-year-old black boy in a laundry where a coin box had been looted. The officer reported that the boy had admitted committing the offense. Public defender waived cross-examination, and the judge found the youth delinquent.

Probation officer then delivered a rather lengthy report on the case. The boy had been sent to the Boys' Training Program and, while no great trouble, did not attend regularly. He had also recently been transferred to the Harris School and had been in trouble there. Probation officer recommended that the prior suspended sentence be revoked and the boy committed to the Youth Correction Authority.

Judge then asked the public defender if he had anything he wanted to say. Public defender: "The record more or less speaks for itself. He does not seem to have taken advantage of the opportunities the court has given him to straighten out." Then, after briefly reconferring with the probation officer, the judge ordered the commitment. Public defender waived the right of appeal.

Second, the denouncer must establish that in "messing up" and not taking advantage of the chances provided him, the denounced has created a situation in which there is *no other alternative open* but commitment to the Youth Correction Authority. In some cases, this may involve showing that the youth is so dangerous that commitment to the Authority is the only effective way he can be restrained; in others, demonstration that by his misbehavior the youth has completely destroyed all possible placements, including the one he has been in. It is only by dramatically showing in these ways that "there is nothing we can do with him" that the proposed commitment can be made to appear as an inevitable and objective necessity.

The fact that many total denunciations concentrate on proving that nothing else can be done with the case reflects the court's basic resistance to unwarrantable agency attempts to "dump" undesirable cases onto them for incarceration. The court feels that most of these institutions are too ready to give up on cases that from the court's point of view are still salvageable. To overcome this suspiciousness, the denouncer must not only present the youth's character as essentially corrupt and "hopeless," but also show that every effort has been made to work with him and every possible opportunity afforded him. The denouncer, in other words, must take pains to avoid appearing to be merely getting rid of a difficult and troublesome case simply to make his own work easier. This requires showing both that persistent efforts have been made to work with the case and that at the present time even extraordinary efforts cannot come up with anything as an alternative to incarceration.

A final aspect of demonstrating that there is no viable alternative to incarceration involves isolating the denounced delinquent from any kind of reputable sponsorship. In the usual case, where a parent acts as sponsor, successful total denunciation requires either that the parent be induced to denounce the youth and declare him fit only for incarceration or that the parent be discredited. In other cases, where the sponsor is a parental substitute, this sponsor must similarly be led to denounce the youth or be

discredited. In this way, for example, sponsors who seek too aggressively to save delinquents considered overripe for commitment by other officials may encounter attacks on their motives, wisdom, or general moral character. This not only undermines the viability of any defense of character made by the sponsor, but also effectively isolates the delinquent by showing the unsuitability of his sponsorship as an alternative to commitment. . . .

Counter-Denunciation

As noted earlier, the courtroom proceeding routinely comes to involve a denunciation of the accused delinquent in the course of a confrontation between him and his accusers. This fact creates the conditions for the use of *counter-denunciation* as a defensive strategy. This strategy seeks to undermine the discrediting implications of the accusation by attacking the actions, motives and/or character of one's accusers.

The underlying phenomenon in counter-denunciation has been noted in a number of other contexts. McCorkle and Korn, for example, have analyzed the concept of the "rejection of the rejectors" as a defensive reaction to imprisonment (1964, p. 520). Similarly, Sykes and Matza explain the "condemnation of the condemners" in the process of neutralization in the following terms: "The delinquent shifts the focus of attention from his own deviant acts to the motives and behaviors of those who disapprove of his violations" (1957, p. 668). The concept of counter-denunciation, in contrast, focuses on the communicative work which accomplishes this shift of attention. Furthermore, it gains relevance as a defense against attempted character discrediting. Use of this strategy, however, is extremely risky in the court setting. While counter-denunciation may appear to the delinquent as a "natural" defense as he perceives the circumstances of his case, it tends to challenge fundamental court commitments and hence, even when handled with extreme care, often only confirms the denunciation.

It is striking that counter-denunciation has the greatest likelihood of success in cases where the complainant or denouncer lacks official stature or where the initiative rests predominantly with private parties who have clearly forced official action. Under these circumstances the wrongful quality of the offense can be greatly reduced if not wholly eliminated by showing that the initiator of the complaint was at least partially to blame for the illegal act. For example:

A 16-year-old black boy, Johnny Haskin, was charged with assault and battery on two teenaged girls who lived near his family in a public housing project. Although a juvenile officer brought the case into court, he was clearly acting on the initiative of the two girls and their mother, for he had had no direct contact with the incident and did not testify about it. He simply put the two girls on the stand and let them tell about what happened. This was fairly confused, but eventually it appeared that Johnny Haskin had been slapping the younger sister in the hall of the project when the older girl had pulled him off. He had then threatened her with a knife. The girls admitted that there had been fighting in the hall for some time, and that they had been involved, but put the blame on Johnny for starting it. Mrs. Haskin, however, spoke up from the back of the room, and told about a gang of boys coming around to get her son (apparently justifying Johnny's carrying a knife). And Johnny himself denied that he had started the fighting, claiming that the younger girl had hit him with a bat and threatened him first.

Judge then lectured both families for fighting, and placed Johnny on probation for nine months, despite a rather long prior record.

In this case, by establishing that the girls had also been fighting, the boy was at least partially exonerated. The success of this strategy is seen in the fact that the judge lectured both families, and then gave the boy what was a mild sentence in light of his prior court record.

Similarly, the possibility of discrediting the victim, thereby invalidating the complaint, becomes apparent in the following "rape" case:

Two black boys, ages 12 and 13, had admitted forcing "relations" on a 12-year-old girl in a schoolyard, the police reported. After a full report on the incidents surrounding the offense, the judge asked the policemen: "What kind of girl is she?" Officer: "I checked with Reverend Frost [the girl's minister and the person instrumental in reporting this incident] and he said she was a good girl."

As the judge's query implies, the reprehensibility of this act can only be determined in relation to the assessed character of the girl victim. Had the police or the accused brought up evidence of a bad reputation or incidents suggesting "loose" or "promiscuous" behavior, the force of the complaint would have been undermined.

In the above cases, successful counter-denunciation of the complainants would undermine the moral basis of their involvement in the incident, thereby discrediting their grounds for initiating the complaint. But this merely shifts part of the responsibility for an offense onto the complaining party and does not affect the wrongful nature of the act per se. Thus, by denouncing the general character of the complainant and the nature of his involvement in the offense, the accused does not so much clear himself as diminish his guilt. If the offense involved is serious enough and the culpability of the complainant not directly related to the offense, therefore, this strategy may have little impact.

For example, in [a] homosexuality-tinged case of car theft, . . . both the accused and his father tried to support their contention that the car owner was lying by pointing to his discredited character. But the "victim's" homosexuality had no real connection with the act of stealing the car nor with the threatened physical violence it entailed, and hence did not affect the judge's evaluation of the act and of the delinquent's character. Under these circumstances, the soiled nature of the victim simply was not considered sufficiently extenuating to dissolve the reprehensibility of the act.[3]

In general, then, a successful counter-denunciation must discredit not only the general character of the denouncer but also his immediate purpose or motive in making the complaint. Only in this way can the counter-denunciation cut the ground out from under the wrongfulness of the alleged offense. For example:

An 11-year-old black boy was charged with wantonly damaging the car of an older black man, Frankie Williams, with a BB gun. With the boy was his mother, a respectably dressed woman, a white lawyer, and a white couple who served as character witnesses.

A juvenile officer brought the case in and then called Mr. Williams up to testify. The witness told of going outside to shovel his car out of the snow several weeks previously and finding his windshield damaged in several places. He had noticed the boy at this time leaning out of the window of his house with a BB gun. Lawyer then cross-examined, getting Williams to admit that he had been bickering with the family for some time, and that a year before the mother had accused him of swearing at her son and had tried to get a court complaint against him. (Judge ruled

this irrelevant after Williams had acknowledged it.) Williams seemed flustered, and grew angry under the questioning, claiming that because of the boy's shooting he would not be able to get an inspection sticker for his car.

Juvenile officer then told judge that although he had not investigated the case, his partner reported that the marks on the windshield were not consistent with a BB gun. Williams had also admitted that he had not looked for any BB pellets. On the basis of this evidence, the judge found the boy not delinquent. He then severely warned all parties in the case: "I'm going to tell you I do not want any more contests between these two families. Do you understand?"

Here, by showing that the complainant had both a selfish motive for complaining about his damaged windshield (to help get it repaired) and a grudge against the defendant and his family, as well as bringing out the lack of concrete evidence to substantiate the charge, the lawyer was able to get the complaint totally dismissed.

Similarly, the circumstances of the following case were such as to suggest initially that complaints had been taken out to intimidate or at least get even with boys against whom there was some resentment:

Two teenaged black boys were brought to court for breaking windows. Case was continued, and policeman gave the following account of what had happened. Several weeks previously there had been a disturbance and some windows broken in a middle class section of the city. There were six boys apparently involved, including these two. One of the occupants of the home had come out and begun shooting at the boys, who were on the other side of the street, "allegedly to protect his property." One of these two boys had been hit in the leg, and another man (apparently a passerby) had also been hit. The shooter, named Barr, "is now up before the grand jury'' for this, but meanwhile had taken out complaints against these two boys. A private attorney representing the two accused then took over, explaining how his clients had just been summoned to testify against Barr. Lawyer next questioned the cop about why complaints had been brought only against these two of the six boys, including the one who had been shot, and the other who had been a witness to the shooting. Cop replied that the other boys had been investigated, but there was nothing against them.

Here the boys' lawyer successfully established that the complaints against his clients had been initiated by the defendant in a related criminal action, suggesting an attempt to discredit in advance their testimony against him. The judge responded by continuing the case, releasing both boys to the custody of their parents, even though one had a long record.

Finally, successful counter-denunciation requires that the denounced provide a convincing account for what he claims is an illegitimate accusation. The court will reject any implication that one person will gratuitously accuse another of something he has not done. The youth in the following case can provide this kind of account:

> Five young boys were charged with vandalism and with starting a fire in a public school. Juvenile officer explained that he had investigated the incident with the school principal, getting two of the boys to admit their part in the vandalism. These two boys had implicated the other three, all of whom denied the charge.
>
> The judge then took over the questioning, trying to determine whether the three accused had in fact been in the school. In this he leaned heavily on finding out why the first two boys should lie. One of the accused, Ralph Kent, defended himself by saying he had not been at the school and did not know the boy who had named him. Judge asked

how this boy had then been able to identify him. Kent replied that he had been a monitor at school, and one of his accusers might have seen him there. And he used to take the other accuser to the basement [lavatory] because the teacher would not trust him alone for fear he would leave the school.

> The two other boys continued to deny any involvement in the incident, but could provide no reason why they should be accused unjustly. The judge told them he felt they were lying, and asked several times: ''Can you give me a good reason why these boys would put you in it?'' Finally he pointed toward Kent and commented: ''He's the only one I'm convinced wasn't there.'' He then asked Kent several questions about what he did as a monitor. When it came to dispositions, Kent was continued without a finding while the four other boys were found delinquent.

In this situation an accused delinquent was able to establish his own reputable character in school (later confirmed by the probation report on his school record), the discredited character of one of his accusers, and a probable motive for their denunciation of him (resentment toward his privileges and position in school) in a few brief sentences. It should be noted, however, that this successful counter-denunciation was undoubtedly facilitated by the fact that denouncers and denounced were peers. It is incomparably more difficult for a youth to establish any acceptable reason why an adult should want to accuse and discredit him wrongfully.

Counter-denunciation occurs most routinely with offenses arising out of the family situation and involving complaints initiated by parents against their own children. Here again it is possible for the child to cast doubt on the parents' motives in taking court action, and on the parents' general character:

A black woman with a strong West Indian accent had brought an incorrigible child complaint against her 16-year-old daughter. The mother reported: "She never says anything to me, only to ask, 'Gimme car fare, gimme lunch money.' . . . As for the respect she gave me I don't think I have to tolerate her!" The daughter countered that her mother never let her do anything, and simply made things unbearable for her around the house. She went out nights, as her mother claimed, but only to go over to a girl friend's house to sleep.

This case was continued for several months, during which time a probation officer worked with the girl and the court clinic saw mother and daughter. The psychiatrist there felt that the mother was "very angry and cold." Eventually an arrangement was made to let the girl move in with an older sister.

In this case the daughter was effectively able to blame her mother and her intolerance for the troubled situation in the home. But in addition, counter-denunciation may also shift the focus of the court inquiry from the misconduct charged to the youth onto incidents involving the parents. This shift of attention facilitated the successful counter-denunciation in the following case.

A 16-year-old white girl from a town some distance from the city was charged with shoplifting. But as the incident was described by the police, it became clear that this offense had occurred because the girl had run away from home and needed clean clothes. Police related what the girl had said about running away: She had been babysitting at home and was visited by her boyfriend, who had been forbidden in the house. Her father had come home, discovered this, and beaten her with a strap. (The girl's face still appeared somewhat battered with a large black-and-blue mark on one cheek, although the court session occurred at least three days after the beating.) She had run away that night.

The rest of the hearing centered not on the theft but on the running away and the incident which precipitated it. After the police evidence, the judge asked the girl: "How did you get that mark on your face?" Girl: "My father hit me." Judge: "With his fist?" Girl (hesitating): "Yes, it must have been his fist." Later in the proceeding, the judge asked the girl specifically why she had run away. She emphasized that she had not tried to hide anything; the kids had been up until eleven and the boy had left his bike out front. "I didn't try to hide it. I told them he'd been there."

With this her father rose to defend himself, arguing with some agitation: ". . . His clothes were loose. Her clothes were loose. Her bra was on the floor. . . . She was not punished for the boy being in the house, but for what she did." Girl (turning toward her father): "What about my eye?" Father: "She got that when she fell out of the bed (angrily, but directed toward the judge)." Girl (just as angrily): "What about the black and blue marks?" Father: "Those must have been from the strap."

The relatively high probability of successful counter-denunciation in cases arising from family situations points up the most critical contingency in the use of this protective strategy, the choice of an appropriate object. Denouncers with close and permanent relations with the denounced are particularly vulnerable to counter-denunciation, as the accusation is apt to rest solely on their word and illegitimate motives for the denunciation may be readily apparent. But again, where relations between the two parties are more distant, counter-denunciation has more chance of success where the denouncer is of more or less equivalent status with the denounced. Thus, the judge can be easily convinced that a schoolmate might unjustly accuse one from jealousy, but will reject any contention that an adult woman would lie about an attempted purse-snatching incident.

While a denounced youth has a fair

chance of successfully discrediting a complainant of his own age, and some chance where the complainant is a family member, counter-denunciations directed against officials, particularly against the most frequent complainants in the juvenile court, the police, almost inevitably fail. In fact, to attempt to counterattack the police, and to a lesser extent, other officials, is to risk fundamentally discrediting moral character, for the court recoils against all attacks on the moral authority of any part of the official legal system.

One reflection of this is the court's routine refusal to acknowledge complaints of *unfair* treatment at the hands of the police. On occasion, for example, parents complain that their children were arrested and brought to court while others involved in the incident were not. Judges regularly refuse to inquire into such practices:

> Two young Puerto Rican boys were charged with shooting a BB gun. After police testimony, their mother said something in Spanish, and their priest-translator explained to the judge: "What they've been asking all morning is why they did not bring the other two boys." The judge replied: "I can only deal with those cases that are before me. I can't go beyond that and ask about these other boys that are not here."

Similarly, in this same case the judge refused to inquire into a complaint of police brutality when the mother complained that one boy had been hit on the head, saying: "The question of whether he was injured is not the question for me right now."

But beyond this, the court will often go to great lengths to protect and defend the public character of the police when it is attacked during a formal proceeding. To accuse a policeman of acting for personal motives, or of dishonesty in the course of his duties, not only brings immediate sanctions from the court but also tends to discredit basically the character of the delinquent accuser. Accusations of this nature threaten the basic ceremonial order of the court proceeding and hence the legitimacy of the legal order itself.

Notes

1. Cavan (1966) employs the concept "normal trouble" to describe aspects of barroom behavior. "Normal trouble" involves "improper activities that are frequent enough to be simply shrugged off or ignored" and hence constitutes "a taken-for-granted aspect of the public drinking place" (p. 18). Cases where the juvenile court feels no special intervention is required involve "normal trouble" in this sense.

2. On occasion, however, the court may find itself in the position of pushing a more severe definition of "trouble" and a more drastic course of action upon some other party. This occurs when the court diagnoses "trouble" where the complainant feels there is none and, more frequently, when parents deny serious trouble in the case of their child.

3. Note, however, that even though this denunciation succeeded, the denouncer suffered both discrediting and penalty. Immediately after the delinquency case had been decided the police took out a complaint for "contributing to the delinquency of a minor" against him, based on his admitted homosexual activities with the youth. This "contributing" case was brought before the juvenile court later that same morning, complainant and accused changed places, and the first denouncer was found guilty, primarily from what he had revealed about his behavior earlier in establishing the delinquency complaint.

References

Cavan, Sherri. 1966 *Liquor License: An Ethnography of Bar Behavior.* Chicago: Aldine.

McCorkle, Lloyd W. and Richard Korn. 1964. "Resocialization within walls." In David Dressler (ed.), *Readings in Criminology and Penology.* New York: Columbia University Press.

Schutz, Alfred. 1964. *Collected Papers, Vol. II: Studies in Social Theory.* Ed. by Maurice Natanson. The Hague: Martinus Nijhoff.

Sykes, Gresham M. and David Matza. 1957. "Techniques of neutralization: A theory of delinquency." *American Sociological Review* 22:664–70.

Prosecuting Juveniles as Adults: The Quest for "Objective Decisions"

25

Lee Ann Osbun
Peter A. Rode

Waiver: Purpose, History, and Major Trends

Since the inception in the United States of a specialized judicial institution for dealing with children and youthful offenders, controversy has surrounded the determination of the boundary between the juvenile and the adult court. In all states, the age of the offender has been the major factor employed in deciding whether juvenile or adult court jurisdiction will attach in a particular case. Although the age specified has varied among states and, over time, within states, most statutes now set 18 as the age of original criminal court jurisdiction,[1] thereby providing that all juveniles 17 or younger initially are subject to the jurisdiction of the juvenile court. In addition to demarcation by age, all states provide for the consideration of other factors in determining jurisdiction in some cases. While age is the initial criterion used to decide a youth's eligibility for juvenile court, other factors (such as seriousness of

the alleged offense, past record, dangerousness, and suitability for treatment within the juvenile system) also may enter into the jurisdiction decision. The additional criteria and the legal mechanisms for making the decision to waive juvenile court jurisdiction vary tremendously from state to state. The intent of these varying standards and mechanisms, however, has been the same: to recognize and to provide for cases in which public safety or individual needs are served better by handling chronological juveniles as adults.

Historically, authority to make decisions regarding the waiver of juveniles to the adult criminal system was granted to the juvenile court judge, who exercised discretion within very broad guidelines set by the state legislature. Consistent with the informal, individualized approach derived from the *parens patriae* doctrine, formal rules of procedure and specific substantive standards rarely were utilized. Prior to reforms beginning in the 1960s then, judges could be said to have "made waiver decisions in an atmosphere of informal procedure and unfettered discretion" (Whitebread and Batey, 1981: 210–211).

From *Criminology,* Vol. 22, No. 1, 1984, pp. 187–202. Reprinted by permission of the American Society of Criminology and the authors.

The United States Supreme Court's 1966 ruling in *Kent v. United States* marked the beginning of major change in the waiver process. In addition to granting basic procedural rights to defendants, the Court in this case also listed eight substantive factors the judges might consider in making waiver decisions *(Kent v. United States,* 1966). In following years, state legislatures offered judges further guidance by specifying the findings needed to justify waiver and by providing lists of criteria to be considered during waiver proceedings (Sorrentino and Olsen, 1977; Simmons, 1978; Wagner, 1979).

Despite the procedural safeguards and substantive criteria enacted in the wake of the Kent decision, judicial discretion in the waiver process has been subjected to continued criticism. The substantive criteria still are considered by many to be too ambiguous to provide an adequate limitation of judicial discretion. Interpretation of the standards remains subjective and "the large number of factors that may be taken into consideration provides ample opportunity for selection and emphasis" as needed to justify the desired outcome (Zimring, 1981: 195). The potential for abuse of discretion continues to be high. The lack of specificity within the standards, for example, may allow judges to legitimate essentially political decisions (such as those made in response to public outrage over a particular crime) in the language of individual rehabilitation (Sorrentino and Olsen, 1977: 510–511; Malmquist, 1979). Others suggest that an ambiguous and discretionary waiver process has contributed substantially to the court's perceived inability to deter serious juvenile crime. Judicial waiver, according to these critics, inherently is unable to provide the certainty of punishment—in this case, the certainty of prosecution as an adult—that they say is an essential element of effective deterrence (Feld, 1981: 515–518).

Additional criticisms of judicial discretion in the waiver decision are directed not at the ambiguity of the standards guiding the decision, but at the fundamental assumptions on which those standards are based. Standards or guidelines for the waiver decision usually are intended to provide indicators of a juvenile's dangerousness or nonamenability to treatment. But critics contend that it currently is impossible to predict with any accuracy whether or not treatment and rehabilitation are possible in a particular case or if a person is dangerous. If this is so, increased clarity and specificity in the standards for judicial waiver will do nothing to improve the decision-making process. According to this argument, the problem lies not in ambiguous language but in a lack of knowledge. If there are no reliable empirical methods for diagnosing, classifying, or treating juvenile offenders, the principles of amenability and dangerousness have no value for the waiver decision and should be abandoned (Feld, 1978).

Partially in response to such criticisms, a number of states have attempted to define a more objective basis for waiver decisions. Although a recent study of juvenile codes effective in 1981 found that 47 states have judicial waiver provisions in their juvenile codes, other transfer mechanisms often co-exist with and affect judicial authority. For example, 14 states specify by statute certain offenses that automatically are excluded from juvenile court jurisdiction. These provisions are referred to as "excluded offense" or "automatic transfer" legislation. In addition. at least four states have attempted to confine judicial discretion by using objective criteria to establish a presumptive or *prima facie* case that certain youths should be transferred (Hamparian et al., 1982: 44–65).[2]

While state legislatures increasingly have been willing in the past several years to consider and to enact both excluded offense provisions and provisions that specify the elements of a presumptive case for waiver, such attempts to reduce discretion in the waiver process are not without fault. Most statutes that attempt to more objectively define those juveniles who should be transferred to criminal court rely only on age and present offense and not prior record. This approach has been criticized as being an overly broad method of effecting transfer (Zimring, 1981: 199–200) and as ignoring research findings that suggest that many juveniles arrested initially for serious, violent offenses will not face repeated charges of the same kind (Hamparian et al.,1978). In general, evidence indicates that when present offense is emphasized in selecting juveniles for transfer, there is a danger of identifying many first-time offenders for whom no treatment has been attempted and who are not likely to recidivate.

The controversies surrounding the process by which juveniles are transferred to the adult legal system point to larger issues in juvenile justice and criminal justice policy. Foremost among these issues is that of the discretionary authority accorded individual decision makers (law enforcement officers, prosecutors, judges, corrections officials) within the juvenile and criminal justice systems. Granted that the particular circumstances of each person and each offense may legitimately influence official decisions, how can equity be achieved while the arbitrary, prejudicial, and inconsistent application of the law is prevented? The more discretion given to individual decision makers, the greater the potential for abuse of that discretion.

In the past several years policymakers have moved to reduce the application of

discretion in the criminal justice system by adopting measures intended to assure the like treatment of like cases. Attention has been directed to "channeling, reducing, and controlling" individual discretion in decisions such as those of pretrial release and of sentencing (Nagel, 1982). As part of this trend, for example, state legislatures have considered, and in some cases adopted, proposals to provide for fixed or determinate sentences imposed on the basis of an offender's current offense and past record. A major justification for mandatory sentencing plans is that reduction of judicial and parole board discretion correspondingly will reduce inequalities and discrepancies in sentencing. Whether or not this objective is likely to be achieved is a matter of continuing debate (Feeley, 1983: 148).

The issue of discretion in the juvenile justice system is even more problematic since the juvenile court was created expressly to provide individual and particularistic treatment to those defined by age as children. Gradually, however, in the face of what some viewed as the harsh and arbitrary treatment of children under its jurisdiction, the juvenile court has been modified to incorporate many of the due process protections found in adult criminal court. Furthermore, in some states objective dispositional guidelines based on current offense and prior record are receiving serious consideration. As the juvenile court shifts from a parens patriae to an increasingly legalistic basis and considers the adoption of dispositional practices common to adult courts, the logic of its continued existence as a separate institution is being questioned (Conrad, 1981).

The present study, while not attempting to address directly the general issues of discretion and of the continued existence of the juvenile court, analyzes a specific policy that bears on them both. By examining the kinds of juvenile cases that are transferred to adult court, something may be learned about the efficacy of age as the primary determinant of juvenile court jurisdiction. By analyzing the kinds of cases in which waiver proceedings were initiated before and after implementation of statutorily defined "objective" criteria for waiver, something may be learned about the effect of such criteria as an alternative to the traditional exercise of discretion.

Revisions in Minnesota Waiver Provisions

Minnesota is one of the states that have moved recently to limit judicial discretion and to establish a more objective basis for the waiver of juvenile court jurisdiction. Prior to 1980 the Minnesota Juvenile Court Act provided that a juvenile 14 years of age or older could be transferred to adult court if the juvenile court judge found that "the child is not suitable to treatment" or that the "public safety is not served" by handling the child within the juvenile court.[3] No further substantive guidance was provided by statute. In 1980 the state legislature established a classification scheme that defined a class of juvenile offenders *presumed* to be unfit for juvenile court treatment. These juveniles are identified on the basis of their age, alleged offense, and record of prior felony offenses. Briefly, a prima facie or presumptive case for waiver can be established if the juvenile was at least 16 years old at the time of the offense and meets one of the combinations of alleged offense and prior record shown in Table 25.1.[4]

The general purpose of the statutory revision was to facilitate the transfer to adult court of juveniles identified as serious offenders. By allowing the prosecutor to establish a presumptive case for waiver in those instances where the specified criteria

are met, the effect of the change is to shift the initial burden of proof from the prosecutor to the defendant in this special category of cases.[5] Cases that do not meet the criteria also may be waived, although the burden of proof then rests on the prosecutor, who must show that the child is unsuitable to treatment or dangerous.

In substance, the presumptive criteria were intended to balance the severity of the alleged offense with the extent of the juvenile's prior record in identifying candidates for adult prosecution. As the severity level of the alleged offense increases, the number of prior felonies required decreases. Property and drug felony offenses require the most extensive prior record; violent felonies require the least extensive prior record.

Minnesota's statutory revisions come at a time when the very foundations of judicial discretion as exercised in the waiver process (and throughout the juvenile system) are being challenged, and when proposals to replace or to limit judicial discretion with objective formulas are being advanced by scholars and practitioners of juvenile justice. However, while the use of objective classification schemes to make waiver decisions has grown rapidly in recent years, these schemes often have been criticized as being imprecise and overly inclusive in defining those juveniles who should be transferred to adult court. Minnesota's 1980 statute attempts to limit judicial discretion while also meeting some of the criticisms directed at objective classification formulas used in other states. Because the statute provides one of the most detailed and balanced formulas enacted to date, Minnesota's recent experience under the revised law provides an important opportunity to assess the utility of objective formulas in identifying those juveniles who require the sanctions of the adult criminal system.

Table 25.1

Requirements for a Presumptive Case for Transfer

Alleged Offense	Prior Record[a]
1. Murder I	No prior record required.
2. Murder II or III Manslaughter I Criminal Sexual Conduct I Assault I	Adjudicated delinquent for *one* felony offense committed in the preceding 24 months.
3. Manslaughter II Kidnapping Criminal Sexual Conduct II Arson I Aggravated Robbery Assault II	Adjudicated delinquent for *two* felony offenses, not in the same behavioral incident, committed in the preceding 24 months.
4. Any other felony (e.g., burglary, auto theft, drug-related felonies)	Adjudicated delinquent for *three* felony offenses, not in the same behavioral incident, committed in the preceding 24 months.

a. One year after the waiver statute was enacted, the legislature modified the prior record requirement by eliminating the requirement that delinquency be adjudicated officially in order for prior offenses to be counted. Since the adjudication requirement was in effect at the time of the study, it is the version used in the following analysis. Additional data collected by the authors indicates that the conclusions reached here would be the same regardless of which version of the criteria was utilized.

Methodology

To evaluate the effect of Minnesota's revised waiver stature, demographic and case history data were obtained from juvenile court files in Hennepin County, an urban county of 900,000 people centered around the city of Minneapolis.[6] Hennepin County was chosen because in Minnesota serious youth crime, the intended target of the new waiver statute, is primarily an urban problem. In 1979, for example, 40.7% of juveniles arrested in Minnesota for major offenses against persons came from Hennepin County.[7] As the state's most populous county, it also has the largest juvenile court caseload and transfers more juveniles to adult court than any other county.

In Hennepin County waiver proceedings are initiated by the county attorney. The prosecutor may choose to initiate waiver proceedings in cases that meet the recently enacted presumptive criteria, but is not required to do so. Furthermore, proceedings may be initiated in cases which do *not* meet the criteria but in which the juvenile's unsuitability to treatment or dangerousness can be claimed on other grounds. Because of these possibilities, demographic and case history data were obtained from juvenile court files for two analytically distinct categories of cases: (1) those in which the juvenile's age, alleged offense, and prior record were sufficient to satisfy the presumptive criteria; and (2) those in which waiver proceedings actually were initiated by the prosecutor. Examination of cases in the first category allows a determination of the number of cases meeting the presumptive criteria that were considered for transfer. Analysis of the second category, however, provides a description of all cases in which transfer proceedings were begun.

Overall 145 cases met either or both of the above conditions during the 18 months covered by the study. The group in which proceedings were initiated was identified readily through log books maintained by the juvenile court and the county attorney's office. Identification of the cases that met the presumptive criteria—out of the thousands of cases petitioned into court each year—was more difficult. The county's computerized tracking system provided an initial list of juveniles who were over 16 years of age and were charged with felony offenses during the designated study periods. The final selection was completed after a case-by-case examination of individual files that had passed the initial screening.

While the county attorney is responsible for initiating waiver proceedings, the judge retains authority for making the waiver decision. Therefore, it was also important to determine which of the initiated cases actually were transferred for criminal prosecution. Each case in the study was followed from initial court petition through final disposition, including trial and sentence in criminal court for those transferred to the adult system. The date of birth, sex, and race of each juvenile were recorded as was information on the juvenile's court record. Court record information included: (1) the date, type, and outcome of all prior and present offenses petitioned into court; and (2) all previous dispositions received by the juvenile.

Data for the study were obtained from three six-month time periods: January 1 through June 30, 1979; January 1 through June 30, 1980; and January 1 through June 30, 1981. The last six-month period followed implementation of the revised statute, while the first two periods occurred during the time before the revisions took effect.

Results

Waiver Decisions and the Presumptive Criteria

General trends in the use of waiver proceedings in Hennepin County from the beginning of 1978 through the middle of 1981 are illustrated in Table 25.2. While the number of waiver motions *filed* by the county attorney during each six-month period remained virtually unchanged, the percentage of waiver motions *granted* increased substantially during the first six months of 1981 following implementation of the presumptive criteria. The increase in transfers granted cannot be attributed primarily to implementation of these criteria, however, as the percentage of waiver motions granted was virtually the same for cases that did not satisfy the presumptive criteria as it was for cases that did (83.3% and 82.6% respectively), indicating that the court's approval of waiver requests had increased across the board.

The next step in the analysis was to compare both cases in which waiver was sought and cases in which waiver was granted with the requirements of the presumptive criteria. As Table 25.3 indicates, a majority of

Table 25.2

Use of Waiver Proceedings in Hennepin County: 1978–1981

Time Period	Motions Filed	Motions Granted	Percentage Granted
January–June 1978	28	14	50.0
July–December 1978	32	15	46.9
January–June 1979	35	19	54.3
July–December 1979	33	20	60.6
January–June 1980	38	17	44.7
July–December 1980	30	19	63.3
Six-month average for 1978–1980:	32.7	17.3	53.1
January–June 1981	35	29	82.9

Table 25.3

Proportion of Cases Initiated and Transferred that Met the Presumptive Criteria

	Before Enactment[a]		After Enactment[b]	
	Number	Percentage	Number	Percentage
Initiated Cases				
Met criteria	15	20.5	12	34.3
Did not meet criteria	58	79.5	23	65.7
Total	73	100.0	35	100.0
Transferred Cases				
Met criteria	8	22.2	10	34.5
Did not meet criteria	28	77.8	19	65.5
Total	36	100.0	29	100.0

a. Cases petitioned into court from January 1 through June 30, 1979 and January 1 through June 30, 1980.

b. Cases petitioned into court from January 1 through June 30, 1981.

cases in both categories failed to meet the presumptive criteria. That is, most juveniles transferred to adult court as well as most for whom waiver proceedings were initiated did not belong to the special class of offenders who are now presumed by law to be unfit for juvenile court treatment. Following enactment of the revised statute, there was a slight increase in the proportion of transferred cases that did satisfy the criteria—from 22.2% before enactment to 34.5% after enactment. Despite this, however, even in the post-implementation period of January through June 1981, two-thirds of the juveniles transferred to adult court did not possess records sufficient to establish an initial presumption in favor of the transfer.

Even though most juveniles transferred do not meet the presumptive criteria, it might be assumed that juveniles who *do* satisfy the criteria are very serious offenders who are always or almost always transferred to adult court. The data do not support this assumption. Many juveniles who met the statutory requirements were never considered formally for transfer. While there was, as Table 25.4 indicates, an increase in

the waivers granted for this group of offenders, this increase may be attributable partly to the previously discussed across-the-board increase in motions granted. Furthermore, even after the revised statute became effective, prosecutors chose to file waiver motions for only about half of the juveniles (54.5%) who met the criteria, while fewer (45.5%) actually were transferred to adult court.

Tables 25.3 and 25.4 suggest that there has been some change in the degree of correspondence between satisfaction of the presumptive criteria and involvement in waiver proceedings. What is more significant, however, is the continuation of large disparities even after the waiver process was modified. Despite legislation that singles out for special consideration those juveniles who meet certain requirements of age, alleged offense, and prior record, prosecutors precluded waiver to adult court in almost one-half of the cases meeting the stated criteria.[8] Conversely, almost two-thirds of the cases in which motions for waiver were filed did not satisfy the criteria. It would appear then that the objective criteria in themselves have not provided

Table 25.4
The Use of Waiver Proceedings in Cases that Satisfy the Presumptive Criteria

	Before Enactment[a]		After Enactment[b]	
	Number	Percentage	Number	Percentage
Total Cases Satisfying the Presumptive Criteria	42	100.0	22	100.0
Waiver Motion Filed	15	35.7	12	54.5
Waiver Granted	8	19.1	10	45.5

a. Cases petitioned into court from January 1 through June 30, 1979 and January 1 through June 30, 1980.
b. Cases petitioned into court from January 1 through June 30, 1981.

prosecutors and judges with an adequate guide for deciding which juveniles should be handled as adults. Their decisions indicate that from their perspective the criteria identify many juveniles who should be retained in juvenile court and fail to identify many who should be transferred to adult court.

The Objective Criteria and Identification of Serious Offenders

Waiver decisions made by juvenile justice officials frequently did not coincide with the waiver decisions suggested by the legislatively defined presumptive criteria. This lack of coincidence does not mean that the criteria are totally useless; it does mean that the objective standards provided by the revised waiver statute do not in themselves give decision makers an adequate definition of juveniles to be transferred to adult court. The question remains as to why the objective criteria are an inadequate substitute for prosecutorial and judicial discretion in waiver decisions. More specifically, it is important to ask whether or not the criteria are effective in identifying those juvenile offenders considered serious, hard-core, or violent.

To address this question profiles were constructed of: (1) those juveniles meeting

the presumptive criteria and (2) those juveniles involved in waiver proceedings. Variables used in constructing the profiles are those commonly accepted as indicative or definitive of serious delinquency: severity of the present offense (violent versus property or drug-related offenses); number of felony offenses charged in the present case; number of offenses, felony offenses, and violent offenses previously admitted or proven in court; length of time covered by the juvenile's official delinquency record (an indicator of the persistence of delinquent behavior and of the amount of time exposed to treatment within the juvenile system); and prior commitment to one of the state's juvenile institutions. No attempt was made to obtain an independent judgment of the youth's dangerousness or amenability to treatment or to measure subjective concepts like sophistication and cruelty. Only objective and verifiable data that can be readily and consistently found in official court records were utilized to construct the profiles.

Table 25.5 compares the profiles of juveniles whose age, offense, and prior record were sufficient to meet the presumptive criteria with those of juveniles who actually became involved in the waiver process. For this table, data from the entire 18-month study period were aggregated. Prosecutorial rather than judicial decisions were used because they represent the initial screening of waiver cases. Essentially the same results were obtained when judicial decisions to grant waiver were analyzed.

The differences between the group profiles presented in Table 25.5 are reduced somewhat by the fact that 27 cases were selected by both methods and therefore were counted in both groups. Even so, it is clear that those juveniles who satisfied the presumptive criteria possessed less serious records (as measured by the variables listed above) than those juveniles who actually became involved in the waiver process. Fewer than half of the juveniles identified by the presumptive criteria were charged with violent felonies or with multiple felonies. While they had, on the average, more prior felony offenses than the waiver group, their prior record was less likely to include violent offenses. Fewer than one-third of the presumptive criteria group had an official delinquency record that spanned more than three years, while almost 60 percent of the waiver group had official records spanning three years or more. Fewer than one-third of the presumptive criteria

group had been placed previously in a state juvenile institution.

To provide an additional perspective, Table 25.6 focuses on cases that satisfied the presumptive criteria, and compares those that were accepted by the prosecutor as appropriate for waiver and those that were rejected. The pattern demonstrated previously in Table 25.5 clearly is repeated. Cases accepted for waiver were on the whole significantly more serious than cases that were rejected. Most importantly, the data indicate that the presumptive criteria identify a rather large subgroup of juveniles who do not on closer examination appear to be very serious offenders. Though technically satisfying the minimum requirements established by the legislature, these youths (left-hand column of Table 25.6) typically are property offenders who have no history of violent offenses, either past or present. They also began their delinquency careers relatively late, have been known to the court for only one or two years, and consequently have been exposed to few of the treatment resources available to the court. While Table 25.5 suggests that the presumptive criteria fail to identify

Table 25.5

Comparison of Waiver Cases and Cases Selected by Objective Criteria

	Presumptive Criteria Satisfied		Motion for Waiver Filed	
	Number	Percentage	Number	Percentage
Total number of cases	64	100.0	108	100.0
Charged with violent felony	24	37.5	60	55.6
Charged with multiple felonies	28	43.8	68	63.0
Avg. number of prior offenses	7.1	—	7.6	—
Avg. number of prior felonies	4.2	—	3.1	—
One or more prior violent felonies	12	18.8	30	27.8
Juvenile court involvement exceeding three years	18	28.1	64	59.3
Avg. length (yrs.) of juvenile court involvement	2.2	—	3.4	—
Prior commitment to state institution	20	31.3	47	43.5

Table 25.6

Prosecutor's Decision to Request Waiver in Cases Satisfying Presumptive Criteria

	Motion for Waiver Not Filed		Motion for Waiver Filed	
	Number	Percentage	Number	Percentage
Total number of cases	37	100.0	27	100.0
Charged with violent felony	8	21.6	16	59.3
Charged with multiple felonies	10	27.0	18	66.7
Avg. number of prior offenses	6.3	—	8.1	—
Avg. number of prior felonies	4.1	—	4.3	—
One or more prior violent felonies	3	8.1	9	33.3
Juvenile court involvement exceeding three years	5	13.5	13	48.2
Avg. length (yrs.) of juvenile court involvement	1.5	—	3.2	—
Avg. age at first delinquency petition	15.5	—	14.3	—
Prior commitment to state institution	6	16.2	14	52.0

many juveniles with serious records, Table 25.6 shows that the criteria identify many juveniles whose overall records could not reasonably be described as serious, violent, or hard-core.

Discussion

Judicial discretion in the making of waiver decisions has been subject to considerable criticism in recent years. Critics claim that the subjective guidelines under which most courts operate are extremely vague, and that the individualized and clinical methods used to determine the desirability of adult prosecution are unreliable. Discretionary waiver procedures therefore invite abuses and result in the faulty identification of hard-core offenders. Support has been garnered for the replacement of subjective criteria with legislatively defined objective standards by those who maintain that "a properly constructed legislative matrix, based on combinations of present offense and prior record, will identify hard-core youth more accurately and objectively than does individualized judicial inquiry" (Feld, 1978: 523).

Several states recently have established objective criteria that either automatically exclude certain juveniles from juvenile court jurisdiction or create a presumption in favor of exclusion. In 1980 Minnesota enacted a detailed statutory formula to govern its waiver process. The formula combines the variables of age, alleged offense, and prior record to identify juveniles presumed to be unfit for retention in the juvenile system.

Contrary to the claims of its supporters, the objective criteria adopted by the Minnesota legislature have not proven to be an adequate means for selecting juveniles for transfer to adult court. The criteria single out many juveniles whose records do not appear to be very serious and fail to identify many juveniles whose records are characterized by violent, frequent, and persistent delinquent activity. Despite its defects and potential for abuse, the traditional discretionary process used by prosecutors and juvenile court judges to make waiver decisions appears to be more successful than the objective criteria alone in identifying the more serious juvenile offenders. Although critics of the discretionary waiver process contend that waiver decisions should be based only on objective variables related to the juvenile's behavior, the present study suggests that objective formulas—even those as sophisticated and balanced as Minnesota's—are too simplistic and too rigid to summarize such behavioral data in a reliable and consistent manner.

Critics of judicial waiver have emphasized the unreliability of clinical predictions of dangerousness and amenability to treatment while failing to recognize that judicial and prosecutorial discretion has never in practice been limited to such predictions. Discretion may, for example, involve the examination of important distinctions regarding the present offense (such as the extent of victimization) that are not captured by the formal charge alone. It may involve the synthesizing of information about the pattern of the juvenile's delinquent career, the nature of his response to prior treatment efforts, and numerous other factors not easily reducible to simplistic objective formulas. Abuses and mistakes undoubtedly occur when the discretionary process is used to determine who should be waived to adult court. The research presented here, however, suggests that objective selection formulas offer no simple solution to this complex problem.

While it might be tempting to believe that the problem lies solely in the quality of the objective criteria devised so far and that further research could help to construct actuarial or objective tables with far greater analytic power, the plausibility of such an approach is questionable. First, while the literature on clinical diagnosis and prediction generally has been quite negative, several studies of actuarial prediction as applied to criminal justice also have produced dismal results (Monahan, 1981:101–104). Second, any effort to reduce the number of false negatives (juveniles who do not meet the criteria and yet are waived) probably would increase the number of false positives (juveniles who do meet the criteria but whose records generally are considered too weak to warrant transfer). Finally, it is important to remember that so-called objective data available from court records are based on previous exercises of discretion (decisions regarding arrest, prosecution, plea-bargaining, and disposition) that pervade the juvenile justice system and that are based only indirectly on the child's actual behavior. In short, there is no indication that further efforts to improve the reliability of objective waiver formulas would obtain significant results.

Notes

1. Eight states set the age at 17 and four states set the original age of criminal court jurisdiction at 16 years of age (Hamparian et al., 1982: 43–44).

2. Seven states plus the District of Columbia allow the prosecutor to file charges in either juvenile or adult court against juveniles at specified ages for specified offenses (Hamparian et al., 1982:62). However, these provisions, known as "concurrent jurisdiction," "direct file," or "prosecutorial choice" provisions,

represent a transfer of discretion rather than an attempt to limit or eliminate discretion through objective criteria.

3. Since 1959 the waiver process has been governed by Minnesota Statute 260.125 as amended.

4. In this study the prima facie criteria refer to the criteria specified in Minnesota Statute 260.125 Subds. 3(2), 3(3), 3(4), and 3(5). Another section of the new waiver statute states that a prima facie case is established if the child

"is alleged by delinquency petition to have committed an aggravated felony against the person and (a) in committing the offense, the child acted with particular cruelty or disregard for the life or safety of another; or (b) the offense involved a high degree of sophistication or planning by the juvenile." This section was excluded from the study because it could not be considered as part of an objective waiver formula due to the highly subjective nature of the factors listed. In any event, no cases that cited this section as a reason for waiver were found in Hennepin County.

5. If the presumptive case is unrebutted—if the defendant does not introduce significant evidence bearing on the issues of suitability for treatment or dangerousness—transfer for adult prosecution will occur (In re Welfare of Givens, 1981). On the introduction of significant evidence bearing on the allegations of unsuitability and dangerousness, the burden of proof moves back to the prosecutor.

6. Data from Hennepin County were collected as part of a larger study of waiver in ten Minnesota counties (Osbun and Rode, 1982). The data base for the larger study includes all cases in which reference proceedings were initiated between January 1, 1978 and June 30, 1981 in ten Minnesota counties.

7. Based on raw figures on Part I offenses against persons supplied by the Minnesota Bureau of Criminal Apprehension.

8. It should perhaps be noted that a wide variety of behaviors are included within the legal definition of a given offense. Thus the offense charged is not always a reliable indicator of the seriousness of the behavior. This fact may help explain prosecutorial choices at the same time that it calls into question the utility of charged offense as an objective criterion for reference.

References

Conrad, J. P. (1981) "Crime and the Child," pp. 179–192 in J. C. Hall et al. (eds.), Major Issues in Juvenile Justice Information and Training: Readings in Public Policy, Columbus, OH: Academy for Contemporary Problems.

Feeley, M. M. (1983) Court Reform on Trial: Why Simple Solutions Fail. A Twentieth Century Fund Report. New York: Basic Books.

Feld, B. C. (1981) "Legislative policies toward the serious juvenile offender: on the virtues of automatic adulthood." Crime and Delinquency 27 (October): 497–521.

————. (1978) "Reference of juvenile offenders for adult prosecution: the legislative alternative to asking unanswerable questions." Minnesota Law Rev. 62 (April): 515–618.

Hamparian, D. M., L. K. Estep, S. M. Muntean, R. R. Priestino, R. G. Swisher, P. L. Wallace, and J. L. White (1982) Youth in Adult Courts: Between Two Worlds. National Institute for Juvenile Justice and Delinquency Prevention. Washington, DC: U.S. Department of Justice.

Hamparian, D. M., R. Schuster, S. Dinitz, and J. P. Conrad (1978) The Violent Few: A Study of Dangerous Juvenile Offenders, Lexington, MA: D. C. Heath.

Kent v. United States (1966) 383 U.S. 541.

Malmquist, C. P. (1979) "Juveniles in adult courts: unresolved ambivalence," pp. 444–456 in S. C. Feinstein and P. L. Giovacchini (eds.), Adolescent Psychiatry: Developmental and Clinical Studies. Vol. 7. Chicago: Univ. of Chicago Press.

Monahan, J. (1981) Predicting Violent Behavior: An Assessment of Clinical Techniques. Beverly Hills, CA: Sage.

Nagel, S. S. (1982) "Discretion in the criminal justice system: analyzing, channeling, reducing, and controlling it." Emory Law J. 31 (Summer): 603–633.

Osbun, L. A. and P. A. Rode (1982) "Changing boundaries of the juvenile court: practice and policy in Minnesota." A Report of the Supreme Court Juvenile Justice Study Commission. Minneapolis: Office of Delinquency Control, University of Minnesota.

Simmons, J. (1978) "Waiver in Indiana—a conflict with the goals of the juvenile justice system" Indiana Law J. 53 (Spring): 601–614.

Sorrentino, J. N. and G. K. Olsen (1977) "Certification of juveniles to adult court." Pepperdine Law Rev. 4: 497–522.

Wagner, J. P. (1979) "Wisconsin's new juvenile waiver statute: when should we wave goodbye to juvenile court protections?" Wisconsin Law Rev. 1979: 190–216.

In re Welfare of Givens (1981) 307 N.W. 2d 489 [Minnesota].

Whitebread, C. H. and R. Batey (1981) "The role of waiver in the juvenile court: questions of philosophy and function," pp. 207–226 in J. C. Hall et al. (eds.), Major Issues in Juvenile Justice Information and Training Readings in Public Policy. Columbus, OH: Academy for Contemporary Problems.

Zimring, F. E. (1981) "Notes toward a jurisprudence of waiver," pp. 193–205 in J. S. Hall et al. (eds.), Major Issues in Juvenile Justice Information and Training: Readings in Public Policy. Columbus, OH: Academy for Contemporary Problems.

A Comparative Analysis of Organizational Structure and Inmate Subcultures in Institutions for Juvenile Offenders

26

Barry C. Feld

The penological debate over the origins, processes, and characteristics of inmate subcultures in correctional facilities has attributed the qualities of subcultures either to features of the formal organization or to preimprisonment characteristics of the incarcerated offenders.[1] Observers of adult and juvenile correctional facilities confirm the emergence of inmate subcultures within institutions, and most studies of prison cultures document their oppositional qualities, with the hostility and antagonism between inmates and staff subsumed in an "inmate code."[2]

The two competing explanations of the inmate social system are commonly referred to as the "indigenous origins" model and the "direct importation" model.[3] The former provides a functionalist explanation that relates the values and roles of the subculture to the inmates' responses to problems of adjustment posed by institutional deprivations and conditions of confinement.[4] Accordingly, the formal organization of the prison shapes the informal inmate social system. While earlier studies of adult maximum-security prisons described a monolithic inmate culture of collective opposition to staff values and goals,[5] more recent studies suggest that a modification of organizational structure in pursuit of treatment goals results in considerably greater variability in the inmate social system and the processes of prisonization.[6]

An alternative interpretation attributes the normative order of adult prisons to the identities, roles, and values held by the inmates before incarceration.[7] Accordingly, inmates' personal characteristics shape the subculture, and in a population of incarcerated offenders an oppositional, criminal value system predominates. Differences in social characteristics such as sex, race, or criminal involvement before incarceration influence both the subculture's qualities and any individual inmate's adaptations to it.[8]

From *Crime and Delinquency,* Vol. 27, No. 3, 1981, pp. 336-363. Reprinted by permission of Sage Publications, Inc. and the author.

Inmate Violence in Institutions

The prevalence of inmate violence and its significance for stratification, role differentiation, and subcultural processes represent a recurring theme.[9] However, the relationships between organizational variables, inmate violence, and other characteristics of the subculture have not been adequately explored.

Physical aggression, verbal abuse, or psychological intimidation can be used to create or reestablish relationships of domination and submission within the subculture.[10] Many maxims of the inmate code are attempts to regulate violence and exploitation among inmates, and many of the "argot" roles differentiate inmates on the basis of their use of or response to aggression.[11] For individual inmates, many of the "pains of imprisonment"—material deprivations, sexual isolation, and threats to status, self-esteem, and personal security — cited in functionalist explanations of subcultures can be alleviated by the use of violence. While imprisonment imposes deprivations, violence and exploitation provide at least some inmates with a potential solution, albeit at the expense of other inmates.[12]

The prevalence of inmate violence also reflects characteristics of the incarcerated. Many adult and juvenile inmates are drawn from social backgrounds or cultures that emphasize toughness, manliness, and the protection of one's own physical integrity.[13] Preincarceration experiences equip in different ways inmates from diverse social, economic, criminal, racial, or sexual backgrounds to participate in the violent subcultures within some institutions.[14] Thus, a predisposition to violence among the inmate subculture also reflects influences of cultural importation which organizational features may aggravate or mitigate.

Neither functionalist nor importation explanations alone adequately explain the characteristics of the inmate subculture or an inmate's adaptations to it. The functionalist model does not account for the influence of pre- and postimprisonment variables on inmates' adaptations, while the importation model does not fully explicate the connections between preprison characteristics and the subcultures that arise within institutions that are not custodial or punitive. Although some recent research attempts to integrate the two perspectives by identifying the ways in which preprison characteristics influence inmates' adaptations to adjustment problems created by the organization,[15] most subculture studies suffer from the common shortcoming of focusing on prisonization within only a single institution. In contrast, a comparison of organizations would permit a fuller exploration of the relationships between formal organizational structure and the ensuing inmate culture, as well as of the influence of preprison characteristics on the adaptations of inmates in diverse settings.[16] Controlling for the effects of preincarceration characteristics on inmates' perceptions and adaptations, this study presents a comparative analysis of the ways in which variations in organizational goals and intervention strategies in institutions for juvenile offenders produce differences in the informal inmate social system.

Organizational features affect the inmate subculture and the prevalence of inmate violence both by creating incentives for inmates to resort to violence and by providing inmates with opportunities to use violence. Organizational variations in the nature and extent of deprivations may motivate inmates in different ways to exploit others. Various organizational control strategies differ in the degree to which they provide an environment conducive to the

use of violence to relieve these deprivations. The deprivations and control strategies also influence many other aspects of
the subculture. This comparative analysis
examines the variations in organizational
goals, staff intervention strategies, and social control practices that influence the levels of violence and the structure of the inmate social system.

Correctional Typology

There are several descriptions of the organizational variations in juvenile and adult
correctional facilities that can be used as
tools to classify systematically and compare the relationships between organizational structure and inmate subculture.[17] A
common classification distinguishes juvenile correctional organizations on the basis
of their custody or treatment goals,[18] distinguishing differences in goals on the basis of
the relative emphases staff place on custody
and containment, and on vocational and academic education versus clinical or group
treatment.[19] The intervention strategies
used to achieve either custodial or therapeutic goals range from group-oriented
practices to those more attuned to individ-

uals' characteristics.[20] Group-oriented
strategies reflect efforts to change or control an inmate through the group of which
he is a member, while individualized methods of intervention focus more directly on
the person, without comparable manipulation of the social environment.

Organizational goals—custody or
treatment—and strategies of change—
group or individual—may vary independently; thus, four different types of correctional organizations may be
distinguished on the basis of both their
correctional goals and the means used to
attain those goals (see Figure 26.1).

Every juvenile correctional institution
confronts the same necessity to explain
both what its clients' problems are and how
the clients should be rehabilitated.[21] The answers to the questions of cause and cure in
turn determine the organizational goals and
the intervention strategies and social control practices required to achieve them. The
typology in Figure 26.1 illustrates four different kinds of correctional solutions to the
problems of juvenile offenders. It also suggests several interrelated organizational
variables: a staff ideology defining inmates
and their needs, organizational goals serv-

Figure 26.1:   Correctional Typology

| *Organizational* | *Organizational Goals* | |
Means	Custody	Treatment
Group-Oriented Intervention Strategy	Group Custody Custodial[a] Obedience/Conformity[b] Protective custody[c]	Group Treatment Group treatment[a] Treatment[b] Therapeutic community[c]
Individual-Oriented Intervention Strategy	Individual Custody Educational[a] Reeducation/Development[b] Protective custody[c]	Individual Treatment Psychotherapeutic[a] Treatment[b,c]

a. Organization corresponding to typology in Studt, Messinger, and Wilson, *C-Unit*, p. 12.
b. Organization corresponding to typology in Street, Vinter, and Perrow, *Organization for Treatment*, p. 12.
c. Organization corresponding to typology in Ohlin, "Organizational Reform in Correctional Agencies," p. 1000.

ing those needs, intervention strategies implemented through programs and social control practices, and the structure of relationships between inmates and staff.

A degree of internal consistency among these organizational variables is necessary. Methods of intervention and social control practices must be complementary, since efforts to ensure compliance that alienate the inmate are incompatible with change strategies requiring commitment on the part of that inmate.[22] Compliance strategies and programs will vary with the correctional goals and inmate changes sought and determine the kinds of relationships staff develop with inmates. Amitai Etzioni's compliance framework provides a basis for a comparative organizational analysis of staff control strategies and inmates' responses in coercive and normative-coercive settings.[23] The primary correctional social control strategies are (1) the threat or use of physical coercion, (2) the threat or use of transfer to less desirable units or isolation cells, (3) the use of a privilege system,[24] and (4) collaboration between inmates and staff, which may be either informal[25] or formal.[26]

Methods

The data for this study were collected in ten cottage units located in four juvenile institutions administered by the Massachusetts Department of Youth Services before the closing of the training schools.[27] A process of institutional decentralization initiated to transform the various cottage settings into small, therapeutic communities[28] provided considerable autonomy and independence for each individual unit. Clinical, vocational, academic, and cottage personnel either formed staff teams or were assigned to cottages to develop coordinated treatment programs. Decentralization resulted in a number of diverse "mini-institutions" in

which staff pursued a variety of goals using different intervention strategies.

Since inmate assignments to the various cottages were not randomized, the ten cottages studied were selected to maximize the comparability of inmate populations and the variety of treatment strategies used. The ten cottages studied included seven units for males, two for females,[29] and one coeducational facility, located in four different state institutions. Cottage populations were matched on the basis of age, race, past criminal histories (both official and self-reported), present commitment offense, age at initial contact and number of prior juvenile court appearances, and prior commitments to institutions. The inmate characteristics in the various cottages are summarized in Table 26.1. The cottages sampled produced comparable inmate groups. Although cottage assignments were not randomized, there was no systematic effort by administrators to match inmate "needs" with particular treatment programs, and the primary determinants were the availability of bed space and the need to maintain a population balance among the various cottages.

In addition to the matching of populations, statistical controls for the effects of background characteristics within each cottage were used to establish cottage comparability. Controls for each background variable were used to determine whether a particular characteristic was systematically associated with differences within each cottage population and whether the differences among cottages were a product of these population differences. In addition to tests for relationships between background variables and attitudes, sign tests were used to allow for interaction effects between inmates' characteristics and cottage treatment strategies. Despite some variations in the respective cottage populations, these

Table 26.1
Inmate Background Characteristics

| | Custody-Oriented Cottages | | | | | Treatment-Oriented Cottages | | | |
| | Group | Individual | | | | Individual | Group | | |
	Cottage 9 (n = 27)	Cottage 8 (n = 15)	Elms (n = 40)	Westview (n = 29)	Lancaster (F) (n = 28+22)[a]	Topsfield (coed) (n = 15)	Sunset (n = 15)	Shirley (n = 16)	"I Belong" (n = 8)
Mean age	15.7	16.3	15.6	15.6	14.9	16.2	15.5	16.3	14.2
Percentage black inmates	19%	27%	35%	21%	11%	32%	25%	19%	25%
Mean age at first juvenile court appearance	12.6	13.2	12.7	13.1	13.1	14.1	12.5	13.8	12.4
Seriousness of present offense (percentage of residents)									
High[b]	24%	36%	35%	27%	9%	0%	23%	21%	29%
Moderate[c]	68	43	60	54	34	60	77	57	43
Low[d]	8	21	5	19	57	40	0	21	28
Prior institutional experience (percentage of residents)	92%	82%	90%	62%	60%	87%	73%	67%	50%

a. Institutional decentralization and the development of cottage-based programs occurred later and, when this study was conducted, were less complete at the Industrial School for Girls, Lancaster, than at the corresponding male institutions. The school still functioned as a traditional training school without any significant program differentiation by cottage. Separate analysis of inmate and staff data in the two cottages sampled ($n = 28+22$) revealed virtually no differences. Consequently, the Lancaster questionnaire data are presented in the aggregate.

b. Offenses against the person—murder, manslaughter, rape, assaults, robbery, and the like.

c. Property offenses—burglary, theft, forgery, unauthorized use of a motor vehicle, and drug offenses.

d. Misdemeanor-level public misbehavior, such as disorderly conduct, as well as juvenile status offenses.

techniques support the conclusion that the substantial differences between cottages were not a function of variations in the inmate populations and are properly attributed to the cottages' social structures.[30] In institutions with young populations (averaging approximately sixteen years of age), who are presumably less committed to criminal careers than are imprisoned adults and who are incarcerated for an average of four months, it is not surprising that background characteristics or preimprisonment experiences are subordinate to the more immediate, organizational imperatives. (Because the sample is not random, no tests of significance are reported.)

Data were collected in each of the ten cottages by a team of five trained researchers who spent about six weeks in each unit administering questionnaires and interview schedules to both staff members and residents. Between 90 and 100 percent of the staff and residents in each cottage completed hour-long closed-ended questionnaires and equally extensive open-ended structured interviews. Most of the researchers' time was spent in participant observation and unstructured interviews, with field notes transcribed onto standardized forms to simplify analysis, coding, and comparison of observations from different settings.

Findings

Organizational Structure

Although the administrators of the Massachusetts Department of Youth Services told the institutional staff to "do good things for kids," they did not specify what the staff members should do or how they should do it. The process of institutional decentralization allowed staff to pursue a variety of goals using diverse treatment strategies within the autonomous cottages. In struc-

turing programs for how their clients should be handled and changed, staff were guided by their own assumptions about the causes of and cures for delinquent behavior. Although there was some diversity among staff within the respective cottages, recruitment, self-selection, and cottage assignments resulted in relatively homogeneous correctional ideologies among cottage personnel; the focus of this study is on the substantial differences among the various units in programs and goals that emerged and the effects of these differences on the respective inmate cultures.

Cottage Programs and Social Control Strategies

Maximum Security (Group Custody)

Cottage Nine was a unit used for juveniles who had run away from the institution and for youths who had committed other disciplinary infractions. About half of all residents escaped from the institution at some time during their stay; there were no significant differences between those who absconded and those who did not. There was no vocational training, academic education, or clinical program in the maximum-security setting. Intervention consisted of punishment and deprivation, with periods of enforced idleness interrupted only for meals, routine clean-up, and cottage maintenance. All the cottage activities took place in a highly controlled, structured environment, and virtually all activities occurred in a group setting. Staff attempted to coerce inmate conformity and obedience, and punished recalcitrance or resistance. As a result, a typical three- to four-week stay in Cottage Nine before return to an open cottage was an unpleasant experience which residents had little choice but to endure.

Staff used physical coercion and isolation cells—"the Tombs"—to enforce obedience, conformity, and respect. These techniques were feasible since there was no program in which staff needed to obtain active inmate participation, and the staff's physical domination made coercion practicable. Staff members used their limited repertoire of controls to counter major forms of deviance such as riots and fights, as well as inmate provocation, disrespect, or recalcitrance. They also used mass lockups and other forms of group punishment. Other control techniques were virtually absent, since there were no amenities or privileges that might be lost, and strategies designed to ensure group control precluded the development of individualized relationships necessary for collaborative controls. The use of coercive tactics alienated inmates, who minimized contacts with staff. Personnel ignored considerable inmate misbehavior that did not challenge their authority, and did not encourage inmates to report deviance that occurred outside the presence of staff members.

Industrial Training School
(Individual Custody)

Despite considerable program diversity, each of the individual custody settings—Cottage 8, Elms, Westview, and the Lancaster Industrial School for Girls—used vocational training as the primary strategy of change. Most of the trades programs consisted of either institutional maintenance or services for residents—a cafeteria program, laundry program, institutional upkeep, painting, landscaping and groundskeeping, and the like. There were limited academic and clinical programs in some of the cottages. However, individual counseling sessions were not scheduled regularly, and inmates initiated contact with clinical staff primarily to secure a weekend furlough or early parole.

Compared with those in the maximum-security unit, residents of the training school cottages enjoyed greater physical freedom within the institution, which rendered staff control more difficult. Inmate cooperation in the work programs was also problematic. Staff used a privilege system to induce conformity, coupling this with the threat of transfer to more punitive, maximum-security settings. The privilege system was a security-graded progression, with inmates at different levels accorded different privileges or governed by different restrictions. Passage from one level to another reflected the amount of time served and an inmate's general behavior and conformity. Because of the relatively limited privileges available, staff members exercised considerable discretion in the rules they enforced, against whom, and under what circumstances. The staff also collaborated informally with inmate leaders to maintain order, manipulating the privilege system to confer additional status and rewards on the elite. Informal collaboration between staff members and the inmate elite is a common training school control strategy because of the availability of privileges, the discretionary bases upon which rewards are manipulated, and the problems of maintaining order posed by program individualization, the need to secure cooperation, and increased inmate freedom.[31]

Individual Treatment

The individual treatment program used all types of clinical treatment, including both individual counseling and individual therapy in a group setting. The cottage program was free and open with few restrictions. Staff minimized deprivations and maximized amenities to encourage inmate commitment and involvement in the clinical process. Staff eschewed universal rules, responding to each inmate on the basis of individualized therapeutic considerations.

Staff relied almost exclusively on a rich privilege system to secure the cooperation and participation of inmates. Although the threat of transfer to a less desirable setting was a possibility, the penalty was never invoked. There was virtually no physical coercion or informal collaboration used to obtain conformity or obedience. In response to inmate deviance, additional clinical sessions were prescribed to reinforce the privilege system—not as sanctions, but to provide additional supports for the recalcitrant resident.

Group Treatment

All of the group treatment cottages used a therapeutic community treatment model,[32] which was supplemented with either vocational or academic educational programs. The therapeutic community treatment model used both daily staff-inmate community meetings and group therapy sessions. A daily log provided the agenda for cottage community discussions, with staff and residents encouraged to record incidents that required the community's attention. At these meetings, staff integrated observations of residents on work, school, or cottage living. They then divided the cottage populations into smaller treatment groups and used a type of guided group interaction to deal with interpersonal problems or to resolve issues raised during the community meetings.

Formal collaboration between staff and inmates was the primary means of social control. Staff used the group problem-solving process to define and enforce cottage norms and to mobilize group pressures to deal with specific instances of deviance. Rules and consequences were elaborated in a privilege system that was jointly enforced; each inmate's privileges and freedoms were more dependent upon performance and participation and were less a function of the length of time served than was the case in the more custodial settings. The gradations of privileges and freedom and the responsibilities associated with each level were consistently and energetically enforced.

The strength of the formal collaboration process was the pressure staff placed upon residents to motivate other inmates to change. The concept of "responsibility" was crucial, and residents were responsible both for their own progress and behavior and for that of others. This principle of third-party responsibility provided a therapeutic rationale that significantly transformed subcultural norms governing informing and greatly increased the amount of information received by staff about the inmate group.

The Relationship Between Staff Correctional Ideology and Cottage Program Characteristics

The differences in correctional programs and control strategies stemmed from various assumptions staff made about appropriate ways to treat inmates. Since staff members were allowed to form their own cottage teams, there was substantial interpersonal and ideological compatibility within units. For purposes of explaining the diversity in the cottage programs and subcultures, the more important differences were among the different units. (See Table 26.2 for a presentation of some of the dimensions on which they differed.)

One component of a correctional ideology is the emphasis placed by staff on inmates' obedience, respect for authority, and submission to external controls. Custodial staff were much more concerned with obedience and respect than were treatment personnel, and subscribed more exten-

Table 26.2
Selected Indicators of Staff Ideology and Goals (as a percentage of total staff in setting)

| Scale | Custody-Oriented Cottages | | | | | | Treatment-Oriented Cottages | | | |
| | Group | Individual | | | | Individual | | Group | |
	Cottage 9 (n = 9)	Cottage 8 (n = 16)	Elms (n = 15)	Westview (n = 10)	Lancaster (F) (n = 14)	Topsfield (coed) (n = 9)	Sunset (n = 5)	Shirley (n = 16)	"I Belong" (n = 8)
Respect for authority	89%	88%	73%	67%	54%	11%	0%	25%	25%
Free will and deterrence	79	81	60	78	50	0	40	38	13
Delinquents cannot be understood	67	75	67	67	43	0	0	19	13
Inmates are dangerous	67	63	47	56	43	0	20	38	13
Conformity to staff orders	56	69	71	63	50		20	6	13
Custody-oriented goals	37	34	32	37	38	15	13	21	10
Personnel acting in clinical capacity	0	18	7	10	21	56	20	44	50

Note: Each scale contains three or more items, with an interitem correlation greater than .5 and significant at the .001 significance level.

sively to the use of external controls to achieve inmate conformity.

Cottage staff members also differed in their views of deviance. Personnel in the treatment-oriented cottages attributed delinquency to emotional or psychological problems, while custody staff rejected psychopathology or emotional dysfunction, emphasizing as a cause of delinquency such factors as a youth's exercise of free will, which could be deterred by punishment. Because the custody staff rejected psychological interpretations, they found delinquent or bizarre inmate behavior considerably more difficult to understand than did treatment staff. Staff members also disagreed over whether delinquents were capable of establishing "normal" relationships, with those emphasizing custody far more likely than treatment personnel to regard the inmates in their cottages as "hard-core delinquents" who were dangerous and untrustworthy.

A correctional ideology both rationalizes deviance and its control and describes the end result sought—the "changed" inmate. Institutional behavior provides the staff with an indicator of an inmate's "rehabilitation" and readiness to return to the community. Custody staff strongly preferred inmates who followed orders, kept to themselves, and stayed out of trouble, which reflected their greater emphasis on external conformity rather than internalized controls. Their more negative perceptions of inmates and apprehension about collusion also led the custody staff members to disrupt informal inmate associations and encourage self-isolation, while treatment personnel encouraged inmate involvement with other inmates.

These alternative analyses of delinquency led staffs to pursue different correctional goals. When personnel were asked to choose among various correctional goals for incarcerated delinquents, significantly more of the custody-oriented staff members subscribed to custodial institutional objectives—isolation, respect and discipline, and training and educating—than did treatment personnel. Allocation of institutional resources provides another indicator of organizational goals; in juvenile institutions, personnel are the primary resource. Organizations pursuing custodial goals assign personnel to control and containment, or vocational and educational functions; treatment-oriented organizations, in contrast, assign more staff members to clinical and treatment functions. The greatest proportion of personnel in the custodial cottages served as guards, work supervisors, and academic instructors, while the treatment-oriented cottages assigned a larger percentage of the staff to treatment roles, with a corresponding reduction in purely supervisory personnel.

The Inmate Subcultures

An inmate subculture develops within the confines of a correctional institution, and its norms and values reflect the focal concerns of institutional life and the inmate population. Inmate roles and subculture stratification reflect conformity to or deviation from these norms, and newly entering inmates are socialized into this system and adapt to the expectations of their fellow inmates. The informal social system often mediates the effectiveness of the formal organization, aiding or thwarting staff members in the pursuit of their goals.[33]

A feature of correctional organization that influences the character of the inmate social systems is the extent to which staff members successfully control inmate violence and exploitation. Institutional characteristics influence the prevalence of inmate aggression by varying the levels of deprivation, a condition that gives some inmates an incentive to direct predatory behavior at others, and by providing the opportunities under which such exploitation may be carried out successfully. Inmate violence is directly related to the quality of relations between inmates and staff and to the information available to personnel about the workings of the subculture. Thus, controlling violence is a sine qua non of effective correctional programming and administration.

There was a clear relationship between the type of formal organization and the informal inmate culture. In the punitive, group custody setting, inmates experienced the greatest deprivation and were the most alienated from other inmates and staff members. Inmate alienation prevented the development of effective staff controls and allowed aggressive inmates to exploit their fellows through diverse forms of violent behavior. In the training school settings, the staff members used a privilege system coupled with informal cooperation of the inmate elite to bring potentially aggressive inmates under some degree of control. This reduced the effectiveness of inmate violence and exploitation, although aggression remained the dominant mode of interaction within the subculture. In the treatment-oriented cottages, especially in the group treatment programs, formal collaboration between inmates and staff members reduced the level of inmate violence and provided a therapeutic rationale for informing that made the workings of the subculture more visible to staff. The greater visibility, combined with significantly reduced deprivation, lowered the necessity for and effectiveness of inmate aggression and exploitation and allowed for the emergence of a more positive inmate culture.

Inmate Perceptions of Staff and Inmates

Problems of institutional living influence inmates' motives for interaction and the types of solutions they can develop. Just as correctional personnel structure their relationships with inmates, residents attempt to structure and control their relationships with staff and other inmates to resolve the problems of the informal organization. The types of relationships and collective solutions available depend upon the inmates' perceptions of the program, staff, and other inmates. Inmate cooperation with staff augers for a more open, visible, and manageable social system. If staff cannot obtain inmate cooperation through either formal or informal collaboration, then a more closed, subterranean, and violent social system emerges.

Cottage Purposes

The cottage goals and programs define the organizational context to which inmates must adapt. Table 26.3 provides a breakdown of inmates' perceptions of the goals, staff, and other aspects of life in the different cottages. When asked about cottage purposes and staff expectations, residents of the custody-oriented cottages described the cottages as places for punishment, while inmates in the treatment-oriented settings regarded the cottages as places for rehabilitation and for gaining self-awareness. As a further indicator of organizational purposes and adaptive constraints, inmates were asked whether staff encouraged them to conform or to gain insight into their own motivation and behavior. Responding to staff expectations (see Table 26.2), inmates in the custody-oriented settings were more than twice as likely to view the staff as demanding obedience and conformity as were those in the treatment cottages, while the latter were almost three times as likely as the residents of custody-oriented settings to describe staff expectations in terms of treatment and self-understanding.

A corollary of the differences in custodi-

anship and punitiveness was the "pain of imprisonment" that inmates described. While some of the problems inmates confront are inherent in incarceration—loss of liberty, separation from family and friends, increased dependency and submission to authority, and the like—other pains of confinement, such as material deprivations, are attributable to characteristics of a particular setting. By virtually every measure, the inmates in the custody-oriented cottages reported far more extensive and severe problems associated with their confinement—boredom, living with other residents, and material deprivations — than did the inmates in the treatment cottages. These reported differences in institutional amenities resulted from staff actions, since treatment personnel tried to minimize the unpleasant, alienating aspects of incarceration to a greater extent than did custody-oriented staff.

Inmate Perceptions of Staff

Inmates' views of staff paralleled staff members' perceptions of inmates. In those settings where staff had negative views of inmates, describing them as dangerous, unreliable, abnormal, or incorrigible, the inmates held correspondingly negative views of staff, regarding them as untrustworthy, unhelpful, or indifferent. In those settings where the staff expressed more favorable views of inmates, residents shared more positive views of the staff. Virtually every inmate in the maximum-security setting and over half the inmates in the individual custody settings, as contrasted with only about one-fifth of those in the treatment settings, regarded staff as neither concerned nor helpful. Inmates readily equated punitive programs with unconcerned staff and therapeutic programs with committed staff. Likewise, residents of the custody-oriented cottages initiated fewer contacts with personnel and talked with them less about personal problems than did those in the treatment settings.

Inmate Perceptions of Other Inmates

Characteristics of the inmate social system also reflect the extent to which inmates can cooperate with one another to ease the hardship of adjusting to the institution. The residents of the custody-oriented cottages reported substantially lower levels of trust and concern on the part of other inmates than did those in the treatment-oriented settings. Residents of the treatment cottages also reported greater inmate solidarity than did their custody cottage counterparts. Since predatory behavior and subcultural violence were more prevalent in the custody-oriented settings, the differences in inmate perceptions also reflect the extent to which inmates were exploited and victimized by others.

Inmate Adaptations

Differences among the programs in staff expectations constitute an additional organizational constraint on inmates' adaptations. Custodial staff emphasized inmate conformity and obedience, whereas treatment staff emphasized gaining insight and solving personal problems (see Table 26.2). In response, inmates in the custody-oriented settings chose either overt conformity and covert deviance or obedience and conformity as adaptive strategies, while those in the treatment-oriented settings chose self-understanding. Similarly, adaptations reflecting elements of prisonization—prompt obedience, conformity, and self-isolation—were chosen by twice as many residents of custody-oriented settings as those in treatment programs, closely paralleling the staff expectations.

Social Structure of the Inmate Subculture

Inmates interact more frequently and intensely with residents of their own cottage than they do with those in other settings, and a set of norms and roles based upon those norms govern their interactions with other inmates and staff. Differences in staff intervention practices are strongly related to variations in inmates' perceptions of other inmates, staff, and institutional adaptation, and to corresponding differences in inmate norms, subculture roles, and interaction patterns.

The inmates' and staff's responses to violence and aggression are among the most important determinants of subculture processes. In the absence of effective controls, violence and aggression underlie most interactions within the inmate subculture.[34] Direct action, toughness, and defense of personal integrity are focal concerns of many delinquent inmates,[35] and even a few aggressive inmates can immediately make the control of violence a major concern within the institution. Moreover, the prevalence of violence is closely related to other subcultural norms, particularly those related to informing.

Inmate norms governing interactions with staff and the acceptability of informing personnel of other inmates' activities have been frequently described.[36] Informing and subcultural violence are closely linked, since uncontrolled violence can deter informing, while informing, if properly encouraged by staff, can reduce it. The regulation of the flow of information between inmates and staff thus emerges as a critical determinant of inmate roles and subculture structure.

Inmates' views of staff and inmates and their adaptations to the institution influence the amount of information staff members receive about the inmate social system,

Table 26.3
Selected Indicators of Inmate Attitudes (as a percentage of total residents)

| | Custody-Oriented Cottages | | | | | Treatment-Oriented Cottages | | | |
| | Group | | Individual | | | Individual | Group | | |
	Cottage 9 (n = 27)	Cottage 8 (n = 15)	Elms (n = 40)	Westview (n = 29)	Lancaster (F) (n = 28+22)	Topsfield (coed) (n = 15)	Sunset (n = 15)	Shirley (n = 16)	"I Belong" (n = 8)
Inmate perceptions of cottage goals: What is this place trying to do for you?									
Gain understanding	11%	20%	23%[a] (23)[a]	24%	28%	73%	53%	63% (64)	86%
Train and educate	11	7	0 (1)	0	0	13	7	13 (8)	0
Respect for authority	0	13	13 (15)	21	13	13	13	13 (13)	14
Punish for the wrong things they did	78	60	64 (61)	55	60	0	27	13 (15)	0
Staff emphasis									
Obey the rules and don't get into any trouble	63	86	74 (78)	79	73	7	46	43 (37)	0
Understand your personal problems	37	14	26	21	27	93	54	57	100
Staff do not help or care about inmates	96	87	46 (58)	59	51	13	20	25 (18)	0
Positive perception of staff	0	0	39	35	40	80	73	63	100

Negative perception of other inmates	70	47 (30)	41 (41)	38	51	7	27 (74)	25 (21)	0
Regardless of what the adults say, the best way to get along here is—									
Stay out of the way of the adults, but get away with what you can	37	7 (18)		17	20	0	13	6 (8)	0
Don't break any rules and keep out of trouble	26	53 (54)		55	33	33	27	44 (38)	50
Show that you are really sorry for what you did	0	7		10	11	13	13	6	13
Try to get an understanding of yourself	37	33 (22)		28	37	53	47	44 (44)	37
Prisonized adaptation	59	60 (51)		38	53	7	40	13 (21)	0
Approval of informing	7	20 (18)		14	36	80	33	50 (51)	88
Positive inmate role	33	33 (45)		48	47	64	60	56 (66)	100
Inmate leaders negative	52	73 (49)		38	48	13	33	31 (26)	0

a. The numbers in parentheses denote the average percentage of residents in each type of cottage responding as shown to the attitudinal indicator. The responses are mutually exclusive; thus, the totals will be 100 percent (with slight variations because of rounding).

which in turn conditions the staff members' ability to control subcultural violence. Residents of the treatment cottages held relatively favorable views of other inmates and staff. Because of the greater availability of privileges and amenities, they had less incentive to engage in covert deviance to relieve deprivations and thus had less to hide. Almost three times as many inmates in the treatment settings as in the custody-oriented settings approved of informing. In fact, a virtual majority of residents of the former approved of informing.

As indicated previously, the treatment inmates' support for informing stemmed, in part, from the staff members' redefinition of informing as "helping" or "being responsible for others" as part of the treatment program. Formal collaboration reinforced the therapeutic rationale for informing and gave inmates greater protection from intimidation by increasing the visibility of informal pressures by other inmates. By legitimating and fostering informing, staff members received an enormous amount of information about the hidden processes of the subculture, which better enabled them to control inmate violence.

Participant observation and structured interviews provided an insight into "strong-arming" and "bogarting"—the subterranean violence among residents. "You have to fight" was a norm in the custody-oriented cottages, and the levels of verbal abuse and physical violence were considerably higher there than in the treatment-oriented settings. Inmates emphasized toughness, resisting exploitation or provocation, and maintaining one's position in the subculture through physical means. Physical and verbal testing and scuffles were daily occurrences, although actual fights were less frequent. The inmate did not have to be a successful fighter, but a willingness to fight to protect himself, his

position, and his property was essential. Fighting and defending against exploitation were as important for female inmates as for males in comparable custodial cottages.

An inmate's readiness and ability to defend personal integrity and property were tested very early during confinement as new residents were subtly or overtly challenged for whatever material goods they possessed. As mentioned above, the greater deprivation in the custody-oriented settings made exploitation a profitable strategy for the more aggressive inmates. Residents who fought back could insulate themselves from chronic exploitation, while failure to do so left them and their possessions vulnerable.

There was significantly less exploitation in the treatment-oriented cottages than in the custody-oriented cottages. The field observers recorded fewer incidents of fights, physical confrontations, or expropriation of property. All the observers commented on the virtual absence here of "ranking"—verbal abuse—as compared with the custody cottages. There was less normative support for fighting, and when it did occur most of the inmates condemned it in the community meetings.

The differences in subcultural violence resulted from the steps staff took to control it. In the custody cottages, inmates retaliated with violence to punish those who informed to staff and to discourage other inmates from doing so. Given their limited social control repertoire, custody staff did not encourage inmates to inform, since it only forced them to confront violent inmates directly. When staff members learned of inmate violence or victimization, they seldom took steps to prevent its recurrence. More frequently, they reinforced the values of the violent subculture by encouraging the resident to fight back and defend himself. In view of the unsympathetic and unsupportive staff response to complaints and the retaliatory inmate violence that followed, inmates had little incentive to cooperate with staff. Custody staff were isolated from the workings of the subculture, and unable to combat the violence that stifled the flow of information. In the treatment-oriented cottages, formal collaboration and inmate support for informing provided channels of communication and a mechanism for coping with incidents of violence.

While inmate approval of informing afforded greater control over inmate violence, there were differences in other subcultural norms as well. Responses to a series of hypothetical stories concerning common incidents in correctional institutions demonstrated a further contrast in the norms that prevailed in the various cottages. About two-thirds of the inmates in the treatment-oriented settings, as compared with less than half of those in the custody-oriented settings, supported "positive" inmate behavior—cooperation with staff, refusal to aid escapes, and the like.

Different inmate roles and subculture stratification accompanied the differences in cottage norms. In the more violent custodial cottages, the roles of superior and inferior were allocated on the basis of an inmate's ability to "out-fight, out-think, or out-talk" fellow inmates. Since most inmates were neither complete successes nor complete failures in out-fighting, out-thinking, or out-talking their peers, the distribution of roles resulted in a stratification system with a few aggressive leaders at the top, a few "punks"—chronic victims—at the bottom, and most of the inmates occupying a more intermediate status, neither "one-up" nor "one-down." In the treatment-oriented settings, inmate roles and stratification were not as tied to physical or verbal prowess.

The differences in cottage norms and inmate relations were reflected in the characteristics of the inmate leadership as well. A majority of inmates in the custody-oriented cottages, as contrasted with about one-quarter of the residents of the treatment cottages, described the leaders as filling a negative and violent role in cottage life. Both observation and interviews revealed that leaders were those inmates who "strong-armed" and exploited lower-status inmates. There was greater normative support for negative inmate behavior in these cottages, and the leaders reflected and perpetuated the dominant values of the subculture.

Norms governing violence and informing constrained inmate leaders in the treatment-oriented cottages. Formal collaboration between inmates and staff reduced the leaders' ability to maintain covert physical control over the inmate group, and they played a more positive and supportive role in the institution. Formal collaboration increased their visibility and required that they at least appear to adopt a cooperative attitude in their relations with staff, which enabled other inmates to establish more positive relationships with inmates and staff.

At the bottom of the custody cottages' social structure were the "punks," inmates who were bullied and exploited and who acquiesced in the role of victim. Since the first rule of survival in the violent subculture was to defend oneself, inmates who were unable or unwilling to fight were at the mercy of those who would do so. Punks were chronically victimized, both psychologically and physically, and were the victims of merciless taunting and pummeling. In the custodial settings, the strong norm against informing prevented either the victims or other inmates from revealing what occurred. The inability of staff to control the violence prevented inmates from revealing their victimization and left them at the mercy of their exploiters.

Homosexual rape was the ultimate act of physical aggression by tough cottage leaders against punks. More than exploitative sexual satisfaction, rape entailed conquest and domination of the victim by the aggressor.[37] Every incident of homosexual assault discovered during this study could be analyzed in terms of leader-punk role relationships; such assaults occurred only in the violent custody-oriented cottages.

In the treatment-oriented settings, punks did not suffer as much physical or verbal abuse. Although other inmates regarded them as weak, immature, and lacking self-respect, formal collaboration provided a substantial check on the extent of their victimization. At least by contrast with those in the custody-oriented settings, low-status inmates in the treatment cottages enjoyed a comparatively benign incarceration experience.

Discussion and Conclusions

Organizational structure has a major effect on the informal inmate social system. The cottage programs varied in both the levels of deprivation and the effectiveness of staff controls and confronted the inmates with markedly different organizations to which to adapt. The respective cottage cultures reflected these differences in inmates' perceptions of cottage purposes and goals, in their adaptations to the institution, in their views of staff and other inmates, and in their norms, values, and interaction patterns.

Punishment and isolation were the reasons given by the inmates in maximum security for their incarceration. They suffered the greatest deprivation within the institution, which gave them the greatest incentive to improve their circumstances through violent exploitation and covert deviance. Staff sought inmate obedience and conformity and used physical control to obtain compliance and suppress challenges to their authority. Inmates were alienated by the staff's repressive controls, and the absence of programs prevented the development of individualized relationships, perpetuating the negative stereotypes of one another held by inmates and staff. Motivated by their poor opinion of inmates, staff attempted to disrupt informal groups. The inmates' isolation hindered them from cooperating with one another in the institutional adjustment or in resisting exploitation, while predatory violence reinforced inmates' negative views of one another. Inmates adapted by isolating themselves, avoiding other inmates and appearing to obey staff. In developing covert deviant solutions to relieve their material deprivation, particularly in exploiting weaker inmates for their possessions, tough inmates reinforced their own dominant status and provided themselves with a measure of safety and security. They discouraged inmate contact that would reveal their own deviant and violent behavior and physically punished inmates who informed to discourage the communication of information that would improve staff control. And the dominance of aggressive inmates reinforced staff efforts to isolate inmates within the culture by making inmates distrustful and fearful of one another. The inmates' ability to use violence determined their various roles within the group, and prevented them from engaging in positive forms of social behavior. The failure of staff to support informing or to control violence forced the inmates to seek accommodation with the primary source of power, the aggressive inmate leaders. This, in turn, reinforced their alienation from one another, precluded collective resistance to aggression, and left each individual inmate at the mercy of those who were more aggressive.

Subculture characteristics in the training school cottages were similar to those in maximum security, although organizational differences reduced the extremes of staff-inmate alienation and antagonism. Program individualization engendered more contacts between staff and inmates that tempered somewhat their negative perceptions of one another. The use of vocational programs required staff to obtain the active cooperation of inmates in productive work. Staff induced at least minimal cooperation and participation in work programs through privileges and rewards that reduced the levels of institutional deprivation. The necessity to obtain voluntary compliance limited the utility of punitive forms of social control, and a privilege system provided staff with a more flexible means of responding to inmates than did the use of force and isolation cells. The forms of adaptation among inmates reflected staff members' primary emphasis on obedience and conformity. Staff informally collaborated with and coopted the potentially violent inmate elite, and thus obtained some control over aggression within the subculture. By coopting the inmate leaders through informal collaboration, staff enlisted their aid in maintaining order within the subculture. In the course of protecting their privileged status, the leaders informally maintained control for staff, suppressed some forms of anti-institutional activities, and reduced the levels of violence within the inmate group. The privileges available reduced the levels of deprivation, and covert inmate deviance declined accordingly. With less to hide, there was less need among the inmates to restrict contact with staff. Although inmates disapproved of informing, this was

not as ruthlessly suppressed as was the case in maximum security. The lesser degree of deprivation and violent exploitation reduced the inmates' isolation and alienation from one another.

The differences in organizational goals and intervention strategies in the treatment-oriented cottages had a significant effect on the inmates' incarceration experience. Staff both elevated treatment expectations over custodial considerations and successfully communicated their expectations to inmates. Rehabilitation, gaining insight, and solving personal problems were seen as the purposes of incarceration, and these goals required change rather than simply conformity. Staff emphasized more rewarding experiences and privileges, and residents of the treatment settings suffered less punishment, deprivation, or alienation than did their custody cottage counterparts. The reduced material deprivation also lowered inmates' incentive to engage in deviant activities within the institution.

In both the individual and group treatment settings, positive contact between staff and inmates was considerable, occurring in individual counseling and through formal collaboration, resulting in markedly more favorable inmate perceptions of staff than in the other settings. Formal collaboration allowed inmates and staff to make decisions collectively about cottage life and provided them with a common context in which to meet. Formal collaboration fostered greater equality among staff members, between staff and inmates, and among inmates, and reduced inmates' alienation from staff and encouraged more favorable views of fellow inmates.

Formal collaboration coupled with individual and group treatment increased the visibility of the inmate subculture and provided staff and inmates with a mechanism for controlling inmate violence. Staff provided a rehabilitation-based rationale for informing, enabling the norm governing this behavior to become more positive than was the case in the custody cottages. Equally important, staff members defined the program itself in such a way as to convince the inmates that personnel were committed to treatment rather than punishment.

The increased communication of information enabled staff to control inmate violence, which reinforced this communication. The reduced deprivation, increased freedom, and support provided by formal collaboration for controlling inmate violence combined to foster more positive, less exploitative inmate relationships.

Notes

1. See Hugh Cline, "The Determinants of Normative Patterns in Correctional Institutions," in *Scandinavian Studies in Criminology*, vol. 2, Nils Christie, ed. (Oslo, Norway: Oslo University Press, 1968), pp. 173–84; Barry Schwartz, "Pre-institutional vs. Situational Influence in a Correctional Community," *Journal of Criminal Law, Criminology and Police Science*, December 1971, pp. 532–42; Charles W. Thomas and Samuel C. Foster, "The Importation Model Perspective on Inmate Social Roles," *Sociological Quarterly*, Spring 1973, pp. 226–34; Charles W. Thomas, "Theoretical Perspectives on Alienation in the Inmate Society," *Pacific Sociological Review*, vol. 18 (1975), pp. 483–99; Charles W. Thomas and Matthew Zingraff, "Organizational Structure as a Determinant of Prisonization," *Pacific Sociological Review*, January 1976, p. 98.

2. Donald Clemmer, *The Prison Community* (Boston: Christopher, 1940); Norman S. Hayner and Ellis Ash, "The Prison as a Community," *American Sociological Review*, vol. 4 (1940), pp. 577–83; Howard Polsky, *Cottage 6* (New York: Russell Sage, 1962); David A. Ward and Gene Kassebaum, *Women's Prison: Sex and Social Structure* (Chicago: Aldine, 1965); Clemens Bartollas, Stuart J. Miller, Simon Dinitz, *Juvenile Victimization: The Institutional Paradox* (Beverly Hills, Sage: 1976).

3. Thomas, "Theoretical Perspectives on Alienation in the Inmate Society"; Charles W. Thomas, "Theoretical Perspectives on Prisonization: A Comparison of the Importation and

Deprivation Models," *Journal of Criminal Law and Criminology*, March 1977, pp. 135–45.

4. Lloyd W. McCorkle and Richard Korn, "Resocialization with Walls," *Annals of the American Academy of Political and Social Science*, May 1954, pp. 88–98; Gresham Sykes, *Society of Captives* (Princeton, N.J.: Princeton University Press, 1958); Gresham Sykes and Sheldon Messinger, "The Inmate Social System," in *Theoretical Studies in Social Organization of the Prison*, Richard Cloward et al., eds. (New York: Social Science Research Council, 1960), pp. 5–19; Irving Goffman, *Asylums* (Garden City, N.Y.: Anchor, 1961).

5. Hayner and Ash, "Prison as a Community"; Clarence Schrag, "Leadership among Prison Inmates," *American Sociological Review*, vol. 19 (1954), pp. 37–42; Clarence Schrag, "Some Foundations for a Theory of Corrections," in *The Prison: Studies in Institutional Organization and Change*, Donald Cressey, ed. (New York: Holt, Rinehart and Winston, 1961), pp. 309–58; Gresham Sykes, "The Corruption of Authority and Rehabilitation," *Social Forces*, vol. 34 (1956), pp. 257–62.

6. Oscar Grusky, "Organizational Goals and the Behavior of Informal Leaders," *American Journal of Sociology*, vol. 65 (1959), pp. 59–67; Oscar Grusky, "Role Conflict in Organizations: A Study of Prison Camp Officials," *Administration Science Quarterly*, March 1959, pp. 452–72; Stanton Wheeler, "Socialization in Correctional Communities," *American Sociological Review*, October 1961, pp. 707–11;

Mayer N. Zald, "Organizational Control Structures in Five Correctional Institutions," *American Journal of Sociology,* November 1962, pp. 335–45; Mayer N. Zald, "Comparative Analysis and Measurement of Organizational Goals: The Case of Correctional Institutions of Juveniles," *Sociological Quarterly,* Summer 1963, pp. 206–30; Peter G. Garabedian, "Social Roles and Processes of Socialization in the Prison Community," *Social Problems,* Fall 1963, pp. 139–52; Peter G. Garabedian, "Social Roles in a Correctional Community," *Journal of Criminal Law, Criminology and Police Science,* September 1964, pp. 338–47; Daniel Glaser, *The Effectiveness of a Prison and Parole System* (Indianapolis, Ind.: Bobbs-Merrill, 1964); Mayer N. Zald and David A. Street, "Custody and Treatment in Juvenile Institutions," *Crime and Delinquency,* July 1964, pp. 249–56; Bernard Berk, Organizational Goals and Inmate Organization," *American Journal of Sociology,* March 1966, pp. 522–34; David A. Street, Robert D. Vinter, and Charles Perrow, *Organization for Treatment* (New York: Free Press, 1966); Ronald L. Akers, Norman S. Hayner, and Werner Gruniger, "Homosexual and Drug Behavior in Prison," *Social Problems,* vol. 21 (1974), pp. 410–22; Ronald L. Akers, Norman S. Hayner, and Werner Gruniger, "Prisonization in Five Countries," *Criminology,* February 1977, pp. 527–54; Barry C. Feld, *Neutralizing Inmate Violence: Juvenile Offenders in Institutions* (Cambridge, Mass.: Ballinger, 1977).

7. John Irwin and Donald Cressey, "Thieves, Convicts, and the Inmate Culture," *Social Problems,* Fall 1962, p. 142; Ward and Kassebaum, *Women's Prison.*

8. Ward and Kassebaum, *Women's Prison;* James Jacobs, "Stratification and Conflict among Prison Inmates," *Journal of Law & Criminology,* vol. 66 (1976), p. 476; Leo Carroll, *Hacks, Blacks, and Cons* (Lexington, Mass.: Lexington Books, 1974); Thomas and Foster, "Importation Model Perspective on Inmate Social Roles"; Thomas, "Theoretical Perspectives on Prisonization."

9. Polsky, *Cottage 6;* Bartollas, Miller, and Dinitz, *Juvenile Victimization;* Jacobs "Stratification and Conflict among Prison Inmates."

10. Social control by inmates within the subculture may be maintained by verbal as well as physical manipulation. Verbal assaults—"ranking"—provide a mechanism by which relative status is fixed by verbal rather than physical aggression. Howard Polsky described ranking as "verbal, invidious distinctions based on values important to the group. . . . Ranking fixes antagonistic positions among three or more persons by placing one member in a target position" (Polsky, *Cottage 6,* p. 62). David Matza describes the same process as "sounding," which entails an "imputation of negative characteristics . . . wherein the recipient concurs with the perpetrator in the negative evaluation of the substance of the remark." (David Matza, *Delinquency and Drift* [New York: John Wiley, 1964], p. 43.) This process of verbal denigration is prevalent in female inmate interactions as well (Rose Giallombardo, *Society of Women* [New York: John Wiley, 1966]; Rose Giallombardo, *Social World of Imprisoned Girls* [New York: John Wiley, 1974]). The target of scornful, mocking, or negative statements made in the presence of a social audience can either concur in the negative imputations, establishing subordination, or resist the characterization. Acquiescence or resistance defines relative social status.

11. Sykes, *Society of Captives;* Sykes and Messinger, "Inmate Social System."

12. Polsky, *Cottage 6;* Bartollas, Miller, and Dinitz, *Juvenile Victimization;* Feld, *Neutralizing Inmate Violence.*

13. Walter Miller, "Lower Class Culture as a Generating Milieu of Gang Delinquency," *Journal of Social Issues,* vol. 14, no. 3 (1958), pp. 5–19; Marvin Wolfgang and Franco Ferracuti, *The Subculture of Violence* (London, England: Tavistock, 1967).

14. Jacobs, "Stratification and Conflict among Prison Inmates"; Giallombardo, *Social World of Imprisoned Girls;* Feld, *Neutralizing Inmate Violence.*

15. Charles W. Thomas and Samuel C. Foster, "Prizonization in the Inmate Contraculture," *Social Problems,* Fall 1972, pp. 229–39; Thomas and Foster, "Importation Model Per-

spective on Inmate Social Roles''; Akers, Hayner, and Gruniger, ''Homosexual and Drug Behavior in Prison''; Feld, *Inmate Violence.*

16. Street, Vinter, and Perrow, *Organization for Treatment;* Akers, Hayner, and Gruniger, ''Homosexual and Drug Behavior in Prison''; Feld, *Neutralizing Inmate Violence.*

17. Donald R. Cressey, ''Prison Organization,'' in *Handbook of Organizations,* J. March, ed. (Chicago: Rand McNally), pp. 1023–70; Street, Vinter, and Perrow, *Organization for Treatment;* Elliot Studt, Sheldon Messinger, and Thomas Wilson, *C-Unit: Search for Community in Prison* (New York: Russell Sage, 1968).

18. Street, Vinter, and Perrow, *Organization for Treatment;* Lloyd Ohlin, ''Organizational Reform in Correctional Agencies,'' in *Handbook of Criminology,* Daniel Glaser, ed. (Chicago: Rand McNally, 1974), pp. 995–1020; Feld, *Neutralizing Inmate Violence.*

19. Zald, ''Organizational Control Structures in Five Correctional Institutions''; Zald, ''Comparative Analysis and Measurement of Organizational Goals''; Zald and Street, ''Custody and Treatment in Juvenile Institutions.''

20. Corresponding to distinctions between custody and treatment, there is also a tension in the organization between tendencies toward bureaucratization and tendencies toward individualization. The pressures of bureaucratization lead personnel to deal with inmates according to gross characteristics. The pull toward individualization leads to nonroutinized treatment with potentially disruptive consequences for the organization. The nonuniform nature of individual behavior results either in individualized, nonroutinized staff responses *or* in an effort to increase predictability through regimentation. While bureaucratization increases regimentation and clearly defined expectations for inmate behavior, individualization requires either specifying norms for every eventuality or delegating discretion and authority to low-level staff to enable them to deal with unpredictable situations and individual variations. The resolution of these countervailing pressures constitutes a primary source of variation in organizations. See

Goffman, *Asylums;* Cressey, ''Prison Organization.''

21. Street, Vinter, and Perrow, *Organization for Treatment.*

22. Amitai Etzioni, *A Comparative Analysis of Complex Organizations* (New York: Free Press, 1961); Amitai Etzioni, *A Comparative Analysis of Complex Organizations* (New York: Free Press, 1975).

23. Ibid.

24. Goffman, *Asylums.*

25. Lacking complete physical domination of inmates, staff members rely upon the inmate elite to maintain social order, in return for which the staff allow the elite certain privileges and immunities. Richard Cloward describes one way in which this process occurs. He notes that the two primary groups in the prison—custodians and inmates—seek, respectively, social order and escape from deprivation. The custodian employs coercion and inducement, force and incentive to secure order from the inmates, but ''in the absence of absolute force, the prisoner must be led to share in the process of social control.'' Disruptive behavior is avoided by guards who provide access to illegitimate means whereby the prisoners can reduce the deprivation. ''The official system accommodates to the inmate system in ways that have the consequence of creating illegitimate opportunity structures.'' To some extent the guards can determine which prisoners will have access to these opportunities, and in turn these prisoners maintain order for the guards as a means of protecting their own privileged positions. This occurs because ''certain prisoners, as they become upwardly mobile in these structures, tend to become progressively conservative. . . . Seeking to entrench their relative advantage over other inmates, they are anxious to suppress any behavior that might disturb the present arrangements.'' Richard Cloward, ''Social Control in Prison,'' in *Theoretical Studies in Social Organization of the Prison* (New York: Social Science Research Council, 1960), pp. 20–48.

This process is also described by Richard McCleary, ''Communication Patterns as Bases of Systems of Authority and Power,'' in *Theoretical Studies in Social Organization of the*

Prison (New York: Social Science Research Council, 1960), pp. 49–77; Richard McCleary, "The Governmental Process and Informal Social Control," in *The Prison,* Donald Cressey, ed. (New York: Holt, Rinehart and Winston, 1961), pp. 149–88; and Sykes, *Society of Captives.* According to Sykes ("Corruption of Authority and Rehabilitation"), the guards must rely on the inmates to maintain order because of the "lack of a sense of duty among those who are held captive, the obvious fallacies of coercion, the pathetic collection of rewards and punishments to induce compliance, the strong pressures toward the corruption of the guard in the form of friendship, reciprocity, and the transfer of duties into the hands of trusted inmates—all are structural defects in the prison's system of power rather than individual inadequacies." The same processes operate in institutions for juvenile offenders. See Polsky, *Cottage 6;* Feld, *Neutralizing Inmate Violence;* Bartollas, Miller, and Dinitz, *Juvenile Victimization.*

26. Formal collaboration between staff and inmates as a means of social control occurs when a social structure allows both to participate, at least to some degree, as members of a common group in defining deviance, determining the appropriate sanctions, or both. Formal collaboration differs from informal collaboration in a number of critical respects. It is explicit and overt, with parties visibly engaged in the process. Since the process is formalized and given organizational sanction, it is legitimate and consistent with the declared principles of the organization, rather than covert, *sub rosa,* and basically subversive of the formal organization. Formal collaboration is universalistic and democratic, with all members of both groups potentially involved, rather than elitist and particularistic, confined only to the inmate leadership.

27. Feld, *Neutralizing Inmate Violence;* Robert Coates, Alden Miller, and Lloyd Ohlin, *Diversity in a Youth Correctional System* (Cambridge, Mass.: Ballinger, 1978); Craig McE-

wen, *Designing Correctional Organizations for Youth* (Cambridge, Mass.: Ballinger, 1978).

28. Maxwell Jones, *Beyond the Therapeutic Community* (New Haven, Conn.: Yale University Press, 1968); Maxwell Jones, *Social Psychiatry in Practice* (Baltimore, Md.: Penguin Books, 1968).

29. The Lancaster Industrial Schools for Girls was not converted to a decentralized, cottage-based institution to nearly the same degree as were the Shirley Industrial School and the Lyman Schools. It still operated as a traditional training school and there were virtually no differences in the social structure of the individual cottages. Accordingly, questionnaire data from Lancaster are aggregated for tabular presentation.

30. Feld, *Neutralizing Inmate Violence,* pp. 207–11.

31. Polsky, *Cottage 6;* Bartollas, Miller, and Dinitz, *Juvenile Victimization;* Feld, *Neutralizing Inmate Violence.*

32. Jones, *Beyond the Therapeutic Community;* Jones, *Social Psychiatry in Practice.*

33. Sykes and Messinger, "The Inmate Social System"; Sheldon Messinger, "Issues in the Study of the Social System of Prison Inmates," *Issues in Criminology,* vol. 4 (1970), pp. 133–44; Street, Vinter and Perrow, *Organization for Treatment.*

34. Polsky, *Cottage 6;* Bartollas, Miller, and Dinitz, *Juvenile Victimization;* Feld, *Neutralizing Inmate Violence.*

35. Miller, "Lower Class Culture as a Generating Milieu of Gang Delinquency"; Wolfgang and Ferracuti, *Subculture of Violence.*

36. Sykes, *Society of Captives;* McCleary, "Communication Patterns as Bases of Systems of Authority and Power"; McCleary, "Governmental Process and Informal Social Control"; Sykes and Messinger, "Inmate Social System."

37. Susan Brownmiller, *Against Our Will: Men, Women and Rape* (New York: Simon & Schuster, 1975).

Juvenile Diversion: A Look at the Record

27

Kenneth Polk

What are the accomplishments of juvenile diversion? In their recent review, Binder and Geis (1984) provide a spirited and provocative defense of diversion, noting that many of those finding fault with the concept base their observations on "polemical and ideological conclusions lacking a firm anchorage in fact" (p. 326). In their attempt to "rehabilitate the record of diversion," Binder and Geis (p. 326) express dismay at the fact that the response to diversion seems to be "inconsistent with the actual record." Their conclusion is that the criticisms of diversion originate in the personal motivations of sociologists and are the result of disciplinary narrowness, distrust of the police, and overidentification with the underdog.

That there have been questions raised about the success of diversion, and that the strongest of these seem to come from sociologists, cannot be disputed. Is it possible, however, that the source of these questions resides not so much in the motivations of

From *Crime and Delinquency*, Vol. 30, No. 4, 1984, pp. 648–659. Reprinted by permission of Sage Publications, Inc. and the author.

sociologists, but in the record of diversion itself? A brief review of some of the empirical work on diversion may help to clarify and give shape to the features of the debate opened up by Binder and Geis.

Diversion and Subsequent Delinquency

A starting point for many analyses of diversion consists of assessing the outcomes of diversion in terms of its impact on subsequent delinquency. What is that record? It is clearly mixed. There are many studies which show that diversion is successful in reducing subsequent deviance (e.g., Duxbury, 1973; Thornton et al., 1972; Forward et al., 1975; Quay and Love, 1977; Palmer et al., 1978; Palmer and Lewis, 1980). These results are at least equally balanced, however, by findings of no impact. One of the most methodologically rigorous evaluations of diversion concluded that: "The hypothesis that diversion leads to lower rates of subsequent delinquent behavior than traditional processing was not supported" (Elliott et al., 1978: 10). In their review of several California diversion programs, Haapanen and Rudisill report that the programs

> were found to have no measurable effect on the self-report delinquency, the attitudes, the family relations, or the minor misbehavior of their clients. Nor did they have a measurable effect on the official delinquency of their clients over a six-month or twelve-month follow-up period [1980:139].

In their evaluation of several programs in Wisconsin, after making comparisons of records of subsequent delinquency between diversion and control clients, it was concluded by Venezia and Anthony (1978:121) that "none of the comparisons resulted in a significant difference being demonstrated." Similarly, in a review of the outcomes of one diversion program it was concluded that "no strong inference can be made" . . . that diversion "had a significant impact on youths' subsequent delinquent behavior" (Quincy, 1981:127; although it should be noted that this investigation did find consistent positive results on self-report measures of delinquency).

Even more important for the present argument, however, are indications of diversion as having harmful effects. In one analysis of a police diversion program, it was concluded that diversion served to aggravate rather than to deter recidivism (Lincoln, 1976). Elliott and colleagues (1978) report that receiving service, regardless of whether the intervention was in a traditional justice setting or in the diversion agency, resulted in higher levels of perceived labeling and self-report delinquency. Similarly, Lincoln (1977) found that although persons who were diverted had lower rates of recidivism than was true for persons who received a court petition, their rates were also higher than those released outright without any form of service.

It further should be noted that these studies suggesting harmful effects of diversion are among the most methodologically rigorous in the diversion literature.

After analyzing this mixed pattern of research, and reviews of evaluations, Alder and Polk (1982:105) suggested that studies showing positive effects "have not stood up under careful scrutiny of their methodology." Binder and Geis profess that it "is inconceivable to us how one can so cavalierly dismiss" the works which show positive results, because this array of research "is no poorer in overall methodology than the array that has produced the negative results upon which the antidiversionists focus their attention" (Binder and Geis, 1984:324–325).

There are three curious features of this response. One, Binder and Geis scrupulously avoid mention of the major empirical investigations which show either negative or harmful effects of diversion. Although they assert that one set of studies is "no poorer," they provide no literature, data, or rationale in support of that assertion. Second, Binder and Geis fail to inform the reader that at least Alder and Polk cite a basis for their conclusion; namely, methodological reviews of diversion research (Alder and Polk, 1982: 105). One of these reviews, after examining a study cited by Binder and Geis as an illustration of the positive effects of diversion, comments:

> The Quay and Love (1977) report presented information on group characteristics, including the mean number of prior arrests for each group within fairly specific categories of offense. Within these narrow categories, the two groups did not differ significantly from one another, and the authors concluded that the two groups were equivalent. However, when the submeans were added together to produce a mean for the total number of priors

in each group, the control group mean was 34% higher than that of clients. Given the importance of prior offenses as a predictor of subsequent offenses, this suggests that the groups cannot be compared without taking this difference into account. There were other problems with this study, the most glaring being the different follow-up periods of clients and controls; the control group had a longer period in which to get arrested. If (a) the proportion of youths arrested in each group and (b) the mean number of arrests per individual are standardized with respect to exposure time, the differences between the groups disappear. Given the fact that clients had fewer prior arrests (were better "risks"), this lack of actual difference calls into question the positive treatment effects that were claimed by the authors (Haapanen and Rudisill, 1980:8).

Similarly, Gibbons and Blake (another source cited by Alder and Polk) carry out an analysis of several evaluations of diversion programs, finding such problems in one typical study as too short a time period for impact assessment, the failure to describe the handling of control cases, and an absence of a range of impact data (Gibbons and Blake, 1976:415). This review concludes:

> Clearly, there is insufficient evidence in the nine studies examined here for one to have much confidence in diversion arguments and contentions (Gibbons and Blake, 1976:420).

Third, is not the posture assumed by Binder and Geis at variance with what is generally accepted within the research community? Assume for a moment that the intervention being proposed were some form of medical treatment. What would the response of the scientific community be if there was evidence that suggests that the form of treatment may be either: (1) beneficial, (2) of no benefit, or (3) potentially

harmful? How compelling would the argument appear, advanced by an obvious advocate of the treatment, that the research showing positive results is "no poorer in overall methodology" than research showing negative or harmful effects? Would not the rules of evidence which apply in such cases place a particular burden of proof on those who advocate the treatment? Is not some caution to be urged, especially when harm has been found in experimentation? How telling is an attack which makes no reference whatsoever to the data and evidence showing negative or harmful results, and instead leaps immediately to challenging the motives of the researchers?

Diversion and Net-Widening

A major feature of the defense of diversion provided by Binder and Geis is their rejection of the concern that diversion may result in a widening of the net of juvenile justice. Their position seems based in the following propositions:

1. Diversion is beneficial in the sense that many or most clients are helped through the services provided by diversion programs.
2. Because diversion is helpful, then the proposition that doing nothing, rather than doing something, is unacceptable. Being precise, Binder and Geis find the argument that it is more desirable to ignore deviant behavior than to seek remedial help in diversion "a dubious proposition at best and a downright harmful one at worst" (Binder and Geis, 1984:316).
3. Diversion programs in most cases are voluntary because "offenders and their families may refuse services without consequences" (Binder and Geis, 1984:313).
4. When coercion is present, we are reminded that coercion has essentially been invited by the offender's choice of behavior. "If he or she wished to retain maximum freedom of choice, it would have been prudent either to

have abstained from the earlier behavior or not to have gotten caught at it'' (Binder and Geis, 1984:313).

5. Because there is actual offense behavior at issue, then some form of social control is desirable and probably inevitable. There is nothing pernicious about social control in the view of Binder and Geis because it consists not simply of law, but of etiquette, norms, regulations, customs and ethics, and takes place in the home, street, school, or family. Not only is social control broadly conceived, but so is the notion of an agent of social control, which consists of the following:

Any person who attempts to influence behavior that is considered unacceptable in a normative sense. This may be a mother, a minister, a friend, indeed anyone with physical or psychological authority, or presumably anyone who interacts with another person, since it is a given of human intercourse that each of us in our actions attempts to influence another to behave in a particular way or to desist from behaving in a certain manner. (Binder and Geis, 1984: 316).

For Binder and Geis, given these premises, diversion becomes a reasonable and responsible form of expanding the devices of social control available to a community for coping with adolescent offense behavior and is worthy of an energetic defense. Because diversion is an effective, voluntary, and appropriate response to delinquent behavior, they find no merit in the concern that net-widening may result from diversion, observing instead:

The phrase "widening the net" is, of course, employed pejoratively, with the intent to evoke an emotional response. It conjures up visions of a mesh net that is thrown over thrashing victims, incapacitating them as they flail about, desperately seeking to avoid captivity. The net is maneuvered by "agents of social control," another image provoking

term, this one carrying a Nazi-like connotation. Both terms are employed for purposes of propaganda rather than to enlighten (Binder and Geis, 1984:315).

Unfortunately, however vivid the imagery, a case rejecting the net-widening argument is built by Binder and Geis which avoids reference to the empirical record. The first two premises are challenged by the evidence of the impact of diversion on subsequent behavior as cited above. If further research confirms either that diversion has no impact or that it is harmful, then the assumption that it is better to do something (in the form of diversion) than to do nothing becomes unsupportable.

Evidence exists which also raises questions about the voluntary nature of diversion services. Early in the development of diversion, Klapmuts (1972) cautioned that if being referred to the diversion program was backed by a threat of referral to court, then the allegedly nonpunitive agency in reality becomes an extension of the justice system and the diversion is a legal fiction. After reviewing the practices of a few diversion programs, Nejelski (1976:410) warned that: "there is a danger that diversion will become a means of expanding coercive intervention in the lives of children and families without proper concern for their rights." A national survey of over 300 youth service bureaus (YSBs), which included more intensive site analyses and interviews with 27 of the diversion agencies, provides some empirical support for such concerns (Polk and Schuchter, 1975:92):

Data from our field visits suggest that diversionary referrals from court intake and courts to YSBs essentially facilitate deferred prosecution; generally are contingent upon admission of guilt without the advice of counsel; that "voluntary agreements" or consent decrees are obtained under coercive circumstances which vitiate the meaning of voluntariness; that throughout the diversionary and referral process the youth inhabits a legal limbo which increases his vulnerability to subsequent punishment for offenses previously committed, and which is a much more subtle and pernicious problem than double jeopardy.

A further problem in the viewpoint of Binder and Geis is their undifferentiated view of the sources of social control. In its original intent, as should be clear from the term "diversion," there was a recognition that control within the juvenile justice system should be sharply differentiated from other forms of social control. The basic assumed thrust of diversion would be to shift responsibility and intervention for some individuals who had entered juvenile justice processing outside of that system into some form of nonjustice, community alternative.

A major concern of many of the researchers who write about net-widening is the question of whether this is, in fact, what diversion programs accomplish. Is diversion serving as a process for moving young persons who have "penetrated" the justice network outward and away from that system, or has it become a device for incorporating a whole new class of clients inside an expanding justice system? Some have questioned whether it is offense behavior at all that brings clients to diversion agencies, pointing out that the attributes of diversion referrals (age, sex, reason for referral) suggest that a population quite different from delinquent offenders is being tapped by diversion programs. From his analysis of evaluations and descriptions of over 50 diversion programs, Klein (1979:165) was able to comment that:

> The conclusion seems unavoidable: among projects reporting on the characteristics of diversion clients, no reasonable case can be

made that these projects are carrying out diversion as its rationale suggested they should. The bulk of "diversion cases" are young people who are normally counseled and released by the police, if indeed they have any dealings with the police. With clients like these, we cannot truly be testing the efficacy of diversion.

Further, Empey (1982) argues that because a majority of diversion projects have actually been connected with, or even operated by, traditional justice agencies, one of the major functional goals of diversion has been subverted:

> Diversion was supposed to turn the flow of juveniles away from the juvenile justice system and back toward the community. But rather than doing that, several studies reveal that as many as half of all referrals have come, not from police and intake officers, but from schools, welfare agencies, and parents—the very people and institutions that were supposed to be mobilized to serve youth in lieu of legal processing (p.482).

One of the persons most closely identified with the origins of the concept of diversion has been concerned enough about the control of the diversion process by the justice system to comment that:

> The cooptation of the diversion movement by law enforcement leaves the rather sour conclusion that not only have the purposes of diversion been perverted but, moreover, police power has been extended over youths and types of behavior not previously subjected to control (Lemert, 1981:43).

Perhaps because the discipline makes them more sensitive to the organizational level of analysis, sociologists then become concerned with two issues. One, does the record of diversion show that responsibility for handling of cases is being shifted away

from the justice system? When the data indicate that the programs are controlled by
justice agencies, that referrals are coming
from rather than to schools, families, and
other community resources, and that the
cases are those that would not under ordinary circumstances come to the attention of
justice authorities, then diversion may be
functioning in quite a different way than its
originators intended and the term would
imply.

Second, if clients come to diversion
agencies for help with personal and social
problems far removed from offense behavior, and if the diversion agency is part
of the justice system, then, whatever the
motivation, young persons are coming under the control of the justice system for behavior that, prior to the introduction of diversion, would not have led to such
control.

The concern for net-widening is, in
short, a concern about whether diversion
is meeting its original goal of deflecting
cases away from juvenile justice processing. A solid, data-grounded argument can
be made which suggests that this goal is
not being met, and that instead the juvenile
justice system, under the banner of diversion, is taking on both more cases and expanded functions (for a recent review, see
Blomberg, 1983). It is not a question of
whether services should be available for
young persons, but one of where those services should be located. The underlying
theory of diversion is that both the individuals served and the community itself
would be better off if more of the responsibility for youth behavior were shifted to
the community and away from juvenile
justice. Is it really inappropriate to discuss
an apparent inconsistency between what
was planned and what resulted when the
inconsistency is revealed by data and evidence?

Diversion and Hidden Sexism

The comments of Binder and Geis regarding the suggestion of Alder and Polk (1982;
see also Alder, forthcoming) [to] examine
such propositions . . . provide a further illustration of their apparent unwillingness to
confront the empirical record of diversion.
In their statement, Alder and Polk . . . examine such propositions as: diversion clients are more likely to be female than are
clients at other points of formal justice
processing; the female clients are being referred to diversion programs disproportionately for the same kinds of behaviors
(status offenses) that have provoked concern for sexism within the juvenile justice
system; diversion programs may be expanding their network of social control; and
finally, diversion may increase the probability of further deviance (and, thus, subsequent formal contact with the juvenile justice system). Literature and extensive data
are presented to substantiate these points.
Alder and Polk warn, however, that the
data are not completely consistent with
each point of their argument. They are
forced to rely on secondary analysis, and
data on some key points of a more complete
argument chain are not available. Accordingly, they alert the reader to the conjectural nature of the argument. They then observe that if the above observations are
accurate (and at least some data are available to support each point), then a reasonable derivative conclusion is that diversion
may represent a form of hidden sexism
which results in an increase in the number
of girls who ultimately come under the control of juvenile justice agencies.

Binder and Geis profess astonishment at
this conclusion, and observe that "in truth,
virtually the entire argument is conjectural
and rhetorical" (1984:324). In what sense
is this the case? Do not Alder and Polk

present evidence at each point of their argument? Is not the conclusion logically consistent with the premises established? This is not to say that Alder and Polk are correct. Binder and Geis may have discussed how the data cited by Alder and Polk are in error or where in the chain of argumentation leading to the conclusion an important flaw or inconsistency exist. This they did not do. Instead, they observe the following:

> What diversion does, according to Alder and Polk, when it is successful in resolving the family, personal, or school problems of females is to contribute to "sex-role maintenance." When it fails to provide help, then, of course, the intervention may be regarded as unsuccessful, and evidence of inflicted labeling harm (p. 324).

Alder and Polk make no such claims. The reader will look in vain for any reference whatsoever in their work to conditions either where diversion is "successful in resolving . . . problems" or where "it fails to provide help." It is difficult to see how this disturbing misrepresentation of the work of others, or a dismissal of several pages of empirical data as "rhetoric" either meets minimal standards of scholarly fairness or serves to clarify the record of diversion.

Conclusion

The contradictory record of juvenile diversion is not easy to read or interpret. Because individuals will approach the evidence from different experiential bases and differential disciplinary paradigms, some disagreements are probably unavoidable. Consider, for example, the following description of diversion (which can be presumed to come from experience) as seen by Binder and Geis (1984:325):

> Some . . . troubling youngsters will be arrested, some will be referred to probation and the courts. Among the group simply arrested and among those referred upward in the justice system, many will be released or redirected to the community. Among those redirected, at least some would benefit from such services as employment counseling, family counseling, a requirement of restitution, a relationship with a Big Brother or Big Sister, substance abuse education, or even psychotherapy. And that is diversion.

This is, of course, precisely the sense of diversion as it was originally intended (i.e., a process which results in removal of individuals from justice system processing, with supportive community experiences substituted). Because Binder and Geis also see the alternative services as both beneficial and voluntary, the vigor with which they defend diversion becomes more explainable.

Unfortunately, the empirical record suggests that this is not diversion in general practice. Study after study suggests that the programs are often run by, or closely connected to, the justice system, and that most of the clients are not offenders being referred outward, but are youngsters with a variety of personal problems far removed from offense behavior who are being referred into this system. The evidence suggests that a large proportion of the programs may be coercive rather than voluntary. The data on impact do not permit us at this time to reject the hypothesis that the services may be either of no benefit or even harmful to the clients experiencing the diversion program. Several bits of evidence can be woven together to suggest that unanticipated consequences of diversion may be occurring in terms of hidden sexist processes.

Despite their professed desire to explain why the response to diversion is "so inconsistent with the actual record," Binder and Geis themselves choose to ignore that record. Crucial evidence contrary to their position receives no mention. Arguments firmly anchored in fact and data are dismissed as "rhetorical," without presentation of alternative evidence. The concerns about diversion are seen as originating not from the research findings, but from the petty motivations of antidiversionist sociologists. There is an alternative view.

Many sociologists, despite what Binder and Geis allege, are firmly committed to the goals of diversion as defined in its original conception. These investigators read the patterns of the empirical record, however, and are dismayed by the drift of diversion from its intended course. They document that drift with data. If Binder and Geis have alternative evidence, they could provide a valuable service by presenting it.

References

Alder, C. "Gender bias in juvenile justice." Crime and Delinquency 30 (forthcoming).

Alder, C. and K. Polk. "Diversion and hidden sexism." Australian and New Zealand J. of Criminology 15: 100–108 (1982).

Binder, A. and G. Geis. "*Ad Populum* argumentation in criminology: juvenile diversion as rhetoric." Crime and Delinquency, 30: 309–333 (1984).

Blomberg, T. G. "Diversions, disparate results, and unresolved questions: an integrative evaluation perspective." J. of Research in Crime and Delinquency 20: 24–38 (1983).

Duxbury, E. Evaluation of Youth Service Bureaus. Sacramento: California Youth Authority, 1973.

Elliott, D. S., F. W. Dunford, and B. Knowles. Diversion: A Study of Alternative Processing Practices. Boulder, CO: Behavioral Research Institute, 1978.

Empey, L. T. American Delinquency: Its Meaning and Construction. Homewood, IL: Dorsey, 1982.

Forward, J. R., M. Kirby, and K. Wilson. Volunteer Intervention with Court-Diverted Juveniles. Denver: Partners' Court Diversion Program, 1975.

Gibbons, D. and G. Blake. "Evaluating the impact of juvenile diversion programs." Crime and Delinquency 22: 411–420 (1976).

Haapanen, R. and D. Rudisill. The Evaluation of Youth Service Bureaus: Final Report, Sacramento: California Youth Authority, 1980.

Klapmuts, N. "Children's rights: the legal rights of minors in conflict with law of social custom." Crime and Delinquency Literature (September, 1972).

Klein, M. W. "Deinstitutionalization and diversion of juvenile offenders: a litany of impediments," pp.145–201 in N. Morris and M. Tonry (eds.), Crime and Justice. Chicago: Univ. of Chicago Press, 1979.

Lemert, E. M. "Diversion in juvenile justice: what hath been wrought?" J. of Research in Crime and Delinquency 18: 34–46 (1981).

Lincoln, S. B. "Juvenile referral and recidivism," in R. M. Carter and M. W. Klein (eds.), Back on the Street: Diversion of Juvenile Offenders. Englewood Cliffs, NJ: Prentice-Hall, 1976.

————. "Recidivism rates of diverted juvenile offenders." Paper presented at the National Conference on Criminal Justice Evaluation, Washington, DC, 1977.

Nejelski, P. "Diversion: the promise and danger." Crime and Delinquency 22: 393–410 (1976).

Palmer, T., M. Bohnstedt, and R. Lewis. The Evaluation of Juvenile Diversion: Final Report. Sacramento: California Youth Authority, 1978.

Palmer, T. and R. Lewis. "A differentiated approach to juvenile diversion." J. of Research in Crime and Delinquency 17: 209–277 (1980).

Polk, K. and A. Schucter. Report: Phase I Assessment of Youth Service Bureaus. A report prepared for the National Institute of Law Enforcement and Criminal Justice, Washington, DC, 1975.

Quay, H. C. and C. T. Love. "The effect of a juvenile diversion program on rearrests." Criminal Justice and Behavior 4: 377–396 (1977).

Quincy, R. L. An Evaluation of the Effectiveness of the Youth Service Bureau Diversion Concept. Unpublished Ph.D. dissertation, Michigan State University at East Lansing, 1981.

Thornton, W., E. Barrett, and L. Musolf. The Sacramento County Probation Department 601 Diversion Project. Sacramento: Sacramento County Probation Department, 1972.

Venezia, P. and D. Anthony. A Program Level Evaluation of Wisconsin's Youth Service Bureaus. Tuscon, AZ: Associates for Youth Development, 1978.

The Politics of Juvenile Justice and Future Directions

As indicated in the introduction to the previous section, ''The Juvenile Justice System'' (Part 6), governmental commitment to funding of community alternatives to secure correctional facilities for juveniles began to increase in the late 1960s and early 1970s. Under the 1974 Juvenile Justice and Delinquency Prevention Act, public training schools were ineligible for federal funds. This funding structure created an incentive for the development of private facilities ''as a supplemental system of youth control and treatment'' that would receive public funds and provide services for governmental agencies (Waegel, 1989:202; Lerman, 1984). While such private organizations also operate institutions that resemble traditional juvenile reformatory or training schools, the most common are community-based group homes, and other residential and nonresidential treatment centers where juveniles receive a variety of mental health, counseling, chemical dependency, and academic and vocational services.[1] However, as Polk suggested in the last chapter (Chapter 27), ''rather than producing a shift of juveniles from public institutions to community alternatives, the result has been to increase the number of juveniles brought under some form of correctional supervision'' (Waegel, 1989:203; Curran, 1988). Private agencies appear to be handling younger, female, and less serious offenders, while traditional public training schools are handling older and more serious offenders (Lerman, 1984). Moreover, about two-thirds of juveniles in private facilities are white, while over half in public training schools are minority youth (Krisberg et al., 1986). Some private residential facilities also appear to have retained some of the coercive features of traditional correctional institutions (Hylton, 1982).

The movement toward community corrections did not take place without opposition. As these new correctional strategies were being implemented on a large scale, the correctional pendulum began to swing in the opposite direction. Beginning in the mid-1970s, a more punishment-oriented "law and order" or "get tough" approach to crime and delinquency began "appealing to substantial segments of the public which had witnessed a rising volume of crime and delinquency" (Waegel, 1989:193; see Hellum, 1979; Wilson, 1975). This approach was reinforced by reports that rehabilitation programs were not working (Martinson, 1974). Some states passed laws that essentially abandoned rehabilitative goals for serious and repeat offenders and endorsed harsher punishment as a means of protecting the public and deterring crime.[2] As a result, by the early 1980s the incarceration rate of juveniles "returned to their highest levels" since the early 1970s, even though "juvenile arrests for serious violent offenses remained stable" (Waegel, 1989:194; Galvin and Polk, 1983; Krisberg et al., 1986).

Reform and Counter-Reform: The Massachusetts Experience

The political constituency for a more conservative counter-reform movement also developed in response to the limitations and problems associated with community-based reform strategies. One of the best examples of the process of reform and counter-reform occurred in the state of Massachusetts. The initial political constituency for reform of the Massachusetts correctional system developed in the late 1960s and early 1970s as a result of various public scandals and governmental investigations of the deplorable conditions in some of the state's secure correctional institutions for juveniles (Miller and Ohlin, 1981). In 1971, after some unsuccessful attempts at reforming the secure correctional system, Jerome Miller, the director of the Division of Youth Services, began to close down all of the state's secure facilities and transfer the inmates to foster homes, group homes, and other community programs. Miller's strategy of *deinstitutionalization* involved an attempt "to replace the institutions with a system of services from private contractors," with an emphasis on doing "good things for kids, . . . linking the youth and the community, and establishing more humane, normal social relationships in [small] living units" (p. 453).

However, Miller's "stress on action was accompanied by a willingness to let administrative concerns catch up later" (p. 453). The closing of the institutions produced some chaos related to problems in tracking youths who had been dispersed throughout the state, in establishing rates of payment and processing payments to private contractors, and in maintaining quality control over the decentralized network of programs (Coates et al., 1978; Miller and Ohlin, 1981; Scull, 1977). Moreover, career goals of different correctional constituencies began to manifest themselves (Miller and Ohlin, 1981). The community-based reforms had replaced many of the old-line staff of the secure correctional institutions with those tied to the newer agencies. Those who had benefitted from employment in the traditional secure facilities began to exploit the public's and legislators' concerns about lapses in security associated with the more open system of community corrections (Ohlin et al., 1974). Proponents of *reinstitutionalization* argued that the "public remains at risk" if serious juvenile offenders are not confined (Coates, 1981:478). They asserted that:

> Community-based services do not provide significant punishment for those violating society's norms, . . . [and they] provide little that would deter youngsters from committing similar crimes again. Incarceration expresses society's intolerance of unlawful behavior, and the fear of punishment can lead the youngster to consider more rationally the consequences of future actions. Youngsters must be taught that they are to be held responsible and accountable for their actions (p. 478).

By 1974, the Massachusetts Department of Youth Services reinstituted a system of secure facilities that appears to operate as a traditional prison devoid of any meaningful program of rehabilitation (Vogel and Thibault, 1981).

On the other hand, the proponents of deinstitutionalization and community corrections believed that "through carefully designed programs and appropriate staff, . . . the vast majority of . . . youth can be effectively and appropriately placed in . . . community-based . . . alternatives without detriment to public protection" (Coates, 1981:478; Wilson, 1978:13). Youths placed in community programs "are not simply turned loose" (Coates, 1981:478).

> For example, tracking programs that have one staff member responsible for two youths living at home provide very close supervision. Group homes frequently place tight restrictions on newcomers during their first two weeks, allowing them time to adjust to the environment and to recognize a need for the program (p. 478).

Moreover, community corrections has fared favorably with secure corrections in protecting the community (see Calhoun and Wayne, 1981; Ohlin et al., 1977).

> Youths frequently run from . . . institutional settings as well as from community programs, . . . [and] many criminal acts take place in institutional settings. They remain unnoticed and unrecorded because they are perpetrated only on a captive population, not on members of the public (p. 478).

According to Coates, decisions regarding placement of juveniles in community versus secure correctional settings "should be guided by the principle that the best choice is the least restrictive alternative appropriate" for a particular youth (p. 481). Clearly, secure corrections remain necessary for some offenders, especially those who have demonstrated a capacity for violence. A Massachusetts task force recommended that about 11 percent of the youth under the Department of Youth Services' jurisdiction needed to be confined in secure correctional facilities (Wilson, 1978). But even violent juvenile offenders will be eventually returned to the community.[3] Thus, for both the community's and the youth's benefit, the offender should be provided with the best possible treatment while confined in a secure correctional environment (Coates, 1981).

The Status Offender Controversy

The policies of diversion and deinstitutionalization have also been accompanied, in some circles, by a call for the *decriminalization* of status offenses. Although diversion and deinstitutionalization policies have led to increased use of community-based corrections, rather than secure corrections, for status offenders (Handler et al., 1982; Kobrin and Klein, 1982), some observers believe that status offenders should be removed from juvenile court jurisdiction altogether. Proponents of this position argue that status offenders require the services of mental health and other youth-serving professionals, not the police, courts, or "strong arm of the law" (Binder et al., 1988:353; Logan and Rausch, 1985). The strategy of separating status offenders from delinquents through statutes designating the former as "Persons in Need of Supervision" (PINS) or "Children in Need of Supervision" (CHINS) has not necessarily resulted in the intended distinctive approaches to treatment (Hickey, 1977). Moreover, status offense statutes are extremely vague,[4] allowing for "flexible interpretations . . . [that] serve as an invitation to arbitrary and capricious enforcement as well as procedural and due process inequities" (Kelly, 1981:365).

Proponents of decriminalization also argue that status offenders are a distinct type of offender and point to research which indicates that many do not go on to commit more serious crimes (Kelly, 1981; Rankin and Wells, 1985). Moreover, Kelly (1981:365) found that status offenders who came before the juvenile court were "somewhat less likely to recidivate" than other offenders, and less likely to commit further serious crimes subsequent to court contact than those youth who were initially charged with felonies or misdemeanors. Kelly attributed some status offenders' escalation to more serious crimes to the negative labeling associated with official court processing.

Opponents of decriminalization counter with a large body of research that has found no clear pattern of offense specialization or escalation among status offenders. That is, most youth engaged in both status offense and other delinquent conduct, with no clear pattern of escalation with or without court contact (Datesman and Aickin, 1985; Rojek and Erickson, 1972; Shelden et al., 1989; Thomas, 1976; Weis, 1979; Wolfgang et al., 1972). Moreover, research on the effects of official labeling, though somewhat inconclusive, has not generally supported the proposition that juveniles experience a decline in their self-image following arrest or juvenile court processing (see Ageton and Elliott, 1974; Anson and Eason, 1986; Forster et al., 1972; Hepburn, 1977; Jensen, 1980; Mahoney, 1974; O'Conner, 1970; Snyder, 1971; Thomas and Bishop, 1984).

Some middle ground regarding the status offender-labeling controversy is suggested by those who encourage researchers to go beyond the vagueness of the status offender category and further differentiate among this group of offenders (Shelden et al., 1989). For instance, Kobrin et al. (1980) identified three types of status offenders who were processed through juvenile court: those with no prior offense history, those with only a prior status offense history, and those with a history of both delinquent and status offenses. Their research indicated that there are different types of status offenders—some who are relatively specialized in their conduct and some who are not.[5] Similarly, some evidence regarding the effects of official labeling has suggested that delinquents' self-image was more likely to decline among youth who were less involved in or committed to delinquency (e.g., first-time middle class offenders) than among youth who were more involved in or committed to delinquency (e.g., high frequency lower-class and minority offenders) and who already possessed "a negative social status, . . . [were] not highly integrated into society, . . . [and were] less sensitive to and less affected by the judgments of officialdom" (Waegel, 1989:113; see Ageton and Elliott, 1974; Liska, 1987; Shoemaker, 1984). Nevertheless, irrespective of research relevant to the status offender-labeling controversy, diversion and deinstitutionalization, rather than decriminalization, remain the predominant strategies for dealing with juvenile status offenders.

Juvenile Restitution: Bridging the Gap Between Rehabilitation and Accountability

Restitution refers to a sanction imposed on an offender whereby he or she "is required to make a service payment or a monetary payment or both to the victim of the crime, to the community, or to both" (Galaway, 1979:57). Although the general concept of paying back victims, or relatives of victims, is an ancient one (Karmen, 1984; Schafer, 1970), it is a relatively new development in the contemporary juvenile justice system. Schneider and Schneider (1975) reported fewer than fifteen formally constituted restitution programs in the U.S. in 1977, but over four hundred in 1985 (Schneider, 1985).

The emergence of restitution as a popular strategy can be traced to a number of developments. It has responded to the growing concern about crime victims who have been the "lost souls" of the criminal and juvenile justice systems, and it has appealed to conservatives who view it as a more severe sanction than probation (Karmen, 1984; Schneider, 1986; Staples, 1986). Restitution has also been touted as having rehabilitative value, especially if the offender is required to pay back the victim directly and confront the victim's "anger, anxiety, and indignation" (Binder et al., 1988:562). In this way, the offender may "develop a more realistic assessment of the consequences of what they have done . . . [and thus] erase one of the strongest defenses . . . to wrongdoing, [the] inability to empathize fully with those who have suffered" (p. 562). Moreover, if youths in restitution programs are provided with positive job experiences under the direction of adult role models, they may acquire a sense of confidence that they can succeed in legitimate social situations (Schneider, 1986).

The major theme of restitution programs has been to make offenders accountable for their behavior and to take responsibility for the harm they have caused to others (Schneider, 1986). The language of "accountability" and "responsibility" transcends both punishment- and treatment-oriented correctional strategies. The accountability-responsibility theme has also been used in conjunction with *reality therapy,* a mode of individualized treatment that attempts to get offenders to understand the consequences of their actions (Cole and Hafsten, 1978; Glasser, 1965). Regardless of the problems they may have encountered in their lives, reality therapy insists that offenders must acknowledge they are responsible for, and must be held accountable for, their behavior.

Thus far, the results of restitution programs have been encouraging. Studies have reported high completion rates of payment to victims (Schneider et al., 1982; Schneider, 1985). Though not all restitution programs have produced lower recidivism rates than other forms of correctional treatment, because of problems in "program management and strategy, community circumstances, or other factors," some do show "a small but important effect on recidivism" (Schneider, 1986:533). Moreover, youths in restitution programs have "never had higher recidivism rates than those in probation or detention conditions" (p. 533; see Rector, 1978).

Do Juveniles Need Religion?

Given the growing popularity of religion in recent years (see Hastings and Hoge, 1986), it may seem surprising how few delinquency textbooks discuss the relationship between religion and delinquent behavior.[6] Religious leaders often blame rising rates of crime and immorality on the decline of religious belief (Hirschi and Stark, 1969). They assume that religion is associated with lower rates of delinquency since it is intended to promote "goodness, morality, concern for the rights and welfare of others, righteousness, and rewards in the hereafter for proper behavior in life" (Binder et al., 1988:465; Fitzpatrick, 1967). But like so many areas of delinquency research, studies on religion and delinquency have produced inconsistent results (Tittle and Welch, 1983). Some studies can be found to suggest that "delinquents do not differ from nondelinquents in their attitudes toward religion, . . . [that] delinquents are more religious than nondelinquents, . . . [and that] nondelinquents are more religious than delinquents (Jensen and Rojek, 1980:230).

In one of the first major studies that raised questions about the religion-delinquency relationship, Hirschi and Stark (1969) found no association between delinquency and church attendance and belief in the supernatural. They explained their findings in terms of churches' inability to instill in their members a "love for their neighbors and because belief in the possibility of pleasure and pain in another world cannot now, and perhaps never could, compete with the pleasures and pains of everyday life" (pp. 212–13).

Burkett and White (1974) offered another interpretation of Hirschi and Stark's findings. They suggested that it was not that religion was irrelevant to delinquency, but that secular institutions may be as effective in controlling delinquent impulses. On the other hand, they did find that religious participation was related to controlling behaviors that were not strongly condemned by secular society, that is, "victimless" crimes such as marijuana and alcohol use. Similar findings were reported in other studies (Albrecht et al., 1977; Jensen and Erickson, 1979; Middleton and Putney, 1962).

Further research indicated that the relationship between religion and delinquency varied by denomination and geographical context. For instance, the relationship between religion and victimless crimes was strongest among "fundamentalist" or highly "ascetic" denominations such as the Church of Christ, Church of God, and Disciples of Christ, and among Baptists and Mormons (Albrecht et al., 1977; Jensen and Erickson, 1979). Other studies found that Jews had lower rates of delinquency than Protestants or Catholics (Austin, 1977; Goldscheider and Simpson, 1967; Rhodes and Reiss, 1970). In addition, the relationship was stronger in rural and southern communities, suggesting varying commitment of church attenders to religious principles (Higgins and Albrecht, 1977; Jensen and Erickson, 1979). Stark et al. (1982:7) argued that:

> in social groups wherein a religious sanctioning system is the mode and is expressed in daily life, the propensity to deviate from the norms will be influenced substantially by the degree of one's commitment to the religious sanctioning system . . . [But] where the religious sanctioning system is not pervasive, the effects of the individual's religious commitment will be muffled and curtailed. In such a setting, religion will not find everyday expression, but will tend to be a highly compartmentalized part of the lives of its adherents.

Importantly, researchers now believe that the effect of religion on delinquency must be understood in the context of a more complex social network and "is so closely tied to the family and other influences that it has little influence that is statistically independent of other predictor variables'' (Elifson et al., 1983:521; Fitzpatrick, 1967). For instance, in a study of marijuana use, Burkett and Warren (1987:127) found that the religion-delinquency relationship was mediated by peer associations, with youth who had ''lower religious commitment . . . [more] . . . vulnerable to . . . involvement with other users.''

However, as indicated above, there are also studies which indicate that religion may be positively related to some types of delinquency (Jensen and Erickson, 1979; Middleton and Fay, 1941; Mizruchi and Perrucci, 1968; Straus and Bacon, 1953). Denominations with strict prohibitions against use of alcohol and other drugs provide adherents with no norms of moderation; so if religious bonds become weakened and individuals become involved in these activities, they have a tendency to engage in excessive use. Jensen and Rojek (1980:233) suggested that:

> when a faith is characterized by a ''hard line'' on certain forms of behavior, those on the fringes may have a higher incidence of those behaviors than those on the fringes of more liberal denominations, possibly as a result of rebellion, stigmatization, or the lack of norms regulating prohibited behavior when it does occur.

Peek et al. (1985) found such a ''deviance amplification'' effect of religion on delinquent behaviors other than alcohol and drugs, especially for Baptists and Methodists.

Binder et al. (1988:478) concluded that ''religion does not produce broadly 'good' boys and girls but that behavior is controlled selectively in accord with the moral priorities of the separate denominations and their modes of interaction with other social processes.'' Similarly, Fitzpatrick (1967:320) suggested that although religion may be ''a major element in social control, . . . [it] does not appear to be necessary for social control. . . . Many of the most law-abiding citizens are people with no religious belief . . . [and] many delinquents are religiously affiliated.''

Nevertheless, for some groups and individuals, religion can clearly have a positive influence. For black Americans, for instance, ''religion has served as a major social support system . . . since the days of slavery, . . . [and it] still remains a force in most communities in terms of offering real aid to families, especially in times of trouble'' (Thornton et al., 1987:430–1; see Frazier, 1974). Williams and Kornblum (1985) have shown that religion can help insulate some poor minority youth from the criminogenic effects of their environment. However, the significance of religion for black youth has been generally ignored by delinquency researchers.

Final Remarks

It would be a serious mistake to assume that a return to religion could become the cornerstone of an overall strategy to reduce delinquency. Clearly, a viable approach to delinquency prevention, as suggested in Part IV of this book, must focus on the family, the schools, peer groups, the economy, and the community. While simply "throwing money" to address problems in these areas is no solution, most observers agree that lack of adequate funds continues to be "a major obstacle to implementing effective programs" (Waegel, 1989:250; Lundman et al., 1976; Williams and Kornblum, 1985). Our society must establish priorities and invest in its people. Those of us who do not live in high crime areas may try to run, but as the saying goes, we cannot hide. Investment in prevention will save money in the long run if we have the foresight to sacrifice short-term tax cuts for long term societal gains.

However, the prospects for establishing such priorities are not good for the immediate future. As Alfred Regnery (1986:40), director of the Office of Juvenile Justice and Delinquency Prevention during the Reagan Administration, remarked, "we have placed less emphasis [than prior administrations] on juvenile crime as a social problem and more emphasis on crime as a justice problem."[7] What this means, in part, is that the Reagan Administration had:

> no preconceptions . . . that the government is going to solve . . . problems. We can improve the law enforcement system somewhat, . . . we can build more prisons, train more police, and help state and local governments improve their enforcement systems. . . . [But the] Administration feels very strongly . . . [about] the necessity of getting government out of people's hair sufficiently for them to live their lives the way they wish and solve their problems in their own way (pp. 42–3).

Regnery suggested the need to abandon the traditional treatment philosophy of the juvenile court and hold juveniles accountable for their conduct. But if he expected that delinquency could be deterred by a strategy that focuses on deterring crime through increased threat of punishment, we are in for "rough sailing." As the deterrent research has shown (see Part 3), crime control strategies need to consider the larger context in which individuals make decisions about violating the law. More attention needs to be given to how punishment risks are evaluated by individuals in the face of various illegal and legal opportunities available to them (see Piliavan et al., 1986).

Such considerations do not mitigate the need, as Regnery (1986) argued, to hold individuals accountable for their behavior, for our society does not have the luxury to wait until broader social problems are resolved. The public demands and deserves to be protected, and some individuals need to be confined. However, we should make every effort to limit confinement to those who pose a danger to the physical well-being of others. And when these individuals are confined, every effort should be made to maximize the likelihood that the incarceration experience will promote commitment to law-abiding behavior rather than to further involvement in a criminal way of life. Decisions to abandon rehabilitative goals in correctional settings represent a cynicism that we cannot afford, for most incarcerated youth will be released at some time to cause further harm to their communities if they are not assisted in developing constructive ways of dealing with their problems.

As for the less serious offenders, who constitute the overwhelming majority of delinquent youth, every effort should be made to minimize their contact with the juvenile justice system. More attention to the strategies of diversion, deinstitutionalization, and decriminalization of status offenders, and to ways of implementing these policies more effectively, would be desirable. Attempts to channel youth into effective treatment programs that are noncoercive and that protect juveniles' rights, and experimentation with innovative alternatives, such as restitution, that offer benefits to both offenders and victims, would also be beneficial.[8] However, we must be cautious about the:

> bifurcated system that has developed, in which public facilities are primarily responsible for institutionalized corrections while the private sector administers the majority of open-environment programs. . . . This situation essentially removes the public and its elected officials from decision-making processes concerning youths and results in an inherent lack of accountability (Curran, 1988:363, 370).

We also need to carefully scrutinize how the waiver procedure is being used. As Osbun and Rode indicated in the previous section (Chapter 25), juveniles who have been transferred to adult court are not necessarily the ones who pose the most serious danger to the public. Bortner (1986) argued that the waiver procedure has served a largely symbolic function: that is, it has allowed juvenile court authorities to portray themselves as responsive to concerns about public safety, while at the same time preserving their traditional mandate to rehabilitate *most* juveniles. "In an era of fiscal uncertainty, when the juvenile justice system is confronted with the necessity of reasserting its worth, maintaining its uniqueness, and redefining its mission," the waiver procedure deflects "more encompassing criticisms of the entire system" and helps juvenile authorities advance their "territorial interest in maintaining jurisdiction over the vast majority" of youthful offenders (pp. 66–7, 70).

Finally, we return to a theme introduced in the first section of this book. Adolescence is more than a stage in the biological life cycle. It is a social construction. We need to rethink the ways we have established adolescence as a marginal period of life where youths' full-fledged adult status is held in abeyance for an extended number of years. More meaningful ways of integrating adolescents with positive adult role models need to be sought (Williams and Kornblum, 1985). As Bortner (1988:378) concluded:

> Young people need to receive the mature and reasoned assistance of adults while simultaneously receiving the opportunities and responsibilities that engender maturity. Much of what they seek—a sense of meaningful contribution to society, a sense of community and friendship, love and support and a measure of individual autonomy—is not unlike what adults seek. The inability of the adult world to assist young people in their transition from infancy to adulthood relates not only to the complexity of such a transition within contemporary society, but it also relates directly to the crisis that plagues most adults. The relationships and roles essential to the well-being of young people do not exist in the lives of many adults, including young people's parents, teachers, jailers, or the gods of mass culture.

Notes

1. Typically, group homes are dormitory-like facilities where juveniles are "supervised during parts of the day and at night, while being allowed limited participation in the larger community either to attend school or work at part-time jobs" (Bynum and Thompson, 1989:415). Foster care programs, where one or two juveniles live in a family with surrogate parents, and rural programs involving "forestry camps, ranches, and farms that provide specific recreational activities or work in a rural setting" are also considered part of community corrections (Siegal and Senna, 1988:508).

2. The trend is also toward increased use of preventive (pretrial) detention for juveniles (Feld, 1984; Lee, 1984–85). See U.S. Supreme Court decision of *Schall v. Martin* (467 U.S. 253, 1984) in Appendix 2.

3. Although the U.S. Supreme Court has ruled that executions of juveniles sixteen years and older is constitutional *(Stanford v. Kentucky,* 109 S. Ct. 2969, 1989), the death penalty is not a viable solution for protecting the public against violent juveniles. Streib (1988) reports that only thirty-eight juveniles in the U.S. were sentenced to death between January 1982 and March 1987. As of March 1987, only three of these youth were actually executed. For discussions of capital punishment generally and for juveniles in particular, see Haas and Inciardi (1987) and Streib (1987, 1988).

4. The reader will recall from Part 1 that juvenile statutes include such offenses as truancy, drinking alcohol, running away from home, curfew violations, immoral behavior, incorrigibility, and being habitually disobedient.

5. Shelden (1989) found that males were more likely than females to escalate from status offenses to more serious conduct.

6. For exceptions, see Binder et al. (1988), Jensen and Rojek (1980), and Thornton et al. (1987).

7. The OJJDP is the federal government's main agency that deals with juvenile justice.

8. Wilderness programs that involve juveniles in outdoor experiences that give them a sense of confidence and accomplishment also show promise as a viable innovation in juvenile corrections (Finckenauer, 1984; Greenwood and Zimring, 1985).

References

Ageton, S.S. and D.S. Elliott. 1974. "The effects of legal processing on delinquent orientations." *Social Problems* 22:87–100.

Albrecht, S.L., B.A. Chadwick, and D.S. Alcorn. 1977. "Religiosity and deviance: Application of an attitude behavior contingent consistency model." *Journal for the Scientific Study of Religion* 16:263–74.

Anson, R. and C. Eason. 1986. "The effects of confinement on delinquent self-image." *Juvenile and Family Court Journal* 37:39–47.

Austin, R. 1977. "Religion and crime control." Paper presented at conference of American Society of Criminology. Atlanta, GA.

Binder, A., G. Geis, and D. Bruce. 1988. *Juvenile Delinquency: Historical, Cultural, and Legal Perspectives*. New York: Macmillan.

Bortner, M.A. 1988. *Delinquency and Justice: An Age of Crisis*. New York: McGraw-Hill.

———. 1986. "Traditional rhetoric, organizational realities: Remand of juveniles to adult court." *Crime and Delinquency* 32:53–73.

Burkett, S.R. and B.O. Warren. 1987. "Religiosity, peer associations, and adolescent marijuana use: A panel study of underlying casual structures." *Criminology* 25:109–34.

Burkett, S.R. and M. White. 1974. "Hellfire and delinquency: Another look." *Journal for the Scientific Study of Religion* 13:455–62.

Bynum, J.E. and W.E. Thompson. 1989. *Juvenile Delinquency: A Sociological Approach*. Boston: Allyn and Bacon.

Calhoun, J.A. and S. Wayne. 1981. "Can the Massachusetts juvenile justice system survive the eighties?" *Crime and Delinquency* 27:522–33.

Coates, R.B. 1981. "Deinstitutionalization and the serious juvenile offender: Some policy considerations." *Crime and Delinquency* 27:477–86.

Coates, R.B., A.D. Miller, and L.E. Ohlin. 1978. *Diversity in a Youth Correctional Setting: Handling Delinquents in Massachusetts*. Cambridge, MA: Ballinger.

Cole, P.Z. and J.W. Hafsten. 1978. "Probation supervision revisited: Responsibility training." *Journal of Juvenile and Family Courts* 29:53–58.

Curran, D.J. 1988. "Destructuring, privatization, and the promise of juvenile diversion: Compromising community-based corrections." *Crime and Delinquency* 34:363–78.

Datesman, S.K. and M. Aickin. 1984. "Offense specialization and escalation among status offenders." *Journal of Criminal Law and Criminology* 75:1246–75.

Elifson, K.W., D.M. Peterson, and C.K. Hadaway. 1983. "Religiosity and delinquency: A contextual analysis." *Criminology* 21:505–27.

Feld, B.C. 1984. "Criminalizing juvenile justice: Rules of procedure for the juvenile court." *Minnesota Law Review* 69:141–276.

Finckenauer, J.O. 1984. *Juvenile Delinquency and Corrections: The Gap Between Theory and Practice.* Orlando, FL: Academic Press.

Fitzpatrick, J.P. 1967. *The Role of Religion in Programs for the Prevention and Correction of Crime and Delinquency. Report of Task Force on Juvenile Delinquency of the President's Commission on Law Enforcement and Administration of Justice, Juvenile Delinquency and Youth Crime.* Washington, DC: U.S. Government Printing Office.

Forster, J., S. Dinitz, and W. C. Reckless. 1972. "Perception of stigma following public intervention for delinquent behavior." *Social Problems* 20:202–11.

Frazier, F.F. 1974. *The Negro Church in America.* New York: Schocken.

Galaway, B. 1979. "Differences in victim compensation and restitution." *Social Work* (Jan.):57–58.

Galvin, J. and K. Polk. 1983. "Juvenile justice: Time for new directions?" *Crime and Delinquency* 29:325–32.

Glasser, W. 1965. *Reality Therapy.* New York: Harper and Row.

Goldscheider, C. and J.E. Simpson. 1967. "Religious affiliation and juvenile delinquency." *Sociological Inquiry* 37:297–310.

Greenwood, P. and F. Zimring. 1985. *One More Chance.* Santa Monica, CA: Rand Corporation.

Haas, K.C. and J.A. Inciardi (eds.). 1988. *Challenging Capital Punishment: Legal and Social Science Approaches.* Newbury Park, CA: Sage.

Handler, J.F., M. Sosin, J.A. Stookey, and J. Zatz. 1982. "Deinstitutionalization in seven states: Principal findings." Pp. 88–126 in J.F. Handler and J. Zatz (eds.), *Neither Angels Nor Thieves: Studies in Deinstitutionalization of Status Offenders.* Washington, DC: National Academy Press.

Hastings, P.K. and D.R. Hoge. 1986. "Religious and moral attitude trends among college students: 1948–84." *Social Forces* 65:370–7.

Hellum, F. 1979. "Juvenile justice: The second revolution." *Crime and Delinquency* 25:299–317.

Hepburn, J.R. 1977. "The impact of police intervention upon juvenile delinquents." *Criminology* 15:235–62.

Hickey, W.L. 1977. "Status offenses and the juvenile court." *Criminal Justice Abstracts* 9:91–122.

Higgins, P.C. and S.L. Albrecht. 1977. "Hellfire and delinquency revisited." *Social Forces* 55:952–8.

Hirschi, T. and R. Stark. 1969. "Hellfire and delinquency." *Social Problems* 17:202–13.

Hylton, J.H. 1982. "Rhetoric and reality: A critical appraisal of community correctional programs." *Crime and Delinquency* 28:341–73.

Jensen, G.F. 1980. "Labeling and identity." *Criminology* 18:121–9.

Jensen, G.F. and M.L. Erickson. 1979. "The religious factor and delinquency: Another look at the hellfire hypothesis." Pp 157–77 in R. Wuthnow (ed.), *The Religious Dimension: New Directions in Quantitative Research.* New York: Academic Press.

Jensen, G.F. and D.G. Rojek. *Delinquency: A Sociological View.* Lexington, MA: D.C. Heath.

Karmen, A. 1984. *Crime Victims: An Introduction to Victimology.* Belmont, CA: Wadsworth.

Kelley, T.M. 1983. "Status offenders can be different: A comparative study of delinquent careers." *Crime and Delinquency* 29:365–80.

Kobrin, S., F. Hellum, and J. Peterson. 1980. "Offense patterns of status offenders." Pp. 203–35 in D. Shichor and D. Kelly (eds.), *Critical Issues in Juvenile Delinquency.* Lexington, MA: Lexington.

Kobrin, S. and M.W. Klein. 1982. *National Evaluation of the Deinstitutionalization of Status Offender Programs: Executive Summary.* Washington, DC: U.S. Department of Justice, Office of Juvenile Justice and Delinquency Prevention.

Krisberg, B., I. Schwartz, P. Litsky, and J. Austin. 1986. "The watershed of juvenile justice reform." *Crime and Delinquency* 32:5–38.

Lee, D.A., 1984–85. "The constitutionality of juvenile preventive detention: Schall v. Martin—Who is preventive detention protecting?" *New England Law Review* 20:341–74.

Lerman, P. 1984. "Child welfare, the private sector, and community-based corrections." *Crime and Delinquency* 30:5–38.

Liska, A.E. 1987. *Perspectives on Deviance.* Englewood Cliffs, NJ: Prentice-Hall.

Logan, C.H. and S.P. Tausch. 1985. "Why deinstitutionalizing status offenders is pointless." *Crime and Delinquency* 31:501–17.

Lundman, R., P.T. McFarlane, and F. R. Scarpitti. 1976. "Delinquency prevention: A description and assessment of projects reported in the professional literature." *Crime and Delinquency* 22:297–308.

Mahoney, A.R. 1974. "The effect of labeling upon youths in the juvenile justice system: A review of the evidence." *Law and Society Review* 8:583–614.

Martinson, R. 1974. "What works—Questions and answers about prison reform." *Public Interest* 35:22–54.

Middleton, R. and P. Fay. 1941. "Attitudes of delinquent and non-delinquent girls toward Sunday observance, the Bible and war." *Journal of Educational Psychology* 32:555–8.

Miller, A.D. and L.E. Ohlin. 1981. "The politics of secure care in youth correctional reform." *Crime and Delinquency* 27:449–67.

Misruchi, E. and R. Perrucci. 1968. "Prescription, proscription and permissiveness: Aspects of norms and deviant drinking behavior." Pp 151–67 in M. Lefton, J.K. Skipper, and C.H. McCaghy (eds.), *Approaches to Deviance.* New York: Appleton-Century-Crofts.

O'Connor, G. 1970. "The effect of detention upon male delinquency." *Social Problems* 18:194–7.

Ohlin, L.E., R.B. Coates, and A. D. Miller. 1974. "Radical correctional reform: A case study of the Massachusetts youth correctional system." *Harvard Educational Review* 44:74-111.

Ohlin, L.E., A.D. Miller, and R.B. Coates. 1977. *Juvenile Correctional Reform in Massachusetts.* National Institute for Juvenile Justice and Delinquency Prevention. Washington, DC: U.S. Government Printing Office.

Peek, C.W., E.W. Curry, and H.P. Chalfant. 1985. "Religiosity and delinquency over time: Deviance deterrence and deviance amplification." *Social Science Quarterly* 66:120-31.

Piliavin, I., R. Gartner, C. Thornton, and R.L. Matsueda. 1986. "Crime, deterrence, and choice." *American Sociological Review* 51:101-19.

Rankin, J.H. and L.E. Wells. 1985. "From status to delinquent offenses: Escalation?" *Journal of Criminal Justice* 13:171-80.

Rector, J.M. 1978. *Restitution by Juvenile Offenders: An Alternative to Incarceration.* Washington, DC: Law Enforcement Assistance Administration, U.S. Department of Justice.

Regnery, A.S. 1986. "A federal perspective on juvenile justice reform." *Crime and Delinquency* 32:39-51.

Rhodes, A.L. and A.J. Reiss. 1970. "The 'religious factor' and delinquent behavior." *Journal of Research in Crime and Delinquency* 7:83-98.

Rojek, D.G. and M.L. Erickson. 1982. "Delinquent careers: A test of the career escalation model." *Criminology* 20:5-28.

Schafer, S. 1970. *Compensation and Restitution to Victims of Crime.* Second edition. Montclair, NJ: Paterson Smith.

Schneider, A.L. 1986. "Restitution and recidivism rates of juvenile offenders: Results from four experimental studies." *Criminology* 24:533-52.

_____. (ed). 1985. *Guide to Juvenile Restitution Programs.* Washington, DC: National Criminal Justice Reference Service and GPO.

Schneider, A.L. and P.R. Schneider. 1977. "Restitution requirements for juvenile offenders: A survey of practices in American juvenile courts." *Juvenile Justice Journal* 18:43-56.

Schneider, P.R., A.L. Schneider, W. Griffith, and M. Wilson. 1982. *Two-Year Report on the National Evaluation of the Juvenile Restitution Initiative: An Overview of Program Performance.* Eugene, OR: Institute of Policy Analysis.

Scull, A.T. 1977. *Decarceration: Community Treatment and the Deviant—A Radical View.* Englewood Cliffs, NJ: Prentice-Hall.

Shelden, R.G., J.A. Norvath, and S. Tracy. 1989. "Do status offenders get worse? Some clarifications on the question of escalation." *Crime and Delinquency* 202-16.

Shoemaker, D.J. 1984. *Theories of Delinquency.* New York: Oxford University Press.

Siegal, L.J. and J.J. Senna. 1988. *Juvenile Delinquency: Theory, Practice, and Law.* Third edition. St. Paul: West.

Snyder, E. 1971. "The impact of the juvenile court hearing on the child." *Crime and Delinquency* 17:180-82.

Staples, W.G. 1986. "Restitution as a sanction in juvenile court." *Crime and Delinquency* 32:177–85.

Stark, R., L. Kent, and D.P. Doyle. 1982. "Religion and delinquency: The ecology of a 'lost' relationship." *Journal of Research in Crime and Delinquency* 19:4–24.

Straus, R. and S.D. Bacon. 1953. *Drinking in College.* New Haven, CT: Yale University Press.

Streib, V.L. 1988. "Imposing the death penalty on children." Pp. 245–67 in K.C. Haas and J.A. Inciardi (eds.), *Challenging Capital Punishment: Legal and Social Science Approaches.* Newbury Park, CA: Sage.

————. 1987. Death Penalty for Juveniles. Bloomington: Indiana University Press.

Thomas, C.W. 1976. "Are status offenders really so different?" *Crime and Delinquency* 22:438–55.

Thomas, C.W. and D.M. Bishop. 1984. "The effect of formal and informal sanctions on delinquency: A longitudinal comparison of labeling and deterrence theory." *Journal of Criminal Law and Criminology* 75:1222–45.

Thornton, W.E., L. Voigt, and W.G. Doerner. 1987. *Delinquency and Justice.* Second edition. New York: Random House.

Tittle, C.R. and M.R. Welch. 1983. "Religiosity and deviance: Toward a contingency theory of constraining effects." *Social Forces* 61:53–80.

Vogel, R.E. and E. Thibault. 1981. "Deinstitutionalization's runaways: The development of a juvenile prison in Massachusetts." *Crime and Delinquency* 27:468–86.

Waegel, W.B. 1989. *Delinquency and Juvenile Control: A Sociological Perspective.* Englewood Cliffs, NJ: Prentice-Hall.

Weis, J.G. 1979. *Jurisdiction and the Elusive Status Offender: A Comparison of Involvement in Delinquent Behavior and Status Offenses. Report of the National Juvenile Justice Assessment Center.* Washington, DC: U.S. Government Printing Office.

Williams, T. and W. Kornblum. 1985. *Growing Up Poor.* Lexington, MA: Lexington.

Wilson, J.Q. 1975. *Thinking About Crime.* New York: Vintage.

Wilson, R. 1978. "The Legacy of Jerome Miller." *Corrections Magazine* 4: 12–18.

Wolfgang, M.E., R.M. Figlio, and T. Sellin. 1972. *Delinquency in a Birth Cohort.* Chicago: University of Chicago Press.

Appendix 1: Note on Statistical Techniques

Students who have never taken a statistics or research methods course may not be familiar with the data analysis techniques used in three of the articles in this book (Chapters 4, 7, and 11). In Chapter 4, Delbert Elliott and Suzanne Ageton use analysis of variance in their study, "Reconciling Differences in Self-Reported and Official Estimates of Delinquency." Elliott and Ageton want to know whether the average rates of delinquency for different groups of youth are "statistically significant." In other words, they want to know whether or not any observed differences between black and white youth and between lower-, working-, and middle-class youth can or cannot be attributed to chance. *Analysis of variance* allows them to measure whether the variation in rates of delinquency *between* the groups is greater than the variation *within* each group. The logic is that only if the between-group variation is greater than the within-group variation can one reach the conclusion that the groups in question exhibit statistically significant differences in their rates of delinquency. *One-way* analysis of variance is used to examine one variable at a time. Thus, Elliott and Ageton calculate the race differences separately from the class differences. *Two-way* analysis of variance is used to test for the interaction between two sets of variables. This enables Elliott and Ageton, for instance, to compare lower-class blacks with working- and middle-class blacks, or lower-class whites with working- and middle-class whites.

In Chapters 7 and 11 respectively, Ronald Akers et al.'s "Social Learning and Deviant Behavior," and Terence Thornberry et al.'s "The Effect of Dropping Out of High School on Subsequent Criminal Behavior," utilize *multiple regression* techniques. Multiple regression allows one to analyze the relationship between a dependent variable and several independent variables. Akers et al. use it to measure the effects of various elements of the social learning process (independent variables) on alcohol/drug use and abuse (dependent variables). Thornberry et al. use it to measure the effects of dropping out of school and other independent variables such as age and social status on subsequent arrest rates. Multiple regression analysis allows Akers et al. and Thornberry et al. to examine the effects on delinquency of particular independent variables while controlling for (taking into account) the effects of other independent variables. Only independent variables with values (regression coefficients) that are statistically significant can be said to have effects on delinquency.

Appendix 2: Major U.S. Supreme Court Decisions on Juvenile Justice

Kent v. U.S., 383 U.S. 541 (1966)
> Juveniles have a right to a separate waiver hearing, with access to legal counsel, before being transferred to the adult criminal justice system.

In re Gault, 387 U.S. 1 (1967)
> Juveniles at the adjudication stage of the juvenile justice system are afforded most, but not all, of the due process protections given to adults, including: notification of charges, right to legal counsel, right to confront and cross-examine witnesses, privilege against self-incrimination, right to transcript of trial, and right to appellate review.

In re Winship, 397 U.S. 358 (1970)
> "Proof beyond a reasonable doubt" rather than a "preponderance of the evidence," is necessary to adjudicate a juvenile as a delinquent.

McKiever v. Pennsylvania, 403 U.S. 528 (1971)
> Juveniles do *not* have a constitutional right to a trial by jury. A jury was not considered essential to the fact-finding capacity of the juvenile court.

Breed v. Jones, 421 U.S. 519 (1975)
> Waiver proceedings do *not* constitute a violation of juveniles' protection against "double jeopardy," but a juvenile cannot be transferred to adult court after being adjudicated in juvenile court. The judges at the waiver hearing and adult court trial must be different.

Schall v. Martin, 104 S.Ct. 2403 (1984)
> Juveniles charged with delinquency may be detained before trial to prevent them from committing additional crimes.

Stanford and Kentucky, 109 S.Ct. 2969 (1989)
> Capital punishment for juveniles sixteen years and older is constitutional.